Lecture Notes in Computer Science 16380

Founding Editors

Gerhard Goos
Juris Hartmanis

Editorial Board Members

Elisa Bertino, *Purdue University, West Lafayette, IN, USA*
Wen Gao, *Peking University, Beijing, China*
Bernhard Steffen, *TU Dortmund University, Dortmund, Germany*
Moti Yung, *Columbia University, New York, NY, USA*

The series Lecture Notes in Computer Science (LNCS), including its subseries Lecture Notes in Artificial Intelligence (LNAI) and Lecture Notes in Bioinformatics (LNBI), has established itself as a medium for the publication of new developments in computer science and information technology research, teaching, and education.

LNCS enjoys close cooperation with the computer science R & D community, the series counts many renowned academics among its volume editors and paper authors, and collaborates with prestigious societies. Its mission is to serve this international community by providing an invaluable service, mainly focused on the publication of conference and workshop proceedings and postproceedings. LNCS commenced publication in 1973.

Neminath Hubballi · Rakesh Verma ·
Shyamasundar Rudrapatna K.
Editors

Information Systems Security

21st International Conference, ICISS 2025
Indore, India, December 16–20, 2025
Proceedings

 Springer

Editors
Neminath Hubballi
Indian Institute of Technology Indore
Indore, Madhya Pradesh, India

Rakesh Verma
University of Houston
Houston, TX, USA

Shyamasundar Rudrapatna K.
Indian Institute of Technology Bombay
Mumbai, Maharashtra, India

ISSN 0302-9743   ISSN 1611-3349 (electronic)
Lecture Notes in Computer Science
ISBN 978-3-032-13713-5   ISBN 978-3-032-13714-2 (eBook)
https://doi.org/10.1007/978-3-032-13714-2

This Springer imprint is published by the registered company Springer Nature Switzerland AG
The registered company address is: Gewerbestrasse 11, 6330 Cham, Switzerland

If disposing of this product, please recycle the paper.

Preface

This book comprises the proceedings of the 21st International Conference on Information Systems Security (ICISS 2025), held at the Indian Institute of Technology Indore (IITI), India, from December 16 to 20, 2025.

This year's conference received a total of 94 submissions from authors across the world. All papers submitted were reviewed following a double-blind review process. Each submission was meticulously reviewed by at least three members of the Program Committee and external reviewers, which consisted of eminent international researchers working in different sub-areas of information security. The PC comprised 41 members and an additional 16 sub-reviewers helped in the review process.

The Program Committee Chairs evaluated and discussed the reviews. After careful consideration of the comments and merits of the papers, 15 full papers and an additional 14 short papers were accepted, resulting in an acceptance ratio of 30.85%. These papers covered a range of topics, including system security, network security, applied cryptography, privacy, and the application of AI to security, among others. The conference program was organized into five technical session tracks: i) Systems Security, ii) Network Security, iii) Privacy, iv) Applied Cryptography, and v) Security Using AI/ML.

This year's conference also included keynotes from eminent speakers, an invited talk, and a PhD Forum speaker.

Keynotes

1. "Smart Contracts, Dumb Mistakes: Understanding and Preventing DeFi Exploits" – Christopher Kruegel, University of California, Santa Barbara, Online
2. "AI Agentic Security: Safeguarding the Next Generation of Autonomous Systems" – Elisa Bertino, Purdue University, Online
3. "Practical resilient efficient quantum key distribution" – Pranab Sen, Tata Institute of Fundamental Research, Mumbai
4. "Threat Modeling for Security of Machine Learning Systems" – Anoop Singhal, National Institute of Standards and Technology

Invited Talk

1. "Reverse Engineering Industrial Control Devices" – Nils Ole Tippenhauer, CISPA Helmholtz Center for Information Security, Online

PhD Forum Talk

1. "Towards developing skills for writing great papers and giving great talks" – Atul Prakash, University of Michigan

We would like to express our appreciation and thanks to all the speakers for delivering their insightful Keynote and Invited talks. A special note of gratitude goes to Pranab Sen, who also contributed a paper to the proceedings.

ICISS 2025 featured two tutorial sessions:

1. "Federated Learning: Architecture, Threat Landscape, and Defence Mechanisms" by Rajiv Ranjan, Devki Nandan Jha, and Tejal Shah of Newcastle University
2. "Vajra-Sandbox: A Robust Framework for Malware Execution and Analysis" by Manjesh Kumar Hanawal (IIT Bombay), Atul Kabra (ReliaQuest), and Prakhar Paliwal (IIT Bombay)

Further, this year's conference also featured two workshops:

1. "Digital Trust for IoT Ecosystems: From Secure Identities to Quantum Resilient Security" – Organized by CDAC Bengaluru
2. "Deep Discovery Challenge Hosting System" – Organized by CAIR, DRDO Bengaluru

Our sincere appreciation to CDAC and DRDO for organizing the workshops.

As in the past, ICISS 2025 had a PhD Forum session where several early and advanced stage PhD students presented their research problems and received invaluable feedback from the expert panel.

It is a pleasure to record our thanks to the session chairs for facilitating the smooth conduct of the sessions, the participants from industry, the organizers, and the PC members for contributing their invaluable time and expertise to the review process. ICISS 2025 would not have been possible without the contributions of the numerous volunteers who gave their time and energy to ensure the success of the conference and its associated events.

Our special thanks go to the Organizing Committee, as well as the faculty, staff, and students of the Indian Institute of Technology Indore for all their efforts and support in the smooth running of the conference.

It is our pleasure to express our gratitude to Springer Nature for assisting us in disseminating the proceedings of the conference in the LNCS series. We also extend our sincere thanks to DRDO and TCS for their generous financial support as Gold Sponsors of this year's conference. We are also thankful to IIT Bombay for the travel grants provided to the PhD forum student participants. Our sincere thanks also go to the other sponsors: Netweb Technologies, Railtel India Ltd, and Samyak Computers.

Finally, we would like to thank all the authors who submitted their papers, the attendees of the tutorials, and the conference participants. We hope you find the proceedings of ICISS 2025 interesting, stimulating, and inspiring for future research.

December 2025   Neminath Hubballi
                                                                Rakesh Verma
                                                   Shyamasundar Rudrapatna K.

Organization

Advisory Steering Committee

Venu Govindaraju   University at Buffalo, USA
Sushil Jajodia   George Mason University, USA
Somesh Jha   University of Wisconsin, USA
Atul Prakash   University of Michigan, USA
Pierangela Samarati   University of Milan, Italy
R. K. Shyamasundar   IIT Bombay, India

Patron

Suhas S. Joshi (Director)   IIT Indore, India

General Chair

R. K. Shyamasundar   IIT Bombay, India

Program Committee Chairs

Neminath Hubballi   IIT Indore, India
Rakesh Verma   University of Houston, USA

Organizing Chair

Neminath Hubballi   IIT Indore, India

Organizing Committee

Bodhisatwa Mazumdar   IIT Indore, India
Gourinath Banda   IIT Indore, India
Soma Saha   PIEMR, India

Finance Chairs

Radha V.	IDRBT Hyderabad, India
Gourinath Banda	IIT Indore, India

Publicity Chairs

Bruno Bogaz Zarpelão	State University of Londrina (UEL), Brazil
Ashok Kumar Das	IIIT Hyderabad, India
Himanshu Agrawal	Curtin University, Australia

PhD Forum Chairs

Radhika B. S.	NIT Surathkal, India
Manjesh Hanawal	IIT Bombay, India

Web Chairs

Meenakshi Tripathi	MNIT Jaipur, India
Yogendra Singh	IIT Indore, India

Tutorial Chairs

Bodhisatwa Mazumdar	IIT Indore, India
Vivek Balachandran	Singapore Institute of Technology, Singapore

Workshop Chairs

Deepak Nadig	Purdue University, USA
Smriti Bhatt	Purdue University, USA

Industry Forum Chairs

Maitreya Natu   TCS, India
Paromita Choudhury   CAIR, DRDO, India

Program Committee

Anoop Singhal   NIST, USA
Ashok Kumar Das   IIIT Hyderabad, India
Ayantika Chatterjee   IIT Kharagpur, India
Barbara Carminati   University of Insubria, Italy
Bhavani Thuraisingham   University of Texas at Dallas, USA
Bodhisatwa Mazumdar   IIT Indore, India
Chandresh Maurya   IIT Indore, India
Claudio Agostino Ardagna   Università degli Studi di Milano, Italy
David Marchette   Naval Surface Warfare Center, USA
Deepak Nadig   Purdue University, USA
Elisa Bertino   Purdue University, USA
Gourinath Banda   IIT Indore, India
Indrajit Ray   Colorado State University, USA
Indrakshi Ray   Colorado State University, USA
K. Gopinath   Rishihood University, India
Luigi V. Mancini   Sapienza University of Rome, Italy
Maniklal Das   ODA-IICT Gandhinagar, India
Manjesh Hanawal   IIT Bombay, India
Maria Francis   IIT Hyderabad, India
Meenakshi Tripathi   MNIT Jaipur, India
Nagendra Kumar   IIT Indore, India
Phu H. Phung   University of Dayton, USA
Pierangela Samarati   Università degli Studi di Milano, Italy
Praveen Tammana   IIT Hyderabad, India
Radhika B. S.   NIT Surathkal, India
Ram Krishnan   University of Texas at San Antonio, USA
Roland Yap Hock Chuan   National University of Singapore, Singapore
Sambuddho   IIIT Delhi, India
Sameer G. Kulkarni   IIT Gandhinagar, India
Sandeep Shukla   IIT Kanpur, India
Sanjit Chatterjee   IISc Bangalore, India
Saravanan Vijayakumaran   IIT Bombay, India
Shuhui Grace Yang   Purdue University Northwest, USA
Somanath Tripathy   IIT Patna, India

Somitra Sanadhya	IIT Jodhpur, India
Srinivas Vivek	IIIT Bangalore, India
Subhra Mazumdar	IIT Indore, India
Venkat Venkatakrishnan	University of Illinois Chicago, USA
Vinay J. Ribeiro	IIT Bombay, India
Vishwas Patil	IIT Bombay, India
Vivek Balachandran	Singapore Institute of Technology, Singapore

External Reviewers Invited by the PC

Aayush Gupta
Arthur Dunbar
Bradley Malin
Bryan Tuck
Houtan Faridi
Mayank Swarnkar
Nikhil Tripathi
Nishath Chandran
Pankaj Chaudhary
Pragya Shrivastava
R. Sekar
Raju Haldar
Shashidhar G. Koolagudi
Shun Cao
Vivekanand Bhat
Vu Minh Hoang Dang

Organizing Executive Committee

Venkata Badarla	IIT Tirupati, India
Neminath Hubballi	IIT Indore, India
Chandrashekar Jatoth	NIT Raipur, India
Jayaprakash Kar	LNMIIT Jaipur, India
Vishwas Patil	IIT Bombay, India
Somanath Tripathy	IIT Patna, India

Gold Sponsors

Other Sponsors

Abstracts of the Keynote Talks

Smart Contracts, Dumb Mistakes: Understanding and Preventing DeFi Exploits

Christopher Kruegel

University of California, Santa Barbara
https://sites.cs.ucsb.edu/~chris/

Abstract. Over the past few years, the Ethereum ecosystem has evolved into the backbone of decentralized finance (DeFi) - a global experiment in programmable money. Billions of dollars now flow through smart contracts that replace traditional intermediaries with code. Yet this vision of transparent, permissionless finance has revealed an uncomfortable truth: when money is software, every bug is a potential heist. In this talk, I will dissect how attackers exploit subtle logic flaws and composability vulnerabilities in smart contracts; issues that go beyond trivial coding errors. I will then introduce Greed, our analysis framework for uncovering such vulnerabilities before they are exploited. Finally, I will outline emerging defenses that aim to detect and even prevent malicious transactions in real time, moving us toward a more secure and resilient on-chain economy.

AI Agentic Security: Safeguarding the Next Generation of Autonomous Systems

Elisa Bertino

Purdue University
https://www.cs.purdue.edu/homes/bertino/

Abstract. The rapid rise of agentic AI—systems capable of autonomous decision-making, goal pursuit, and dynamic interaction with digital and physical environments—ushers in unprecedented opportunities and challenges for security. Unlike traditional AI models, agentic systems operate continuously, adapt to evolving contexts, and often integrate with external tools, APIs, and critical infrastructures. This shift redefines the security landscape: agents may be both powerful defenders and novel attack vectors. This talk will explore the emerging field of AI Agentic Security, focusing on three dimensions: (1) security principles for AI agents; (2) securing AI agents themselves against prompt manipulation, goal hijacking, and adversarial environments; (3) leveraging agentic AI to enhance defensive capabilities, from adaptive intrusion detection to automated incident response; and (4) establishing trustworthy foundations through formal verification, policy alignment, and resilience against adversarial coordination. I will highlight recent advances, open research challenges, and pathways for integrating security-by-design principles into the agentic AI lifecycle.

Practical Resilient Efficient Quantum Key Distribution

Pranab Sen

Tata Institute of Fundamental Research, Mumbai, India
https://www.tcs.tifr.res.in/~pgdsen

Abstract. Quantum key distribution (QKD) is a uniquely quantum way to generate a secure uniformly random secret key of n bits between two remote parties Alice and Bob who share only polylog n bits of prior uniformly random secret key. The final secret key should be secure even under eavesdropping action by a third party Eve who can listen in to and tamper with all communication between Alice and Bob in a limited fashion. Almost all known QKD protocols use two-way communication, including the earliest and most famous one, viz. Bennett-Brassard 1984 (BB84). Also most known QKD protocols have an information reconciliation step where Alice and Bob go from their respective raw keys, which are slightly different due to Eve's actions, to their reconciled raw keys, which are exactly the same. No provably correct efficient algorithm for information reconciliation suitable for QKD was known. All experimental implementations of QKD suffer significant channel losses, instrument imperfections etc., which have to be handled by additional classical two-way communication. One-way QKD becomes important in some critical / military scenarios. We design a strictly one-way QKD protocol that is end-to-end efficient, resilient and practical to implement on today's hardware. Using the 4 BB84 quantum states, it can ideally tolerate up to 50% losses without eavesdropping bit and instrument errors, or 11% bit and instrument errors without losses. A tradeoff exists between losses and bit errors, e.g. loss of 20% and bit error of 2% is tolerable in practice, which is a realistic figure. We also design new efficient resilient and practical two-way protocols with much lesser communication overhead than earlier works.

Threat Modeling for Security of Machine Learning Systems

Anoop Singhal

National Institute of Standards and Technology (NIST), Gaithersburg, USA
https://www.nist.gov/people/anoop-singhal

Abstract. In this presentation, we will present Threat Modeling techniques for security of ML systems using Causality Graphs. Threat Modeling looks at a system from an adversary's perspective to anticipate attack goals, and at a system's entry points to determine the functionality an adversary can exercise on the assets of a system. Vulnerabilities are discovered when a threat is investigated. Security experts can then propose defense mechanisms to mitigate the threats and thereby improve the overall security of the system.

Abstracts of Invited Talks and Tutorials

Reverse Engineering Industrial Control Devices

Nils Ole Tippenhauer

CISPA Helmholtz Center for Information Security, Saarbrücken, Germany
https://tippenhauer.de/

Abstract. Industrial Control Systems are the foundation of critical infrastructure systems such as the power grid or manufacturing. In such systems, Programmable Logic Controllers (PLCs) collect sensor information, compute appropriate control reactions in real time, and transmit these to actuators. Both hosts and network protocols in this context are usually proprietary, with unclear resilience against malicious manipulations. In this talk, I will provide an overview of recent work on the security assessment of such hosts and protocols, and discuss how the related unique challenges can be overcome.

Towards Developing Skills for Writing Great Papers and Giving Great Talks

Atul Prakash

University of Michigan, Ann Arbor, MI, USA
https://web.eecs.umich.edu/~aprakash/

Abstract. A huge aspect of being a Ph.D. student and becoming a researcher is communicating your research to others in your community via research papers and presentations. These skills of writing great papers and giving great talks take time to develop and can be a lifelong endeavor. This talk, primarily meant for Ph.D. students, is about some of the strategies to adopt towards developing those skills.

Federated Learning: Architecture, Threat Landscape, and Defence Mechanisms

Rajiv Ranjan[a] Devki Nandan Jha[b], and Tejal Shah[c]

Newcastle University, UK
[a]https://www.ncl.ac.uk/computing/people/profile/rajranjan.html
[b]https://www.ncl.ac.uk/computing/people/profile/devjha.html
[c]https://www.ncl.ac.uk/computing/people/profile/tejalshah.html

Abstract. Federated Learning (FL) is an emerging machine learning paradigm that enables collaborative model training across decentralized devices or servers holding local data, without exchanging the raw data itself. This privacy-preserving approach is increasingly adopted in applications such as mobile computing, healthcare, and finance, where data sensitivity and regulatory constraints are paramount. This tutorial will provide a comprehensive overview of FL, beginning with its core architecture, including the client-server model, communication protocols, and aggregation techniques such as Federated Averaging (FedAvg). We will delve into the practical challenges of FL, particularly those arising from non-IID data distributions, limited communication bandwidth, and device heterogeneity. A key focus of the tutorial will be the threat landscape in FL. We will explore a range of attacks including poisoning attacks, inference attacks, and model inversion, illustrating how adversaries can compromise model integrity or extract private information. The session will then transition into defence mechanisms, covering state-of-the-art techniques such as differential privacy, secure aggregation, and anomaly detection frameworks.

Kaniz Raisa, David Nandan Raju* and Iqbal Sarkar†

Newcastle University, UK

*https://www.ncl.ac.uk/computing/people/profile/profile.html
†https://www.ncl.ac.uk/computing/people/profile/profile.html
‡https://www.ncl.ac.uk/computing/people/profile/profile.html

Abstract. Federated Learning (FL) is an emerging machine learning paradigm that enables collaborative model training across decentralized devices or servers (including mobile), without exchanging the raw data itself. This privacy-preserving approach is increasingly adopted in applications such as mobile keyboard prediction and finance, where data sensitivity and regulatory constraints are paramount. This tutorial will provide a comprehensive overview of FL, from its core architecture, including the characteristics of its communication protocols and aggregation techniques such as federated averaging (FedAvg). We will dive into the practical enablement of FL, including its orchestration from FL deployment using unified communication frameworks, and describe the opportunities it offers to the industry with its decentralised nature. As this new approach of machine learning processing at the edge brings privacy, attacks and ... threat landscape, from new adversarial attacks which compromised model integrity or exfiltration of information. The section will then transition into defence mechanisms, discussing the range of state-of-the-art techniques — such as differential privacy, secure aggregation, and anomaly detection/mitigation.

Vajra-Sandbox: A Robust Framework for Malware Execution and Analysis

Manjesh Kumar Hanawal[a], Atul Kabra[b], and Prakhar Paliwal[a]

[a]Indian Institute of Technology Bombay,
[b]ReliaQuest
{mhanawal, 25D2020, prakhar.paliwal}@iitb.ac.in
https://www.ieor.iitb.ac.in/mhanawal

Abstract. Modern malware shows complex behavior and often uses clever tricks to avoid being detected by traditional setups designed to run the malware in safe and isolated environments. In this tutorial we will discuss design and implementation of a strong, high-fidelity malware sandbox that can safely run malicious binaries while resisting their anti-evasion strategies. Our sandbox, named Vajra-Sandbox, is built on VirtualBox-based virtualization with automated orchestration. It uses Osquery, an open-source operating system instrumentation framework, for in-depth system-level monitoring.

We discuss various hardening techniques used by Vajra-Sandbox to prevent the malware from detecting the isolation environment and performing evasions. This includes hiding the hypervisor, using realistic hardware settings, simulating user activity, aging systems, and quietly deploying logging agents. Vajra-Sandbox collects both dynamic and static data, such as process behavior, file system actions, registry changes, network communication, and memory snapshots. These behaviors are linked to the MITRE ATT&CK framework for tactical classification and further enhanced with threat intelligence from MISP.

After execution, a detailed malware report is automatically generated. This report includes visuals of the process tree, indicators of compromise related to files and networks, screenshots, and full-simulation video recordings. This framework improves malware visibility for security researchers, helps create detection rules, and integrates into machine learning processes for future threat classification. The resulting system shows high reliability in logging evasive malware behavior while keeping strong isolation and forensic depth.

Workshop

A Workshop on Digital Trust for IoT Ecosystems: From Secure Identities to Quantum Resilient Security

Centre for Development of Advanced Computing (C-DAC)
https://www.cdac.in/

Abstract. In today's hyperconnected world, every "thing" on the Internet must be validated before it can be trusted. This tutorial dwells on the evolving landscape of Digital Trust for IoT Ecosystems, from establishing secure device identities to managing digital certificates in dynamic environments. We also look ahead to the quantum era, where post-quantum cryptography (PQC) will redefine how devices authenticate and communicate securely. The participants will gain insights into designing end-to-end trustworthy IoT ecosystems through Public Key Infrastructure (PKI) that integrate identity, attestation, and cryptographic agility, ensuring long-term security in the face of evolving digital and quantum-era threats.

Contents

Access Control

An ML-Driven Adaptive Risk-Based Access Control for the Internet
of Drones (IoD) 3
    V. P. Jithu Vijay, Sabu M. Thampi, and T. Alwin Varghese

Optimizing Machine Learning Based Access Control Administration
Through Data Distillation 14
    Mohammad Nur Nobi, Md Shohel Rana, and Ram Krishnan

AI for Security

The Hidden Risks of LLM-Generated Web Application Code:
A Security-Centric Evaluation of Code Generation Capabilities in Large
Language Models 27
    Swaroop Dora, Deven Lunkad, Naziya Aslam, S. Venkatesan,
    and Sandeep Kumar Shukla

Frequency-Aware Deepfake Detection: Transformers vs. CNNs 38
    Aditi Panda, Srijit Kundu, Tanusree Ghosh, and Ruchira Naskar

NEXUS: Neuron Activation Scores Exploits for Unveiling Sensitive
Attributes 49
    Debasmita Manna and Somanath Tripathy

MazeNet: Protecting DNN Models on Public Cloud Platforms With TEEs 65
    Kripa Shanker, Vivek Kumar, Aditya Kanade, and Vinod Ganapathy

Automation and Risk: Transformers Models Reshape Sensitive
Information Management 85
    Wellington Fernandes Silvano, Maurício Konrath, Lucas Mayr,
    and Ricardo Felipe Custódio

A Secure Federated Learning Using Differential Privacy Mondrian
Clustering 104
    Rojalini Tripathy, Paladri Pranitha, B. U. Tejonath,
    and Padmalochan Bera

Attack Resilient Federated Learning Framework 115
    Sushant Kumar, Kasturi Routray, and Padmalochan Bera

SANVector: SBERT-APTNet Vector Framework for Cyber Threat Attack
Attribution Using Diversified CTI Logs 136
   Sougata Dolai, Annu Kumari, and Mayank Agarwal

Applied Cryptography

Cryptanalysis of Two Outsourced Ciphertext-Policy Attribute-Based
Encryption Schemes 151
   Koshalesh Meher and Y. Sreenivasa Rao

Dynamic Key-Constant Aggregate Encryption (DKCAE) for Secure Data
Sharing in Contemporary Computing 168
   Inarat Hussain, Devrikh Jatav, Gaurav Pareek, and B. R. Purushothama

Adversarial Attack on CryptoEyes from INFOCOM 2021 188
   Jashwanth Kadaru, Imtiyazuddin Shaik, and Srinivas Vivek

Randomness Efficient Algorithms for Estimating Average Gate Fidelity
via k-Wise Classical and Quantum Independence 208
   Aditya Nema and Pranab Sen

DoPQM: Devices Oriented Post-quantum Cryptographic Migration
Strategies for an Enterprise Network 231
   Amit Bhowmick, Divyesh Saglani, Lakshmi Padmaja Maddali,
   Akhila Rayala, Meena Singh Dilip Thakur,
   and Rajan Mindigal Alasingara Bhattachar

Cyber Security Case Study

Cyber Warfare During Operation Sindoor: Malware Campaign Analysis
and Detection Framework 245
   Prakhar Paliwal, Atul Kabra, and Manjesh Kumar Hanawal

Fraud Detection

Genetic-LAD: A Hybrid Approach for Financial Fraud Detection 269
   Nikhil Katiyar, Sneha Chauhan, Sugata Gangopadhyay,
   and Aditi Kar Gangopadhyay

Intrusion Detection

Curriculum Learning with Image Transformation and Explainable AI
for Improved Network Intrusion Detection 285
  Sathwik Narkedimilli, C. Pavan Kumar, and Raghavendra Ramachandra

SAAT: Stealthy Adversarial Attack on IDS in Cyber Physical Systems
Using Control Logic Induction 299
  Rajneesh Kumar Pandey and Tanmoy Kanti Das

Malware Detection

Enhancing Android Malware Detection with Federated Learning:
A Privacy-Preserving Approach to Strengthen Cyber Resilience 323
  Monalisa Meena, Jyoti Gajrani, Meenakshi Tripathi, Dhruv Suthar,
  Chetan Rawat, and Sweety Singhal

Network Security

Uncovering Security Weaknesses in srsRAN with CodeQL: A Static
Analysis Approach for Next-Gen RAN Systems 337
  Garrepelly Manideep, Sriram Sankaran, and Altaf Shaik

Systematic Literature Review of Vulnerabilities and Defenses in VPNs,
Tor, and Web Browsers 357
  Neha Agarwal, Ethan Mackin, Faiza Tazi, Mayank Grover,
  Rutuja More, and Sanchari Das

Security-Centric NWDAF Module for Threat Detection and Mitigation
in 5G Core Networks 376
  Lakshmi R. Nair, Adithya Anil, Preetam Mukherjee, and Manuj Aggarwal

Privacy

SoK: Evaluation of Methods for Privacy Preserving Edge Video Analytics 389
  Arun Joseph and Vinod Ganapathy

Privacy-Preserving Fair Text Summarization Using Federated Learning 411
  Aman Lachhiramka, Nibhrant Vaishnav, and Dheeraj Kumar

System Security

Self-learning Digital Twin for Kubernetes Security 433
  N. S. Devnath, Aayushman Singh, Adarsh Sasikumar,
  and Sriram Sankaran

Security and Privacy Assessment of U.S. and Non-U.S. Android
E-Commerce Applications 444
  Urvashi Kishnani and Sanchari Das

Adaptive MQTT Honeypots for IIoT Security Using Extended Mealy
Machines 455
  Saurabh Chamotra, Navdeep Singh, and Piyali Dutta

Modular Analysis of Attack Graphs for Smart Grid Security 466
  B. S. Smitha Rani, Preetam Mukherjee, and Mathias Ekstedt

Author Index 477

Access Control

An ML-Driven Adaptive Risk-Based Access Control for the Internet of Drones (IoD)

V. P. Jithu Vijay$^{(\boxtimes)}$ ⓘ, Sabu M. Thampi ⓘ, and T. Alwin Varghese

School of Computer Science and Engineering (SoCSE), Digital University Kerala, Technopark Phase IV, Pallippuram, Thiruvananthapuram 695317, Kerala, India
`{jithu.csres22,sabu.thampi,alwin.cs23}@duk.ac.in`

Abstract. The Internet of Drones (IoD) are rapidly gaining attraction due to their adaptability and diverse range of uses. However, the dynamic and distributed nature of IoD networks presents major security challenges, especially in managing access control. Traditional static access control methods are insufficient for adapting to the constantly changing scenarios and threats in drone operations. To address this limitation, dynamic access control approaches have been explored, where access decisions are based on real-time context. In this paper, we propose an ML-Driven Adaptive Risk-Based Access Control framework for the IoD, which continuously updates access permissions based on fluctuating risk levels from various drone operation parameters. The framework has been implemented, estimating the risk value from contextual features, drone-specific features, and Ground Control Station (GCS) parameters. Based on the estimated risk value, the access decision is made. A comparative analysis was performed between various ML models and their performance was evaluated using standard metrics. The results show that our proposed model is more effective in making accurate access decisions under varying environmental and operational conditions.

Keywords: Internet of Drones (IoD) · Unmanned Aerial Vehicles (UAV) · Risk-Based Access Control (RBAC) · Machine Learning · Security

1 Introduction

In recent years, the Internet of Drones (IoD) has gained significant attention for its flexibility, remote operability, and ability to function in diverse environments. Unlike traditional aircraft, drones are remotely or autonomously controlled using embedded sensors and onboard systems. A typical Unmanned Aircraft System (UAS) consists of multiple drones or Unmanned Aerial Vehicles (UAV) and a Ground Control Station (GCS) that coordinates their movement and data exchange [15]. As drones become more intelligent and interconnected, real-time communication with GCS and other drones introduces new security challenges,

N. Hubballi et al. (Eds.): ICISS 2025, LNCS 16380, pp. 3–13, 2026.
https://doi.org/10.1007/978-3-032-13714-2_1

especially when it comes to controlling which drone can access a particular region during different phases of their operation.

Access control refers to the security process that determines which drone is permitted to access specific regions, ensuring that only authorized drones can interact with sensitive regions, while denying access to unauthorized drones. Traditional models such as Discretionary Access Control, Mandatory Access Control, and Role-Based Access Control rely on fixed rules that cannot adapt to changing conditions. For instance, a drone initially assigned to a normal mission may require immediate access to a restricted area during an emergency. Static mechanisms cannot handle such changes effectively, leading to mission delays or incorrect denials. Real-world IoD systems require access decisions that respond dynamically to operational and contextual factors, such as battery level, payload, and environmental conditions [7].

Dynamic access control mechanisms address these limitations by continuously evaluating contextual and operational parameters to make real-time decisions. Techniques such as attribute-based, trust-based, and risk-based access control have been explored for such environments. Among these, Risk-Based Access Control (RBAC) stands out as the most suitable for IoD because it considers the current operational risks before granting access. By continuously assessing factors such as battery level, payload, and environmental conditions, it improves decision accuracy, safety, and reliability. In this paper, we propose an ML-Driven Adaptive RBAC framework for the IoD, which continuously updates access permissions based on the fluctuating risk value from various drone operation parameters.

The main contributions of this paper are as follows:

- This work introduces an adaptive risk-based access control framework utilizing machine learning to evaluate the real-time risk value of each drone and determine whether access is granted or denied.
- The final risk score is computed by analyzing contextual features, drone-specific attributes, and Ground Control Station parameters using a combination of Random Forest and Fuzzy Logic.
- A comparative analysis was performed among multiple machine learning models, and their performance was evaluated using standard evaluation metrics.

The rest of the paper is organized as follows. Section 2 describes the literature review of various RBAC models. The proposed methodology is discussed in Sect. 3 and Sect. 4 discusses the results obtained. Finally, the conclusion and future work are presented in Sect. 5.

2   Related Works

The IoD is a growing field that introduces new security threats, primarily due to unauthorized access. Therefore, strong access control mechanisms are essential to protect it from such vulnerabilities. Since there is no research on RBAC for the IoD yet, this section explores how RBAC has evolved in IoT networks over the past few years. Several works have focused on improving access control in the IoT by introducing risk-based and adaptive security techniques.

Hany et al. [3] proposed a Neuro-Fuzzy model that dynamically estimates risk in IoT systems using real-time data. It addressed the limitations of static access control but suffered from limited datasets, reducing its reliability in practical scenarios. Habib et al. [6] emphasized the use of contextual information (user location, device status, environment) in adaptive security decisions. Their method improved responsiveness but was prone to errors if the context was misread, leading to unintended access denials. Atlam et al. [4] introduced a fuzzy logic-based model incorporating user attributes, action severity, and past behavior to determine access. Although flexible, it heavily relies on expert knowledge and fine-tuning of fuzzy logic rules, which introduce bias.

In another study, Hany et al. [2] proposed a dynamic risk-based access control model with smart contracts to track user actions and dynamically adjust access during sessions. While effective in improving security, this method is complex and might struggle with performance and scalability issues. Finally, Rath et al. [12] proposed a behavior-based dynamic access control system for IoT, where permissions are determined by risk levels. However, the method is quite complex and slow down performance, especially when used in large IoT systems where quick and accurate risk calculations are necessary.

From the reviewed studies, it is clear that RBAC techniques used in IoT systems provide valuable direction to improve security in the IoD. Approaches such as neuro-fuzzy models, context-aware frameworks, and adaptive decision-making systems show promising results in dynamically managing access decisions based on real-time data. These methods can be adapted to suit the rapidly changing conditions faced in drone operations. The addition of environmental context, user behavior, and mission-specific parameters can help to adjust access permissions more accurately. By applying these techniques to the IoD, access control systems can become more responsive, flexible, and capable of handling access decisions effectively in rapidly changing IoD environments.

3 Proposed Methodology: ML-Driven Adaptive Risk-Based Access Control for the Internet of Drones (IoD)

Risk can be defined as the loss or damage that may arise from future events, often resulting in adverse outcomes. Mathematically, risk is often quantified using the formula (1):

$$\text{Quantified Risk} = \text{Likelihood} \times \text{Impact} \tag{1}$$

Here, likelihood represents the probability of an incident occurring in a specific sub-region based on real-time contextual, drone-specific features, and GCS parameters. The impact refers to the severity of the incident, which depends on the sensitivity of the sub-region. By combining these two components, the proposed system computes the risk value for each requesting drone in real-time.

Figure 1 shows the proposed ML-driven adaptive risk-based access control framework. We consider a city with different entities such as hospitals, schools, government offices, private organizations, military facilities, and major junctions. A drone-based surveillance system is used to monitor the entire city, which is divided into four sub-regions based on the sensitivity level of each area. For that we have an IoD network to monitor these four sub-regions, and it is connected to the GCS. Each sub-regions in the city is associated with a certain risk value based on the sensitivity level. Initially, the identity of each drone is verified using a suitable authentication mechanism. Assuming the drone is already authenticated, and it requests access to monitor a particular sub-region.

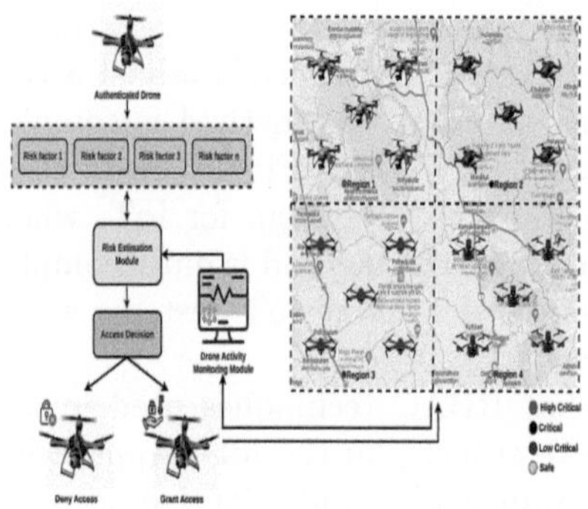

Fig. 1. Proposed framework of ML-Driven Adaptive RBAC for the IoD.

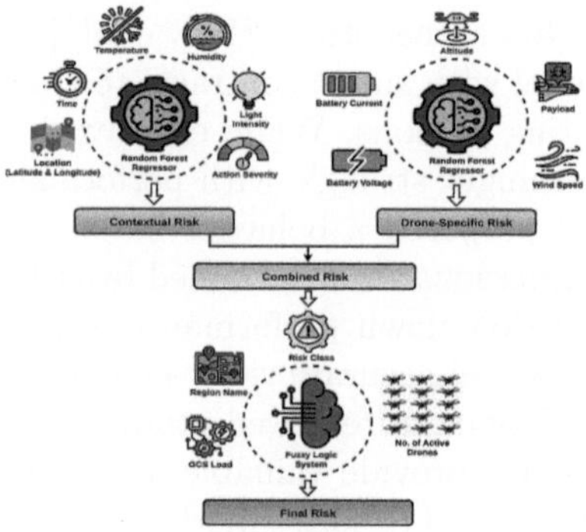

Fig. 2. Risk Estimation Module.

The risk estimation module shown in Fig. 2 computes the overall risk based on three components (contextual, drone-specific, and GCS), each comprising different risk factors. In the first phase, a Random Forest Regressor is trained on the contextual dataset (includes risk factors such as location, time, temperature, humidity, light intensity, and the action severity of the specific sub-region) to model the relationship between contextual features and risk values. Similarly, in the second phase, another Random Forest Regressor is trained on the drone-specific dataset (includes risk factors such as battery voltage, current battery level, altitude, payload, and wind speed) to predict the risk based on drone parameters. The risks from these two components are then combined and mapped to a risk class (ranging from 1 to 8). Finally, using the GCS parameters, which include risk factors such as the no. of drones, GCS load, and access region, along with the risk class, the final risk value is computed using fuzzy logic. Based on this final risk value, an access decision is made to determine whether access is granted or denied. If access is granted, the drone is added to the IoD network of the corresponding authorized sub-region. Algorithm 1 outlines the procedure for calculating the overall risk value for each drone. The drone activity module shown in Fig. 1 will monitor the authorized drones movements in real-time. If any drone deviates from its authorized sub-region to another unauthorized sub-region, this module will generate an alert, and the risk estimation module again recalculates the risk based on the current context. The new estimated risk value is again analyzed and dynamically adjusts the permission in real-time.

Algorithm 1. Risk Prediction and Access Control

1: **Load Datasets:** Load contextual dataset $D_c = \{X_c, y_c\}$ and drone-specific dataset $D_d = \{X_d, y_d\}$.

2: **Contextual Risk Prediction:** Train RF RF_c on D_c.

3: For input x_c, predict $\hat{y}_c = \frac{1}{T} \sum_{t=1}^{T} h_t(x_c)$.
   Drone Risk Prediction: Train RF RF_d on D_d.
   For input x_d, predict $\hat{y}_d = \frac{1}{T} \sum_{t=1}^{T} h_t(x_d)$.

4: **Combine Risks:**
   Compute $\hat{y}_{comb} = \alpha \hat{y}_c + (1 - \alpha)\hat{y}_d$ and map to class $C_i = \lceil 8 \cdot \hat{y}_{comb} \rceil$.

5: **Fuzzy Logic System:** Define membership functions for risk class, number of drones, control station load, requested region, and access chance.
   Construct fuzzy rules using these parameters.

6: **Access Control Decision:** Provide input values (combined risk class, no. of drones, ground control station load, access region) to the fuzzy engine. Compute access score S_{access} and compare with threshold $\theta = 50$.

7: **if** $S_{access} \geq \theta$ **then**
   Grant access.

8: **else**
   Deny access.

9: **end if**=0

---

4 Experimental Results

4.1 Experimental Setup

In this section, the proposed risk prediction framework is evaluated using various ML models that predict the risk value based on both contextual and drone-specific features. The evaluated models include Random Forest, Gradient Boosting, Linear Regression, Ridge Regression, Decision Tree, K-Nearest Neighbour (KNN), and Support Vector Regression (SVR). For each model, R^2, Root Mean Square Error (RMSE), Accuracy, and F1-score are computed. The best performing model, Random Forest, is then integrated with a Fuzzy Logic system to compute the final risk value, based on which the access decision is made.

Dataset: Here, we use two datasets to predict the initial risk: one from contextual features and the other from drone-specific features. The contextual feature dataset is prepared by selecting a specific region on the map. This region is divided into four sub-regions, namely R1, R2, R3, and R4, based on the sensitivity of the area. Latitude and longitude data for each sub-region were randomly collected. Using DHT11 and LDR sensors connected to Arduino, we collected temperature, humidity, and light intensity data for the selected region at regular intervals over one week, along with time records (0 for day and 1 for night). We also considered an extra parameter, called action severity, which evaluates how a specific action impacts a particular region concerning confidentiality, integrity, and availability in drone operations. These features were chosen because previous studies [6,10,11] have shown that contextual information has an important role in making better access decisions. To create the risk labels, each data record was assigned a value between 0 and 1 depending on the sensitivity of the sub-region it belongs to. We divided the risk values into four ranges: 0 to 0.25 for safe regions, 0.25 to 0.5 for low-critical regions, 0.5 to 0.75 for critical regions, and 0.75 to 1.0 for high-critical regions. Thus, the contextual dataset includes features such as Latitude, Longitude, Time, Temperature, Humidity, Light Intensity, and Action Severity as independent variables, while the risk value (ranging from 0 to 1) is considered the target variable.

For creating the drone-specific dataset, the work in [13] involved conducting 209 autonomous flights of a small quadcopter package delivery drone. In each flight, the drone was programmed to take off, follow a predefined route, and land, while altering various operational parameters. The drone carried onboard sensors, including GPS, IMU, voltage and current sensors, as well as an ultrasonic anemometer to capture detailed measurements of inertial motion, wind speed, and power usage. Parameters such as ground speed, payload weight, and cruising altitude were systematically changed during each flight. From this large dataset, we sorted the drones from high to low performance based on features such as flight time, battery voltage, battery current, speed, payload, and altitude. The top 20 high-performing drone feature sets are assigned to the high-critical region. Similarly, the next 20 are assigned to the next critical region, the following 20 to the low-critical region, and the final 20 to the safe region.

The drone-specific dataset includes a wide range of independent variables, including Drone Type, Flight Time, Wind Speed, Wind Angle, Battery Voltage, Battery Current, Position X, Position Y, Position Z, Orientation X, Orientation Y, Orientation Z, Orientation W, Velocity X, Velocity Y, Velocity Z, Angular X, Angular Y, Angular Z, Linear Acceleration X, Linear Acceleration Y, Linear Acceleration Z, Speed, Payload, and Altitude. From these, we selected features such as battery voltage, battery current, altitude, payload, and wind speed for drone-specific risk modeling because each of these factors has been shown to deeply influence drone performance and safety. Battery voltage and battery current reflect the battery health and power capacity, which are essential for maintaining flight integrity and avoiding mid-air failures [1,5,8]. Payload weight influences lift, balance, and power draw, thereby increasing strain on propulsion systems and battery under heavier loads [5]. Altitude affects aerodynamics and control responsiveness, influencing how drones behave under environmental stress [9]. Wind speed is a major external factor that disrupts stability, trajectory, and flight feasibility, especially under adverse conditions [14]. The risk value, which ranges from 0 to 1, is used as the target variable for modeling and is assigned to each record in a similar way as in the contextual dataset.

4.2   Results and Discussion

This section presents the experimental findings obtained from the proposed adaptive risk evaluation framework. It demonstrates the effectiveness of different ML algorithms in estimating risks based on contextual and drone-specific features, outlines the reason behind the chosen model, and explains how the final access decision is determined using a fuzzy logic-based control system.

Contextual and Drone-Specific Risk Model Performance: The main objective was to build reliable models for estimating two distinct types of risk. To achieve this, we evaluated and compared the performance of seven different regression algorithms for both tasks. The detailed results of this comparison are shown in Table 1.

Table 1. Performance metrics of different ML models for predicting Contextual and Drone-specific risk.

Model	Contextual				Drone-Specific			
	R^2	RMSE	Accuracy	F1	R^2	RMSE	Accuracy	F1
Gradient Boosting	0.9825	0.0380	0.8802	0.8729	0.8794	0.0999	0.8117	0.8115
Linear Regression	0.9837	0.0368	0.8854	0.8779	0.8374	0.1161	0.7896	0.7910
Ridge Regression	0.9837	0.0368	0.8854	0.8779	0.8374	0.1161	0.7895	0.7909
SVR (RBF)	0.9717	0.0484	0.8750	0.8748	0.8937	0.0938	0.8252	0.8260
Decision Tree	0.9695	0.0502	0.8542	0.8535	0.9106	0.0861	0.8461	0.8459
KNN	0.9777	0.0429	0.8698	0.8642	0.9470	0.0662	0.8680	0.8660
Random Forest	**0.9802**	**0.0405**	**0.8724**	**0.8671**	**0.9486**	**0.0652**	**0.8697**	**0.8680**

For contextual risk prediction, the initial results showed Linear Regression performed the best on the test set with an R^2 of 0.9837 and an RMSE of 0.0368, which was the lowest. Despite these strong performance metrics, the model exhibited a major drawback: it frequently generated risk values outside the acceptable range of $[0, 1]$ when exposed to new data. This lack of constraint make it not suitable for real-world application. The Random Forest model, on the other hand, performed well at the cost of a slightly lower R^2 of 0.9802 by producing predictions within the valid range consistently. Due to its robustness and reliability, Random Forest was selected over Linear Regression. Feature analysis showed 'Action_Severity' and location parameters (latitude and longitude) to be the strongest predictors, confirming the expectation that the intended action and location are important determinants of contextual risk.

In the case of drone-specific risk prediction, the Random Forest model also emerged as the most effective among all the evaluated algorithms. It achieved the highest R^2 score of 0.9486 and the lowest RMSE value of 0.0652, demonstrating strong predictive capability. As observed in the contextual risk scenario, linear regression-based models lacked the reliability needed for consistent performance. The strong results from the Random Forest model can be attributed to its strength in capturing complex, and non-linear interactions among the various drone-specific parameters.

Figures 3 and 4 present the classification and discriminative power of the Random Forest models for both contextual and drone-specific risk prediction tasks. The confusion matrices (Fig. 3) present high accuracy for all risk classes, with dominant diagonal values reflecting minimal misclassification. In contrast, the ROC curves (Fig. 4) confirm the models' good discriminative power, with AUC values all greater than 0.98 in both contexts.

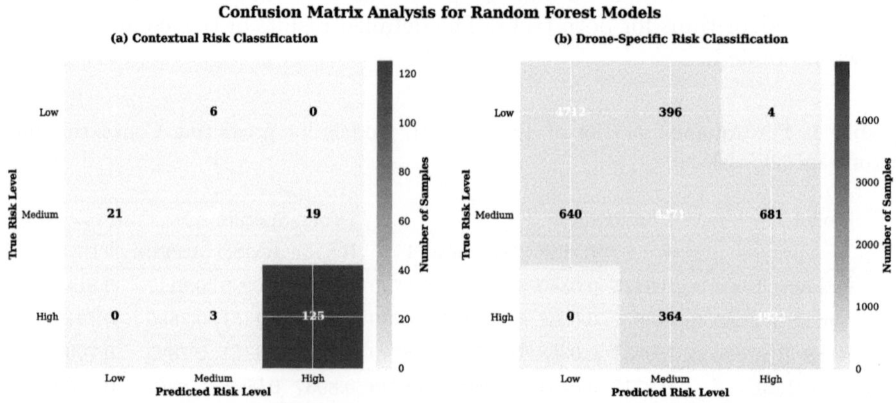

Fig. 3. Confusion Matrix Analysis for Random Forest Models: (a) Contextual Risk Classification shows strong diagonal dominance with minimal misclassifications. (b) Drone-Specific Risk Classification effectively captures risk even at larger scales.

Integration of Risk Assessment model with Fuzzy Logic System: In the final stage, contextual and drone-specific risk values are combined by taking their average, and this combined value is mapped to a risk class from 1 to 8. This mapped risk class, along with three other inputs such as the no. of active drones, the current GCS load, and the requested region, is given to a fuzzy inference system. For each of these inputs, we define triangular membership functions. The risk is divided into low, medium, high, and very high; the number of drones is divided into few, moderate, many, and full; the control room load is categorized as low, medium, and high; and the regions are represented as R1 to R4.

A set of fuzzy rules is then applied to make decisions. For instance, if the risk is low, the number of drones is few, the control room load is low, and the region is R1, then the access chance is high. As the risk level, number of drones, and GCS load increase, the access chance decreases. If the risk is very high or the drone capacity is full, the rules assign a low access chance, meaning access is denied. These rules are applied using Mamdani fuzzy inference to handle different uncertain conditions.

The fuzzy system gives a linguistic output (low, medium, or high access chance), which is then converted into a single numerical value using the centroid defuzzification method. This value is called the Access Score. If the Access Score is greater than or equal to the threshold value (50 in our case), the drone is granted access; otherwise, access is denied.

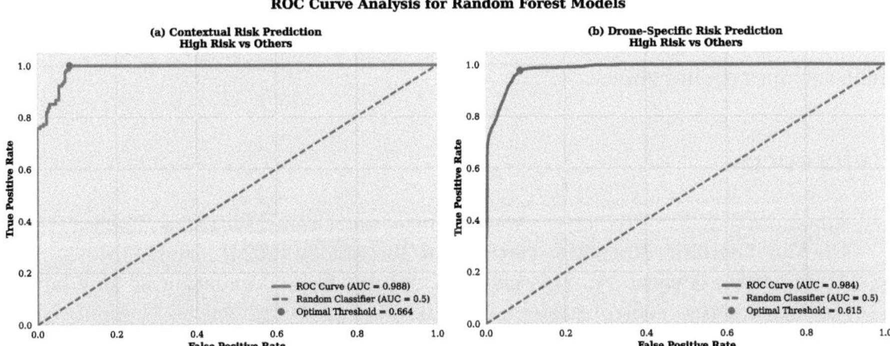

Fig. 4. ROC Curve Analysis for Random Forest Models: (a) Contextual Risk Prediction exhibits excellent discriminative power (AUC = 0.988). (b) Drone-Specific Risk Prediction also performs well with AUC = 0.984, indicating strong binary risk classification capabilities.

5   Conclusion and Future Scope

In this paper, we proposed an ML-driven adaptive risk-based access control framework for the IoD systems. The proposed framework dynamically adjusts drone access permissions based on the real-time estimation of operational risk, incorporating both contextual and drone-specific features. Risk evaluation was performed using Random Forest regressor model, and final access decisions were made through a fuzzy logic-based inference system that considers Ground Control Station parameters. The framework shows improved adaptability over traditional static models by continuously evaluating real-time contextual features such as location, time, temperature, humidity, light intensity and action severity, along with drone-specific features including battery status, altitude, payload and wind speed, and Ground Control Station parameters such as the number of drones, control room load and access region, to dynamically adjust access decisions in response to changing drone behavior and surroundings. Experimental evaluation shows that the proposed framework is capable of making accurate and context-aware access decisions in real time, thereby improving the overall security and resilience of IoD networks. In the future, this framework can be extended to handle new and emerging threats in IoD systems more effectively. The capability of the proposed framework can be further enhanced by integrating traditional Role-Based Access Control mechanisms. By combining role assignments with real-time risk evaluation, the IoD system can enforce more context-aware and fine-grained access decisions, improving both security and operational flexibility. Also, the optimization of the fuzzy logic rules, which currently rely on manual tuning. Automating this process using adaptive techniques such as reinforcement learning could improve accuracy and reduce human bias. As IoD systems scale up, ensuring computational efficiency will be important, especially when handling multiple drones and continuous data streams in real time. Incorporating federated learning models would allow decentralized nodes to collaboratively update risk estimations while preserving data privacy across different operational zones.

References

1. Almannaei, K.J.: Predictive Maintenance on Drone Batteries Failure Using Machine Learning. Rochester Institute of Technology (2024)
2. Atlam, H.F., Alenezi, A., Hussein, R.K., Wills, G.B.: Validation of an adaptive risk-based access control model for the internet of things. Int. J. Comput. Netw. Inf. Secur. **15**(1), 26 (2018)
3. Atlam, H.F., Azad, M.A., Fadhel, N.F.: Efficient NFS model for risk estimation in a risk-based access control model. Sensors **22**(5), 2005 (2022)
4. Atlam, H.F., Walters, R.J., Wills, G.B., Daniel, J.: Fuzzy logic with expert judgment to implement an adaptive risk-based access control model for IoT. Mob. Netw. Appl. **26**(6), 2545–2557 (2021)
5. Gatscher, J., Breitenbach, J., Buettner, R.: Machine learning-based power consumption prediction for unmanned aerial vehicles in dynamic environments (2023)
6. Habib, K., Leister, W.: Context-aware authentication for the internet of things. In: Eleventh International Conference on Autonomic and Autonomous Systems Fined, pp. 134–139 (2015)
7. Jithu Vijay, V.P., Thampi, S.M.: Navigating the Skies: Exploring Dynamic Access Control in the Internet of Drones (IoD), pp. 345–380. Springer, Cham (2025). https://doi.org/10.1007/978-3-031-82826-3_10
8. Kulkarni, C., Hogge, E., Quach, C.C.: Remaining flying time prediction implementing battery prognostics framework for electric UAV's. Technical report (2018)
9. Mahadi, A.M., Kamal, N.L.M., Omran, A., Sahwee, Z., Norhashim, N., Shah, S.A.: Altitude effects on cellular-connected UAV performance and video transmission efficiency: empirical analysis and recommendations. Defence S&T Tech. Bull. **17**(2) (2024)
10. Merlec, M.M., In, H.P.: SC-CAAC: a smart-contract-based context-aware access control scheme for blockchain-enabled IoT systems. IEEE Internet Things J. **11**(11), 19866–19881 (2024)
11. Nguyen, P., Nguyen, H.H., Phung, P., Truong, H.L., Cheung, T.: Advanced context-sensitive access management for edge-driven IoT data sharing as a service. ACM Trans. Internet Technol. **25**(2), 1–31 (2025)
12. Rath, T.A., Colin, J.N.: Adaptive risk-aware access control model for internet of things. In: 2017 International Workshop on Secure Internet of Things (SIoT), pp. 40–49. IEEE (2017)
13. Rodrigues, T.A., et al.: In-flight positional and energy use data set of a DJI Matrice 100 quadcopter for small package delivery. Sci. Data **8**(1), 155 (2021)

14. Wang, B.H., Wang, D.B., Ali, Z.A., Ting Ting, B., Wang, H.: An overview of various kinds of wind effects on unmanned aerial vehicle. Measur. Control **52**(7–8), 731–739 (2019)
15. Zuo, Z., Liu, C., Han, Q.L., Song, J.: Unmanned aerial vehicles: control methods and future challenges. IEEE/CAA J. Autom. Sinica **9**(4), 601–614 (2022)

Optimizing Machine Learning Based Access Control Administration Through Data Distillation

Mohammad Nur Nobi[1(✉)], Md Shohel Rana[2], and Ram Krishnan[3(✉)]

[1] Institute for Cyber Security (ICS), The University of Texas at San Antonio (UTSA), San Antonio, TX 78249, USA
`mohammadnur.nobi@my.utsa.edu`
[2] School of Computing, Georgia Southern University, Statesboro, GA 30460, USA
`mrana@georgiasouthern.edu`
[3] ICS, Department of Computer Engineering, UTSA, San Antonio, TX 78249, USA
`ram.krishnan@utsa.edu`

Abstract. Machine learning-based access control (MLBAC) shows promise in effectively determining access in complex scenarios where a trained ML model makes decisions. When access policies change, the underlying ML model must be updated to accommodate these changes. This process requires a portion of past training data, known as *Replay Data*, along with the new changes to retain existing knowledge and avoid challenges like catastrophic forgetting. Traditionally, Replay Data is selected randomly, constituting a large portion (approximately 25%) of the historical data, and often does not adequately represent the overall data distribution. This paper proposes a systematic approach to selecting Replay Data using active learning-based data distillation, resulting in a more compact (approximately 10% of the training data) and representative dataset. We thoroughly examine the proposed method and assess the effectiveness of the developed Replay Data. Our evaluation demonstrates that, even with this more compact Replay Data, the ML model can retain its past knowledge with impressive accuracy, ranging from 96.5% to 98.5%.

Keywords: Access control · MLBAC Administration

1 Introduction

As technology continues to evolve in areas such as big data, the Internet of Things (IoT), cloud computing, and edge computing, there is a growing need for dynamic and highly efficient access control systems to keep up with these advancements. The application of machine learning (ML) to solve different access control problems, such as policy mining and attribute engineering for ABAC [1,2], or role mining for RBAC [10] systems, is significant. Beyond optimizing problems with legacy access control systems, researchers have recently proposed using trained

N. Hubballi et al. (Eds.): ICISS 2025, LNCS 16380, pp. 14–24, 2026.
https://doi.org/10.1007/978-3-032-13714-2_2

ML models to make more robust and generalized access control decisions, supplementing or eventually replacing legacy systems [11,13]. These systems, known as machine learning-based access control (MLBAC) [8,11,13], can capture the access control state with significantly higher accuracy than traditional models such as ABAC or RBAC [8,11,13]. We provide a further overview of these models in Sect. 2.

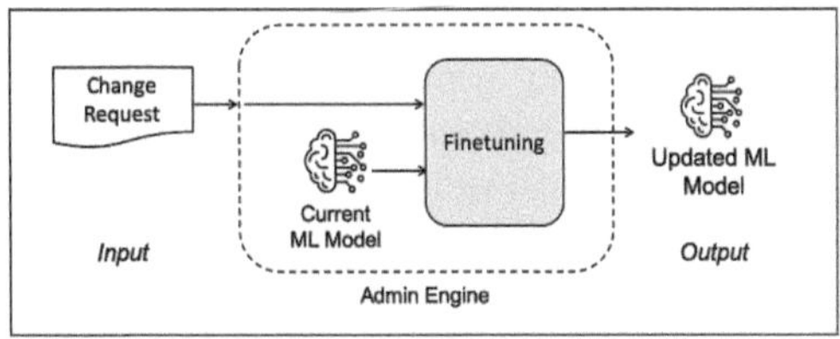

Fig. 1. Overview of the MLBAC Administration.

Access control policies, like many systems, are dynamic and require ongoing updates to reflect changes in users, resources, or organizational structure. For instance, if a user's access must be revoked due to a change, the administrator updates the policy accordingly–a process known as *access control administration* [7,17]. Unlike ABAC or RBAC, which update policies or roles, MLBAC handles changes by adjusting the weights and parameters of its ML model.

As proposed by Nobi et al. [12] and illustrated in Fig. 1, the administration framework (Admin Engine) takes a change request and the current ML model–responsible for existing access control decisions–as input. Over time, the model requires frequent updates to reflect system changes. However, this continual learning process is complex and presents several challenges. A major issue, highlighted by Nobi et al. [12], is catastrophic forgetting, where the updated model loses its prior access control knowledge. This well-known ML problem has prompted various solutions [6,16]. State-of-the-art MLBAC administration addresses this by using Replay Data–a subset of access control history–alongside new changes during model updates [12,16].

Nobi et al. [12] proposed randomly selecting about 25% of training data as Replay Data to reduce storage and security concerns. However, this method may fall short for two key reasons: First, random selection might not adequately represent the full dataset, potentially biasing the model toward certain classes or inputs. Second, storing a quarter of the data remains burdensome for many systems. Thus, further minimizing Replay Data size is essential.

To address both issues, this paper proposes a more effective alternative to random selection: distilling the access control history into a compact, representative Replay Data set, as shown in Fig. 2. Here, the change request is expressed through Tasks and Criteria, defined in detail in Sect. 3.1. This approach ensures that distilled data preserves the essence of the original dataset, maintains comparable or improved performance, and significantly reduces Replay Data size.

To our knowledge, this is the first data distillation method designed specifically for training and administration in ML-based access control systems. Our key contributions are summarized below.

- We introduce an active learningbased data distillation method using uncertainty to generate Replay Data, addressing catastrophic forgetting in access control administration.
- Our framework produces a compact and representative Replay Data set–just 10% of the training data, compared to 25% in prior work.
- We validate our approach using a publicly available synthetic access control dataset, demonstrating its effectiveness.
- Evaluation shows that even with reduced Replay Data, the ML model retains prior knowledge with high accuracy (96.5%98.5%), highlighting the quality of the distilled data.

Paper Organization. Section 2 reviews related work on access control administration and data distillation. Section 3 introduces an active learning-based framework for generating replay data. Section 4 presents experimental results and key findings. Finally, Sect. 5 concludes the paper.

2   Related Study

This section reviews research on data distillation and MLBAC, where ML models replace traditional access control policies. We first examine data distillation in access control, noting that our approach is the first in this domain. Distillation has gained traction for optimizing ML systems by reducing data needs. Rana et al. introduced DEEPDISTAL [15], applying active learning to select informative samples for Deepfake detection, reducing computation while maintaining accuracy in resource-limited settings. Active learning enhances distillation by lowering labeling costs. Hino et al. [4] surveyed key trends, while Konyushkova et al. [9] and Hsu and Lin [5] developed adaptive and meta-learning frameworks for task-specific systems. We then explore ML models for access control. Karimi et al. [8] proposed a reinforcement learning (RL) framework where an agent learns access policies via user feedback. Nobi et al. [13] introduced DLBAC, using deep neural networks trained on authorization tuples to improve decision accuracy. Chhetri et al. [3] extended this with $DLBAC_{Env}$, incorporating environmental metadata for context-aware access decisions. For MLBAC administration, Nobi et al. [12] pioneered a framework addressing challenges like catastrophic forgetting, where updated models lose prior knowledge. Our work builds on theirs, focusing on systematic Replay Data generation to mitigate this issue. We compare our results with their framework in Sect. 4.2.

3   Methodology

Figure 2 illustrates the MLBAC administration framework and contrasts our proposed method with the state-of-the-art. Originally introduced by Nobi et

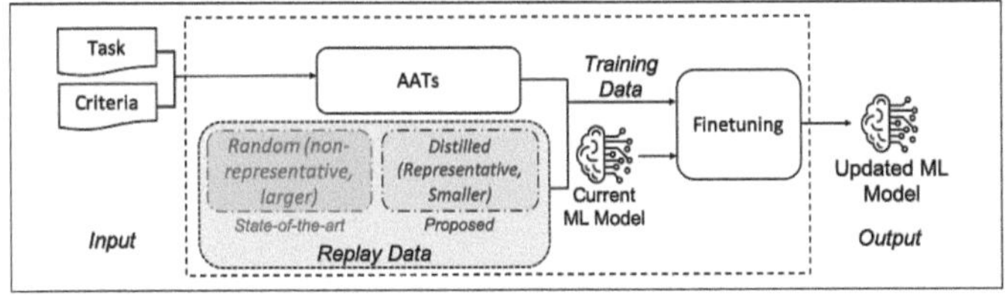

Fig. 2. Comparison of Replay Data Mechanism in MLBAC Administration.

al. [12], we adopt this framework with key modifications to the Replay Data generation process. Rather than relying on random sampling, we introduce a systematic approach using a distillation framework. The goal is to extract a compact subset that preserves the essential features of the original data. Our active learning-based distillation method produces highly representative training data with minimal size. Section 3.2 provides further details on this framework.

3.1 Terminologies

This section introduces several terminologies, defined in [12], that are repeatedly used in the explanation of administration in MLBAC.

- **Authorization Tuple.** An Authorization Tuple is a user-permissions tuple $\langle user, resource, permissions \rangle$ that specifies the permissions of a *user* to a *resource*. For example, an Authorization Tuple $\langle Alice, Document1, \{read, write\} \rangle$ indicates that a user *Alice* has operations *read* and *write* access to a resource *Document1*.
- **Task.** A **Task** is a change request represented as a tuple $\langle user, resource, operation, access \rangle$, where *access* can be either *permit* or *deny*. For example, the Task $\langle Alice, Document1, write, deny \rangle$ represents a request to revoke Alice's write access to Document1.
- **Criteria.** A *Criteria* is defined as a tuple of user and resource metadata namevalue pairs, expressed as $\langle \{umeta_0 \in \{val_0, \ldots, val_i\}, \ldots, umeta_m \in \{val_0, \ldots, val_j\}\}, \{rmeta_0 \in \{val_0, \ldots, val_k\}, \ldots, rmeta_n \in \{val_0, \ldots, val_l\}\} \rangle$, where $\{umeta_0, umeta_1, \ldots, umeta_m\}$ is a set of user metadata names, $\{rmeta_0, rmeta_1, \ldots, rmeta_n\}$ is a set of resource metadata names, and each $\{val_0, \ldots\}$ represents possible values for the corresponding metadata. For example, a sample *Criteria* could be $\langle umeta1 \in \{val_0, val_1\}, rmeta4 \in \{val_2\} \rangle$, meaning that $umeta1$ can be val_0 or val_1, and $rmeta4$ can be val_2.
- **AAT.** AAT (Admin Authorization Tuple) is an updated Authorization Tuple generated from an existing one based on a Task. For example, $\langle Alice, Document1, \{write, deny\} \rangle$ is a given *Task*. Suppose that the existing Authorization Tuple in the system for user *Alice* and resource *Document1* is $\langle Alice, Document1, \{read, \{write\}\} \rangle$. The AAT with respect to the given Task would be $\langle Alice, Document1, \{read\} \rangle$. AAT, in effect, is the change that

the admin seeks to make. The Admin Engine internally generates some similar AAT based on users and resources similar to the user and resource in the Task and the input Criteria. All the changes are combined as **AATs**.

3.2   Active Learning Framework for Replay Data Distillation

The proposed algorithm applies active learning to iteratively distill a dataset by querying the most uncertain samples from an unlabeled pool. This reduces labeling effort, improves model performance, and ensures representativeness. The workflow includes initialization, learner setup, uncertainty-based querying, and dataset construction. Unlike static feature-based methods (e.g., Feature Ranking, Feature-Weighted Sampling), our approach dynamically computes uncertainty per iteration, enabling balanced selection across feature and label spaces while reducing redundancy.

Given a dataset (e.g., access control logs), the framework requires an initial labeled fraction ($\leq 10\%$), a query budget, and batch size. These determine the number of iterations and queried samples. While empirically chosen in this study, they can be tuned using Bayesian optimization, grid search, or adaptive stopping. Smaller datasets used budgets of 10–50; larger ones used up to 100.

The process begins by splitting the dataset D into D_{train} (labeled, $m\%$) and D_{pool} (unlabeled, $(100-m)\%$), with an empty set D_{queried} to store selected samples. A base classifier h (e.g., Random Forest) is trained on D_{train}. The uncertainty for a sample $x_i \in D_{\text{pool}}$ is computed as $u(x_i) = 1 - \max_k p_k$ for single-label classification, or $u_{\text{mean}}(x_i) = \frac{1}{L} \sum_{l=1}^{L} (1 - \max p_k^{(l)})$ for multi-label tasks, where L is the number of labels. At each iteration t, the most uncertain samples in the top B form the query set Q_t, which is added to D_{train} and D_{queried}, and removed from D_{pool}. The model is retrained on the updated D_{train}. The loop continues until the query budget is exhausted or D_{pool} is empty. The final evaluation is conducted on a held-out test set D_{test}. The distilled dataset is then defined as $D_{\text{distilled}} = D_{\text{train-initial}} \cup D_{\text{queried}}$, with size $|D_{\text{distilled}}| = |D_{\text{train-initial}}| + \sum_{t=1}^{N} |Q_t|$. While $D_{\text{distilled}}$ and the final D_{train} are equivalent, we define it separately to emphasize its role as a curated replay buffer for MLBAC policy updates.

These adaptations enable a 60% reduction in replay size (from 25% to 10%) while retaining 96.5–98.5% accuracy, directly addressing the catastrophic forgetting challenge in MLBAC administration.

4   Evaluation

4.1   Implementation

Active Learning Parameters and Configuration. To evaluate the proposed active learning-based distillation method, we conducted experiments on the public dataset described in Sect. 4.1, aiming to assess how well the distilled replay set preserves model performance while reducing labeling and storage costs.

Algorithm 1. MLBAC-Tailored Active Learning for Replay Data Distillation

---

Input: Initial dataset, $D = \{X, Y\}$, where X represents input features, and Y represents labels; Fraction of data for initial training set, m; Maximum number of iterations, N; Uncertainty scoring function (single- or multi-label), $u(\cdot)$; Batch size, B (number of samples queried per iteration); Base classifier, c (e.g., Random Forest).

Output: Final distilled replay dataset, $D_{\text{distilled}}$

Steps:

1: Split D into:
   - **Training pool:** $D_{\text{train-initial}} = \{X_{\text{train}}, Y_{\text{train}}\}$, contains $m\%$ of D.
   - **Query pool:** $D_{\text{pool}} = \{X_{\text{pool}}, Y_{\text{pool}}\}$, contains remaining $(D - m)\%$ of D.
   - Set $D_{\text{train}} \leftarrow D_{\text{train-initial}}$ and initialize $Q \leftarrow \varnothing$ (aggregated queried samples).
2: **Train initial model:** Train classifier C on D_{train}
3: Iterative Active Learning Loop
   - **Score uncertainties:** For each $x_i \in D_{\text{pool}}$, compute:
       1. Single-label: $u(x_i) = 1 - \max_k p_k$
       2. Multi-label: $u_{\text{mean}}(x_i) = \frac{1}{L} \sum_{l=1}^{L} \left(1 - \max_k p_k^{(l)}\right)$
   - **Select queried set:** $Q_t \leftarrow$ Top-B samples with highest uncertainty
   - **Update datasets:** $D_{\text{train}} \leftarrow D_{\text{train}} \cup Q_t$; $Q \leftarrow Q \cup Q_t$; $D_{\text{pool}} \leftarrow D_{\text{pool}} \setminus Q_t$
   - **Retrain model:** Train C on updated D_{train}
   - **Early stopping:** Stop if accuracy improvement $< \tau$ over last two iterations
4: **Construct distilled dataset:** $D_{\text{distilled}} \leftarrow D_{\text{train-initial}} \cup Q$
5: **return** $D_{\text{distilled}}$

The dataset was preprocessed following [12], with full reproducibility details provided herein. Samples were normalized and encoded into feature vectors compatible with a Random Forest classifier. The full dataset D was partitioned as follows: (i) $D_{\text{train-initial}}$ (10%) for model initialization, (ii) D_{pool} (90%) for iterative querying, and (iii) D_{test} (20 %) as a separate holdout set for final evaluation.

Parameter Selection and Automation. As discussed in Sect. 3.2, the query budget (N) and batch size (B) determine the number of iterations and samples selected per round. While initially set empirically based on validation performance, these parameters can be automated using Bayesian optimization (to balance cost and accuracy), adaptive stopping (e.g., halting when accuracy gain falls below 0.5% over two rounds), or dataset-size scaling (smaller N and B for compact datasets to reduce redundancy, larger values for broader coverage in larger datasets).

Active Learning Loop Execution. The base classifier h was trained on D_{train} and refined iteratively via uncertainty sampling. At each iteration t, the top B most uncertain samples from D_{pool} were selected as Q_t, labeled, and added to the training set. The total queried set is defined as $Q = \bigcup_{t=1}^{N} Q_t$, representing the union of all queried samples across iterations, distinguishing per-round sets (Q_t) from the aggregated replay set (Q). Uncertainty was computed as $u(x_i) = 1 - \max_k p_k$ for single-label classification, where p_k is the predicted probability for class k, and as $u_{\mathrm{mean}}(x_i) = \frac{1}{L}\sum_{l=1}^{L}(1 - \max p_k^{(l)})$ for multi-label tasks, where L is the number of labels and $p_k^{(l)}$ denotes the predicted probabilities for label l. After each iteration, queried samples were removed from D_{pool} to avoid duplication, and the classifier was retrained on the updated D_{train}. The loop continued until the query budget was exhausted or D_{pool} was empty.

Distilled Dataset Construction After the loop, the distilled dataset is defined as $D_{\mathrm{distilled}} = D_{\mathrm{train\text{-}initial}} \cup Q$. Though identical to the final D_{train}, $D_{\mathrm{distilled}}$ serves as a compact replay set for future MLBAC updates. Model performance is evaluated on D_{test} using accuracy, precision, recall, and F1-score—validating the representativeness of $D_{\mathrm{distilled}}$ and the role of active learning in mitigating catastrophic forgetting with minimal replay size.

Training Dataset. To simulate continuous changes in access control, we developed 18 distinct changes, defined as Task, and their respective data, known as Admin Authorization Tuples (AATs), for a simulated dataset *u5k-r5k-auth12k* in [12]. This *u5k-r5k-auth12k* data was originally proposed as part of DLBAC [13], which is being used in many other works [3,14]. The initial model training dataset and administration-related change data are publicly available[1], and we rely on them for the experimentation in this work. As described in [12], AATs are built based on a change request (Task) and a set of criteria representing the proposed change in terms of authorization tuples. Also, Other Authorization Tuples (OATs) refer to authorization tuples in the system that are not part of the proposed change.

Replay Data Generation. We generate Replay Data using the proposed method described in Sect. 3.2. This work simulates a multi-Task administration and performs three different administrations sequentially. To do that, we need three different Replay Data. We use *oats_task1_6.sample* as the input data to generate Replay Data for Tasks t1 to t6. For the Tasks t7 to t12, we use *oats_task7_12.sample* as input. For the final three Tasks, t13 to t18, we take *oats_task13_18.sample* as input. We generate three sets of Replay Data of different sizes (25% of the input file, 15% of the input file, and 10% of the input file) for each Task set to demonstrate the efficacy of utilizing distilled data as the Replay Data. We maintain the Replay Data name convention as <Replay Data Size>-distill-<respective Tasks>. For example, the Replay Data *25-distill-t1-t6* indicates that the size of the Replay Data is 25% of input OATs, and it was generated for Tasks t1 to t6. If accepted, we will publicly share the source code and datasets in our GitHub repository.

MLBAC Sequential Administration Using Fine-Tuning. We conducted experiments using a ResNet-based convolutional neural network with sequential

---

[1] https://github.com/dlbac/MLBAC-Administration/tree/main/datasets/six_tasks.

learning. Following the multi-task administration strategy from [12], multiple changes are grouped and applied via fine-tuning. This process is repeated for each task set, enabling efficient model adaptation across evolving requirements.

In this work, we train the same ResNet model based on the entire *u5k-r5k-auth12k* dataset to simulate the access control administration idea. We perform administration using the Replay Data that is of 25% size. To evaluate the performance of the MLBAC for continuous learning, we perform **three sequential** administrations (**t1-t6, t7-t12, t13-18**) using respective AATs and Replay Data. For the first administration, we finetune the model using AATs (dataset: aats_task1_6.sample) that combines six different Tasks (t1 to t6) and their Replay Data (*25-distill-t1-t6*). Next, we administer the next set of Tasks (t7 to t12) using respective AATs (dataset: aats_task7_12.sample) and Replay Data (*25-distill-t1-t6*). Finally, we administer Tasks t13 to t18. We repeat the same exercise for Replay Data size 15% and 10% using the same set of AATs.

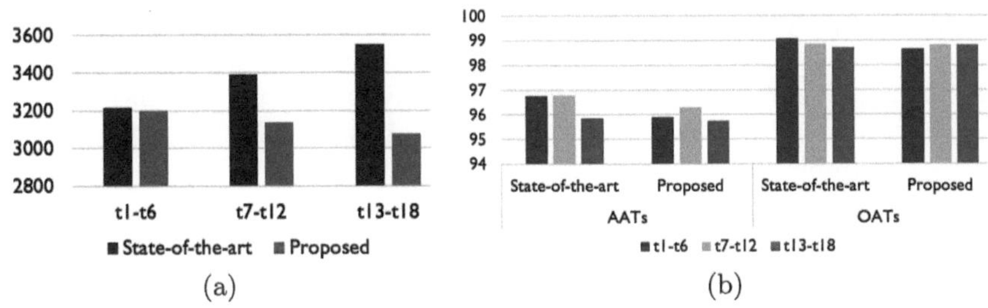

Fig. 3. Performance Comparison Between State-of-the-art and Proposed method. (a) Sample Count Comparison. (b) Accuracy Comparison.

4.2   Results

To evaluate the proposed method, we compare its performance with the state-of-the-art MLBAC administration approach [12]. Although various Replay Data sizes are generated, we use the largest (25%) for comparison to match their setup. Our goal is to show that similar performance can be achieved with significantly less data. We also present results for smaller Replay Data sizes. Further details are provided in the following sections.

Comparison with State-of-the-Art Work Figure 3 compares the proposed method with the state-of-the-art. Figure 3(a) shows Replay Data sizes, where the state-of-the-art consistently uses larger sets–especially for t13t18, exceeding 500 samples ($\approx$5% of the original training data). Our method aims to minimize Replay Data size. Despite using less data, Fig. 3(b) shows no performance drop. While the state-of-the-art performs slightly better on AATs, our method remains competitive. For OATs, our approach achieves similar or slightly better accuracy, highlighting its strength in retaining prior knowledge and mitigating catastrophic forgetting–even with smaller Replay Data.

Proposed Method's Performance Comparison Across Different-Sized Replay Data As outlined in Sect. 4.1, we generated three sets of Replay Data, representing 25%, 15%, and 10% of the original training data. It is important to note that the smaller the dataset, the more difficult it becomes to mitigate catastrophic forgetting. Therefore, careful design of the Replay Data is essential to ensure that the existing access control state can be preserved even with fewer samples. Figure 4 illustrates the outcomes for all three sets of Replay Data. Overall, the performance of AATs remains consistently stable across different sizes of Replay Data, falling within the range of 95.5% to 96.5%. In contrast, the performance of OATs is higher than that of AATs, ranging from approximately 96.5% to 98.5% across all OATs. This indicates that even with a very limited subset of data (10%) used as Replay Data, performance was not adversely affected, demonstrating the high quality of the selected samples within the 10% Replay Data set. Table 1 further demonstrates the evaluation across several other metrics such as precision, recall, and F1-score. As shown, in all cases, the performance is around 96% to 99%, except for the precision of the **t7-t12** and **t13-t18** administrations for 10% size Replay Data.

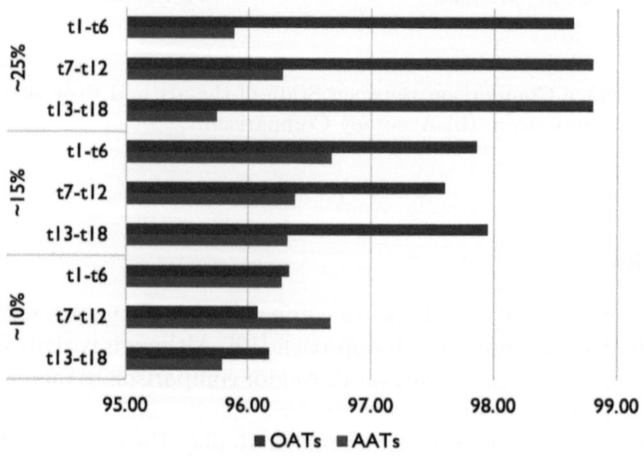

Fig. 4. Comparative Performance of Replay Data by Administration.

Table 1. Accuracy, Precision, Recall, and F1-score Across Different Administrations for Various Replay Data.

Rep. Data Size	Tasks	Accuracy		Precision		Recall		F1-Score	
		AATs	OATs	AATs	OATs	AATs	OATs	AATs	OATs
$\tilde{2}5\%$	t1–t6	95.88	98.64	96.08	98.65	95.83	98.41	95.95	98.53
	t7–t12	96.28	98.80	99.00	97.98	94.47	99.45	96.74	98.71
	t13–t18	95.74	98.80	98.40	98.07	94.33	99.38	96.32	98.72
$\tilde{1}5\%$	t1–t6	96.68	97.86	96.96	97.93	96.54	97.45	96.75	97.69
	t7–t12	96.38	97.60	98.95	95.68	94.79	99.31	96.82	97.46
	t13–t18	96.32	97.95	98.53	96.65	95.28	99.00	96.88	97.81
$\tilde{1}0\%$	t1–t6	96.28	96.34	97.39	96.45	95.17	95.60	96.27	96.02
	t7–t12	96.67	96.08	98.88	92.92	95.42	99.12	97.12	95.92
	t13–t18	95.79	96.17	97.61	93.77	95.25	98.31	96.41	95.98

5   Conclusion

This paper presents a framework for generating effective Replay Data in machine learning-based access control administration (MLBAC). It aims to reduce catastrophic forgetting during sequential learning using smaller Replay Data, while adapting to changes in MLBAC. The approach is evaluated on a widely used synthetic dataset. Results show it preserves prior knowledge across administrations, maintaining high accuracy with less Replay Data.

This work is partially supported by the National Institute of Standards and Technology grant 70NANB23H133 and the National Science Foundation (NSF) CREST grant 1736209.

References

1. Abu Jabal, A., Bertino, E., Lobo, J., Law, M., Russo, A., et al.: Polisma-a framework for learning attribute-based access control policies. In: ESORICS (2020)
2. Alohaly, M., Takabi, H., Blanco, E.: A deep learning approach for extracting attributes of abac policies. In: ACM SACMAT (2018)
3. Chhetri, P., Bhatt, S., Bhatt, P., Nobi, M.N., Benson, J., Krishnan, R.: Environment aware deep learning based access control model (2024)
4. Hino, H.: Active learning: problem settings and recent developments. ArXiv preprint arXiv:2012.04225 (2020)
5. Hsu, W.N., Lin, H.T.: Active learning by learning. In: AAAI (2015)
6. Hu, W., Lin, Z., Liu, B., Tao, C., Tao, Z., Ma, J., et al.: Overcoming catastrophic forgetting for continual learning via model adaptation. In: ICLR (2018)
7. Jha, S., Sural, S., Atluri, V., Vaidya, J.: An administrative model for collaborative management of abac systems and its security analysis. In: IEEE CIC (2016)
8. Karimi, L., Abdelhakim, M., Joshi, J.: Adaptive abac policy learning: a reinforcement learning approach. arXiv (2021)

9. Konyushkova, K., et al.: Learning active learning from data. In: NeurIPS (2017)
10. Ni, Q., Lobo, J., Calo, S., Rohatgi, P., Bertino, E.: Automating role-based provisioning by learning from examples. In: ACM SACMAT (2009)
11. Nobi, M.N., Gupta, M., Praharaj, L., Abdelsalam, M., Krishnan, R., Sandhu, R.: Machine learning in access control: a taxonomy and survey (2022)
12. Nobi, M.N., Krishnan, R., Huang, Y., Sandhu, R.: Administration of machine learning based access control. In: ESORICS. Springer, Heidelberg (2022). https://doi.org/10.1007/978-3-031-17146-8_10
13. Nobi, M.N., Krishnan, R., Huang, Y., Shakarami, M., Sandhu, R.: Toward deep learning based access control. In: ACM CODASPY (2022)
14. Nobi, M.N., Krishnan, R., Sandhu, R.: Adversarial attacks in machine learning based access control (2022)
15. Rana, M.S., Nobi, M.N., Sung, A.H.: Deepdistal: deepfake dataset distillation using active learning. In: CVPR Workshops. IEEE (2024)
16. Shin, H., et al.: Continual learning with deep generative replay. arXiv (2017)
17. Stoller, S.D.: An administrative model for relationship-based access control. In: DBSec. Springer, Heidelberg (2015). https://doi.org/10.1007/978-3-319-20810-7_4

AI for Security

The Hidden Risks of LLM-Generated Web Application Code: A Security-Centric Evaluation of Code Generation Capabilities in Large Language Models

Swaroop Dora[1], Deven Lunkad[2], Naziya Aslam[1(✉)], S. Venkatesan[1],
and Sandeep Kumar Shukla[3]

[1] Department of IT, IIIT Allahabad, Allahabad, India
`{iit2022052,prf.naziya,venkat}@iiita.ac.in`
[2] Department of ECE, IIIT Allahabad, Allahabad, India
`iec2022125@iiita.ac.in`
[3] Cyber MANTHAN Centre, IIIT Hyderabad, Hyderabad, India
`sandeeps@iiit.ac.in`

Abstract. The rapid advancement of Large Language Models (LLMs) has enhanced software development processes, minimizing the time and effort required for coding and enhancing developer productivity. However, despite their potential benefits, code generated by LLMs has been shown to be insecure in controlled environments, raising critical concerns about their reliability and security in real-world applications. This paper uses predefined security parameters to evaluate the security compliance of LLM-generated code across multiple models, such as `ChatGPT`, `DeepSeek`, `Claude`, `Gemini` and `Grok`. The analysis reveals critical vulnerabilities in authentication mechanisms, session management, input validation and HTTP security headers. Although some models incorporate security measures to a limited extent, none fully align with industry best practices, highlighting the associated risks in automated software development. Our findings underscore that human expertise is crucial to ensure secure software deployment or review of LLM-generated code. Also, there is a need for robust security assessment frameworks to enhance the reliability of LLM-generated code in real-world applications.

Keywords: Web Security · LLM · Web Development · Generative AI · Automated Code Development · Risk Assessment

1 Introduction

Large Language Models are considered essential tools for software engineering operations, including code generation and content summarization alongside debugging qualities and programming query responses [1]. LLMs, particularly

N. Hubballi et al. (Eds.): ICISS 2025, LNCS 16380, pp. 27–37, 2026.
https://doi.org/10.1007/978-3-032-13714-2_3

GPT from OpenAI [2], `Claude` from Anthropic [3], and `Llama` from Meta [4], have revolutionized problem-solving through their conversational interface. Developers use models to outline problems, explain their requirements and get solutions. According to a survey by Shani et al. [5], generative models help 92% of US developers to support their daily operations.

The habitual utilization of LLMs among software developers activates substantial doubts about software security levels. Perry et al. [6] found that developers using AI assistants produced code with higher security vulnerabilities. Notably, they also displayed greater confidence in the security of their code, increasing the likelihood of introducing vulnerabilities into real-world applications. Fu et al. [7] found that GitHub Copilot introduced security vulnerabilities in 32.8% of Python code and 24.5% of JavaScript code. Security vulnerabilities in LLM-generated code can severely compromise systems, similar to critical exploits like Log4Shell [8]. The CVE Program documented over 34,000 vulnerabilities in 2024, becoming increasingly common and destructive to software systems' safety, security, and reliability.

Hence, it is essential to analyze and highlight the security issues associated with autogenerated code to raise awareness among developers and enhance the security of LLM-based web application code generation. To address these concerns, this paper presents the following key contributions:

- Created a checklist for evaluating the security of LLM-generated Web Applications: We have created a comprehensive checklist along with risk for systematic analysis of web applications generated by LLMs.
- Comparative Security Analysis of Various LLM Capabilities in Generating Secure Web Applications: We evaluated multiple LLMs (`ChatGPT`, `Claude`, `DeepSeek`, `Gemini` and `Grok`) against a comprehensive set of security parameters, identifying their strengths and weaknesses in authentication, session management, input validation and injection attack protection.
- Risk Assessment: Performed the risk assessment of LLMs' generated web code through both manual evaluation and automated analysis using the OWASP ZAP scanner to present the security risk.

The rest of the paper is organized as follows. Section 2 highlights the state-of-the-art associated works. Section 3 presents the methodology, including the security evaluation parameters and the security risk. Section 4 presents the security analysis of LLMs generated code with respect to compliance and risk. Section 5 discusses the outcomes and presents the recommendations. Finally, Sect. 6 presents the conclusion along with the future work.

2   Related Work

LLMs have emerged as powerful tools for code generation, significantly enhancing developer productivity. However, their ability to produce secure code remains a critical concern, as LLM-generated code can introduce vulnerabilities if not properly evaluated. Several studies have analyzed the security implications of

LLM-generated code, highlighting potential risks and the need for improved safeguards.

Toth et al. [9] investigated the security of PHP code generated by GPT-4, analyzing for vulnerabilities such as SQL Injection and XSS. They found that 11.56% of the sites could be compromised, with 26% having at least one exploitable vulnerability, highlighting significant risks in using LLM-generated code in real-world applications. Perry et al. [6] examined the security implications of AI code assistants, highlighting that while these tools enhance productivity, they may also introduce vulnerabilities in the generated code. A user study involving 47 participants was conducted to assess security-related programming tasks in Python, JavaScript, and C.

Khoury et al. [10] examined the security of code generated by ChatGPT, revealing that it frequently produces insecure programs unless explicitly prompted for security improvements. Through an analysis of 21 programs across five programming languages, they found that only five were initially secure, with vulnerabilities such as SQL injection and path traversal being common. While ChatGPT could identify and explain security flaws when prompted, its ability to generate inherently secure code remained limited.

Despite these contributions, prior work has primarily evaluated the security of LLM-generated code in isolation without systematically analyzing authentication, session management, or HTTP security headers. Moreover, these studies do not provide a structured security benchmarking approach for LLMs or explore proactive security enhancement techniques. Our research addresses these gaps by conducting a comprehensive security analysis of multiple LLMs across critical security parameters, identifying systemic weaknesses, and proposing improvements to enhance the security posture of LLM-assisted development.

3 Methodology

This work systematically evaluates the security compliance of web application code generated by multiple LLMs using the proposed checklist for assessing security in LLM-generated web applications. The objective is to determine which LLMs adhere more closely to secure coding practices and to highlight potential security gaps that users should be aware of before directly deploying the generated code. The five state-of-the-art LLMs selected for evaluation are GPT (4o), DeepSeek (v3), Claude (3.5 Sonnet), Gemini (2.0 Flash Experimental), and Grok (3).

A set of standardized prompts was designed to elicit code generation for web-based authentication and user management systems, where security is paramount. These prompts ensured that the LLMs were tested on their ability to implement security best practices. Each LLM was provided with identical input prompts to generate web application code, ensuring consistency in testing conditions. Table 1 outlines the structured prompts used to evaluate the security aspects of LLM-generated web code in the development of an authentication system for an e-commerce platform.

Table 1. Prompts given to LLMs

Prompts	Description
Prompt 1	Set the context for developing a modern, responsive, and secure authentication system for an e-commerce website using PHP, HTML, and MySQL, following industry-standard security practices
Prompt 2	Provide an optimized database schema for user credentials, authentication logs, and security measures for an e-commerce website's authentication system using MySQL
Prompt 3	Provide secure backend code in PHP for authentication, registration, password management, and session handling with robust validation and error handling for an e-commerce website
Prompt 4	Provide frontend code in HTML for intuitive and accessible login/signup pages with email, password, and image upload, ensuring a seamless user experience for an e-commerce website

Using these structured prompts, we systematically examine whether LLMs generate secure code that aligns with security standards, particularly in authentication, session management, input validation and injection attack protection.

3.1   Security Evaluation Parameters

As the adoption of LLMs for generating web application code increases, ensuring that these models produce secure and reliable implementations is crucial. LLMs are trained on vast datasets but do not inherently guarantee security compliance unless explicitly prompted and guided. This evaluation aims to assess security vulnerabilities in LLM-generated code and determine whether critical security best practices are followed. We categorize security parameters into six broad domains to systematically analyze security compliance: Authentication Security, Input Validation & Protection Against Injection Attacks, Session Security, Secure Storage, Error Handling & Information Disclosure, and HTTP Security Headers. To assess the security of the LLM-generated web code, we employed a standard risk assessment model where risk is given in Eq. 1 [11].

$$\text{Risk} = \text{Likelihood} \times \text{Impact} \tag{1}$$

We measured the Likelihood based on possibility of occurrence by analyzing how easy an attack is to perform, its chance of success, and the potential existence of a vulnerability these days in the implementations. This detailed likelihood analysis was combined with an Impact assessment categorized as *Severe, Major, Significant, Minor, and Insignificant* to produce a final risk rating. The proposed impact measure is given in Table 2. The risks were then classified into *Extreme, Very High, High, Medium, Low and Very Low*. The risk of non-fulfilment of each security parameter is presented in Table 3. The risk associated with each security parameter is computed based on the likelihood of vulnerability exploitation and its potential impact. This methodology highlighted critical weaknesses in the generated code, particularly within Authentication Security, Input Validation & Protection Against Injection Attacks, and Session Security.

Table 2. Impact Measurement

Level	Impact Measure
Severe	Causes immediate and complete account compromise, resulting in irreversible data loss, financial damage, and unauthorized system access
Major	Enables large-scale data exfiltration and account/session hijacking requiring immediate mitigation
Significant	Enables large-scale automated attacks or account takeovers/lock, primarily exploiting weak authentication mechanisms rather than direct application vulnerabilities
Minor	Elevates the risk of client-side exploits such as MitM or clickjacking, potentially exposing session data or enabling limited user manipulation without direct system compromise
Insignificant	Exposes limited non-critical information, such as valid usernames or error responses, slightly weakening the application's ability to detect or resist attacks

4   Analysis

In this section, we analyze different LLMs generated web application code with respect to security compliance based on the created security checklist and the risk of using it in real-world applications.

4.1   Security Compliance Analysis

Table 4 presents the summary of the security requirements compliance by the various LLMs while generating the web application code based on security parameters presented in Sect. 3.1. The evaluation identifies security strengths and weaknesses in authentication, session management, input validation, logging, and HTTP security headers.

1. **Authentication Security:** The security implementations across tested AI models are critically weak, marked by a universal absence of essential protections like MFA, CAPTCHA, and lockout notifications. While Gemini is the only model to enforce brute-force protection and Grok maintains the strictest password policy, these are exceptions in an otherwise insecure landscape. Only Claude offers email verification as an additional layer. This widespread failure to implement standard security features leaves user accounts across all platforms highly vulnerable to common attacks.

2. **Rate Limiting:** Essential access controls are poorly and inconsistently implemented across the models. Only Grok enforces rate-limiting, and only Claude has CSRF protection, while a universal vulnerability exists as no model enforces a secure CORS policy, creating a significant attack surface for common threats.

3. **Session Security:** Session management security is inconsistent across the models. While ChatGPT, Gemini, and Grok correctly implement secure cookie flags, and most protect against session fixation, critical gaps remain. Notably, only Gemini enforces session timeouts, and Claude is the only model lacking both secure cookie flags and session fixation protection. This creates

Table 3. Security Parameters and Risk

Broader Categories	Category	Security Parameter	Likelihood	Impact	Risk
Authentication Security	Brute Force Protection	Lockout after max failed login attempts	Almost certain	Significant	Very High
		CAPTCHA triggered after failed attempts	Almost Certain	Significant	Very High
		Account lockout notification sent	Moderate	Insignificant	Low
	Password Policy	Password complexity (Uppercase, Lowercase, Numbers, Symbols, Length)	Moderate	Significant	Medium
		Password expiration	Moderate	Insignificant	Low
		Password reuse restriction (last N passwords disallowed)	Unlikely	Minor	Low
	MFA	MFA Enabled	Likely	Major	Very High
		Type of MFA (TOTP, OTP, Push Notification)	Moderate	Insignificant	Low
		Backup code available	Moderate	Significant	Medium
	Rate Limiting	Max login attempts per second/IP	Almost Certain	Significant	Very High
		Response after rate limit exceeded (Error code, CAPTCHA, Lockout)	Unlikely	Insignificant	Very Low
Input Validation & Protection Against Injection Attacks	Email Validation	Email Verification	Unlikely	Insignificant	Very Low
	SQL Injection Protection	Parameterized Queries Used	Likely	Major	Very High
		Special characters properly escaped	Likely	Major	Very High
	XSS Protection	JavaScript execution inside input fields	Likely	Major	Very High
		HTML tag injection possible (<script>alert(1) </script>)	Moderate	Major	High
		Login API uses the POST method only	Unlikely	Minor	Low
		CORS policy configured properly	Unlikely	Minor	Low
		CSRF token present in requests	Likely	Major	Very High
		CSRF token validation enforced	Likely	Major	Very High
	HPP Protection	Handling of multiple identical parameters (e.g., ? user=admin & user=guest)	Unlikely	Minor	Low
Session Security	Secure Cookies	Session creation enabled	Unlikely	Insignificant	Very Low
		Session cookie has a Secure flag	Almost Certain	Major	Extreme
		Session cookie has a HttpOnly flag	Almost Certain	Major	Extreme
		Session cookie has SameSite flag	Almost Certain	Major	Extreme
	Session Expiry	Session timeout duration (minutes)	Unlikely	Minor	Low
	Session Hijacking Protection	Session ID regenerated after login	Moderate	Severe	Very High
		Session Fixation Protection	Almost Certain	Major	Extreme
		Session ID stored only in cookies, not in URLs	Moderate	Severe	Very High
Secure Storage	Password Hashing	Hashing Algorithm Used (bcrypt, Argon2, PBKDF2, NA)	Unlikely	Severe	High
		Salted hashes used	Unlikely	Severe	High
Error Handling & Information Disclosure	Generic Error Messages	Does the error message reveal if the username exists?	Unlikely	Insignificant	Very Low
		Does the error message reveal password complexity rules?	Unlikely	insignificant	Very Low
	Logging & Monitoring	Failed login attempts logged	Unlikely	insignificant	Very Low
		Unusual login attempts flagged	Unlikely	insignificant	Very Low
		Logs stored securely	Moderate	Minor	Medium
HTTP Security Headers	CSP Protection	CSP header present	Unlikely	Minor	Low
		CSP policy blocks inline scripts	Moderate	Minor	Medium
		CSP blocks data URIs for scripts	Moderate	Minor	Medium
		CSP restricts external script sources	Moderate	Minor	Medium
	Clickjacking Protection	X-Frame-Options set	Moderate	Minor	Medium
	MIME Type Sniffing Protection	X-Content-Type-Options set to nosniff	Moderate	Minor	Medium
	HSTS	Strict-Transport-Security header present	Moderate	Minor	Medium
		HSTS max-age value (seconds)	Unlikely	Minor	Low
	Referrer Policy Protection	Referrer-Policy header set	Moderate	Minor	Medium
		Referrer-Policy set to "no-referrer" or "strict-origin-when-cross-origin"	Moderate	Minor	Medium
	Feature Policy & Permissions Policy	Permissions-Policy header present	Moderate	Minor	Medium
		Restrictions on camera, microphone, geolocation access set	Moderate	Minor	Medium

a fragmented security posture where no single model is fully secure, with Claude exhibiting the most significant weaknesses.

4. **Input Validation and Injection Attacks:** While all models effectively prevent SQL injection through parameterized queries and proper escaping, frontend security is inconsistent. A significant vulnerability exists in DeepSeek and Gemini, which are vulnerable to cross-site scripting (XSS) attacks due to their failure to prevent JavaScript execution and HTML tag injection in input fields.

5. **Logging and Error Handling:** Logging and error handling are inconsistent, with critical gaps. While Gemini and Grok log failed login attempts, Gemini's error messages leak sensitive information, aiding enumeration attacks. Most critically, no model detects unusual logins or stores logs securely, indicating a widespread failure in proactive threat detection and information leak prevention.

6. **Security Headers:** The analysis reveals a critical and universal lack of essential HTTP security headers across all models. This widespread omission leaves them vulnerable to a host of common web-based threats, including cross-site scripting (XSS), clickjacking, and man-in-the-middle (MITM) attacks, creating a significant and easily exploitable attack surface.

Table 4 highlights that the vulnerabilities exist across all broader categories except the secure storage in the generated code. It is worth noting that `Claude` fails even in the secure storage category. All models require substantial improvements in authentication security, session management, error handling and HTTP security headers to align with current industry best practices and established frameworks, such as the NIST cybersecurity guidelines [12].

Table 4. Security Requirements Coverage of LLMs

Broader Categories	Grok	ChatGPT	DeepSeek	Claude	Gemini
Authentication Security	3/11	1/11	0/11	0/11	2/11
Input Validation Protection Against Injection Attacks	5/10	5/10	3/10	8/10	3/10
Session Security	7/8	7/8	4/8	3/8	8/8
Secure Storage	2/2	2/2	2/2	0/2	2/2
Error Handling Information Disclosure	3/5	2/5	2/5	2/5	1/5
HTTP Security Headers	0/12	0/12	0/12	0/12	0/12

Note: x/y: y is the total number of security parameters in that category, and x indicates how many each LLM is implementing

4.2   Risk Analysis

The security evaluation based on Table 3 reveals that the LLM-generated code has significant non-compliance with essential security requirements, resulting in inherent risks. Figure 1a shows the extreme risks in the different LLMs' generated code. It shows that the `Claude` and `DeepSeek` generated code with extreme risk, not others. Figure 1b shows that all LLMs' generated code has very high risks. Figure 1c shows that all LLMs' generated code except **Grok** has high risks. Figure 1d and Fig. 1e show that all LLMs' generated code has medium and low risk, respectively. Figure 1f shows the presence of very low risks in all the LLM's generated code. The web application code that all LLMs generate has a security risk; hence, there is a need for a security test before deploying it in a real environment.

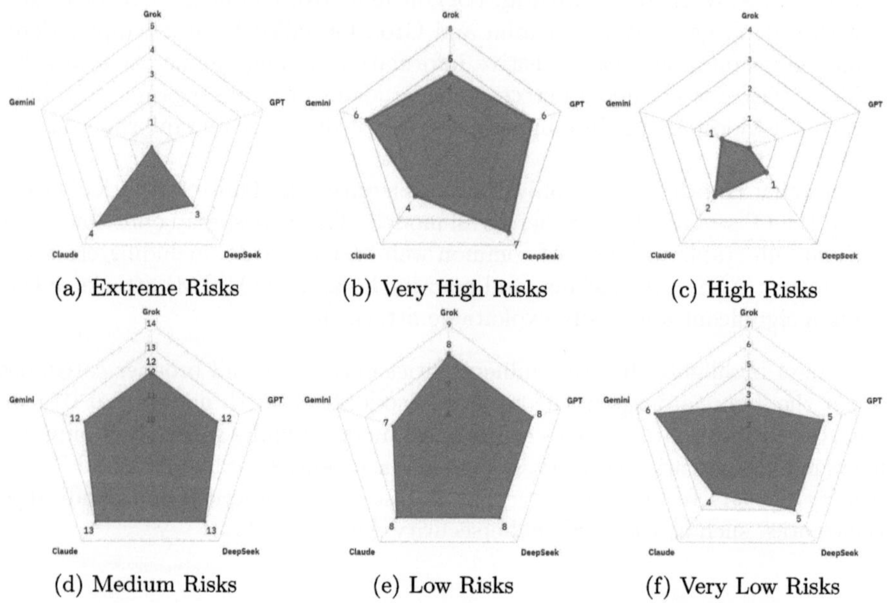

(a) Extreme Risks   (b) Very High Risks   (c) High Risks

(d) Medium Risks   (e) Low Risks   (f) Very Low Risks

Fig. 1. Risk Levels Comparison: Risk Assessment of LLMs Across Different Risk Levels. This radar chart visualization compares various LLMs– **Grok**, **GPT**, **Gemini**, **Claude**, and **DeepSeek** across six risk categories: Extreme, Very High, High, Medium, Low, and Very Low. The red-shaded regions indicate the relative risk scores for each model in the respective risk categories.

4.3   Risk Analysis Using OWASP Zed Attack Proxy (ZAP) Scanner

We also analysed the security risk of code generated by **ChatGPT**, **DeepSeek**, **Claude**, **Gemini** and **Grok** using OWASP Zed Attack Proxy (ZAP) scanner [13]. It is a free and open-source web application security scanner. The risk levels classified by the ZAP scanner include: *High, Medium, Low* and *Informational*. The *Informational* risk level indicates findings that do not pose an immediate, direct security threat but may still be relevant for security analysis to control future combinational exploits. The code generated by the five LLMs was given to the ZAP tool, and a report was generated. Based on the reports, we plotted radar graphs for the four risk levels in Fig. 2. Figure 2a indicates that **Claude**,

`DeepSeek` and `GPT` generated code with high risk, while the other two did not. Figures 2b, 2c and 2d show that all LLMs generated code with medium, low and informational risks, respectively, except `Gemini`. Hence, the security test is needed before deploying the code in real time applications. Additionally, we discovered that during the general scan, the ZAP tool flagged the HTTPOnly attribute as missing, despite it being implemented in the codebase. Also, ZAP has not covered all the security requirements as per Table 3.

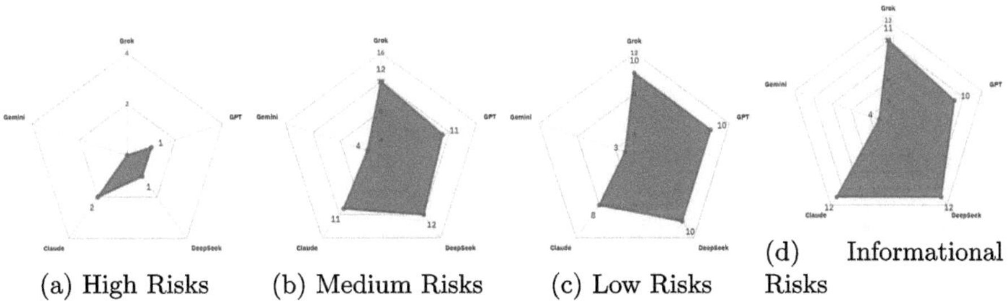

(a) High Risks   (b) Medium Risks   (c) Low Risks   (d) Informational Risks

Fig. 2. A comparison of the automated tool identified risk levels

5   Discussion

The analysis of LLMs presented in Sect. 4 indicates that human intelligence or an automated testing tool is required to ensure the development of secure web applications. While LLMs can automate security enforcement and anomaly detection, they lack contextual awareness, adaptive reasoning, and proactive threat mitigation qualities inherent to human security experts. The systematic vulnerabilities observed in LLMs, such as the absence of MFA and the lack of essential HTTP security headers, suggest that LLM-driven systems still fall short in implementing comprehensive security frameworks. Unlike humans, who can analyze emerging threats, identify novel attack patterns, and adapt security protocols dynamically, LLMs operate within predefined constraints and are prone to adversarial exploits. Thus, while LLMs can assist in security tasks, human expertise remains indispensable for designing, auditing, and maintaining secure systems. The LLMs can generate the secure code by avoiding the identified risk if the prompt specifically mentions every security requirement; however, it should not be taken to justify LLMs' capability since many users may not be aware of all the security requirements. The recommendations based on the analysis are as follows:

- **Improve the prompt**: The user should improve the prompt by indicating each and every aspect of the security parameters to derive the secure web application code from the LLMs.
- **Security Testing**: The LLM-generated web application code should undergo security testing through a security assessment framework to identify vulnerabilities. Security experts can perform this testing manually or using different security tools.

– **LLM Improvement**: The LLMs need to be improved considering the security standards, even though the prompts do not specifically ask for the security requirements.

6   Conclusion and Future Work

Our work highlights critical security gaps in large language models (LLMs) generated web application code, emphasizing vulnerabilities in authentication, session management, and HTTP security headers. Although models like `Grok` and `Gemini` offer marginal improvements in authentication and error handling as per ours and automated security analysis, no LLM currently implements a comprehensive security framework. The absence of multi-factor authentication and strict session management policies underscores the need for rigorous security enhancements. These findings reinforce the necessity for continuous assessment to ensure LLM-generated code aligns with security standards. As LLMs are increasingly used in software development and automation, a robust security assessment framework is essential to mitigate risks and prevent exploitation. Additionally, integrating human expertise with LLM-driven security mechanisms can improve reliability, ensuring these models evolve to meet cybersecurity standards. Future research will focus on expanding the security requirements analysis and incorporating anomaly detection to improve security evaluations.

References

1. Belzner, L., Gabor, T., Wirsing, M.: Large language model assisted software engineering: prospects, challenges, and a case study. In: International Conference on Bridging the Gap between AI and Reality, pp. 355–374. Springer, Heidelberg (2023)
2. OpenAI. Openai. https://www.openai.com/. Accessed 20 Mar 2025
3. Claude. Meet Claude—anthropic.com. https://www.anthropic.com/claude. Accessed 20 Mar 2025
4. Llama. Llama—llama.meta.com. https://llama.meta.com/. Accessed 20 Mar 2025
5. Shani, I.: Survey reveals ai's impact on the developer experience (2023). https://github.blog/2023-06-13-survey-reveals-ais-impact-on-the-developer-experience/. Accessed 20 Mar 2025
6. Perry, N., Srivastava, M., Kumar, D., Boneh, D.: Do users write more insecure code with ai assistants?. In: Proceedings of the 2023 ACM SIGSAC Conference on Computer and Communications Security, pp. 2785–2799 (2023)
7. Fu, Y., et al.: Security weaknesses of copilot generated code in github. *arXiv preprint*arXiv:2310.02059 (2023)
8. log4j, What is the Log4j Vulnerability? — IBM—ibm.com. https://www.ibm.com/think/topics/log4j. Accessed 20 Mar 2025
9. Tóth, R., Bisztray, T., Erdődi, L.: Llms in web development: evaluating llm-generated php code unveiling vulnerabilities and limitations. In: International Conference on Computer Safety, Reliability, and Security, pp. 425–437. Springer, Heidelberg (2024)

10. Khoury, R., Avila, A.R., Brunelle, J., Camara, B.M.: How secure is code generated by chatgpt?. In: 2023 IEEE International Conference on Systems, Man, and Cybernetics (SMC), pp. 2445–2451. IEEE (2023)
11. Kovačević, N., Stojiljković, A., Kovač, M.: Application of the matrix approach in risk assessment. Oper. Res. Eng. Sci. Theory Appl. **2**(3), 55–64 (2019)
12. NIST. Nist. https://www.nist.gov/news-events/news/2024/02/nist-releases-version-20-landmark-cybersecurity-framework. Accessed 20 Mar 2025
13. ZAP. Zed attack proxy (zap) (2025). https://www.zaproxy.org/. Accessed 25 June 2025

Frequency-Aware Deepfake Detection: Transformers vs. CNNs

Aditi Panda[1]([✉]), Srijit Kundu[2], Tanusree Ghosh[3], and Ruchira Naskar[3]

[1] Birla Institute of Technology, Mesra, Ranchi, Jharkhand, India
`panda38aditi@gmail.com`
[2] SRM Institute of Science and Technology, Chennai, India
`sk1899@srmist.edu.in`
[3] Indian Institute of Engineering Science and Technology, Shibpur, India
`2021itp001.tanusree@students.iiests.ac.in, ruchira@it.iiests.ac.in`

Abstract. Deepfakes have become commonplace due to the rise of GANs and LLM based generative models. With this, there has also been a rise in research towards effective deepfake-detection. In this work, we propose a transformer based model for deepfake-detection, operating on frequency-domain image features. Alongside, we also test the effectiveness of our solution with a smaller CNN-based model, for the sake of comparing model complexity vis-a-vis feature set effectiveness. In this paper, we focus on detection of Diffusion Model (DM) generated deepfake images. We train our models on an extensive dataset of diffusion modelgenerated images. We also demonstrate their generalization capabilities and report that while smaller models work well for in-domain testing, we do need larger, deeper neural networks for improved generalization. Our experiments on the recently proposed *DeepFakeEval* dataset corroborate our findings.

Keywords: AI Images · Deepfakes · Generalized detection

1 Introduction

Deepfakes have emerged as a formidable threat in the modern digital era, enabling the creation of highly realistic synthetic images and videos. Although these technologies have diverse applications in entertainment, media, and education, they simultaneously pose serious digital security and privacy risks. It can easily be used to spread misinformation, manipulate individuals' identities, and invade privacy[1]. A growing body of researchers is now focusing on developing universal detectors that can effectively detect synthetic images from any generative model. Several studies reveal that frequency-based features are more efficient in classifying images properly than features in the spatial domain.

Several studies have revealed that synthetic images contain detectable artifacts, particularly in the frequency domain [1]. Researchers found that GAN-generated images possess severe anomalies in their Fourier spectra, often linked to

---

[1] https://www.npr.org/2024/12/21/nx-s1-5220301/deepfakes-memes-artificial-intelligence-elections.

upsampling operations [2]. This has inspired various detection methods, including patch-level analysis [3], auto-correlation [4], enhancing Self-Blended Images (SBI) with frequency extractors [3], and architectures like FreqNet that focus on high-frequency features to improve generalization [5].

More recently, research has shifted from GANs to Diffusion Models (DMs), as models trained to detect GAN-generated images perform poorly on DM-generated content [6,7]. This highlights the need for detection algorithms specifically designed for the unique artifacts produced by DMs.

This study presents a deepfake-detection system that utilizes frequency-domain features and assesses its efficacy through two distinct classifiers: a lightweight CNN architecture named *DM-Net* [8] and a cutting-edge Vision Transformer namely, the *Swin Transformer* [9]. Instead of evaluating these models solely as a performance benchmark, our objective is to comprehend the interaction between model complexity and architectural type with frequency-based representations in the realm of diffusion-based deepfakes. We seek to determine if simpler models, equipped with robust frequency features, can equal or surpass deep transformer-based designs, especially in cross-domain contexts. The major contributions of our work can be summarized as follows.

- We examine and contrast three unique frequency representations primarily, viz., Discrete Cosine Transform (DCT), Discrete Fourier Transform (DFT), and Power Spectral Density (PSD), for deepfake image detection.
- We establish that PSD features possess the capability of achieving high accuracy in detecting synthetic images using two separate models, varying in terms of model complexity: a CNN based lightweight *DM-Net* and a cutting-edge *Swin Transformer* based model.
- We test our high performing models on the *Deepfake-EVAL* [10] and the DF^3 [11] datasets and establish that the *PSD* feature set operated with the *Swin Transformer* model can effectively identify deepfakes with high accuracy.
- Our *PSD + Swin Tiny* model provides an accuracy of over 99% even in a cross-dataset scenario (trained on *DiffusionFace* [12], tested on *Deepfake-EVAL*, also beating most of the State-of-the-Art (SOTA) models when tested on the DF^3).

The rest of the paper is organized as follows. Section 2 describes the proposed architecture. Section 3 presents and discusses the results of our experiments covering in-domain and cross-domain testing. Section 4 summarizes our findings.

2   Proposed Methodology

In this section, we present the proposed classification method for identifying deepfakes from real images. We choose the DiffusionFace dataset [12] and first perform a statistical analysis to identify artifacts and irregularities in the synthetic images of this dataset. After the statistical analysis, we present our classification network architecture. It takes as input the frequency features computed in the first step and learns their discriminative patterns. After training we perform two types of evaluation: in-domain testing for finding how the classification model works on the DiffusionFace dataset and cross-domain testing on the DeepFakeEval dataset [10] for understanding how frequency features help in improving the generalization performance.

Frequency-Domain Feature Analysis: We analyze five frequency-domain characteristics to identify artifacts in synthetic images. The key features are:

- **Discrete Fourier Transform (DFT):** Decomposes the image into sine and cosine components to identify periodic structures.
- **Discrete Cosine Transform (DCT):** Concentrates image energy into a few low-frequency coefficients for efficient localized analysis.
- **Power Spectral Density (PSD):** Measures the energy distribution across frequencies to reveal dominant textural patterns.
- **Angular & Radial Spectral Density (ASD/RSD):** Measure energy distribution along specific angular directions (ASD) or as a function of frequency magnitude (RSD).

The formulations [13] are:

$$X_{u,v} = \sum_{m,n} x_{m,n} \cdot e^{-2\pi i\left(\frac{um}{M} + \frac{vn}{N}\right)} \tag{1}$$

$$X_{k,\ell} = \sum_{m,n} x_{m,n} \cos\left[\frac{\pi}{M}(m + \tfrac{1}{2})k\right] \cos\left[\frac{\pi}{N}(n + \tfrac{1}{2})\ell\right] \tag{2}$$

$$P_{u,v} = |X_{u,v}|^2 \tag{3}$$

where $x_{m,n}$ is the pixel value at spatial coordinates (m, n); $X_{u,v}$ and $X_{k,\ell}$ are the complex DFT and DCT coefficients at frequency indices (u, v) and (k, ℓ) respectively; the terms $e^{(\cdot)}$ and $\cos(\cdot)$ are the 2D complex exponential and cosine basis functions; and $P_{u,v}$ is the PSD, or the squared magnitude of the DFT coefficient. Additionally, by converting the 2D Fourier Transform $F(u, v)$ of an image from Cartesian (u, v) to polar (r, θ) coordinates, we define ASD and RSD as:

$$ASD(\theta) = \int_0^{\infty} |F(r, \theta)|^2 \, dr \tag{4}$$

$$RSD(r) = \int_0^{2\pi} |F(r, \theta)|^2 \, d\theta \tag{5}$$

Statistical Feature Analysis: Earlier studies have shown that frequency-domain analysis is highly effective for synthetic image detection because generative models leave distinct artifacts in the spectral domain. Our analysis of the DiffusionFace dataset [12] reveals these patterns clearly as well on diffusion images. In the Power Spectral Density (PSD) plots (Fig. 1a), synthetic images display tell-tale artifacts such as central line patterns or grid-like structures

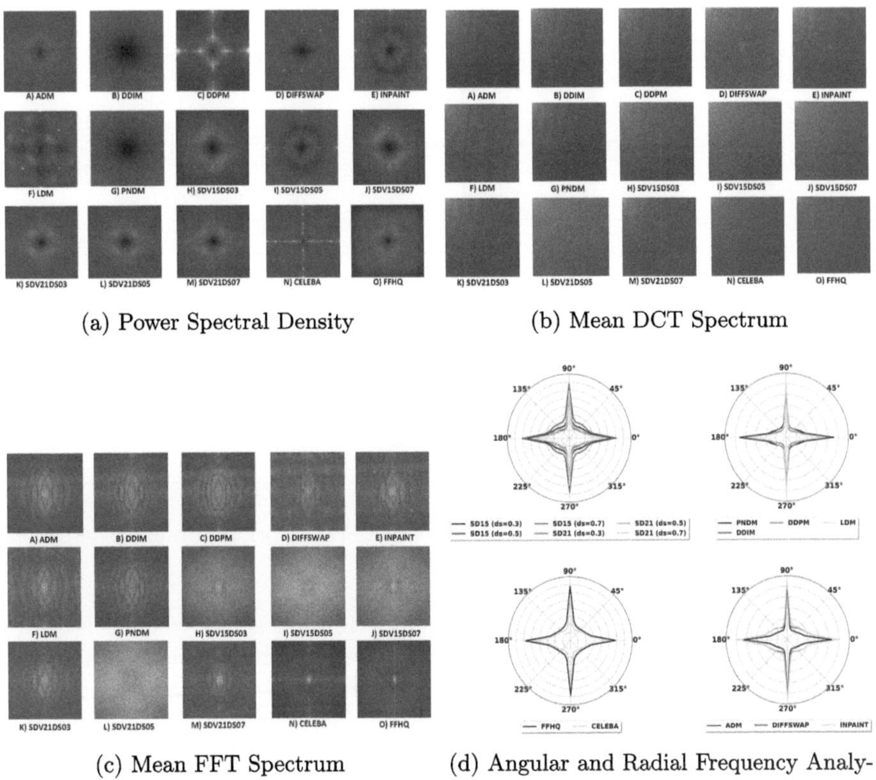

(a) Power Spectral Density   (b) Mean DCT Spectrum

(c) Mean FFT Spectrum   (d) Angular and Radial Frequency Analysis

Fig. 1. Statistical Feature Analysis of Synthetic Images from the DiffusionFace Dataset alongside Real Images from Celeb-A and FFHQ.

reminiscent of GANs. Similarly, in the Mean DCT Spectrum (Fig. 1b), synthetic images are marked by scattered high-frequency components, which are absent in real images. The most visible ones are found near the high frequency range of ADM, DDIM, DDPM, PNDM, and SD 2.1. We also find grid-like artifacts in DiffusionSwap, Inpainting, LDM, and SD 1.5 spectra. Here, the similarity of DM spectra to real images is limited to the amount or volume of purple dots. ADM, DDIM, DDPM, Inpainting and LDM have the maximum volume of artifacts, while DiffusionSwap, and all Stable Diffusion models have lesser amount of artifacts. Similar patterns are visible in Fig. 1c and 1d.

Proposed Architecture for Deepfake Detection: Of the five frequency-domain features examined, three—DCT, DFT, and PSD—were selected for training the classification networks. The selection of these three representations was guided by their complementary spectral characteristics. DFT captures global periodic structures and amplitude variations across the entire image spectrum, DCT highlights dominant low-frequency components while suppress-

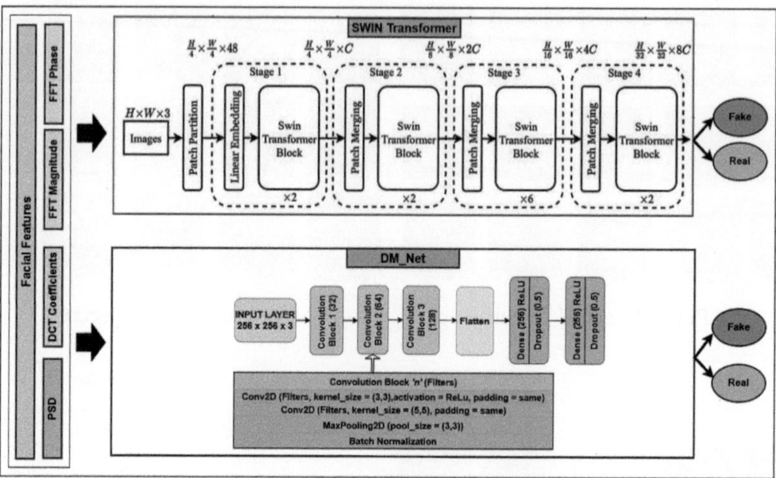

Fig. 2. Proposed Frequency-Based Classification Framework for deepfake-detection

ing noise, and PSD quantifies the energy distribution across frequencies in an orientation-independent manner. Preliminary experiments revealed that ASD and RSD introduced redundant information and did not improve accuracy. Also, DFT, DCT, and PSD produce the most discerning differences between real and synthetic images, as evident in Fig. 1. Most noticeable artifacts are evident in these DCT, DFT and PSD, but not in ASD and RSD. For our experiments, we employed two classifiers to distinguish between real and synthetic images : a Swin Transformer and a custom Convolutional Neural Network (CNN) as illustrated in Fig. 2.

- **Swin Transformer:** The first model is the Swin Transformer ('tiny' variant) [9], which balances performance and computational efficiency. It utilizes a hierarchical structure with shifted window-based self-attention, reducing complexity from quadratic to linear with respect to image size. This design efficiently captures both local and long-range dependencies by enabling cross-window communication. The model, trained from scratch on 224×224 inputs, uses a fully connected layer for binary classification.
- **Custom CNN:** The second model is a custom CNN [8] designed for 256×256 images. It features three main convolutional blocks, each containing dual-kernel convolutions (3×3 and 5×5), max-pooling, and batch normalization. This design allows for the simultaneous capture of fine-grained and broader contextual features. Across the three blocks, the number of feature channels increases from 32 to 64 to 128. In all cases, ReLU has been used as activation function. The extracted features are then flattened and passed through two dense layers with dropout and a final sigmoid activation for binary classification.

Implementation Details: Both the model architectures process tensors with a batch size of 32 samples, training for 20 epochs using binary cross-entropy loss. For DM-Net, we employ the Adagrad optimizer with an initial learning rate of 0.01, chosen for its adaptive learning rate properties that automatically adjust parameter updates based on historical gradients. This approach provides stable convergence for our binary classification task without requiring manual learning rate scheduling. Additionally, we implement a *ReduceLROnPlateau* callback that reduces the learning rate by a factor of 0.5 when validation loss plateaus for 5 consecutive epochs, with a minimum threshold of 1e-6. For the Swin Tiny, we use the AdamW optimizer with a learning rate of 1e-4, as AdamW is well-suited for transformer-based models due to its adaptive learning rate and decoupled weight decay, which helps improve generalization and stability during training. The learning rate of 1e-4 is chosen to provide a good balance between convergence speed and stability. The training pipeline incorporates callbacks to save the best-performing model based on validation accuracy, ensuring optimal generalization performance. All training and evaluation code, including model checkpoints are available at our public repository: https://github.com/SrijitK10/DM-Net.

3 Experimental Results and Analysis

In this section, we present and analyze our experimental results. We quantify the detector performance in terms of evaluation metrics like: Accuracy, Precision, Recall, F1-Score, ROC-AUC, presented in Table 1.

Datasets Used: We have primarily used the *DiffusionFace* dataset, which was curated by Chen et al. [12] for statistical analysis and training and validation of the models. Each image-generating method, whether conditional or unconditional, consists of 30,000 images. The real images used for training were taken from the FFHQ dataset. The statistical analysis for each method, as well as the Celeb-A and FFHQ datasets, was carried out on 3000 images. We used 3000 images from each method of the DiffusionFace dataset for training and 1000 images for validation and testing. To match the synthetic images , we made a set of 39,000 images from the FFHQ dataset for training and 13,000 images for validation and testing. In summary, the training set consisted of 78,000 images, and the validation and testing sets contained 26,000 images each.

For cross-domain testing, we used the DeepFake-Eval dataset [10]. It consists of 1975 synthetic images collected from a variety of sources from the Internet. Unlike DiffusionFace, the DeepFake-Eval dataset is not an academic dataset, it was built to test generalization performance of state-of-the-art deepfake detector models.

Visualization of Useful Features: We use t-distributed Stochastic Neighbor Embedding (t-SNE) to visualize the feature separability of our four best models in a lower-dimensional space. The resulting plots show that PSD features provide superior class separation compared to DCT for both the DM-Net(Fig. 3a

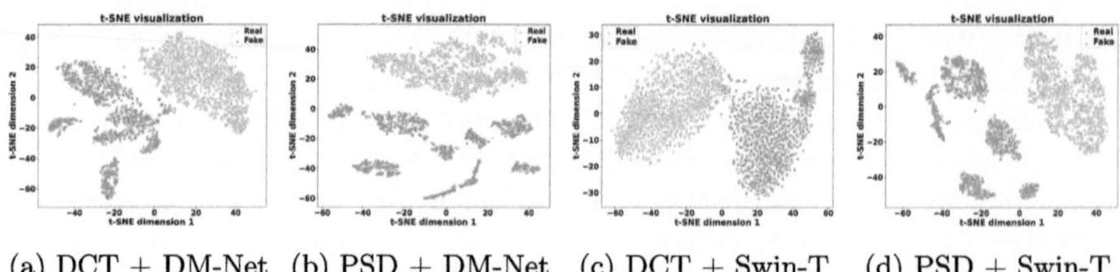

(a) DCT + DM-Net   (b) PSD + DM-Net   (c) DCT + Swin-T   (d) PSD + Swin-T

Fig. 3. Comparison of feature separation by DCT and PSD frequency features in DM-Net and Swin-T detection models.

Table 1. In-Domain and Cross-Domain Detection Performance Evaluation

Setting	Model	Feature	Accuracy	Precision	Recall	F1-score	AUC
In-Domain Testing	Swin-T	DCT	98.60	98.59	98.61	98.60	99.88
		DFT	97.78	98.09	97.45	97.77	99.65
		PSD	99.99	99.99	99.98	99.99	100
	DM-Net	DCT	99.69	99.74	98.64	99.69	99.99
		DFT	99.06	99.11	99.02	99.06	99.94
		PSD	99.99	99.98	99.99	99.99	99.99
Cross-Domain Without Finetuning	Swin-T	DCT	62.77	94.36	37.12	42.13	80.03
		DFT	60.52	91.05	33.56	39.85	74.12
		PSD	99.99	100.0	99.99	99.99	100.0
	DM-Net	DCT	54.71	97.44	19.63	27.53	75.05
		DFT	71.23	98.28	43.13	59.95	87.97
		PSD	50.58	93.21	21.12	22.21	74.14

and Fig. 3b) and Swin-T architectures (Fig. 3c and Fig. 3d). The combination of the Swin-T model with PSD features yields the most compact and well-defined clusters, visually confirming its enhanced ability to capture discriminative structural and spectral differences.

In-Domain vs. Cross-Domain Performance: For in-domain testing, we observe that the PSD combined with the DM-Net and Swin Transformer perform the best out of all the other combinations, achieving an accuracy of 99.99 % in both cases. The models that uses DCT as the primary feature show a slight dip in the performance, followed by the DFT feature of the images.

To test generalization, we evaluate our trained models on the DeepFake-EVAL dataset [10]. DCT and DFT variants perform better for Swin-T and DM-Net respectively. Without fine-tuning the networks, the recall and F1 values are low, however, the precision value remains impressive for both detectors with both DCT and DFT. The PSD variants perform best for the Swin-T model even without finetuning. This can be attributed to the huge number of parameters of the deep transformer architecture, which contributes to the decent generalization

Table 2. Performance evaluation on post-processed images

Operations	Parameters	None +Swin-T	None +DM-Net	PSD +Swin-T	DCT + Swin-T	PSD + DM-Net	DCT + DM-Net	DFT + DM-Net	DFT + Swin-T
Median Filter	3 × 3	99.45	97.02	100.0	94.95	99.99	99.91	97.80	86.53
	5 × 5	99.70	92.79	100.0	84.23	100.0	99.80	87.60	73.88
Gaussian Noise	1.0	99.03	99.24	100.0	98.25	99.98	99.67	98.76	97.30
	2.0	98.93	96.55	100.0	94.79	100.0	99.18	97.88	95.71
CLAHE	–	97.06	99.32	100.0	95.20	99.99	99.49	96.79	82.45
Average Blurring	3 × 3	99.88	99.20	100.0	98.95	99.99	99.98	96.66	98.24
	5 × 5	99.93	79.94	100.0	97.28	99.99	97.73	65.27	95.20
Gamma Correction	0.8	98.45	99.96	100.0	98.12	99.99	99.76	98.77	91.22
	0.9	98.44	99.71	100.0	98.45	99.99	99.78	98.93	97.46
	1.2	98.28	99.63	100.0	97.55	99.99	99.68	98.88	91.92

Table 3. Evaluation Results (AUC) on DF^3

Test Data	CNN- aug [7]	GAN- DCT [2]	Nodown [14]	Beyond Spectrum [15]	PSM [16]	GLFF [11]	PSD+ Swin-T	DFT+ DM-Net
Unprocessed	0.723	0.656	0.970	0.819	0.901	0.906	0.925	0.694
Common Post-processing	0.710	0.443	0.823	0.624	0.878	0.887	0.992	0.984
Face Blending	0.795	0.483	0.888	0.558	0.877	0.905	1.000	0.517
Anti- forensics	0.605	0.504	0.894	0.644	0.863	0.834	0.999	0.999
Multi-image Compression	0.217	0.646	0.105	0.577	0.411	0.547	0.963	0.977
Mixed	0.528	0.497	0.468	0.470	0.724	0.801	1.000	0.999
Average	0.596	0.538	0.691	0.616	0.775	0.813	0.980	0.862

performance. While smaller networks offer simplicity, deeper models ultimately generalize better due to their sheer capacity to translate the extensive learning of their million parameters to unknown images/in the wild images. The DM-Net model with PSD performs the worst for cross-domain/ generalization in terms of recall and F1 scores. This further proves that smaller number of parameters are not well-suited for generalization purposes.

Robustness Analysis: To assess model resilience against common image perturbations, we applied various post-processing operations (e.g., median filtering, Gaussian noise, blurring) to the test data. The results, presented in Table 2, show that frequency-domain features significantly enhance robustness.

Models using PSD features were remarkably resilient, consistently achieving near-perfect accuracy (∼100%) across all perturbations for both Swin-T and DM-Net. DCT features also provided considerable robustness, performing only slightly worse than PSD. In contrast, models trained without frequency features showed a significant drop in performance, especially under heavy blurring. While DFT features offered moderate improvements, their efficacy was inconsistent and contingent on the model architecture. In summary, PSD is the most effective feature for improving robustness against post-processing attacks, followed closely by DCT.

Comparison with State-of-the-Art: We compared our two best cross-domain models (PSD + Swin-T and DFT + DM-Net) against various state-of-the-art (SOTA) detectors on the challenging DF^3 dataset. The Area Under the Curve (AUC) results, detailed in Table 3, show that our proposed methods achieve superior performance across all post-processing scenarios.

Table 4. Ablation Study of the models with and without using frequency features

Training Set	Testing Set	Feature	Swin-T	DM-Net
DiffusionFace	DiffusionFace	None	99.91	99.78
		DCT	98.60	99.69
		DFT	97.78	99.06
		PSD	100.00	99.99
DiffusionFace	DeepFake-EVAL	None	50.33	63.50
		DCT	62.77	54.71
		DFT	60.52	71.23
		PSD	100.00	50.58

Our primary model, PSD + Swin-T, consistently outperforms all competing methods. It achieves a state-of-the-art average AUC of 0.980, significantly surpassing the next-best model, GLFF (0.813). Notably, it scores near-perfectly (AUC $\approx$ 1.000) on challenging tasks like face blending, anti-forensics, and mixed perturbations. Our second model, DFT + DM-Net, also demonstrates strong robustness with an average AUC of 0.862, outperforming all other baselines. In contrast, traditional detectors like GAN-DCT [2] and CNN-aug [7] fail on heavily processed media, underscoring their limited generalization capabilities.

Ablation Study: We performed an ablation study to measure the impact of frequency-domain features (DCT, DFT, and PSD) on the Swin-T and DM-Net models. The results, detailed in Table 4, are evaluated in both in-domain and cross-domain settings.

For **in-domain testing**, baseline models already achieve high accuracy (>99.7%), which is further improved to near-perfect scores with the inclusion of frequency features, especially PSD.

The critical role of these features is highlighted in the **cross-domain setting**. Without frequency inputs, model performance drops sharply (e.g., Swin-T to 50.33%). The integration of PSD features dramatically boosts the Swin-T model's generalization accuracy to 100%. However, the lighter DM-Net model shows an architectural dependency, performing inconsistently and achieving its best cross-domain result with DFT. This confirms that while frequency features are vital for generalization, the optimal feature choice can be model-dependent.

4   Conclusion

In this paper, we assessed frequency-domain features for detecting synthetic images with both a lightweight CNN and a Vision Transformer. Our experiments consistently show that frequency-aware representations, particularly Power Spectral Density (PSD), significantly enhance detection performance and robustness against post-processing attacks.

While our lightweight CNN performed well on in-domain data, it failed to generalize. In contrast, the deeper Swin Transformer, when paired with PSD features, demonstrated exceptional generalization and resilience. Our findings emphasize the essential importance of model complexity and feature selection in the development of deepfake detectors. Although basic CNNs can perform adequately in controlled environments, attaining generalization and resilience in practical applications requires utilizing the learning potential of deeper models in conjunction with meticulously designed frequency-domain inputs.

References

1. Dzanic, T., Shah, K., Witherden, F.D.: Fourier spectrum discrepancies in deep network generated images. In: Proceedings of the 34th International Conference on Neural Information Processing Systems, NIPS '20, Red Hook, NY, USA. Curran Associates Inc (2020)
2. Frank, J., Eisenhofer, T., Schönherr, L., Fischer, A., Kolossa, D., Holz, T.: Leveraging frequency analysis for deep fake image recognition. In: International Conference on Machine Learning, pp. 3247–3258. PMLR (2020)
3. Chai, L., Bau, D., Lim, S.-N., Isola, P.: What makes fake images detectable? Understanding properties that generalize. In: Vedaldi, A., Bischof, H., Brox, T., Frahm, J.-M. (eds.) ECCV 2020. LNCS, vol. 12371, pp. 103–120. Springer, Cham (2020). https://doi.org/10.1007/978-3-030-58574-7_7
4. Corvi, R., Cozzolino, D., Zingarini, G., Poggi, G., Nagano, K., Verdoliva, L.: On the detection of synthetic images generated by diffusion models. In: ICASSP 2023 - 2023 IEEE International Conference on Acoustics, Speech and Signal Processing (ICASSP), pp. 1–5 (2023)
5. Tan, C., Zhao, Y., Wei, S., Guanghua, G., Liu, P., Wei, Y.: Frequency-aware deepfake detection: Improving generalizability through frequency space domain learning. In: Proceedings of the AAAI Conference on Artificial Intelligence, vol. 38, pp. 5052–5060 (2024)
6. Ricker, J., Damm, S., Holz, T., Fischer, A.: Towards the detection of diffusion model deepfakes. arXiv preprint arXiv:2210.14571 (2022)
7. Wang, S.Y., Wang, O., Zhang, R., Owens, A., Efros, A.A.: Cnn-generated images are surprisingly easy to spot... for now. In: Proceedings of the IEEE/CVF Conference on Computer Vision and Pattern Recognition, pp. 8695–8704 (2020)
8. Kundu, S., Ghosh, T., Naskar, R.: Using local phase quantization to identify fake faces in online social networks. In: TENCON 2024 - 2024 IEEE Region 10 Conference (TENCON), pp. 323–326 (2024)
9. Liu, Z., et al.: Swin transformer: hierarchical vision transformer using shifted windows. In: 2021 IEEE/CVF International Conference on Computer Vision (ICCV), Los Alamitos, CA, USA, October 2021, pp. 9992–10002. IEEE Computer Society (2021)
10. Chandra, N.A., et al.: Deepfake-eval-2024: a multi-modal in-the-wild benchmark of deepfakes circulated in 2024 (2025)
11. Yan, J., Jia, S., Cai, J., Guan, H., Lyu, S.: Glff: global and local feature fusion for ai-synthesized image detection. IEEE Trans. Multimedia **26**, 4073–4085 (2023)
12. Chen, Z., et al.: Diffusionface: towards a comprehensive dataset for diffusion-based face forgery analysis. arXiv preprint arXiv:2403.18471 (2024)

13. Gonzalez, R.C., Woods, R.E.: Digital Image Processing, 2nd edn. Addison-Wesley Longman Publishing Co., Inc, Boston (1992)
14. Gragnaniello, D., Cozzolino, D., Marra, F., Poggi, G., Verdoliva, L.: Are gan generated images easy to detect? A critical analysis of the state-of-the-art. In: 2021 IEEE International Conference on Multimedia and Expo (ICME), pp. 1–6. IEEE (2021)
15. He, Y., Yu, N., Keuper, M., Fritz, M.: Beyond the spectrum: detecting deepfakes via re-synthesis. In: 30th International Joint Conference on Artificial Intelligence (IJCAI) (2021)
16. Ju, Y., Jia, S., Ke, L., Xue, H., Nagano, K., Lyu, S.: Fusing global and local features for generalized ai-synthesized image detection. In: 2022 IEEE International Conference on Image Processing (ICIP), pp. 3465–3469. IEEE (2022)

NEXUS: Neuron Activation Scores Exploits for Unveiling Sensitive Attributes

Debasmita Manna and Somanath Tripathy[✉]

Department of Computer Science and Engineering, Indian Institute of Technology Patna, Patna, India
{debasmita_2121cs18,som}@iitp.ac.in

Abstract. Neural network models have been widely used to make critical decisions across diverse applications. However, these models are susceptible to inference attacks that can expose sensitive information such as gender, race, and other personal attributes from the private data used during training. We focus on a particular variant of this attack, known as sensitive value inference, where the adversary aims to reliably pinpoint records within a candidate pool that possess a specific value for the sensitive attribute. We exploit neuron activation values to frame this attack, to infer sensitive attributes. The attack is based on the observation that some neurons are strongly correlated with specific sensitive attribute values in the input. After identifying the most important neurons, the attacker selects the top-k and uses their activation values to train an attack model that can predict the sensitive attribute. We construct the attack based on two distinct threat scenarios: (a) where the model creator incorporates sensitive attributes in both the training data and model inputs, and (b) where these sensitive attributes are intentionally excluded from both the training data and input to censor them. We evaluated our attack on the *COMPAS, CENSUS, and Texas-100x, and UCI credit card* datasets. It is observed that the proposed attack achieves an inference precision of 72% when the sensitive attribute is omitted from the training data, and this precision increases to 93% when the sensitive attribute is included during training.

Keywords: Attribute inference attack · Privacy · Sensitive attribute · Neuron activations

1 Introduction

Deep neural network has become an integral part in the decision making of modern *IT* services, advances in personalized medicine, product recommendations, finance, law and criminal justice, etc. Leading technology companies offer *ML* services through platforms such as *Google Cloud AI, Amazon SageMaker, Microsoft Azure ML and IBM Watson* etc. However, the models are also susceptible to inference attacks that may reveal confidential details embedded in the data used during training. These include membership inference [16], attribute inference [9], property inference [10], and partial memorization [5].

In this work, we investigate attribute inference attacks, where adversaries aim to uncover sensitive details about individuals such as gender, ethnicity, or political affiliation by analyzing a model's outputs, even if these attributes were not explicitly included in the training data. Attribute inference attacks compromise privacy, also threaten model security by facilitating reverse engineering and intellectual property theft. This attack can be used to violate privacy and discriminate against individuals based on their sensitive attributes. According to the report [1], Google and Alphabet face a class action lawsuit for allegedly misusing personal data and copyrighted material to train AI models, including Bard. Similar cases have been filed against Meta, Microsoft, and OpenAI for unauthorized data usage. Nowadays, overly used large language models (LLMs) can also expose sensitive data, including PII, financial details, business secrets, and proprietary algorithms [2]. For instance, an LLM-powered email assistant needs read access to summarize messages but uses a plugin that also allows sending emails, creating a security risk. A malicious email could exploit this by injecting a prompt that tricks the LLM into searching the inbox for sensitive data and forwarding it to an attacker.

Veale et al. [17] highlighted the risk that privacy attacks particularly membership inference attacks (MIAs) might lead to machine learning models being classified as personal data under the European Union's General Data Protection Regulation (GDPR). As MIAs may allow adversaries to determine whether specific individuals' data were used in training, potentially making those individuals identifiable. Although current GDPR regulations do not explicitly categorize trained models as personal data, this perspective may shift if such risks persist. Additionally, model extraction attacks add complexity to the issue, as they can be used to reconstruct models and enable further privacy violations. Additionally, in statistical disclosure control, the Dalenius Desideratum suggests that using a model should not reveal more information about an individual's input than what could be learned without the model [16]. However, it has been shown that this level of privacy is impossible to achieve for any model that provides useful output [7]. Motivated by these challenges we focus on attribute inference attacks.

In [9] Fredrikson et al. introduced an approach where an adversary who knows some non sensitive attributes of a specific individual and seeks to infer that individual's sensitive attribute(s), assuming their data was part of the model's training set. This method is relevant in contexts where each record corresponds to a single person. Later, in [8], the same authors proposed Typical Instance Reconstruction (TIR), where they assume that the attacker has access to the model and a given class label and aims to reconstruct a typical example representative of that class [8].

Previous works on attribute inference, such as [8,9,14], have primarily focused on black-box settings. However, many of these approaches fail to outperform standard imputation methods that rely solely on statistical correlations without requiring access to the target model. Notably, the studies in [9,14] assume that the adversary has full knowledge of all attribute values in the training data except the sensitive attribute being inferred, which may not reflect realistic constraints. In contrast, methods like those in [6,13,15] rely on access to feature importance scores derived from model explanations, assuming that the attacker is provided with or can query the importance values corresponding to the training data features. But, companies may restrict access to explanation details to protect trade secrets. Jayaraman et al. [12] performed attribute inference attacks under the assumption that the sensitive attribute is included during training. However, such approaches are limited in practical scenarios where the model is trained without access to the sensitive attribute.

To address all these gaps, we propose a white box attack that leverages access to the parameters of the model to infer sensitive attributes, even when those attributes were not explicitly part of the training data. Our method operates in two scenarios: when the sensitive attribute is included in the trained model and when it is excluded. Attributing a model's predictions to its input features is well-studied. We extend this analysis to hidden units (neurons), and measure how much a hidden unit contributes to a model's decision. The rationale behind this attack is that the flow of attribution through a neuron helps to identify its influence on individual predictions or across multiple inputs. Based on that, it is observed that a subset of neurons in the target model are associated to different values of the input records. The adversary can detect neurons that respond more strongly i.e., show higher activation when the input data includes certain sensitive attribute values. This threat is realistic in settings where models are distributed as packaged pretrained modules, such as via Apple's Core ML or Google's TensorFlow Mobile, and deployed on edge devices. In such scenarios, the model recipient becomes the attacker: (i) Insider Attacker: A trusted entity (e.g., a hospital) receives a diagnostic model, but a developer within reverse-engineers it to uncover sensitive correlations in the training data. (ii) External Attacker: An adversary gains access to a user's device, extracts the model from an app binary, and analyzes it to reveal private patterns (e.g., biases or demographic links).

The primary innovations of this paper are the following:

- In this work, we propose *NEXUS* (**N**euron Activation **EX**ploits for **U**nveiling **S**ensitive Attributes) an attribute inference attack exploiting the neuron activation of the corresponding model.
- We present an attack that determines the neurons most strongly correlated with the sensitive values of a target attribute, enabling precise analysis of the model's internal representations. Two context of the attack is considered. In Threat Model 1, we demonstrate that our attack effectively infers the sensitive attribute directly from neuron activations. In Threat Model 2, we show that the attack can infer the sensitive attribute by leveraging neuron activations associated with other non-sensitive attributes.
- We perform the attack on four datasets including *CENSUS, COMPASS, UCI Credit, and Texas-100x*. Our approach achieves inference accuracies between

0.79 and 0.94 when the target attribute is included, and between 0.74 and 0.90 when it is excluded from the dataset.

Organization: Sect. 2 reviews the related work in this domain. Section 3 outlines the methodology of *NEXUS*. Section 4 provides a detailed overview of the experimental results along with their analysis. Section 5 discusses the privacy, and proposed work effectiveness and provides the conclusions of this work.

2   Related Work

Table 1 presents a comparison between the proposed method and existing approaches. Fredrikson et al. [8,9] proposed two types of model inversion attacks: one aimed at inferring sensitive attributes, and the other focused on reconstructing representative inputs from the model. In [9], the adversary knows the non-sensitive attributes $n(x)$ and the true label y for a training record. The attacker constructs a set of candidate inputs $x_i = (n(x), s_i)$, where $s_i \in \{s_0, s_1, \ldots, s_{k-1}\}$ are possible values of the sensitive attribute. For each x_i, the model prediction $\hat{y}_i = M(x_i)$ is obtained. A score is computed for each candidate as $S(s_i) = C[y, \hat{y}_i] \cdot p_{s_i}$, where $C[\cdot]$ is a compatibility function and p_{s_i} is the prior probability of s_i. The sensitive value s_i with the highest score is selected as the inferred attribute. In the Typical Instance Reconstruction (TIR) attack [8], the adversary targets a specific class and queries the model to generate a prototypical input (e.g., a facial image), potentially revealing sensitive patterns learned during training.

Mehnaz et al. [14] proposed an attribute inference attack framework that employs two distinct strategies to infer sensitive attributes. In *CSMIA*, the adversary tries to determine the sensitive value of a record x that has a known class label y. To do this, the adversary constructs several variants x_i of x, where the non-sensitive attributes $n(x_i)$ remain the same as $n(x)$, but the sensitive attribute $s(x_i)$ is replaced with possible values s_i from a known set. Each x_i is then queried on the target model, which returns a prediction y_i and a confidence score conf_i for each query. If only one y_i matches the true label y, the corresponding s_i is inferred as the sensitive value. If multiple y_i's match y, the s_i with the highest confidence score conf_i is chosen. If none match y, the s_i associated with the lowest confidence score is selected as the inferred sensitive value. In *LOMIA* the adversary generates predictions for each variant x_i, similar to the approach used in *CSMIA*, but without utilizing confidence scores. An attack dataset is constructed by collecting all inputs x for which only one x_i yields the correct class label y. Each such instance is added to the attack dataset as a pair (x, y) as input and the corresponding sensitive value s_i as the target output. This dataset is then used to train an attack model, which is subsequently employed to infer the sensitive attribute values for other records.

Duddu et al. [6] proposed two different methods for inferring a sensitive attribute $s(x)$ using model explanations, assuming black-box access to a target model. In both methods, the adversary possesses an auxiliary dataset

Table 1. Comparison with SOTA

Scheme	Access	Training dataset	Attribute Importance	Sensitive Attribute
Mehnaz et al. [14]	■	✓	✗	✓
Fredrikson et al. [9]	■	✓	✗	✓
Luo et al. [13]	■	✗	✓	✓
Duddu et al. [6]	■	✗	✓	✓, ✗
Jayaraman et al. [12]	□	✗	✗	✓
Nexus (Proposed)	□	✗	✗	✓, ✗

Access: Type of access to the target model ■: black-box, □: white-box. Training dataset: Whether attacker has an access to training dataset (attacker knows all the attributes value except only one that he wants to infer) or not. Attribute importance: Whether attribute importance score of the training dataset is leveraged to the attacker or not. Sensitive attribute: Either the sensitive attribute is included or excluded during training

$D_{\text{aux}} = \{(x, s(x))\}$. In the first method, the target model is trained with the sensitive attribute $s(x)$ included in the input. The adversary queries the model with x and obtains explanation vectors $\phi(x \cup s(x))$, which reflect feature importance. These are then used to train an attack model that maps $\phi(x \cup s(x)) \rightarrow s(x)$. In the second method, the model is trained without including $s(x)$. The adversary queries the model with input x and receives explanation vectors $\phi(x)$, which are used to train the attack model $\phi(x) \rightarrow s(x)$, allowing inference of the sensitive attribute even though it was not part of the target model's training process. In another work, feature inference attacks [13] use Shapley-based explanations to infer sensitive attributes. The adversary queries the target model using the auxiliary dataset to obtain explanation vectors $\phi(x)$, which encode feature importance. Assuming that $\phi(x)$ preserves sufficient information to approximate a one-to-one mapping with input features, an attack model is trained. In [3], an attacker leverages a synthetic dataset with quasi-identifiers and applies linear reconstruction to infer missing attributes by minimizing query error. In [18], a black-box attack uses Zeroth-Order Gradient Estimation to train a generative model that infers private features (e.g., gender, age) by perturbing inputs and observing output changes, enabling inference without internal model access.

In [12], the attacker utilizes an auxiliary dataset D_{aux} containing samples with known sensitive attribute values. To assess neuron importance with respect to a specific target sensitive value s^*, the attacker flips each $s(x)$ in D_{aux} to s^* while keeping the non-sensitive attributes $n(x)$ unchanged, and queries the target model to obtain neuron activations. For each neuron, the Pearson correlation coefficient between its activation and the binary sensitive label (flipped to s^*) is computed. Neuron activation values are scaled and combined using a weighted average, with weights based on absolute correlation values, to compute an aggregated score op $\in [0, 1]$ indicating the model's confidence in predicting the sensitive attribute $s(x) = s^*$.

3   *NEXUS: The Proposed Methodology*

3.1   Threat Model

We consider a passive adversary $\mathcal{A}_{dv}$ who does not attempt to modify the model's architecture, parameters, or outputs. The adversary has white-box access to the model, granting visibility into internal parameters such as weights and neuron activations. Although $\mathcal{A}_{dv}$ has no access to the model's original training dataset, it possesses an auxiliary dataset drawn from the same domain. The goal of $\mathcal{A}_{dv}$ is to infer the value of a sensitive attribute $s(x) \in \mathcal{S}$ of a target input (x) that was used during training of the target model. We consider two threat models such as $\mathbf{TM}_S$ and $\mathbf{TM}_{\neg S}$.

$\mathbf{TM}_S$: The target model (f_{target}) is trained on a dataset that includes the sensitive attribute s. The adversary leverages the neuron activations $\mathcal{H}^*(\mathbf{x} \cup s(x))$ to construct an attack model f_{adv} that predicts the value of the sensitive attribute:

$$f_{\text{attack}} : \mathcal{H}^*(\mathbf{x} \cup s(x)) \rightarrow \hat{s}$$

$\mathbf{TM}_{\neg S}$: The target model is trained on a dataset that excludes the sensitive attribute s. The adversary constructs an attack model f_{adv} that maps the neuron activations induced by all the non-sensitive attributes to an estimate of the sensitive attribute:

$$f_{\text{attack}} : \mathcal{H}^*(\mathbf{x}) \rightarrow \hat{s}$$

This scenario represents a worst-case inference condition for the adversary $\mathcal{A}_{dv}$, where the sensitive attribute s is intentionally excluded from the model training pipeline in an effort to preserve privacy.

3.2   The Proposed Method

The adversary creates an auxiliary dataset $\mathcal{D}_{\text{aux}} = \{(x^{(i)}, y^{(i)}, s(x^{(i)}))\}_{i=1}^{z}$, where $x^{(i)} \in \mathbb{R}^m$ is the input feature vector, $y^{(i)} \in \mathcal{Y}$ is the true class label, and $s(x^{(i)}) \in \mathcal{S} = \{s_0, s_1, \ldots, s_{k-1}\}$ is the sensitive attribute (e.g., gender). The dataset consists of z samples, and each instance contains both the label and the corresponding sensitive attribute. Figure 1 demontrates the proposed diagram of *NEXUS*.

We consider a trained machine learning model (f_{target}), composed of a set of n elements $\mathcal{N} = \{m_i\}_{i=1}^{n}$, such as filters in a convolutional neural network where $n = \sum_{l=1}^{L} n_l$ across L layers. The performance of the full model is denoted $V(\mathcal{N})$, and our goal is to assign a contribution score $\phi_i \in \mathbb{R}$ to each neuron m_i such that $\sum_{i=1}^{n} \phi_i = V(\mathcal{N})$, where i is the index of that neuron. To evaluate the importance of each neuron, we consider subnetworks $S \subseteq \mathcal{N}$ by zeroing out all elements in $\mathcal{N} \backslash S$, where zeroing is done by replacing a filter's output with its mean activation to preserve layer statistics. This neuron-level contribution estimation is inspired by the Neuron Shapley framework proposed in [11], which adapts the Shapley

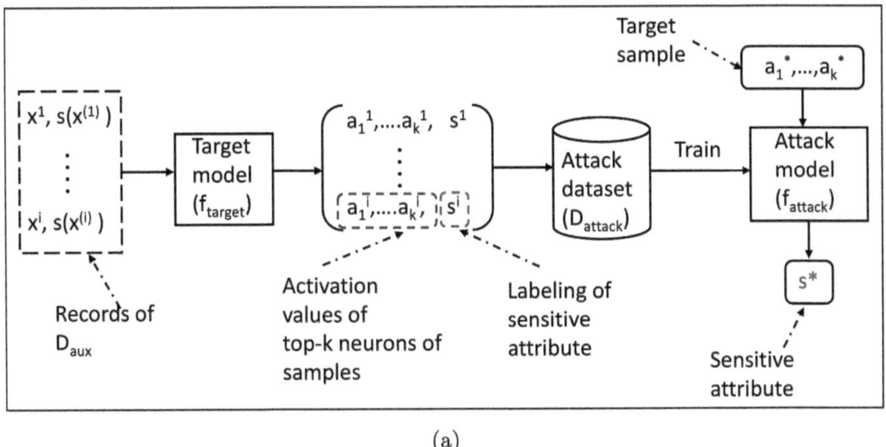

Fig. 1. Attack diagram

value from cooperative game theory to quantify individual neuron contributions. The model is not retrained, and the performance of each subnetwork is denoted $V(S)$. We adopt the Shapley value as our valuation framework, which uniquely satisfies three desirable properties such as (i) *Zero contribution*, where $\phi_i = 0$ if adding neuron i to any subnetwork S does not change performance; (ii) *Symmetry*, where two neurons with identical impact on all subsets receive equal scores such as $\phi_i = \phi_j$; and (iii) *Additivity*, where neuron contributions are additive across performance metrics, i.e., $\phi_i(V_1 + V_2) = \phi_i(V_1) + \phi_i(V_2)$. The Shapley value for neuron i is given by:

$$\phi_i = \frac{1}{|\mathcal{N}|} \sum_{S \subseteq \mathcal{N} \setminus \{i\}} \frac{1}{\binom{|\mathcal{N}|-1}{|S|}} [V(S \cup \{i\}) - V(S)] \tag{1}$$

which represents the average marginal contribution of neuron i across all possible subsets S.

We select the top-k most influential neurons, denoted by $\mathcal{N}_k = \{m_{(1)}, m_{(2)}, \ldots, m_{(k)}\}$, based on their Shapley values, such that $\phi_{(1)} \geq \phi_{(2)} \geq \cdots \geq \phi_{(k)}$. Using these neurons, we construct an attack dataset where each sample is represented by the activation values of the top-k neurons from the (f_{target}). Specifically, for each input $x^{(i)}$ (i-th input sample) from the auxiliary dataset, we extract the corresponding activation vector $\mathbf{a}_k^{(i)} = [a_{(1)}^{(i)}, a_{(2)}^{(i)}, \ldots, a_{(k)}^{(i)}]$, where $a_{(j)}^{(i)}$ is the contribution score of neuron $m_{(j)} \in \mathcal{N}_k$ for input $x^{(i)}$. So, the resulting attack dataset is defined as:

$$\mathcal{D}_{\text{attack}} = \left\{ \left(\mathbf{a}_k^{(i)}, \ s^{(i)} \right) \right\}_{i=1}^{N} \tag{2}$$

where $\mathbf{a}_k^{(i)}$ serves as the input feature vector, $s^{(i)}$ is the corresponding sensitive attribute value, and N is the number of samples we consider. The value of $s^{(i)}$

for each sample is set as the label of $\mathcal{D}_{\text{attack}}$. The attack dataset is then used to train an attack model f_{attack}, which learns to infer the sensitive attribute based solely on the activations of the top-k most contributive neurons. Once f_{attack} is trained on the attack dataset $\mathcal{D}_{\text{attack}} = \{(\mathbf{a}_k^{(i)}, s^{(i)})\}_{i=1}^N$, it can be used to infer the sensitive attribute of any target input record. For a new target sample $x^{(*)}$, we first extract its top-k neuron activation values $\mathbf{a}_k^{(*)} = [a_{(1)}^{(*)}, a_{(2)}^{(*)}, \ldots, a_{(k)}^{(*)}]$, corresponding to the previously selected top-k neurons $\mathcal{N}_k$. Then pass this activation vector $\mathbf{a}_k^{(*)}$ to the trained attack model f_{attack}, which outputs the inferred sensitive attribute value:

$$\hat{s}^{(*)} = f_{\text{attack}}(\mathbf{a}_k^{(*)}) \tag{3}$$

This inference $\hat{s}^{(*)}$ represents the adversary's prediction of the sensitive attribute for the target input $x^{(*)}$. Algorithm 1 describes the step-by-step procedure of our proposed method, *Nexus*.

Algorithm 1: *NEXUS*: Neuron Activation Scores Exploits for Unveiling Sensitive Attributes

---

Input: f_{target}: Target model with neurons $\mathcal{N} = \{n_i \mid i \in [1, m]\}$,
    Auxiliary dataset $\mathcal{D}_{\text{aux}} = \{(\mathbf{x}_i, y_i, s_i)\}_{i=1}^z$, where
$s_i \in \mathcal{S} = \{s_0, s_1, \ldots, s_{k-1}\}$ is the sensitive attribute.
Output: Inferred sensitive attribute $\hat{s^*}$ for a target input $\mathbf{x}^*$
for $n_i \in \mathcal{N}$ **do**

> $\phi_i \leftarrow \sum_{S \subseteq \mathcal{N} \setminus \{i\}} \frac{|S|!(m-|S|-1)!}{m!} [V(S \cup \{i\}) - V(S)]$ // Compute contribution score of each neurons

    $\mathcal{N}_k \leftarrow$ Top-k neurons from $\mathcal{N}$ based on ϕ_i // Select top-k influential neurons with highest contribution scores
$\mathcal{D}_{\text{attack}} \leftarrow \emptyset$ // Initialize attack dataset
for $(\mathbf{x}_i, y_i, s_i) \in \mathcal{D}_{\text{aux}}$ **do**

> $\mathbf{a}^{(i)} \leftarrow [n_j(\mathbf{x}_i) \mid n_j \in \mathcal{N}_k]$
> // Extract the activation values of top-k influential neurons for the samples of auxiliary dataset
> $\mathcal{D}_{\text{attack}} \leftarrow \mathcal{D}_{\text{attack}} \cup \{(\mathbf{a}^{(i)}, s_i)\}$ // Creates the attack dataset

for $\mathbf{x}^*$ **do**

> $\mathbf{a_k} \leftarrow [n_j(\mathbf{x}) \mid n_j \in \mathcal{N}_k]$ // Extract top-k neurons activation values
> $\hat{s^*} \leftarrow f_{attack}(\mathbf{a_k}; \boldsymbol{\theta}_{\text{adv}}^*)$ // Infer the value of the sensitive attribute of the target record (x^*)

In this work, to infer the value of the sensitive attribute neuron activation score is utilized. The core intuition of this work is that a white box adversary can exploit neuron activation patterns to infer sensitive attributes. The intuition of this work is that a sub group of neurons are highly activated for different values of the sensitive attribute of several samples. So, we utilize few neurons among them to perform the attribute inference attack.

4   Experimental Result

4.1   Datasets

Adult Income (CENSUS): The dataset used in this work [4] contains 48,842 entries with 14 features describing individuals from the 1994 U.S. Census. Its primary purpose is to predict whether a person earns more than 50 K annually. Features include education level, marital status, occupation, weekly working hours, and others. For the purpose of this work, the 'marital status' attribute has been simplified into two groups: Married (combining Married-civ-spouse, Married-spouse-absent, and Married-AF-spouse) and Single (including Divorced, Never-married, Separated, and Widowed). The attributes 'marital status', 'race', and 'gender' are considered sensitive and are the targets of inference by the adversary. After filtering out records with missing data, the dataset is reduced to 45,222 instances. From this, 31,655 records are used to train the target model. The remaining 13,567 are split evenly: 6,783 are used as auxiliary data for training the attack model, and 6,784 are used to test the attack on previously unseen samples. To maintain a realistic attack scenario and avoid making sensitive attribute inference too obvious, the 'relationship' attribute (e.g., values like husband, wife, or unmarried), which strongly correlates with 'marital status', is excluded from the dataset.

UCI Credit Card: The dataset used in this work [19] is an anonymized collection from the UCI Machine Learning Repository, containing details about credit card applicants. It includes 30,000 records, each with 24 features. After eliminating entries with missing data, 29,601 records remain. Out of these, 20,720 are allocated for training the target model, 4,440 are used as auxiliary data for training the attack model, and the remaining 4,441 are set aside for testing the attack's effectiveness. The problem is approached as a binary classification task, where the goal is to predict whether a credit card application is approved. In this context, the attributes 'gender' and 'marital status' are treated as sensitive information that the adversary attempts to infer.

COMPAS Recidivism: This dataset[1], commonly used in commercial risk assessment systems, is designed to predict the probability that a criminal defendant will reoffend. It initially contains 60,843 entries, and following preprocessing and removal of invalid records, 60,798 valid samples are retained. Of these, 42,558 are used to train the target model, 9,120 are assigned as auxiliary data to train the attack model, and the remaining 9,120 are reserved for testing the attack's performance. The task is structured as a binary classification problem, where the objective is to determine whether an individual is likely to reoffend. In this scenario, the attributes 'marital status' and 'gender' are regarded as sensitive and are the targets of inference by the adversary.

---

[1] https://www.kaggle.com/datasets/danofer/compass.

Texas-100X: The Texas-100X dataset[2] is an enhanced version of the Texas-100 hospital dataset, originally introduced by Shokri. Each entry includes comprehensive patient information, covering both demographic data (such as age, gender, and race) and medical details (including length of stay, type and source of admission, diagnosis codes, discharge status, medical expenses, and primary surgical procedures). The primary task is to predict one of 100 surgical procedures based on a patient's health profile. Unlike the anonymized Texas-100 dataset which contains 60,000 records with binary-encoded attributes and is unsuitable for fine grained analysis Texas-100X is compiled from the same public files to retain 10 original, interpretable features. It comprises 925,128 records from 441 hospitals. For experimentation, 647,589 records are used for training the target model, 138,769 for training the attack model, and 138,770 for testing. To avoid confounding effects due to the strong overlap between race and ethnicity, the ethnicity attribute is excluded, allowing the analysis to focus on inferring race and gender as sensitive attributes.

For all the datasets, we use 70% of dataset $\mathcal{D}$ to train the target model (f_{target}) and the remaining 30% for testing. Half of the test data (D_{aux}) is used for training the attack model, while the other half is reserved for evaluation.

4.2   Target Model

The neural network comprises two hidden layers, each with 256 neurons and ReLU activation. The output layer is a softmax layer with one neuron per output class. All hidden layers utilize the Rectified Linear Unit (ReLU) activation function to introduce non-linearity and facilitate gradient flow. The network is trained using the cross-entropy loss function and optimized with the Adam optimizer at a learning rate of 0.001. On the *CENSUS* dataset the accuracy of the model on the test dataset is 86.27%, on *UCI Credit* dataset the model accuracy is 82.03%, on *COMPAS* dataset the accuracy is 83.76%, and on *TEXAS-100x* dataset the accuracy is 46.8%.

4.3   Evaluation Metrics

The evaluation metrics are given below:

– Precision: The proportion of correctly predicted positive cases out of all cases that were predicted as positive. This metric reflects the proportion of instances predicted by the adversary as having the sensitive attribute in the positive class that are actually correct.

$$\text{Precision} = \frac{\text{TP}}{\text{TP} + \text{FP}}$$

---

[2] https://drive.google.com/drive/folders/1nDDr8OWRaliIrUZcZ-0I8sEB2WqAXdKZ.

- Recall: The proportion of true positives to the sum of true positives and false negatives. This quantifies the proportion of actual positive instances of the sensitive attribute that are correctly identified by the adversary.

$$\text{Recall} = \frac{\text{TP}}{\text{TP} + \text{FN}}$$

- Accuracy: The ratio of correctly inferred sensitive attributes out of all instances. It measures how many predictions made by the adversary are correct, regardless of class.

$$\text{Accuracy} = \frac{\text{TP} + \text{TN}}{\text{TP} + \text{FP} + \text{TN} + \text{FN}}$$

where TP, FP, TN, and FN are true positive, false positive, true negative and false negative.

4.4 Experimental Result

Table 2. Performance of *NEXUS*

Datasets	Attribute	TM_S									$TM_{\neg S}$		
		P			R			A			P	R	A
		Our	[12]	[14]	Our	[12]	[14]	Our	[12]	[14]	Our	Our	Our
Census	$\mathcal{G}$	.93	.87	.86	.94	.88	.87	.94	.89	.87	.88	.9	.9
	$\mathcal{R}$	.83	.77	.76	.93	.87	85	.93	.89	88	.7	86	.89
	$\mathcal{M}$	.93	.87	.89	.93	.87	.9	.93	.87	.89	.91	.9	.92
Uci	$\mathcal{G}$	.93	.86	.86	.93	.87	.87	.93	.87	.87	.89	.9	.9
	$\mathcal{M}$	.93	.85	.86	.94	.85	.86	.94	.85	.86	.89	.88	.9
Compas	$\mathcal{G}$	.9	.87	.85	.94	.9	.87	.94	.92	. 9	.85	.91	.94
	$\mathcal{M}$	.92	.84	.85	.92	.88	.89	.92	.88	.87	.86	.9	.92
Texas	$\mathcal{G}$	.78	.62	.59	.79	.63	.6	.79	.64	.61	.73	.74	.75
	$\mathcal{R}$	.76	.63	.6	.79	.63	.62	.79	.64	.61	.72	.74	.74

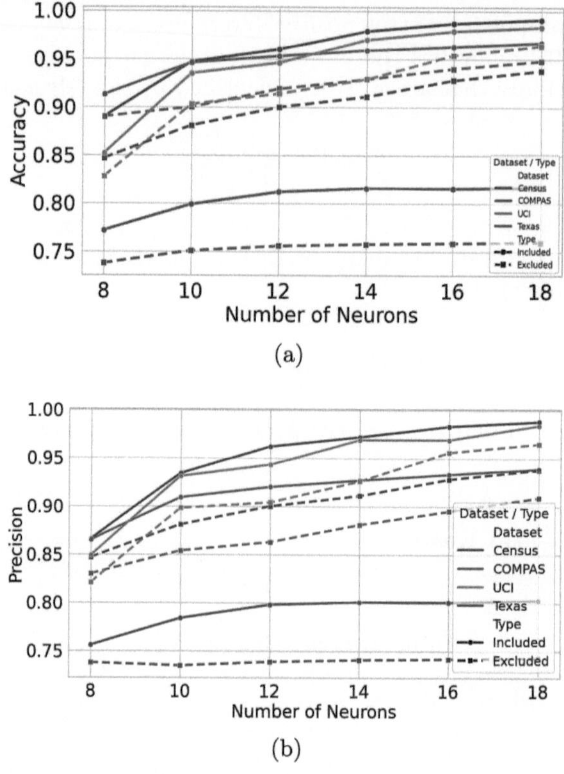

Fig. 2. (a) Accuracy, and (b) Precision of inferring the sensitive attribute value (gender) of (*Census, UCI, Compas, Texas-100x*) datasets with respect to number of neurons

Table 2 summarizes the results of the proposed method, evaluated on *CENSUS, COMPAS, UCI, and TEXAS-100* under two threat models $\mathbf{TM}_S$ and (with) and $\mathbf{TM}_{\neg S}$ (without) the sensitive attribute during training. Precision $\mathcal{P}$, recall $\mathcal{R}$, and accuracy $\mathcal{A}$, are reported to infer gender, marital status, and race, and are compared with existing methods. In this table, we used the following abbreviations for sensitive attributes: gender $\mathcal{G}$, race $\mathcal{R}$, and marital status $\mathcal{M}$. In the *Adult Census* dataset, where *Gender* is treated as sensitive attribute, existing methods [12, 14] report precision values of 0.87 and 0.86, and recall values of 0.88 and 0.87. In comparison, *NEXUS*, achieves higher precision of 0.93 and recall of 0.94. The overall classification accuracy also improves from 0.89 in previous works to 0.94 with our method. These results are obtained when the sensitive attribute is included during model training. Furthermore, even when the sensitive attribute is excluded from the training dataset, *NEXUS* maintains strong performance with a precision of 0.88, recall of 0.90, and accuracy of 0.90. Similarly, when *Marital Status* is treated as the sensitive attribute, existing methods by [12, 14] report precision values of 0.87 and 0.89, recall values of 0.87 and 0.90, and accuracy scores of 0.87 and 0.89, respectively. In contrast, our proposed method *NEXUS* achieves improved performance with a precision, recall, and accuracy of 0.93 across all three metrics. On the other hand, by excluding the sensitive attribute from the training dataset, *NEXUS* has been observed to maintain performance such as precision, recall and precision of .88, .9, and .9 respectively. When *Race* is considered as the sensitive attribute, the existing method by Jayaraman et al. [12] reported a precision of 0.77, recall of 0.87, and accuracy of 0.88. Also, the existing method by Mehnaz et al. [14] the precision, recall, and the accuracy is 0.76, 0.85, and 0.88 respectively. In contrast, *NEXUS* could achieve higher performance with a precision of 0.83, recall of 0.93, and accuracy of 0.93. Furthermore, even when the sensitive attribute is excluded from the training dataset, *NEXUS* maintains comparable performance, achieving a precision of 0.7, recall of 0.86, and accuracy of 0.89.

On the *UCI Credit* dataset, when *Gender* is considered as the sensitive attribute, existing methods [12,14] report a precision of 0.86, 0.86, recall of 0.87, 0.87 and accuracy of 0.87, 0.87. In contrast, our proposed method *NEXUS* achieves significantly improved results with a precision of 0.93, recall of 0.93, and accuracy of 0.93. Similarly, when *Marital Status* is treated as the sensitive attribute, existing methods achieve a precision, recall, and accuracy of 0.85, while *NEXUS* outperforms them with scores of 0.93, 0.94, and 0.94, respectively. Even when the sensitive attribute is excluded from the training dataset, *NEXUS* maintains strong performance. For *Gender*, the precision, recall, and accuracy are 0.89, 0.90, and 0.90; for *Marital Status*, all three metrics reach 0.90.

On the *COMPAS* dataset, when *Gender* is used as the sensitive attribute, existing methods by [12,14] report a precision of 0.87, 0.85, recall of 0.90, 0.87 and accuracy of 0.92, .9. In comparison, our proposed method *NEXUS* achieves improved performance with a precision of 0.90, recall of 0.94, and accuracy of 0.94. When *Marital Status* is considered the sensitive attribute, existing methods [12,14] yield precision of 0.84, and 0.85, recall 0.88, 0.89 and accuracy 0.88, 0.87 respectively whereas *NEXUS* attains 0.9, 0.94, and 0.94 for all three metrics such as precision, recall, accuracy respectively. Even when the sensitive attribute is excluded from the training dataset, *NEXUS* continues to perform effectively. For *Gender*, it achieves a precision of 0.85, recall of 0.91, and accuracy of 0.94. For *Marital Status*, the corresponding values are 0.86, 0.90, and 0.92.

On the *Texas 100X* dataset, when *Gender* is considered the sensitive attribute, existing methods [12,14] achieve a precision of 0.62, 0.59 recall of 0.63, 0.6 and accuracy of 0.64, 0.61. In contrast, our proposed method *NEXUS* significantly improves these metrics, achieving a precision of 0.78, recall of 0.79, and accuracy of 0.79. When *Race* is used as the sensitive attribute, existing approach by [12] yield precision, recall, and accuracy values of 0.63, 0.63, and 0.64 respectively, while *NEXUS* attains higher values of 0.76, 0.79, and 0.79. Even in the absence of the sensitive attribute from the training data, *NEXUS* continues to perform robustly. When *Gender* is excluded, it achieves a precision of 0.73, recall of 0.74, and accuracy of 0.75. For *Race*, the corresponding results are 0.72, 0.74, and 0.74.

Figure 2b shows the precision for all four datasets *Census, COMPAS, UCI Credit, and Texas 100X* when the sensitive attribute Gender is either included or excluded from the training data, with the exclusion case considering the top 8 to 18 most important neurons. For the Census dataset, precision ranges from 0.86 to 0.98 when Gender is included, and from 0.76 to 0.93 when excluded. In the COMPAS dataset, precision varies from 0.86 to 0.93 with inclusion, and from 0.83 to 0.90 with exclusion. For the UCI Credit dataset, the range is 0.84 to 0.98 when included, and 0.87 to 0.96 when excluded. In the Texas 100X dataset, precision ranges from 0.75 to 0.80 with inclusion and from 0.72 to 0.74 with exclusion.

Figure 2a shows the accuracy for all four datasets *Census, COMPASS, UCI Credit, and Texas 100X* when the sensitive attribute Gender is either included or excluded from the training dataset. In the exclusion setting, the top 8 to 18 most important neurons are considered. For the Census dataset, accuracy ranges from 0.89 to 0.99 when Gender is included, and from 0.89 to 0.95 when excluded. In the COMPASS dataset, accuracy varies from 0.91 to 0.96 with inclusion and from 0.89 to 0.94 with exclusion. For the UCI Credit dataset, accuracy ranges from 0.85 to 0.98 when the sensitive attribute is included, and from 0.90 to 0.96 when excluded. In the Texas 100X dataset, accuracy lies between 0.77 and 0.81 with inclusion and between 0.73 and 0.76 with exclusion.

5   Conclusion

In this work, we proposed *NEXUS*, an attribute inference attack targeting neural network models. Our approach identifies the most influential neurons with respect to a given sensitive attribute using Shapley analysis. By selecting the top-k neurons with the highest contributions, an attack dataset is constructed, in which each sample is represented by the activation values of these top-k neurons, and the corresponding sensitive attribute serves as the label. This dataset is then used to train an attack model that learns to infer sensitive attributes solely from neuron activations, without requiring explicit access to the sensitive attribute during inference. We evaluated the effectiveness of NEXUS across four diverse benchmark datasets *Census, COMPASS, UCI Credit, and Texas-100X* and demonstrated that our method could successfully recover sensitive attribute values with better accuracy. These results highlight the vulnerability of deep neural networks to internal representation leakage and underscore the need for robust privacy-preserving techniques in model deployment. Further, our method demonstrated high inference accuracy for certain attributes, ranging from 0.79 to 0.94 when the attribute is included in the dataset, and from 0.74 to 0.90 when the attribute is excluded.

Acknowledgement. We acknowledge the Ministry of Education (MoE), Government of India, and Ministry of Electronics and Information technology for funding this research under the project ISEA Phase-III.

References

1. Case 3:23-cv-03440-lb document 1 filed 07/11/23 page 1 of 90. https:// fingfx.thomsonreuters.com/gfx/legaldocs/myvmodloqvr/GOOGLE%20AI %20LAWSUIT%20complaint.pdf. Accessed July 2023
2. Llm02:2025 sensitive information disclosure, https://genai.owasp.org/llmrisk/ llm022025-sensitive-information-disclosure/. Accessed July 2025
3. Annamalai, M.S.M.S., Gadotti, A., Rocher, L.: A linear reconstruction approach for attribute inference attacks against synthetic data. In: 33rd USENIX Security Symposium (USENIX Security 24), pp. 2351–2368 (2024)
4. Becker, B., Kohavi, R.: Adult. UCI Machine Learning Repository (1996). https:// doi.org/10.24432/C5XW20.
5. Carlini, N., Liu, C., Erlingsson, U., Kos, J., Song, D.X.: The secret sharer: evaluating and testing unintended memorization in neural networks. In: USENIX Security Symposium (2018)
6. Duddu, V., Boutet, A.: Inferring sensitive attributes from model explanations. In: Proceedings of the 31st ACM International Conference on Information & Knowledge Management, CIKM '22, New York, NY, USA, pp. 416–425. Association for Computing Machinery (2022)
7. Dwork, C., Naor, M.: On the difficulties of disclosure prevention in statistical databases or the case for differential privacy. J. Priv. Confident. **2**, 09 (2010)
8. Fredrikson, M., Jha, S., Ristenpart, T.: Model inversion attacks that exploit confidence information and basic countermeasures. In: Proceedings of the 22nd ACM SIGSAC Conference on Computer and Communications Security, CCS '15, New York, NY, USA, pp. 1322–1333. Association for Computing Machinery (2015)
9. Fredrikson, M., Lantz, E., Jha, S., Lin, S.M., Page, D., Ristenpart, T.: Privacy in pharmacogenetics: an end-to-end case study of personalized warfarin dosing. In: Fu, K., Jung, J. (eds.) Proceedings of the 23rd USENIX Security Symposium, San Diego, CA, USA, 20–22 August 2014, pp. 17–32. USENIX Association (2014)
10. Ganju, K., Wang, Q., Yang, W., Gunter, C.A., Borisov, N.: Property inference attacks on fully connected neural networks using permutation invariant representations. In: Proceedings of the 2018 ACM SIGSAC Conference on Computer and Communications Security, CCS '18, New York, NY, USA, pp. 619–633. Association for Computing Machinery (2018)
11. Ghorbani, A., Zou, J.: Neuron shapley: discovering the responsible neurons. In: Proceedings of the 34th International Conference on Neural Information Processing Systems, NIPS '20, Red Hook, NY, USA. Curran Associates Inc. (2020)
12. Jayaraman, B., Evans, D.: Are attribute inference attacks just imputation? In: Proceedings of the 2022 ACM SIGSAC Conference on Computer and Communications Security, CCS '22, New York, NY, USA, pp. 1569–1582. Association for Computing Machinery (2022)
13. Luo, X., Jiang, Y., Xiao, X.: Feature inference attack on shapley values. In: Proceedings of the 2022 ACM SIGSAC Conference on Computer and Communications Security, CCS '22, New York, NY, USA, pp. 2233–2247. Association for Computing Machinery (2022)
14. Mehnaz, S., Dibbo, S.V., Kabir, E., Li, N., Bertino, E.: Are your sensitive attributes private? Novel model inversion attribute inference attacks on classification models. In: USENIX Security Symposium (2022)
15. Shokri, R., Strobel, M., Zick, Y.: On the privacy risks of model explanations. In: Proceedings of the 2021 AAAI/ACM Conference on AI, Ethics, and Society, AIES

'21, New York, NY, USA, pp. 231–241. Association for Computing Machinery (2021)

16. Shokri, R., Stronati, M., Song, C., Shmatikov, V.: Membership inference attacks against machine learning models. In: 2017 IEEE Symposium on Security and Privacy (SP), pp. 3–18 (2017)

17. Veale, M., Binns, R., Edwards, L.: Algorithms that remember: model inversion attacks and data protection law. Phil. Trans. R. Soc. A: Math. Phys. Eng. Sci. **376**(2133), 20180083 (2018)

18. Yang, R., Ma, J., Zhang, J., Kumari, S., Kumar, S., Rodrigues, J.P.C.: Practical feature inference attack in vertical federated learning during prediction in artificial internet of things. IEEE Internet Things J. **11**(1), 5–16 (2023)

19. Yeh, I.C.: Default of Credit Card Clients. UCI Machine Learning Repository (2009). https://doi.org/10.24432/C55S3H.

MazeNet: Protecting DNN Models on Public Cloud Platforms With TEEs

Kripa Shanker[1(✉)], Vivek Kumar[1], Aditya Kanade[2], and Vinod Ganapathy[1]

[1] Department of Computer Science and Automation, Indian Institute of Science, Bengaluru, India
{kripashanker,vg}@iisc.ac.in, vivekkumar13@alum.iisc.ac.in
[2] Microsoft Research India,Bengaluru, India
kanadeaditya@microsoft.com

Abstract. Machine Learning-as-a-Service (MLaaS) enables deep learning (DL) model owners to outsource inference tasks to a public cloud platform. A model owner trains a DL model in-house and uploads the trained model to a MLaaS. For the uploaded model, the MLaaS platform exposes an API to query the uploaded model with inputs and obtain predictions. However, uploading the trained model to public cloud platforms exposes the model owner to security and privacy risks, as the model is available in plaintext to the cloud provider during inference.

In this work, we present techniques to secure DL models with trusted execution environments and propose a secure outsourcing scheme to offload portions of the DL model computations during inference to faster untrusted processors. We implement the presented techniques in MazeNet, a framework to transform pretrained models into MazeNet models and deploy them on a public cloud platform to provide inference services.

We evaluate MazeNet on popular convolutional neural networks, and the results demonstrate that MazeNet improves the performance of DNN models as compared to a secure baseline model, where the model runs within a trusted environment. MazeNet increases the throughput of the inference task up to 30x and decreases the latency up to 5x for the benchmark models in our experimental evaluation.

Keywords: Privacy · Intel SGX · Machine learning

1 Introduction

Machine Learning-as-a-Service (MLaaS) enables deep learning (DL) model owners to deploy trained models on public cloud platforms to provide inference services. A model owner pretrains a model in-house and uploads the trained model to a public cloud platform. In turn, MLaaS exposes an API endpoint to the uploaded model to query the model with inputs and obtain predictions.

However, moving the model to a public cloud platform exposes the model owner and the uploaded model to various security and privacy risks. First, a

---

V. Kumar and A. Kanade—Work done while at the Indian Institute of Science, Bangalore, India.

N. Hubballi et al. (Eds.): ICISS 2025, LNCS 16380, pp. 65–84, 2026.
https://doi.org/10.1007/978-3-032-13714-2_6

compromised or malicious MLaaS provider can easily steal the deployed models as the model is available in plaintext during the inference because the cloud vendor controls the entire hardware and software stack at its data centres. A stolen model leads to financial losses and legal troubles for the model owner. Often, organisations invest significant financial resources to train state-of-the-art models [21] that solve critical business problems. Second, having access to model parameters and intermediate states, the DL model can leak sensitive information about their private training dataset through membership inference attacks [44]. Often, these models are trained on private datasets to improve the accuracy of the learning task. Legal laws in many countries require that private data, such as financial transactions [1], electronic health records [2], insurance, etc., be protected. Otherwise, the defaulting organisation will be penalised heavily [1,2]. Third, the MLaaS provider can tamper with the uploaded model to influence the results. Therefore, it becomes crucial to protect the integrity and confidentiality of the uploaded models on public cloud platforms.

A naive solution to protect the model on an MLaaS platform would be to run the model within a Trusted Execution Environment (TEE) such as Intel Software Guard Extensions (SGX). The TEE will be responsible for ensuring the confidentiality and integrity of the DL model during the inference process. However, directly running the DL model within the TEE is suboptimal.

First, TEEs often have fixed and usually smaller protected memory than the main memory. For example, SGXv1 offers only 128 MB of protected memory. Therefore, a DL model larger than protected memory incurs a performance penalty. Second, TEEs cannot securely utilise untrusted but powerful resources such as co-located processors, main memory, and storage available on the system.

In this work, we present MazeNet, a framework to transform pre-trained models into MazeNet models and securely run them on heterogeneous and distributed systems consisting of trusted execution environments and untrusted runtimes. MazeNet uses three key techniques to overcome the limitations of TEEs and provides a secure and fast inference solution.

First, to overcome the fixed protected memory of SGX enclaves, MazeNet splits the DNN model into smaller models, referred to as submodels, such that the maximum memory usage of each submodel during inference is less than the size of the protected memory offered by the SGX enclaves. During inference, MazeNet distributes the submodels to different SGX enclaves. Splitting avoids the performance penalty due to swapping when submodels execute within SGX enclaves. Figure 1a shows an illustration of splitting, where a model $\mathcal{M}$ is split ① into five submodels $\mathcal{S}_1 \ldots \mathcal{S}_5$.

Second, running submodels only within TEEs leaves other untrusted resources underutilised. Therefore, to maximise the system utilisation and improve the performance, a subset of submodels is outsourced to untrusted runtime environments. However, outsourcing to an untrusted environment raises privacy risks for the outsourced submodels. Therefore, MazeNet employs its second technique, cloaking, a secure outsourcing scheme to offload submodel evaluation to untrusted hardware. In cloaking, synthetic layers and neurons are added to

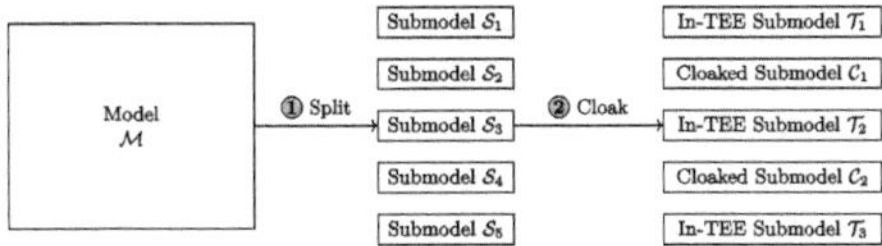

(a) On-premises, a Model Builder splits ① the pre-trained model and cloaks ② a subset of submodels to produce a MazeNet model.

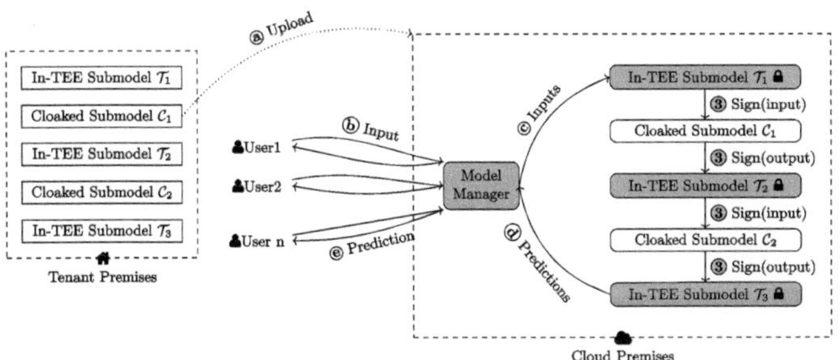

(b) On the cloud, a Model Manager deploys the MazeNet model, and exposes an API for users to query the model. During the inference, the MLaaS provider signs inputs and outputs of cloaked submodels ③ that are outsourced to untrusted environments.

Fig. 1. End-to-end workflow of MazeNet system.

the submodel, which hides the original weights within the synthetic weights to protect the privacy of the outsourced submodel. In the Fig. 1a, after splitting, submodel $\mathcal{S}_2, \mathcal{S}_4$ are cloaked ② to produce final MazeNet Model.

Third, during inference, the adversary can tamper with any data or computation outside the TEEs, including cloaked submodel weights. MazeNet employs digital signatures to detect tampering in offloaded computations. It requires the cloud vendor to sign ③ both the inputs and the outputs of the cloaked submodels, as shown in Fig. 1b, to commit to submodel evaluation results. The signatures are later used during an audit phase, where MazeNet independently verifies some of the outsourced computations by re-executing some of them.

Figure 1 shows the end-to-end MazeNet workflow. First, a cloud tenant transforms a pretrained model into a MazeNet model with *Model Builder* and uploads the generated model to a public cloud platform, where a *Model Manager* securely deploys the uploaded model and exposes an API to query the model.

Prior works [16,46,50] have proposed secure outsourcing schemes to outsource linear layers of DL models to hardware accelerators. However, outsourcing only linear layers is suboptimal, as linear layers are frequently followed by nonlinear layers. As a result, the intermediate state needs to be constantly moved between the TEE and the GPUs. Table 1 shows the data transferred between TEE and non-TEE for prior works. MazeNet overcomes this limitation by outsourcing both the linear and the non-linear layers to GPUs, thereby reducing communication costs. MazeNet can reduce up to 90% of the data transfer cost. Figure 2 compares MazeNet with prior works.

Table 1. Data transfers between the TEE and GPU when only linear layers are outsourced to GPUs, while non-linear layer executes within the TEE.

| | Data transfer (MB) | | |
Model	TEE→GPU	GPU→TEE	Total
VGG16	34.77	51.71	86.48
ResNet50	38.70	40.39	79.09
DenseNet201	91.43	29.96	121.39

To evaluate the benefits and costs of the proposed techniques, we have built a prototype of the MazeNet framework on top of TensorFlow [14]. We transform popular convolutional neural networks (CNN), VGG16 [45], ResNet50 [17], and DenseNet201 [18], into MazeNet models and compare them against a secure baseline model, where the whole unmodified model runs within a TEE. Our evaluation shows that MazeNet can improve the throughput up to 30x and reduce the latency up to 5x for the models considered in our experimental evaluation.

To summarise, the following are the main contributions of this work:

- This work presents MazeNet, a framework to secure trained deep learning models on public cloud with trusted execution environments.
- It proposes an outsourcing scheme to outsource both linear and non-linear layers to untrusted environments to accelerate the model inference.
- Our evaluation shows that MazeNet can significantly improve the throughput and the latency of DL models as compared to the secure baseline models.

2   Background

Trusted Execution Environments. Trusted Execution Environments (TEEs) provide an isolated environment that is protected against software and hardware-based attacks from privileged adversaries, including the OS, BIOS, and firmware. Silicon vendors have introduced support for TEEs [11, 28, 31, 32]. This work uses Intel SGX as a TEE because its threat model is most suitable for cloud workloads, as it has a minimal trusted computing base. With SGX, applications can build enclaves within their program address space, whose contents are protected from privileged adversaries.

Threat Model. MazeNet admits a strong adversary based on the standard threat model of Intel SGX. We only trust the code and data residing in enclaves and the Intel CPU. The adversary controls the privileged system software, including the OS, firmware, and BIOS. It can read and modify data located outside SGX enclaves. The main goal of this work is to protect the privacy of trained parameters of a deep learning model. We assume that the cloud vendor is not aware of the pretrained model architecture. This work does not aim to protect the privacy of user inputs, as it is orthogonal to the goal of model privacy.

Prior research has demonstrated several side-channel attacks against SGX [7, 52], and Intel is actively working to fix those side-channel attacks [20]. Therefore, side-channel attacks are outside the scope of this work.

Prior Work	Model Privacy (server)	Input Privacy (server)	Outsource to Untrusted Hardware	Scalable to Large Models	Platform / Technique
Securenets [8]	✓	✓	✓		SMM
Cryptonets [13]					FHE
Chameleon [38]		✓			GC
DeepSecure [39]	✓	✓			GC
Crypflow [25]	✓			✓	MPC
SecureML [35]		✓			MPC
MiniONN [29]		✓			FHE and GC
Gazelle [23]	✓				FHE and MPC
Shadownet [46]	✓		✓		ARM TrustZone
DarknetTZ [34]				✓	ARM TrustZone
OMG [5]	✓				ARM TrustZone
Occlumency [27]		✓			SGX
TensorScone [26]	✓				SGX
DarkNight [16]	✓		✓		SGX
MLCapsule [15]	✓	✓			SGX
Slalom [50]			✓		SGX
MazeNet	✓		✓	✓	SGX

Fig. 2. Feature comparison of prior works with respect to the privacy of models and user inputs. SMM: Secure Matrix Multiplication, SGX: Intel Software Guard eXention. FHE: Fully Homomorphic Encryption. MPC: Multi-Party Compuation. GC: Garbled Circuits.

3   Building MazeNet Models

A pre-trained model is transformed in two stages. First, the model is split into smaller models. Then, a subset of models is cloaked to produce a MazeNet model.

3.1   Splitting DNN Models

The size of DNN models is increasing as new state-of-the-art architectures are introduced, and larger models are trained to achieve higher accuracy on the learning task. Recent report [4] states that computing resources needed for DNNs doubles every 3.4 months, with GPT-3 model reaching 175 billion parameters. Due to their large size, many DNN models do not fit within the fixed protected memory offered by TEEs. In case of SGX enclaves, the hardware can only cryptographically protect a small portion of main memory [16,49]. Models larger than the size of protected memory incur a performance penalty due to swapping.

Intel SGX reserves a portion of main memory, Enclave Page Cache (EPC), to store the encrypted pages of the enclaves in the main memory, which are protected by the hardware. As this is a fixed portion of memory, enclave applications and DNN models that have higher memory requirements than the size of the protected memory incur EPC swapping, where the SGX driver in the kernel

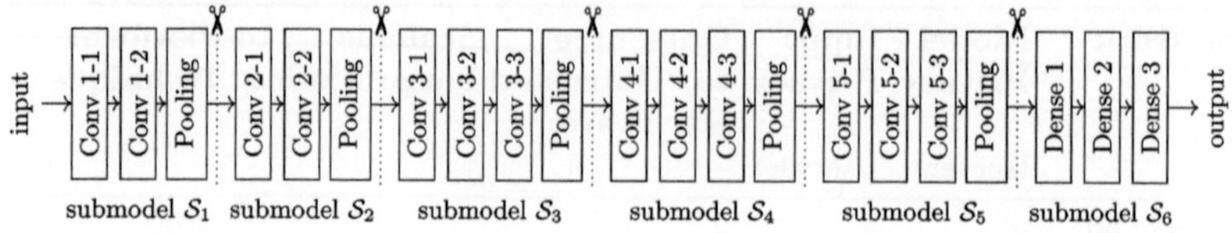

Fig. 3. Splitting the VGG16 [45] model into smaller submodels.

seals a few pages of EPC and stores them on the unprotected memory. Thus freeing a few pages in the EPC for enclave applications. Due to EPC swapping, the performance of enclave applications is severely degraded, as swapping is computationally expensive due to the cryptographic operations required to ensure confidentiality and integrity of swapped pages in untrusted memory. Further, applications stall if they needs any of the swapped-out pages.

To overcome this limitation of fixed protected memory, MazeNet splits large DNN models into smaller models referred to as submodels, such that each submodel fits within the protected memory offered by SGX. After splitting, each submodel can be deployed on different TEEs to avoid EPC swapping.

Figure 3 shows one such splitting of the VGG16 model, where the splits are performed after the pooling layers. In the case of functional models, where the output of one layer can be input to more than one following layers, the splits can be performed at block levels.

3.2   Submodel Cloaking

The submodels obtained from splitting can be hosted on TEEs to provide secure inference services. However, deploying submodels only on TEEs leaves other powerful but untrusted system resources, such as CPUs and GPUs, underutilised. Therefore, a subset of the submodels is deployed in the untrusted runtime environment to improve the performance of the inference service. The submodels deployed within TEEs are referred to as in-TEE submodels, while the submodels deployed outside the TEEs are referred to as non-TEE submodels.

However, outsourcing submodels to untrusted environments poses the following security and privacy risks, which were earlier mitigated by TEEs. First, passive adversaries can observe the delegated submodels in plaintext and therefore they can learn the connection between different layers along with their parameters and weights. Second, an active adversary can tamper with outsourced computation. It can replace the weights of outsourced submodels, change the results, or perform replay attacks on outsourced computations.

To protect the privacy of outsourced submodels, MazeNet employs its second technique of cloaking, where the submodels are cloaked before deploying them to untrusted environments. In cloaking, synthetic layers and neurons are added to the submodel to produce a cloaked submodel, where the original submodel is embedded within the cloaked submodel. Cloaking hides the existing weights within synthetic weights.

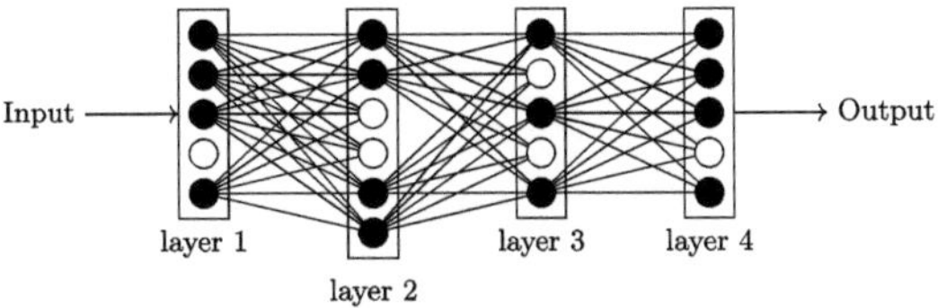

Fig. 4. Phase 1: Adding synthetic neurons (O) between existing neurons (●) in a four layer submodel.

Key idea. The key idea behind cloaking is that parameters or weights of a layer are a set of matrices, and it is difficult to distinguish whether a given matrix is part of a pre-trained model or not. For example, filters in convolutional layers detect different features. Given two filters, each detecting a different feature, it is difficult to determine which one is part of the trained model.

Prior work on model explanations that tries to reason about the working of DL models suggests that individual filters and units (neurons) need a global view of the entire model to reason about the usefulness or role of individual neurons in the predictions [48]. Thus, when synthetic weights are added in submodels, an adversary cannot distinguish between the embedded weights and the newly added synthetic weights. It can only observe the partial computation, which contains a mix of actual and synthetic computation. The keys to recover the results from cloaked submodels are securely stored within the TEEs.

For cloaking, a subset of submodels are marked as in-TEE, which are deployed within TEEs, while the remaining are marked as non-TEE, which are cloaked to produce cloaked submodels. The first and the last layer in the pre-trained model are always part of in-TEE submodels. The remaining submodels are alternatively marked as in-TEE and non-TEE. In the previous example of splitting VGG16 model in the Fig. 3, submodels S_1, S_3, S_5 are marked as in-TEE submodels, while submodels S_2, S_4 are labelled as non-TEE and cloaked.

3.3 Cloaking Process

Non-TEE submodels are cloaked in two phases. In the first phase, synthetic neurons are inserted into existing (embedded) layers to hide embedded neurons. Then, in the second phase, synthetic layers are added to hide embedded layers.

Sample weight distributions. The weights of the synthetic neuron and layers are drawn from sample weight distributions. However, the probability distribution of weights for each layer is unknown beforehand, and during the training, layers learn one of the instances of these weights from the distributions. The weight distributions differ across layers, as each layer learns a different feature. For example, in convolutional networks, initial layers learn simple features such as edge detection, while deeper layers learn complex features such as facial expression. A sample distribution can be created for layers during the training and hyperparameter tuning phase by recording the weights of each layer. More-

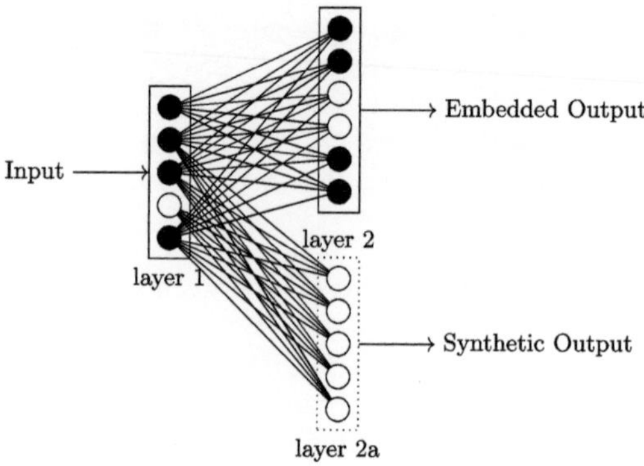

Fig. 5. Phase 2: Adding a synthetic layer, `layer 2a`, to a two layer submodel.

over, the sample distribution can be extended by training the model multiple times with different initial weights.

Phase 1: Adding Synthetic Neurons. In the first phase, synthetic neurons are added to the convolutional and dense layers. In case of convolutional layers, synthetic filters compatible with existing filters in the layer are sampled and appended to the existing filters. For dense layers, weight matrices compatible with the size of the input tensor are sampled and appended to existing weights. Finally, the weights are shuffled to hide the existing weights from the newly added weights.

Adding synthetic neurons and filters makes the layers incompatible with the following layers as the size of the outputs increases. For example, consider a dense layer containing 64 neurons. Suppose 32 neurons are added to the layer during the first phase of cloaking. Then, it will produce output of length 96 instead of 64. Thus, the following layer will become incompatible as it expects input size to be 64. Therefore, the outputs from cloaked layers are filtered before feeding them to following following layers. Figure 4 shows that the output of synthetic neurons is filtered before feeding them to the following layer. The output of synthetic neurons is used later in the second phase of cloaking when synthetic layers are added. Similarly, shuffling the filter and weight matrices results in incorrect results produced by layers. Therefore, the weights of the following layers are also reordered such that dot products compute the same results as before the weights were shuffled.

After synthetic neurons are added, embedded weights are hidden from the adversary. However, the adversary still knows that a subset of the weights are from the embedded model for any given layer. Therefore, to further hide the embedded layer as well, synthetic layers are added.

Phase 2: Adding Synthetic Layers. During the second phase, synthetic layers are added to the submodels obtained from the first phase of cloaking to build the final cloaked submodels. Adding synthetic layers embeds the existing submodel within a bigger model (cloaked submodel).

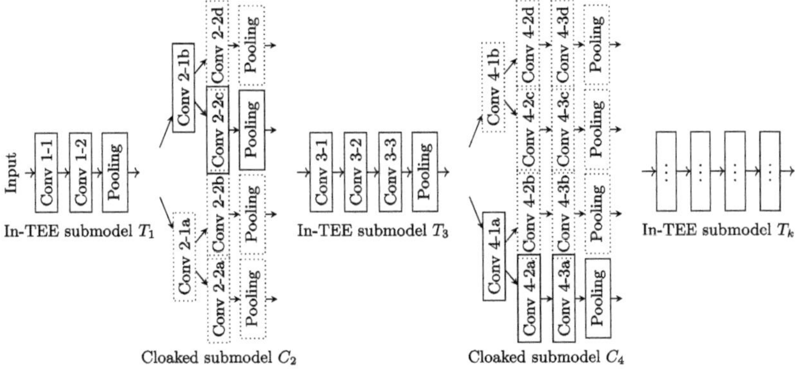

Fig. 6. One of the instances of the VGG16 MazeNet model obtained after splitting and cloaking. Layer represents embedded layers, while Layer represent synthetic layers.

A submodel can be hidden in another model as new architectures have been introduced which moves away from the traditional sequential architecture where the output of one layer is input to the immediately following layer. State-of-the-art models differ widely in their architecture from introduction of skip connection in ResNet [17], densely connected layer in DenseNet [18], parallel layers in Inception module of GoogleNet [47], and ensemble models, [12,17] which combine multiple independent models to form a bigger model. Thus, a submodel may appear to be part of multiple architectures. Further, adding synthetic layers increases the difficulty of identifying embedded layers based on the input-output relationship between the layers in the cloaked submodels.

The model owner provides the architecture of the synthetic layers for the second phase of cloaking, which specifies the location and the type of synthetic layers to be added in the cloaked submodels. To attach synthetic layers, intermediate inputs are selected from the submodel, and they are filtered. In contrast to embedded layer, the inputs to synthetic layers contain outputs of synthetic neurons as well as shown in Fig. 5, which were added in the first phase of cloaking. Then, the weights for the synthetic layers are drawn from the sample distributions, and the layers are added to the submodel.

The synthetic outputs produced by the synthetic layers are later eliminated by the TEEs. During cloaking, MazeNet uses taints to track the status of each value produced by the layers in the cloaked submodel. A taint tensor is maintained for each input, intermediate, and output tensor. The values in the taint tensor indicate whether the corresponding value in the actual tensor is **real** or **synthetic**. For the initial user input, the taint tensor is initialised with **real** label. As the input passes through the synthetic layers and synthetic neurons, the corresponding value in the taint tensor is set to **synthetic**. Similarly, **real** label is set for values produced by embedded layers or neurons.

Figure 6 shows one of the instances of generated MazeNet model corresponding to the VGG16 model. It consists of three in-TEE submodels, T_1, T_3, and T_5, and two cloaked submodels, C_2 and C_4.

4   Running MazeNet Models

A Model Manager on the cloud deploys the MazeNet models generated from pre-trained models. It deploys in-TEE submodels within Intel SGX enclaves and cloaked submodels on untrusted environments. Then, it exposes an API to query the deployed model. On receiving input from a user, it routes the input through a series of in-TEE and cloaked submodels to compute the inference results.

However, during the inference, an adversary on the cloud can read and modify any data and computations that are outsourced to the untrusted runtime to compromise the inference process or results. To detect integrity violations during cloaked submodel evaluation, MazeNet relies on digital signatures. The enclaves are built with the public key of the cloud provider. Thus, the public key cannot be modified or replaced during the inference. If the cloud vendor tampers with the private key that it controls, the signature verification will fail.

Outside the enclave, MazeNet requires the cloud vendor to compute signatures $Sign_{sk}(C_{input})$, where sk is the cloud vendor's private key, for each input C_{input} and output C_{output} of the cloaked submodels $C \in \mathcal{C}$. The enclave, which receives the intermediate output C_{output} as input for the in-TEE submodel, verifies the intermediate outputs and corresponding signatures. On successful verification, the enclave filters embedded outputs from synthetic outputs with taint obtained during cloaking and feeds the filtered output to the in-TEE submodel to proceed with the inference process. Then, the enclave sends both signatures to the Model Manager for auditing.

During an audit phase, the Model Manager can randomly verify some of the outsourced computation by re-executing those computations within a TEE, or outsource them to a non-colluding party, such as other cloud vendors or on-premises execution. The audit phase does not influence the throughput or latency of the system, as it happens when the system is idle or in an offline phase.

Security Analysis of MazeNet Models. All the in-TEE submodels run within TEEs; therefore, in-TEE submodel weights are secured by the hardware from adversaries. In the case of non-TEE submodels, each non-TEE submodel $\hat{T} \in \hat{\mathcal{T}}$ is cloaked to get a corresponding cloaked submodel $C \in \mathcal{C}$. To steal the weights of the embedded non-TEE submodel $\hat{T}$ from the cloaked submodel C, the adversary needs to correctly identify embedded neurons from synthetic ones. Equivalently, the adversary can steal the submodel if it can correctly guess the synthetic outputs from the embedded outputs, which are filtered by the enclaves.

Each subset of output from the cloaked model corresponds to a unique model. However, only one of them corresponds to the embedded model. Thus, the problem of submodel stealing for the adversary reduces to correctly identifying a subset from all possible subsets of a given set. For a set of size $|S|$, there are $2^{|S|} - 1$ possible subsets, excluding the empty subset. Therefore, if a cloaked submodel produces N tensors as outputs, then the probability that an adversary can correctly guess the embedded non-TEE submodel $\hat{T}$ is:

$$P(\hat{T}) = \frac{1}{2^N - 1}$$

For the entire model, the number of expected weights that would be presented in randomly extracted submodels would be the sum of expected weights in the individual cloaked submodels. Therefore, the number of weights present in a randomly extracted model by the adversary would be:

$$E[\text{Embedded Weights}] = \sum_{C \in \mathcal{C}} \frac{|W_C|}{2^{||C||} - 1}$$

Here, $|W_C|$ is the number of embedded weights or parameters present in cloaked submodel C, and $||C||$ is the number of output tensor produced by the cloaked submodel C.

5   Implementation

We have built the MazeNet framework on TensorFlow [14]. It consists of two components: Model Builder and Model Manager. Model Builder accepts a pre-trained model in TensorFlow `SavedModel` format, and produces a MazeNet model consisting of in-TEE and cloaked submodels. The in-TEE submodels are exported in `TFLite` format, and the cloaked submodel in `SavedModel` format. In addition to the MazeNet model, the Model Builder produces taint tensors that are required during the inference process.

On the cloud, Model Manager manages the life cycle of MazeNet models. It is responsible for securely deploying in-TEE submodels within the TEEs and cloaked submodels in untrusted environments. The enclave hosting in-TEE submodels has secure access to taint tensors during the inference process to filter embedded outputs.

Our implementation relies on Intel SGX as a TEE. As applications do not run out-of-the-box on Intel SGX, the research community and industry have developed multiple frameworks to run applications on SGX. These include Graphene-SGX [51], Porpoise [42], Panoply [43], SGX-LKL [36]. Among these, we have selected Graphene-SGX (v1.0) as it supports the Python programming environment and the TensorFlow deep learning framework.

To implement the MazeNet framework, we have added cloaking support for popular layers in the TensorFlow framework, which were present in our benchmark models – VGG16, ResNet50, and DenseNet201. In total, TensorFlow has around 150 types of layers, and we implemented cloaking support for 20 TensorFlow layers for the benchmark models.

In the implementation, adding cloaking support for TensorFlow layers required 715 lines of Python code in Model Builder, and 550 lines for Model Manager as reported by `pygount` [3]. Further, MazeNet can be extended to other models by implementing cloaking for unsupported layers present in the model.

Table 2. Configuration parameter used to generate MazeNet models.

Model	Cloak factor	Submodel width	In-TEE layers
VGG16	10%	10	1, 11, 22
ResNet50	10%	10	1–7, 92–102, 174–177
DenseNet201	10%	10	1–7, 49–137, 477–709

6   Evaluation

To find the benefits and costs of the presented techniques, we transformed popular convolutional neural networks, VGG16 [24], ResNet50 [17], and DenseNet201 [18], into MazeNet models.

Generating MazeNet models. We have used pre-trained model weights present in Keras library [9] to produce MazeNet models. In MazeNet, the model developer provides the set of synthetic layers to be added during the cloaking phase. For the evaluation, we duplicated existing layers to produce cloaked submodels.

There are three key configuration parameters (split, cloak factor, cloaked submodel width) for building a MazeNet model. Table 2 lists the configuration parameters used in our evaluation.

1. **Split** states how the given model should be split into smaller submodels. According to the Table 2, layer $1, 11$ and 22 of the VGG16 model are designated as in-TEE layers. Therefore, the Model Builder produces three in-TEE submodels, each containing one layer, while the remaining layers $\{L_2, \ldots, L_{10}\}, \{L_{12}, \ldots, L_{21}\}$ are part of two cloaked submodels.
2. **Cloak factor** represents the percentage of synthetic weights to be added to build a cloaked layer. For example, a convolutional layer with 64 filters and 10% cloak factor will result in 72 filters in the cloaked convolutional layer.
3. **Cloaked submodel width** limits the maximum width during cloaking, as duplicating layers increases the width of the submodel, where width is the number of layers present at a given depth d.

6.1   Experimental Setup

Based on the parameters in Table 2 to build MazeNet models, the Model Builder produces three in-TEE and two cloaked submodels. The in-TEE submodels are deployed on three TEE systems that are equipped with an Intel i7-7700 desktop-class CPU, which supports SGXv1 with 128 MB of cryptographically protected memory, and 32 GB of main memory. The remaining two cloaked submodels are deployed on non-TEE systems without SGX support. The non-TEE system is equipped with server-class Xeon Gold 6150 CPU, having 36 cores and 72 threads, along with 256 GB of main memory. As the server-class machine has a high core count and sufficient main memory, both the cloaked submodels are deployed on

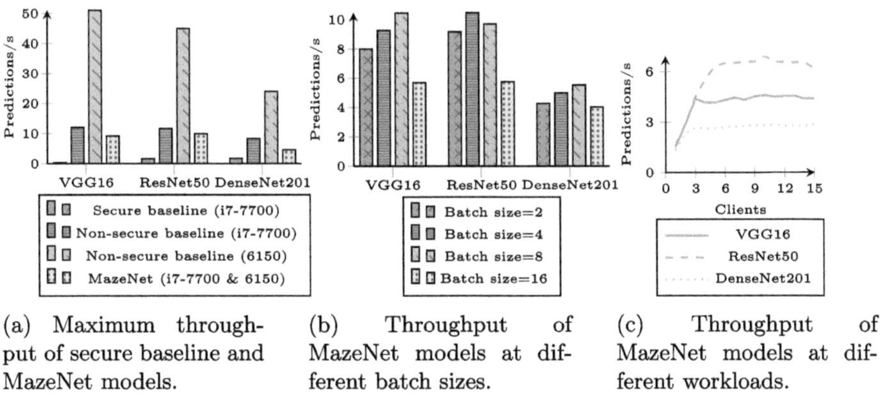

(a) Maximum throughput of secure baseline and MazeNet models.

(b) Throughput of MazeNet models at different batch sizes.

(c) Throughput of MazeNet models at different workloads.

Fig. 7. Throughput of MazeNet models generated from parameters in Table 2.

the same machine. Our evaluation focuses on throughput and latency, where the inference service performs classification on images from the ImageNet [40].

Baseline models. We compare the performance of MazeNet models against *secure baseline* models where the whole unmodified model executes within a TEE. The secure baseline model executes on one of the TEE systems (i7-7700) described above. As the non-TEE system does not support any TEE, we cannot report secure baseline performance for the 6150 CPU. Similarly, for *non-secure baseline*, we run unmodified models in the standard untrusted environment.

The accuracy of MazeNet models is similar to unmodified models, as MazeNet performs the same set of computations in addition to synthetic computations.

6.2 Throughput Results

To evaluate throughput, we query the models with 128 input samples that are split across eight clients, where each client simulates a single user and query the models in parallel. We repeat this experiment with different batch sizes, where multiple inputs are grouped to form a batch, and report the maximum throughput across batch sizes, for each model in Fig. 7a. The results demonstrate that MazeNet models achieve higher throughput when compared to the secure baseline models. MazeNet models benefit from the faster untrusted processors, whereas the secure baseline models are limited by the weak trusted CPU. However, the speedup observed across models differs significantly from 30x in VGG16 to 2x in DenseNet201. The speedup is more significant in VGG16 as it is computationally expensive, requiring 30.96 GFLOPs as compared to ResNet50 and DenseNet201 models, which require 7.73 and 8.58 GFLOPs, respectively. Thus, the VGG16 MazeNet model benefits more from untrusted processors.

During the experiments, we observed that each MazeNet model achieved maximum throughput at a different batch size. Therefore, we next measure the role of batch size in the throughput of MazeNet models. To measure the impact

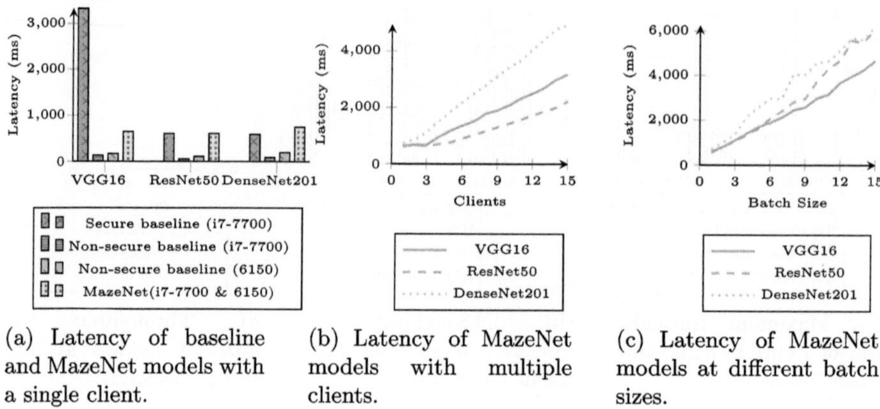

(a) Latency of baseline and MazeNet models with a single client.

(b) Latency of MazeNet models with multiple clients.

(c) Latency of MazeNet models at different batch sizes.

Fig. 8. Latency trends of MazeNet models.

of batch size, eight clients query the model at different batch sizes, and the results are presented in Fig. 7b. Increasing the batch size improves the throughput of MazeNet models. However, increasing the batch size beyond the optimal point leads to a significant decline in throughput. The primary reason for this degradation of throughput is EPC swapping in enclaves due to the large intermediate state produced by in-TEE submodels at higher batch sizes.

Finally, we evaluate how the throughput scales with increasing workload. Initially, a single client queries the model with a fixed batch size of one. Then, the number of clients is progressively increased, while keeping the batch size fixed, to simulate the increasing workload. Figure 7c shows the throughput of MazeNet models at varying workloads. Initially, the overall throughput of MazeNet inference system increases with an increase in workload. However, the throughput saturates when the number of clients crosses six.

6.3 Latency Results

Latency is the time duration a client has to wait for results after sending the inputs to the model. To measure the latency of models, we query the model with a single client that queries the model with a single input. The observed latency for different models is reported in Fig. 8a. The results show a significant improvement in latency for the VGG16 MazeNet model compared to the secure baseline, with latency dropping from 3 to 0.6 s – a 5x improvement.

However, there is no latency improvement for the ResNet50 and DenseNet201 MazeNet models. There are two main sources that contribute to the latency of MazeNet models, in addition to computational operations. First is the time spent on computing the digital signatures by cloaked submodels and verification of signatures by enclaves. Second is the time spent on data transfers between cloaked and in-TEE submodels. As compared to the VGG16 MazeNet Model, the ResNet50 and DenseNet201 MazeNet models spend more time on computing

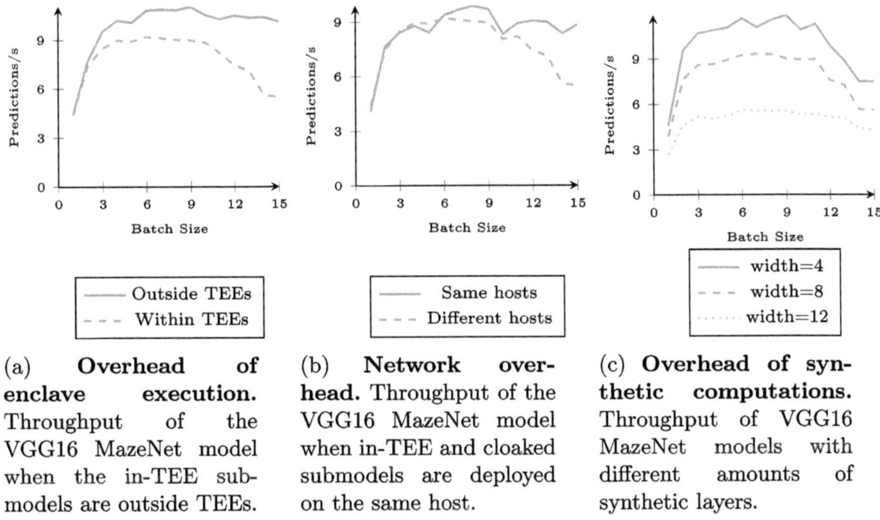

(a) **Overhead of enclave execution.** Throughput of the VGG16 MazeNet model when the in-TEE submodels are outside TEEs.

(b) **Network overhead.** Throughput of the VGG16 MazeNet model when in-TEE and cloaked submodels are deployed on the same host.

(c) **Overhead of synthetic computations.** Throughput of VGG16 MazeNet models with different amounts of synthetic layers.

Fig. 9. Overheads arising from different sources during MazeNet inference.

digital signatures and data transfers than performing deep learning operations, which can be accelerated by untrusted hardware.

Next, we evaluate how the latency changes with increasing workload. We began with a single client which queries the model with a single input. Then, progressively, we increase the number of clients over time. Figure 8b presents the latency trends of MazeNet models under the varying number of clients. Initially, the Latency increases slightly when the number of clients is increased from one to five. As the number of clients increases, the number of active models in the inference pipeline increases. However, when the pipeline is full or saturated, further increasing the number of clients proportionally increases the latency as the input queries are queued by the Model Manager.

Next, we investigate the impact of batch size on the latency of MazeNet models. We measure the latency of MazeNet models at different batch sizes while keeping the number of clients constant (one). Initially, the client sends the query with a single input. Then, it gradually increases the number of input samples within the batch. Figure 8c reports the latency for the entire batch. For all the models, the latencies at different batch sizes follow the same pattern. The batch latency increases with an increase in batch size. However, the average time spent per input sample within a batch reduces from 0.60 to 0.30 s when the batch size is increased from one to fifteen. Similarly, it decreases from 0.56 to 0.40 s for ResNet50, and 0.71 to 0.41 s for DenseNet201. The results show that batching can reduce the time spent per input during inference.

6.4   Overheads

Overhead of enclave execution. Applications run slowly within enclaves due to the overheads intrinsic to enclave execution. To quantify the overhead of enclave execution, we measure the throughput of MazeNet models in two configurations: in-TEE submodels within TEEs and in-TEE submodels outside TEEs. In the first configuration, we run MazeNet models in the standard configuration as per the experimental setup described in Sect. 6.1. In the second configuration, in-TEE submodels are deployed in an untrusted environment to avoid the overheads of enclave execution, while the remaining setup remains the same.

Figure 9a plots the throughput of the VGG16 MazeNet model in both configurations. The throughput of the standard configuration, in-TEE submodels with TEEs, is within 20% of the other configuration for batch sizes up to eight, as the throughput is bottlenecked by cloaked submodel execution time instead of the enclave execution. However, at higher batch sizes, EPC swapping occurs due to the larger intermediate state produced by the in-TEE submodels, which shifts the bottleneck from the cloaked submodel to EPC swapping in enclaves. Consequently, the throughput of in-TEE submodels within TEE starts to decrease at higher batch sizes. Thus, the overhead of enclave execution is more prominent when there is EPC swapping, while it is minimal without EPC swapping.

Network Overhead. Intermediate results of submodels are transferred over the network, which introduces overhead during the inference process. We evaluate the overhead due to the 1 Gigabit Ethernet network in our experimental setup. To isolate network overhead, we run both the in-TEE submodels and cloaked submodels and in-TEE submodels on the same non-TEE system, the server machine described in the experimental setup, Sect. 6.1. This eliminates the need for network transfers during the inference process. As the in-TEE submodels runs outside the enclave, similar to the previous experiment, we can offset the performance gains from running in-TEE submodels outside the enclave, up to 20% at smaller batch sizes. We compare the throughput of the VGG16 MazeNet model in the above two configurations. The throughput in both cases is similar, as the inference process is compute-bound. During inference, VGG16 submodels transfer around 10 MB of data per single input inference. As the MazeNet model in standard configuration achieves around eight inferences per second, the network bandwidth of one Gigabit does not introduce any significant overhead.

Overhead of synthetic computations.: To quantify the overhead due to the synthetic computations present in the cloaked submodels, we compare the number of floating-point operations required to compute inference results in unmodified models and MazeNet models. Table 3 lists the number of floating point operations (FLOPs) in unmodified and MazeNet models, which were generated from the parameters given in Table 2. Next, we evaluate the impact of different amounts of synthetic layers on the throughput of MazeNet models. Figure 9c shows the throughput trends for three models, each having different widths.

Table 3. Number of Floating-Point Operations (FLOPs) in standard and Mazenet models when models were cloaked with parameters in Table 2.

Model	Standard	MazeNet Submodels			
		in-TEE	Cloaked	Total	Increase
		(GFLOPs)			
VGG16	30.96	1.85	151.76	153.60	5x
ResNet50	7.73	0.684	60.85	61.54	8x
DenseNet201	8.58	3.17	51.18	54.36	6x

7 Related Works

Prior works have used trusted execution environments to protect the privacy and confidentiality of training and inference of deep learning models [5,6,19,26]. Another line of research has focused on offloading deep learning computation to hardware accelerators [16,46,50,53]. The main limitation of these works is that they outsource only linear layers. However, often linear layers are followed by a non-linear layer. Therefore, the intermediate outputs of the linear layers need to be constantly moved between the TEE and the GPUs. MazeNet overcomes this by outsourcing both linear and non-linear layers to untrusted environments, thus reducing the constant need to transfer data between TEE and GPUs.

Another line of works has presented cryptography-based solutions that use homomorphic encryption schemes [10,13,41] and multi-party computation [25,30,35,37–39] protocols or a combination of both techniques [23,33] to protect deep learning workloads. Recent work [22] reports sub-second latency for the VGG16 model with GPUs on a smaller CIFAR dataset, while MazeNet achieves sub-second latency with CPUs on the larger ImageNet dataset. Cryptography-based techniques face two primary challenges when applied in real-world deployments. The first is the significant computational overhead associated with cryptographic operations. The second is the high communication cost incurred by interactive protocols. Together, these limitations make such approaches less practical for applications where low latency and high throughput are critical.

8 Conclusion

In this work, we presented MazeNet to protect the privacy models on public cloud platforms with TEEs, and introduced methods to outsource portions of computation during inference to untrusted hardware. Our outsourcing scheme outsources both the linear and non-linear layers. We implemented the presented techniques in a prototype framework, MazeNet, to build MazeNet models from given pre-trained models and deploy the MazeNet models on a public cloud platform to provide inference services. Our evaluation of popular convolutional networks demonstrates that MazeNet models can improve the throughput by up to 30x and the latency by up to 5x as compared to the secure baseline models.

Acknowledgements. This work is funded by the Foundation for Science Innovation and Development (FSID), Indian Institute of Science, through the "Security and Privacy of Smart Cities, Sub-Project: Secure Enclaves for Sensitive Applications in Smart Cities" project, managed by IUDX, and "Secure Digital Enclaves for Sensitive Applications" grant. Vivek Kumar is currently affiliated with Goldman Sachs, Bangalore, India, but was a student at the Indian Institute of Science while working on this project.

References

1. Right to financial privacy act of 1978, 12 USC 3401 – 3422
2. Health insurance portability and accountability act of 1996 (1996), pUBLIC LAW 104–191—AUG. 21 (1996)
3. Aglassinger, T.: Pygount. https://pypi.org/project/pygount/
4. Amodei, D., Hernandez, D.: Ai and compute. https://openai.com/blog/ai-and-compute/
5. Bayerl, S.P., et al.: Offline model guard: secure and private ml on mobile devices. In: DATE 2020 (2020)
6. Brasser, F., Gens, D., Jauernig, P., Sadeghi, A.R., Stapf, E.: Sanctuary: arming trustzone with user-space enclaves. In: NDSS (2019)
7. Chen, G., Chen, S., Xiao, Y., Zhang, Y., Lin, Z., Lai, T.H.: Sgxpectre: stealing intel secrets from SGX enclaves via speculative execution. In: 2019 IEEE European Symposium on Security and Privacy (EuroS&P), pp. 142–157. IEEE (2019)
8. Chen, X., Ji, J., Yu, L., Luo, C., Li, P.: Securenets: Secure inference of deep neural networks on an untrusted cloud. In: Proceedings of The 10th Asian Conference on Machine Learning (2018)
9. Chollet, F.: Keras. https://keras.io/api/applications/
10. Dathathri, R., et al.: Chet: an optimizing compiler for fully-homomorphic neural-network inferencing. In: Proceedings of the 40th ACM SIGPLAN conference on programming language design and implementation, pp. 142–156 (2019)
11. Kaplan, D., Jeremy Powell, T.W.: AMD memory encryption. https://www.amd.com/content/dam/amd/en/documents/epyc-business-docs/white-papers/memory-encryption-white-paper.pdf (2021)
12. Ganaie, M.A., Hu, M., Malik, A.K., Tanveer, M., Suganthan, P.N.: Ensemble deep learning: a review. Eng. Appl. Artif. Intell. **115**, 105151 (2022)
13. Gilad-Bachrach, R., Dowlin, N., Laine, K., Lauter, K., Naehrig, M., Wernsing, J.: Cryptonets: applying neural networks to encrypted data with high throughput and accuracy. In: Proceedings of The 33rd International Conference on Machine Learning (2016)
14. Google: tensorflow. https://github.com/tensorflow/tensorflow
15. Hanzlik, L., et al.: Mlcapsule: guarded offline deployment of machine learning as a service. In: 2021 IEEE/CVF Conference on Computer Vision and Pattern Recognition Workshops (CVPRW) (2021)
16. Hashemi, H., Wang, Y., Annavaram, M.: Darknight: an accelerated framework for privacy and integrity preserving deep learning using trusted hardware. In: MICRO-54: 54th Annual IEEE/ACM International Symposium on Microarchitecture (2021)

17. He, K., Zhang, X., Ren, S., Sun, J.: Deep residual learning for image recognition. In: 2016 IEEE Conference on Computer Vision and Pattern Recognition (CVPR) (2016)
18. Huang, G., Liu, Z., Van Der Maaten, L., Weinberger, K.Q.: Densely connected convolutional networks. In: Proceedings of the IEEE conference on computer vision and pattern recognition, pp. 4700–4708 (2017)
19. Hunt, T., Song, C., Shokri, R., Shmatikov, V., Witchel, E.: Chiron: privacy-preserving machine learning as a service (2018)
20. Intel: Q3 2018 speculative execution side channel update. https://www.intel.com/content/www/us/en/security-center/advisory/intel-sa-00161.html
21. Jagielski, M., Carlini, N., Berthelot, D., Kurakin, A., Papernot, N.: High accuracy and high fidelity extraction of neural networks. In: 29th USENIX Security Symposium (USENIX Security 20) (2020)
22. Jawalkar, N., Gupta, K., Basu, A., Chandran, N., Gupta, D., Sharma, R.: Orca: FSS-based secure training and inference with gpus. In: 2024 IEEE Symposium on Security and Privacy (SP). pp. 597–616 (2024)
23. Juvekar, C., Vaikuntanathan, V., Chandrakasan, A.: Gazelle: a low latency framework for secure neural network inference. In: Proceedings of the 27th USENIX Conference on Security Symposium, pp. 1651–1668. SEC'18, USENIX Association, USA (2018)
24. Krizhevsky, A., Sutskever, I., Hinton, G.E.: Imagenet classification with deep convolutional neural networks. In: Proceedings of the 25th International Conference on Neural Information Processing Systems - Volume 1, pp. 1097–1105. NIPS'12, Curran Associates Inc., Red Hook, NY, USA (2012)
25. Kumar, N., Rathee, M., Chandran, N., Gupta, D., Rastogi, A., Sharma, R.: Cryptflow: secure tensorflow inference. Cryptology ePrint Archive, Paper 2019/1049 (2019)
26. Kunkel, R., Quoc, D.L., Gregor, F., Arnautov, S., Bhatotia, P., Fetzer, C.: Tensorscone: a secure tensorflow framework using intel SGX (2019)
27. Lee, T., et al.: Occlumency: privacy-preserving remote deep-learning inference using SGX. In: The 25th Annual International Conference on Mobile Computing and Networking (2019)
28. Limited, A.: Building a secure system using trustzone technology. https://documentation-service.arm.com/static/5f212796500e883ab8e74531   (December 2008)
29. Liu, J., Juuti, M., Lu, Y., Asokan, N.: Oblivious neural network predictions via minionn transformations. In: Proceedings of the 2017 ACM SIGSAC Conference on Computer and Communications Security (2017)
30. Liu, J., Juuti, M., Lu, Y., Asokan, N.: Oblivious neural network predictions via minionn transformations. In: Proceedings of the 2017 ACM SIGSAC conference on computer and communications security, pp. 619–631 (2017)
31. Ltd., A.: Arm Confidential Compute Architecture (2021). https://developer.arm.com/documentation/den0125/0300. Accessed 2 April 2025
32. McKeen, F., et al.: Innovative instructions and software model for isolated execution. In: HASP (2013)
33. Mishra, P., Lehmkuhl, R., Srinivasan, A., Zheng, W., Popa, R.A.: Delphi: a cryptographic inference system for neural networks. In: Proceedings of the 2020 Workshop on Privacy-Preserving Machine Learning in Practice, pp. 27–30 (2020)
34. Mo, F., et al.: Darknetz: towards model privacy at the edge using trusted execution environments. In: Proceedings of the 18th International Conference on Mobile Systems, Applications, and Services (2020)

35. Mohassel, P., Zhang, Y.: Secureml: a system for scalable privacy-preserving machine learning. In: IEEE Symposium on Security and Privacy (SP) (2017)
36. Priebe, C., et al.: SGX-LKL: Securing the host OS interface for trusted execution. In: arXiv:1908.11143 (2019)
37. Rathee, D., et al.: Cryptflow2: practical 2-party secure inference. In: ACM CCS 2020 (2020)
38. Riazi, M.S., Weinert, C., Tkachenko, O., Songhori, E.M., Schneider, T., Koushanfar, F.: Chameleon: a hybrid secure computation framework for machine learning applications. Cryptology ePrint, pp .2017/1164 (2017)
39. Rouhani, B.D., Riazi, M.S., Koushanfar, F.: Deepsecure: scalable provably-secure deep learning. In: Annual Design Automation Conference (2018)
40. Russakovsky, O., et al.: ImageNet large scale visual recognition challenge. Int. J. Comput. Vision **115**(3), 211–252 (2015). https://doi.org/10.1007/s11263-015-0816-y
41. Sanyal, A., Kusner, M., Gascon, A., Kanade, V.: Tapas: tricks to accelerate (encrypted) prediction as a service. In: International conference on machine learning, pp. 4490–4499. PMLR (2018)
42. Shanker, K., Joseph, A., Ganapathy, V.: An evaluation of methods to port legacy code to SGX enclaves. In: Proceedings of the 28th ACM Joint Meeting on European Software Engineering Conference and Symposium on the Foundations of Software Engineering (2020)
43. Shinde, S., Le Tien, D., Tople, S., Saxena, P.: Panoply: low-TCB linux applications with SGX enclaves. In: NDSS (2017)
44. Shokri, R., Stronati, M., Song, C., Shmatikov, V.: Membership inference attacks against machine learning models. In: 2017 IEEE symposium on security and privacy (SP), pp. 3–18. IEEE (2017)
45. Simonyan, K., Zisserman, A.: Very deep convolutional networks for large-scale image recognition. In: 3rd International Conference on Learning Representations (ICLR 2015) (2015)
46. Sun, Z., Sun, R., Liu, C., Chowdhury, A.R., Jha, S., Lu, L.: Shadownet: a secure and efficient system for on-device model inference (2020)
47. Szegedy, C., et al.: Going deeper with convolutions. In: Proceedings of the IEEE conference on computer vision and pattern recognition, pp. 1–9 (2015)
48. Szegedy, C., et al.: Intriguing properties of neural networks. In: International Conference on Learning Representations (ICLR) (2014)
49. Taassori, M., Shafiee, A., Balasubramonian, R.: Vault: reducing paging overheads in SGX with efficient integrity verification structures. SIGPLAN Not. (2018)
50. Tramer, F., Boneh, D.: Slalom: fast, verifiable and private execution of neural networks in trusted hardware. In: International Conference on Learning Representations (2019)
51. Tsai, C., Porter, D.E., Vij, M.: Graphene-SGX: a practical library OS for unmodified applications on SGX. In: USENIX Annual Technical Conference (2017)
52. Van Bulck, J., et al.: Foreshadow: extracting the keys to the intel SGX kingdom with transient out-of-order execution. In: Proceedings FO the 27th USENIX Security Symposium (2018)
53. Zhang, Z., et al.: No privacy left outside: On the (in-) security of tee-shielded DNN partition for on-device ml. In: 2024 IEEE Symposium on Security and Privacy (SP), pp. 3327–3345. IEEE (2024)

Automation and Risk: Transformers Models Reshape Sensitive Information Management

Wellington Fernandes Silvano[✉][iD], Maurício Konrath[iD], Lucas Mayr[iD], and Ricardo Felipe Custódio[iD]

Computer Security Laboratory (LabSEC), Federal University of Santa Catarina (UFSC), Florianópolis, SC 88040-900, Brazil
{wellington.fernandes,lucas.mayr}@posgrad.ufsc.br,
mauricio.konrath@grad.ufsc.br, ricardo.custodio@ufsc.br
https://labsec.ufsc.br

Abstract. The automation of sensitive information classification using AI is critical for modern security, yet a singular focus on accuracy metrics dangerously obscures the risks posed by residual errors. False Negatives can lead to catastrophic data breaches, creating an unmanaged attack surface. This paper bridges the gap between formal security theory and applied machine learning by proposing a framework to operationalize principles of conditional secrecy. We demonstrate how the confidence scores from Transformer models can be used as a practical mechanism to enforce a principled secrecy policy, segmenting data into dynamic security levels. This approach allows organizations to manage the trade-off between automation coverage and risk exposure by treating low-confidence classifications as a controlled transfer to a trusted group of human reviewers. We validate this framework on the expert-annotated Monsanto Papers corpus, showing that Transformer-based classification, unlike traditional methods, provides the necessary discriminative power to make this principled approach viable. Our work offers a new, risk-aware methodology for the secure deployment of AI in high-stakes information governance.

Keywords: Information Security · Secrecy · Risk Management · Natural Language Processing · Transformer Models · Document Classification

1 Introduction

Effective large-scale information governance relies on a foundational security principle: the ability to apply differentiated protection controls based on content sensitivity [1,2]. The formal security literature has long explored models for this purpose, such as **conditional secrecy**, where a secret is maintained unless specific security levels are compromised [3], and **secrecy by typing**, which restricts

N. Hubballi et al. (Eds.): ICISS 2025, LNCS 16380, pp. 85–103, 2026.
https://doi.org/10.1007/978-3-032-13714-2_7

information flow to trusted "groups" of entities [4]. However, the practical and scalable application of these principles to vast repositories of unstructured data (e.g., documents and emails) remains a significant operational challenge, often depending on slow, expensive, and error-prone manual processes.

The recent rise of Artificial Intelligence (AI) models, particularly Transformer architectures [5], offers an unprecedented promise to automate text classification at scale. While the Natural Language Processing (NLP) field has demonstrated the high performance of these models, the information security community has only begun to explore their profound operational implications. AI-driven automation introduces a new paradigm and, with it, a new type of vulnerability: the inherent risk from probabilistic classification errors. A blind reliance on aggregate accuracy metrics overlooks the distinct impacts of False Positives (FPs), which create operational overhead, and False Negatives (FNs), which can lead to catastrophic secrecy violations [6–8].

This paper argues that the key to secure automation lies not merely in pursuing marginally higher performance but in actively managing these residual errors. We identify a critical gap in the literature: a bridge is needed between established security principles, such as conditional secrecy [9], and the practical mechanisms offered by the probabilistic outputs of modern AI models. How can a security manager reliably use a confidence model to implement a segmented data protection policy, where the ensuring that the critical secret remains computationally infeasible to infer?

To address this question, we propose a framework that operationalizes the principle of conditional secrecy through confidence threshold analysis. Our contributions are: i) We demonstrate how the confidence thresholds of AI classifiers can be used to **operationalize the security principle of "secrecy by type"** at scale by defining dynamic security levels for information handling [3]. ii) We propose a risk management methodology that uses this technique to segment information flows, enabling an explicit trade-off between automation coverage and error exposure, treating the low-confidence stream as a controlled access to a trusted "group" [4]. iii) We validate the framework through a comparative analysis on a real-world, expert-annotated corpus (the Monsanto Papers), showing that Transformer models, due to their superior discriminative power, are fundamentally better suited to implement this security policy than traditional approaches. iv) We provide our open-source code and evaluation dataset for reproducibility and future benchmarking.

2   Background

This section establishes the theoretical foundations for our proposed framework, bridging formal security principles with the practical application of machine learning for classification. We begin by reviewing foundational concepts from the formal security literature, such as conditional secrecy and secrecy by typing, and posit that their practical implementation presents a significant challenge for unstructured data. Subsequently, we delve into the specifics of sensitive information classification, detailing the operational and security risks posed by misclassifications (False Negatives and Positives). Finally, we introduce the machine learning models evaluated in this study, contrasting traditional classifiers with modern Transformer-based architectures whose probabilistic outputs are central to our risk management approach.

2.1   From Secrecy Principles to Automated Governance

The challenge of protecting sensitive data is fundamentally about applying differentiated protection controls, a concept formally explored in the security literature. A key approach is through models of *conditional secrecy*, which posit that a secret is maintained unless specific, predefined security levels are compromised. This allows for a granular security posture where the compromise of one component does not lead to a total system failure. Gordon and Jeffrey formalize this via dynamically generated security levels and an ordering that governs information flow, ensuring secrets only flow to levels of equal or higher security [3].

A practical mechanism for enforcing such policies is through *secrecy by type*, which restricts the dissemination of information to trusted "groups" or a defined "reach". In this model, a distinction is made between "honest clients," who adhere to verifiable rules, and a potentially dishonest adversary. A well-typed system can statically guarantee that a secret intended for a specific group of honest clients is never revealed to outsiders [4]. Furthermore, the notion of **relative secrecy** acknowledges that absolute non-interference is often impractical. Instead, security can be defined by computational intractability: a controlled "leak" is acceptable if the effort required for an adversary to deduce the full secret from it is prohibitive, such as learning a secret in polynomial time [9].

Despite the theoretical elegance of these models, their operationalization on large-scale, unstructured enterprise data remains a major hurdle. Manually assigning security levels or defining secrecy groups for millions of documents is infeasible. This paper posits that the probabilistic outputs of modern AI classifiers offer a novel and practical mechanism to bridge this theory-practice gap. We propose that a classifier's confidence score can be used to dynamically instantiate these security principles.

Specifically, a confidence threshold (τ) acts as a mechanism for controlled declassification or risk segmentation. Documents classified with high confidence $(\geq \tau)$ can be treated as belonging to a high security level, suitable for automated processing. Conversely, documents with low confidence $(< \tau)$ are relegated to a lower security level, requiring handling by a trusted "group" of human reviewers [4], thus operationalizing the principle of conditional secrecy [3]. This approach transforms a statistical metric into an actionable security control, enabling a scalable implementation of differentiated protection.

2.2 Sensitive Information Classification

Sensitive information governance refers to the policies, processes, and technologies designed to protect sensitive data throughout its lifecycle, from creation and storage to processing and destruction. Document classification is a crucial aspect of this governance framework, as it enables organizations to identify, label, and safeguard sensitive content within documents. By ensuring that sensitive data is classified in accordance with legal, regulatory, and organizational standards, document classification plays a pivotal role in maintaining the integrity and confidentiality of sensitive information. Classifying sensitive information involves both identifying personally identifiable information, trade secrets, or confidential business data, and applying appropriate security controls to protect this information. Misclassifications of sensitive information can result in serious security risks, including data breaches, unauthorized access, and non-compliance with data protection regulations.

Data classification serves as the first line of defense in sensitive information governance. By accurately distinguishing between sensitive and non-sensitive information, organizations can apply the appropriate level of security controls with better granularity. Furthermore, effective document classification enhances the ability to implement DLP systems. This distinction allows for the efficient and secure management of vast amounts of data, ensuring that sensitive content is properly protected against unauthorized access, while non-sensitive information can be more flexibly handled [10]. These systems rely on accurate classification to monitor and restrict the exchange of sensitive data within and outside the organization, preventing potential leaks or unauthorized transfers [11].

Risks of Misclassification. The consequences of misclassification can be severe, and the two most critical errors in this context are False Negatives (FNs) and False Positives (FPs), which can significantly impact data security and organizational operations.

False Negatives (FNs): Occurs when sensitive information is incorrectly classified as non-sensitive. This leads to the unintended exposure of confidential data to unauthorized individuals. For example, personal health information or financial data may be mistakenly shared with individuals or organizations not authorized to access it, resulting in data breaches and violations of privacy regulations [12]. FNs can also cause sensitive data to bypass essential security measures, such as encryption or access controls, which are necessary to maintain data confidentiality and protect against unauthorized access.

False Positives (FPs): Occurs when non-sensitive information is mistakenly flagged as sensitive. This can disrupt business operations by leading to unnecessary redactions, where information is hidden even though it is non-sensitive. Over-application of security controls, such as encryption, might also occur, resulting in operational inefficiencies and wasted resources. In sensitive sectors like healthcare or finance, such errors could severely impact workflow, productivity, and decision-making, including patient care or financial transactions [13].

Minimizing Security Risks. The classification confidence thresholds are essential for balancing coverage and minimizing security risks. A low threshold increases coverage but may lead to excessive False Positives, overwhelming security teams with unnecessary alerts. Conversely, a high threshold reduces FPs but may result in False Negatives, potentially compromising data security. The challenge is to find the optimal threshold that minimizes errors in security-critical environments. Dynamic thresholding, which adjusts thresholds based on document type, risk level, or operational context, offers a more flexible solution. Additionally, confidence-aware systems, which combine classifier confidence with human review, have been shown to enhance review accuracy and efficiency, reducing the likelihood of critical misclassifications [12,13]. Techniques like confidence calibration and uncertainty quantification further refine these thresholds, providing more reliable confidence estimates and supporting more secure, risk-aware deployments [10,14]. In our context, fine-tuning confidence thresholds is crucial to reduce security risks while ensuring operational efficiency. Furthermore, implementing dynamic, confidence-aware strategies ensures that sensitive data is accurately classified without overburdening manual reviewers, leading to more secure and efficient systems. This threshold-based balancing act is the practical mechanism through which the formal principles of conditional secrecy and risk segmentation, discussed in Sect. 2.1, can be operationalized.

2.3 Models

The task of automated sensitive information classification leverages a spectrum of machine learning models. These can be broadly categorized into traditional approaches, such as Support Vector Machines and Random Forest, which typically rely on manually engineered features from text, and modern Transformer-based architectures like BERT and ELECTRA, which utilize self-attention mechanisms and large-scale pretraining to capture complex linguistic patterns with minimal feature engineering [5,15]. While Transformer models often achieve state-of-the-art performance on various NLP benchmarks, their operational characteristics, particularly concerning computational resources and error profiles, can differ significantly from traditional models, especially in scenarios with smaller or imbalanced datasets [16,17]. To operationalize our risk management methodology, it is essential to understand the architectural differences between machine learning models. This study evaluates two distinct model classes not only on standard performance metrics but, more importantly, on their security implications arising from misclassification patterns when applied to sensitive document governance. Much of the existing research tends to focus on aggregate metrics like accuracy and F1-score, often overlooking the nuanced security risks posed by FPs and FNs in real-world, high-stakes applications [15]. This section outlines the specific models evaluated in this work.

Support Vector Machine (SVM). Support Vector Machines (SVM) are a class of supervised learning algorithms commonly used for classification tasks.

SVM works by finding the optimal hyperplane that maximizes the margin between two classes in a high-dimensional space. The decision boundary is determined by the support vectors, which are the data points closest to the hyperplane. SVM is particularly known for its effectiveness in high-dimensional feature spaces, making it suitable for text classification tasks where the number of features (e.g., words or n-grams) can be very large. However, SVM requires manual feature engineering and may struggle with non-linear relationships in data without kernel functions, which makes it less flexible compared to deep learning models. The use of SVM for text classification tasks has been well-documented in the literature. It has shown strong performance in various domains, including spam detection and sentiment analysis [18].

Random Forest. Random Forest is an ensemble learning method that combines the outputs of multiple decision trees to improve classification accuracy. Each tree in the forest is trained on a random subset of the data, and the final prediction is made based on the majority vote across all trees. This approach helps mitigate overfitting, which is a common problem with individual decision trees. Random Forest is widely used in classification tasks because it handles both numerical and categorical data well, requires less feature engineering, and is relatively robust against overfitting. However, it may not perform as well as deep learning models when capturing complex, hierarchical patterns in large datasets. Random Forest has been successfully applied to various text classification problems, including topic detection and sentiment analysis [19].

Bidirectional Encoder Representations for Transformers. BERT Base[1] is a pre-trained Transformer model that has set new benchmarks in natural language processing tasks. BERT Base is unique in that it uses a bidirectional attention mechanism, meaning it considers both the left and right context of a word in a sentence, which enables it to understand the full meaning of a word based on its surrounding words. BERT Base is pre-trained on a large corpus of text using unsupervised learning tasks, such as Masked Language Modeling (MLM), and then fine-tuned for specific tasks like text classification, question answering, and named entity recognition. BERT's ability to capture contextual information has made it particularly effective in complex classification tasks involving unstructured text data, including the classification of sensitive information in legal, medical, and financial documents [5].

ELECTRA. ELECTRA[2] is a more efficient variant of Transformers that utilizes a new pre-training objective, where the model learns to distinguish between real and fake tokens generated by a smaller generator network. This approach improves training efficiency by allowing the use of the same amount of data as BERT Base but with a lower computational cost. ELECTRA's discriminative

---

[1] https://huggingface.co/docs/transformers/en/model_doc/bert.
[2] https://huggingface.co/docs/transformers/v4.13.0/model_doc/electra.

training method helps the model learn more effectively from fewer labeled examples. This makes a suitable option for environments with limited computational resources or smaller datasets, while still achieving competitive performance in text classification tasks. ELECTRA has demonstrated strong performance in several NLP benchmarks in many cases despite using fewer resources [20].

General Models Characteristics. This study evaluates these models for sensitive information classification: Support Vector Machines (SVM), Random Forest, BERT Base, and ELECTRA. SVM and Random Forest represent traditional machine learning approaches, while BERT Base and ELECTRA are Transformer-based models. SVM and Random Forest rely on manually engineered features, whereas BERT Base and ELECTRA utilize self-attention mechanisms and pretraining to capture complex semantic relationships.

3   Methodology

This section outlines the methodology employed to evaluate the performance of distinct classification models for sensitive information detection. The experimental objective is presented first, followed by a detailed description of the dataset used for training and testing. We then describe the models that were evaluated in this study. Finally, the evaluation metrics used to assess model performance are explained.

Experimental Objective. This study's objective is to introduce and validate a risk management methodology for sensitive information governance. The methodology operationalizes the principle of conditional secrecy by leveraging AI classifier confidence thresholds to segment information flows. To demonstrate its viability and underscore the importance of model architecture in its implementation, we conduct a comparative analysis. We evaluate how Transformer-based models (BERT Base, ELECTRA) and traditional classifiers (Support Vector Machines, Random Forest) differ in their ability to enable this risk-aware methodology, focusing on their fine-grained False Negative and Positive error profiles.

Dataset Description. This study utilizes the *Monsanto Papers*[3], a corpus of documents made public as part of the litigation surrounding Monsanto's herbicide product, Roundup. These publicly accessible documents provide a rare and valuable window into sensitive information pertaining to corporate practices and legal strategies. A significant hurdle in advancing research on sensitive information classification is the scarcity of relevant, annotated, real-world datasets. Such data are often proprietary, subject to strict legal frameworks, or contain operationally critical information, thus severely limiting their use in academic settings. We remark that the *Monsanto Papers* directly address this scarcity, offering an exceptional opportunity for this investigation.

---

[3] https://www.wisnerbaum.com/toxic-tort-law/monsanto-roundup-lawsuit/
monsanto-depositions-and-court-docs/.

The annotations in the dataset, which classify information according to various legal sensitivity categories, were carefully **prepared by qualified legal professionals**. This expert annotation adds authenticity and domain-specific relevance. Thus, we selected 972 annotated sentences. Our dataset includes a balanced distribution, with each class containing exactly 243 examples.

The categories defined by the legal annotations are:

i) **TOXIC**: Documents concerning the toxicity of glyphosate, including discussions on carcinogenicity and related regulatory concerns;

ii) **CHEMI**: Communications about the chemical properties of Roundup, including internal and external studies on its ingredients and environmental impact;

iii) **GHOST**: Documents related to ghostwriting, particularly instances where Monsanto employees influenced scientific papers without proper attribution; and

iv) **REGUL**: Interactions with regulatory bodies, including attempts to influence rulings or manage public perception regarding Roundup's safety and environmental impact.

This dataset was used to evaluate models for their ability to classify sensitive information in documents, with each model trained and tested using consistent parameters shown in Tables 1 and 2. The dataset's design, combined with its real-world legal context, enables a thorough investigation of model behavior in scenarios that reflect typical limitations associated with sensitive data.

Table 1. Experimental parameters for transformer-based models. The experiments were conducted using Google Colab with a Tesla T4 GPU.

Parameter	Value
Learning rate	2×10^{-5}
Batch size	16
Maximum sequence length	128 tokens
Training epochs	20
Train/test split	80%/20% (stratified)
Hardware	NVIDIA Tesla T4 GPU

Traditional Metrics. We propose a set of evaluation metrics designed to move beyond aggregate performance and illuminate the specific security risks associated with misclassification. To evaluate the classification performance of the models, we utilize a suite of standard metrics commonly used in the literature, such as Accuracy, Precision, Recall, and F1-score. While these metrics are important, our primary focus in this study is on confusion matrices, confidence per class and threshold optimization.

Table 2. Experimental parameters for traditional machine learning models SVM and Random Forest.

Parameter	SVM	Random Forest
Feature extraction	TF-IDF	TF-IDF
Max features	5000	5000
N-gram range	(1, 2)	(1, 2)
Kernel	Linear	N/A
Regularization (C)	1.0	N/A
Number of estimators	N/A	100
Class weight	Balanced	Balanced
Train/test split	80%/20% (fixed)	80%/20% (fixed)

Confusion Matrix. The confusion matrix provides a detailed breakdown of predicted versus actual class assignments, enabling fine-grained analysis of classification performance. For a multi-class classification problem with n classes, the confusion matrix C is an $n \times n$ matrix where each element $C_{i,j}$ represents the number of instances from class i that were predicted as class j. The confusion matrix is calculated as:

$$C_{i,j} = \sum_{x \,\in\, \text{Test Set}} \mathbb{1}(y(x) = i \wedge \hat{y}(x) = j)$$

where $y(x)$ is the true class of instance x, $\hat{y}(x)$ is the predicted class, and $\mathbb{1}$ is the indicator function that returns 1 if the condition is true and 0 otherwise. The implementation of confusion matrix calculation and visualization uses scikit-learn's `confusion_matrix` function and seaborn's `heatmap` for visualization.

Confidence by Class. The confidence by class provides critical insights into model calibration and class-specific performance. For each class c in the dataset:

$$\text{Conf}_{\text{correct}}(c) = \{\text{conf}(x) \mid x \in \text{Test Set}, y(x) = c, \hat{y}(x) = c\}$$
$$\text{Conf}_{\text{incorrect}}(c) = \{\text{conf}(x) \mid x \in \text{Test Set}, y(x) = c, \hat{y}(x) \neq c\}$$

where $\text{conf}(x)$ is the prediction confidence (probability) assigned by the model to the predicted class for instance x. The implementation of calculation and visualization involves separating correctly and incorrectly classified examples, then plotting them using distinct markers for better distinction. This visualization provides several important insights: i) Class-specific Accuracy: By comparing the count of circular markers (correct) and 'x' markers (incorrect) for each class, we visually assess class-specific accuracy. ii) Misclassification Patterns: Classes with a higher proportion of 'x' markers indicate higher error rates, suggesting potential areas for model improvement. iii) Confidence Distribution: The vertical spread of markers reveals the distribution of confidence scores, with tightly clustered points suggesting consistent confidence and widely dispersed points indicating variable confidence.

Through this visualization, we identify classes that are particularly challenging for the model and gain insights into potential strategies for refinement.

Threshold Optimization. The implementation of confidence thresholds in intent classification systems represents a critical strategy for balancing classification accuracy against coverage. We implement a systematic approach to threshold optimization: i) Threshold Scanning: We evaluate model performance across confidence thresholds from 0 to 1; ii) Performance Curves: For each model, we analyze two curves: a) Accuracy-Threshold Curve: Shows how accuracy changes with increasing confidence threshold; and b) Coverage-Threshold Curve: Illustrates the proportion of instances meeting each confidence threshold. iii) Operating Point Selection: Optimal threshold selection depends on the balance between accuracy and coverage. We identify key points: a) Maximum F1 Point: The threshold that maximizes the F1-score. b) High-Reliability Point: The threshold where accuracy exceeds 95%. c) Balanced Point: The threshold offering a compromise between accuracy and coverage.

Dataset Generality. Although the Monsanto Papers dataset provided an authentic context for evaluation, the proposed framework is inherently dataset-agnostic. Because the core mechanism relies on probabilistic confidence outputs rather than domain-specific features, it can be applied to any corpus, such as legal, medical, companies or financial text collections. This property positions the methodology as a general risk-management layer that can be deployed across diverse data governance pipelines.

Illustrative Example of the Risk Segmentation Process. To illustrate the proposed methodology, consider a simplified example where a Transformer model classifies corporate emails into *sensitive* or *non-sensitive*. For a given confidence threshold $\tau = 0.8$, messages predicted with confidence $\geq \tau$ are automatically processed under high-security controls, such as encryption and restricted access. Messages with confidence below τ are flagged for human review, implementing the "conditional secrecy" principle. For instance, an email mentioning an unpublished product formula with 0.97 confidence would be automatically quarantined, while one with ambiguous phrasing and 0.63 confidence would be sent to a restricted reviewer group. This toy example demonstrates how confidence thresholds can translate formal secrecy principles into operational control policies.

In summary, while standard metrics like Accuracy, Precision, Recall, and F1-score provide valuable insights, they do not always capture the nuances of classification errors that directly impact security. Therefore, by focusing on confusion matrices, confidence per class, and threshold optimization, we aim to obtain a more comprehensive understanding of model performance, particularly in relation to the security risks associated with misclassifications.

4   Analysis and Results

This section presents the evaluation results of models on sensitive information detection, focusing on their ability to minimize False Positives and False Negatives. First, we summarize the overall model performance; then, we analyze the confusion matrices and error patterns. Next, confidence-by-class visualizations reveal prediction certainty and areas of weakness. Finally, threshold analysis explores how adjusting confidence levels affects accuracy and error rates. The experiments conducted in this study are fully reproducible and have been made publicly available for the research community[4].

4.1   Overall Performance

The overall performance of the models was evaluated using key classification metrics: Accuracy, F1-Score, Precision, and Recall. These metrics provide a comprehensive overview of how well each model performs in identifying and classifying sensitive information, with particular focus on both the effectiveness and the balance of the models' predictions. In Table 3, we present the performance comparison of the four models based on these metrics.

Table 3. Overall performance comparison of models.

Model	Accuracy	F1-Score	Precision	Recall
SVM	0.9538	0.9539	0.9552	0.9538
Random Forest	0.9487	0.9490	0.9506	0.9487
BERT Base	0.9641	0.9641	0.9642	0.9641
ELECTRA	0.9795	0.9794	0.9797	0.9795

The ELECTRA model achieved the highest performance across all metrics, with Accuracy, F1-Score, Precision, and Recall all exceeding 97%. This demonstrates ELECTRA's ability to accurately classify sensitive information while minimizing misclassifications, making it the most reliable model for both security and operational efficiency. BERT Base also performed well, with an Accuracy and F1-score of 96.41%, showing strong contextual understanding, and positioning it as a solid second in performance. Traditional models achieved competitive results, with SVM at 95.38% Accuracy and Random Forest slightly lower at 94.87%. While effective, these models fall short in capturing complex relationships compared to BERT and ELECTRA. These results highlight the growing dominance of Transformer models in sensitive information classification.

These aggregate performance metrics, while confirming the superior capability of Transformer models, serve as a foundational step. Unlike traditional models, Transformer architectures derive their advantage not merely from size or depth, but from their contextual self-attention mechanism, which dynamically captures inter-token dependencies and semantic nuances. This allows them to assign more calibrated confidence values, crucial for our risk-segmentation framework. In contrast, SVM and Random Forest models rely on sparse lexical

---

[4] https://anonymous.4open.science/r/SBSEG2025-3351/README.md.

cues, limiting their ability to represent contextual ambiguity. The key security question, which our methodology addresses, is not just overall accuracy but how the underlying confidence distributions of these models can be leveraged for risk control. This will be explored in the following sections

4.2   Confusion Matrices

The Confusion Matrices presented in the sub-figures of Fig. 1 offer a granular view of each model's classification behavior and error tendencies across the four categories of the dataset. These matrices are essential for understanding how well the models distinguish between the different classes and highlight areas where the models struggle. Therefore, the subsequent analysis delves into the class-specific confidence profiles of these classifiers, as this is the core mechanism our methodology uses to manage the identified risks.

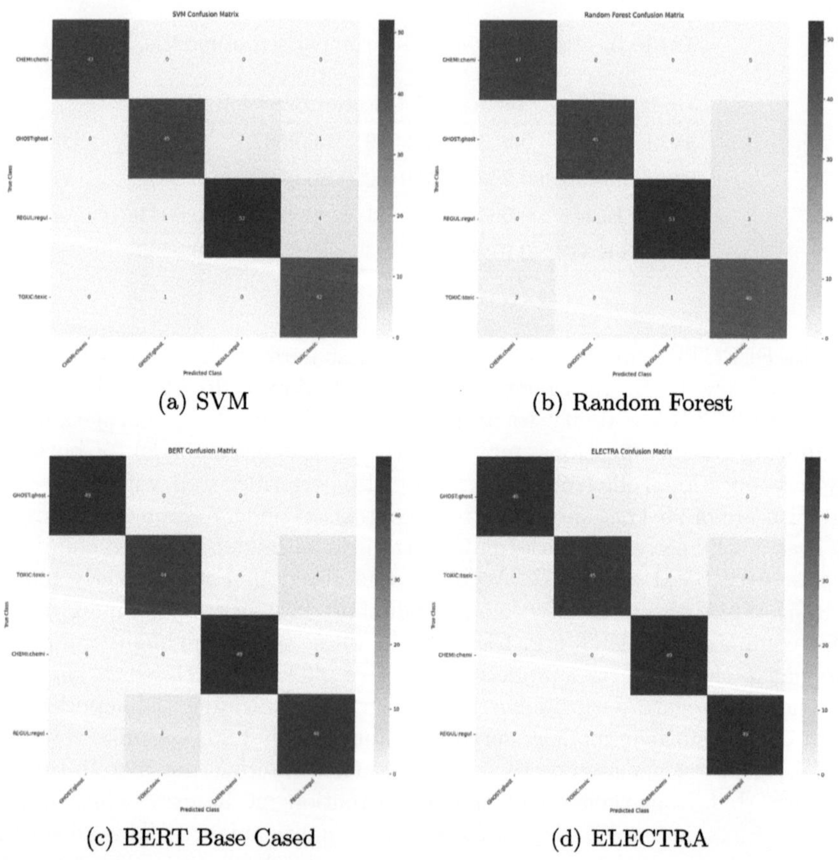

(a) SVM   (b) Random Forest

(c) BERT Base Cased   (d) ELECTRA

Fig. 1. Confusion matrices for the four evaluated models in document classification across four categories.

The confusion matrices reveal that while all models correctly classify many instances, critical misclassifications remain. The SVM model performs well in the CHEMI and GHOST classes, correctly identifying most examples. However, it struggles with REGUL and TOXIC categories, where several False Negatives appear, especially in REGUL. These results indicate that the SVM model fails to capture the latent semantic distinctions required to resolve class-specific boundaries, particularly under overlapping lexical distributions. Random Forest exhibits a similar pattern, with strong performance in CHEMI and GHOST, but notable misclassifications in TOXIC, including False Positives. While errors in REGUL are fewer than in SVM, the model still shows weaknesses in accurately handling categories.

Conversely, Transformers models showed improved performance, with the BERT base exhibiting fewer errors overall. It correctly classifies most instances across all classes, benefiting from its contextual understanding. Nevertheless, some FNs persist in the TOXIC category, reflecting challenges in eliminating critical misclassifications in high-stakes environments. ELECTRA surpasses all other models with minimal errors across every class. It achieves the lowest rates, particularly in the difficult TOXIC and REGUL categories.

From a security perspective, the error patterns elucidated by the confusion matrices are paramount. The tendency of traditional models to exhibit higher False Negative rates in REGUL and TOXIC categories signifies a tangible risk of sensitive data exposure. While Transformer-based models, notably ELECTRA, substantially mitigate these specific errors, the persistence of any misclassification warrants further investigation. Nevertheless, we argue that understanding the confidence with which models make predictions is crucial for assessing their reliability in operational security scenarios. Therefore, the subsequent analysis delves into the class-specific confidence profiles of these classifiers.

4.3 Confidence by Class

The Confidence by Class shown in the sub-figures of Fig. 2 provides a deeper insight into how each model approaches classification across the different categories. This analysis focuses not only on the models' prediction accuracy but also on their confidence in making correct or incorrect classifications. They show the confidence levels for each model in classifying data into the four categories of the dataset: CHEMI, GHOST, REGUL, and TOXIC. The confidence values are plotted for each example in the test set, providing a visual representation of how confident the model was when making each prediction.

The visualizations clearly illustrate the models' confidence levels in their predictions. Notably, SVM and Random Forest exhibit lower and more dispersed confidence values in the TOXIC and REGUL classes, as evidenced by the more scattered data points in these categories. This dispersion reflects greater uncertainty and less consistency in these models' predictions, which corresponds to the higher rates of False Positives and False Negatives observed in the confusion matrices.

In contrast, BERT Base and ELECTRA demonstrate significantly higher and more consistent confidence levels, with fewer isolated points. This indi-

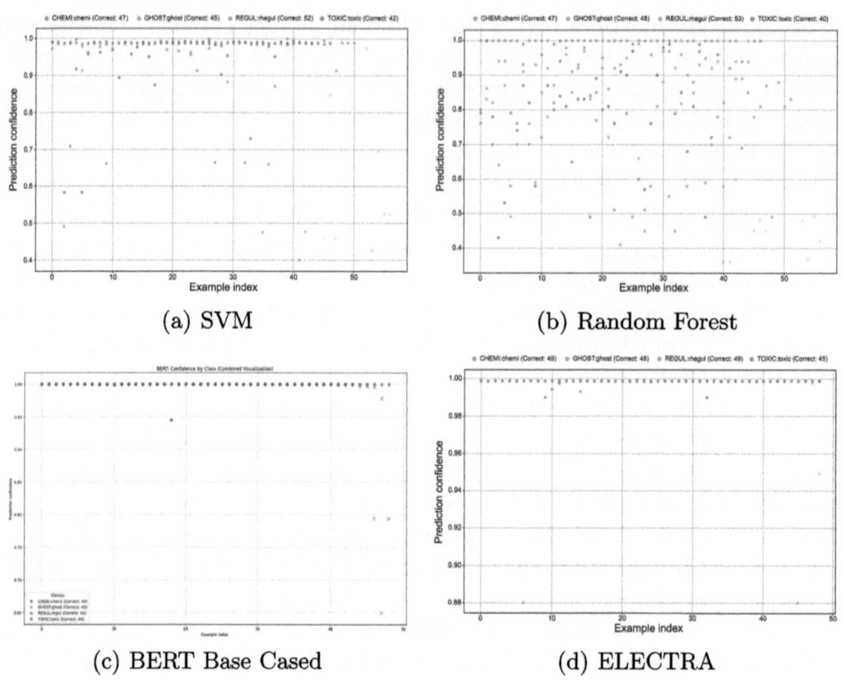

(a) SVM   (b) Random Forest

(c) BERT Base Cased   (d) ELECTRA

Fig. 2. Confidence by Class for SVM, Random Forest, BERT, and ELECTRA.

cates a stronger capacity of these Transformer-based architectures to capture complex textual nuances and deliver more reliable classifications. Specifically, ELECTRA maintains high confidence across all classes, including the more challenging TOXIC and REGUL categories, thereby substantially reducing the risk of misclassification.

Therefore, the dispersion of confidence scores highlighted in Figs. 2(a)–2(d) underscores a critical limitation of traditional models. Although SVM and Random Forest can achieve competitive accuracy, their generally lower and more inconsistent confidence levels introduce greater uncertainty. Accordingly, this heightened uncertainty poses significant security and reliability risks in real-world sensitive information classification, a concern potentially amplified in scenarios involving a higher number of distinct sensitive categories. In stark contrast, Transformer-based models like BERT Base and ELECTRA typically enhance operational security by minimizing both uncertainty and classification errors. However, a crucial observation is that both BERT Base and, particularly, ELECTRA also exhibited instances of high confidence in their (albeit infrequent) misclassifications. This tendency might be partly attributed to the inherent ambiguity in classifying certain documents, a challenge that can confound even human experts. Nevertheless, the pronounced ELECTRA inclination towards high-confidence predictions, even for incorrect outcomes, is a noteworthy characteristic demanding careful consideration, especially in high-stakes deployments where poor model calibration could mask underlying risks. Crucially, the inconsistent confidence levels of traditional models make it difficult to define a meaningful and stable threshold (τ) to reliably segment information into different security levels.

4.4   Threshold Impact on Model Performance and Security Posture

This subsection presents the core of our proposed methodology in action. We analyze the critical impact of varying confidence thresholds τ on model performance, specifically examining the trade-off between classification accuracy on items meeting the threshold and the overall coverage. This analysis is pivotal because the choice of τ directly dictates the operational security posture. To quantify this, we consider two key factors derived from the accuracy-coverage trade-off curves and plot them in Figs. 3(a)-3(d).

Automated Classification Error Rate. ($\mathrm{Err}_{\mathrm{auto}}(\tau)$) for sentences processed with confidence $\geq \tau$:

$$\mathrm{Err}_{\mathrm{auto}}(\tau) = 1 - \mathrm{Accuracy}_{\mathrm{covered}}(\tau) \tag{1}$$

where $\mathrm{Accuracy}_{\mathrm{covered}}(\tau)$ is the accuracy of predictions for items meeting the threshold τ. A high $\mathrm{Err}_{\mathrm{auto}}(\tau)$ indicates significant risk within the automated classifications, particularly if these errors are False Negatives (FNs).

Manual Review Workload Rate. ($W_{\mathrm{manual}}(\tau)$), representing the proportion of sentences falling below the threshold τ and thus requiring human intervention:

$$W_{\mathrm{manual}}(\tau) = 1 - \mathrm{Coverage}(\tau) \tag{2}$$

where $\mathrm{Coverage}(\tau)$ is the proportion of sentences with confidence $\geq \tau$. A high $W_{\mathrm{manual}}(\tau)$ increases reliance on manual processes, which are resource-intensive and have their own potential for error, including missing FNs. The interplay between $\mathrm{Err}_{\mathrm{auto}}(\tau)$ and $W_{\mathrm{manual}}(\tau)$ defines the security challenge: minimizing errors in automated decisions while managing the workload and inherent risks of manual review.

For SVM (Fig. 3(a)), achieving a low $\mathrm{Err}_{\mathrm{auto}}(\tau)$, and therefore a high $\mathrm{Accuracy}_{\mathrm{covered}}(\tau)$, typically requires setting a *high* confidence threshold τ. However, this results in a low $\mathrm{Coverage}(\tau)$ and consequently a high $W_{\mathrm{manual}}(\tau)$ (Eq. 2). If τ is lowered to reduce $W_{\mathrm{manual}}(\tau)$ (e.g., to its optimal F1-score threshold around 0.47), $\mathrm{Accuracy}_{\mathrm{covered}}(\tau)$ degrades, increasing $\mathrm{Err}_{\mathrm{auto}}(\tau)$ (Eq. 1). This presents a difficult security trade-off: either risk FNs within a large manual review workload or risk higher error rates in the automated stream.

Similarly, Random Forest (Fig. 3(b)) shows a comparable dynamic. Its optimal F1-score at a low threshold of 0.37 yields a high $\mathrm{Coverage}(\tau)$ and thus a lower $W_{\mathrm{manual}}(\tau)$. However, this reliance on lower-confidence predictions increases $\mathrm{Err}_{\mathrm{auto}}(\tau)$. Attempting to reduce $\mathrm{Err}_{\mathrm{auto}}(\tau)$ by raising τ quickly increases $W_{\mathrm{manual}}(\tau)$, again posing a security challenge in balancing automated risk versus manual review burden and its associated fallibility.

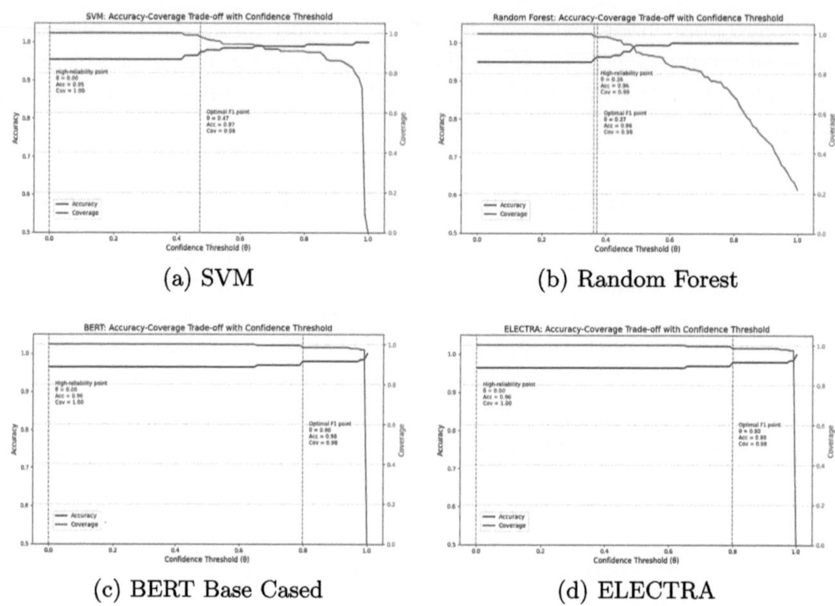

(a) SVM

(b) Random Forest

(c) BERT Base Cased

(d) ELECTRA

Fig. 3. Accuracy-Coverage trade-off curves for SVM, Random Forest, BERT Base, and ELECTRA with varying confidence thresholds.

Conversely, BERT Base (Fig. 3(c)) offers a significantly improved security profile. It maintains a low $\mathrm{Err}_{\mathrm{auto}}(\tau)$ across a much wider range of $\mathrm{Coverage}(\tau)$ values, with an optimal F1-score threshold around 0.8. This implies a broader "safe operating window" where $W_{\mathrm{manual}}(\tau)$ can be substantially reduced without a drastic increase in $\mathrm{Err}_{\mathrm{auto}}(\tau)$. For security concerns, this means more reliable automation on account of a lower chance of FNs in the automated flow and a more manageable $W_{\mathrm{manual}}(\tau)$ for human review.

Objectively, ELECTRA (Fig. 3(d)) exhibits particularly advantageous characteristics in this threshold analysis. It sustains high accuracy, which implies low rates of False Positives and False Negatives within the set of automatically classified sentences, even as its $\mathrm{Coverage}(\tau)$ extends significantly across a wide range of thresholds, also achieving an optimal F1-score around a τ of 0.8. This superior capability signifies that ELECTRA can automate a larger proportion of classifications while maintaining a low error rate. From a security risk perspective, this performance is highly beneficial; ELECTRA minimizes the likelihood of False Negatives being erroneously accepted by the automated system, and by reducing the load on manual reviewers, also curtails opportunities for human error in the subsequent process. However, we highlight that for ELECTRA's automated classifications to reach their peak observed accuracy, effectively minimizing residual errors within the covered set, an operational threshold exceeding $\tau = 0.95$ is indicated by its accuracy curve, which is comparable to that of BERT Base.

In summary, this threshold analysis provides the core validation for our methodology. It demonstrates that Transformer models are not merely more accurate; their well-calibrated and discriminative confidence scores make them a superior substrate for implementing a policy of conditional secrecy. The "safe operating window" they provide allows for a practical segmentation of information into a high-security automated level and a manageable low-security level for human review, effectively operationalizing the principles outlined in Sect. 2.1. In contrast, the volatile confidence scores of traditional models render them less reliable for such a security-critical task.

5   Final Considerations

This research introduced a security risk methodology to address the critical challenge of managing residual errors in automated sensitive information classification. By operationalizing principles of secrecy by type through a threshold-based methodology, we demonstrated that modern Transformer models offer a significant advantage that extends beyond raw accuracy. Their superior discriminative ability is not an end in itself, but rather a necessary condition that unlocks a more granular and effective risk control strategy, allowing for a practical implementation of security policies previously confined to formal theory.

While our experiments were conducted on a single, albeit highly relevant, expert-annotated dataset, the conceptual methodology we propose is broadly applicable. For practitioners, our core recommendation is not simply to adopt Transformers, but to adopt a risk-aware deployment methodology. Before integration into live security architectures, organizations must perform a threshold impact analysis, as demonstrated here, to define an explicit operational security posture that aligns with their risk appetite. This involves quantifying the cost of manual review for low-confidence items against the potential impact of automated errors, particularly critical False Negatives.

We anticipate that the application of high-precision classifiers will have a profound impact on the design of practical information security systems. While the capabilities of Transformer models are well-established within the NLP community, to the best of our knowledge, this is the first works to analyze their potential to reshape security models and resource management. The ability to classify information with high fidelity enables a paradigm shift in how security resources are allocated, allowing organizations to direct stronger, more expensive layers of protection to what is critical. This move towards data-driven, granular security is a recent and significant novelty, promising more efficient and effective governance.

It is also crucial to contextualize model fallibility. The literature reports only moderate agreement even among human experts on nuanced sensitivity review tasks [12], highlighting the inherent ambiguity of the problem. When viewed against this baseline, the consistency and scalability of Transformer models, coupled with a framework to manage their uncertainty, represent a significant step forward.

Future work should explore integrating this threshold-based risk framework with other techniques like cost-sensitive learning and model calibration to further refine the risk-coverage trade-off. Ultimately, the goal is not to achieve perfect, infallible automation, but to engineer the most effective and secure **human-machine system** for protecting our most sensitive information.

In practice, threshold values need not remain static. Organizations can implement adaptive threshold calibration, periodically updating τ based on observed false negative rates, domain drift, or feedback from human reviewers. Such continuous recalibration ensures that the automationrisk balance remains aligned with evolving operational conditions and your own organizational risk definitions.

Acknowledgments. The authors would like to express their deepest gratitude to the Operador Nacional do Registro Civil of Brazil (ON-RCPN) for funding and institutional support, essential for carrying out this research and fostering innovation in the Brazilian civil registry ecosystem. This study was also supported by the Conselho Nacional de Desenvolvimento Científico e Tecnológico (CNPq) and by the Coordenação de Aperfeiçoamento de Pessoal de Nível Superior Brazil (CAPES) Finance Code 001.

References

1. Karabin, S.J.: Data classification for security and control. EDPACS EDP Audit Control Secur. Newsl. **13**(6), 1–20 (1985)
2. Tankard, C.: Data classification-the foundation of information security. Netw. Secur. **2015**(5), 8–11 (2015)
3. Gordon, A.D., Jeffrey, A.: Secrecy despite compromise: types, cryptography, and the pi-calculus. In: Abadi, M., de Alfaro, L. (eds.) CONCUR 2005. LNCS, vol. 3653, pp. 186–201. Springer, Heidelberg (2005). https://doi.org/10.1007/11539452_17
4. Chaudhuri, A., Abadi, M.: Secrecy by typing and file-access control. In: 19th IEEE Computer Security Foundations Workshop (CSFW'06), p. 12. IEEE (2006)
5. Devlin, J., Chang, M.W., Lee, K., and Toutanova, K.: BERT: pre-training of deep bidirectional transformers for language understanding. In: Proceedings of the 2019 Conference of the North American Chapter of the Association for Computational Linguistics: Human Language Technologies, vol. 1 (Long and Short Papers), pp. 4171–4186. Association for Computational Linguistics (2019)
6. Kaul, D.: AI-powered autonomous compliance management for multi-region data governance in cloud deployments. J. Curr. Sci. Res. Rev. **2**(03), 82–98 (2024)
7. Freund, J., Jorion, N.: The true cost of a data breach. ISACA J. **1** (2023)
8. IBM Security: Relatório do custo das violações de dados 2024. IBM Security (2024)
9. Volpano, D., Smith, G.: Verifying secrets and relative secrecy. In: Proceedings of the 27th ACM SIGPLAN-SIGACT Symposium on Principles of Programming Languages, pp. 268–276 (2000)
10. Neerbek, J.: Sensitive information detection: recursive neural networks for encoding context. arXiv preprint arXiv:2008.10863 (2020)
11. Peters, M.E., et al.: Deep contextualized word representations. arXiv preprint. arXiv preprint arXiv:1802.05365 (2018)

12. Mcdonald, G., Macdonald, C., Ounis, I.: How the accuracy and confidence of sensitivity classification affects digital sensitivity review. ACM Trans. Inf. Syst. (TOIS) **39**(1), 1–34 (2020)
13. Kongsgård, K.W., Nordbotten, N.A., Mancini, F., Engelstad, P.E.: Data loss prevention based on text classification in controlled environments. In: Ray, I., Gaur, M.S., Conti, M., Sanghi, D., Kamakoti, V. (eds.) ICISS 2016. LNCS, vol. 10063, pp. 131–150. Springer, Cham (2016). https://doi.org/10.1007/978-3-319-49806-5_7
14. Vaswani, A., et al.: Attention is all you need. Adv. Neural. Inf. Process. Syst. **30**, 5998–6008 (2017)
15. Aydın, N., Erdem, O.A., Tekerek, A.: Comparative analysis of traditional machine learning and transformer-based deep learning models for text classification. J. Polytech. **28**(2), 445–452 (2025)
16. Yang, E., et al.: Transformer versus traditional natural language processing: how much data is enough for automated radiology report classification? Br. J. Radiol. **96**(1149), 20220769 (2023)
17. Gupta, C., Johri, I., Srinivasan, K., Hu, Y.C., Qaisar, S.M., Huang, K.Y.: A systematic review on machine learning and deep learning models for electronic information security in mobile networks. Sensors **22**(5), 2017 (2022)
18. Cortes, C., Vapnik, V.: Support-vector networks. Mach. Learn. **20**, 273–297 (1995)
19. Breiman, L.: Random forests. Mach. Learn. **45**, 5–32 (2001)
20. Clark, K., Luong, M.T., Le, Q.V., and Manning, C.D.: Electra: pre-training text encoders as discriminators rather than generators. arXiv preprint arXiv:2003.10555 (2020)

A Secure Federated Learning Using Differential Privacy Mondrian Clustering

Rojalini Tripathy[(✉)], Paladri Pranitha, B. U. Tejonath,
and Padmalochan Bera

Indian Institute of Technology Bhubaneswar, Bhubaneswar, India
{a22ee09003,21cs01037,21cs01024,plb}@iitbbs.ac.in

Abstract. Federated Learning (FL) is a decentralized machine learning
approach that enables model training over distributed nodes without sharing the private data. However, FL faces various challenges, such as limited scalability, handling data heterogeneity, and the impact of malicious
clients on model performance. In this paper, we propose a hierarchical
FL framework using gossip protocol and Differential Privacy Mondrian
(DPM) clustering. Our framework follows a three-level architecture that
consists of a central server, cluster heads, and data owners to ensure scalability. The proposed framework addresses data heterogeneity by grouping clients based on statistical properties of data. It also assigns weights
to clients based on their contribution to the global model, thereby mitigating the impact of malicious clients. To evaluate the performance of our
proposed framework, we experimented on three well-known FL datasets,
MNIST, FMNIST, and CIFAR-10. The results show that our framework
achieves 2.1% higher accuracy, reduces training loss by 15.46%, and has
less execution time compared to the standard FedAvg algorithm. The
results demonstrate that the framework performs better in terms of training efficiency and model accuracy while preserving privacy.

Keywords: Hierarchical Federated Learning · Differential Privacy ·
Malicious Clients · DPM Clustering · Gossip Protocol

1 Introduction

Today, Artificial Intelligence (AI) based distributed training is extensively being
used in different security applications such as healthcare, smart surveillance,
financial fraud identification, malware analysis, etc. However, such systems face
various challenges, including handling data volume and privacy. Moreover, in
privacy-preserving distributed learning, participants do not wish to share their
data with the collaborators. Federated Learning (FL) [13] addresses these challenges by offering a decentralized training approach that enhances privacy in
collaborative learning. Instead of exchanging raw data, FL enables participants
to share only model parameters, reducing the risk of data leakage while allowing
effective model training over distributed devices. The secure data sharing approach of FL makes it suitable for many sensitive applications, such as intrusion

N. Hubballi et al. (Eds.): ICISS 2025, LNCS 16380, pp. 104–114, 2026.
https://doi.org/10.1007/978-3-032-13714-2_8

detection in IoT networks, smart homes [12], intelligent transportation systems [16], remote healthcare [14], etc.

In FL, each client trains a local model and shares only the updated model parameters to the central server for aggregation. However, the participating clients belong to a variety of users or environments, generating heterogeneous data. Handling such a large volume of heterogeneous data remains a potential challenge in FL. Studies [1, 4] suggest that clients can be grouped into clusters based on dataset similarity and perform cluster-level aggregation to mitigate heterogeneity. However, when the dataset contains sensitive information, the clustering algorithm must preserve data privacy. While many privacy-preserving clustering algorithms are available in the literature [7, 10, 11], the study [9] states that these algorithms do not produce accurate cluster centers, which impacts model accuracy. Differential Privacy Mondrian (DPM) clustering addresses this based on the principle of data separation. DPM partitions the data space using a recursive multidimensional splitting strategy and adds noise using differential privacy in each iteration. This motivates the use of DPM clustering in our proposed framework to group sensitive datasets. As the number of clients and their diversity increase, the system becomes more vulnerable to malicious clients. These clients may send tempered model gradients to the server, leading to potential attacks on the global model. To address this, we assign weights to the clients based on their contribution to the central model using the gossip protocol [6]. The gossip protocol is a decentralized communication method used for information dissemination among nodes in a network. Inspired by social networks, this protocol allows clients to share their model updates with other participating clients that limits central server communications.

In this paper, we propose a hierarchical FL framework that implements DPM clustering and gossip protocol to enhance scalability and handle data heterogeneity while minimizing the impact of malicious clients. We use DPM clustering algorithm to group clients with similar data distributions into clusters, ensuring that clients within a cluster train models on homogeneous data. Our framework consists of a central server, cluster-heads, and end-clients, which can be effectively deployed in large-scale networks. We use a client-level gossip protocol, where the cluster head detects potential malicious clients by analyzing their model updates and assigns lower weights to clients with suspicious data, thereby minimizing malicious client impact. We summarize the key contributions of this research as follows:

- Hierarchical Federated Learning: We propose a scalable framework that uses a hierarchical architecture consisting of a central server, cluster heads, and end-clients to effectively deploy it for large-scale networks.
- Handling Data Heterogeneity: The clients are grouped based on their data distribution using DPM clustering to ensure that each cluster's clients train models on homogeneous data.
- Minimizing Malicious Client Impact: We use a client-level gossip protocol to detect and minimize the impact of malicious clients by assigning lower weights to the detected clients.

- Enhanced Model Performance: Our experiments on benchmark FL datasets show that the proposed framework improves model accuracy by 2.1%, minimizes overall training loss by 15.46% and has less computation time compared to the FedAvg algorithm.

2 Related Work

FL introduced by McMahan et al. in 2016 [13], is a distributed machine learning environment that preserves data privacy by sharing model parameters. Despite providing data privacy, FL faces statistical heterogeneity, i.e., clients having non-independent identically distributed (non-i.i.d.) data can negatively impact model performance [15]. To address this, several FL frameworks [5,7,10,11] use clustering algorithms to group clients based on their statistical properties. In [7], Kim et al. proposed a dynamic clustering approach, where after each round clients are grouped into clusters based on model gradient similarities. In [10], Long et al. proposed a multi-center FL framework, where clients are clustered based on model characteristics to improve personalization. In [11], Ma et al. proposed an optimization based clustering algorithm for FL. Instead of applying a predefined clustering algorithm, clients are dynamically assigned to clusters based on how well each cluster model minimizes the client's local loss. This allows the framework to form clusters and train personalized models simultaneously, improving convergence in non-IID data. However, these clustering algorithms require high computations, making it unsuitable for large-scale networks.

To improve scalability, [1,4] proposed hierarchical FL, where clients do not send their updates directly to the central server. Instead, they are divided into multiple tiers. In [1], Abad et al. proposed a hierarchical FL for cellular networks, where mobile users train under Small-cell Base Stations (SBSs), and SBSs then forward aggregated updates to a macro-cell base station. In [4], Chen et al. proposed collaborative FL to overcome centralized bottlenecks in large-scale IoT environments. This allows edge devices to form a topology and selects which devices participate per round, reducing overall central server communication. These frameworks improve scalability and are capable of handling data heterogeneity; however, the client grouping approaches do not use privacy-preserving clustering algorithm, making it vulnerable to malicious client attacks.

To detect and minimize malicious clients, several studies are available in the literature [3,8]. In [8], Li et al. designed a FL defense mechanism that detects malicious clients by filtering abnormal updates through a variational autoencoder. However, this framework assumes the central server has information about the overall training data distribution, which is practically difficult. Cao et al. [3] proposed FLTrust, where the server assigns trust scores to clients using a small clean dataset and aggregates updates based on cosine similarity. However, obtaining such a dataset is often not practical in dynamic environments.

Through this study, we observe that clustering based FL approaches handle non-i.i.d. data but has high computational overhead, which affects model scalability. Hierarchical FL frameworks improve scalability but lack privacy-preserving client grouping mechanisms. This emphasises the need for a unified model that addresses data heterogeneity, scalability, data privacy, and minimizes the impact of malicious clients.

3   Background

3.1   DPM Clustering

DPM clustering [9] is a recursive partitioning algorithm that identifies clusters by separating data along sparse regions, while providing privacy. Let M denote the number of clients $\{C_1, C_2, \ldots, C_M\}$, each holding a private dataset D_i, where $1 \leq i \leq M$. Each client C_i is represented by a feature vector $F_i \in \mathbb{R}^d$, constructed from statistical summaries such as mean, variance, skewness, or other domain specific descriptors. The set of all client feature vectors is denoted as $\mathcal{F} = \{F_1, F_2, \ldots, F_M\}$. At each recursion step, DPM operates on a working subset $\mathcal{S} \subseteq \mathcal{F}$. For each feature dimension $j \in \{1, 2, \ldots, d\}$, the values are sorted, and candidate split points $\{s_1, s_2, \ldots, s_L\}$ are identified as midpoints between adjacent sorted values in that dimension. These split candidates represent potential decision boundaries for partitioning. For each candidate split s in dimension j, a utility function is evaluated based on two parameters, emptiness and centreness, i.e., $u(\mathcal{S}, s) = \mathrm{emptiness}(s) + \mathrm{centreness}(s) + \mathrm{Lap}\left(\frac{1}{\epsilon}\right)$. Here, ϵ is the DP privacy budget and $\mathrm{Lap}(\cdot)$ denotes Laplace noise. In DPM, the emptiness score quantifies the sparsity of the region around s. It can be represented as:

$$\mathrm{emptiness}(s) = \frac{\min(|\mathcal{S}_L|, |\mathcal{S}_R|)}{|\mathcal{S}|} \tag{1}$$

Here, $\mathcal{S}_L$ is the subset of feature vectors where the value in dimension j is less than or equal to s and $\mathcal{S}_R$ is the complementary subset where the value in dimension j is greater than s. A higher emptiness score indicates a more balanced and sparser split. The centreness score favors splits close to the median of the projected values. It can be represented as

$$\mathrm{centreness}(s) = 1 - \frac{|\mathrm{median}(\mathcal{S}_j) - s|}{\max(\mathcal{S}_j) - \min(\mathcal{S}_j)} \tag{2}$$

Here, $\mathcal{S}_j$ is the set of all values in $\mathcal{S}$ projected onto dimension j. $\mathrm{median}(\mathcal{S}_j)$, $\max(\mathcal{S}_j)$, and $\min(\mathcal{S}_j)$ represent the median, maximum, and minimum of the projected values, respectively. The probability of selecting a split point s is $P(s)$, which is calculated as:

$$P(s) \propto \exp\left(\frac{\epsilon \cdot u(\mathcal{S}, s)}{2\Delta u}\right) \tag{3}$$

Here, Δu denotes the global sensitivity of the utility function $u(\mathcal{S}, s)$, i.e., the maximum possible change in utility caused by modifying a single input feature vector. The selected split s^* is then used to partition the subset $\mathcal{S}$ into: $\mathcal{S}_L = \{x \in \mathcal{S} \mid x[j] \leq s^*\}$, $\mathcal{S}_R = \{x \in \mathcal{S} \mid x[j] > s^*\}$. The algorithm recursively continues on $\mathcal{S}_L$ and $\mathcal{S}_R$ until condition $|\mathcal{S}| \leq T$ is met, where T is a predefined minimum cluster size threshold. The final output is a set of clusters $\{K_1, K_2, \ldots, K_n\}$.

4   Proposed Framework

In this section, we describe the working procedure of our proposed hierarchical FL framework. Let us consider M clients, denoted as $C_1, C_2, \ldots, C_M$, where each client C_i holds a local dataset D_i, and $1 \leq i \leq M$. Now we present the working procedure as follows:

Cluster Formation and Head Selection: Each client C_i represent their dataset D_i by a feature vector $F_i = [\mu_i, \sigma_i^2]$. Where μ_i and σ_i^2 denote the mean and variance of D_i. Then DPM clustering is applied on the feature vector set $\mathcal{F}$, resulting in clusters $\{K_1, K_2, \ldots, K_n\}$. For cluster head selection, the central server S broadcasts the initialized model parameter P_{glob} to all clients. This is the only phase where the server communicates with all clients directly. In subsequent phases, the server communicates only with the selected cluster heads. After receiving the initialized model parameters, each client C_i trains its local model using a batch of data from D_i and sends local model parameters P_i to the server. For cluster K_ℓ, S selects a client as the cluster head whose local model parameters are closest to the global average P_{avg}. For every client $C_i \in K_\ell$, the distance from the global model d_i is calculated using the Euclidean distance $d_i = \|P_i - P_{\mathrm{avg}}\|_2$. S assigns a weight w_i to client C_i based on the calculated distance. When a cluster head fails or drops out, S selects the next closest client within the same cluster as the new cluster head. From this point onward, cluster heads are denoted as CH_ℓ, and clients within each cluster K_ℓ are denoted as $C_{\ell j}$, where j indexes the client within cluster ℓ.

Initial Model Broadcast and Local Training: The server S performs weighted averaging on the local updates received from clients. The aggregated model parameters P_{glob} are calculated using the following equation:

$$P_{glob} \leftarrow \sum_{i=1}^{M} w_i P_i \tag{4}$$

Then, S broadcasts P_{glob} to all cluster heads and cluster heads distribute in their respective clusters. Each client trains a local model using the local dataset and the global model parameters received. After training, clients send local model parameters $P_r^{\ell j}$ to the cluster head CH_ℓ for further aggregation.

Cluster-Level Aggregation: After receiving local model parameters, the cluster head assigns weights to each client using the gossip protocol. It calculates the distance between each client's model and its own model as $d_r^{\ell j} = \|P_r^{\ell j} - P_{CH_\ell}\|_2$. Then, the CH_ℓ assigns $w_{\ell j}$ weights to the clients based on the $d_r^{\ell j}$. The cluster head assigns weights dynamically in each round and stores them for use in the next round. Further, the cluster head performs intra-cluster aggregation, which is represented as:

$$P_{\mathrm{agg}}^{(\ell)} \leftarrow \frac{1}{p+1} \left(P_{CH_\ell} + \sum_{j=1}^{p} w_{\ell j} P_r^{\ell j} \right) \tag{5}$$

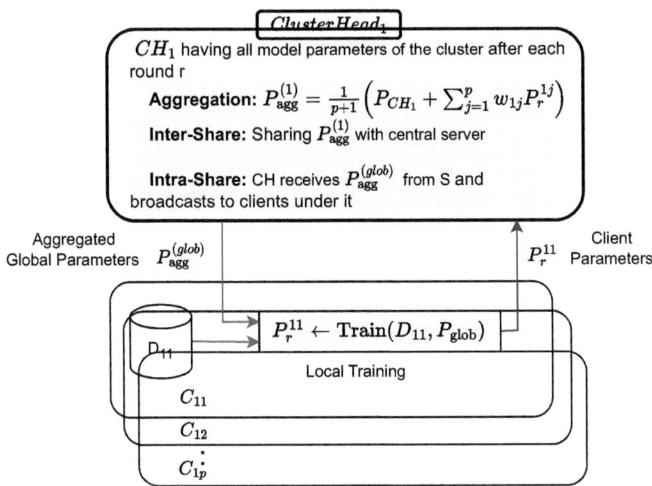

Fig. 1. Cluster Level Aggregation in Proposed Hierarchical FL Framework

Here, P_{CH_ℓ} is the model parameters of the cluster head CH_ℓ, $w_{\ell j}$ is the weight assigned to $C_{\ell j}$ and p is the number of clients in cluster K_ℓ excluding the cluster head. The cluster head CH_ℓ then transmits $P_{agg}^{(\ell)}$ to S for global aggregation. The Fig. 1 illustrates the cluster-level aggregation in the proposed framework.

Central Aggregation: Then server S receives the cluster-level aggregated model parameters from each cluster head CH_ℓ, where $\ell \in \{1, 2, \ldots, n\}$. Then S performs central aggregation over all cluster-level updates. This global model $P_{glob}^{(r)}$ for round r is computed as:

$$P_{glob}^{(r)} \leftarrow \frac{1}{n}\sum_{\ell=1}^{n} w_{CH_\ell} P_{agg}^{(\ell)} \tag{6}$$

Then, S broadcasts the updated global model to all cluster heads CH_ℓ. Subsequently, the cluster heads disseminate the global updates to the clients $C_{\ell j}$ within their respective clusters K_ℓ for the next training round. This process continues until convergence or until a specified number of training rounds. Figure 2 illustrates the central aggregation in the proposed framework.

5   Evaluation

In this section, we present the experimental results of our proposed hierarchical FL framework and evaluate its performance metrics by comparing model accuracy, training loss, and execution time with FedAvg.

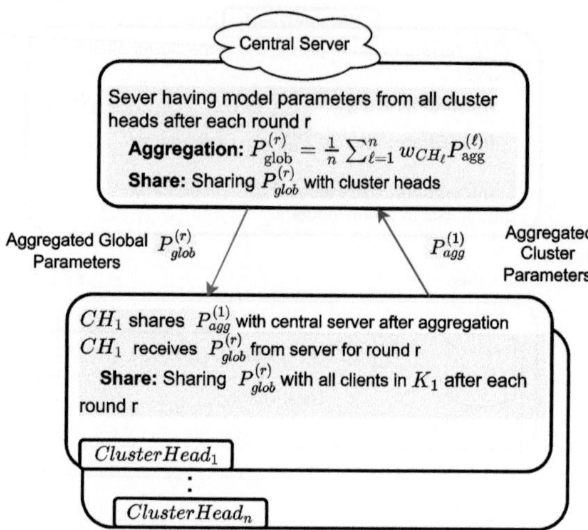

Fig. 2. Central Aggregation in Proposed Hierarchical FL Framework

5.1   Experimental Setup

We implemented using the Flower framework [2] and executed it in Jupyter Notebook with Python 3.10.12. The training dataset is evenly partitioned among clients, representing each client by the mean and variance of its local data. Experiments conducted on a system with NV164/Mesa Intel® UHD Graphics 630 (CFL GT2), Intel® Core™ i7-9700K CPU @ 3.60 GHz (8 cores), 1.3 TB storage, and 31.2 GiB RAM. We experimented on three benchmark datasets for FL MNIST, FMNIST, and CIFAR-10.

5.2   Performance Analysis

To evaluate the performance of the proposed algorithm, we experimented under two setups: (1) varying the number of clients, and (2) varying the number of training rounds. In both experiments, we observed model accuracy, training loss, and training time, and compared the results with the benchmark FedAvg algorithm.

Model Accuracy: Figures 3a, Fig. 4a, and Fig. 5a illustrate the accuracy comparison for varying numbers of rounds and clients. In MNIST, our proposed framework achieves the highest accuracy of 96.91% while FedAvg observes 96.6%. In FMNIST, our framework observes 94.61%, while FedAvg observes 92.9%. In CIFAR-10, the proposed algorithm achieves 55.01%, whereas FedAvg reaches 50.0%. The proposed framework shows an average improvement of 2.1% in training accuracy compared to FedAvg on all three datasets with 10 and 15 clients. The results demonstrate that when the communication round increases, the model accuracy increases, and when the number of clients increases, the accuracy decreases for all the experiments. However, in all experiments, the proposed framework achieves better accuracy than FedAvg.

Training Loss: Figures 3b, Fig. 4b, and Fig. 5b show the training loss for varying numbers of rounds and clients. In MNIST, our framework has a minimum training loss of 0.1100 while FedAvg has of 0.1700. In FMNIST, our framework has 0.4137 loss, whereas FedAvg has a higher final loss of 0.4870. In CIFAR-10, the proposed framework has a loss of 1.3367, while FedAvg has 1.4820. From the results, we observe that our framework achieves a 15.46% reduction in training loss compared to FedAvg across all datasets. In summary, our proposed FL framework provides faster convergence, consistently minimizing training loss than FedAvg across datasets.

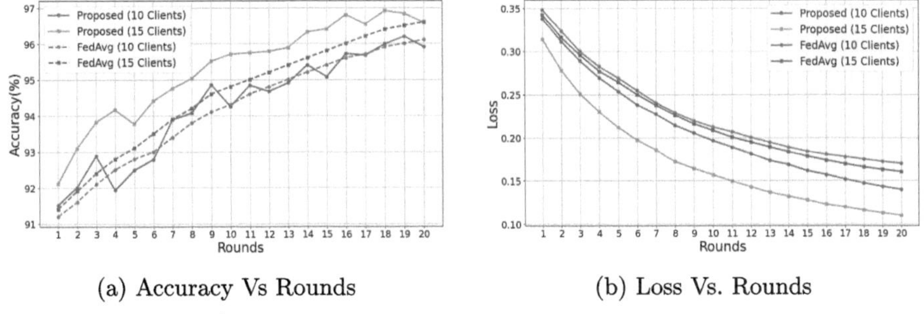

(a) Accuracy Vs Rounds (b) Loss Vs. Rounds

Fig. 3. Training loss and model accuracy on MNIST dataset for 20 rounds

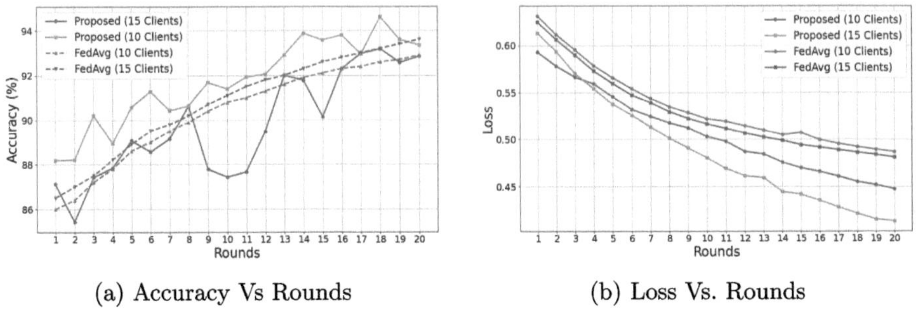

(a) Accuracy Vs Rounds (b) Loss Vs. Rounds

Fig. 4. Training loss and model accuracy on FMNIST dataset for 20 rounds

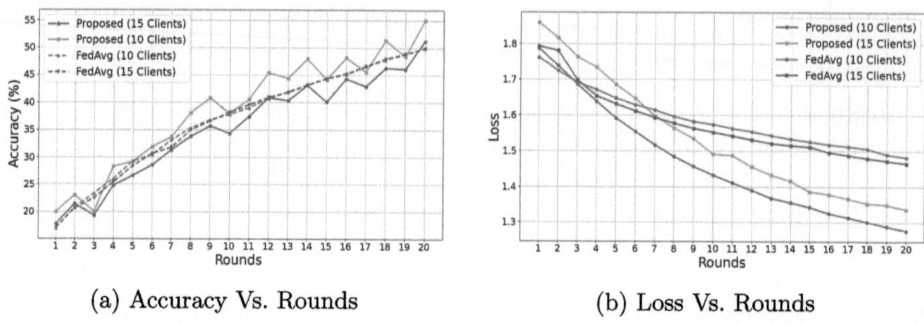

(a) Accuracy Vs. Rounds   (b) Loss Vs. Rounds

Fig. 5. Training loss and model accuracy on CIFAR-10 dataset for 20 rounds

Training Time: We observe the training time is consistent across rounds for all three datasets, however, it is lower with fewer clients. In MNIST, with 10 clients, the average time taken per round is 61.34 s. Similarly, for FMNIST is 61.98 s, and for CIFAR-10 is 85.52 s. The total simulation time and other performance metrics are presented in Table 1. The results show that simulation time is directly influenced by both the number of participants and the complexity of the dataset.

Table 1. Performance comparison of the proposed framework.

Dataset	Clients	Accuracy(%)	Loss	Simulation Time (s)	Time per Round (s)
MNIST	15	96.48	0.1393	1464.08	61.34
	10	97.12	0.1102	1429.59	60.08
FMNIST	15	95.16	0.3177	1507.41	63.59
	10	92.84	0.3492	1488.92	61.98
CIFAR-10	15	55.01	1.6440	2147.41	91.41
	10	51.98	2.2831	1992.83	85.52

6   Conclusion

In this paper, we propose a scalable hierarchical FL framework that supports data heterogeneity while controlling the impact of malicious clients on training. Clients are clustered using the DPM clustering algorithm that doesn't require server communication, thereby securing the model from malicious server attacks. The framework follows intra-cluster and inter-cluster aggregation to enhance scalability and model performance. Clients are grouped into clusters based on the similarity in their data distributions, which addresses data heterogeneity. We use a client-level gossip protocol in each cluster to detect and minimize the impact of malicious clients. Experimental results on the MNIST, FMNIST, and CIFAR-10 datasets demonstrate that our proposed framework achieves 2.1% higher accuracy and reduces training loss by 15.46%. We also observe an improvement in execution time compared to the standard FedAvg algorithm. The proposed framework can be deployed in large-scale networks, and it is capable of controlling malicious clients. In the future, we plan to integrate different secret sharing techniques in the parameter exchange.

Acknowledgement. This research was partially supported by Virtual and Augmented Reality Center of Excellence (VARCoE), IIT Bhubaneswar under the project VARCoE/23/06.

References

1. Abad, M.S.H., Ozfatura, E., Gunduz, D., Ercetin, O.: Hierarchical federated learning across heterogeneous cellular networks. In: 2020 IEEE International Conference on Acoustics, Speech and Signal Processing (ICASSP), ICASSP 2020, pp. 8866–8870. IEEE (2020)
2. Beutel, D.J., et al.: Flower: a friendly federated learning research framework. arXiv preprint arXiv:2007.14390 (2020)
3. Cao, X., Fang, M., Liu, J., Gong, N.Z.: Fltrust: Byzantine-robust federated learning via trust bootstrapping. arXiv preprint arXiv:2012.13995 (2020)
4. Chen, M., Poor, H.V., Saad, W., Cui, S.: Wireless communications for collaborative federated learning. IEEE Commun. Mag. **58**(12), 48–54 (2021)
5. Diaa, A., Humphries, T., Kerschbaum, F.: {FastLloyd}: federated, accurate, secure, and tunable {k-Means} clustering with differential privacy. In: 34th USENIX Security Symposium (USENIX Security 2025), pp. 2733–2752 (2025)
6. Hu, C., Jiang, J., Wang, Z.: Decentralized federated learning: a segmented gossip approach. arXiv preprint arXiv:1908.07782 (2019)
7. Kim, Y., Al Hakim, E., Haraldson, J., Eriksson, H., da Silva, J.M.B., Fischione, C.: Dynamic clustering in federated learning. In: IEEE International Conference on Communications, ICC 2021, pp. 1–6. IEEE (2021)
8. Li, S., Cheng, Y., Wang, W., Liu, Y., Chen, T.: Learning to detect malicious clients for robust federated learning. arXiv preprint arXiv:2002.00211 (2020)
9. Liebenow, J., Schütt, Y., Braun, T., Gehrke, M., Thaeter, F., Mohammadi, E.: DPM: clustering sensitive data through separation. In: Proceedings of the 2024 on ACM SIGSAC Conference on Computer and Communications Security, pp. 273–287 (2024)
10. Long, G., Xie, M., Shen, T., Zhou, T., Wang, X., Jiang, J.: Multi-center federated learning: clients clustering for better personalization. World Wide Web **26**(1), 481–500 (2023)
11. Ma, J., Long, G., Zhou, T., Jiang, J., Zhang, C.: On the convergence of clustered federated learning. arXiv preprint arXiv:2202.06187 (2022)
12. Malik, I., Bhardwaj, A., Bhardwaj, H., Sakalle, A.: IoT-enabled smart homes: architecture, challenges, and issues. In: Revolutionizing Industrial Automation Through the Convergence of Artificial Intelligence and the Internet of Things, pp. 160–176 (2023)
13. McMahan, B., Moore, E., Ramage, D., Hampson, S., Arcas, B.A.: Communication-efficient learning of deep networks from decentralized data. In: Artificial Intelligence and Statistics, pp. 1273–1282. PMLR (2017)

14. Tripathy, R.: A hybrid federated learning for medical cyber physical systems. In: Proceedings of the 25th International Conference on Distributed Computing and Networking, pp. 377–381 (2024)
15. Wang, L., Xu, S., Wang, X., Zhu, Q.: Addressing class imbalance in federated learning. In: Proceedings of the AAAI Conference on Artificial Intelligence, vol. 35, pp. 10165–10173 (2021)
16. Zhang, R., Mao, J., Wang, H., Li, B., Cheng, X., Yang, L.: A survey on federated learning in intelligent transportation systems. IEEE Trans. Intell. Veh. (2024)

Attack Resilient Federated Learning Framework

Sushant Kumar, Kasturi Routray$^{(\boxtimes)}$, and Padmalochan Bera

Indian Institute of Technology Bhubaneswar, Bhubaneswar, India
{sk91,s21ee09001,plb}@iitbbs.ac.in

Abstract. Federated learning (FL) stands out as a promising paradigm for collaborative training of machine learning models where a server supervises the learning process while keeping sensitive data on the user devices. Here, training is decentralized and conducted on edge devices beyond the control of a server. This increases the potential for malicious clients to tamper with the learning process and compromise the global model, resulting in a significant security risk. The majority of existing solutions are designed for scenarios where data exhibits independent and identically distributed (IID) characteristics across devices. A notable performance degradation is observed when the data distribution deviates from the independent and identically distributed (non-IID) scenario. In this paper, we first evaluate the performance of existing Byzantine robust aggregation schemes in non-IID settings within an adversarial scenario. Then, we introduce a novel attack-resilient aggregation scheme named *FedResil* with the objective of enhancing performance in the same adversarial environment. It leverages non-private data, which is collectively agreed upon by the participating clients before the training process begins, to delineate clusters of clients. Subsequently, the server applies existing Byzantine robust aggregation rules to each cluster independently, generating model updates within each cluster. The model update from each cluster is then aggregated to construct the final global model. Through extensive experimentation, we demonstrate that *FedResil* in malicious settings achieves performance similar to that in scenarios where there is no malicious client.

Keywords: Federated Learning · Security · Adversarial Attacks · Malicious Clients

1 Introduction

Federated learning [20], a transformative paradigm in machine learning, serves as a crucial solution to the evolving challenges of data privacy, accessibility, and collaborative learning. Unlike traditional central machine learning methods, where data is transported to a server for computation, federated learning ingeniously

---

This research was partially supported by the Virtual and Augmented Reality Center of Excellence (VARCoE), IIT Bhubaneswar under the project VARCoE/23/06.

N. Hubballi et al. (Eds.): ICISS 2025, LNCS 16380, pp. 115–135, 2026.
https://doi.org/10.1007/978-3-032-13714-2_9

flips this approach by moving computation to the data itself. This addresses critical concerns associated with data privacy, making it a necessary evolution in the field. More specifically, it comprises multiple rounds, each encompassing distinct steps. First, the server initializes the global model with random parameters. Subsequently, the server distributes these model parameters to all participating clients. Following this, clients individually train the model using their local data. Once the local training is complete, the updated model from each client is transmitted back to the server. Finally, the server consolidates these updated models using predefined aggregation rules.

The conventional model of central machine learning encounters significant limitations while dealing with distributed data sources, especially in sensitive domains like healthcare and finance. Federated learning, however, emerges as a solution that not only preserves privacy but unlocks unprecedented collaboration opportunities. It empowers diverse entities, such as hospitals, financial institutions, and organizations, to collectively learn and improve machine learning models without compromising the confidentiality of their individual datasets [19,28]. However, the decentralized structure of federated learning creates opportunities for various attacks by malicious clients since the server lacks control over the local training process. The majority of attacks can be classified into two categories: targeted attacks and untargeted attacks. Targeted attacks [2,9,25] involve the goal of introducing a secondary task to the model, such as generating incorrect predictions for specific input data. In contrast, untargeted attacks [12,13,24] aim to degrade the overall model performance and impede convergence. Given that untargeted attacks present a significant risk to the federated learning process by hindering convergence, our focus in this paper is directed towards addressing these attacks. A good number of studies in the literature have aimed to mitigate the impact of such attacks, including notable methods like Krum [5], Trimmed Mean [29], and Median [29] by discarding statistical outliers. However, the majority of these approaches have been developed and assessed within the context of identically and independently distributed (IID) data scenarios.

In this paper, we examine the effectiveness of current aggregation schemes designed to withstand Byzantine faults in settings where data distribution is non-IID. Our findings reveal that these schemes exhibit poor performance when confronted with non-IID data distributions. Subsequently, we propose a more robust scheme, namely, *FedResil*, which introduces a collaborative approach where clients jointly determine and share non-private data features such as data statistics and device specifications. Utilizing this shared information, the server organizes clients into clusters and applies existing Byzantine robust aggregation techniques within each cluster. The final model is derived by computing a weighted average of the aggregated models from each cluster, with the weights equal to the size of the cluster. Our proposed scheme introduces an intermediary step to the existing schemes, enhancing their performance while maintaining compatibility with most existing approaches. In the context of federated learning, clustering-based approaches [6,8,18,23] have gained considerable attention.

However, existing works often operate in vastly different settings or impose strict constraints on the sources behind non-IID data distribution, which might not always be the case. Our framework stands out by providing a more flexible and resilient solution. Clients are given the autonomy to determine the pertinent non-private features for clustering, anticipating the complexities associated with non-IID data. The adaptability and resilience of our framework make it a promising advancement in the field of Byzantine robust aggregation.

2   Related Work

2.1   Attacks in Federated Learning

Adversarial attacks pose a significant challenge in federated learning (FL) due to the multitude of existing attack strategies and the complexity of defense mechanisms. Adversarial attacks are typically categorized as either targeted or untargeted, depending on the adversaries' objectives. Targeted attacks [2,9,25] aim to introduce additional tasks to the model, such as generating inaccurate predictions for specific input data. Conversely, untargeted attacks [12,13,24] seek to diminish overall model performance and hinder convergence. Furthermore, attacks can be classified based on the approach adversaries employ to disrupt the learning process. These can manifest as either data poisoning attacks or model poisoning attacks. In data poisoning attacks [14,30], malicious clients possess access to data and can manipulate it to compromise the integrity of the global model. Conversely, in model poisoning attacks [3,21,27], malicious clients directly alter the model updates transmitted to the server with the intent of compromising model security. Below, we provide a brief discussion of some of the most renowned attacks:

- Data Poisoning Attacks:
    - **Label Flipping Attack** [14]: The adversaries intentionally flip the labels of their data samples. This attack aims to corrupt the training process by introducing mislabeled data so that local training produces poisoned updates to the server.
    - **GAN based attack** [30]: In this approach, the adversaries use Generative Adversarial Nets (GANs) to generate poisoned data samples to corrupt the training process while maximizing their disguise.
- Model Poisoning Attacks:
    - **Bit Flip Attack** [27]: In this attack, the adversaries flip some of the bits of some individual floating point numbers in the representation of the model.
    - **Little is Enough Attack** [3]: In this attack, adversaries collaborate to compute the mean (μ) and standard deviation (σ) for each coordinate in the model. They then craft a malicious model by computing $\mu + z_{max}\sigma$ for each coordinate, where z_{max} represents the maximal change that can be applied by them without being detected.

- **Gaussian Noise Attack** [21]: Here, the adversaries craft model updates by sampling model weights from a Gaussian distribution that results from other adversaries' model updates.

While our analysis can be applied to many types of attacks, in this paper, we present a thorough analysis on Label Flipping Attack, Little is Enough Attack, and Gaussian Noise Attack in non-IID settings.

2.2   Byzantine Robust Aggregation Schemes in FL

In the literature, several defense mechanisms have been proposed to counter the aforementioned attacks. Among these, Byzantine robust aggregation emerges as one of the most promising approaches. Given that the server is typically more trusted and accessible than the distributed clients, implementing robust aggregation at the server level proves to be both effective and feasible. Here, we discuss some of the state-of-the-art schemes designed to enhance resilience against malicious clients:

Krum [5]: In this method, each local model update is viewed as a point in hyperspace. The algorithm selects a local model V to serve as the representative vector by minimizing the sum of squared distances between V and its $n - f - 2$ closest neighbors, where n represents the total number of clients and f denotes the maximum number of tolerable adversaries.

Trimmed Mean [29]: For each local model update dimension from the clients, it excludes the largest $k\%$ and smallest $k\%$ of values and calculates the mean of the remaining values to form the global model.

Median [29]: For each local model update dimension from the clients, it selects the median of the values to form the global model with the aim of keeping it closer to the centre of the distribution.

FL Trust [7]: The fundamental concept involves treating a model update as a vector, defined by both its direction and magnitude, where malicious clients can manipulate both aspects. The server defines an ideal model by training it over a clean dataset owned by the server. Trust scores are calculated using the ReLU-clipped cosine similarity between the server's model update and each client's model update. Ultimately, the global model is derived by averaging the normalized local model updates, weighted by their respective trust scores.

Spectral Anomaly Detection [17]: In this scheme, the authors initially train a variational autoencoder using model weights generated during training on a clean dataset. This variational autoencoder serves as the anomaly detection model. When local model updates are passed through the encoder and decoder, they incur reconstruction errors. Model updates with high reconstruction errors are subsequently excluded from the aggregation process, thereby enhancing the overall robustness of the aggregation mechanism.

Since FL Trust and Spectral Anomaly Detection rely on access to a clean dataset on the server, which may not always be practical, we exclude them from our analysis. So, in this paper, we conduct an analysis of Krum, Trimmed Mean, and Median in non-IID settings across two different scenarios: one without utilizing our *FedResil* framework and the other incorporating our *FedResil* framework under the attacks as presented in Sect. 2.1.

2.3 Clustering Based Approaches in Federated Learning

Recently, clustering-based approaches [6,8,18,23] have been extensively discussed in the literature as a means to address the heterogeneity of data among clients. However, we find that most of these studies examine scenarios different from the one we focus on in our work.

Federated Learning with Hierarchical Clustering [6]: This paper considers a benign environment where the objective is to reach higher accuracy by training specialized models for clusters of clients. Initially, conventional FL is carried out until a predefined round. At this juncture, clusters of clients are determined using the similarity between the updated local model updates from all clients. Subsequently, these identified client clusters undergo independent but simultaneous training, each initialized with the joint model's current state, resulting in multiple models to achieve higher accuracy.

Clustered Federated Learning [23]: It begins with the server computing pairwise cosine similarities α among clients. Cluster candidates $c1$ and $c2$ are then identified by minimizing the maximum similarity between pairs of clients from different clusters α_{cross}. If α_{cross} drops below a predefined threshold $\alpha_{\text{cross}}^{\text{thresh}}$, updates from the smaller cluster are considered malicious and excluded from the aggregation process. The approach, however, does not account for the non-IID nature of the data.

Dynamic Clustering for Non-IID Data [8]: This paper focuses on employing clustering-based methods utilizing distribution characteristic data obtained from individual clients (such as mean, variance, and standard deviation) to tackle the challenges presented by dynamic environments in federated learning. In these environments, clients may join and leave frequently, leading to fluctuations in data distribution. However, it operates under the assumption of a benign environment.

Mini FL [18]: Our work most closely resembles to Mini FL. In this approach, the authors address the non-IID distribution of data by considering Geo-feature, Time-feature, and User-feature as the basis for clustering clients. Each feature is evaluated individually to determine which one forms the most effective clusters. Once the best feature for clustering is identified, existing Byzantine-robust schemes are applied to each cluster to generate model updates. These updates are then aggregated to form the global model.

In our work, we extend the Mini FL framework, which suffers from a significant limitation due to its lack of generalizability. Specifically, Mini FL only considers three specific features (Geo-feature, Time-feature, and User-feature) separately as sources of non-IIDness. To overcome this limitation and improve robustness, we propose a more generalized approach. In our method, clients collaboratively determine a set of non-private features to serve as the basis for clustering. Additionally, we leverage all available features simultaneously to facilitate more effective clustering. Notably, we do not conduct an analysis of Mini FL within our settings because it does not address non-IIDness resulting from features other than the aforementioned three.

3   Proposed FedResil Framework

3.1   Problem Definition

We consider a generic federated learning scenario having a central server S and N clients, denoted as $C = \{C_1, C_2, ..., C_N\}$. The dataset $D = \bigcup_{i=1}^{N} D_i$ is partitioned across the clients, and each client C_i holds a portion of the dataset, denoted as D_i. Let $M = \{i \mid C_i \text{ is malicious}\}$ be the set of malicious clients. In round t of federated learning, each client C_i sends local updates w_i^t to the server after training the global model w^t received in the previous round on its local dataset D_i. The server S iteratively computes the global model using an aggregate rule from the local model updates w_i^t as: $w^{t+1} = \text{Aggregate}(\{w_i^t\}_{i=1}^{N})$, where w^{t+1} represents updated global parameters for the next iteration.

Let $L(w; D)$ represent the global loss function computed on the dataset D. The objective is to find a robust aggregation method denoted as Aggregate that iteratively learns w such that the following value is minimized:

$$L_{non-malicious} = \sum_{j \in \{1,2,...,N\} \setminus M} L(w, D_j)$$

where $L_{non-malicious}$ denotes the sum of losses over the datasets of non-malicious clients.

3.2   Workflow of FedResil Framework

The motivation behind our proposed scheme stems from the limitations observed in existing Byzantine robust aggregation schemes. These schemes exhibit effectiveness in mitigating the impact of malicious clients when data distribution follows an independent and identically distributed (IID) pattern. The underlying principle of many Byzantine robust aggregation schemes relies on the assumption that updates from benign clients cluster around the mean, while updates from malicious clients deviate significantly from the mean. However, recent research highlighted by the authors of [3] has demonstrated that even small perturbations around the mean can evade many existing defenses proposed in [5, 15, 29], rendering them ineffective. This vulnerability becomes particularly high in scenarios where the data distribution is non-IID. In such cases, updates from benign clients are centered around different points according to the underlying data distribution, leading to challenges in accurately identifying malicious updates. To address this issue, we propose a novel approach where we partition the larger non-IID domain into smaller IID-like domains. By applying Byzantine robust aggregation schemes independently to each of these smaller domains, we aim to enhance the resilience of existing algorithms, thereby improving their efficacy in non-IID settings.

To address the challenge of breaking down larger non-IID domains into smaller IID-like clusters without compromising privacy, clients in our proposed approach agree in advance to share a set of p non-private features denoted as f. These features, encapsulated in a one-dimensional vector, contain information about the dataset that can aid in the segmentation of the larger non-IID cluster. The shared features encompass various data statistics and device-specific details relevant to the task at hand. For instance, in a simple image classification task aimed at distinguishing between airplanes, trucks, and cars, the non-private feature vector may include details such as the total number of images for each category (e.g., airplanes, trucks, cars), camera model specifications, average image resolution, and other pertinent attributes. These features are accumulated into a single 1-dimensional vector of size p, facilitating collaborative clustering without compromising individual privacy as the actual images are not shared with the server. Similarly, for a regression healthcare problem such as predicting blood glucose levels using variables such as blood pressure, age, body weight, height, and gender, the set of non-private features may include a count of underage and overage persons, percent of overweight persons, the machine model used to measure blood pressure, and so on. These features offer statistical summaries of the dataset, protecting the privacy of individual data stored on edge devices.

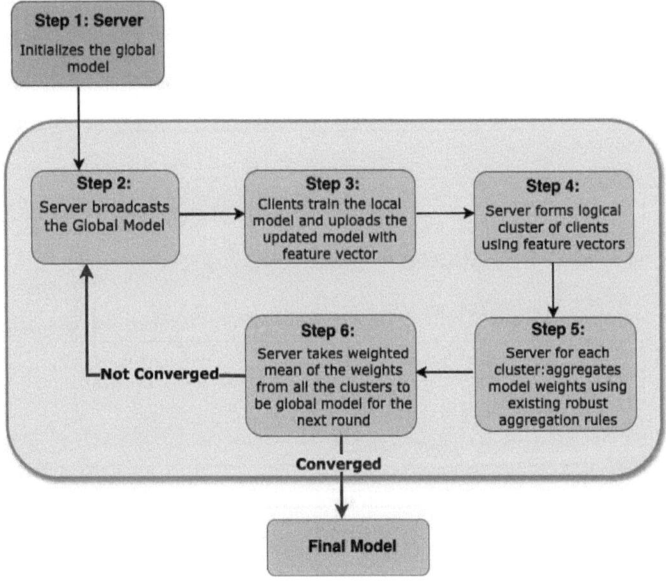

Fig. 1. Flowchart of FedResil Framework

In accordance with the aforementioned context, we introduce our algorithm with greater precision, as illustrated in Fig. 1. Following the standard FL procedure, the server initializes the global model w^0 with random parameters in step 1. Subsequently, in step 2, the server sends the model w^t (for the initial round $t = 0$) to all clients. Step 3 involves each client C_i conducting local model training on its dataset D_i and uploading a set of non-private features f_i^t, alongside local model updates w_i^t. In steps 4 through 6, the server applies our proposed dynamic clustering scheme, *FedResil*, utilizing $\bigcup_{i=1}^{N}\{w_i^t, f_i^t\}$ as inputs to derive the final model updates, as detailed below, comprising three crucial steps:

Dynamic Clustering Based on Feature Vectors: The server utilizes the feature vectors $f^t = \bigcup_{i=1}^{N} f_i^t$ received from all the clients in round t to parition them into k-clusters, $CL = \{CL_1, CL_2, \ldots CL_k\}$, using the k-means clustering algorithm [16]. Here, f^t has dimensions $N \times p$, where N is the number of clients and p is the number of non-private features. We utilize the silhouette index [22] to choose the optimal k for the k-means clustering algorithm.

Algorithm 1. FedResil

Require: $\{(w_i^t, f_i^t) : C_i \in C\}$
1: $f \Leftarrow []$
2: $w \Leftarrow []$
3: **for all** (w_i^t, f_i^t) in $\{(w_i^t, f_i^t) : C_i \in C\}$ **do**
4:     f.append(f_i^t)
5:     w.append(w_i^t)
6: **end for**
7: optimal_k = find_optimal_k(f, $[2 \ldots N - 1]$)
8: labels $\Leftarrow$ k_means_algorithm(f, n_clusters=optimal_k) $\triangleright$ Step 4
9: CL $\Leftarrow$ {} $\triangleright$ Clusters of model weights
10: **for** $i = 1$ to N **do**
11:     CL[label[i]].append(w[i])
12: **end for**
13: $w_{CL} \Leftarrow []$ $\triangleright$ Aggregated model updates from each cluster
14: **for** $j = 1$ to optimal_k **do**
15:     w_{CL}.append(Existing_Robust_Aggregation(CL[j])) $\triangleright$ Step 5
16: **end for**
17: $w^{t+1} \Leftarrow$ WeightedMean(w_{CL}) $\triangleright$ Step 6

Aggregation of Model Weights within Clusters: For each of the k clusters $CL_j \in CL$, the server uses existing Byzantine robust aggregation schemes to form a model update $w_{CL_j}^t$ within each cluster.

Global Model Generation: The server takes the weighted mean of the model updates $w_{CL_j}^t$ from each cluster, weighted by number of clients $|CL_j|$ in that cluster, to form the global model for the next iteration as: $w^{t+1} =$

WeightedMean($\{w^t_{CL_j}\}^k_{j=1}$) $= \frac{\sum^k_{j=1} w^t_{CL_j} \times |CL_j|}{\sum^k_{j=1} |CL_j|}$. The precise steps of our proposed framework are delineated in Algorithm 1. This algorithm first finds the optimal number of clusters (optimal_k) using the procedure find_optimal_k. Using the optimal_k value and set of non-private features f, it utilizes the k-means clustering algorithm to partition the clients. Then, it assigns each client's model weights to the corresponding cluster. Next, it aggregates model updates from each cluster using a robust aggregation method. Finally, it computes the new global model weights for the next iteration by taking the weighted mean of the aggregated updates. The procedure find_optimal_k outlined in Algorithm 2 iteratively applies the k-means clustering algorithm with different cluster counts $k \in [2, N - 1]$, calculates the average silhouette score for each, selects the k with the highest silhouette score, and returns it as the optimal number of clusters.

4   Performance Evaluation

4.1   Experimental Setup

In our experiments, we consider a generic FL scenario where a server coordinates training across clients. Specifically, we designate a total of 16 clients denoted as $C_0, C_1, \ldots, C_{15}$. For conducting our simulations, we utilize the FL framework named Flower [4], in conjunction with the TensorFlow library [1].

Algorithm 2. find_optimal_k

Require: f: Set of non-private features from all the clients
Require: *search_range*: Set of possible values for optimal_value of k
1: silhouette_scores $\Leftarrow []$
2: **for** $k \in$ search_range **do**
3:      labels $\Leftarrow$ k_means_algorithm(f, n_clusters=k)
4:      silhouette_avg $\Leftarrow$ silhouette_score(f, labels)
5:      silhouette_scores.append(silhouette_avg)
6: **end for**
7: max_silhouette_score $\Leftarrow$ max(silhouette_scores)
8: max_silhouette_score_index $\Leftarrow$ index_of(max_silhouette_score, silhouette_scores)
9: optimal_k $\Leftarrow$ search_range[max_silhouette_score_index]
10: **return** optimal_k

Datasets: We have used three prominent datasets to demonstrate the efficacy of our framework: **MNIST** [10], **Fashion-MNIST** [26], and **NSL-KDD** [11]. MNIST and Fashion-MNIST serve as standard benchmarks for FL evaluation. We specifically selected the NSL-KDD dataset to demonstrate the versatility of our framework, showcasing its applicability beyond image data to diverse data types, including non-image datasets. MNIST comprises 60k training and 10k testing grey-scale images of handwritten digits (0 to 9) with labels. Similarly, Fashion-MNIST includes 60k training and 10k testing grey-scale images depicting clothing items like T-shirts, trousers, pullovers, dresses, etc., spanning a total of ten distinct classes. NSL-KDD is a benchmark dataset widely used for intrusion detection system evaluation. It includes around 125k training and 22k testing samples comprising input features like duration, protocol type, source IP, destination IP, etc. The output feature is a label indicating the type of attack. We categorised the attack label into five major categories, namely Normal, DOS, Probe, R2L and U2R, for a multi-class classification task. To remove the imbalance between the train and the test dataset, we combine and shuffle them before we split them into a 70–30 train-test for the rest of our analysis. To induce non-IID characteristics, the training data for MNIST and Fashion-MNIST (labels 0–9) are partitioned among 16 clients according to the distribution in Table 1. For NSL-KDD, the same partitioning scheme is applied with labels 0–4 corresponding to Normal, DoS, R2L, Probe, and U2R, respectively.

Model Architecture: For MNIST and Fashion-MNIST datasets, we train a model with two CNN layers. The first CNN layer consists of 32 filters of 3×3 dimension with a Rectified Linear Unit (ReLU) activation function, followed by a max-pooling layer with a pool size of 2×2. The second CNN layer follows a similar architecture with 64 filters of size 3×3 and ReLU activation. Again, a max-pooling layer with a 2×2 pool size is applied to reduce the spatial dimensions

Table 1. Data distribution across clients for different datasets

	MNIST and Fashion-MNIST										NSL-KDD				
	0	1	2	3	4	5	6	7	8	9	0	1	2	3	4
C_0	10	10	5	15	10	0	0	0	0	0	10	10	0	0	10
C_1	20	10	10	5	15	0	5	0	0	0	10	10	0	0	15
C_2	10	20	10	10	5	0	5	0	0	0	10	20	0	0	5
C_3	20	10	20	10	10	0	5	0	0	0	20	10	0	0	10
C_4	10	20	10	20	10	0	5	0	0	0	10	20	0	0	10
C_5	15	10	20	10	20	0	5	0	0	0	15	10	0	0	20
C_6	5	15	10	20	10	0	5	0	0	0	5	15	0	0	10
C_7	10	5	15	10	20	20	15	0	0	0	20	5	0	0	20
C_8	0	0	0	0	0	20	15	0	0	0	0	0	5	15	0
C_9	0	0	0	0	0	10	10	0	20	0	0	0	10	5	0
C_{10}	0	0	0	0	0	10	20	0	10	0	0	0	10	10	0
C_{11}	0	0	0	0	0	40	10	25	15	0	0	0	25	20	0
C_{12}	0	0	0	0	0	0	0	20	10	20	0	0	5	10	0
C_{13}	0	0	0	0	0	0	0	20	15	30	0	0	20	10	0
C_{14}	0	0	0	0	0	0	0	25	20	30	0	0	10	20	0
C_{15}	0	0	0	0	0	0	0	10	10	20	0	0	15	10	0

Note: Each element at the i, j location indicates the percentage of data samples with label j that C_i possesses of the feature maps. Then, a flattening layer is introduced to convert the 2D feature maps into a 1D vector, followed by a dense layer of 64 units with ReLU activation. Finally, a dense layer of 10 units is applied with softmax activation to get the output probabilities corresponding to each label.

For the NSL-KDD dataset, we train a multilayer perceptron, comprising a dense layer with 128 units and ReLU activation as the initial layer. Subsequently, a dropout layer with a dropout rate of 20% was introduced to mitigate overfitting. Following this, two additional dense layers with 64 and 16 units, respectively, were incorporated, both utilizing ReLU activation. Finally, a dense layer of 5 units with softmax activation was applied to generate output probabilities corresponding to each label. During training, only the protocol_type, service, flag, duration, src_bytes, and dst_bytes input features were considered to avoid overfitting. We use Adam Optimizer for training all the above models, with the loss function being categorical cross-entropy. We train our models for 50 FL rounds with a batch size of 32 and 10 steps per epoch.

Attack Models: In our simulations, the goal of malicious clients is to disrupt the learning process by following one of the below attacks as presented in Sect. 2.1:

Label Flipping Attack: In this attack [14], all malicious clients in M engage in label swapping belonging to classes 2–3 and 7–8 for MNIST and Fashion-MNIST datasets and 0–4 and 3–2 for NSL-KDD dataset. Specifically, label exchange for classes 2–3 entails converting dataset instances with label 2 to label 3, and vice versa, where instances labelled as 3 are transformed to label 2.

Little is Enough Attack: In this attack, all malicious clients in M craft and upload a malicious model by computing $\mu + z_{\max}\sigma$ for each coordinate following Algorithm 3 of [3].

Gaussian Noise Attack: We employ a modified form of the Gaussian Noise Attack, as described in [21]. Here, malicious clients within the set M introduce Gaussian noise $\mathcal{N}(\sigma, \sigma^2)$, derived from the distribution of all malicious clients, into their model updates.

Non-private feature vectors: Let us denote the number of output labels by num_labels. For dynamic clustering of clients, we adopt a 1-dimensional vector of size p = num_labels. The value at the jth position represents the number of data points with label j. Therefore, each client uploads a feature vector of size num_labels. As the actual data, whether images or records, are retained by the client, privacy is ensured. For example, a client C_i may upload a feature vector as $f_i^t = [10, 20, 30, 20, 10, 40, 50, 50, 40, 10]$ for MNIST dataset, indicating that it has trained on a dataset having 10 images with label 0, 20 images with label 1, and so on in the current FL round t. The server has the capability to perform post-processing on feature vectors prior to employing the k-means algorithm. In our case, the server divides the value at the jth position of f_i^t by the total number of images with label j, a calculation that can be readily derived from the received feature vectors.

Table 2. List of malicious clients under different settings

Malicious Clients Count	Malicious Clients List
1	5
2	5, 7
4	5, 7, 11, 14
6	1, 5, 7, 8, 11, 14
8	0, 1, 5, 7, 8, 10, 13, 14

Evaluation Metrics: As discussed in Sect. 3.1, the primary goal is to establish a robust framework wherein the cumulative losses across datasets from non-malicious clients are minimized. In classification tasks, loss minimization directly translates to improved accuracy. Therefore, we choose accuracy as the primary metric for evaluating our framework. To ensure a comprehensive evaluation, we assess the efficiency of our framework on the test dataset that was not distributed to clients for training purposes. These test data points are considered representative of clean data associated with non-malicious clients for evaluation purposes, albeit not manually distributed to clients, as it does not impact our analysis.

As our framework incorporates an additional dynamic clustering step onto existing Byzantine robust aggregation schemes, we aim to assess its performance by comparing it against established algorithms such as Krum, Trimmed Mean, and Median. Our analysis consists of two parts. Firstly, we conduct a detailed examination of the performance of existing schemes with and without our framework when the number of malicious clients is set to 4. We track the performance across each federated learning round to assess both stability and final model performance. Secondly, we analyse how performance evolves as the number of malicious clients is incrementally increased. For this part of the analysis, we vary the number of malicious clients as follows: 1, 2, 4, 6, and 8. Table 2 enumerates the clients exhibiting malicious behaviour under these specified conditions.

For the initial part of the analysis, we set f (maximum number of malicious clients) to 4 for Krum and k (proportion_cut) to 0.25 for Trimmed Mean. However, for the subsequent analysis involving varying numbers of malicious clients, we set f to the number of malicious clients and maintain k at 0.25. This comparison is conducted across various attack environments, including Label Flipping Attack, Little is Enough Attack, and Gaussian Noise Attack.

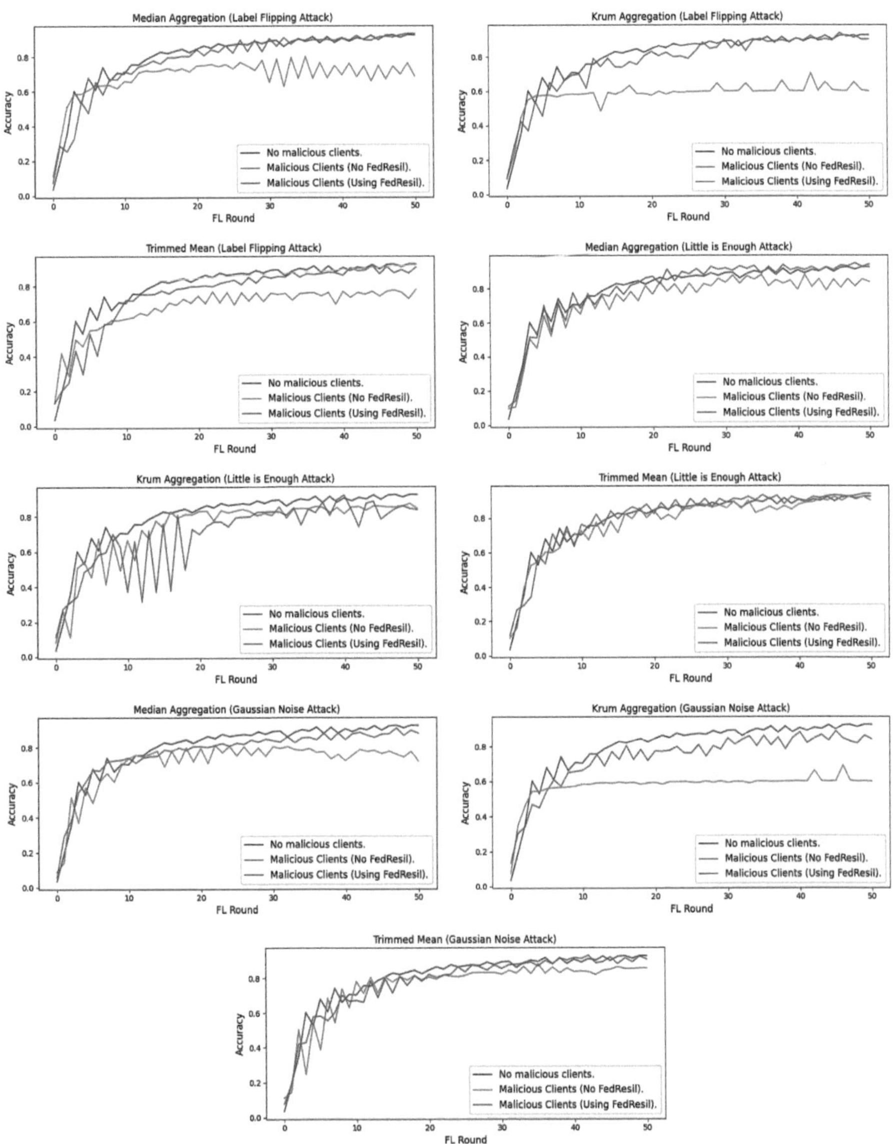

Fig. 2. Performance Evaluation on MNIST dataset with four malicious clients

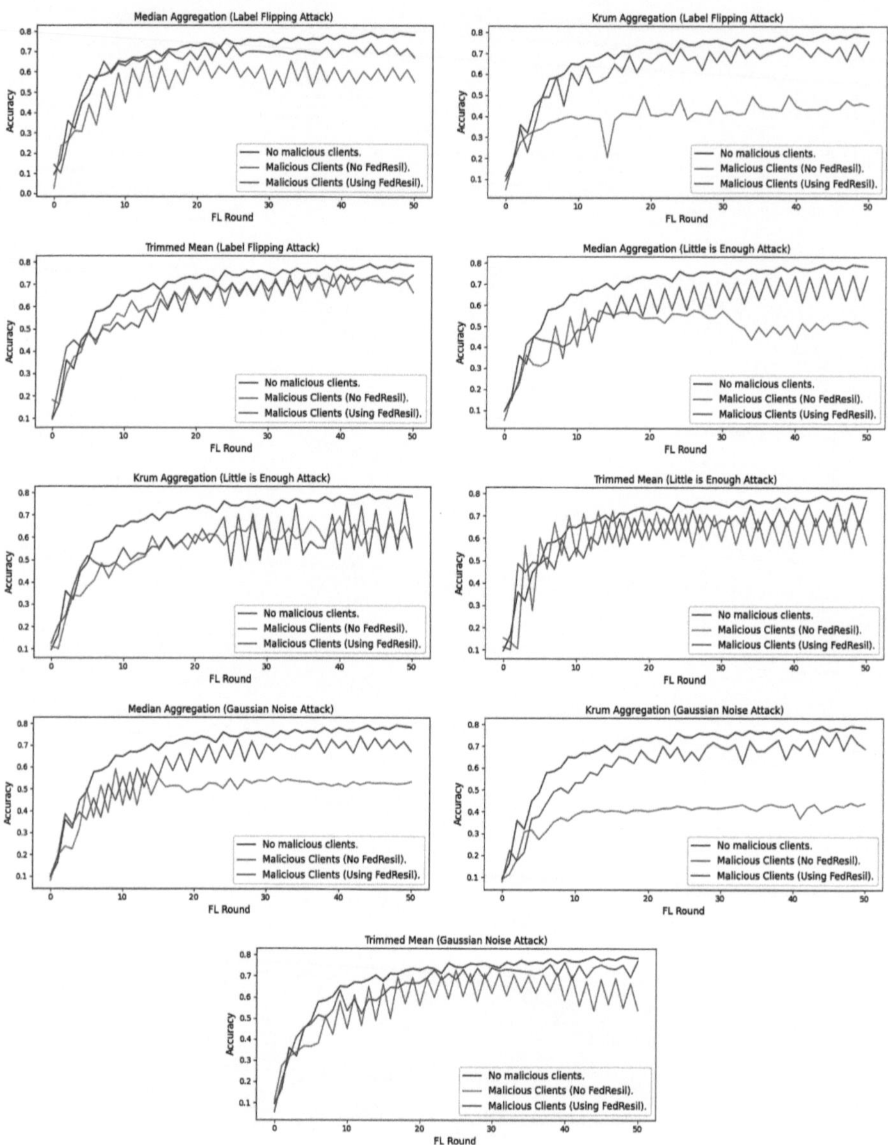

Fig. 3. Performance Evaluation on Fashion-MNIST dataset with four malicious clients

4.2   Results

For the first part of our analysis, we first establish a baseline for accuracy comparison by conducting vanilla federated learning without any malicious clients. Next, we evaluate the performance of various existing Byzantine robust aggregation rules under different attack scenarios with number of malicious clients = 4 and record the outcomes. Finally, we integrate our dynamic clustering approach,

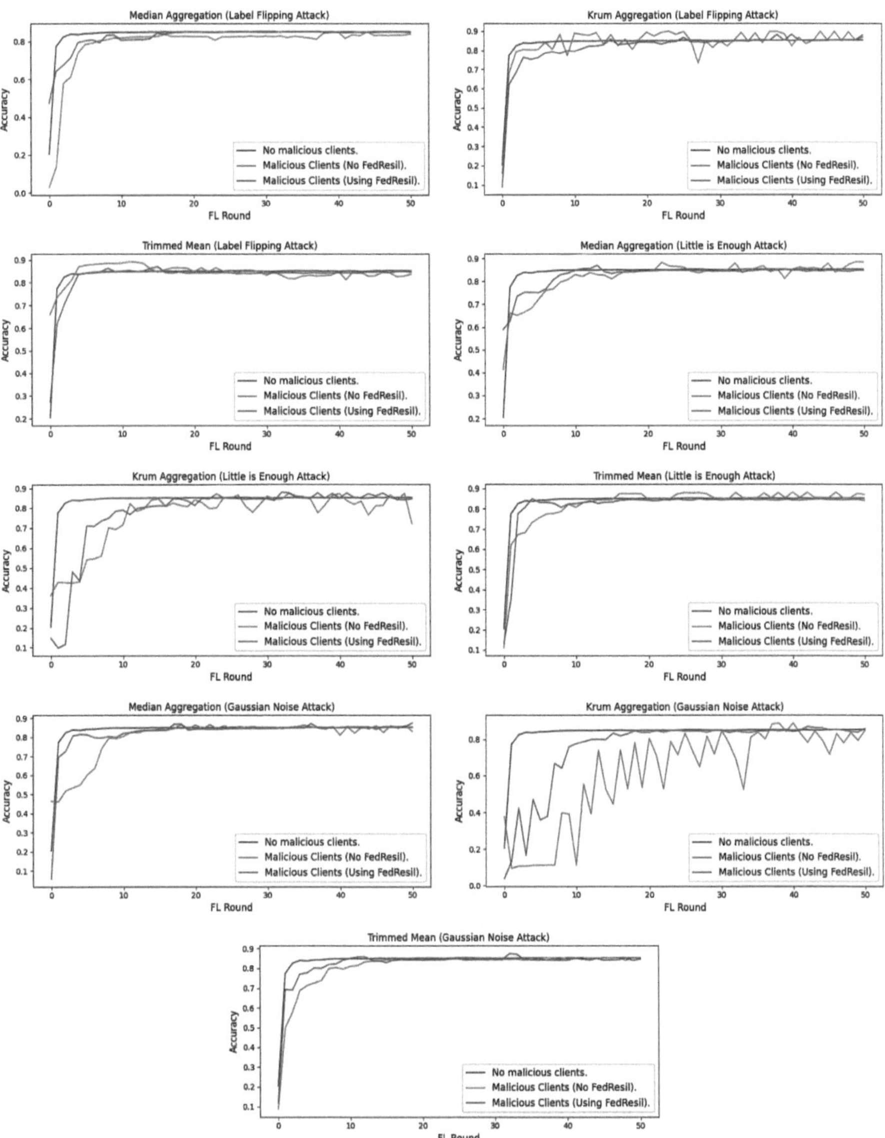

Fig. 4. Performance Evaluation on NSL-KDD dataset with four malicious clients

FedResil, with these existing methods and assess their performance under the same attack scenarios. For the second part of our analysis, we vary the number of malicious clients as mentioned in Table 2 and record the final accuracy after 50 FL rounds for the same Byzantine robust aggregation rules with and without utilizing our framework.

Table 3. Performance Summary with four malicious clients

	MNIST			Fashion-MNIST			NSL-KDD		
Benign Environment	92.46			78.43			85.22		
Aggregation Rules	LF[a]	LE[b]	GN[c]	LF[a]	LE[b]	GN[c]	LF[a]	LE[b]	GN[c]
Median	68.59	83.80	71.89	55.20	49.55	53.38	83.94	88.38	83.12
Median - FedResil	93.16	94.13	88.00	67.27	73.92	67.58	84.85	84.80	87.46
Krum	59.92	84.37	59.97	45.04	55.92	43.79	86.90	72.22	84.88
Krum - FedResil	89.93	83.80	83.98	75.79	55.51	68.90	88.05	84.59	85.88
TMean[d]	78.06	90.17	85.50	66.50	57.26	53.92	83.70	87.05	84.86
TMean[d] - FedResil	90.71	94.11	90.53	74.29	77.17	77.09	84.64	84.22	84.70

Accuracy (in percentage) after 50 rounds of FL for Benign Environment (without any malicious clients with standard FL) and under various attacks with Byzantine robust schemes.
[a] Label Flipping Attack.
[b] Little is Enough Attack.
[c] Gaussian Noise Attack.
[d] Trimmed Mean.

Figures 2, 3 and 4 illustrate the performance, i.e., accuracy with FL rounds, of existing schemes, both with and without our framework, across various attack scenarios for the MNIST, Fashion-MNIST and NSL-KDD datasets, respectively. In all these figures, the blue line corresponds to the baseline achieved with vanilla federated learning without any malicious clients. The orange line represents the performance of the selected algorithm without our framework within a specific attack scenario involving four malicious clients, while the green line represents the performance of the chosen algorithm with our *FedResil* framework under the same attack scenario. The final accuracy of each scheme under different attack scenarios is presented as a performance summary in Table 3.

The experimental findings indicate a significant degradation in the performance of existing Byzantine robust aggregation rules when applied to non-IID version of MNIST and Fashion-MNIST datasets. For instance, under Gaussian noise attack for the Fashion-MNIST dataset, the accuracy drops to approximately 43.79% with Krum aggregation. Similarly, for the MNIST dataset under Label Flipping Attack, the accuracy decreases to 59.92% with Krum aggregation. In contrast, our proposed *FedResil* framework demonstrates a notable increase in performance under the same conditions, achieving accuracies of about 68.9% and 89.93%, respectively. For the NSL-KDD dataset, we observe that accuracy remains almost the same in most of the cases. This consistency can be attributed to the limited impact of attacks on the training process. Specifically, we observe that the training accuracies with malicious clients, without the integration of our framework, closely resemble those in benign environments. Consequently, there is minimal opportunity for significant improvements in model performance. However, we do note significant improvement under Little is Enough Attack with Krum Aggregation where accuracy increases from 72.22 % to 84.59 %. The limited impact of attacks on performance can be attributed to the inherent bias present in the dataset. Approximately 87% of the data points consist of Normal and DoS type attacks. Even if the model accurately learns to classify between these points, the resulting accuracy would still be relatively high. Given the majority presence of these points in the dataset, the model can effectively learn from benign clients, even when malicious clients introduce poisonous updates.

Figures 5, and 6 depict the performance of *FedResil* with varying numbers of malicious clients. They represent the final accuracy achieved after 50 FL rounds across different numbers of malicious clients. In all these figures, the orange line represents the performance of the selected algorithm without our framework within a specific attack scenario, while the green line represents the performance of the chosen algorithm with our *FedResil* framework under the same attack scenario. The graphs clearly demonstrate that our framework consistently improves the performance in nearly all cases. As anticipated, the accuracies exhibit a declining trend with an increase in the number of malicious clients, regardless of whether our framework is utilized. However, even with this decrease, the accuracy remains notably higher when our framework is employed compared to scenarios where it is not utilized. For some cases, where there is no scope for improvements, it maintains accuracy comparable to existing robust aggregation schemes. From Figs. 2, 3, 4, 5 and 6, it becomes clear that our framework substantially improves the performance of existing schemes in the majority of scenarios. In a few cases where it does not lead to significant improvement, our framework maintains comparable performance to existing schemes. The superior performance of our framework stems from the assumptions underlying existing schemes, which are designed under the premise that the data distribution across clients is IID. In contrast, our framework excels by breaking down the larger non-IID domain into smaller IID domains suited for their respective applications.

4.3 Discussion

In this section, we examine how our proposed *FedResil* framework can be extended and scaled to achieve improved performance and efficiency. *FedResil* framework utilizes non-private features of the dataset to transform a non-IID dataset into simpler IID-like datasets. This enables the efficient application of existing Byzantine robust aggregation schemes. Below, we explore some key facets of our approach.

Extensibility: Currently, our framework discards model updates that seem to be malicious updates to ensure the higher performance of the trained model. This capability can be further expanded to detect malicious clients in adversarial scenarios. Essentially, we can monitor the frequency of rejected model updates attributed to each client over a certain number of rounds. Clients with higher rejection frequencies can then be flagged as potentially malicious. Subsequently, we can disregard their updates and proceed with regular federated learning procedures.

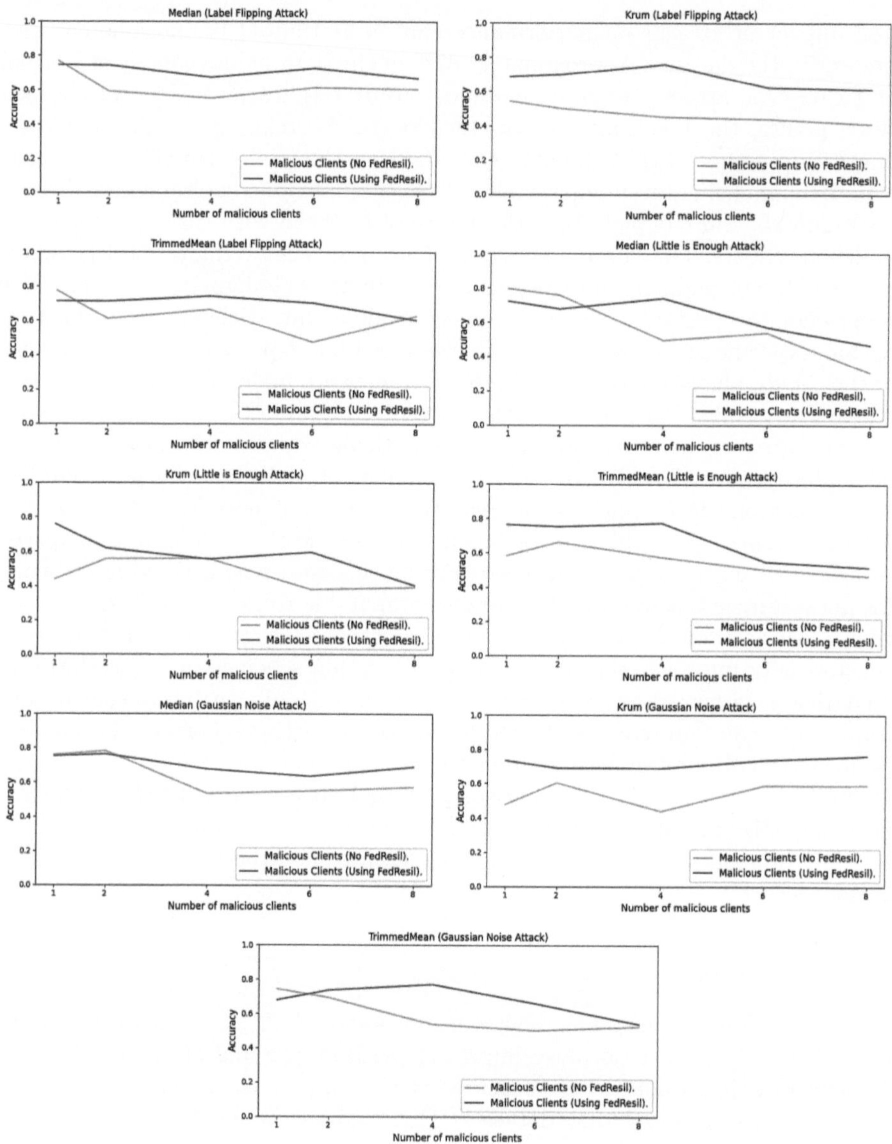

Fig. 5. Effect of varying number of malicious clients on Fashion-MNIST dataset

Scalability: In our framework, we follow the standard FL approach, but with the addition of clients uploading non-private features, f_i^t, alongside their local model updates, w_i^t. This doesn't affect complexity on the client side. However, on the server side, we leverage these non-private features for clustering the clients. To find the optimal number of clusters, we iterate through each $k \in [2, N-1]$ using the k-means algorithm and evaluate the silhouette score for each. This

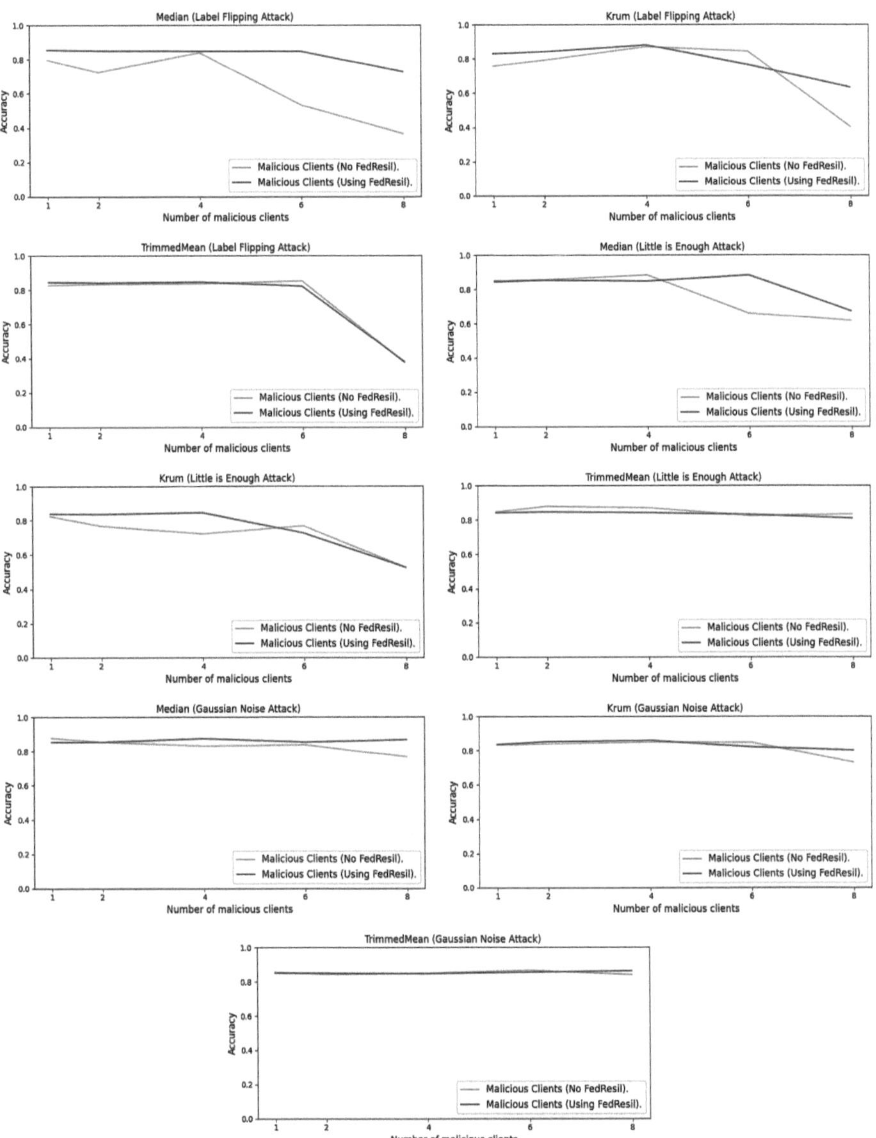

Fig. 6. Effect of varying number of malicious clients on NSL-KDD dataset

increases clustering complexity for each FL round, ensuring effective client partitioning as the dataset evolves over time. To manage this, we can perform re-clustering at intervals rather than every round, balancing computational costs with accurate clustering, making it suitable for large-scale applications.

5   Conclusion

In our study, we investigated the efficacy of existing Byzantine robust aggregation schemes and identified a decrease in model performance under non-IID settings, primarily attributed to the fact that most of the existing Byzantine robust algorithms work by discarding statistical outliers. Moreover, by leveraging non-private features of the dataset, we introduced *FedResil* framework which effectively partitions clients into clusters with similar data distributions. Subsequently, existing Byzantine robust aggregation schemes are applied under each cluster, leveraging their proficiency in IID conditions. Through extensive experimentation with various attack types and algorithms, *FedResil* framework shows significant performance enhancements, often reaching levels comparable to those observed in non-adversarial environments.

References

1. Abadi, M., et al.: {TensorFlow}: a system for {Large-Scale} machine learning. In: 12th USENIX Symposium on Operating Systems Design and Implementation (OSDI 2016), pp. 265–283 (2016)
2. Bagdasaryan, E., Veit, A., Hua, Y., Estrin, D., Shmatikov, V.: How to backdoor federated learning. In: International Conference on Artificial Intelligence and Statistics, pp. 2938–2948. PMLR (2020)
3. Baruch, G., Baruch, M., Goldberg, Y.: A little is enough: circumventing defenses for distributed learning. In: Advances in Neural Information Processing Systems, vol. 32 (2019)
4. Beutel, D.J., et al.: Flower: a friendly federated learning research framework. arXiv:2007.14390 (2020)
5. Blanchard, P., El Mhamdi, E.M., Guerraoui, R., Stainer, J.: Machine learning with adversaries: Byzantine tolerant gradient descent. In: Advances in Neural Information Processing Systems, vol. 30 (2017)
6. Briggs, C., Fan, Z., Andras, P.: Federated learning with hierarchical clustering of local updates to improve training on non-IID data. In: 2020 International Joint Conference on Neural Networks (IJCNN), pp. 1–9. IEEE (2020)
7. Cao, X., Fang, M., Liu, J., Gong, N.Z.: Fltrust: Byzantine-robust federated learning via trust bootstrapping. arXiv:2012.13995 (2020)
8. Chen, M., Wu, J., Yin, Y., Huang, Z., Liu, Q., Chen, E.: Dynamic clustering federated learning for non-IID data. In: CAAI International Conference on Artificial Intelligence, pp. 119–131. Springer, Cham (2022)
9. Chen, X., Liu, C., Li, B., Lu, K., Song, D.: Targeted backdoor attacks on deep learning systems using data poisoning. arXiv:1712.05526 (2017)
10. Deng, L.: The MNIST database of handwritten digit images for machine learning research. IEEE Signal Process. Mag. **29**(6), 141–142 (2012)
11. Mohi-ud din, G.: NSL-KDD (2018). https://doi.org/10.21227/425a-3e55
12. Fang, M., Cao, X., Jia, J., Gong, N.: Local model poisoning attacks to {Byzantine-Robust} federated learning. In: 29th USENIX Security Symposium (USENIX Security 2020), pp. 1605–1622 (2020)
13. Fraboni, Y., Vidal, R., Lorenzi, M.: Free-rider attacks on model aggregation in federated learning. In: International Conference on Artificial Intelligence and Statistics, pp. 1846–1854. PMLR (2021)

14. Fung, C., Yoon, C.J., Beschastnikh, I.: The limitations of federated learning in sybil settings. In: 23rd International Symposium on Research in Attacks, Intrusions and Defenses (RAID), pp. 301–316 (2020)
15. Guerraoui, R., Rouault, S., et al.: The hidden vulnerability of distributed learning in Byzantium. In: International Conference on Machine Learning, pp. 3521–3530. PMLR (2018)
16. Hartigan, J.A., Wong, M.A.: Algorithm as 136: a k-means clustering algorithm. J. R. Stat. Soc. Ser. C (Appl. Stat.) **28**(1), 100–108 (1979)
17. Li, S., Cheng, Y., Wang, W., Liu, Y., Chen, T.: Learning to detect malicious clients for robust federated learning. arXiv:2002.00211 (2020)
18. Li, Y., Yuan, D., Sani, A.S., Bao, W.: Enhancing federated learning robustness in adversarial environment through clustering non-IID features. Comput. Secur. **132**, 103319 (2023)
19. Long, G., Tan, Y., Jiang, J., Zhang, C.: Federated learning for open banking. Federated Learn.: Priv. Incentive 240–254 (2020)
20. McMahan, H.B., Moore, E., Ramage, D., Arcas, B.A.: Federated learning of deep networks using model averaging. arXiv:1602.05629, **2**, 2 (2016)
21. Pillutla, K., Kakade, S.M., Harchaoui, Z.: Robust aggregation for federated learning. IEEE Trans. Signal Process. **70**, 1142–1154 (2022)
22. Rousseeuw, P.J.: Silhouettes: a graphical aid to the interpretation and validation of cluster analysis. J. Comput. Appl. Math. **20**, 53–65 (1987)
23. Sattler, F., Müller, K.R., Wiegand, T., Samek, W.: On the byzantine robustness of clustered federated learning. In: 2020 IEEE International Conference on Acoustics, Speech and Signal Processing (ICASSP), ICASSP 2020, pp. 8861–8865. IEEE (2020)
24. Shi, J., Wan, W., Hu, S., Lu, J., Zhang, L.Y.: Challenges and approaches for mitigating byzantine attacks in federated learning. In: IEEE International Conference on Trust, Security and Privacy in Computing and Communications (TrustCom), pp. 139–146 (2022)
25. Sun, Z., Kairouz, P., Suresh, A.T., McMahan, H.B.: Can you really backdoor federated learning? arXiv:1911.07963 (2019)
26. Xiao, H., Rasul, K., Vollgraf, R.: Fashion-MNIST: a novel image dataset for benchmarking machine learning algorithms. arXiv:1708.07747 (2017)
27. Xie, C., Koyejo, O., Gupta, I.: Generalized byzantine-tolerant SGD. arXiv:1802.10116 (2018)
28. Xu, J., Glicksberg, B.S., Su, C., Walker, P., Bian, J., Wang, F.: Federated learning for healthcare informatics. J. Healthcare Inform. Res. **5**, 1–19 (2021)
29. Yin, D., Chen, Y., Kannan, R., Bartlett, P.: Byzantine-robust distributed learning: towards optimal statistical rates. In: International Conference on Machine Learning, pp. 5650–5659. PMLR (2018)
30. Zhang, J., Chen, J., Wu, D., Chen, B., Yu, S.: Poisoning attack in federated learning using generative adversarial nets. In: 18th IEEE International Conference on Trust, Security and Privacy in Computing and Communications/13th IEEE International Conference on Big Data Science and Engineering (TrustCom/BigDataSE), pp. 374–380. IEEE (2019)

SANVector: SBERT-APTNet Vector Framework for Cyber Threat Attack Attribution Using Diversified CTI Logs

Sougata Dolai[ID], Annu Kumari[ID], and Mayank Agarwal[✉][ID]

Department of Computer Science and Engineering, IIT Patna, Bihar 801103, India
{sougata_2411ai20,annu_2411ai68,mayank265}@iitp.ac.in

Abstract. Advanced Persistent Threat (APT) is a type of cyberattack where intruders gain unauthorized access and remain undetected for an elongated period of time. The main purpose of an APT is to steal sensitive information, spy on operations, or disrupt systems. To overcome these challenges, in this paper, we have proposed a novel modular and scalable architecture SANVector (SBERT-APTNet Vector) framework that uses fine-tuned SBERT embeddings, contrastive learning, and multi-view features to automatically identify the threat actors from unstructured reports about cyber threats. For that, we have focused on attributing APT activities to known threat actor groups such as APT28, APT29, Lazarus Group, Turla, and others extracted from various log report sources such as FireEye, Crowdstrike, Unit42, Mandiant, and Kaspersky. In all we analyze a total of 11 APT groups. To begin, our model incorporates a strong preprocessing pipeline that normalizes attacker aliases, extracts deep semantic features, and masks indicators of compromises using a trained SBERT model. Furthermore, these features are classified using the traditional model with K-Nearest Neighbor (KNN) to achieve high performances of 93.17% accuracy and a perfect F1 score across various threat groups. Moreover, we compare the performance of fine-tuned SBERT with SBERT models using classifiers, such as KNN, SVM, AdaBoost, XGBoost, and DNN. In addition, this study provides a practical solution to the critical problem of APT attribution, with implications for enhancing cyber defense operation, national security, and threat intelligence workflows.

Keywords: APT attribution · Cyber threats · Fine-tuned SBERT · KNN

1 Introduction

In the era of rapid evolving cyber-threat attack, Advance Persistent Threats (APTs) are one of the major hazardous and sophisticated cyber-attack that often linked to nation-states or organized cybercriminal groups. These attacks are hard to detect, identify pattern, and remain hidden for an elongated time and also work in a coordinated way. They often reuse distinct Tactics, Techniques,

N. Hubballi et al. (Eds.): ICISS 2025, LNCS 16380, pp. 136–148, 2026.
https://doi.org/10.1007/978-3-032-13714-2_10

and Procedures (TTPs) which are cataloged in frameworks such as MITRE ATT&CK. Despite the increasing availability of lots of unstructured data in forms of text reports, blogs and advisories, major of this data is not used effectively due to lack of automated semantic analysis framework. Prior research often focused on analyzing code or Indicators of Compromise (IoCs) for attribution but these techniques possess challenges including actor impersonation, repeated use of the same tools and limited to semantic interpretability. In contrast, to address these challenges we have proposed SBERT-APTNet Vector(which explicitly connects SBERT and APT classification), a novel deep learning framework which uses advanced semantic techniques. It works by fine-tuning a significant model SBERT with a distinctive kind of learning to perform attack attribution directly from textual threat intelligence reports.

SANvector introduces various novel contributions. To begin, first it implements robust preprocessing step that helps to standardized all information like modify distinct names to same form, conceal significant details, and filtering out noise. Furthermore, we have fine-tuned a state-of-the-art model SBERT using techniques that enhance the model ability to effectively distinguish between distinct threat groups. Lastly, it uses KNN classifier trained on these all feature to accurately identify threat groups, achieving 93.17% accuracy and perfect F1-scores (1.00) in the best-performing fold. In summary, SANvector is powerful tool that helps to summarize unstructured text reports into machine-readable intelligence. It provides readymade framework for cybersecurity teams to quickly and accurately identify and understand the groups behind cyber-attacks. While, prior research in APT attribution has mostly focused on small sets of threat actors, but our research tackles this issues by using a larger number of APT group instances for a thorough analysis. To overcome this limitation, we incorporate a wide range of threat intelligence sources, such as MITRE ATT&CK, Unit42, Mandiant, and kaspersky to gather and examine unstructured reports about threats. This approach helps our model recognize more diverse threat behaviour patterns, which improves the accuracy and broad applicability of our attribution results. We chose SBERT as the core model because it generates sentence-level embeddings that capture more detailed semantic meaning compared to word2vec or TF-IDF. Unlike standard BERT, SBERT creates dense vectors that are specifically designed to measure similarity, which is crucial for matching CTI reports that describe similar TTPs. Additionally, our fine-tuned SBERT model employs contrastive learning to better align the embeddings with the CTI domain and address the limitations of earlier NLP-based attribution methods such as Attack2Vec.

The main contribution of this research are:

1. We have proposed SANvector, a novel framework that uses fine-tuned SBERT embedding, contrastive learning and multi-view features to automatically identify the threat actors from unstructured cyber threat intelligence reports.
2. We have analyzed APT29, Lazarus Group, APT28, Sandworm Team, OilRig, Kimsuky, Turla, Wizard Soider, Magic Hound, Muddy Water and Threat

Group 3390 with their aliases, focusing on patterns derived from unstructured threat intelligences sources.
3. We performed a comparative evaluation with other ML techniques, typically used for cyber attack attribution.

2   Related Work

Cyber threat attribution has been studied from various perspectives over time and the existing research can generally be grouped into three main categories: framework-based methods, approaches using natural language processing and feature engineering and solutions that rely on deep learning or embeddings. Below, we outline the major contributions in each of these categories as well as their respective limitations. Although these studies have made important contributions and face challenges like limited scalability, reliance on manually designed features and difficulties in dealing with unstructured threat intelligence data.

Qiang et al. [1] introduced a framework that integrates the Intrusion Kill Chain with F2T2EA (Find, Fix, Track, Target, Engage, and Access) model to identify cyber attacks using CTI. Although this method is well- structured and systematic but it is not fully automated and relies on the quality of available threat data. Similarly, Hettema [2] developed a rationality-based model that applies belief revision principles to incident the attribution. However, this model lacks clear steps for practical use. These rule and framework based methods offer conceptual clarity but suffer from limitations in scalability and automation.

Irshad and Siddiqui [3] proposed Attack2vec, an embedding model which extracts structured features from unstructured CTI reports to automate actor attribution. A major limitation of this method is the lack of standardized formats in CTI reports, which affects consistency. Furthermore, Shin et al. [4] introduced ART, a Python tool that reclassifies APT groups using MITRE ATT&CK and cosine similarity. Although, its effectiveness is limited by the incomplete coverage of ATT&CK. Lee and Choi [5] developed MuCamp, which generates variations of cyber campaigns by substituting TTP synonym. The accuracy of this method depends on the reliability of the synonym sets. Edie et al. [6] used association rule mining and weighted Jaccard similarity for attack attribution to achieve high accuracy. However, their method remains sensitive to the completeness of CTI data.

Recent studies increasingly uses deep learning and pretrained embeddings in cyber threat attribution. Wang et al. [7] proposed ThreatInsight, which combines Honeypoint-collected IPs addresses and threat knowledge graphs for early detection of APT activities. However, its performance is highly dependent on the coverage of the graph. Tang et al. [8] developed a CNN-based model which enhanced with self-attention and SPP-net features for detecting APT malware variants but it requires large high-quality labeled datasets. Perry et al. [9] proposed NO-DOUBT, which used SMOBI word embeddings to attribution attacks from textual reports CTI. Though, the method applicability is limited by its reliance on labeled intelligence. Moreover, Permana et al. [10] explored POS-tagging and BiLSTM-CRF for automatic data labeling, though their work incomplete. Cheng et al. [11] proposed DeBERTaIC, a hybrid model combining DeBERTa, BiGRU, CRF, and LightGBM for cyber threat analysis in consumer electronics networks. However, the resource heavy design restricts deployment. Zhang et al. [12] have recently attempted to combine hierarchical systems with large language models (LLMs) to identify the source of cyber attacks. However, human involvement is still needed to check and confirm the information which is extracted.

3   Datasets

Cyber threat attack attribution heavily depends upon the availability and quality of labeled threat intelligence data. In this paper, we have created two stage of automated data collection using MITRE ATT&CK framework. The objective was to collect threat group metadata and their associated references content, which would help with tasks such as threat classification, attribution, and language model fine-tuning. Each report had a plain text description of the threat activity, and each was labeled with the corresponding APT group. In total, the dataset consists of 11 well-known threat groups like APT29, Lazarus Group, APT28, Turla, OilRig.

We obtained structured data about threat actor from MITRE ATT&CK resources, which offers each group name, brief description, and curated external references to threat intelligence reports. To gather this data, we developed a custom web crawler that collected metadata for each group, including the group name, profile URL, and reference links from sources such as Crowdstrike, Mandiant, Unit42, FireEye, and Kaspersky. The newspaper3k library was used to extract article titles and contents, while BeautifulSoup served as a fallback for dynamic or irregular HTML structures. Non-text formats like PDFs, slides, and multimedia files were filtered out to maintain data quality. The cleaned text was stored as plain files organized by group, enabling downstream NLP tasks such as NER, token classification, and threat actor attribution.

4   Proposed Work

This research proposes SANvector, a thorough and adaptable framework for precisely classifying cyber threat reports into their specific APT groups. This framework combines NLP, contrastive learning (refers to self-supervised representation learning technique that trains model to differentiate between similar and dissimilar data points for example "APT28" used "spear-phishing" and "Fancy Bear" sent a targeted phishing email refers to similar attack, however contrastive learning can teach the model to place these in same vector space neighborhood), fine-tuned sentence embeddings, and traditional machine learning classifiers. It can handle real-world cyber threat intelligence data, and deals with challenges like sparse data, noise and distinctive naming conventions. The main objective of this paper is to create a framework that is semantically aware, adaptable and easy to understand. This framework able to identify and attribute threat actors using unstructured CTI reports and learn semantically detailed representation of threat group behaviors even with limited labeled data. Figure 1 illustrates the flow diagram of our proposed framework which consists of data collection, data preprocessing, model fine-tune, feature extraction and classification. These five steps pipeline is discussed in details below.

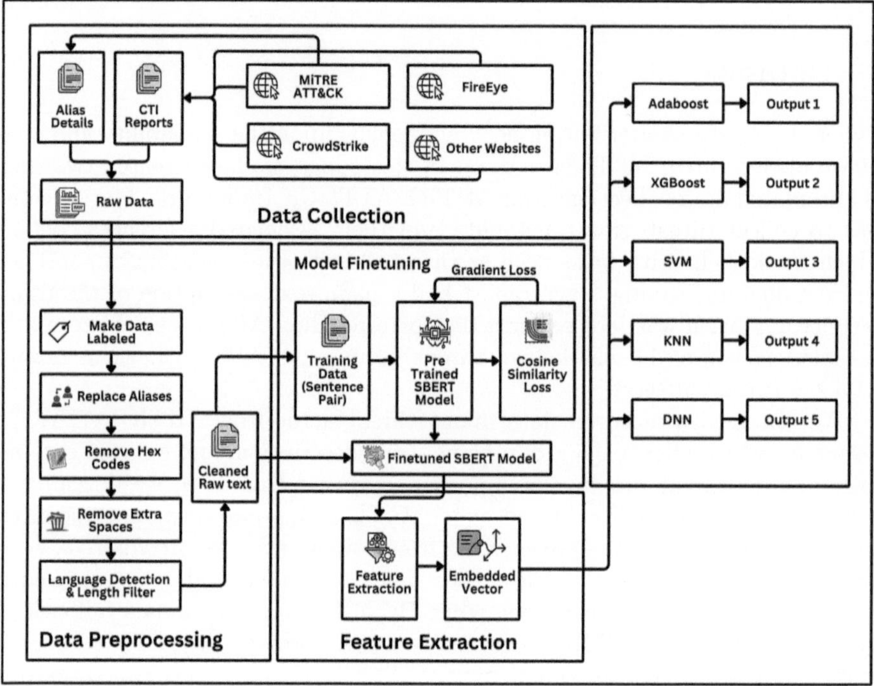

Fig. 1. Proposed Architecture for Attack Attribution.

Data Collection: Data collection is the important part for gathering relevant data for processing. It involves gathering raw data from CTI reports from publicly available sources like MITRE ATT&CK and other websites. Each report was labeled with correct APT group either manually or using semi-automated methods based on the context and known attack indicators. Alias dictionaries were built from MITRE ATT&CK and other public databases to connect similar APT names. Threat actor groups are often recognized by different names across various cyber security vendors and researchers. For example, "APT28" has aliases "Fancy Bear", "Sofacy", "Sednit" and "Lazarus Group" has "Hiden Cobra", "Guardians of Peace". However, we have collected 11 label data and number of labels per data are demonstrated in Table 1 and their aliases.

Table 1. Distribution of APT Labels in the Dataset and Their Aliases

Label	No. of Samples	Aliases
APT29	32	IRON RITUAL, IRON HEMLOCK, NobleBaron, Dark Halo, NOBELIUM, UNC2452, YTTRIUM
Lazarus Group	32	Labyrinth Chollima, HIDDEN COBRA, Guardians of Peace
APT28	26	IRON TWILIGHT, SNAKEMACKEREL, Swallowtail, Group 74, Sednit, Sofacy
Sandworm Team	25	ELECTRUM, Telebots, IRON VIKING, Voodoo Bear, Seashell Blizzard
OilRig	23	COBALT GYPSY, IRN2, APT34, Helix Kitten, Evasive Serpens, Hazel Sandstorm
Kimsuky	15	Black Banshee, Velvet Chollima, Emerald Sleet, THALLIUM, APT43, Springtail
Turla	15	IRON HUNTER, Group 88, Waterbug, WhiteBear, Snake, Krypton
Wizard Spider	13	UNC1878, TEMP.MixMaster, Grim Spider, FIN12, GOLD BLACKBURN, ITG23
Magic Hound	11	TA453, COBALT ILLUSION, Charming Kitten, ITG18, Phosphorus, Newscaster
Muddy Water	9	Earth Vetala, MERCURY, Static Kitten, Seedworm, TEMP.Zagros, Mango Sandstorm
Threat Group 3390	8	Earth Smilodon, Emissary Panda, BRONZE UNION, APT27, Iron Tiger

Data Preprocessing: For data preprocessing, firstly we have collected a raw data from text reports and then processed it through multi-step approach to improve the text quality and remove irrelevant noise. Figure 1 is overall framework, which includes various steps for data preprocessing. The reports were assemble from open-source CTI feeds, as well as MITRE ATT&CK mappings and other websites. Each report was saved as a .txt file, with associated metadata in a CSV file that linked the APT group to the report. A total of 209 reports were labeled for use in the training and testing the model. This ensured a balanced mix of both well-known and less documented APT groups. Here, we have used multi-step cleaning process to prepare the data. Distinct names for the same APT group aliases were standardized using a list of known interpretation (like "APT28" being the same as "Fancy Bear" or "Sofacy"). Apart from that, we have used regular expressions to remove patterns like SHA and MD5 hashes, hexadecimal code as well as IPv6 addresses, to prevent overfitting to file-specific data. We removed extra spaces, control characters, non-English documents and other non-meaningful symbols to keep text clean. Thus, these steps helped to ensure that our pipeline would generalize well to real-world reports and not rely on simple word matches.

Model Fine-tuning: To convert CTI narratives into meaningful vector representations, we have used a fine-tuned version of SBERT model. Reports originating from the same APT group are considered as positive, whereas reports from different APT groups are considered as negative pairs. This approach allows the model to understand and learn the similarities in behavioral traits and language patterns associated with specific threat groups. Here, cosine similarity is used to ensure that similar reports have high similarity in their embeddings. This fine-tuned SBERT model is then used to generate downstream embedding generation for classification.

Feature Extraction/Embeddings: In feature extraction, each CTI reports is cleaned and turned into a dense, fixed-length vector using the fine-tuned SBERT model. This creates a high-dimensional representation that captures the meaning and key elements of the report, such as TTPs and behaviors used by the APT group. The proposed framework is designed to support multi-view fusion, dimensionality reduction and semantic representation. SBERT, is a version of BERT model designed to generate semantically sentence embeddings. SBERT uses a siamese or triplet network structure to produce fixed-size sentence vectors that can be compared directly using cosine similarity or other distance metrics. It enables efficient and scalable semantic similarity computations. SBERT achieves this by fine-tuning BERT using supervised objectives such as classification or contrastive loss on labeled sentence pairs. We fine-tune a pre-trained SBERT model using a contrastive learning approach on labeled similar or dissimilar sets of sentence. With each pair, we have created embeddings and then used cosine similarity to calculate a contrastive loss. This loss is then backpropagated to update the model and improving its embedding space to match domain-specific semantic similarity. The resulting model performs better on downstream clustering and classification tasks in CTI.

Classification: The embeddings are then given to the traditional machine learning classifiers for assigning group-level attribution. Here, several models are tested like K- Nearest Neighbor (KNN), Support Vector Machine (SVM), AdaBoost, XGBoost and Deep Neural Network (DNN) to improve classification. The classification process uses 5-fold cross-validation to ensure the model works well on new data. We chose k-fold cross-validation to achieve a more reliable and robust evaluation of our model. This method involves splitting dataset into k subsets and rotating the training and validation process across all folds to reduces the risk of biased results from single train-test split. This approach helps to detect overfitting, ensures the model performs well across various data segments, and offers a better estimate of model performance. As shown in Table 2 we have mentioned that KNN perform well because KNN does not overfit on small datasets and it does not need to learn complicated boundaries because SBERT already separates different groups in the embedding space. Apart from that, KNN uses distances like cosine or Euclidean, it directly follows what the embeddings were trained for, without needing extra steps.

In summary fine-tuned SBERT model helps to differentiate between similar and different threat actors. Furthermore, aliases resolution engine helps to solve the problem of inconsistent naming of APT groups. Moreover, semantic embedding representation avoid the needs for manually creating features and offers a flexible solution that works across various threat intelligence areas.

SANvector uses SBERT embeddings but adds several important improvements that set it apart from other SBERT-based methods used for attribution. Unlike prior approaches that uses standard SBERT models but SANvector performs domain specific fine-tuning with contrastive learning. This helps the model better understand and align with the tactics, techniques, and procedures (TTPs) used by attackers in CTI reports. Additionally, SANvector includes a process for resolving aliases and preprocessing data. This helps standardize names of threat actors such as matching "APT28" with "Fancy Bear", and hides indicators of compromise (IoCs) which reduces errors caused by similar but misleading word choices. The model also uses a multi-view approach that combines semantic embeddings with structured information about threat actors giving a more complete picture for accurate attribution. Finally, by combining these fine-tuned embeddings with a KNN classifier SANvector achieves high accuracy (93.17%) and low variability and performing better than traditional methods that use SBERT with a classifier. These improvements make SANvector a strong, reliable, and scalable solution that goes beyond typical uses of SBERT.

5   Results and Discussion

In this section, we have evaluated results to analyze the performance of our proposed model, we did an experiment using CTI report of labeled data and have collected 209 relevant reports among 290 reports. To explore our proposed framework capability we have used only 11 labeled CTI reports in real-word attack

Table 2. Result of Fine-tuned SBERT Model with KNN Classifier

Threat Group	Precision	Recall	F1-score	Support
APT28	0.92	0.92	0.92	26
APT29	0.85	0.94	0.89	31
Kimsuky	0.76	0.93	0.84	14
Lazarus_Group	0.94	0.97	0.95	32
Magic_Hound	1.00	0.73	0.84	11
MuddyWater	1.00	1.00	1.00	9
OilRig	0.96	0.96	0.96	23
Sandworm_Team	1.00	0.96	0.98	23
Threat_Group-3390	1.00	0.88	0.93	8
Turla	1.00	0.93	0.97	15
Wizard_Spider	1.00	0.92	0.96	13
Accuracy	-	-	**0.93**	**205**
Macro avg	0.9488	0.9207	0.9312	205
Weighted avg	0.9376	0.9317	0.9322	205

campaign. For evaluation metrics we have used precision, recall, F1-Score, macro and weighted average to measure the performance and accuracy of our model as shown in Table 2. In this research, we have proposed a fine-tuned SBERT-based framework that uses APT classification for cyber threat attribution which helps to identify APT group reports through semantic analysis. The results indicate that our method works much better than the baseline models, especially when compared to regular SBERT embeddings.

Performance and Accuracy: Our experiments show that when we use fine-tuned SBERT embeddings along with KNN or SVM classifiers, we get best results with an average accuracy of 93.17% and F1-score exceeding 0.93 across most threat groups. On the other hand, models that use SBERT embeddings performed poorly due to their inadequacy in catching sentence-level semantics. **Scalability and Additional Threat Groups:** The current evaluation uses data from 11 APT groups and 209 reports but scalability remains a concern. The system is modular in design allow for the addition of more threat groups and CTI sources. Still, a larger and more diverse set of data is needed to ensure robustness and applicability to broad range of threat actor behaviour and linguistic patterns. **Data Collection and Limitations:** One of the major challenges in our study was limited availability of high-quality CTI reports. We have collected 290 reports among which only 209 relevant reports were gathered, which require manual curation due to noisy and unstructured nature of open-source intelligence. This restricts the diversity of threat behaviour captured in dataset and may affect the performance in real world scenarios that involve less-documented or emerging threat groups.

Illustrated in Tables 3 and 4 we evaluated multiple classifiers, including SVM, AdaBoost, XGBoost, DNN, and KNN. Among them, KNN consistently outperformed the others, achieving 93.17% accuracy with a perfect F1-score for multiple APT groups. This demonstrates that the fine-tuned SBERT embeddings effectively distinguish between different groups in vector space and KNN leverages effectively without overfitting. In addition to this, the model not only enhance APT group attribution using semantic learning, but also offers a framework that can be used for future Cyber threat Intelligence tasks.

The fine-tuned SBERT outperforms the base SBERT because it is specifically trained for the CTI domain. The base SBERT creates general sentence embeddings but it is not customized for CTI text. The fine-tuned SBERT uses contrastive learning on CTI-related data, allowing it to better understand relationships within threat reports. This training enables it to differentiate between reports that appear similar but describe different threat actors. As a result, the fine-tuned SBERT shows higher accuracy, precision, and consistency in classification tasks.

Table 3. Performance Comparison Using SBERT Model

Model	Avg Accuracy (%)	Std Dev Accuracy	Macro Precision	Macro Recall	Macro F1-score	Weighted Precision	Weighted Recall	Weighted F1-score
Adaboost	20.49	±1.95	0.1361	0.1531	0.1409	0.1673	0.2049	0.1809
XGBoost	60.49	±8.51	0.5848	0.5452	0.5500	0.6239	0.6049	0.6023
SVM	71.71	±7.00	0.7414	0.6300	0.6540	0.7290	0.7171	0.7013
KNN	72.20	±5.25	0.7456	0.6718	0.6910	0.7417	0.7220	0.7194
DNN	14.63	±5.12	0.0862	0.1134	0.0831	0.1160	0.1463	0.1089

Table 4. Performance Comparison Using Fine-Tuned SBERT Model

Model	Avg Accuracy (%)	Std Dev Accuracy	Macro Precision	Macro Recall	Macro F1-score	Weighted Precision	Weighted Recall	Weighted F1-score
Adaboost	41.46	±7.40	0.7014	0.3725	0.3826	0.6408	0.4146	0.3673
XGBoost	91.71	±4.78	0.9347	0.9114	0.9214	0.9215	0.9171	0.9179
SVM	92.68	±2.67	0.9250	0.9142	0.9174	0.9364	0.9268	0.9302
KNN	93.17	±2.39	0.9488	0.9207	0.9312	0.9376	0.9317	0.9322
DNN	91.22	±3.96	0.9175	0.9050	0.9090	0.9222	0.9122	0.9157

While our proposed framework show high performance across various CTI processing tasks but some limitation persist. Initially, the dataset currently includes a limited number of APT groups. Adding more groups could help the model generalize better. Secondly, We have saved 209 unique CTI reports, obtaining high-quality, unstructured reports from diverse and reliable sources remains a challenges. The lack of these resources could impact the model's training strength. Moreover, the system has not fully incorporated real-time updates and diverse CTI sources in multiple languages. This opens up opportunities for additional research on real-time and cross- language threat detection.

The comparison of the SBERT and fine-tuned SBERT visualizations are shown in Fig 2 that fine-tuned makes embeddings better in t-SNE projections. In the fine-tuned t-SNE chart the data points are grouped closely together and form clear clusters showing stronger connections between similar words. On the other hand, the original SBERT t-SNE plot has points that are more spread out and the cluster are not as clear. Overall, fine-tuning enhance both the compactness and separability of embeddings. Moreover, t-SNE does a better capturing differences between groups because it handles more complex, non-linear relationships. Additionally, the reduced overalp in fine-tuned embeddings indicates better discriminative power for downstream classification task. The stability of class boundaries in fine-tuned t-SNE visualization highlights a more consistent embedding space that could improve model generalization.

6   Security Analysis

SANvector exhibit various advantages according to the threat model and also efficiently handles aliases due to its initial processing step cleans and standardizes the names that are obtained from different CTI sources. Moreover, it is less likely to be deceived by impersonation attempts due to fine-tuned embeddings

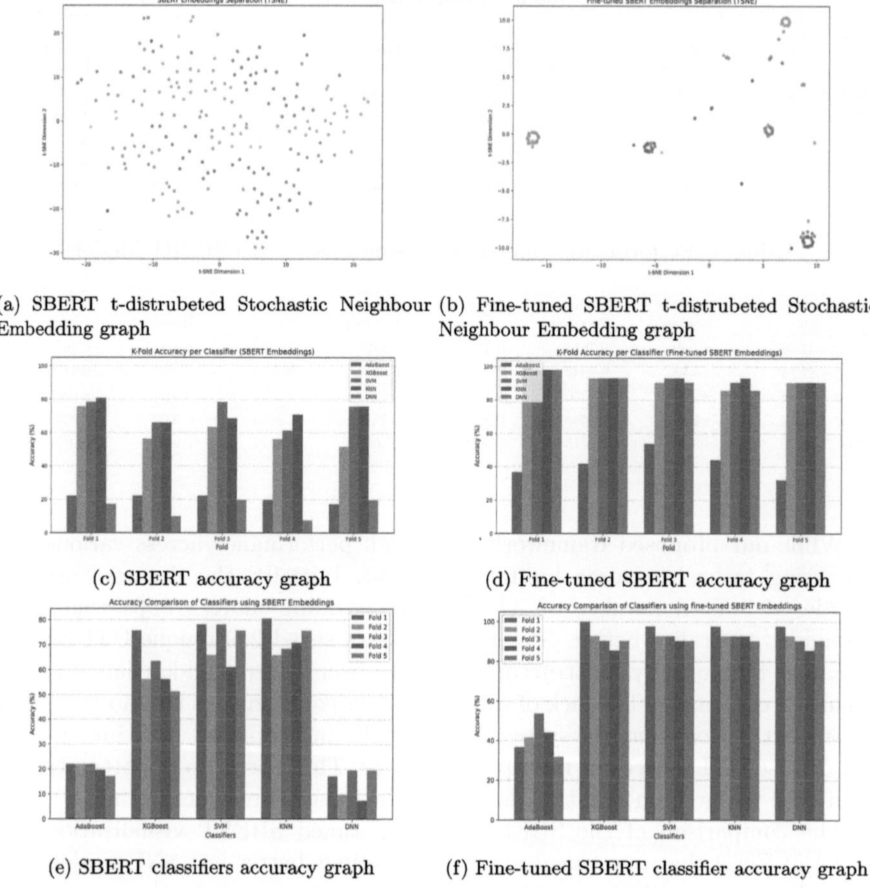

(a) SBERT t-distrubeted Stochastic Neighbour Embedding graph

(b) Fine-tuned SBERT t-distrubeted Stochastic Neighbour Embedding graph

(c) SBERT accuracy graph

(d) Fine-tuned SBERT accuracy graph

(e) SBERT classifiers accuracy graph

(f) Fine-tuned SBERT classifier accuracy graph

Fig. 2. Comparison of SBERT and Fine-tuned SBERT results using different visualization and accuracy metrics

which focus on deeper behavioral patterns rather than just surface-level features. Additionally, SANvector can handle noisy or incomplete reports by using contrastive learning across multiple CTI reports. Despite these advantages, it still faces challenges with CTI text that is intentionally altered to mislead the system. In the future, integrating adversarial training and anomaly detection could help to improve its security further.

7 Conclusion

In this paper, we have discussed APT which are complex and targeted cyber attacks often carried out by highly skilled adversaries. Effectively, identifying APT actors in order to enhance and improve preventive measures in cyber security. For that, we have proposed a novel SANvector framework which uses fine-tuned sentence embeddings model with APT classification, contrastive learning and multi-step data processing. The framework was created to resolve major challenges that occur in cyber threat intelligence, particularly for those arising from unstructured text reports, inconsistent APT group aliases, and for the scarcity of labeled data. Our framework consists of data collection, preprocessing and aliases normalization. This ensures high quality, semantic and reliable input for training model. We used modified version of SBERT model to understand the meaning of the text better and create high-quality embeddings. These embeddings were then used with traditional machine learning models to assign threats to specific threat groups. Apart from that, these models tested among various classifier in which KNN performed well, achieving an accuracy of 93.17% with standard deviation of $\pm$ 2.39% and perfect F1-scores for various APT groups. We compared our results with standard SBERT embeddings and other classifiers demonstrated that our approach is more effective, reliable and stable. Overall, SANvector demonstrate reliable, accurate and easy to implement and understand to identify threat actors using CTI reports. It provides reasonable foundation for use in real-world settings like security operations centers, national cyber security efforts and advance malware defense systems.

References

1. Qiang, L., Zeming, Y., Baoxu, L., Zhengwei, J., Jian, Y.: Framework of cyber attack attribution based on threat intelligence. In: Mitton, N., Chaouchi, H., Noel, T., Watteyne, T., Gabillon, A., Capolsini, P. (eds.) InterIoT/SaSeIoT -2016. LNICST, vol. 190, pp. 92–103. Springer, Cham (2017). https://doi.org/10.1007/978-3-319-52727-7_11
2. Hettema, H.: Rationality constraints in cyber defense: incident handling, attribution and cyber threat intelligence. Comput. Secur. **109**, 102396 (2021)
3. Irshad, E., Siddiqui, A.B.: Cyber threat attribution using unstructured reports in cyber threat intelligence. Egypt. Inf. J. **24**(1), 43–59 (2023)
4. Shin, Y., Kim, K., Lee, J.J., Lee, K.: Art: automated reclassification for threat actors based on ATT&CK matrix similarity. In: World Automation Congress (WAC) 2021, pp. 15–20 (2021)
5. Lee, I., Choi, C.: Mucamp: generating cyber campaign variants via TTP synonym replacement for group attribution. IEEE Trans. Inf. Forensics Secur. **20**, 6162–6174 (2025)
6. Edie, K., Mckee, C., Duby, A.: Extending threat playbooks for cyber threat intelligence: a novel approach for APT attribution. In: 2023 11th International Symposium on Digital Forensics and Security (ISDFS), pp. 1–6 (2023)
7. Wang, Z., Zhou, Y., Liu, H., Qiu, J., Fang, B., Tian, Z.: Threatinsight: innovating early threat detection through threat-intelligence-driven analysis and attribution. IEEE Trans. Knowl. Data Eng. **36**(12), 9388–9402 (2024)
8. Tang, B., Leng, P., Shen, X., Wei, Y.: Deep learning-based apt malware and variants detection with attribution analysis. In: 2023 IEEE 6th International Conference on Pattern Recognition and Artificial Intelligence (PRAI), pp. 996–1003 (2023)

9. Perry, L., Shapira, B., Puzis, R.: No-doubt: attack attribution based on threat intelligence reports. In: IEEE International Conference on Intelligence and Security Informatics (ISI) 2019, pp. 80–85 (2019)

10. Permana, D.R., Stiawan, D., Rini, D.P., Afifah, N., Ningrum, S.K., Budiarto, R.: An enhanced method with part of speech tagging and named entity recognition techniques towards advanced persistent threat in cyber threat intelligence: work in progress. In: 2024 11th International Conference on Electrical Engineering, Computer Science and Informatics (EECSI), pp. 493–498 (2024)

11. Cheng, K., Tang, W., Tan, L., Li, X., Yang, J.: Debertaic: a framework for cyber threat analysis integrating deberta model and attack intelligence chain. IEEE Trans. Consum. Electron. 1 (2025)

12. Zhang, J., Cheng, K., Xiong, X., Dong, R., Huang, J., Jie, S.: Construction of cyber-attack attribution framework based on LLM. In: 2024 IEEE 23rd International Conference on Trust, Security and Privacy in Computing and Communications (TrustCom), pp. 2250–2255 (2024)

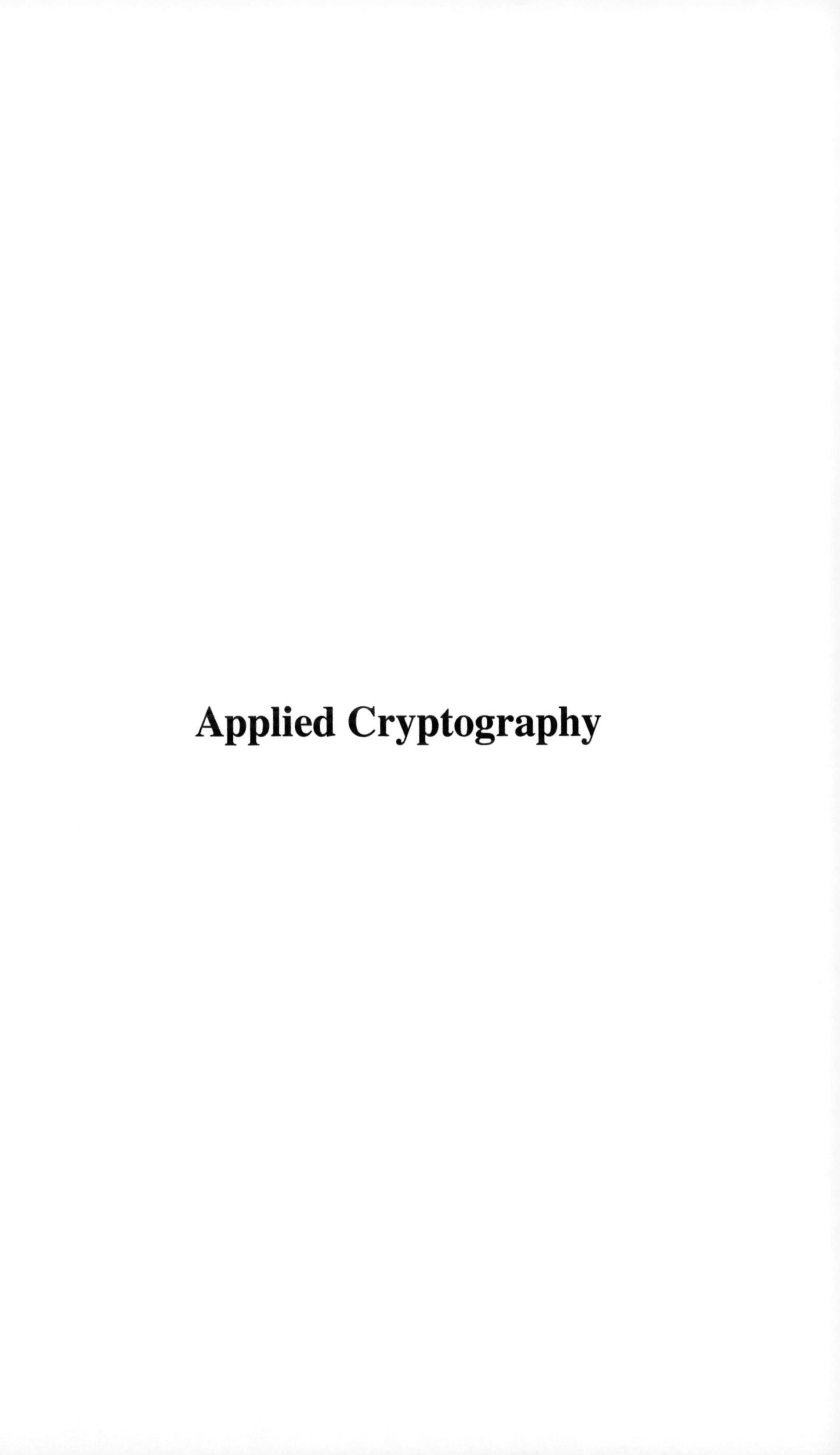

Applied Cryptography

Cryptanalysis of Two Outsourced Ciphertext-Policy Attribute-Based Encryption Schemes

Koshalesh Meher and Y. Sreenivasa Rao[✉]

Department of Mathematics, National Institute of Technology Warangal,
Warangal 506004, Telangana, India
`km23mar1r05@student.nitw.ac.in`, `ysr@nitw.ac.in`

Abstract. Outsourced Ciphertext-Policy Attribute-Based Encryption (CP-ABE) has emerged as a promising solution that enables fine-grained access control over encrypted data, making it well-suited for cloud-based data storage and sharing systems, especially when resource-constrained devices delegate computationally intensive tasks to cloud servers. To address the computational overhead of encryption, several outsourced CP-ABE schemes have been proposed, allowing heavy encryption computations to be offloaded to cloud servers. However, outsourcing encryption to potentially untrusted cloud servers introduces new security challenges, particularly regarding data confidentiality. Recently, Zhang et al. and Miao et al. independently proposed two outsourced CP-ABE schemes. The Zhang et al. scheme is a proxy re-encryption scheme, where the cloud server converts an identity-based encryption ciphertext into a CP-ABE ciphertext to establish a fine-grained data sharing mechanism in the Industrial Internet of Things environments. The scheme proposed by Miao et al. is an outsourced CP-ABE with verifiable encryption that establishes a fine-grained data sharing mechanism in the cloud-assisted mobile electronic health system, and later they extend it for verifiable decryption. The authors in both the schemes claimed that their proposed schemes preserve data confidentiality against the semi-trusted cloud server and unauthorized users. However, after a comprehensive security analysis of these two prominent outsourced CP-ABE schemes, we identify that the two schemes fail to provide data confidentiality. After carefully revisiting Zhang et al. and Miao et al. schemes, in this paper, we demonstrate that their schemes fail to provide data confidentiality by proposing message recovery attacks. Our attacks show that the semi-trusted cloud server can successfully extract the plaintext encoded in a ciphertext.

Keywords: Outsourced CP-ABE · proxy re-encryption · identity-based encryption · verifiable outsourced ABE · data confidentiality · message recovery attack

N. Hubballi et al. (Eds.): ICISS 2025, LNCS 16380, pp. 151–167, 2026.
https://doi.org/10.1007/978-3-032-13714-2_11

1   Introduction

With the growing need for secure data sharing over open and distributed networks such as the internet and cloud-based platforms, advanced cryptographic techniques have become essential. One such technique is Identity-Based Encryption (IBE) [2], a form of public key encryption in which a user's public key can be derived from a unique identifier. However, IBE provides only coarse-grained access control, which limits its applicability in scenarios requiring more flexible and fine-grained access policies. To overcome this limitation, Attribute-Based Encryption (ABE) [5] was introduced. ABE extends IBE by associating encryption or decryption capabilities with a set of descriptive attributes rather than fixed identities. It supports fine-grained access control, making it highly suitable for applications such as cloud storage, electronic health (e-health), and the Industrial Internet of Things (IIoT). ABE comes in two main variants, Key-Policy Attribute-Based Encryption (KP-ABE) [3,11] and Ciphertext-Policy Attribute-Based Encryption (CP-ABE) [7,9,15]. In KP-ABE, the ciphertext is associated with a set of attributes, and the user's private key is embedded with an access policy. In CP-ABE, the roles are reversed, i.e., the ciphertext is encrypted under an access policy, and the user's private key is tied to a set of attributes. In both encryption schemes, decryption is possible only if the set of attributes satisfies the access policy. Among these, CP-ABE has gained particular attention for enabling data owners to enforce expressive and flexible access control policies directly in the encryption process. In recent years, outsourced CP-ABE schemes [1,12,14,18] have been developed to reduce the computational burden on resource-constrained devices by delegating intensive operations to cloud servers. These schemes often incorporate additional mechanisms, such as proxy re-encryption [4,17] or verifiability [8,10,13], to improve performance and functionality.

A Proxy Re-Encryption (PRE) scheme that transforms IBE ciphertext to ABE ciphertext is proposed by He et al. [6]. However, their scheme does not achieve non-interactive transformation, and the data owner needs to bear complex computational overhead to generate a re-encryption key. Zhang et al. [17] proposed a scheme on the similar concept of He et al. [6] in the IIoT environment while achieving fine-grained data sharing with intended IIoT devices. As a result, a non-interactive PRE scheme is proposed in which computationally intensive operations are off-loaded to a semi-trusted cloud (proxy server) in order to reduce the computational cost of both data owners and data consumers.

Since the outsourced encryption and decryption are performed by malicious cloud server, it is crucial to verify the correctness of these operations. To verify the outsourced decryption mechanism, the schemes [8,14,16] have been proposed. Although these schemes support verifiable outsourced decryption mechanism, they cannot achieve verifiable outsourced encryption. To address this, Miao et al. [13] proposed an Outsourced CP-ABE (OABE) with verifiable encryption scheme, and then they extended OABE to develop outsourced CP-ABE with verifiable decryption (OABE+) to reduce the encryption and decryption complexities of mobile users and also ensure that the cloud server has accurately performed the ciphertext transformation and encryption operations.

The outsourced CP-ABE schemes proposed by Zhang et al. [17] and Miao et al. [13] are designed for cloud-based applications for efficient and secure data sharing. The authors in [17] and [13] claimed that their schemes are secure against unauthorized access. However, on the security analysis of these two outsourced CP-ABE schemes, we find a significant security vulnerability.

1.1 Our Contribution

The authors in [17] and [13] claimed that their schemes preserve data confidentiality against malicious cloud server. Despite their claims of preserving data confidentiality against malicious cloud server and unauthorized users, our in-depth analysis reveals critical vulnerabilities that undermine these assurances. In this paper, we show that the PRE scheme proposed by Zhang et al. [17] lacks data confidentiality by proposing an attack where the semi-trusted proxy server can extract the plaintext from a ciphertext. We propose two message recovery attacks (Attack 1 and Attack 2) by the malicious cloud server on both OABE and OABE+ schemes of Miao et al.'s [13], which show that these schemes fail to provide data confidentiality. In each of the OABE and OABE+ schemes, the cloud server launches Attack 1 without interacting with the public verifier, while Attack 2 by interacting with the public verifier.

1.2 Paper Organization

The rest of this paper is organized as follows. We provide the necessary preliminaries in Sect. 2. In Sect. 3, we review Zhang et al.'s [17] PRE scheme and present its cryptanalysis. In Sect. 4, we provide a quick review of Miao et al.'s [13] OABE and OABE+ schemes and present their cryptanalysis. The paper is concluded in Sect. 5.

2 Preliminaries

In this section, we present the definition of bilinear map and review the concept of access structure and Linear Secret-Sharing Scheme (LSSS).

2.1 Bilinear Map

Given two cyclic groups $\mathbb{G}$ and $\mathbb{G}_T$ of prime order p, and a generator g of $\mathbb{G}$, a bilinear map is a function $e : \mathbb{G} \times \mathbb{G} \to \mathbb{G}_T$ satisfying the following three properties.

- *Bilinearity*: $\forall u, v \in \mathbb{Z}_p^*$, we have $e\left(g^u, g^v\right) = e\left(g, g\right)^{uv}$, where $\mathbb{Z}_p$ is a field of prime order p.
- *Non-degeneracy* : $\exists\, g \in \mathbb{G}$ such that $e(g, g) \neq 1$.
- *Computability*: $e\left(g, g\right)$ can be computed efficiently.

2.2 Access Structure

The formal definition of access structure is as follows.

Definition 1. Let U be the universe of attributes. Let $\mathcal{P}(U)^*$ be the collection of all non-empty subsets of U. Each nonempty subset of $\mathcal{P}(U)^*$ is called an access structure. An access structure Γ is said to be Monotone Access Structure (MAS) if $\{C \in \mathcal{P}(U)^* : C \supseteq B \text{ for some } B \in \Gamma\} \subseteq \Gamma$. The sets in Γ are called authorized sets, and the sets not in Γ are called unauthorized sets with respect to the MAS Γ.

By the definition, every superset of an authorized set is again an authorized set in MAS.

2.3 LSSS

The formal definition of LSSS realizing a MAS is as follows.

Definition 2. Let Γ be a MAS. An LSSS for Γ (over a field $\mathbb{Z}_p$) is an $l \times n$ matrix M (with entries in $\mathbb{Z}_p$) along with a row labeling function $\rho(\cdot)$ which associates each row i of M with an attribute $\rho(i)$ in Γ that consists of the following features.

- The share for each attribute forms a vector over $\mathbb{Z}_p$.
- Let $s \in \mathbb{Z}_p^*$ be a secret and $y_2, y_3, \ldots, y_n$ be randomly chosen from $\mathbb{Z}_p$. Set $\boldsymbol{v} = (s, y_2, y_3, \ldots, y_n) \in \mathbb{Z}_p^n$. $\{\lambda_i : \lambda_i = \mathsf{M}_i \boldsymbol{v}\}_{i \in [l]}$ is a set of l shares of the secret s, where $\mathsf{M}_i \in \mathbb{Z}_p^n$ is the ith row of the matrix M. The share λ_i belongs to the attribute $\rho(i)$. For any authorized attribute set $S \in \Gamma$, we can compute a set of secret reconstruction constants $\{\omega_i\}_{i \in I} \subset \mathbb{Z}_p$, where $I = \{i \in [l] : \rho(i) \in S\}$, satisfying $\sum_{i \in I} \omega_i \mathsf{M}_i = \boldsymbol{\epsilon} = (1, 0, \ldots, 0)$. Hence, $\sum_{i \in I} \omega_i \lambda_i = \sum_{i \in I} \omega_i (\mathsf{M}_i \boldsymbol{v}) = \boldsymbol{\epsilon} \cdot \boldsymbol{v} = s$.

Note that the constants $\{\omega_i\}$ can be computed in time polynomial in the size of the matrix M using Gaussian elimination.

We denote Γ by the LSSS $(\mathsf{M}_{l \times n}, \rho(\cdot))$ and is called LSSS realizable access structure.

3 Cryptanalysis of Zhang et al.'s PRE Scheme

In this section, we first review the PRE scheme proposed by Zhang et al.'s [17] and then show how the scheme fails to provide data confidentiality.

3.1 Review of Zhang et al.'s [17] PRE Scheme

In Zhang et al.'s [17] system model, there exist four entities: Data Owner (DO), Private Key Generator (PKG), Cloud, and Data Receiver (DR). The organization of these entities is depicted in Fig. 1. PKG sets up the system by generating public keys (PP_{IBE}, PP_{ABE}) and master secret keys (MSK_{IBE}, MSK_{ABE}).

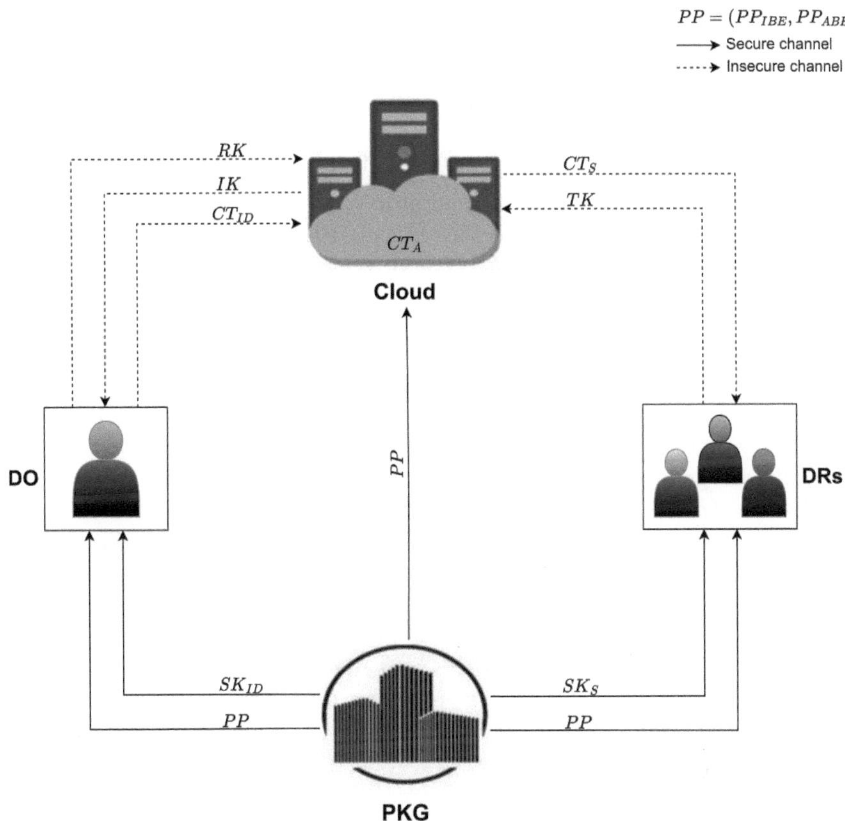

Fig. 1. System model of Zhang et al.'s PRE scheme.

It sends public keys to all other entities in the system and keeps master secret keys confidential. PKG creates secret keys (SK_{ID}, SK_S) and provides to the respective users. DO encrypts data using IBE, generates the ciphertext (CT_{ID}), and uploads it to the cloud. The cloud generates an intermediate re-encryption key (IK) corresponding to an access policy specified by the DO and outputs it to the DO. To re-encrypt the original ciphertext, the DO generates a re-encryption key (RK) and sends it to the cloud. The cloud re-encrypts or transforms the IBE ciphertext (CT_{ID}) to ABE ciphertext (CT_A) and stores it for data sharing. When a DR wants to access the data, it sends a transformation key (TK) to the cloud. The cloud partially decrypts the ciphertext and sends the transformed ciphertext (CT_S) to the DR, who can recover the original data using the retrieval key.

The basic construction of Zhang et al.'s PRE is as follows.

1. *Setup*: PKG initializes the system by first executing the following two algorithms to generate public parameters and master secret keys for IBE and ABE schemes.

   - **Setup$_{\mathbf{IBE}}$**$(\lambda) \to (PP_{IBE}, MSK_{IBE})$: Given a security parameter λ, PKG executes the bilinear generator $\mathcal{G}$ to generate a tuple of bilinear pairing parameters $\mathcal{BP} = (p, \mathbb{G}, \mathbb{G}_T, e)$. PKG chooses random elements $\alpha_0 \in \mathbb{Z}_p^*$ and $g_1, g_2, g_3, g_4 \in \mathbb{G}$ and assigns the public parameters and master secret key, respectively, as

   $$PP_{IBE} = (\mathcal{BP}, g_1, g_1^{\alpha_0}, g_2, g_3, g_4), \ MSK_{IBE} = \alpha_0.$$

   - **Setup$_{\mathbf{ABE}}$**$(\lambda, U) \to (PP_{ABE}, MSK_{ABE})$: Taking the security parameter λ and an attribute universe $U \subseteq \mathbb{Z}_p$ as input, PKG executes the bilinear generator $\mathcal{G}$ to produce a tuple of bilinear pairing parameters $\mathcal{BP} = (p, \mathbb{G}, \mathbb{G}_T, e)$. Then, it chooses random elements $\alpha, a \in \mathbb{Z}_p^*$ and $h_{x'} \in \mathbb{G}$ for each attribute $x' \in U$. Besides, it chooses a collision-resistant hash function $H : \mathbb{G}_T \to \mathbb{G}$. It sets the public parameters and master secret key, respectively, as

   $$PP_{ABE} = \big(\mathcal{BP}, g, g^a, e(g, g)^\alpha, \{h_{x'}\}_{x' \in U}, H\big), \ MSK_{ABE} = g^\alpha.$$

2. *Key Generation*: In this phase, PKG executes the following two key generation algorithms to generate secret keys for data users.

   - **KeyGen$_{\mathbf{IBE}}$**$(PP_{IBE}, MSK_{IBE}, ID) \to SK_{ID}$: Upon receiving an input of PP_{IBE}, MSK_{IBE}, and an identity ID, PKG chooses a random $u \in \mathbb{Z}_p^*$ and computes
   $$SK_1 = g_2^{\alpha_0}\big(g_1^{\alpha_0 ID} g_4\big)^u, \ SK_2 = g_1^u.$$

   It sets the IBE secret key as $SK_{ID} = \big(SK_1, SK_2\big)$.

   - **KeyGen$_{\mathbf{ABE}}$**$(PP_{ABE}, MSK_{ABE}, S) \to SK_S$: Given input PP_{ABE}, MSK_{ABE}, and an attribute set S, PKG randomly chooses $t \in \mathbb{Z}_p^*$ and computes
   $$K' = g^\alpha g^{at}, L' = g^t, \forall x \in S : K_x' = h_x^t.$$

   It sets the ABE secret key as $SK_S = \big(S, K', L', \{K_x'\}_{x \in S}\big)$.

3. *Data Encryption*: The DO first encrypts the data using IBE scheme and then uploads the resulting ciphertext to the cloud.

   - **Encrypt$_{\mathbf{IBE}}$**$(PP_{IBE}, ID, \mathcal{M}) \to CT_{ID}$: Taking PP_{IBE}, ID, and a message $\mathcal{M} \in \mathbb{G}_T$ as input, the DO chooses a random $w \in \mathbb{Z}_p^*$ and computes

   $$C_0 = g_1^w, C_1 = (g_1^{\alpha_0 ID} g_4)^w, C_2 = \mathcal{M} \cdot e(g_1^{\alpha_0}, g_2)^w, C_3 = g_3^w.$$

   It sets the IBE ciphertext as $CT_{ID} = (C_0, C_1, C_2, C_3)$ and stores it in the cloud.

4. *Intermediate Re-encryption Key Generation*: In this phase, the cloud generates an intermediate re-encryption key and sends it to the DO.

- **RKGen$_{\mathbf{out}}$**$(PP_{ABE}, (M, \rho)) \rightarrow IK$: On input PP_{ABE} and an LSSS access structure (M, ρ), where M is a matrix of size $l \times n$ and ρ is a function that associates each row of M with an attribute, the cloud chooses r' and λ'_i, r'_i for $i = 1$ to l randomly from $\mathbb{Z}_p^*$ and computes

$$D_0 = g^{r'}, D_{i,1} = g^{a\lambda'_i} h_{\rho(i)}^{-r'_i}, D_{i,2} = g^{r'_i}.$$

It sets the intermediate re-encryption key as $IK = \big((M, \rho), r', D_0, \{\lambda'_i, r'_i, D_{i,1}, D_{i,2}\}_{i \in [l]}\big)$.

5. *Re-encryption Key Generation*: In this phase, the DO generates a re-encryption key and sends it to the cloud for further re-encryption.
   - **RKGen$_{\mathbf{user}}$**$(PP_{IBE}, PP_{ABE}, SK_{ID}, IK) \rightarrow RK$: Given PP_{IBE}, PP_{ABE}, SK_{ID}, and IK as input, the DO chooses t', r randomly from $\mathbb{Z}_p^*$ and computes

$$D_3 = SK_1 g_3^{t'}, D_4 = SK_2, D_5 = H(e(g,g)^{\alpha r}) g_1^{t'}, D_6 = r - r'.$$

It again chooses $r_1, \ldots, r_l, v_2, \ldots, v_n \in \mathbb{Z}_p^*$ at random and computes

$$(\lambda_1, \lambda_2, \ldots, \lambda_l)^T = M(r, v_2, \ldots, v_n)^T, D_{i,7} = \lambda_i - \lambda'_i, D_{i,8} = r_i - r'_i$$

where T denotes the transpose of a matrix. sets the re-encryption key as $RK = \big(D_0, D_3, D_4, D_5, D_6, \{D_{i,1}, D_{i,2}, D_{i,7}, D_{i,8}, \}_{i \in [l]}\big)$.
6. *Re-encryption*: Upon receiving the re-encryption key, cloud re-encrypts the IBE ciphertext to ABE ciphertext by executing the following algorithm.
   - **ReEnc**$(PP_{ABE}, CT_{ID}, RK) \rightarrow CT_A$: On taking PP_{ABE}, CT_{ID}, and RK as input, cloud computes

$$E = \frac{e(D_4, C_1)}{e(D_3, C_0)}, \ C = C_2 \cdot E.$$

It sets the re-encrypted ciphertext as $CT_A = \big(C, C_3, D_0, D_5, D_6, \{D_{i,1}, D_{i,2}, D_{i,7}, D_{i,8}\}_{i \in [l]}\big)$.
7. *Transformation Key Generation*: During this phase, the DR generates a transformation key for partial decryption of ABE ciphertext and a retrieval key for final decryption.
   - **KeyGen$_{\mathbf{out}}$**$(SK_S) \rightarrow (TK, RtK)$: Taking SK_S as input, the DR chooses a random $z \in \mathbb{Z}_p^*$ and computes

$$K'' = K'^{\frac{1}{z}}, \ L'' = L'^{\frac{1}{z}}, \ \forall x \in S : K''_x = K'^{\frac{1}{z}}_x.$$

It sets the transformation key as $TK = \big(K'', L'', \{K''_x\}_{x \in S}\big)$ and retrieval key as $RtK = z$.
8. *Data Decryption*: This phase consists of two algorithms **Decrypt$_{\mathbf{out}}$**, executed by the cloud to decrypt the ciphertext partially, and **Decrypt$_{\mathbf{user}}$**, executed by the DR for final decryption.

- **Decrypt$_{\text{out}}$**$(PP_{ABE}, CT_A, TK) \rightarrow CT_S/\perp$: On input PP_{ABE}, CT_A associated with (M, ρ), and TK connected with S, the cloud first checks whether S satisfies (M, ρ) or not. If not, it outputs $\perp$. Otherwise, it defines $I = \{i \,|\, \rho(i) \in S\}$ and calculates $\omega_i \in \mathbb{Z}_p$ such that $\sum_{i \in I} \omega_i \lambda_i = r$, and computes

$$A = \frac{e\left(D_0 g^{D_6}, K''\right)}{\prod_{i \in I} \left(e(D_{i,1} g^{a D_{i,7}} h_{\rho(i)}^{-D_{i,8}}, L'') \, e(D_{i,2} g^{D_{i,8}}, K''_{\rho(i)})\right)^{\omega_i}}.$$

It sets the transformed ciphertext as $CT_S = (C, D_5, A, C_3)$.
- **Decrypt$_{\text{user}}$**$(PP_{ABE}, RtK, CT_S) \rightarrow \mathcal{M}$: Upon receiving PP_{ABE}, RtK, and CT_S as input, the DR recovers the message by computing

$$\mathcal{M} = C \cdot e\left(\frac{D_5}{H(A^z)}, C_3\right).$$

3.2   Message Recovery Attack by the Cloud

Here, we show that after receiving the re-encryption key RK, the semi-trusted cloud can recover the message $\mathcal{M}$ from the ciphertext CT_{ID} stored in it by any DO.

Interaction between a DO and the cloud, till receiving the RK (shown in Fig. 2), is as follows.

① A DO first encrypts a message $\mathcal{M}$ using the IBE encryption algorithm **Encrypt$_{\text{IBE}}$** and uploads the resulting ciphertext CT_{ID} to the cloud.
② When the DO wishes to implement the fine-grained data sharing with other DRs, it creates an access policy (M, ρ) over the DRs' attributes and delegates the same to the cloud.
③ Upon receiving (M, ρ), using the **RKGen$_{\text{out}}$** algorithm, the cloud generates an intermediate re-encryption key IK corresponding to (M, ρ).
④ Now, the DO combines this IK with its IBE private key SK_{ID} and builds a re-encryption key RK (using the **RKGen$_{\text{user}}$** algorithm), and sends this RK to the cloud.

At this stage, the cloud has the following information Δ.

$$\Delta = \left\{ \begin{array}{l} PP_{IBE} = (\mathcal{BP}, g_1, g_1^{\alpha_0}, g_2, g_3, g_4) \\ PP_{ABE} = (\mathcal{BP}, g, g^a, e(g,g)^\alpha, \{h_{x'}\}_{x' \in U}, H) \\ CT_{ID} = (C_0, C_1, C_2, C_3) \\ IK = ((M, \rho), r', D_0, \{\lambda'_i, r'_i, D_{i,1}, D_{i,2}\}_{i \in [l]}) \\ RK = (D_0, D_3, D_4, D_5, D_6, \{D_{i,1}, D_{i,2}, D_{i,7}, D_{i,8}\}_{i \in [l]}) \end{array} \right\}$$

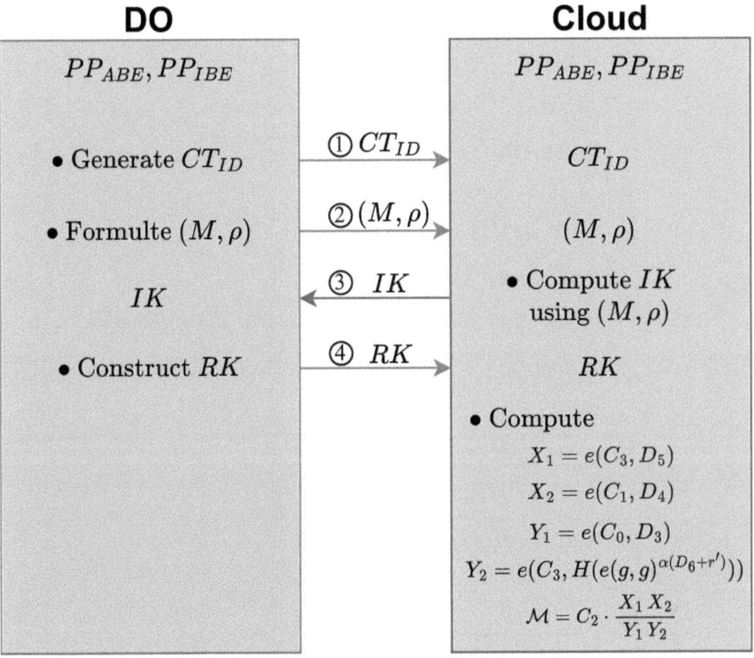

Fig. 2. Message recovery attack by the cloud.

Now, using Δ, the cloud can extract the message $\mathcal{M}$ embedded in the ciphertext CT_{ID} as described below.

– Compute
$$X_1 = e(C_3, D_5), \ X_2 = e(C_1, D_4), \ Y_1 = e(C_0, D_3)$$

– Set
$$Y_2 = e\big(C_3, H\big(e(g,g)^{\alpha(D_6+r')}\big)\big)$$

– Recover the message $\mathcal{M}$ as
$$\mathcal{M} = C_2 \cdot \frac{X_1 X_2}{Y_1 Y_2}$$

Correctness of Our Attack. The cloud can calculate
$$\begin{aligned}
X_1 &= e(C_3, D_5) \\
&= e\big(g_3^w, H(e(g,g)^{\alpha r})\, g_1^{t'}\big) \\
&= e(g_3^w, H(e(g,g)^{\alpha r}))\, e(g_3^w, g_1^{t'}) \\
&= e(g_3^w, H(e(g,g)^{\alpha r}))\, e(g_3, g_1)^{wt'}
\end{aligned}$$

$$X_2 = e(C_1, D_4)$$
$$= e\big((g_1^{\alpha_0 ID} g_4)^w, g_1^u\big)$$
$$= e(g_1^{\alpha_0 IDw}, g_1^u)\, e(g_4^w, g_1^u)$$
$$= e(g_1, g_1)^{\alpha_0 IDwu}\, e(g_4, g_1)^{wu}$$

$$Y_1 = e(C_0, D_3)$$
$$= e\big(g_1^w, g_2^{\alpha_0}(g_1^{\alpha_0 ID} g_4)^u g_3^{t'}\big)$$
$$= e(g_1^w, g_2^{\alpha_0})\, e(g_1^w, g_1^{\alpha_0 IDu})\, e(g_1^w, g_4^u)\, e(g_1^w, g_3^{t'})$$
$$= e(g_1, g_2)^{w\alpha_0}\, e(g_1, g_1)^{w\alpha_0 IDu}\, e(g_1, g_4)^{wu}\, e(g_1, g_3)^{wt'}$$

$$Y_2 = e\big(C_3, H\big(e(g, g)^{\alpha(D_6 + r')}\big)\big)$$
$$= e\big(g_3^w, H\big(e(g, g)^{\alpha(r - r' + r')}\big)\big)$$
$$= e\big(g_3^w, H(e(g, g)^{\alpha r})\big)$$

$$\frac{X_1 X_2}{Y_1 Y_2} = \frac{1}{e(g_1, g_2)^{w\alpha_0}}$$

$$C_2 \cdot \frac{X_1 X_2}{Y_1 Y_2} = \mathcal{M} \cdot e(g_1^{\alpha_0}, g_2)^w \frac{1}{e(g_1, g_2)^{w\alpha_0}}$$
$$= \mathcal{M} \cdot e(g_1, g_2)^{\alpha_0 w} \frac{1}{e(g_1, g_2)^{w\alpha_0}}$$
$$= \mathcal{M}.$$

4   Cryptanalysis of Miao et al.'s OABE Scheme

In this section, we first review the Miao et al.'s [13] OABE scheme. Subsequently, we present two possible attacks on the OABE scheme, highlighting its failure to preserve data confidentiality.

4.1   Review of Miao et al.'s [13] OABE Scheme

The system model of the OABE scheme consists of five entities, namely Trusted Authority (TA), Data Owner (DO), Public Verifier (PV), Cloud Server (CS), and Data Users (DUs). The organization of these entities is presented in Fig. 3. TA sets up the system by generating public key pk and master secret key msk. It makes pk publicly available to all entities in the system and keeps msk confidential. It then generates the public/secret key pair $(\mathsf{pk}_{PV}, \mathsf{sk}_{PV})$ for PV and secret keys $(\mathsf{sk}_{CS,u}, \mathsf{sk}_u)$ for CS and mobile user u, respectively. For sharing e-health data with authorized DUs, each DO produces an intermediate ciphertext

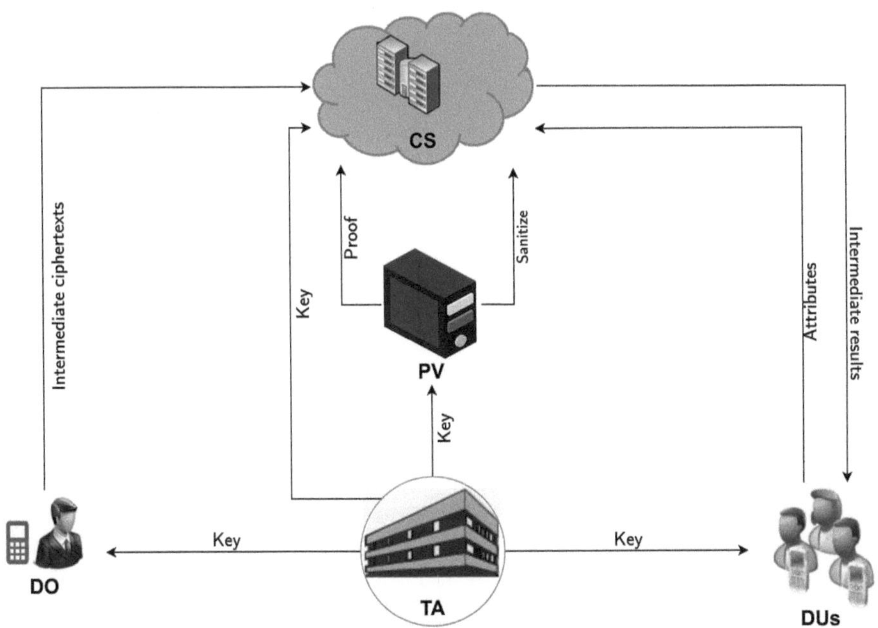

Fig. 3. System model of OABE scheme.

cph* for each e-health data $\mathcal{R}$ and sends it to the CS. CS further encrypts cph*
to generate the final ciphertext cph and then sends cph to PV. Upon receiving
cph, PV chooses a random attribute set as challenging information and sends it
to CS. Then, CS generates the proof information proof and returns it to PV.
If proof is valid, PV generates the sanitized ciphertexts $\overline{\text{cph}}$ for CS. Otherwise,
PV aborts cph. To access encrypted e-health data, a DU needs to submit his
attributes to CS. CS performs partial decryption after verifying DU's attributes
and returns the intermediate results to DU, from which DU can retrieve the
plaintext e-health data $\mathcal{R}$ using its secret key.

We present only the necessary algorithms of Miao et al.'s [13] OABE scheme,
using which the CS is able to recover the original e-health data from the corresponding ciphertext sent by any DO. For detailed construction, readers can
refer to [13].

Setup (1^λ). Given the security parameter λ, TA runs this algorithm to output
the public bilinear parameters $\mathcal{BP} = (\mathbb{G}, \mathbb{G}_T, e, p, g)$, and chooses random ele-
ments $h_1, \ldots, h_{|\mathsf{U}|} \in \mathbb{G}$ for the system attribute set U, where $|\mathsf{U}|$ is the size of sys-
tem attributes. Then, TA chooses random elements $h, w \in \mathbb{G}, \alpha, \alpha_1, \alpha_2, a, b \in \mathbb{Z}_p^*$
and a collision-resistant hash function $H : \{0,1\}^* \to \mathbb{Z}_p^*$, where $\alpha_1 + \alpha_2 = \alpha$.
Finally, TA computes $e(g,g)^\alpha, e(g,g)^{\alpha_1}, g^a, g^b$, and outputs the public key pk

and master key msk by (1).

$$\mathsf{pk} = \left(\mathcal{BP}, e(g,g)^{\alpha}, e(g,g)^{\alpha_1}, h, w, g^a, g^b\right)$$
$$\mathsf{msk} = (\alpha, \alpha_1, \alpha_2, b) \tag{1}$$

KeyGen(pk, msk). Given the public key pk and master key msk, TA needs to generate keys for both PV and mobile user u. The two sub-algorithms are shown as follows.

1. $\mathsf{KeyGen}_{PV}(\mathsf{pk}, \mathsf{msk})$. TA chooses a random element $c \in \mathbb{Z}_p^*$ and generates the public-secret key pair $(\mathsf{pk}_{PV}, \mathsf{sk}_{PV})$ for PV, which is shown by (2).

$$\mathsf{pk}_{PV} = g^c, \mathsf{sk}_{PV} = c \tag{2}$$

2. $\mathsf{KeyGen}_u(\mathsf{pk}, \mathsf{msk}, \mathsf{ID}_u, \mathsf{S}_u)$. Let ID_u and S_u be, respectively, the identity and attribute set of mobile user u, such as DO or DU. When u registers with the system, TA first selects a random element $t_u \in \mathbb{Z}_p^*$ and generates the complete secret key $\mathsf{sk} = (\mathsf{sk}_{CS,u}, \mathsf{sk}_u)$. The secret key component sk_u is sent to the mobile user u, and the secret key component $\mathsf{sk}_{CS,u} = \left(K_u, L_u, R_u, \{K_{u,x}\}_{x \in \mathsf{S}_u}\right)$ is sent to CS. The secret key sk is defined by (3).

$$K_u = g^{\alpha_1} g^{at_u} w^{1/(b+H(\mathsf{ID}_u))}, L_u = g^{t_u},$$
$$R_u = g^{1/(b+H(\mathsf{ID}_u))}, K_{u,x} = h_x^{t_u},$$
$$\mathsf{sk}_u = g^{\alpha_2} g^{at_u} \tag{3}$$

Enc(pk, $\mathcal{R}$). Given the e-health data set $\mathcal{R} = \{R\}$ and public key pk, this encryption process is divided into two sub-algorithms. DO conducts the lightweight encryption operations and outsources the time-consuming operations to CS. The concrete sub-algorithms are demonstrated as follows.

1. $\mathsf{Enc}_{DO}(\mathsf{pk}, \mathcal{R}, \Gamma)$. For each e-health data $R \in \mathcal{R}$, DO first chooses a key $K_R \in \mathbb{G}_T$ and encrypts R as $C_R = \mathsf{Enc}_{K_R}(R)$ by using the traditional symmetric encryption algorithm Enc such as AES. Then, DO encrypts K_R by specifying an access structure $\Gamma = (\mathsf{M}_{l \times n}, \rho(\cdot))$ for preventing unauthorized access permissions. Specifically, DO first chooses a random vector $\boldsymbol{v} = (s, y_2, \ldots, y_n) \in \mathbb{Z}_p^n$ and computes $\lambda_i = \mathsf{M}_i \boldsymbol{v}$, then computes (C, C', C'') by (4). Finally, DO sends the intermediate ciphertexts $\mathsf{cph}^* = (\Gamma, C_R, C, C', C'', \{\lambda_i\})$ to CS.

$$C = K_R \cdot e(g,g)^{\alpha s} \cdot e(g, \mathsf{pk}_{PV})^s,$$
$$C' = g^s, C'' = w^s \mathsf{pk}_{PV}^s \tag{4}$$

2. $\mathsf{Enc}_{CS}(\mathsf{pk}, \mathsf{cph}^*)$. Upon receiving each record ciphertext uploaded by DO, CS first chooses a random element $r_i \in \mathbb{Z}_p^*$ and computes $\{C_i, D_i\}$ by (5), where $i \in [1, l]$, $\{\rho(i)\} \subset S_{DO}$. Finally, CS stores the final ciphertexts $\mathsf{cph} = (\Gamma, C_R, C, C', C'', \{C_i, D_i\})$.

$$C_i = g^{a\lambda_i} h_{\rho(i)}^{-r_i} \mathsf{pk}_{PV}^{-r_i}, \ D_i = g^{r_i} \tag{5}$$

$\mathsf{Sanitize}(\mathsf{pk}, \mathsf{sk}_{PV}, \mathsf{cph})$. For checking whether CS has correctly generated the final ciphertexts cph, PV first chooses a random attribute set $S_{DO}^* \subset S_{DO}$ (S_{DO} is DO's attribute set) that satisfies Γ, and sends it to CS.

4.2   Cryptanalysis of Miao et al.'s [13] OABE Scheme

Before proposing our message recovery attacks, called Attack 1 and Attack 2, we first describe some important observations on the process of constructing a ciphertext. The process happens as an interaction between DO and CS.

The e-health data file R is encrypted using a symmetric-key encryption algorithm Enc such as AES with the help of the secret key $K_R \in \mathbb{G}_T$ in $C_R = \mathsf{Enc}_{K_R}(R)$. The key K_R is blinded in C as $C = K_R \cdot e(g,g)^{\alpha s} \cdot e(g, \mathsf{pk}_{PV})^s$, where s is a secret random exponent, and $e(g,g)^\alpha$ and pk_{PV} are publicly known parameters. Hence, the mask $e(g,g)^{\alpha s} \cdot e(g, \mathsf{pk}_{PV})^s$ needs to be obtained to recover the data file R.

The DO shares the secret s among the attributes involved in the access structure. And, the corresponding shares $\{\lambda_i\}_{i \in [l]}$ are made available to the CS in order to construct the final ciphertexts. Now the CS can reconstruct the secret s using the shares $\{\lambda_i\}$ and the corresponding access structure Γ. Since $e(g,g)^\alpha, g$ and pk_{PV} are public, the CS can compute the mask $e(g,g)^{\alpha s} \cdot e(g, \mathsf{pk}_{PV})^s$ using the reconstructed s. Lastly, the key K_R can be extracted from the intermediate ciphertext component C as

$$K_R = \frac{C}{e(g,g)^{\alpha s} \cdot e(g, \mathsf{pk}_{PV})^s}.$$

Based on these observations, we suggest two attacks subsequently on the security notion of data confidentiality.

4.2.1   Attack 1: Message Recovery Attack by CS (Without Interacting with PV)

We demonstrate, without interacting with the PV, how the CS can recover the e-health data R embedded in an intermediate ciphertext cph^*, sent by a DO.

Once DO uploads the cph^* to the CS, the CS has the following information Δ_2.

$$\Delta_2 = \left\{ \begin{array}{l} \mathsf{pk} = \left(\mathcal{BP}, e(g,g)^\alpha, e(g,g)^{\alpha_1}, h, w, g^a, g^b\right) \\ \mathsf{cph}^* = (\Gamma, C_R, C, C', C'', \{\lambda_i\}) \end{array} \right\}$$

Now, using Δ_2, the malicious CS can extract the e-health data R embedded in cph^* as described below.

- If A is the set of all attributes used in the access structure Γ, then A satisfies Γ. Hence, CS can obtain the secret reconstruction constants $\{\omega_i\}_{i \in [l]}$ using LSSS.
- Next, it computes the secret s as $s = \sum_{i \in [l]} \omega_i \lambda_i$ with the help of the secret shares $\{\lambda_i\}_{i \in [l]}$ available in Δ_2.
- Now, it can recover the key K_R used in $C_R = \mathsf{Enc}_{K_R}(R)$ by performing the following computation

$$K_R = \frac{C}{(e(g,g)^\alpha)^s \cdot e(g, \frac{C''}{w^s})} \tag{6}$$

- Finally, CS retrieves the original e-health data R by performing the symmetric decryption algorithm

$$\mathsf{Dec}_{K_R}(C_R) = R.$$

Correctness of Attack 1. Here, we present the correctness of Eq. (6).

$$\frac{C}{(e(g,g)^\alpha)^s \cdot e(g, \frac{C''}{w^s})} = \frac{K_R \cdot e(g,g)^{\alpha s} \cdot e\left(g, \mathsf{pk}_{PV}\right)^s}{e(g,g)^{\alpha s} \cdot e\left(g, \frac{w^s \mathsf{pk}_{PV}^s}{w^s}\right)}$$

$$= \frac{K_R \cdot e\left(g, \mathsf{pk}_{PV}^s\right)}{e\left(g, \mathsf{pk}_{PV}^s\right)}$$

$$= K_R$$

4.2.2 Attack 2: Message Recovery Attack by CS (Interacting with PV)

We present here how the CS can recover the e-health data R encoded in an intermediate ciphertext cph^* by interacting with PV.

Interaction between DO, CS, and PV is (presented in Fig. 4) as follows.

① Using an access structure $\Gamma = (\mathsf{M}_{l \times n}, \rho(\cdot))$, DO produces an intermediate ciphertext cph^* and uploads it to the CS.
② CS re-encrypts the intermediate ciphertext cph^* according to Γ and sends the final ciphertext cph to PV .
③ PV verifies whether CS has correctly generated cph by sending a random attribute set $S_{DO}^* \subset S_{DO}$ $\left(S_{DO}^* \text{ satisfies } \Gamma\right)$ to CS as challenging information.

At this stage, the CS has the following information Δ_1.

$$\Delta_1 = \left\{ \begin{array}{l} \mathsf{pk} = (\mathcal{BP}, e(g,g)^\alpha, e(g,g)^{\alpha_1}, h, w, g^a, g^b) \\ \mathsf{cph}^* = (\Gamma, C_R, C, C', C'', \{\lambda_i\}) \\ S_{DO}^* \text{ satisfies } \Gamma \end{array} \right\}$$

Now, using Δ_1, the malicious CS can extract the e-health data R embedded in the intermediate ciphertext cph^* as described below.

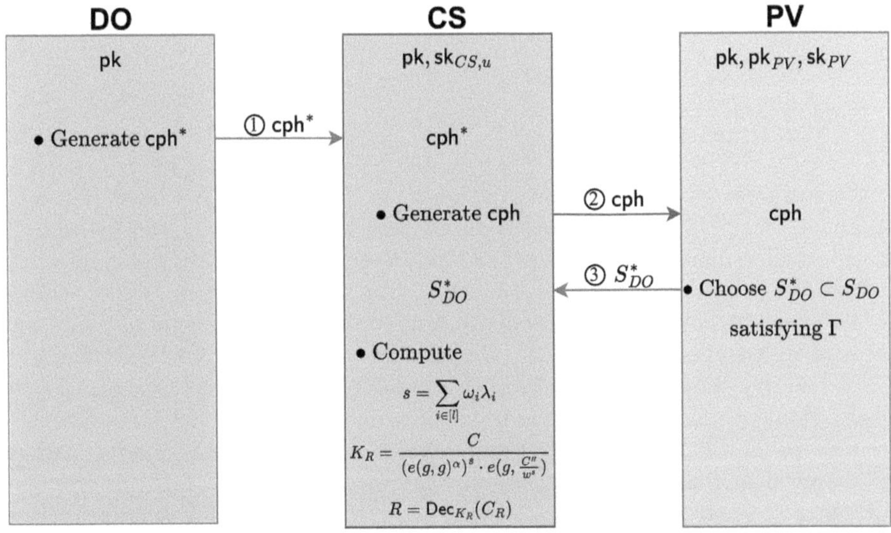

Fig. 4. Attack 2: Message recovery attack by CS.

- Upon receiving S^*_{DO} from PV, CS obtains the secret reconstruction constants $\{\omega_i\}_{i \in I}$, where $I = \{i \in [l] : \rho(i) \in S^*_{DO}\}$ and computes the secret s as $s = \sum_{i \in I} \omega_i \lambda_i$. This is possible because S^*_{DO} satisfies Γ.
- It recovers the key K_R used in $C_R = \mathsf{Enc}_{K_R}(R)$ by performing the following computation

$$K_R = \frac{C}{(e(g,g)^\alpha)^s \cdot e(g, \frac{C''}{w^s})}.$$

- Finally, CS retrieves the original e-health data R by performing the symmetric decryption algorithm

$$\mathsf{Dec}_{K_R}(C_R) = R.$$

The correctness of Attack 2 is same as that of Attack 1.

4.3 Cryptanalysis of Miao et al.'s [13] OABE+ Scheme

The OABE+ scheme is an enhancement of the OABE scheme, incorporating verifiable outsourced decryption into its framework. KeyGen of the OABE+ scheme is same as that of the OABE scheme. Only there is some modification in Setup, Enc, Sanitize, and Dec algorithms. For detailed construction of the OABE+ scheme, readers can refer to [13].

By applying the same mechanism used in Attack 1 for the OABE scheme to the OABE+ scheme, the CS can extract the session key r_R and correspondingly the symmetric encryption key K^*_R, using which it can retrieve the original e-health data R. The Attack 2 for the OABE scheme can also be used in a similar fashion for the OABE+ scheme to retrieve the original e-health data R. So, both the message recovery attacks for the OABE scheme are applicable to the OABE+ scheme as well.

5   Conclusion

In this work, we cryptanalyze the security of the IBE-ABE PRE scheme proposed by Zhang et al. [17] and the OABE and OABE+ schemes proposed by Miao et al. [13]. Unfortunately, we found that the schemes in [17] and [13] are insecure, as they fail to provide data confidentiality. Our proposed attack for the scheme in [17] shows that the semi-trusted cloud server can extract the actual message encoded in a ciphertext. Similarly, the attacks we presented for the schemes in [13] reveal that a malicious cloud server is capable of extracting the underlying e-health data encoded in every ciphertext. Since data confidentiality is the essential security property of every encryption scheme, their proposed schemes cannot be deployed in real-life applications. In our future work, we will construct an efficient and secure outsourced CP-ABE scheme with verifiable encryption and decryption capabilities.

Acknowledgement. The authors would like to thank the anonymous reviewers of this paper for their valuable comments and suggestions.

References

1. Abdollahi, S., Mohajeri, J., Salmasizadeh, M.: Highly efficient and revocable CP-ABE with outsourcing decryption for IoT. In: 2021 18th International ISC Conference on Information Security and Cryptology (ISCISC), pp. 81–88. IEEE (2021)
2. Boneh, D., Franklin, M.: Identity-based encryption from the Weil pairing. In: Kilian, J. (ed.) CRYPTO 2001. LNCS, vol. 2139, pp. 213–229. Springer, Heidelberg (2001). https://doi.org/10.1007/3-540-44647-8_13
3. Ferrer-Rojas, A., Maharaj, B.: Multiauthority KP-ABE access model with elliptic curve cryptography. SAIEE Africa Res. J. **116**(2), 59–67 (2025)
4. Ge, C., Susilo, W., Baek, J., Liu, Z., Xia, J., Fang, L.: A verifiable and fair attribute-based proxy re-encryption scheme for data sharing in clouds. IEEE Trans. Dependable Secure Comput. **19**(5), 2907–2919 (2021)
5. Goyal, V., Pandey, O., Sahai, A., Waters, B.: Attribute-based encryption for fine-grained access control of encrypted data. In: Proceedings of the 13th ACM Conference on Computer and Communications Security, pp. 89–98 (2006)
6. He, K., et al.: A new encrypted data switching protocol: bridging IBE and ABE without loss of data confidentiality. IEEE Access **7**, 50658–50668 (2019)
7. Li, H., Yu, K., Liu, B., Feng, C., Qin, Z., Srivastava, G.: An efficient ciphertext-policy weighted attribute-based encryption for the internet of health things. IEEE J. Biomed. Health Inform. **26**(5), 1949–1960 (2021)
8. Li, J., Wang, Y., Zhang, Y., Han, J.: Full verifiability for outsourced decryption in attribute based encryption. IEEE Trans. Serv. Comput. **13**(3), 478–487 (2017)
9. Li, X., Wang, H., Ma, S.: An efficient ciphertext-policy weighted attribute-based encryption with collaborative access for cloud storage. Comput. Standards Interfaces **91**, 103872 (2025)

10. Li, Z., Li, W., Jin, Z., Zhang, H., Wen, Q.: An efficient ABE scheme with verifiable outsourced encryption and decryption. IEEE Access **7**, 29023–29037 (2019)
11. Luo, F., Wang, H., Yan, X., Wu, J.: Key-policy attribute-based encryption with switchable attributes for fine-grained access control of encrypted data. IEEE Trans. Inf. Forensics Secur. (2024)
12. Luo, W., Lv, Z., Yang, L., Han, G., Zhang, X.: FOC-PH-CP-ABE: an efficient CP-ABE scheme with fully outsourced computation and policy-hidden in the industrial internet of things. IEEE Sens. J. (2024)
13. Miao, Y., et al.: Verifiable outsourced attribute-based encryption scheme for cloud-assisted mobile e-health system. IEEE Trans. Dependable Secure Comput. (2023)
14. Wang, H., He, D., Han, J.: VOD-ADAC: anonymous distributed fine-grained access control protocol with verifiable outsourced decryption in public cloud. IEEE Trans. Serv. Comput. **13**(3), 572–583 (2017)
15. Waters, B.: Ciphertext-policy attribute-based encryption: an expressive, efficient, and provably secure realization. In: Catalano, D., Fazio, N., Gennaro, R., Nicolosi, A. (eds.) PKC 2011. LNCS, vol. 6571, pp. 53–70. Springer, Heidelberg (2011). https://doi.org/10.1007/978-3-642-19379-8_4
16. Zhang, L., You, W., Mu, Y.: Secure outsourced attribute-based sharing framework for lightweight devices in smart health systems. IEEE Trans. Serv. Comput. **15**(5), 3019–3030 (2021)
17. Zhang, Q., Fu, Y., Cui, J., He, D., Zhong, H.: Efficient fine-grained data sharing based on proxy re-encryption in IIoT. IEEE Trans. Dependable Secure Comput. (2024)
18. Zhang, R., Ma, H., Lu, Y.: Fine-grained access control system based on fully outsourced attribute-based encryption. J. Syst. Softw. **125**, 344–353 (2017)

Dynamic Key-Constant Aggregate Encryption (DKCAE) for Secure Data Sharing in Contemporary Computing

Inarat Hussain[1], Devrikh Jatav[1], Gaurav Pareek[1(✉)] [iD],
and B. R. Purushothama[2] [iD]

[1] Indian Institute of Information Technology Vadodara, Vadodara, India
{inarat_h22,devrikh_j22,gaurav}@diu.iiitvadodara.ac.in
[2] National Institute of Technology Karnataka, Surathkal, India
puru@nitk.edu.in

Abstract. Key-aggregate encryption (KAE) is a cryptographic technique suitable for data sharing in a secure manner for a wide range of application scenarios. Each ciphertext is associated with a distinct class index, and the owner can efficiently generate an aggregate key that grants access only to the selected classes without revealing information about others. Each user gets only a constant-size secret called the aggregate key, regardless of the number of data items for which the user is authorized. One of the important problems with conventional KAE schemes is that they do not support dynamic updates in access rights. In some of the early schemes, the cost of enforcing dynamic update is almost as much as the cost of initializing the whole cryptosystem. Furthermore, most of the dynamic KAE schemes enforce full user revocation. However, a much more practically applicable feature is to partially revoke the user for only a subset of data items in its authorization set. This paper proposes a novel provably secure cryptosystem called dynamic key-constant aggregate encryption (DKCAE) which securely and efficiently enforces partial revocation of a user for any given data class from its aggregate set. The proposed DKCAE scheme achieves this without updating any secret aggregate key(s) and consequently without needing any secure transmissions. The paper formally proves that the proposed DKCAE scheme is secure under the standard model assumption and the existence of target collision-resistant hash functions. A detailed theoretical and practical comparative analysis of performance further confirms that the proposed DKCAE scheme enforces dynamic access control more efficiently than other existing dynamic KAE schemes.

Keywords: Dynamic Access Control · User Revocation · Key-Aggregate Encryption

1 Introduction

Key-aggregate encryption (KAE) [1] has garnered considerable interest in recent times due to its efficiency in data sharing for a range of application scenarios.

KAE allows a data owner to partition its data into n classes $\{1, 2, \ldots, n\}$ and delegate the decryption rights to a subset of these data classes, called an aggregate set, to any data user. This delegation is made possible through a unique constant-size secret key called an aggregate key. Each different aggregate set S has a different aggregate key, denoted as $\mathcal{K}_S$. The schematic description of KAE is shown in Fig. 1. KAE is directly applicable to secure data sharing across a broad spectrum of modern computing environments [2–4]. KAE derives its efficiency from three core properties: (1) the aggregate key has a constant size, regardless of how many data classes it can decrypt; (2) the public parameters stored by the data owner grow linearly with the number of data items or classes; and (3) the ciphertext size for any data class remains constant, irrespective of the number of aggregate sets it belongs to. These properties are collectively termed as key-aggregate efficiency requirements [7], which every KAE scheme is expected to satisfy. Dynamic access control is a critical requirement in secure data sharing, enabling the selective and partial revocation or reinstatement of a user's access rights. In the context of KAE, this means the ability to add or remove data classes from an aggregate set at any time [4]. We refer to such modifications as fine-grained dynamic updates. Figure 2 illustrates the concept of a KAE scheme supporting fine-grained dynamic updates. Although the original KAE framework lacks support for dynamic updates, several dynamic KAE variants have been proposed, each with certain limitations.

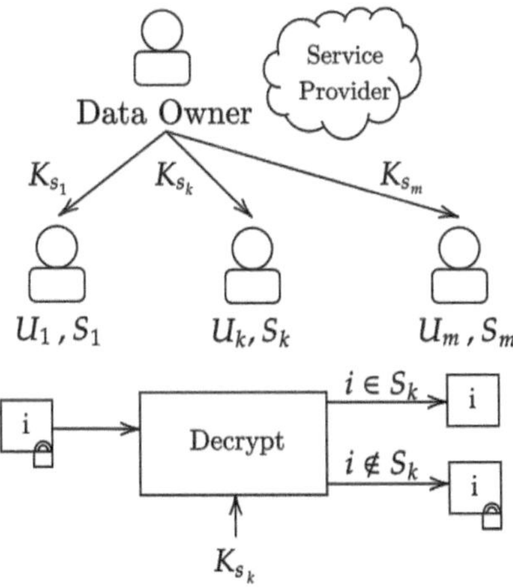

Fig. 1. KAE system operation.

Patranabis et al. [5] were the first to formalize the security frameworks for KAE and did the first work in the area of dynamic KAE schemes. In their scheme, the data owner changes the access rights of users by updating a random parameter, which each user stores privately in addition to the usual aggregate key; the same random parameter is used for encrypting the messages under data

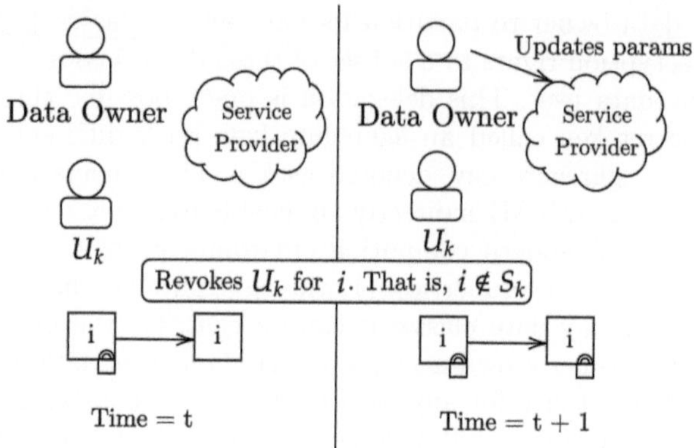

Fig. 2. Example of fine-grained dynamic updates in KAE.

classes that are present in the user's aggregate set. Whenever the data owner wants to update a user's access privileges, it calculates a new random parameter and securely sends it to all the users except the revoked one(s). The future messages under the revoked data class(es) are encrypted under the updated random parameter. To highlight the limitations of the scheme in [5], consider users with non-disjoint (or overlapping) aggregate sets. After revocation of one or more data classes from one of the users' aggregate set requires updating the random parameter corresponding to the revoked data class. Now, the random parameter is required to be sent to all the users who still have the data class i in their aggregate sets. This cost is extremely high and sometimes impractical. Similar limitations exist in the subsequent works by [4,6] and [7]. However, the difference between the work by Patranabis et al. [5] and the remaining aforementioned works is that while the former worked on full revocation, the latter aimed both partial and full revocation of users. That said, all the aforementioned purportedly dynamic KAE schemes suffer from impractical secure communication cost. Recently, Liu et al. [8] introduced a KAE scheme that uses threshold cryptography to allow the data owner to revoke any given user completely from the system. That is, the scheme in [8] supports full user revocation. The interesting point about this scheme is that it does not require any secure transmissions for carrying out full revocation. However, we note that the scheme enforces both partial and full revocation of users despite not needing any secure transmissions. Moreover, the scheme in [8] requires calculating and updating a large number of parameters corresponding to each non-revoked user. The computational overhead is notably high, as generating each non-revoked user's key incurs a cost that is linear in the number of data classes in the associated aggregate set. Another scheme which claims to be dynamic is by Gan et al. [9], which requires multi-linear mapping for its design. The scheme is considered computationally impractical due to the absence of any efficient instantiations of multi-linear pairings.

To summarize the discussion above, there are KAE schemes that enforce partial revocation but they come with impractical communication costs [4–7,9].

A scheme that does not require such a large number of secure communications, does not support partial revocation and subjects the data owner to very high computation overhead [8]. Efficiently enforcing partial revocation of access rights of data users is an important requirement in most computing scenarios. Since most schemes support full revocation, it may seem that it is possible to enforce partial revocation by first revoking the user fully from the system and then re-instating the same user using different randomization and for an updated authorization set. However, it is trivial to verify that it will render the data items shared before the revocation operation non-decryptable to the user that is partially revoked using this method.

In view of the discussion presented above, a KAE scheme that efficiently supports fine-grained dynamic updates is well-motivated. The KAE scheme proposed in this paper enforces both partial and full user revocation without the need for any secure communications at all. This is the first scheme to simultaneously achieve both properties while also meeting all key-aggregate efficiency requirements highlighted earlier in this section. In particular, public storage cost linear in the number of data classes, constant user's and data owner's private storage cost, and constant ciphertext size corresponding to a message under a given data class.

1.1 Our Contributions

We propose a novel provably-secure Dynamic Key-Constant Aggregate Encryption (DKCAE) scheme to address the problem of partial user revocation. The proposed scheme requires no secure communications to enforce either full or partial revocation of the data users. The proposed DKCAE scheme enforces fine-grained dynamic updates more efficiently than the existing KAE schemes that claim to be dynamic while meeting all key-aggregate efficiency requirements. The accompanying theoretical and practical comparative analysis of our scheme with the existing ones further affirms our claims regarding the performance. The scheme is provably-secure in the standard model. Proposed is the first KAE scheme that securely enforces fine-grained dynamic updates without needing any secure transmissions.

1.2 Paper Organization

Section 2 presents the construction syntax along with the correctness and security definitions of the proposed scheme. Section 3 details the core idea and provides the concrete construction of the DKCAE scheme, including analyses of its correctness, security, and performance. Section 4 reviews recent related work on key-aggregate encryption schemes. Finally, Sect. 5 concludes the paper.

2 The Proposed DKCAE Scheme

This section details the construction syntax, correctness and security definitions of the proposed DKCAE scheme. Also, we define some mathematical preliminaries used to design the scheme.

2.1 Construction Syntax

We define the proposed DKCAE construction as a collection of polynomial-time procedures Π:

$$\Pi = \{\mathbf{Set}, \mathbf{Gen}, \mathbf{Extract}, \mathbf{AggEnc}, \mathbf{AggDec}, \mathbf{AggSetUpdate}\}$$

1. $\mathbf{Set}(1^\lambda, n) \to \mathbf{genpar}$: Given a security parameter λ and the total number of data classes n, this algorithm outputs the public parameters $\mathbf{genpar}$.
2. $\mathbf{Gen}(\mathbf{genpar}) \to (\mathbf{SK}, \mathbf{PK}, \mathbf{DK})$: Takes the public parameters $\mathbf{genpar}$ as input and generates a master secret key $\mathbf{SK}$, a public key $\mathbf{PK}$, and a dynamic key $\mathbf{DK}$.
3. $\mathbf{Extract}(\mathbf{genpar}, \mathbf{SK}, \mathbf{DK}, set(u)) \to (AK, par(u))$: Outputs a constant-size aggregate key AK and a set of public parameters $par(u)$, based on the input parameters and the aggregate set $set(u)$.
4. $\mathbf{AggEnc}(i, \mathbf{PK}, \mathbf{DK}, M) \to C_i$: Applies the public and dynamic keys to transform message M into ciphertext C_i corresponding to data class i.
5. $\mathbf{AggDec}(C_i, AK_u, par(u), set(u)) \to M$: Decrypts the ciphertext C_i to retrieve the message M, using the aggregate key and public parameters. Decryption is successful if and only if $i \in set(u)$.
6. $\mathbf{AggSetUpdate}(i, set(u), \mathbf{genpar}, \mathbf{type}) \to (\mathbf{DK}', par'(u))$: Depending on the operation type (addition or revocation), this algorithm updates the aggregate set $set(u)$ by adding or removing data class i, and returns the updated dynamic key $\mathbf{DK}'$, revised public parameters $par'(u)$. All future ciphertexts are produced using the updated values $\mathbf{DK}'$ and $par'(u)$.

2.2 Correctness

The DKCAE scheme is correct if the following holds true:

The decryption outputs the correct underlying plaintext message. The decryption is correct if for every $i \in set(u)$:

$$\Pr \left[\begin{array}{c} \mathbf{AggDec}(C_i, AK, \\ par(u), set(u)) \\ = M \end{array} \middle| \begin{array}{c} C_i \leftarrow \mathbf{AggEnc}(i, \mathbf{PK}, \mathbf{DK}, M), \\ \{AK_u, par(u)\} \leftarrow \mathbf{Extract}(\mathbf{genpar}, \mathbf{SK}, set(u)), \\ i \in set(u) \end{array} \right] = 1$$

After revoking the access rights of the user u_r, the revoked user u_r with updated set $set'(u_r) \leftarrow set(u_r) \setminus \{i\}$ cannot decrypt ciphertexts encrypted under the new dynamic key $\mathbf{DK}'$:

$$\Pr\left[\begin{array}{c|c} \mathbf{AggDec}(C'_i, AK_{u_r}, \\ par'(u_r), set'(u_r)) = M \end{array} \middle| \begin{array}{c} C'_i \leftarrow \mathbf{AggEnc}(i, \mathbf{PK}, \mathbf{DK}', M), \\ (par'(u_r)) \leftarrow \mathbf{ExtractPub}(\mathbf{DK}', set'(u_r), \\ \mathbf{DK}', par'(u_r) \leftarrow \mathbf{AggSetUpdate}(i, \\ set(u'_r), \mathbf{genpar}, \text{`Remove'}), \\ i \notin set'(u_r) \end{array}\right] = 0.$$

2.3 Security Definitions

We characterize the chosen-plaintext attack (CPA) resilience of the proposed DKCAE construction through a formal game between a PPT adversary $\mathcal{A}$ and a challenger $\mathcal{C}$.

- **CPAInit:** $\mathcal{A}$ selects a set $S^* \subseteq \{1, \ldots, n\}$ as target and submits S^* to $\mathcal{C}$. The latter then selects a target data class label $i^* \in S^*$ at random.
- **CPASetup:** $\mathcal{C}$ executes the **Set** and **Gen** algorithms to generate (**genpar**, **PK**, **SK**), and sends (**genpar**, **PK**) to $\mathcal{A}$ while keeping the master secret key **SK** private.
- **CPAQuery-I:** $\mathcal{A}$ may adaptively issue **Extract** queries for any subset $S \subseteq \{1, \ldots, n\}$, with the constraint that $S = \{1, \ldots, n\} \setminus S^*$ and $i^* \notin S$. The challenger responds with the corresponding aggregate key AK and public parameters $par(u)$.
- **Challenge:** The adversary $\mathcal{A}$ produces two messages m_0 and m_1 of identical length, each selected from the prescribed message space. The challenger $\mathcal{C}$ then randomly chooses a bit $b \in \{0, 1\}$ and encrypts m_b for the target class i^* using the existing public parameters **genpar**:

$$C = \mathbf{AggEnc}(i^*, \mathbf{PK}, \mathbf{DK}, m_b).$$

  The challenger then revokes i^* from S^* and obtains an updated set $S' = S^* \setminus \{i^*\}$. It then updates the public parameters accordingly and re-encrypts m_b under i^* using the newly updated parameters **genpar**:

$$C' = \mathbf{AggEnc}(i^*, \mathbf{PK}, \mathbf{DK}', m_b).$$

  Both ciphertexts C and C' are sent to $\mathcal{A}$.
- **Guess:** Finally, $\mathcal{A}$ outputs a guess b' for b and succeeds if it is correct in its guess for b.

  The adversary's advantage in this CPA security game is defined as:

$$\mathsf{Adv}_{\mathcal{A}}^{\mathrm{CPA}} = \left| \Pr[b' = b] - \tfrac{1}{2} \right|.$$

Definition 1 ((ε, t, n)-CPA Security). *A Key-Aggregate Encryption (KAE) over n data classes is said to be (ε, t, n)-CPA secure if no probabilistic polynomial-time (PPT) adversary $\mathcal{A}$ running in time t can win the CPA game with advantage at least ε, i.e.,*

$$\mathsf{Adv}_{\mathcal{A}}^{CPA} < \varepsilon.$$

2.4   Preliminaries

Definition 2 (Bilinear Pairing).   *Let $\mathbb{G}_1$ and $\mathbb{G}_2$ be cyclic multiplicative groups of prime order p, and let $g \in \mathbb{G}_1$ be a generator. A function $e : \mathbb{G}_1 \times \mathbb{G}_1 \to \mathbb{G}_2$ is called a* bilinear pairing *if it satisfies the following properties:*

(a) **Bilinearity:** *For all $a, b \in \mathbb{Z}_p$, we have*

$$e(g^a, g^b) = e(g, g)^{ab} = e(g^b, g^a).$$

(b) **Non-degeneracy:** *The value $e(g, g)$ is not equal to the identity element of $\mathbb{G}_2$; i.e., $e(g, g) \neq 1$.*

(c) **Efficient Computability:** *The map e can be computed efficiently.*

Definition 3 (Decision n-BDHE Problem).   *Let $\alpha \in \mathbb{Z}_p$ be a randomly chosen exponent with $g_i = g^{\alpha^i} \in \mathbb{G}_1$ for $i \in \{1, 2, \ldots, n, n+2, \ldots, 2n\}$. Considering the tuple*

$$(h, P = (g, g_1, \ldots, g_n, g_{n+2}, \ldots, g_{2n}), Z),$$

where $h \in \mathbb{G}_1$ and $Z \in \mathbb{G}_2$, the goal is to determine whether $Z = e(h, g_{n+1})$ or Z is a random element in $\mathbb{G}_2$.

   An algorithm $\mathcal{A}$ is said to have advantage ϵ in solving the Decision n-BDHE problem if it runs in at most time τ and satisfies:

$$|\Pr\left[\mathcal{A}(h, P, e(h, g_{n+1})) = 0\right] - \Pr\left[\mathcal{A}(h, P, Z) = 0\right]| \geq \epsilon.$$

Definition 4 (Decision (τ, ϵ, n)-BDHE Assumption).   *The Decision (τ, ϵ, n)-BDHE assumption holds in the bilinear setting $(\mathbb{G}_1, \mathbb{G}_2)$ if no algorithm $\mathcal{A}$ running in time at most τ can solve the Decision n-BDHE problem with advantage at least ϵ.*

3   The Concrete DKCAE Scheme

We begin by outlining the core idea underlying the proposed DKCAE construction. This is followed by detailing the concrete construction, along with the correctness proof and formal security analysis. Finally, we provide a practical comparative performance evaluation of the proposed scheme against several notable existing dynamic KAE schemes.

3.1   Principal Idea

The DKCAE scheme uses the ciphertext transformation presented in [10], which outputs an aggregate re-encryption key to delegate the decryption capabilities of one aggregate key to another different aggregate key. The authors in [10] present two ways in which the notion of KAE and proxy re-encryption can be augmented to obtain the so-called key-aggregate proxy re-encryption (KAPRE). We use their second variant to achieve the goals listed for the current work. We

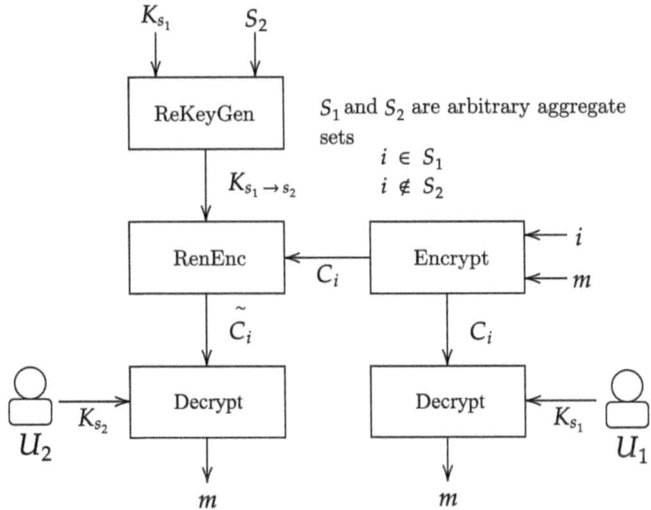

(a) The concept of key-aggregate proxy re-encryption (KAPRE) [10]

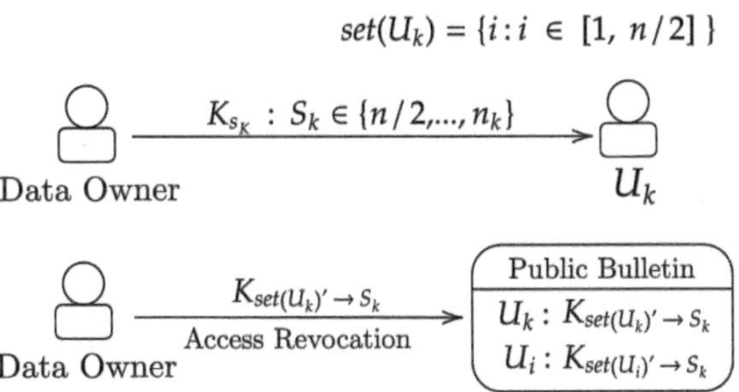

(b) Schematic flow of the proposed scheme

Fig. 3. Principal idea behind the proposed DKCAE scheme.

first briefly review the second variant of KAPRE [10] and then discuss how we adapt the ciphertext transformation in KAPRE to construct DKCAE scheme.

Suppose there are two users U_1 and U_2, and they have access to their respective aggregate keys K_{S_1} and K_{S_2}. Suppose that U_1 wishes to delegate her decryption capabilities to U_2. U_1 first outputs a aggregate re-encryption key $K_{S_1 \rightarrow S_2}$ so that a semi-trusted service provider (proxy) re-encrypts all data items under data class $i \in S_1$ using this key. These re-encrypted data items can now be decrypted by U_2 using her aggregate key K_{S_2}. This transformation of a ciphertext C_i under class $i \in S_1$ to C_j under class $j \in S_2$ allows U_1 to delegate her decryption capabilities to U_2. As a result, delegation of access rights does not require any reissue of new aggregate keys and only the ciphertexts are updated. Figure 3(a) illustrates this delegation process.

Figure 3(b) illustrates the dynamic update mechanism using the ciphertext transformation technique explained above, without the need to securely transmit any new aggregate keys. All updates to the access rights of a user U_k are made to the public bulletin. When revocation is required, the data owner updates the dynamic key and public parameters associated with that user. Notably, even if multiple users share overlapping access rights, revocation of one user's rights does not affect others. This is achieved by taking twice the class labels compared to the case with the conventional KAE schemes, i.e., for n data items take $2n$ class labels ($4n$ numbers of g_i's) as opposed to n labels ($2n$ numbers of g_i's) in case of traditional KAE schemes. In DKCAE, the first n class labels are used to encrypt the data items and the remaining n class labels are used to create aggregate keys. For this, the authorization set $\mathrm{set}(u)$ containing data classes from the last n class labels is computed for any user u as $\mathrm{set}(u) = \{n + i : i \in S\}$. Now the aggregate key is computed using these newly computed aggregate sets corresponding to each user u. Obviously, these aggregate keys will not be able to correctly decrypt the encryptions under the class labels $i = 1, \ldots, n$. For decryption to be possible, an aggregate re-encryption key $K_{S \to \mathrm{set}(u)}$ is output along with the aggregate key corresponding to u. While the user retains the aggregate key as a confidential value, the re-encryption key functions as a public parameter linked to that user. In this way, the set of data classes that u is authorized to access is also represented in the aggregate re-encryption key instead of the aggregate key alone. As a result, whenever a partial revocation of u for data class i is to be carried out, the corresponding re-encryption key can be updated without having to update the aggregate key. In order to invalidate the previously computed aggregate re-encryption keys, freshness is ensured by including a random dynamic key which is updated every time there is update in the corresponding aggregate re-encryption key(s). This way, the fine-grained dynamic updates can be enforced by updating only the public parameter corresponding to the user i.e. the aggregate re-encryption key. This saves us the overhead/cost of securely transmitting updated aggregate keys more than once and preventing one-affects-all updates. For the concrete construction, we modify the KAPRE construction given in [10] so as to remove the random oracle assumption and prove semantic security of the DKCAE scheme in standard model with target collision-resistant hash function assumption.

3.2   Concrete Construction

The concrete construction of the proposed DKCAE scheme is based on the bilinear pairings introduced in Definition 2. The notations used throughout the construction are summarized in Table 1. For simplicity, the construction in this section assumes $n/2$ data classes, requiring a total of $2n$ elements g_i which is consistent with conventional KAE schemes. We also assume that n is even; however, in cases where n is odd, a dummy data class identifier can be introduced without impacting the functionality of the system.

Table 1. Summary of Notations Used

Notation	Description
SK	Master secret key $= \{\gamma_1, \gamma_2\}$
PK	Master public key $= g_{n/2}^{\gamma_1}$
DK	Dynamic key $= g^{\gamma_2}$
AK_u	Aggregate key for user u
$par(u)$	Public parameters for user u
$set(u)$	Aggregate set authorized for user u, where $set(u) \subseteq \{1, 2, \ldots, n\}$
$par_{u,0}$	Public value used in construction of $par(u)$
$par'(u)$	Updated public parameters for user u
C_i	Cipher text for class i
$x \xleftarrow{\$} X$	An element selected from X uniformly at random and stored in x

1. **Set**$(1^\lambda, n/2) \to$ **genpar**: Following is our setup procedure:
   - Let $\mathbb{G}_1$ and $\mathbb{G}_2$ be cyclic groups of prime order p, where p satisfies $2^\lambda \leq p < 2^{\lambda+1}$. Let g be a randomly chosen generator of $\mathbb{G}_1$.
   - Select a secret exponent $\alpha \in \mathbb{Z}_p$ uniformly at random. For each index $i \in \{1, 2, \ldots, n, n+2, \ldots, 2n\}$, compute $g_i = g^{\alpha^i} \in \mathbb{G}_1$. Discard the value of α after computation.
   - Choose a hash function $H : \mathbb{G}_2 \to \mathbb{G}_1$ that is target collision-resistant (TCR).
   - Define the public parameters as:

$$\mathbf{genpar} \leftarrow \langle g, p, \mathbb{G}_1, \mathbb{G}_2, H, g_1, g_2, \ldots, g_n, g_{n+2}, \ldots, g_{2n} \rangle.$$

2. **Gen(genpar)** $\to \{\mathbf{SK}, \mathbf{PK}, \mathbf{DK}\}$: Generation of the master-public and master-secret keys and the dynamic key as follows:
   - Randomly sample two elements $\gamma_1, \gamma_2 \in \mathbb{Z}_p$.
   - Store $\mathbf{SK} \leftarrow \{\gamma_1, \gamma_2\}$, $\mathbf{PK} \leftarrow g_{n/2}^{\gamma_1}$ and $\mathbf{DK} \leftarrow g^{\gamma_2}$.

3. **Extract(genpar, PK, SK, DK,** $set(u)) \to \{AK_u, par(u)\}$: Derive the aggregate key and associated parameters for the authorized class set $set(u) \subseteq \{1, 2, \ldots, n\}$ by invoking the sub-procedures **ExtractPriv** and **ExtractPub** as described below:

(a) **ExtractPriv:** Compute

$$AK_u = \left(\prod_{b \in set(u)} g_{n/2+1-b} \right)^{\gamma_1}$$

and send it to the authorized user via a secure transmission channel. Additionally, compute and publish:

$$par_{u,0} = \prod_{j \in set(u)} g_{n/2+j}.$$

Both AK_u and $par_{u,0}$ will not change and remain same throughout.

(b) **ExtractPub:** Randomly sample $r, s \in \mathbb{Z}_p$ and $R_1 \in \mathbb{G}_2$. These values are then used to compute the public parameter tuple $par(u) = (par_1, \ldots, par_5)$ associated with the aggregate key AK_u as follows:

$$par_1 = \left(\prod_{a \in set(u)} g_{n+1-a} \right)^{\gamma_1} \cdot (\mathbf{DK})^s,$$

$$par_2 = (g_{n/2})^r,$$

$$par_3 = (\mathbf{PK} \cdot par_{u,0})^r,$$

$$par_4 = R_1 \cdot e(g_1, g_n)^r,$$

$$par_5 = g^s \cdot H(R_1)$$

4. **AggEnc**$(i, \mathbf{PK}, \mathbf{DK}, M) \rightarrow C_i$: The plaintext message M is encrypted for data class i to generate the ciphertext $C_i = \langle C_1, C_2, C_3, C_4 \rangle$ in the following manner:

   – We select a value at random $t \xleftarrow{\$} \mathbb{Z}_p$ and compute:

$$C_1 = g^t, \quad C_2 = (\mathbf{PK} \cdot g_i)^t, \quad C_3 = M \cdot e(g_1, g_n)^t, \quad C_4 = (\mathbf{DK})^t,$$

5. **AggDec**$(C_i, AK_u, par(u), set(u)) \rightarrow M$: The ciphertext $C_i = \langle C_1, C_2, C_3, C_4 \rangle$ is decrypted utilizing AK_u to recover the original plaintext message M as follows:

   – Compute $\mathbf{A}$ as:

$$\mathbf{A} = \frac{C_3 \cdot e\left(par_1, \prod_{\substack{a \in set(u) \\ a \neq i}} g_{n+1-a+i}, C_1 \right)}{e\left(C_2, \prod_{a \in set(u)} g_{n+1-a} \right)}$$

   – Compute $\mathbf{B}$ as:

$$\mathbf{B} = \frac{par_4 \cdot e(AK_u, par_2) \cdot e\left(\prod_{j \in set(u)} \prod_{\substack{b \in set(u) \\ b \neq j}} g_{n/2+1-b+j}, par_2 \right)}{e\left(par_3, \prod_{b \in set(u)} g_{n/2+1-b} \right)}$$

   – Then we use $\mathbf{A}$ and $\mathbf{B}$ that we had earlier computed to obtain the plaintext message M:

$$M = \mathbf{A} \cdot e(par_5 \cdot (H(\mathbf{B}))^{-1}, C_4)^{-1}$$

6. $\mathbf{AggSetUpdate}(i, set(u), \mathbf{genpar}, \mathbf{type}) \rightarrow \{\mathbf{DK'}, par'(u)\}$:
   - Depending on the value of $\mathbf{type}$, modify the authorized set $set(u)$ as follows: If $\mathbf{type} = $ 'Remove', then compute the new set as $set'(u) = set(u) \setminus \{i\}$. If $\mathbf{type} = $ 'Add', update the set as $set'(u) = set(u) \cup \{i\}$.
   - Generate a fresh random value $\gamma_2' \in \mathbb{Z}_p$ and compute the renewed dynamic key as $\mathbf{DK'} = g^{\gamma_2'}$. Update the second component of the master secret key with γ_2', while keeping γ_1 unchanged.
   - Run the subroutine $\mathbf{ExtractPub}$ using the updated dynamic key $\mathbf{DK'}$ and the revised set $set'(u)$ to obtain the new public parameter $par'(u)$ corresponding to the modified access set.
   - For every other user in the system, re-execute the $\mathbf{ExtractPub}$ subroutine with their existing authorized sets and the new dynamic key $\mathbf{DK'}$ to ensure consistency.
   - All ciphertexts associated with data class i generated in the future must now be encrypted using the updated dynamic key $\mathbf{DK'}$. Specifically, compute $C_i' \leftarrow \mathbf{AggEnc}(i, \mathbf{PK}, \mathbf{DK'}, M)$.

3.3   Correctness Analysis

In the algorithm $\mathbf{AggDec}$, we compute $\mathbf{A}$ and $\mathbf{B}$ which is further simplified as follows:

$$
\mathbf{A} = \frac{C_3 \cdot e\left(par_1 \cdot \prod_{\substack{a \in set(u) \\ a \neq i}} g_{n+1-a+i}, C_1 \right)}{e\left(C_2, \prod_{a \in set(u)} g_{n+1-a} \right)}
$$

$$
= \frac{M \cdot e(g_1, g_n)^t \cdot e\left(\prod_{a \in set(u)} g_{n+1-a}^{\gamma_1} \cdot g^{\gamma_2 s} \cdot \prod_{\substack{a \in set(u) \\ a \neq i}} g_{n+1-a+i}, g^t \right)}{e\left(g^{\gamma_1 t} g_i{}^t, \prod_{a \in set(u)} g_{n+1-a} \right)} = M \cdot e(g^{\gamma_2 s}, g^t)
$$

$$
\mathbf{B} = \frac{par_4 \cdot e(AK_u, par_2) \cdot e\left(\prod_{j \in set(u)} \prod_{\substack{b \in set(u) \\ b \neq j}} g_{n/2+1-b+j}, par_2 \right)}{e\left(par_3, \prod_{b \in set(u)} g_{n/2+1-b} \right)}
$$

$$
= \frac{R_1 \cdot e(g_1, g_n)^r \cdot e\left(\prod_{b \in set(u)} g_{n/2+1-b}^{\gamma_1}, g_{n/2}^r \right) \cdot e\left(\prod_{j \in set(u)} \prod_{\substack{b \in set(u) \\ b \neq j}} g_{n/2+1-b+j}, g_{n/2}^r \right)}{e\left(g_{n/2}^{\gamma_1 r} \cdot \prod_{j \in set(u)} g_{n/2+j}^r, \prod_{b \in set(u)} g_{n/2+1-b} \right)}
$$

$$= R_1 \cdot e(g_1, g_n)^r \cdot \prod_{j \in set(u)} e(g_{n/2+1}, g_{n/2}^r)^{-1} = R_1 \cdot e(g_1, g_n)^r \cdot e(g_1, g_n)^{-r} = R_1$$

Finally,

$$\mathbf{A} \cdot e(par_5 \cdot (H(B))^{-1}, C_4)^{-1} = M \cdot e(g^{\gamma_2 s}, g^t) \cdot e(g^s \cdot H(R_1) \cdot H(R_1)^{-1}, g^{\gamma_2 t})^{-1}$$
$$= M \cdot e(g^{\gamma_2 s}, g^t) \cdot e(g^s, g^{\gamma_2 t})^{-1} = M.$$

After revocation, the correctness of the scheme holds. Below, we show how a revoked user u_r will not be able to obtain the plaintext message M due to invalid decryption of the updated ciphertext C_i'. The new values of $\mathbf{A}$ and $\mathbf{B}$ are computed as follows:

$$\mathbf{A} = \frac{C_3' \cdot e\left(par_1' \cdot \prod_{\substack{a \in set'(u_r) \\ a \neq i}} g_{n+1-a+i}, C_1'\right)}{e\left(C_2', \prod_{a \in set'(u_r)} g_{n+1-a}\right)} = M \cdot e(g^{\gamma_2' s'}, g^{t'})$$

$$\mathbf{B} = \frac{par_4' \cdot e(AK_{u_r}, par_2') \cdot e\left(\prod_{j \in set'(u_r)} \prod_{\substack{b \in set'(u_r) \\ b \neq j}} g_{n/2+1-b+j}, par_2'\right)}{e\left(par_3', \prod_{b \in set'(u_r)} g_{n/2+1-b}\right)} \neq R_1'$$

Now, since $set(u_r) \neq set'(u_r)$, the above terms do not further cancel out to produce R_1'. Hence, $\mathbf{B} \neq R_1'$. Instead, $\mathbf{B}$ is equal to some value ρ. Assuming the hash is collision resistant, we get $H(R_1') \neq H(\rho)$ and hence,

$$\mathbf{A} \cdot e(par_5' \cdot (H(B))^{-1}, C_4')^{-1} = M \cdot e(g^{\gamma_2' s'}, g^{t'}) \cdot e(g^{s'} \cdot H(R_1') \cdot H(\rho)^{-1}, g^{\gamma_2' t'})^{-1}$$
$$\neq M$$

3.4   Security Analysis

Theorem 1 (IND-CPA Security of the DKCAE). *Let n be the number of data classes and λ the security parameter. If the Decision n-BDHE assumption (as defined in Definition 4) holds in the bilinear setting $(\mathbb{G}_1, \mathbb{G}_2)$, then the DKCAE construction introduced in Sect. 3.2 achieves CPA security as formalized in Definition 1. Specifically, for any PPT adversary $\mathcal{A}$ attempting to win the CPA game, its advantage is bounded by a negligible function:*

$$\mathsf{Adv}_{\mathcal{A}}^{CPA}(\lambda) \leq negl(\lambda).$$

Proof. We prove the security of our scheme by reducing it to the Decision n-BDHE problem. Suppose a PPT adversary $\mathcal{A}$ exists that can achieve a non-negligible advantage ε in breaking the CPA security of our construction. In that case, we can devise a polynomial-time algorithm $\mathcal{C}$ that incorporates $\mathcal{A}$ as a subroutine to solve the Decision n-BDHE problem with the same advantage, contradicting the assumed computational hardness of the n-BDHE assumption.

- **CPAInit:** $\mathcal{A}$ outputs a target set $S^* \subset \{1,\ldots,n\}$. $\mathcal{C}$ selects a random $i^* \in S^*$ as the challenge class. We define the set S as $S = \{1,\ldots,n\} \setminus S^*$. $\mathcal{C}$ aims to simulate the encryption under i^* without knowing $g^{\alpha^{n+1}}$.
- **CPASetup:** $\mathcal{C}$ simulates the system parameters using the challenge:
  - Chooses $\gamma_1 \in \mathbb{Z}_p$ at random and sets $\mathbf{PK} = g_{n/2}^{\gamma_1}$.
  - Chooses $\gamma_2 \in \mathbb{Z}_p$ at random and sets $\mathbf{DK} = g^{\gamma_2}$.
  - Publishes public parameters:

$$\mathbf{genpar} = \left\langle g, g^{\alpha}, g^{\alpha^2}, \ldots, g^{\alpha^n}, H : \mathbb{G}_2 \to \mathbb{G}_1 \right\rangle.$$

- **CPAQuery-I:** $\mathcal{A}$ may issue **Extract** queries for sets S_i such that $S_i \cap S^* = \varnothing$. For each such query, $\mathcal{C}$ returns the corresponding aggregate key AK_{S_i} and relevant public parameters. $\mathcal{C}$ uses the known BDHE terms to simulate the aggregate key:

$$AK_{S_i} = \prod_{j \in S_i} (g^{\alpha^{(n/2)+1-j}})^{\gamma_1} \cdot \prod_{j \in S_i} (g^{\alpha^{(n/2)+1-j+i^*}})^{-1}.$$

All such exponents are computable since $j \neq i^*$ and α^{n+1} is never explicitly needed. Then the public parameters $par(u) = (par_1, par_2, par_3, par_4, par_5)$ are calculated as follows:

$$par_1 = \left(\prod_{a \in S_i} g_{n+1-a} \cdot g_{n+1-a+i^*}^{-1} \right)^{\gamma_1} \cdot (\mathbf{DK})^s,$$

$$par_2 = (g_{n/2})^r,$$

$$par_3 = (\mathbf{PK} \cdot \prod_{j \in S_i} g_{n/2+j})^r,$$

$$par_4 = R_1 \cdot e(g_1, g_n)^r,$$

$$par_5 = g^s \cdot H(R_1)$$

where $R_1 \xleftarrow{\$} \mathbb{G}_2$ and $r, s \xleftarrow{\$} \mathbb{Z}_p$
- **Challenge:** Given two messages (m_0, m_1) submitted by the adversary $\mathcal{A}$, the challenger $\mathcal{C}$ selects at random a bit $b \in \{0, 1\}$ and a value $t \in \mathbb{Z}_p$, and initializes:

$$C_1 = g^t, C_2 = (\mathbf{PK} \cdot g_{i^*})^t = g^{\gamma_1 t} \cdot g^{\alpha^{i^*} t}, C_3 = m_b \cdot Z, \quad C_4 = \mathbf{DK}^t = g^{\gamma_2 t},$$

where $Z = e(g_1, g_n)^t$ and $C = (C_1, C_2, C_3, C_4)$

Then, $\mathcal{C}$ revokes i^* from S^* and sets $S' = S^* \setminus \{i^*\}$. A new dynamic key is generated as:

$$\mathbf{DK}' = g^{\gamma_2'},$$

for random $\gamma_2' \in \mathbb{Z}_p$. New public parameter is computed. The second ciphertext is computed as:

$$C_1' = g^t, C_2' = (\mathbf{PK} \cdot g_{i^*})^t, C_3' = m_b \cdot Z, C_4' = (\mathbf{DK}')^t,$$

where $C' = (C_1', C_2', C_3', C_4')$
$\mathcal{C}$ sends both C and C' to $\mathcal{A}$.

- **Guess:** $\mathcal{A}$ produces a guess b' for the secret bit b, and $\mathcal{C}$ returns 0 when $b = b'$, and 1 otherwise.

Let $\mathsf{Adv}_{\mathcal{A}}^{\mathrm{CPA}} = \left| \Pr[b' = b] - \frac{1}{2} \right|$.

If the BDHE challenge element $Z = e(g, g)^{\alpha^{n+1}t}$, then both ciphertexts C (before revocation) and C' (after revocation) are well-formed and valid encryptions of m_b under class i^*. Otherwise, C_3 and C_3' contain a random group element, making both ciphertexts independent of b. Therefore, $\mathcal{A}$ has a non-negligible advantage in getting a correct guess of b, while in the random case, its advantage is negligible. Thus, the advantage of $\mathcal{C}$ in solving the BDHE instance is:

$$\mathsf{Adv}_{\mathcal{A}}^{\mathrm{CPA}} \geq \varepsilon \Rightarrow \mathsf{Adv}_{\mathcal{C}}^{\mathrm{BDHE}} \geq \varepsilon.$$

Note that after i^* is revoked from S^*, the updated ciphertext C' is generated using a fresh dynamic key $\mathbf{DK}'$ and updated public parameters. Since $\mathcal{A}$ never obtains an aggregate key for any set containing i^*, and cannot compute $g^{\alpha^{n+1}}$, it cannot decrypt either ciphertext, nor distinguish whether C or C' is encrypted using pre- or post-revocation parameters.

This indistinguishability of C and C' implies that the aggregate key AK_{S_i} (issued before revocation) does not leak any information about ciphertexts encrypted under the revoked class i^*. Hence, revocation ensures that access to i^* is effectively removed. Therefore, the scheme remains CPA-secure even in the presence of dynamic revocation.

If $\mathcal{A}$ can distinguish between m_0 and m_1 with a non-negligible advantage, then $\mathcal{C}$ can distinguish the BDHE challenge term $Z = e(g, g)^{\alpha^{n+1}t}$ from random with the same advantage, contradicting the assumed hardness of the n-BDHE problem. Therefore, no such adversary exists, and the proposed KAE is CPA-secure.

Table 2. System Configuration and Cryptographic Parameters

Category	Specification
Hardware	AMD Ryzen 5 5500U with Radeon Graphics @2.10GHz
OS	64-bit Ubuntu 24.04.2 LTS (WSL)
Compiler	gcc 13.3.0
Program Library	pbc-0.5.14
Curve	$y^2 = x^3 + x$
Group Order	160 bits
Base Field	512 bits
DLog Security	1024 bits (approx.)

3.5   Performance Analysis

This section presents an evaluation of the DKCAE scheme, focusing on the time complexity of its core operations and the overall storage requirements for different system entities. As previously noted, the scheme satisfies all key-aggregate efficiency properties. Consequently, the private storage required by each data user remains constant and corresponds to the size of the aggregate key issued by the data owner. Furthermore, the public bulletin board stores a constant-size public key for each user. In particular, the private and public storage overheads in our scheme are $|\mathbb{G}_1|$ and $|\mathbb{G}_2| + 4\,|\mathbb{G}_1|$, respectively, where $|X|$ denotes the bit-length required to represent an element from set X. Beyond user-specific public keys, the data owner also posts public parameters on the bulletin board: two per data class, resulting in an additional storage cost of $2n\,|\mathbb{G}_1|$, where n is the number of data classes. Hence, the total public storage overhead grows at most linearly with the greater of the two parameters: the number of users or the number of data classes. This linear bound stands in contrast to certain existing schemes such as [4], where public storage may grow as a high-degree polynomial (not necessarily linear) in the security parameter, depending on the complexity of dynamic update operations. Another important efficiency feature of our scheme is its support for constant-size ciphertexts. Specifically, each ciphertext has a size of $4\,|\mathbb{G}_1| + |\mathbb{G}_2|$.

Table 3. Variation of time-costs (in milliseconds) of the procedures involved in the proposed scheme with n and N_{avg}

Procedure	$n = 100$ $N_{\mathrm{avg}} = 10$	$n = 200$ $N_{\mathrm{avg}} = 20$	$n = 300$ $N_{\mathrm{avg}} = 30$	$n = 400$ $N_{\mathrm{avg}} = 40$	$n = 500$ $N_{\mathrm{avg}} = 50$
Extraction	3.154	4.070	4.177	2.683	3.075
Encryption	5.064	2.956	2.981	1.384	1.576
Decryption (Private)	0.266	0.355	0.358	0.215	0.239
Decryption (Public)	3.115	8.555	13.627	13.274	19.806
AggSetUpdate	3.694	9.078	12.970	5.493	2.872

Table 4. Variation of time-costs of operations with the overlapping factor (OF)

	$OF = 10$	$OF = 20$	$OF = 30$	$OF = 40$	$OF = 50$
Extraction	2.428	2.386	2.399	2.372	2.348
Encryption	1.390	1.360	1.370	7.213	1.345
Decryption (Private)	0.222	0.218	0.220	0.219	0.214
Decryption (Public)	3.392	3.345	3.135	3.109	3.080
Update	2.484	2.417	2.438	2.414	2.380

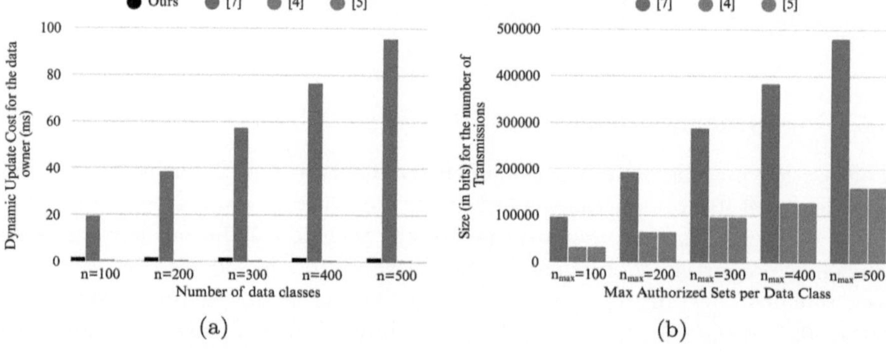

Fig. 4. (a) Dynamic update cost for different number of data classes, (b) Size of the number of transmissions for different maximum authorized sets per data class.

$$OF = \text{Average}\left(\frac{|set(i) \cap set(j)|}{max\{|set(i)|, |set(j)|\}} \times 100\right)$$

For assessing the time costs of different operations, the scheme was implemented using the Pairing-Based Cryptography (PBC) library [20] on a system configured as detailed in Table 2. Experiments were conducted by varying the number of data classes (n), the average number of classes per user's aggregate set (N_{avg}), and the overlap factor (OF)—defined as the percentage of common data classes between any two distinct users u_i and u_j. The overlap factor is calculated as:

$$OF = \text{Average}\left(\frac{|set(i) \cap set(j)|}{\max\{|set(i)|, |set(j)|\}} \times 100\right)$$

The parameters N_{avg} and OF are critical in performance analysis, as the computational cost in several existing dynamic KAE schemes depends on both the size of aggregate sets and the number of aggregate sets containing the revoked data class. Specifically, in the schemes proposed by [4] and [7], revoking a data class i from an aggregate set S_k necessitates updating all aggregate keys associated with any set that includes i. These updated keys must then be securely transmitted to the respective data users. In contrast, our scheme eliminates the need for such key updates, even for users whose access rights have changed thereby avoiding any secure communication overhead. The only requirement is for the data owner to update the public parameters on the public bulletin board. The computational time costs associated with key extraction, encryption, decryption, and dynamic updates (revocation) are summarized in Table 3. It is important to note that, in our scheme, most decryption-related operations can be outsourced to a semi-trusted computation service provider, significantly reducing the computational burden on the end users. Furthermore, Table 4 illustrates how the time costs of various operations vary with the parameter OF, using fixed values of $n = 100$ and $N_{avg} = 10$, and varying OF. The results confirm that, within the proposed DKCAE scheme, the computational time for all operations remains consistently stable irrespective of changes in the overlap factor.

Finally, we analyze the variation in dynamic update costs of the proposed scheme in comparison with existing dynamic KAE schemes [4, 5, 7], as illustrated in Fig. 4a. For this analysis, the number of users (m) is fixed at 100, and the overlap factor (OF) is chosen such that each data class belongs to an average of 50 aggregate sets. Our findings reveal that the dynamic update cost of our approach stacks up favorably against the referenced schemes. Figure 4b presents a comparison of the secure transmission overheads (measured in bits) required during dynamic updates in our scheme versus existing dynamic KAE schemes. In these existing schemes, the secure transmission size is proportional to the number of aggregate sets containing a given data class, denoted by $n_{\max}$. In contrast, our scheme requires no secure transmissions during dynamic updates. As a result, our scheme is excluded from Fig. 4b. This key advantage demonstrates the high performance of our approach, as it eliminates the need for the data owner to securely transmit any parameters during revocations. In conclusion, the proposed DKCAE scheme achieves security and efficiency on par with existing dynamic and non-dynamic KAE schemes while offering a significant performance enhancement. It effectively addresses a critical cryptographic challenge by enabling dynamic access control without modifying any user's secret and without requiring any secure communication during updates.

4   Related Works

The concept of Key-Aggregate Encryption (KAE), introduced by Chu et al. [1], aims to provide scalable and flexible mechanisms for data sharing in cloud storage, allowing users to enforce fine-grained access control on encrypted data. Unlike traditional public-key encryption methods that require sharing either a single decryption key (which risks overexposure) or multiple keys (which are inefficient to manage), KAE enables a data owner to lend their decryption rights for an arbitrary subset of encrypted data classes through a single, constant-size aggregate key.

Ever since the work by [1], KAE has gained significant attention for enabling fine-grained, scalable access control in cloud storage systems. However, dynamic revocation remains a challenging aspect in practical deployments. Several extensions have been proposed to incorporate revocation mechanisms within the KAE framework. To this end, numerous schemes have appeared in the literature that use key-aggregation for applications like secure data sharing and service authentication [6]. Some have worked towards enhancing the efficiency of enforcing dynamic access control using KAE [4,5,7–9,11,12]. However, all of them either do not support partial user revocation, or if they do, these schemes subject the data owner to substantial computation and storage overhead. A detailed explanation has been given in Sect. 1 while presenting for the motivation of the proposed DKCAE scheme. There exist some works that extend key-aggregate encryption in other cryptographic primitives and models like searchable encryption [13,14], proxy re-encryption [10], identity-based encryption [15], Blockchain-based access control [16] and searchable encryption [17–19]. These works are important extensions of the KAE primitive.

5   Conclusions and Future Works

We have proposed the notion and a provably-secure concrete construction of dynamic key-constant-aggregate encryption (DKCAE) in this paper. The unique feature of DKCAE is that it supports selective and partial revocation of a user for a subset of the data classes for which a user is initially authorized. That is, the users can be revoked for specific data class(es) from their aggregate sets without affecting other access rights of the partially revoked user or other users in the system. This is achieved despite satisfying all the key-aggregate performance requirements. The proposed construction presents an interesting application of the well-known ciphertext transformation technique using proxy re-encryption but in key-aggregate encryption scenario. The scheme has been analyzed for its correctness, security and practical performance. A comparative analysis with other existing schemes suggests that our scheme is much more efficient in enforcing fine-grained dynamic updates while satisfying all classical performance requirements. The aforementioned characteristics of DKCAE may be useful for authentication and/or access control in many practical contemporary computing scenarios. Refining the notion of DKCAE, its practical implementation on an experimental testbed simulating the internet-scale traffic continues to be a focus of future work.

References

1. Chu, C.K., Chow, S.S., Tzeng, W.G., Zhou, J., Deng, R.H.: Key-aggregate cryptosystem for scalable data sharing in cloud storage. IEEE Trans. Parallel Distrib. Syst. **25**(2), 468–477 (2013)
2. Liu, L., Huang, C., Zhu, D., Liu, D., Ni, J., Shen, X.: Enabling efficient and distributed access control for pervasive edge computing services. IEEE Trans. Mob. Comput. **23**(12), 11342–11356 (2024)
3. Liu, L., Huang, C., Zhu, D., Liu, D., Ni, J., Shen, X.S.: Secure and distributed access control for dynamic pervasive edge computing services. In: 2022 IEEE Global Communications Conference, GLOBECOM 2022, pp. 5487–5492. IEEE (2022)

4. Pareek, G., Purushothama, B.R.: Secure and efficient revocable key-aggregate cryptosystem for multiple non-predefined non-disjoint aggregate sets. J. Inf. Secur. Appl. **58**, 102799 (2021)

5. Patranabis, S., Shrivastava, Y., Mukhopadhyay, D.: Dynamic key-aggregate cryptosystem on elliptic curves for online data sharing. In: Biryukov, A., Goyal, V. (eds.) INDOCRYPT 2015. LNCS, vol. 9462, pp. 25–44. Springer, Cham (2015). https://doi.org/10.1007/978-3-319-26617-6_2

6. Patranabis, S., Shrivastava, Y., Mukhopadhyay, D.: Provably secure key-aggregate cryptosystems with broadcast aggregate keys for online data sharing on the cloud. IEEE Trans. Comput. **66**(5), 891–904 (2016)

7. Pareek, G., Maiti, S.: Efficient dynamic key-aggregate cryptosystem for secure and flexible data sharing. Concurr. Comput.: Pract. Exp. **35**(19), e7553 (2023)

8. Liu, J., Qin, J., Zhang, X., Wang, H.: Efficient key-aggregate cryptosystem with user revocation for selective group data sharing in cloud storage. IEEE Trans. Knowl. Data Eng. **36**(11), 6042–6055 (2024)

9. Gan, Q., Wang, X., Wu, D., et al.: Revocable key-aggregate cryptosystem for data sharing in cloud. Secur. Commun. Netw. **2017** (2017)

10. Pareek, G., Purushothama, B.R.: Kapre: key-aggregate proxy re-encryption for secure and flexible data sharing in cloud storage. J. Inf. Secur. Appl. **63**, 103009 (2021)

11. Padhya, M., Jinwala, D.C.: BTG-RKASE: privacy preserving revocable key aggregate searchable encryption with fine-grained multi-delegation & break-the-glass access control. In: ICETE (2), pp. 109–124 (2019)

12. Liu, Z., Li, T., Li, P., Jia, C., Li, J.: Verifiable searchable encryption with aggregate keys for data sharing system. Futur. Gener. Comput. Syst. **78**, 778–788 (2018)

13. Cui, B., Liu, Z., Wang, L.: Key-aggregate searchable encryption (KASE) for group data sharing via cloud storage. IEEE Trans. Comput. **65**(8), 2374–2385 (2015)

14. Li, T., Liu, Z., Li, P., Jia, C., Jiang, Z.L., Li, J.: Verifiable searchable encryption with aggregate keys for data sharing in outsourcing storage. In: Liu, J.K., Steinfeld, R. (eds.) ACISP 2016. LNCS, vol. 9723, pp. 153–169. Springer, Cham (2016). https://doi.org/10.1007/978-3-319-40367-0_10

15. Kajita, K., Ohtake, G.: Encpds: encrypted personal data stores via key-aggregate id-based proxy re-encryption. In: 2024 17th International Conference on Security of Information and Networks (SIN), pp. 1–8. IEEE (2024)

16. Zhang, K., Hu, X., Zhao, J., Wei, L., Ning, J.: Blockchain-based revocable key-aggregate searchable encryption for group data sharing in cloud-assisted industrial IoT. IEEE Internet Things J. (2025)

17. Lee, J., Kim, M., Oh, J., Park, Y., Park, K., Noh, S.: A secure key aggregate searchable encryption with multi delegation in cloud data sharing service. Appl. Sci. **11**(19), 8841 (2021)

18. Basudan, S., Alamer, A.: Verifiable key-aggregate searchable encryption scheme for fog-based internet of autonomous vehicles. Appl. Sci. **15**(6), 3081 (2025)

19. Wang, H., Ning, J., Wu, W., Lin, C., Zhang, K.: KA-SE: key-aggregation authorized searchable encryption scheme for data sharing in wireless sensor networks. IEEE Trans. Serv. Comput. (2024)

20. PBC: Pairing-Based Cryptography. https://crypto.stanford.edu/pbc/

Adversarial Attack on CryptoEyes from INFOCOM 2021

Jashwanth Kadaru[(✉)], Imtiyazuddin Shaik, and Srinivas Vivek

IIIT, Bangalore, Bengaluru, India
{Jashwanth.Kadaru095,shaik.imtiyazuddin,srinivas.vivek}@iiitb.ac.in

Abstract. Privacy-Preserving classification of Machine Learning (PPML) models has gained traction, owing to strict data privacy regulations. One such work, CryptoEyes (Wenbo et al., INFOCOM 2021) enables users to encrypt images using AES in ECB mode and store it at the server for processing. The authors claimed that their protocol have two advantages: (i) service provider could extract enough information in the form of (encrypted) contour, which gives it the ability to perform machine learning classification on encrypted images, and (ii) use of secret permutation known only to user and server, this prevents man-in-the-middle adversary from reconstructing meaningful image content or accurately map encrypted data to its original class distribution even after having access to a train dataset, thereby achieving privacy. However, in this paper we demonstrate an adversarial attack, which surpass claimed classification accuracy for an adversary against CryptoEyes. Our attack approach uses new data transformation techniques for better feature identification and then train an ML model on image pixels encrypted *and* permuted. We identify the key vulnerabilities enabling this data leakage and show how an adversary can exploit these weaknesses. The training of our learning model is key agnostic. The results show that with our attack the adversary is able to train a model on MNIST dataset with at least 74.2% classification accuracy on encrypted and permuted image pixels.

Keywords: Privacy-Preserving Machine Learning · Encrypted Image Classification · Adversarial Machine Learning · Deep Learning Security · Cryptanalysis · AES-ECB

1 Introduction

Third-party service providers offering cloud-based storage and image processing services often seek to categorize vast collections of user-uploaded images to derive valuable demographic insights. Meanwhile, users or organizations uploading images to these servers prioritize privacy, while still benefiting from the analytical capabilities of cloud platforms. Ensuring privacy in such applications is a critical requirement, necessitating solutions that balance data utility and security. The service provider should be able to extract broad demographic trends, such as popular locations, emerging hobbies, or prevailing clothing styles, without accessing or inferring any sensitive user-specific information.

© The Author(s), under exclusive license to Springer Nature Switzerland AG 2026
N. Hubballi et al. (Eds.): ICISS 2025, LNCS 16380, pp. 188–207, 2026.
https://doi.org/10.1007/978-3-032-13714-2_13

This is typically achieved through privacy-preserving techniques such as homomorphic encryption [7], secure multi-party computation [5], perturbation-based approaches [22], etc. In the context of privacy-preserving image classification, one of the approaches involves encrypting images on the client's device, ensuring that only the authorized service provider can process the encrypted data to generate insights while remaining restricted from directly accessing raw image content or personal identifiers of the users.

Existing privacy-preserving methods, such as homomorphic encryption and secure multi-party computation, provide strong security guarantees but often come with significant computational overhead and latency. Additionally, new techniques rely on explicitly identifying and masking sensitive regions within images [24], which can be subjective and error-prone.

Wenbo et al. [9] proposed a protocol, called CryptoEyes, that enhances computational efficiency and reduces errors in privacy-preserving image classification. It also eliminates the need for identifying, masking, blurring, or obfuscating sensitive regions, an inherently subjective and error-prone process. Privacy is achieved by encrypting a group of pixel blocks, ensuring that the service provider cannot infer fine-grained details about the image contents. The encryption process employs AES block encryption [6], along with permutation of encrypted pixels. It is important to note the resultant ciphertext after encryption read by the server is still an image, refer Fig. 1b. The paper [9] also introduces a two-stream convolutional model that outperformed then state-of-the-art classifiers such as Deep Neural Networks (DNN) [14], Stacked Autoencoders (SAE) [21], Deep Belief Networks (DBN) [10], and Convolutional Neural Networks (CNN) [15] on encrypted image data. Notably, CryptoEyes exhibits key-agnostic behavior, allowing image classification by a third-party service provider without requiring knowledge of the AES decryption key. AES block-wise encryption in Electronic CodeBook (ECB) mode is responsible for the contour-preserving characteristics of the encryption, ensuring service provider model can train an ML model to classify the encrypted images. The end result is that the images are both encrypted in blocks, and blocks are permuted to provide privacy guarantees.

In addition, the paper [9] also claims in the result section [9][Section IV.D] that an adversary with enough training data cannot train a model to classify the encrypted images, without the knowledge of the permutation sequence order used. The paper [9] claims that permutation of encrypted images prevents the unauthorized users from successfully attempting a classification attack to obtain category information of encrypted images, and without pre-shared permutation sequence order the unauthorized party cannot perform the classification successfully. Therefore, presenting a strong claim that the permutation sequence functions as a countermeasure against adversarial classification.

Our Contribution in this paper is to present attacks on the CyrptoEyes protocol where a man-in-the-middle eavesdropping adversary can classify and label previously unseen plaintext images with high accuracy. This is despite the fact that the image pixels are encrypted and are sent to the server in a randomly permuted order unknown to the adversary. To enable such an attacks by the adversary, we equip the adversary with the following tools:

- A naive attack, by comparing pixel-by-pixel encrypted and permuted images.
- A data transformation technique which helps in maintaining structural patterns in the encrypted and permuted image. This helps in providing key independent transformation of ciphertexts to enable contour detection and classification. This is done to break the security provided by the permutation of blocks of ciphertexts.
- Two additional methods for the above mentioned data transformation technique to make the adversary's model more robust under limited training data.
- An advanced attack, by using a CNN based model, inspired by CryptoEyes model itself, and do the classification, thus breaking the security of CryptoEyes. This approach is key agnostic.

We briefly present the overview of two attack scenarios by the adversary here. Details can be found from Sect. 3 onwards. For all the scenarios, we describe an eavesdropping adversary, who gets access to labeled encrypted and permuted images, we call this the train set. It is important to note that the CryptoEyes [9, Section IV.D] claims a maximum accuracy for adversary with a train set as 25.5% for MNIST dataset even after training on labeled data, provided the images are encrypted using permutation sequence which is not shared with adversary. We propose two strategies by the adversary to get better accuracy, and hence, break the security guarantees promised by CryptoEyes.

Naive attack: The adversary has the train set and now tries to classify a previously unseen encrypted and permuted image (test image) by comparing it with the entries in the train set, label wise. i.e. the train set is divided using the labels and for each label images we compare the test image, pixel-by-pixel. The highest matching score gives the class label of test image. Using this approach our adversary was able to achieve an accuracy of 33%, surpassing CryptoEyes's claims.

Advanced Attack: To improve adversary's classification accuracy, we use a block map transformation on the train set. This is done by replacing ciphertext image blocks with pixel values based on frequency analysis. A benefit of this approach is that it makes it easier for the adversary for contour detection and matching of images (as described in Fig. 5a). This transformation of ciphertext image block by the adversary is key agnostic, and hence, powerful and practical, and the output is (for MNIST dataset) Black and White image blocks (which are still permuted). Key agnostic means the client could change to a different AES encryption key, but the attack will still work as long as the permutation is fixed. So there is no need for any re-training because the AES encryption key got changed! The adversary can then use two additional data transformation approaches we proposed namely: Ciphertext Occlusion Replacement and Markov-Based White Block Estimation. The advantage of these transformation methods is that they preserve the consistency with encrypted image structures while introducing controlled modifications. These transformation techniques also help in making the model more robust to changes in inputs (for MNIST dataset, changes in handwriting etc., which we suspect is the reason for less accuracy of adversary in the naive approach).

Now, to improve adversary's classification accuracy further, we propose using an ML model that can classify the transformed permuted black and white images. Our proposed model for classification is inspired by the CryptoEyes, with a two-stream convolutional neural network (CNN) along with a Long Short-Term Memory (LSTM) head. We use the LSTM head, different from the dense layers in CryptoEyes, to improve the classification performance. One stream of input to CNN is the transformed permuted images themselves, the other stream is obtained as the gradient maps which provide better feature extraction capabilities of the encrypted contour. This way a man-in-the-middle adversary is able to train a model on the MNIST dataset and break the security of the CryptoEyes protocol in under a few minutes, with 74.9% accuracy. The experimental results can be found in Sect. 5.

The rest of the paper can be summarized as follows: Sect. 2 gives an overview of the CryptoEyes protocol, the adversarial attack model, and handshake phase between the user and service provider, as presented in [9]. Explanation of the attack methodology, followed by the naive attack method in Sect. 3. Section 4 goes in detail of the model architecture of the adversary for the advanced attack method, the training process and hyper-parameters setup. The detailed results are presented in Sect. 5 before concluding the paper in Sect. 6.

2   Background on CryptoEyes

2.1   CryptoEyes Protocol

The privacy-preserving classification scheme proposed in the CryptoEyes paper [9] utilizes AES encryption in the ECB mode on the image, followed by segmentation into fixed-size blocks, permutation of these blocks, and their subsequent reassembly of resulting ciphertext into the final image. The AES key and permutation sequence are kept secret and the permutation sequence is shared only with the service provider.

After encrypting the images (encryption and then permutation) the user sends the encrypted images over the channel to service provider. The service provider receives the encrypted and permuted ciphertext. The service provider can undo permutation and obtain the AES encrypted images in the original order using the secret shared permutation sequence. A ciphertext block is organized as blocks of images at the server's end. In the context of MNIST, this will be a 28×28 ciphertext read as an encrypted image by the server. The service provider now trains a model to classify these AES encrypted images. We now recall the CryptoEyes model in detail as we need it later in the paper (Fig. 2).

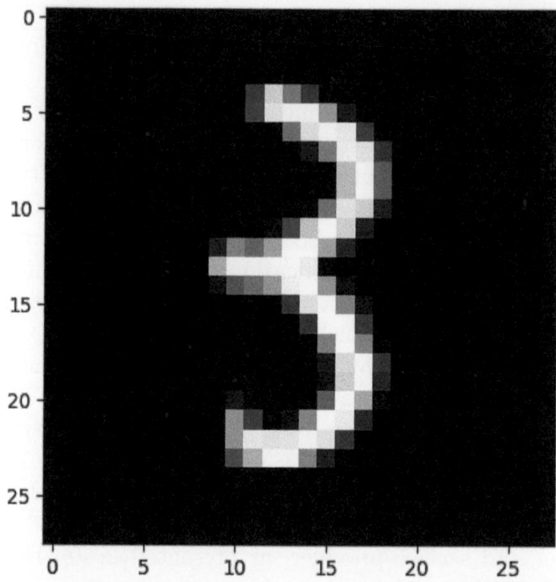

(a) Plaintext 28x28 grayscale MNIST image of the digit 3, where each pixel represents an intensity value ranging from 0 (black) to 255 (white). This dataset is commonly used in handwritten digit classification tasks.

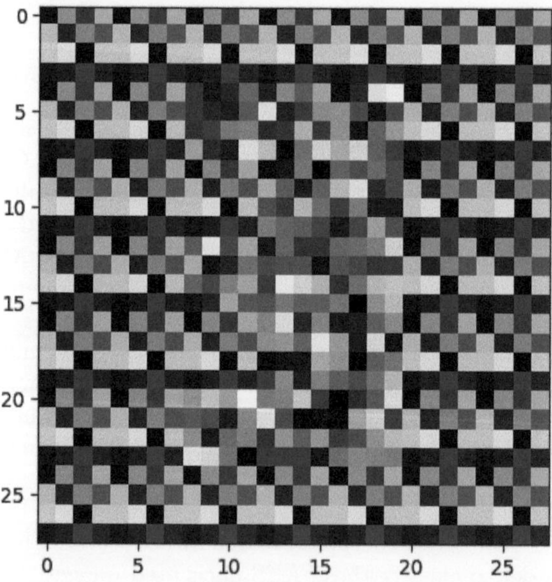

(b) AES encrypted 28x28 grayscale version of Image 1.(a). Each encryption block is of dimension 4x4 and is encrypted using a fixed AES key.

Fig. 1. .

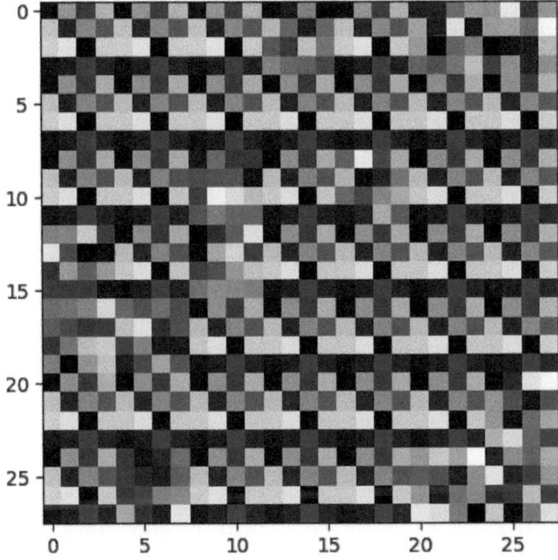

Fig. 2. Final permuted encrypted 28×28 grayscale image of MNIST image in 1.(a). The image was divided into 7×7 grid of 4×4 blocks and permuted using a randomly generated permutation sequence

2.2   Machine Learning Classification Model by CryptoEyes

The CryptoEyes paper proposed a novel architecture to learn classification over the unpermuted (ordered as in the original image) but encrypted images, that can extract the contour information from the blocks and exhibit AES-key agnostic properties that allow the model to suppress the noise in the image present due to encryption.

The CryptoEyes model leverages a two-stream convolutional neural network (CNN) that extracts implicit contour information retained in encrypted images. AES encryption operates at a block level, where substitution and permutation occur within each block, allowing coarse-grained contour structures to persist despite encryption. The proposed model of CryptoEyes processes encrypted images through one stream and their corresponding gradient maps through another, effectively capturing critical contour features for classification. This dual-stream architecture enhances performance by allowing interaction between the encrypted image representation and its gradient-based contour information.

To extract contours from encrypted images, the model utilizes a gradient map, computed using horizontal and vertical kernels to highlight regions of intensity variation. This process generates horizontal (Gx) and vertical (Gy) gradient components, which are combined to obtain a gradient magnitude representation. Feeding the encrypted image into one CNN stream and the gradient map into the second stream enables the network to learn distinguishing features that remain intact after AES encryption. This method addresses the challenge of working with encrypted data by exploiting structural patterns embedded in the encryption process.

Furthermore, the model incorporates a specialized kernel design that aligns with the AES encryption structure. Instead of conventional convolutional kernels, it employs one-dimensional kernels of size 1×16 pixels, corresponding to the AES block size of 128 bits, to maximize feature extraction within encrypted blocks while minimizing unrelated inter-block dependencies. Additionally, a weighted-average gate mechanism inspired by gated neural networks is employed to effectively merge feature representations from both streams, improving classification accuracy. This approach ensures that the model captures relevant encrypted image features without introducing unnecessary artifacts, making it more robust for privacy-preserving classification tasks.

2.3   Encoding of Image and Permutation in CryptoEyes

The AES block cipher (in ECB mode) can only encrypt plaintexts of size 128-bit at a time, which is equal to 16 bytes or 16 pixels of single channel image. Assuming the size of encrypted image and plaintext image is the same (which is generally the case to avoid data loss or storage loss), during encryption the underlying encrypting block must align itself with size of 16 bytes. This limits the encryption-block dimensions to 1×16, 2×8, 4×4, 8×2, 16×1 for a single channel image.

The permutation key size is equal to the number of permutation blocks the image is divided into. If the image is divided into n rows of n blocks each, then we have a total of n^2 blocks. The set of all possible permutations has a cardinality of $n^2!$, which grows rapidly with n. Here, ! stands for the factorial.

For a single channel image of size $m \times m$, the secret permutation sequence (secret key) size can be approximately given by $(m^2/16) \log(m^2/16)$ (assuming each individual ciphertext is treated as a permutation block). Table 1 is a listing of estimated permutation key sizes vs image resolutions. Table 1 shows that the permutation key size grows rapidly with growing image size. This leads to challenges in secure storage and maintenance. Also, implementing secure data computing for large key sizes is a challenge. Hence, it is safe to assume that the number of permutation blocks created within an image is always smaller than the number of ciphertext blocks (4×4 or 2×8 or 1×16 blocks). We also assume that the permutation blocks do not have dimensions that undercut all the ciphertexts contained within a block, as this destroys the contour information in the image significantly. See Fig. 3 & 4.

Table 1. Key size for different image resolutions

Image size	64×64	256×256	512×512	1024×1024
Key size	0.077 KB	1.850 KB	8.631 KB	39.456 KB

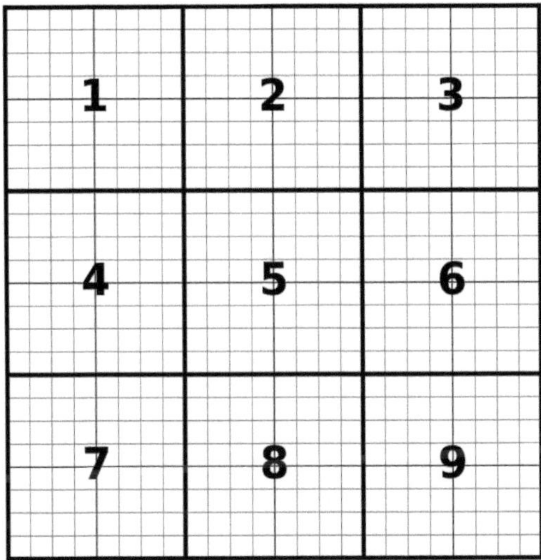

(a) Encryption blocks align perfectly within grid blocks, preserving structure after permutation. (24x24 image, 8x8 grid block size, 4x4 encryption block size.)

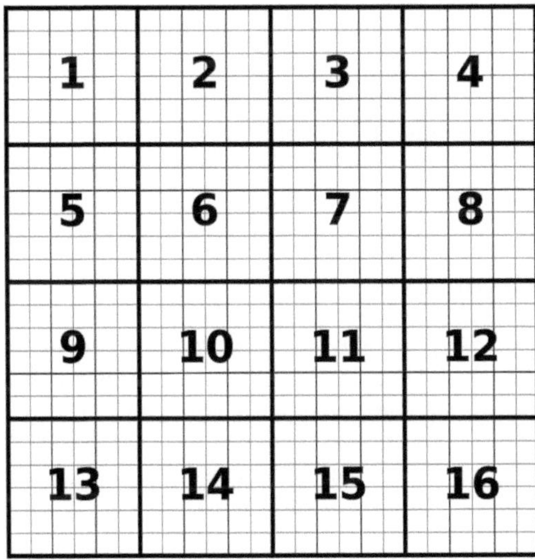

(b) Encryption blocks completely disrupt grid alignment and vice-versa, causing severe distortion when permuted. (24x24 image, 6x6 grid block size, 2x8 encryption block size.)

Fig. 3. Comparison of encryption and grid alignment: (a) Perfect alignment vs. (b) Completely destructive alignment

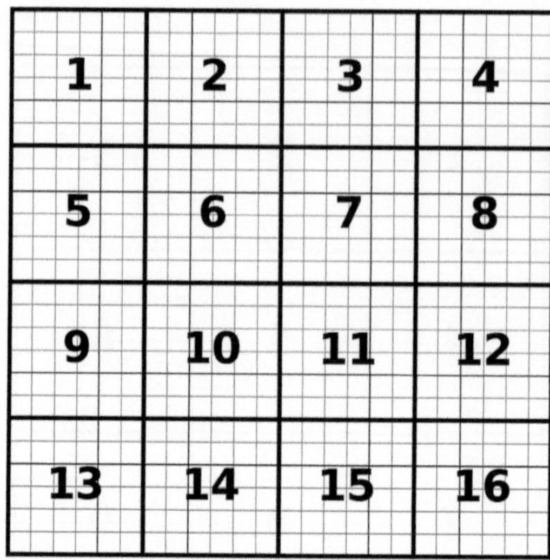

Fig. 4. Partial misalignment of encryption and grid blocks, leading to moderate distortion when permuted. Structural properties are preserved partially. (24×24 image, 6×6 grid block size, 4×4 encryption block size).

This is assumption forms the basis for classification over permuted encrypted images. CryptoEyes [9] did not mention any guidelines as to how a grid size must be chosen relative to the ciphertext dimensions. This could provide many configurations of grid size and encryption block size that have clear cryptographic weaknesses which reveal significant information and aid adversary in almost achieving complete classification accuracy.

2.4   Attacking CryptoEyes

Recall the encryption step in the CryptoEyes scheme in Sect. 2. We can say that every plaintext consisting of the same bit-sequence has been mapped to the same ciphertext, under the given AES key. Thus, the resulting image after AES encryption, has the properties of a segmented image. Different regions of repeating patches (say 4×4 pixels for MNIST) are preserved in the encrypted image and remapped to a patch with different pixel values (Look at Fig. 1b). This is the basis for classification on the service provider's end, since service provider can undo the permutation operation (using the secretly shared-key with user) and train a model to learn features spread across the encrypted image.

Now, the challenge for the adversary remains training a model over encrypted-permuted images, to classify the user's images with high accuracy. If the adversary overcomes this challenge, then the privacy of users is breached and the service provider is at a risk. Under the attack model & security claims made in the CryptoEyes paper [9], the adversary can potentially obtain enough training data, just as much as the service provider. This is stated in Section III.D of the paper [9]. The permutation transformation over the encrypted images functions as the only layer of protection against the adversary. If the adversary is able to train the model on limited data to learn the inter-block relationships encoded via the transformation, then the security of the system is at risk. We present three such attacks from an adversary in this paper.

We will be designing an eavesdropping, computationally bounded adversary, i.e., the adversary can access all information in exchange between user and service provider. We assume that the adversary knows about the encryption algorithm and hyper-parameters, namely, grid size and encryption block size, which is realistic. We define the terms as follows: 1) grid size refers to the $m \times n$ grid of blocks into which the image is divided for permutation, 2) block size is the number of pixels in a row, times the number of pixels in a column of each block defined by the grid, and 3) encryption block size is the size of pixel-array (4×4) that is chosen for encrypting the image, 128-bit plaintext at a time. We use MNIST-digits dataset $(28 \times 28$ grayscale images, 10-labels) to test the hypothesis.

The objective of the adversary is to classify encrypted and permuted user images from CryptoEyes. The goal of the adversary is to achieve the following:

- Classify the encrypted permuted images of a user, without knowing the contents of secret keys (AES key and permutation sequence).

We would like to reiterate that our attacks on CryptoEyes are based on their claims in [9, Section III.D] that the adversary can have access to training data. A successful attack would demonstrate vulnerabilities in the encryption-permutation pipeline of CryptoEyes [9], highlighting potential risks in the privacy-preserving image classification system.

3 Attack Methodology

The protocol of CryptoEyes [9] explicitly defines that each user adheres to a fixed permutation sequence and AES encryption key. In practical implementations, users have the flexibility to vary their AES keys arbitrarily without sharing them with the service provider. However, the permutation sequence cannot be altered arbitrarily and necessitates a key agreement protocol between the user and the service provider to ensure synchronization. Consequently, a labeled dataset of fully encrypted user images may contain images encrypted with different AES keys, yet the permutation order of grid blocks remains consistent across all samples. This consistency preserves structural patterns within the images, which can be effectively visualized by applying a color-based representation to the ciphertexts, as demonstrated in the following Fig. 5.

In this section, we first propose a naive attack by adversary to break the CryptoEyes system. In the next section we will talk about the advanced attack in detail. The setup is same for both attack approaches, where the adversary has a train set, which is the set of images (encrypted and permuted) captured by adversary during interaction between client and server. We reiterate that this

(a) An arbitrarily chosen MNIST grayscale image of the digit 6, which has close structural similarity with the digit in fig. 3(b). The images are labelled with respective version names on the top.

(b) A different arbitrarily chosen MNIST grayscale image of the digit 6, which has close structural similarity with the digit in fig. 3(a). The images are labelled with respective version names on the top.

Fig. 5. Visualization of structural properties in encrypted-permuted MNIST images using a ciphertext-based coloring scheme (Image size: 28×28, encryption block size: 4×4, grid block size: 7×7, grayscale images). Frequently occurring ciphertext blocks (likely from uniform background regions) are mapped to black, while infrequent ones (corresponding to distinct foreground objects) are mapped to white. Structurally similar plaintext images yield structurally similar encrypted-permuted images, preserving spatial correlations. In images with non-uniform backgrounds (or) multiple background regions, with ciphertexts exceeding the threshold, are assigned different colors to distinguish them from each other. This scheme can be easily extended to RGB images, where encryption can be applied independently per channel or jointly using multichannel encryption.

train set also contains labels in plaintext. The task of the adversary is to classify an unseen, unlabeled image. The CryptoEyes paper claims that the best the adversary can do for MNIST dataset is 25.5% accuracy.

3.1   Naive Attack

First the adversary buckets each encrypted and permuted image (train images) depending on the class label. Now, the adversary compares the test image with each image in the bucket for respective label and assigns a matching score depending on number of matches (pixel-by-pixel) for that label. We computed the score for a respective label as the number of pixels matched divided by the total number of pixels. This method works only if all images of a label, have very close & identical properties, which is partly the case for MNIST. However, we note that this naive attack cannot be generalized or used in real world scenarios.

This attack experiment is just to prove that the permutation operation is a weak encryption. Finally, the highest of average matching scores for all labels, gives the class label of test image. In our testing, the adversary using this approach could achieve an accuracy of 33%, which exceeds the claims of CryptoEyes [9]. However this is still low. We suspect this might be due to the case that there are different writing styles for each digit in MNIST dataset. A single change in pixel can result in completely different ciphertext image after encryption and permutation. To overcome this, we propose an advanced attack with a few data transformation approaches to make our attack more robust and key agnostic, without having to generate large datasets with different AES keys to train the model in a key agnostic manner.

4   Advanced Attack

Data transformation for image datasets typically involves applying transformations to create modified versions of images while preserving their key features. These transformations, also called transformation operations, include geometric transformations (rotation, scaling, translation, mirroring), brightness adjustment (color jittering, Gaussian noise addition, brightness/pixel-level intensity adjustment), blurring, occlusion-based transformations, elastic deformation, and etc. For our application, the permutation of blocks in the image restricts the use of most of these transformations. Since the images are both permuted and encrypted at the block level, geometric transformations and elastic deformations would disrupt the underlying structure, making reconstruction meaningless. Noise addition alters pixel values, which in an encrypted space corresponds to unpredictable changes to underlying plaintext, breaking the integrity of the data. As a result, these transformations cannot be directly applied without compromising the encrypted representation. We propose key-agnostic data transformations on permuted images to make the attack more robust.

4.1   Block Map Transformation

Instead of working directly with ciphertexts, we convert encrypted images into block map representations, which are key agnostic, where each encryption block is mapped to a pixel value based on its frequency and threshold. This intermediate representation enables easy transformation while allowing us to preserve characteristics of the encrypted image.

Encrypted images consist of permuted blocks of ciphertexts, where each block corresponds to a specific region of the plaintext image. The transformation process involves counting the frequency of each ciphertext and assigning unique pixel values to them. Ciphertexts that occur frequently are assigned distinct colors, while less frequent ones are mapped to a default white value of 255. The resulting block map maintains a structural relationship with the encrypted image and allows transformation methods to operate at a more meaningful level.

In our experiments, encrypted permuted MNIST image dataset consists only of black and white ciphertext blocks due to the presence of a single majority ciphertext. The transformation is particularly effective for datasets with multiple frequently occurring ciphertexts, as it facilitates controlled transformation while maintaining the structural patterns in the image. This block map transformation effectively neutralizes the impact of rotating AES keys (if the user chooses to switch AES keys, the service provider trained model is already able to handle it due to its key-agnostic property. Hence, this modification is crucial to ensure the adversarial model remains effective across AES keys), enabling our attack to remain robust across key variations and make our attack effective on CryptoEyes. We apply two more advanced data transformations to make our model more robust at learning underlying contour information, while reducing the burden on the adversary to obtain a prohibitively large dataset.

4.2   Advanced Data Transformation for Labeled Encrypted Images

We discuss two advanced but effective, key-agnostic transformation methods on the permuted encrypted images, based on simple principles: 1) *Ciphertext Occlusion Replacement (COR)* Replacing minority ciphertext blocks with majority ciphertext, simulating occlusion in the underlying plaintext space. 2) *Markov-Based White Block Estimation (MWBE)* Using a Markov chain model to estimate white block placements and reconstruct label images while maintaining a controlled number of white blocks and maximizing likelihood. This method is especially effective on MNIST dataset.

4.3   Ciphertext Occlusion Replacement (COR)

The Ciphertext Occlusion Replacement (COR) method modifies the block map representation by replacing minority ciphertexts with the most frequently occurring ciphertext. This simulates occlusion in the underlying plaintext, where digit markings are masked by dominant ciphertext blocks. The process ensures that the transformed image remains within the encrypted domain, while introducing meaningful variations.

The COR transformation ensures that less frequent ciphertext representations are occluded by dominant ones, maintaining consistency with encrypted image structures while introducing controlled modifications.

4.4   Markov-Based White Block Estimation (MWBE)

The Markov-based White Block Estimation (MWBE) method generates transformed block maps by leveraging spatial dependencies within a given set of block maps corresponding to a fixed label (0–9). The process begins by computing the probability of each block being white across all provided block maps. It then selects an initial white block based on high probability and iteratively expands the white region using a Markov-based selection rule. The approach ensures

---

Algorithm 1. Ciphertext Occlusion Replacement (COR)

1: **Input:** Block map B of size $m \times n$, occlusion fraction ρ
2: **Output:** New occluded block map B'
3:
4: Compute the frequency of each pixel value in B
5: Identify the majority pixel value P_{maj} with the highest frequency
6: Identify the set of minority pixel values $\mathcal{P}_{min}$ occurring less frequently
7: Compute the total number of pixels to replace: $N_{occ} = \rho$
8: Initialize $B' \leftarrow B$
9: Randomly select N_{occ} pixels from $\mathcal{P}_{min}$
10: **for** each selected pixel (i, j) in B' **do**
11:      Replace $B'[i, j]$ with P_{maj}
12: **end for**
13: **return** B'

---

that the generated block maps align with the structural properties observed in the dataset while maintaining variability. This method as described, works well enough on MNIST dataset as seen in the results section. However, on datasets with multiple majority ciphertext blocks (ciphertexts with frequency greater than threshold), this method will need some modifications to adapt to the dataset.

We acknowledge that, given a moderately large dataset, advanced generative models such as Generative Adversarial Networks (GANs) [18,20,23], Variational Autoencoders (VAEs) [3,4,8], diffusion models [2,13,19], and normalizing flows can enhance block map generation by capturing intricate data distributions. These models learn complex dependencies within the data, facilitating the synthesis of encrypted images by learning to model the encrypted images provided in the training data. However, in this paper, we focus on simpler, home-brewed methods to demonstrate that significant results can be achieved without the computational complexity of more sophisticated models. The efficacy of these methods can be seen from the test accuracies, in the results section.

The block-map helps reduce the noise coming from block-wise AES encryption of the original images & make it simpler for generation of new encrypted images. After the block map transformation, the adversary can choose to apply any technique (COR, MWBE, VAE, GAN) for generating synthetic images from the block maps of train images, without having these methods to simulate the random AES encryption process which was used to generate the original train images. Later on, during training the adversary can choose to map these blocks back to original image sizes or apply the same transformation on test images during inference, to predict the class labels using the model trained on block maps.

Now we discuss the adversaries model to process the transformed, encrypted and permuted images to break the security of the CryptoEyes scheme.

Algorithm 2. Markov-based White Block Estimation (MWBE)

1: **Input:** Set of block maps $\mathcal{B} = \{B_1, B_2, \ldots, B_k\}$ of size $m \times n$ of label l, white block range $K_{\min}, K_{\max}$, maximum retries R

2: **Output:** New probabilistically generated block map B' for label l

3: Initialize B' as an empty block map of size $m \times n$

4: Compute initial probabilities $P(W_{i,j})$ for each block (i, j) across $\mathcal{B}$

5: Select an initial block (i_0, j_0) with high $P(W_{i,j}) > 0.6$

6: Initialize selected set $S = \{(i_0, j_0)\}$

7: Randomly sample $K \sim \mathcal{U}(K_{\min}, K_{\max})$

8: Set retry counter $r = 0$

9: **while** $|S| < K$ and $r < R$ **do**

10:     Compute conditional probabilities $P(W_{i,j}|W_{i',j'})$ for unselected (i, j) based on last selected $(i', j') \in S$

11:     **if** valid candidate blocks exist **then**

12:         Select next block (i, j) from top-ranked candidates

13:         Add (i, j) to S

14:     **else**

15:         Restart from (i_0, j_0) and increment retry counter r

16:     **end if**

17: **end while**

18: **for** each $(i, j) \in S$ **do**

19:     Set $B'[i, j] = 1$

20: **end for**

21: **return** B'

4.5   Model Architecture and Training Hyper-Parameters

The adversary's model design is inspired by the CryptoEyes framework (as deployed at server's end), particularly in its approach to handling encrypted images and extracting meaningful features from gradient maps. The proposed model follows a two-stream convolutional neural network (CNN), along with a LSTM head to improve classification performance on permuted images. The 2-stream CNN architecture is designed to process both encrypted image data and extracted gradient maps. This architecture is structured to leverage both raw encrypted features and contour-based representations to enhance classification performance. This also provides the model with AES key agnostic capabilities, which allow the model to classify images encrypted with new AES keys, as long as the secret permutation key is fixed and the same.

4.6   Processing via Gradient Map Computation

The contour-based features present in the encrypted images are crucial for classification task. To extract the contour features from the raw encrypted images, for better feature extraction capabilities, we use gradient maps. The gradient computation is based on the Sobel operator [11], applied via 3×3 convolutional kernels to compute horizontal and vertical gradients. The resulting gradient map is obtained using the Euclidean norm of these gradients, highlighting crucial structural elements within the encrypted input: $G_x(i,j) = \sum_{i,j} [k_1(i,j) \otimes I(i,j)]$ and $G_y(i,j) = \sum_{i,j} [k_2(i,j) \otimes I(i,j)]$, where I is the image, $I(i,j)$ is the pixel value, k_1 is horizontal kernel (3×3 Sobel operator), k_2 is vertical kernel (3×3 Sobel operator), G_x and G_y are the encrypted horizontal and vertical component, respectively. $\otimes$ is the tensor product. The gradient magnitude G (i.e., the gradient map) is given by: $G = \sqrt{G_x^2 + G_y^2}$.

4.7   Dual Stream Feature Extraction and Feature Fusion

The CNN architecture of the adversary processes two different input streams: the encrypted image stream and the gradient map stream. Each stream passes through multiple gated convolutional layers, where a primary convolution operation extracts features, and a parallel gating mechanism using a sigmoid activation function refines feature selection. Instead of standard ReLU [17] activations, we employ LeakyReLU [16] to allow for better gradient flow. The extracted feature maps undergo average pooling and max pooling operations to retain relevant information while reducing dimensionality.

After extracting features independently from both streams, the representations are flattened and concatenated to form a unified feature vector. This vector undergoes a reshaping operation to ensure compatibility with the recurrent classification head. By combining spatial and edge-based features, this fusion mechanism allows the model to leverage complementary information from both encrypted and gradient-enhanced representations.

4.8   LSTM-Based Classification Head

To effectively capture sequential dependencies and high-level feature interactions, we employ a Long Short-Term Memory (LSTM) network. Unlike a standard Multi-Layer Perceptron (MLP) head used in CryptoEyes, which processes features independently, LSTM effectively captures temporal dependencies and structured patterns within the fused feature representations. Its ability to retain long-range dependencies enables better discrimination of complex features, making it particularly suited for handling sequential or structured inputs derived from encrypted images and gradient maps. The output of the LSTM is passed through a fully connected softmax layer, which generates probability distributions over the target classes.

4.9   Training and Optimization

The model is trained using the Adam optimizer [12] with a learning rate of 0.00005 to ensure stable convergence. We use sparse categorical cross-entropy as the loss function to accommodate integer-based labels while optimizing classification performance. By leveraging gated convolutions, an optimized LSTM configuration, and an efficient feature extraction pipeline, the proposed model achieves robust performance in classifying encrypted visual data, without needing access to the secret keys.

4.10 Dataset and Training Setup

MNIST dataset consists of 60,000 training and 10,000 testing grayscale images of handwritten digits (0–9), each of size 28×28 pixels. It serves as benchmark in the image classification task. Each image represents a single digit, with pixel intensity values ranging from 0 to 255. Despite its relatively small size and simpler images, MNIST remains a fundamental dataset for testing pattern recognition algorithms, feature extraction techniques, and model generalization in various machine learning applications.

Our experiments were conducted on Kaggle's free tier that use an NVIDIA Tesla P100 GPU with 16GB VRAM, a vCPU (Intel Xeon), and 13GB of available RAM, running on a cloud-based Linux environment. Our models and training code is implemented on TensorFlow [1] framework.

We consider 10 image labels for training and testing the proposed model on MNIST dataset. The model can be trained using standard back propagation algorithm and stochastic gradient descent. The batch size in the conducted training experiments is 64 samples per batch, and the validation set size is 5% of MNIST train dataset (60,000 images).

Encrypting Train Images. Before training and inference, plaintext images undergo a two-layered transformation: (1) AES 128-bit block-wise encryption and (2) a fixed random permutation of $m \times m$ image blocks. We experiment with AES key sizes of 128, 192, and 256 bits while maintaining a fixed permutation sequence across train and test datasets. Varying the permutation sequence per batch introduces genuine randomness, preventing the model from learning permutation-specific patterns.

The grid size, a crucial hyperparameter, determines the number of blocks per image and the permutation sequence length. We fix a 7×7 grid with 4×4 encryption blocks, requiring a 49-length permutation randomly selected from 49! possible choices ($\sim 6 \times 10^{62}$). The encryption process remains consistent with CryptoEyes, ensuring reproducibility and robustness in our experiments. We randomly selected AES keys.

Encrypting Test Images. The test dataset consists of the standard 10,000 images from MNIST, encrypted using the same fixed permutation key as the training data to maintain consistency in spatial transformations. However, to ensure that the model learns features independent of specific AES keys, the encryption keys for test images are drawn from a different pool than those used for training. This setup evaluates the model's ability to generalize across varying encryption keys while preserving the structural constraints imposed by the fixed permutation. All other encryption parameters, including the grid size and encryption block size, remain unchanged from the training phase.

5   Results

In this section, we will show the classification accuracies of adversarial model on permuted encrypted images, in comparison to the classification accuracy of CryptoEyes model on (unpermuted) encrypted images of MNIST dataset. We consider all 10 labels in all the experiments and also show the results for few-shot learning scenario where the adversary is given few images per label. Our attack code is publicly available at https://github.com/JashwanthKadaru/Adversarial-Attack-on-Crypto-Eyes.

Table 2. Accuracy Over MNIST Across different AES Key sizes

Model	AES-128		AES-192		AES-256	
	Train	Test	Train	Test	Train	Test
Adversary	78.7%	74.9%	83.1%	74.2%	81.5%	73.8%
CryptoEyes	85.5%	84.9%	82.9%	82.4%	80.4%	80.0%

The results in Table 2 show that adversary can learn classification over permuted encrypted images and produce performance very similar to the service provider's Crypto Eyes model on encrypted images.

Table 3 presents the accuracy of the adversary's model trained with a limited number of image-label pairs, evaluated across different training set sizes after applying the 3 data transformation techniques discussed. The AES-key length used for encryption is 128 bits. This models a scenario where the adversary operates under practical constraints, with access to only a limited set of labeled training images.

Table 3. Accuracy of Adversary's Model with Varying Training Sizes and 128-bit AES key

	Images per Label				
	10 per label	30 per label	50 per label	100 per label	500 per label
Test Accuracy	36.6%	44.2%	46.4%	51.6%	60.7%
Train Accuracy	43.3%	54.4%	53.8%	56.3%	69.4%

6   Conclusion

The findings presented in this study underscore the adversary's ability to achieve competitive classification performance despite the 2-fold protection of images: encryption and permutation of image blocks, highlighting potential vulnerabilities in CryptoEyes. We have shown 3 attacks to demonstrate that the adversary can achieve higher accuracy than claimed by CryptoEyes. In the naive attack, the AES encryption key needs to be the same for the train and the test set. However, our advanced attack is key agnostic, making it more powerful and realistic. While CryptoEyes demonstrates superior robustness, the results suggest that additional security mechanisms may be required to further mitigate adversarial efficacy. For future work, it will be interesting to mount an attack on the CryptoEyes protocol that does not have access to the training data set as such attacks are more realistic.

Acknowledgment. This work was partially funded by the Privacy-Preserving Data Processing and Exchange for Sensitive Data in the National Digital Public Infrastructure (P3DX) project, and the Infosys Foundation Career Development Chair Professorship grant for Srinivas Vivek.

References

1. Abadi, M., et al.: TensorFlow: large-scale machine learning on heterogeneous systems (2015). https://www.tensorflow.org. Accessed 22 Feb 2025
2. Bot66: MNIST diffusion (2023). https://github.com/bot66/MNISTDiffusion
3. Chollet, F.: Variational autoencoder (2020). https://keras.io/examples/generative/vae/
4. Chou, J.: Generated loss and augmented training of MNIST VAE. arXiv preprint arXiv:1904.10937 (2019)
5. Cramer, R., Damgård, I., Nielsen, J.B.: Multiparty computation from threshold homomorphic encryption. In: Pfitzmann, B. (ed.) EUROCRYPT 2001. LNCS, vol. 2045, pp. 280–300. Springer, Heidelberg (2001). https://doi.org/10.1007/3-540-44987-6_18
6. Daemen, J., Rijmen, V.: The Design of Rijndael: AES-the Advanced Encryption Standard. Springer, Heidelberg (2002). https://doi.org/10.1007/978-3-662-60769-5
7. van Dijk, M., Gentry, C., Halevi, S., Vaikuntanathan, V.: Fully homomorphic encryption over the integers. In: Gilbert, H. (ed.) EUROCRYPT 2010. LNCS, vol. 6110, pp. 24–43. Springer, Heidelberg (2010). https://doi.org/10.1007/978-3-642-13190-5_2
8. Fisher, C.K., Kansal, R.: Variational autoencoders with keras and MNIST (2018). https://fnallpc.github.io/machine-learning-hats/notebooks/5-vae-mnist.html
9. He, W., Wei, M., Li, S., Qiu, B., Wang, W.: CryptoEyes: privacy preserving classification over encrypted images. In: IEEE INFOCOM 2021 - IEEE Conference on Computer Communications. IEEE (2021). https://doi.org/10.1109/INFOCOM42981.2021.9488738

10. Hinton, G.E., Osindero, S., Teh, Y.W.: A fast learning algorithm for deep belief nets. Neural Comput. **18**(7), 1527–1554 (2006). https://doi.org/10.1162/neco.2006.18.7.1527
11. Kanopoulos, N., Vasanthavada, N., Baker, R.: Design of an edge detection filter using the sobel operator. IEEE J. Solid-State Circuits **23**(2), 358–367 (1988)
12. Kingma, D.P., Ba, J.: Adam: a method for stochastic optimization. arXiv preprint arXiv:1412.6980 (2014)
13. Kong, Z., Ping, W., Huang, J., Catanzaro, B.: Effective data augmentation with diffusion models. arXiv preprint arXiv:2302.07944 (2023)
14. LeCun, Y., Bengio, Y., Hinton, G.: Deep learning. Nature **521**(7553), 436–444 (2015). https://doi.org/10.1038/nature14539
15. LeCun, Y., Bottou, L., Bengio, Y., Haffner, P.: Gradient-based learning applied to document recognition. Proc. IEEE **86**(11), 2278–2324 (1998). https://doi.org/10.1109/5.726791
16. Maas, A.L., Hannun, A.Y., Ng, A.Y.: Rectifier nonlinearities improve neural network acoustic models. In: Proceedings of the 30th International Conference on Machine Learning (ICML), pp. 3–8 (2013)
17. Nair, V., Hinton, G.E.: Rectified linear units improve restricted Boltzmann machines. Proceedings of the 27th International Conference on Machine Learning (ICML), pp. 807–814 (2010)
18. Nguyen, T.T., Le, T., Tran, H., Phung, D.: On data augmentation for GAN training. arXiv preprint arXiv:2006.05338 (2020)
19. Saha, E., Tran, G.: Diffusion random feature model. arXiv preprint arXiv:2310.04417 (2023)
20. Valle, R., Shih, K.J., Lee, H.Y., Essa, I.: Evaluation of generative networks through their data augmentation capacity. OpenReview (2018). https://openreview.net/forum?id=HJ1HFlZAb
21. Vincent, P., Larochelle, H., Lajoie, I., Bengio, Y., Manzagol, P.A.: Stacked denoising autoencoders: learning useful representations in a deep network with a local denoising criterion. J. Mach. Learn. Res. **11**, 3371–3408 (2010)
22. Wang, X., Reeves, D.S.: Robust correlation of encrypted attack traffic through stepping stones by manipulation of inter-packet delays. In: Proceedings of the 10th ACM Conference on Computer and Communications Security. ACM (2003)
23. Yao, Y., et al.: Conditional variational autoencoder with balanced pre-training for generative adversarial networks. arXiv preprint arXiv:2201.04809 (2022)
24. Yu, J., Wang, J., Tao, D., Song, X., Wang, M.: iPrivacy: image privacy protection by identifying sensitive objects via deep multi-task learning. IEEE Trans. Inf. Forensics Secur. **12**(5), 1005–1016 (2017)

Randomness Efficient Algorithms for Estimating Average Gate Fidelity via k-Wise Classical and Quantum Independence

Aditya Nema[1,2,3] and Pranab Sen[3(✉)]

[1] Indian Institute of Technology Gandhinagar , Palaj, Gandhinagar 382055, India
`aditya.nema@iitgn.ac.in`
[2] Institute for Quantum Information, RWTH Aachen University, 52074 Aachen, Germany
[3] Tata Institute of Fundamental Research, Mumbai 400005, India
`pranab.sen.73@gmail.com`

Abstract. We present three new algorithms for efficient in-place estimation of average fidelity of a d dimensional quantum logic gate, without using ancilla qubits. The main advantage of our algorithms is the much smaller usage of truly random bits compared to what was known so far. Reducing the requirement of classical seed randomness increases the reliability of estimation, as high quality random bits are usually an expensive computational resource. Commonly used sources of random bits are strictly speaking either pseudorandom or have a non-trivial bias.

Previous approaches for this task replaced Haar random unitaries in the naive estimation algorithm by approximate unitary 2-designs by sampling them uniformly and independently. In contrast, in our first algorithm we sample the unitaries of the approximate unitary 2-design uniformly using a limited independence pseudorandom generator, highlighting the usage of computational derandomization theory for quantum computation. This algorithm uses $O((\log d)(\log \epsilon^{-1}))$ random bits in contrast to $\Omega(\epsilon^{-2}(\log d)(\log \epsilon^{-1}))$ random bits used in the previous works, with the same number of gate evaluations (c.f. [Dankert et al., Physical Rev. A **80**, 012034 (2009)]).

Our second efficient algorithm, uses a quantum 4-tensor product expander, in the regime of large gate dimension d and not "too small" estimation error. It uses even lesser random bits than the first algorithm, and has the added advantage that it needs to implement only one unitary from an approximate 4-design as opposed to potentially all unitaries from an approximate 2-design in previous algorithms. This is significantly advantageous for NISQ machines and early fault tolerant quantum computers where one wants to minimize the number of times the quantum RAM needs to be loaded due to coherence time limitations.

Our third efficient algorithm, based on an l-quantum tensor product expander for moderately large values of l, works for all values of the parameters. It uses slightly more random bits than the other algorithms but has the advantage that it needs to implement only a small number

N. Hubballi et al. (Eds.): ICISS 2025, LNCS 16380, pp. 208–230, 2026.
https://doi.org/10.1007/978-3-032-13714-2_14

of unitaries from an approximate l-design versus potentially all the unitaries of an approximate 2-design in previous algorithms. This advantage can be of great importance to the experimental implementations in the near future.

Keywords: Average gate fidelity · randomized benchmarking · approximate unitary t-designs · classical derandomization theory

1   Introduction

Unitary quantum logic gates serve as the basic building blocks of quantum circuits implementing quantum algorithms. They are nothing but unitary operators chosen from a predetermined set. Implementation of any quantum algorithm is achieved by application of an appropriate sequence of these gates. However, in practice there is always some error between the ideal gate output given a particular input state and the actual gate output because of noise. Thus if we want to apply a quantum gate, it is desirable that the noisy experimental version Λ be close to the ideal gate $\mathbf{U}$ with respect to some measure. Most works use the so-called *fidelity* as a measure of closeness. This leads to the notion of gate fidelity for a particular input state. Notice that this characterisation depends on the quantum state inputted to the gate. However when the gate is used as part of a quantum circuit, it may not be feasible to figure out the states that may possibly be inputted to the gate during the course of operation of the circuit. One would like to remove this state dependence in the definition of gate fidelity and instead come up with a quantity that serves as a general measure of the quality of the gate implementation. One way to do this is to consider the gate fidelity averaged over the Haar probability measure on all possible pure input states. This quantity is called the *average gate fidelity* [1].

Estimating average gate fidelity has become especially urgent these days due to the spectacular advances in experimental quantum computation. Exciting demonstrations of quantum computing power are already being given by the 50–150 qubit processors at Google, IBM, Quantinuum etc. If a fully fault tolerant quantum computer is brought to fruition, then current worldwide standard cryptography and cybersecurity protocols will collapse due to Shor's algorithms for integer factoring and discrete logarithm [23]. Hence it is important to calibrate and measure progress in quantum computation by sound benchmarking. Average gate fidelity estimation, and its close cousin randomized benchmarking, are the best methods we have at present for benchmarking experimental quantum computers. They can also be used to benchmark sources and detectors for quantum key distribution (QKD) protocols, which ideally give unbreakable cybersecurity guaranteed by the fundamental laws of physics, independent of any computational assumptions.

Emerson et al. [1] gave an algorithm for estimating the average fidelity of a unitary d-dimensional gate using several independent samples of $d \times d$ Haar random unitaries. While they did not explicitly bound the number of samples required in order to obtain an estimate of the average fidelity to within an additive error of ϵ, their method can be analyzed to show that $O(\epsilon^{-2})$ independent Haar random samples of unitaries suffice. This is prohibitively expensive, both in terms of the computational cost required to implement the Haar random unitaries as well as in terms of the number of random bits required to do the sampling. Both these quantities are at least $\Omega(\epsilon^{-2}\frac{d^2}{\log d}\log(1/\epsilon))$ [21, Corollary 4.2.13]. Later works [2,3] showed that the computational cost and the number of random bits can be drastically brought down by choosing independent uniform samples from a unitary 2-design. Again, these papers did not rigorously estimate the running time and the usage of random bits of their algorithm, but nevertheless those can be analysed to obtain a bound of $O(\epsilon^{-2}\text{polylog}(d/\epsilon))$ for both.

In this paper, we treat the usage of classical random bits as a resource and try to minimize it. One of the reasons behind this is that high quality random bits are an expensive computational resource, a realisation that has roots going back to the classic work of Knuth [25] from the 1960s. Classical random number generators are either pseudo-random or have a bias or are limited by the energy constraints of the underlying hardware. These limitations have led to the development of quantum random number generators (QRNGs); see the review article by Mannalath et al. [24] for an up to date summary of QRNGs. Thus, reducing random bits while preserving the efficiency of the algorithm and the estimation error would generally lead to more reliable estimation in practice. In fact, one of the motivations for QRNGs is precisely more accurate estimation of parameters and simulation of complex physical systems. However, high quality device independent QRNGs secure against quantum adversaries often have low random bit rates [24]. In view of this, it becomes especially important to reduce the requirement of true random bits for average gate fidelity estimation. Currently we have experimental realizations of quantum circuits on 50 to 150 qubits, and they have to be benchmarked accurately and reliably so as to carry out a reliable computing task practically.

Another reason behind reducing the number of random bits is that it often gives us deep insights into the algorithms involved, leading to serendipitous additional optimizations that may have otherwise escaped our attention. In this paper, we shall actually see an example of such a serendipitous optimization. Our second and third algorithms not only use far less random bits that what was known earlier; they also require the algorithms to implement a much smaller set of unitaries from approximate designs than potentially all unitaries of an approximate 2-design in earlier works [2,3]. This is very important for the near future because implementing a wide range of unitaries is technologically fraught with immense challenges. One major challenge will be loading a quantum random access memory (RAM) with new samples repeatedly owing to its fragility.

We give three new algorithms for efficient in-place estimation, without using ancilla qubits, of the average fidelity of a quantum logic gate acting on a d dimensional system using much fewer random bits than what was known so far. We consider in-place algorithms only because good quality qubits are likely to remain a very expensive resource in near-term experimental implementations, and so we want to avoid ancilla qubits as much as possible. Our algorithms use some cutting edge tools from both classical as well as quantum derandomization theory. An excellent introduction to classical derandomization techniques can be found in Goldreich's book [20].

In our first algorithm, in contrast to earlier works, we sample the unitaries of the approximate unitary 2-design uniformly using a limited independence pseudorandom generator [15,16], a powerful tool from derandomization theory. This algorithm uses $O(\epsilon^{-2}(\log \delta^{-1})(\log d)(\log \epsilon^{-1}))$ number of basic operations in order to estimate the average gate fidelity to within an additive error ϵ with confidence $1 - \delta$, which is the same as [2]. However, it only uses $O((\log \delta^{-1})((\log d)(\log \epsilon^{-1}) + \log\log \delta^{-1}))$ random bits, which is much lesser number than the $\Omega(\epsilon^{-2}(\log d)(\log \epsilon^{-1}))$ random bits used in the previous works.

Our second efficient algorithm, based on a 4-quantum tensor product expander [19], works if the gate dimension d is large and the estimation error requirement is not too tiny. It uses even lesser random bits than the first algorithm, and has the added advantage that it needs to implement only one unitary from an approximate 4-design versus potentially all the unitaries of an approximate 2-design in the first algorithm. Our third efficient algorithm, based on an l-quantum tensor product expander [19] for moderately large values of l, works for all values of the parameters. It uses slightly more random bits than the other algorithms but has the advantage that it needs to implement only a small number of unitaries from an approximate l-design versus potentially all the unitaries of an approximate 2-design in the first algorithm.

2   Notation and Preliminaries

Throughout the paper, $\mathcal{H}$ denotes a complex Hilbert space of finite dimension d and $\mathcal{H}^{\otimes m}$ denotes the m fold tensor product of $\mathcal{H}$. The notation $\bar{a}$ is used to denote complex conjugate of the underlying complex number a. We use $\mathbf{1}$ to denote the identity operator on $\mathcal{H}$. $\mathcal{M}_{k,d}$ denotes the vector space of $k \times d$ linear operators over complex field and $\mathcal{M}_d = \mathcal{M}_{d,d}$. Note that $\mathcal{M}_d$ is itself a Hilbert space of dimension d^2 with Hilbert-Schmidt inner product, defined as: $\langle A, B \rangle \triangleq Tr(A^\dagger B)$. For $p > 0$, we let $\|\cdot\|_p$ denote the Schatten p-norm of operators in $\mathcal{M}_d$, defined as: $\|A\|_p \triangleq [\mathrm{Tr}\,(A^\dagger A)^{p/2}]^{1/p}$. This is nothing but the ℓ_p-norm of the vector of singular values of A. The case $p = 1$ is called the *trace norm*. The case $p = 2$ is the Frobenius norm or the Hilbert-Schmidt norm induced from the eponymous inner product. Letting $p \to \infty$ gives us the Schatten ℓ_∞-norm which is nothing but the largest singular value of A, aka operator norm or spectral norm of A. Often, we use ρ to denote a quantum state or a density matrix which is a Hermitian, positive semidefinite matrix with unit trace. We let $\mathcal{D}(d)$ denote the set of all $d \times d$ density matrices. A pure quantum state is a rank-one density matrix. We denote by $\mathbb{CP}^{d-1}$ the set of pure quantum states in $\mathcal{H}$. The notation $|\cdot\rangle$ denotes a vector of unit ℓ_2-length.

We use Λ to denote the noisy experimental realization of an ideal unitary quantum gate $\mathbf{U}$. For a bipartite Hilbert space $\mathcal{H}_1 \otimes \mathcal{H}_2$, the partial trace $\mathrm{Tr}\,_{\mathcal{H}_2}$

denotes the operation of tracing out $\mathcal{H}_2$. We use X to denote a random variable and $\bar{X}$ to denote its expected value with respect to a probability measure μ, i.e., $\bar{X} \triangleq \int X \, d\mu$. The notation $\mathrm{Var}(X)$ denotes the variance of random variable X, i.e. $Var(X) = \overline{(X - \bar{X})^2}$. The symbol $\mathbb{U}(d)$ stands for the the unitary group on $\mathcal{H}$ i.e. the group of $d \times d$ complex unitary matrices. We tacitly assume that the ceiling is taken of any formula that provides dimension or value of t in unitary t-design. The symbol Haar is used to denote the unique unitarily invariant Haar probability measure on $\mathbb{U}(d)$, or $\mathbb{CP}^{d-1}$ as appropriate. Expectation with respect to a measure μ is denoted by $\mathbb{E}_\mu[\cdot]$.

Fidelity between two quantum states ρ and σ is defined as: $F(\rho, \sigma) \triangleq \|\sqrt{\rho}\sqrt{\sigma}\|_1^2 = (\mathrm{Tr}\sqrt{\sqrt{\rho}\sigma\sqrt{\rho}})^2$. Fidelity is a measure of distinguishabilty of two states. It is easy to see that $F(\rho, \sigma) = 1$ implies ρ and σ are identical, and $F(\rho, \sigma) = 0$ implies that ρ and σ have orthogonal support and there exists a single measurement that distinguishes them perfectly. Fidelity is related to trace distance via the following inequality, also known as Fuchs-Van de Graaf inequalities.

$$1 - \sqrt{F(\rho, \sigma)} \leq \frac{\|\rho - \sigma\|_1}{2} \leq \sqrt{1 - F(\rho, \sigma)}. \tag{1}$$

A linear mapping $\Lambda : \mathcal{M}_m \to \mathcal{M}_d$ is called a super operator, and a super operator which is completely positive and trace preserving is considered as a quantum operation. The vector space of superoperators is denoted by $L(\mathcal{M}_m, \mathcal{M}_d)$ or just $L(\mathcal{M}_m)$ if $m = d$. Let $\mathbf{U} \in \mathbb{U}(d)$. Then $\mathbf{U}$ is also a quantum operation defined as $\mathbf{U}(\rho) = U\rho U^\dagger$. Suppose Λ is a 'noisy' implementation of the unitary quantum operation $\mathbf{U}$. Then Λ is a quantum operation from $\mathcal{M}_d$ to $\mathcal{M}_d$, and so it can be represented using *Kraus operators* as $\Lambda(\rho) = \sum_k A_k \rho A_k^\dagger$, where $\{A_k\}_k$ are $d \times d$ matrices called Kraus operators of Λ, with the property that $\Sigma_k A_k^\dagger A_k = \mathbf{1}$. It turns out that d^2 Kraus operators suffice to describe any quantum operation from $\mathcal{M}_d$ to $\mathcal{M}_d$. We shall measure the distance between two superoperators via the so-called *diamond norm* [18]. The diamond norm of a superoperator $\Lambda : \mathcal{M}_d \to \mathcal{M}_d$ is defined as follows:

$$\|\Lambda\|_\diamond := \sup_m \max_{X \in \mathcal{M}_{dm} : \|X\|_1 = 1} \|(\mathbb{I}_m \otimes \Lambda)(X)\|_1 = \max_{X \in \mathcal{M}_{d^2} : \|X\|_1 = 1} \|(\mathbb{I}_d \otimes \Lambda)(X)\|_1,$$

where $\mathbb{I}_m$ is the identity superoperator on $\mathcal{M}_m$. A quantum operation Λ always has $\|\Lambda\|_\diamond = 1$.

Gate fidelity between Λ and $\mathbf{U}$ for an input state ρ is defined as:

$$\mathcal{F}_{\Lambda, \mathbf{U}}(\rho) \triangleq F(\Lambda(\rho), \mathbf{U}(\rho)) = (\mathrm{Tr}\sqrt{\sqrt{\Lambda(\rho)}\mathbf{U}(\rho)\sqrt{\Lambda(\rho)}})^2.$$

The average gate fidelity $\bar{\mathcal{F}}_{\Lambda, \mathbf{U}}$ is now defined to be the expectation of the gate fidelity $\mathcal{F}_{\Lambda, \mathbf{U}}(|\psi\rangle\langle\psi|)$ for pure input states $|\psi\rangle\langle\psi|$ chosen from the Haar probability measure on $\mathbb{CP}^{d-1}$:

$$\bar{\mathcal{F}}_{\Lambda, \mathbf{U}} := \int_{\mathbb{CP}^{d-1}} (\mathrm{Tr}\sqrt{\sqrt{\Lambda(\rho)}\mathbf{U}(\rho)\sqrt{\Lambda(\rho)}})^2 \, d\,\mathrm{Haar}(\psi)$$

In practice, when one wants to benchmark the quality of the experimental implementation of a unitary quantum logic gate $\mathbf{U}$, one runs the implementation twice, first in the forward direction followed by the backward direction. If the implementation were indeed perfect, this would just do the quantum operation $\mathbf{U}^{-1}\mathbf{U} = \mathbf{1}$. But because the implementation is noisy what we get is a quantum operation, which we will again denote by Λ, that is close to the identity quantum operation. Let $|\psi\rangle$ be a unit length vector in $\mathcal{H}$. Define

$$\mathcal{F}_\Lambda(|\psi\rangle) \triangleq \langle\psi|\Lambda(|\psi\rangle\langle\psi|)|\psi\rangle.$$

Alternately, let $V \in \mathbb{U}(d)$. Define

$$\mathcal{F}_\Lambda(V) \triangleq \langle 0|V^{-1}\Lambda(V|0\rangle\langle 0|V^{-1})V|0\rangle.$$

Then the average gate fidelity of Λ is given by

$$\bar{\mathcal{F}}_\Lambda \triangleq \bar{\mathcal{F}}_{\Lambda,\mathbf{1}} = \int_{\mathbb{CP}^{d-1}} \langle\psi|\Lambda(|\psi\rangle\langle\psi|)|\psi\rangle d\,\mathrm{Haar}(\psi) = \int_{\mathbb{U}(d)} \mathcal{F}_\Lambda(V) d\,\mathrm{Haar}(V).$$

The average gate fidelity defined above has a nice expression in terms of the Kraus operators of Λ [1]:

$$\bar{\mathcal{F}}_\Lambda = \sum_k \frac{|\mathrm{Tr}\, A_k|^2 + d}{d^2 + d}.$$

The variance of the gate fidelity under the Haar measure on $d \times d$ unitaries V happens to satisfy the following inequality [11, Equation 18].

$$\mathrm{Var}_V[\mathcal{F}_\Lambda(V)] \leq \frac{26}{d}. \tag{2}$$

The gate fidelity is an example of a function from the unit ℓ_2-norm sphere S^{2d-1} in $\mathbb{C}^d$ to $\mathbb{R}$. More generally, consider a function $f : (S^{2d-1})^{\times t} \to \mathbb{R}$ defined on a direct product of t spheres. Let $\eta > 0$. The function f is said to be η-*Lipschitz* if for all unit length vectors $v_1, \ldots v_t, w_1, \ldots, w_t \in S^{2d-1}$, we have

$$|f(v_1, \ldots v_t) - f(w_1, \ldots, w_t)| \leq \eta \sqrt{\sum_{i=1}^{t} \|v_i - w_i\|_2^2}.$$

The following fact was proved in [17, Lemma 2.7].

Fact 1. *Let $\eta > 0$. Let $f : (S^{2d-1})^{\times t} \to \mathbb{R}$ be η-Lipschitz. Consider the probability distribution on points $(v_1, \ldots, v_t) \in (S^{2d-1})^{\times t}$ where the v_is are chosen independently from the Haar measure on S^{2d-1}. Define*

$$\mu \triangleq \mathbb{E}_{(v_1,\ldots,v_t)}[f(v_1, \ldots, v_t)].$$

Let $\delta > 0$. Then,

$$\Pr_{(v_1,\ldots,v_t)}[|f(v_1, \ldots, v_t) - \mu| > \delta] \leq 4\exp(-\frac{\delta^2 d}{16\eta^2}).$$

Now let f be the following function

$$f(|\psi_1\rangle, \ldots, |\psi_t\rangle) \triangleq t^{-1} \sum_{i=1}^{t} F_\Lambda(|\psi_i\rangle).$$

Trivially,

$$\mu \triangleq \mathbb{E}_{|\psi_1\rangle,\ldots,|\psi_t\rangle}[f(|\psi_1\rangle, \ldots, |\psi_t\rangle)] = \bar{\mathcal{F}}_\Lambda.$$

It is easy to see that

$$|f(|\psi_1\rangle, \ldots, |\psi_t\rangle) - f(|\phi_1\rangle, \ldots, |\phi_t\rangle)|$$

$$= t^{-1}|\sum_{i=1}^{t}(\mathcal{F}_\Lambda(|\psi_i\rangle) - \mathcal{F}_\Lambda(|\phi_i\rangle))| \leq t^{-1}\sum_{i=1}^{t}|\mathcal{F}_\Lambda(|\psi_i\rangle) - \mathcal{F}_\Lambda(|\phi_i\rangle)|$$

$$\leq t^{-1}\sum_{i=1}^{t}(|\mathrm{Tr}\,[\Lambda(|\psi_i\rangle\langle\psi_i|)|\psi_i\rangle\langle\psi_i|] - \mathrm{Tr}\,[\Lambda(|\psi_i\rangle\langle\psi_i|)|\phi_i\rangle\langle\phi_i|]| + |\mathrm{Tr}\,[\Lambda(|\psi_i\rangle\langle\psi_i|)|\phi_i\rangle\langle\phi_i|]$$

$$- \mathrm{Tr}\,[\Lambda(|\phi_i\rangle\langle\phi_i|)|\phi_i\rangle\langle\phi_i|]|)$$

$$\leq t^{-1}\sum_{i=1}^{t}(\||\psi_i\rangle\langle\psi_i|] - |\phi_i\rangle\langle\phi_i|\|_1 + \|\Lambda(|\psi_i\rangle\langle\psi_i|) - \Lambda(|\phi_i\rangle\langle\phi_i|)\|_1)$$

$$\leq 2t^{-1}\sum_{i=1}^{t}\||\psi_i\rangle\langle\psi_i| - |\phi_i\rangle\langle\phi_i|\|_1 \leq 4t^{-1}\sum_{i=1}^{t}\||\psi_i\rangle - |\phi_i\rangle\|_2 \leq 4t^{-1/2}\sqrt{\sum_{i=1}^{t}\||\psi_i\rangle - |\phi_i\rangle\|_2^2},$$

which shows that the Lipschitz constant $\eta \leq 4t^{-1/2}$. Let $\delta > 0$. Consider the probability distribution on points $(V_1, \ldots, V_t) \in \mathbb{U}(d)^{\times t}$ obtained by choosing each V_i independently from the Haar measure. Define $f(V_1, \ldots, V_t)$ in the natural fashion i.e. now the arguments to the function consist of linear operators and function definition remains the same. By Fact 1,

$$\Pr_{(V_1,\ldots,V_t)}[|f(V_1, \ldots, V_t) - \mu| > \delta] \leq 4\exp(-\frac{\delta^2 dt}{256}). \tag{3}$$

Now, we define an approximate unitary 2-design via the so-called *twirling operation* as in [2]. Let ν be a probability measure on $\mathbb{U}(d)$. Let Λ be a superoperator on $\mathcal{M}_d$. Define the ν-twirling operation $E_\nu : L(\mathcal{M}_d) \to L(\mathcal{M}_d)$ as follows:

$$E_\nu(\Lambda) \triangleq \left(X \to \int_{\mathbb{U}(d)} V^\dagger\Lambda(VXV^\dagger)V \, d\nu(V)\right), \tag{4}$$

where $\Lambda \in L(\mathcal{M}_d)$ and $X \in \mathcal{M}_d$. When ν is the Haar probability measure on $\mathbb{U}(d)$, we shall write the above superoperator as $E_{\mathrm{Haar}}(\Lambda)$.

Definition 1. *The probability measure ν is an ϵ-approximate unitary 2-design if:*

$$\|E_\nu(\Lambda) - E_{\mathrm{Haar}}(\Lambda)\|_\diamond \leq \epsilon\|\Lambda\|_\diamond \tag{5}$$

for all superoperators $\Lambda \in L(\mathcal{M}_d)$. If $\epsilon = 0$, then ν is said to be an exact unitary 2-design.

We now recall the definition of a quantum tensor product expander [19].

Definition 2. *A quantum t-tensor product expander (t-qTPE) in $\mathcal{H}$, $|\mathcal{H}| = d$, of degree s can be defined as a quantum operation $\mathcal{G} : L(\mathcal{H}^{\otimes t}) \to L(\mathcal{H}^{\otimes t})$ that can be expressed as $\mathcal{G}(M) = \frac{1}{s}\sum_{i=1}^{s}(U_i)^{\otimes t}M(U_i^{-1})^{\otimes t}$, for any matrix $M \in L(\mathcal{H}^{\otimes t})$, where $\{U_i\}_{i=1}^{s}$ are $d \times d$ unitary matrices. The qTPE is said to have second singular value λ if $\|\mathcal{G}-\mathcal{I}\|_\infty \leq \lambda$, where $\mathcal{I}$ is the 'ideal' quantum operation defined by its action on a matrix M by $\mathcal{I}(M) := \int_{U \in \mathbb{U}(D)} U^{\otimes t}M(U^\dagger)^{\otimes t}\,d\,\mathrm{Haar}(U)$. In other words, if $M \in L(\mathcal{H}^{\otimes t})$, then $\|\mathcal{G}(M) - \mathcal{I}(M)\|_2 \leq \lambda\|M\|_2$. We use the notation (d, s, λ, t)-qTPE to denote such a quantum tensor product expander.*

From the above definition, it is easy to see that a (d, s, λ, t)-qTPE is also simultaneously a (d, s, λ, t')-qTPE for any $t' < t$.

Let $X_1, X_2, \ldots, X_n$ be a sequence of $\{0, 1\}$-valued random variables. Let $2 \leq k \leq n$. Let $S \subseteq \{1, 2, \ldots, n\}$, $S = \{s_1, s_2, \ldots, s_k\}$. Let $X_{s_1}X_{s_2}\cdots X_{s_k}$ denote the actual joint distribution of the corresponding random variables. Let $0 < p < 1$. Let $B(k, p)$ denote the Bernoulli distribution i.e. the distribution of k fully independent identical coin tosses with probability of a coin turning up HEAD equal to p. The sequence $X_1, X_2, \ldots, X_n$ is said to be *θ-approximate p-biased k-wise independent* if for any subset $S = \{s_1, \ldots, s_k\}$,

$$\|X_{s_1}X_{s_2}\cdots X_{s_k} - B(k, p)\|_1 \leq \theta,$$

i.e. the joint probability distribution of any subset of the random variables of size k is θ-close to the Bernoulli distribution in ℓ_1-distance.

We first state a Chernoff bound for a fully independent (i.e. 0-approximate n-wise independent) sequence of random variables. This bound can be derived from [7, Corollary A.1.14].

Fact 2. *Let $X_1, X_2, \ldots, X_n$ be a fully independent sequence of identically distributed $\{0, 1\}$-valued random variables. Let $p \triangleq \mathbb{E}[X]$. Let $0 < \epsilon < p$. Let $X \triangleq n^{-1}\sum_{i=1}^{n} X_i$. Then*

$$\Pr[|X - p| > \epsilon] \leq 2\exp(-\frac{\epsilon^2 n}{3}).$$

We now state a Chernoff-like bound for θ-approximte k-wise independent random variables. This bound can be derived from [16, Theorem 5].

Fact 3. *Let $X_1, X_2, \ldots, X_n$ be a θ-approximate p-biased k-wise independent sequence of $\{0, 1\}$-valued random variables. Let $0 < \epsilon < p$. Let $X \triangleq n^{-1}\sum_{i=1}^{n} X_i$. Suppose $k = e^{-1/3}\epsilon^2 n$. Then,*

$$\Pr[|X - p| > \epsilon] \leq \exp(-k/2) + \theta(\frac{n}{\epsilon})^k.$$

We now recall that a θ-approximate $1/2$-biased k-wise independent sequence of random bits can be efficiently constructed by spending only a small amount of truly random bits [15, Theorem 3].

Fact 4. *Let k, n be positive integers, $\theta > 0$ and $r \triangleq k + 2\log\log k + 2\log\log n + 2\log\theta^{-1}$. Then there is a function $f : \{0,1\}^r \to \{0,1\}^n$ such that, if the uniform distribution on $\{0,1\}^r$ is provided at the input, the resulting sequence $X_1, X_2, \ldots, X_n$ at the output is a θ-approximate $1/2$-biased k-wise independent sequence of random bits. Moreover there is a deterministic algorithm that, given an input string $z \in \{0,1\}^r$ and a bit position $i \in \{1, 2, \ldots, n\}$, computes the output bit $f(z)_i$ in time $\mathrm{poly}(r)$.*

Facts 3 and 4 allow us to prove the following easily.

Fact 5. *Let $\mathcal{Y}$ be a set and g a function $g : \mathcal{Y} \to [0,1]$. Let $p \triangleq \mathbb{E}_Y[g(Y)]$, where the expectation is taken over the random variable Y uniformly distributed on $\mathcal{Y}$. Let n be a positive integer, $\epsilon, \theta > 0$ and $r \triangleq 4\epsilon^2 n \log |\mathcal{Y}|) + 2\log\theta^{-1}$. Then there is a function $f : \{0,1\}^r \to \mathcal{Y}^n$ such that, if the uniform distribution on $\{0,1\}^r$ is provided at the input, the resulting sequence $X_1, X_2, \ldots, X_n$ of random bits at the output, where $X_i = 1$ with probability $g(Y_i)$ and 0 otherwise, satisfies*

$$\Pr[|X - p| > \epsilon] \leq \exp(-\epsilon^2 n/4) + \theta(\frac{n}{\epsilon})^{\frac{\epsilon^2 n}{4}},$$

X being defined as $n^{-1}\sum_{i=1}^n X_i$. Moreover, there is a deterministic algorithm that, given an input string $z \in \{0,1\}^r$ and a position $i \in \{1, 2, \ldots, n\}$, computes the output element $f(z)_i \in \mathcal{Y}$ in time $\mathrm{poly}(r)\log|\mathcal{Y}|$.

3 Bounding the Tail of the Gate Fidelity Distribution

In this section, we show how to bound the tail of the gate fidelity distribution, both under the Haar measure as well as under the uniform measure on a qTPE. As a warm up, we first show that approximate unitary 2-designs and 2-qTPEs are related.

Fact 6. *A $(d, s, \lambda, 2)$-qTPE is a (λd^4)-approximate unitary 2-design consisting of s unitaries.*

Proof. Let S denote the swap operator on $\mathcal{H}^{\otimes 2} \otimes \mathcal{H}^{\otimes 2}$ which swaps the two multiplicands of the central tensor product symbol. Swap is a unitary operation. Let V be a unitary operator, and X a linear operator on $\mathcal{H} \otimes \mathcal{H}$. Let $\mathbf{1}$ denote the identity operator on $\mathcal{H}$. Let $\mathbb{I}$ be the identity superoperator on $L(\mathcal{H})$. Let $\Lambda : L(\mathcal{H}) \to L(\mathcal{H})$ be a superoperator. Then,

$$\left| \mathrm{Tr}\left[\left(\left(s^{-1} \sum_{i=1}^s (U_i^{-1} \otimes \mathbf{1}) ((\Lambda \otimes \mathbb{I})((U_i \otimes \mathbf{1}) X (U_i^{-1} \otimes \mathbf{1}))) (U_i \otimes \mathbf{1}) \right) \right. \right.$$

$$\left. \left. - \left(\int_{\mathbb{U}(d)} (U^{-1} \otimes \mathbf{1}) ((\Lambda \otimes \mathbb{I})((U \otimes \mathbf{1}) X (U^{-1} \otimes \mathbf{1}))) (U \otimes \mathbf{1})\, d\,\mathrm{Haar}(U) \right) V \right] \right|$$

$$= \left| s^{-1} \sum_{i=1}^s \mathrm{Tr}\left[((\Lambda \otimes \mathbb{I})((U_i \otimes \mathbf{1}) X (U_i^{-1} \otimes \mathbf{1}))) (U_i \otimes \mathbf{1}) V (U_i^{-1} \otimes \mathbf{1}) \right] \right.$$

$$\left. - \int_{\mathbb{U}(d)} \mathrm{Tr}\left[((\Lambda \otimes \mathbb{I})((U \otimes \mathbf{1}) X (U^{-1} \otimes \mathbf{1}))) (U \otimes \mathbf{1}) V (U^{-1} \otimes \mathbf{1}) \right] d\,\mathrm{Haar}(U) \right|$$

$$= \left| s^{-1} \sum_{i=1}^{s} \mathrm{Tr}\left[((((\Lambda \otimes \mathbb{I})((U_i \otimes \mathbf{1})X(U_i^{-1} \otimes \mathbf{1}))) \otimes ((U_i \otimes \mathbf{1})V(U_i^{-1} \otimes \mathbf{1})))S\right] \right.$$

$$\left. - \int_{\mathrm{U}(d)} \mathrm{Tr}\left[((((\Lambda \otimes \mathbb{I})((U \otimes \mathbf{1})X(U^{-1} \otimes \mathbf{1}))) \otimes ((U \otimes \mathbf{1})V(U^{-1} \otimes \mathbf{1})))S\right] d\,\mathrm{Haar}(U) \right|$$

$$= \left| \mathrm{Tr}\left[((((\Lambda \otimes \mathbb{I}) \otimes (\mathbb{I} \otimes \mathbb{I}))(s^{-1} \sum_{i=1}^{s}((U_i \otimes \mathbf{1}) \otimes (U_i \otimes \mathbf{1}))(X \otimes V)((U_i^{-1} \otimes \mathbf{1}) \otimes (U_i^{-1} \otimes \mathbf{1})))S\right] \right.$$

$$\left. - \mathrm{Tr}\left[((((\Lambda \otimes \mathbb{I}) \otimes (\mathbb{I} \otimes \mathbb{I}))(\int_{\mathrm{U}(d)}((U \otimes \mathbf{1}) \otimes (U \otimes \mathbf{1}))(X \otimes V)((U^{-1} \otimes \mathbf{1}) \otimes (U^{-1} \otimes \mathbf{1})) d\,\mathrm{Haar}(U)))S\right] \right|$$

$$= |\mathrm{Tr}\left[((((\Lambda \otimes \mathbb{I}) \otimes (\mathbb{I} \otimes \mathbb{I}))(((\mathcal{G} \otimes' (\mathbb{I} \otimes'' \mathbb{I})) - (\mathcal{I} \otimes' (\mathbb{I} \otimes'' \mathbb{I}))) (X \otimes V)))S\right]|$$

$$\leq \|((\Lambda \otimes \mathbb{I}) \otimes (\mathbb{I} \otimes \mathbb{I}))(((\mathcal{G} \otimes' (\mathbb{I} \otimes'' \mathbb{I})) - (\mathcal{I} \otimes' (\mathbb{I} \otimes'' \mathbb{I})))(X \otimes V))\|_1$$

$$\leq \|\Lambda\|_{\diamond} \cdot \|((\mathcal{G} \otimes' (\mathbb{I} \otimes'' \mathbb{I})) - (\mathcal{I} \otimes' (\mathbb{I} \otimes'' \mathbb{I})))(X \otimes V)\|_1$$

$$\leq d^2 \|\Lambda\|_{\diamond} \cdot \|X \otimes V\|_1 \cdot \|(\mathcal{G} \otimes' (\mathbb{I} \otimes'' \mathbb{I})) - (\mathcal{I} \otimes' (\mathbb{I} \otimes'' \mathbb{I}))\|_{\infty}$$

$$= d^4 \|\Lambda\|_{\diamond} \|X\|_1 \cdot \|\mathcal{G} - \mathcal{I}\|_{\infty} \ = \ \lambda d^4 \|\Lambda\|_{\diamond} \|X\|_1.$$

Above, we used the so-called *swap trick* $\mathrm{Tr}\,[MN] = \mathrm{Tr}\,[(M \otimes N)S]$ in the second equality, $\otimes'$, $\otimes''$ in the fourth equality indicate that the splitting of the tensor multiplicands is different from the splitting in $X \otimes V$, the fact that $\|\mathcal{G}(X)\|_1 \leq \sqrt{|\mathcal{H}|}\|X\|_1 \|\mathcal{G}\|_{\infty}$ for an operator $X \in L(\mathcal{H})$ and superoperator $\mathcal{G} : L(\mathcal{H}) \to L(\mathcal{H})$ in the third inequality, and $\|V\|_1 = d^2$ in the fifth equality. Since

$$\|E_{\mathcal{G}}(\Lambda) - E_{\mathrm{Haar}}(\Lambda)\|_{\diamond}$$

$$= \max_{X:\|X\|_1=1} \|((E_{\mathcal{G}}(\Lambda) - E_{\mathrm{Haar}}(\Lambda)) \otimes \mathbb{I})(X)\|_1$$

$$= \max_{X:\|X\|_1=1} \max_{V:\mathrm{unitary}} |\mathrm{Tr}\left[(((E_{\mathcal{G}}(\Lambda) - E_{\mathrm{Haar}}(\Lambda)) \otimes \mathbb{I})(X))V\right]|$$

$$= \max_{X:\|X\|_1=1} \max_{V:\mathrm{unitary}} \left| \mathrm{Tr}\left[((s^{-1} \sum_{i=1}^{s}(U_i^{-1} \otimes \mathbf{1})((\Lambda \otimes \mathbb{I})((U_i \otimes \mathbf{1})X(U_i^{-1} \otimes \mathbf{1})))(U_i \otimes \mathbf{1})) \right. \right.$$

$$\left. \left. - (\int_{\mathrm{U}(d)}(U^{-1} \otimes \mathbf{1})((\Lambda \otimes \mathbb{I})((U \otimes \mathbf{1})X(U^{-1} \otimes \mathbf{1})))(U \otimes \mathbf{1}) d\,\mathrm{Haar}(U)))V\right] \right|,$$

we get $\|E_{\mathcal{G}}(\Lambda) - E_{\mathrm{Haar}}(\Lambda)\|_{\diamond} \leq \lambda d^4 \|\Lambda\|_{\diamond}$. This completes the proof.

We now prove four lemmas that will help us relate the tail of the distribution of gate fidelity calculated with respect to a unitary chosen from the Haar measure versus chosen from a t-qTPE.

Lemma 1. *Let $\{A_k\}_k$ be Kraus operators of quantum operation Λ, i.e., $\Lambda(\rho) = \sum_k A_k \rho A_k^{\dagger}$. We will use $\mathcal{F}(V)$ as a shorthand for $\mathcal{F}_{\Lambda}(V)$. Let l be a positive integer. Let $a \in \mathbb{C}$. Define $M \triangleq (\sum_k A_k \otimes A_k^{\dagger}) - a\mathbf{1}_{d^2}$. Then,*

$$\mathcal{F}(V) - a = \mathrm{Tr}\left[(V^{\dagger})^{\otimes 2} M V^{\otimes 2})|00\rangle\langle 00|\right],$$

and $(\mathcal{F}(V) - a)^l = \mathrm{Tr}\left[((V^{\dagger})^{\otimes 2l} M^{\otimes l} V^{\otimes 2l})|0^{2l}\rangle\langle 0^{2l}|\right].$

Proof. We have

$$\mathcal{F}(V) - a = \langle 0|V^{-1}\Lambda(V|0\rangle\langle 0|V^{-1})V|0\rangle - a$$

$$= \langle 0|V^{\dagger}(\sum_k A_k V|0\rangle\langle 0|V^{\dagger}A_k^{\dagger})V|0\rangle - a$$

218   A. Nema and P. Sen

$$= \Big(\sum_k \langle 0|V^\dagger A_k V|0\rangle \cdot \langle 0|V^\dagger A_k^\dagger V|0\rangle\Big) - a$$

$$= \Big(\sum_k \mathrm{Tr}\,[(V^\dagger A_k V)|0\rangle\langle 0|]\mathrm{Tr}\,[(V^\dagger A_k^\dagger V)|0\rangle\langle 0|]\Big) - a$$

$$= \Big(\sum_k \mathrm{Tr}\,[((V^\dagger A_k V)|0\rangle\langle 0|) \otimes ((V^\dagger A_k^\dagger V)|0\rangle\langle 0|)]\Big) - a$$

$$= \Big(\sum_k \mathrm{Tr}\,[(V^\dagger \otimes V^\dagger)(A_k \otimes A_k^\dagger)(V \otimes V)(|0\rangle \otimes |0\rangle)(\langle 0| \otimes \langle 0|)]\Big) - a$$

$$= \sum_k \mathrm{Tr}\,[(V^\dagger \otimes V^\dagger)(A_k \otimes A_k^\dagger)(V \otimes V)|00\rangle\langle 00|] - a\mathrm{Tr}\,[\mathbf{1}_{d^2}|00\rangle\langle 00|]$$

$$= \mathrm{Tr}\,[(V^\dagger)^{\otimes 2}MV^{\otimes 2}|00\rangle\langle 00|].$$

This proves the first equality. For the second equality,

$$(\mathcal{F}(V) - a)^l = (\mathrm{Tr}\,[(V^\dagger)^{\otimes 2}MV^{\otimes 2}|00\rangle\langle 00|])^l = \mathrm{Tr}\,[((V^\dagger)^{\otimes 2}MV^{\otimes 2}|00\rangle\langle 00|)^{\otimes l}]$$
$$= \mathrm{Tr}\,[(V^\dagger)^{\otimes 2l}M^{\otimes l}V^{\otimes 2l}|0^{2l}\rangle\langle 0^{2l}|].$$

This completes the proof.

Lemma 2. *Under the notation of Lemma 1, $\|M\|_2 \le (1 + |a|)d$ and $\|M^{\otimes l}\|_2 \le ((1 + |a|)d)^l$.*

Proof. Define $N \triangleq \sum_k A_k \otimes A_k^\dagger$. We have

$$\|N\|_2 = \sqrt{\mathrm{Tr}\,[NN^\dagger]} = \sqrt{\mathrm{Tr}\,\Big[\sum_{j,k}(A_j \otimes A_j^\dagger)(A_k^\dagger \otimes A_k)\Big]}$$

$$= \sqrt{\sum_{j,k} \mathrm{Tr}\,[A_j A_k^\dagger]\mathrm{Tr}\,[A_j^\dagger A_k]} = \sqrt{\sum_{j,k} \mathrm{Tr}\,[A_j^\dagger A_k]\overline{\mathrm{Tr}\,[A_j^\dagger A_k]}}$$

$$= \sqrt{\sum_{j,k}|\langle A_j, A_k\rangle|^2} \le \sqrt{\sum_{j,k}\|A_j\|_2^2\|A_k\|_2^2} = \sum_k\|A_k\|_2^2 = \mathrm{Tr}\,\Big[\sum_k A_k^\dagger A_k\Big] = \mathrm{Tr}\,[\mathbf{1}_d] = d,$$

where the inequality is obtained by applying Cauchy-Schwarz to the Hilbert-Schmidt inner product. The notation $\bar{\cdot}$ denotes complex conjugate of the complex number represented by $\cdot$. Then

$$\|M\|_2 \le \|N\|_2 + |a|\|\mathbf{1}_{d^2}\|_2 = (1 + |a|)d.$$

This completes the proof of the lemma.

Lemma 3. *Let d, l, s be positive integers and $\lambda > 0$. Let $a \in \mathbb{C}$. The notation $\mathbb{E}_{V:\mathrm{qTPE}}[\cdot]$ denotes the expectation with respect to a $d \times d$ unitary V chosen uniformly at random from a $(d, s, \lambda, 2l)$-qTPE. The notation $\mathbb{E}_{V:\mathrm{Haar}}[\cdot]$ denotes the expectation with respect to a $d \times d$ unitary V chosen from the Haar measure. Then,*

$$|\mathbb{E}_{V:\mathrm{qTPE}}[(\mathcal{F}(V) - a)^l] - \mathbb{E}_{V:\mathrm{Haar}}[(\mathcal{F}(V) - a)^l]| \le \lambda((1 + |a|)d)^l.$$

Proof. Using Lemmas 1 and 2, we get

$$
\begin{aligned}
&|\mathbb{E}_{V:\mathrm{qTPE}}[(\mathcal{F}(V)-a)^l] - \mathbb{E}_{V:\mathrm{Haar}}[(\mathcal{F}(V)-a)^l]| \\
&= |\mathbb{E}_{V:\mathrm{qTPE}}[\mathrm{Tr}\,[((V^\dagger)^{\otimes 2l} M^{\otimes l} V^{\otimes 2l})|0^{2l}\rangle\langle 0^{2l}|]] - \mathbb{E}_{V:\mathrm{Haar}}[\mathrm{Tr}\,[((V^\dagger)^{\otimes 2l} M^{\otimes l} V^{\otimes 2l})|0^{2l}\rangle\langle 0^{2l}|]]| \\
&= |\mathrm{Tr}\,[(\mathbb{E}_{V:\mathrm{qTPE}}[(V^\dagger)^{\otimes 2l} M^{\otimes l} V^{\otimes 2l}] - \mathbb{E}_{V:\mathrm{Haar}}[(V^\dagger)^{\otimes 2l} M^{\otimes l} V^{\otimes 2l}])|0^{2l}\rangle\langle 0^{2l}|]| \\
&\leq \|\mathbb{E}_{V:\mathrm{qTPE}}[(V^\dagger)^{\otimes 2l} M^{\otimes l} V^{\otimes 2l}] - \mathbb{E}_{V:\mathrm{Haar}}[(V^\dagger)^{\otimes 2l} M^{\otimes l} V^{\otimes 2l}]\|_2 \\
&\leq \lambda \| M^{\otimes l} \|_2 \;\leq\; \lambda((1+|a|)d)^l.
\end{aligned}
$$

This completes the proof of the lemma.

Lemma 4. *Let t be a positive integer. Let d, l, s be positive integers and $\lambda > 0$. Let $0 \leq a \leq 1$. The notation $\mathbb{E}_{V_1,\ldots,V_t:\mathrm{qTPE}}[\cdot]$ denotes the expectation with respect to independently choosing $d \times d$ unitaries $V_1,\ldots,V_t$ uniformly at random from a $(d,s,\lambda,2l)$-qTPE. The notation $\mathbb{E}_{V_1,\ldots,V_t:\mathrm{Haar}}[\cdot]$ denotes the expectation with respect to independently choosing $d \times d$ unitaries $V_1,\ldots,V_t$ from the Haar measure. Define the function $f : \mathrm{U}(d)^{\times t} \to \mathbb{R}$ as*

$$
f(V_1,\ldots,V_t) \triangleq t^{-1}\sum_{i=1}^{t}\mathcal{F}_\Lambda(V_i),
$$

i.e., f is the average of t gate fidelities. Then,

$$
|\mathbb{E}_{(V_1,\ldots,V_t):\mathrm{qTPE}}[(f(V_1,\ldots,V_t)-a)^l] - \mathbb{E}_{(V_1,\ldots,V_t):\mathrm{Haar}}[(f(V_1,\ldots,V_t)-a)^l]| \leq \lambda(2d)^l.
$$

Proof. From Lemma 3, it is easy to see that

$$
\begin{aligned}
&|\mathbb{E}_{(V_1,\ldots,V_t):\mathrm{qTPE}}[(f(V_1,\ldots,V_t)-a)^l] - \mathbb{E}_{(V_1,\ldots,V_t):\mathrm{Haar}}[(f(V_1,\ldots,V_t)-a)^l]| \\
&= t^{-l}|\mathbb{E}_{(V_1,\ldots,V_t):\mathrm{qTPE}}[(\sum_{i=1}^{t}\mathcal{F}_\Lambda(V_i)-a)^l] - \mathbb{E}_{(V_1,\ldots,V_t):\mathrm{Haar}}[(\sum_{i=1}^{t}\mathcal{F}_\Lambda(V_i)-a)^l]| \\
&\leq t^{-l}\sum_{i_1,\ldots,i_t:\sum_{j=1}^{t}i_j=l}\binom{l}{i_1\cdots i_t}|\prod_{j=1}^{t}\mathbb{E}_{V_j:\mathrm{qTPE}}[(\mathcal{F}_\Lambda(V_j)-a)^{i_j}] - \prod_{j=1}^{t}\mathbb{E}_{V_j:\mathrm{Haar}}[(\mathcal{F}_\Lambda(V_j)-a)^{i_j}]| \\
&\leq t^{-l}\sum_{i_1,\ldots,i_t:\sum_{j=1}^{t}i_j=l}\binom{l}{i_1\cdots i_t}\sum_{m=t}^{1}|\prod_{j=1}^{m}\mathbb{E}_{V_j:\mathrm{qTPE}}[(\mathcal{F}_\Lambda(V_j)-a)^{i_j}]\prod_{j=m+1}^{t}\mathbb{E}_{V_j:\mathrm{Haar}}[(\mathcal{F}_\Lambda(V_j)-a)^{i_j}] \\
&\qquad\qquad - \prod_{j=1}^{m-1}\mathbb{E}_{V_j:\mathrm{qTPE}}[(\mathcal{F}_\Lambda(V_j)-a)^{i_j}]\prod_{j=m}^{t}\mathbb{E}_{V_j:\mathrm{Haar}}[(\mathcal{F}_\Lambda(V_j)-a)^{i_j}]| \\
&= t^{-l}\sum_{i_1,\ldots,i_t:\sum_{j=1}^{t}i_j=l}\binom{l}{i_1\cdots i_t}\sum_{m=t}^{1}|\prod_{j=1}^{m-1}\mathbb{E}_{V_j:\mathrm{qTPE}}[(\mathcal{F}_\Lambda(V_j)-a)^{i_j}]\prod_{j=m+1}^{t}\mathbb{E}_{V_j:\mathrm{Haar}}[(\mathcal{F}_\Lambda(V_j)-a)^{i_j}] \\
&\qquad\qquad (\mathbb{E}_{V_m:\mathrm{qTPE}}[(\mathcal{F}_\Lambda(V_j)-a)^{i_m}] - \mathbb{E}_{V_m:\mathrm{Haar}}[(\mathcal{F}_\Lambda(V_j)-a)^{i_m}])| \\
&\leq t^{-l}\sum_{i_1,\ldots,i_t:\sum_{j=1}^{t}i_j=l}\binom{l}{i_1\cdots i_t}\sum_{m=t}^{1}|(\mathbb{E}_{V_m:\mathrm{qTPE}}[(\mathcal{F}_\Lambda(V_j)-a)^{i_m}] - \mathbb{E}_{V_m:\mathrm{Haar}}[(\mathcal{F}_\Lambda(V_j)-a)^{i_m}])| \\
&\leq t^{-l}\lambda((1+a)d)^l\sum_{i_1,\ldots,i_t:\sum_{j=1}^{t}i_j=l}\binom{l}{i_1\cdots i_t} \\
&\leq \lambda(2d)^{2l},
\end{aligned}
$$

where in the fourth inequality we used the fact that if $(i_1, \ldots, i_p)$ is a partition of l where each $i_m \neq 0$, $1 \leq m \leq p$, then for any $x > 1$, $\sum_{m=1}^{p} x^{i_m} \leq \prod_{m=1}^{p} x^{i_m} \leq x^l$. This completes the proof of the lemma.

We now prove the following important result giving a tail bound on the uniform average of t gate fidelity functions, when the t unitaries are chosen independently and uniformly from a qTPE.

Proposition 1. *Let t, d, s, l be positive integers and $\delta, \lambda > 0$. Consider the probability distribution on points $(V_1, \ldots, V_t) \in \mathbb{U}(d)^{\times t}$ obtained by choosing each V_i independently and uniformly from a $(d, s, \lambda, 4l)$-qTPE. Define the function $f : \mathbb{U}(d)^{\times t} \to \mathbb{R}$ as*

$$f(V_1, \ldots, V_t) \triangleq t^{-1} \sum_{i=1}^{t} \mathcal{F}_\Lambda(V_i),$$

i.e., f is the average of t gate fidelities. Then,

$$\Pr_{(V_1, \ldots, V_t):\text{qTPE}}[|f(V_1, \ldots, V_t) - \bar{\mathcal{F}}_\Lambda| > \delta] \leq \delta^{-2l}\left(4\left(\frac{256l}{dt}\right)^l + \lambda(2d)^{2l}\right).$$

For the special case where $l = 1$, we get

$$\Pr_{(V_1, \ldots, V_t):\text{qTPE}}[|f(V_1, \ldots, V_t) - \bar{\mathcal{F}}_\Lambda| > \delta] \leq \delta^{-2}\left(\frac{26}{dt} + \lambda(2d)^2\right).$$

Proof. By Lemma 4, $|\mathbb{E}_{(V_1, \ldots, V_t):\text{qTPE}}[(f(V_1, \ldots, V_t) - \bar{\mathcal{F}}_\Lambda)^l] - \mathbb{E}_{(V_1, \ldots, V_t):\text{Haar}}[(f(V_1, \ldots, V_t) - \bar{\mathcal{F}}_\Lambda)^l]| \leq \lambda(2d)^l$.
From Eq. 2, we get that

$$\mathbb{E}_{(V_1, \ldots, V_t):\text{Haar}}[(f(V_1, \ldots, V_t) - \bar{\mathcal{F}}_\Lambda)^2] = t^{-1}\mathbb{E}_{V:\text{Haar}}[(\mathcal{F}_\Lambda(V) - \bar{\mathcal{F}}_\Lambda)^2] = \frac{26}{dt}.$$

Observe that

$$\Pr_{(V_1, \ldots, V_t):\text{qTPE}}[|f(V_1, \ldots, V_t) - \bar{\mathcal{F}}_\Lambda| > \delta] \leq \delta^{-2l}\mathbb{E}_{(V_1, \ldots, V_t):\text{qTPE}}[(f(V_1, \ldots, V_t) - \bar{\mathcal{F}}_\Lambda)^{2l}]$$

$$\leq \delta^{-2l}\left(\mathbb{E}_{(V_1, \ldots, V_t):\text{Haar}}[(f(V_1, \ldots, V_t) - \bar{\mathcal{F}}_\Lambda)^{2l}] + \lambda(2d)^{2l}\right).$$

Now for $l = 1$ we have

$$\Pr_{(V_1, \ldots, V_t):\text{qTPE}}[|f(V_1, \ldots, V_t) - \bar{\mathcal{F}}_\Lambda| > \delta] \leq \delta^{-2l}\left(\frac{26}{dt} + \lambda(2d)^2\right).$$

For larger values of l, we employ the l-moment method of [4] as adapted into the quantum setting by Low [5], combined with the tail bound of Eq. 3 for the Haar measure. We obtain

$$\mathbb{E}_{(V_1, \ldots, V_t):\text{Haar}}[(f(V_1, \ldots, V_t) - \bar{\mathcal{F}}_\Lambda)^{2l}] \leq 4\left(\frac{256l}{dt}\right)^l.$$

This gives us

$$\Pr_{(V_1, \ldots, V_t):\text{qTPE}}[|f(V_1, \ldots, V_t) - \bar{\mathcal{F}}_\Lambda| > \delta] \leq \delta^{-2l}\left(4\left(\frac{256l}{dt}\right)^l + \lambda(2d)^{2l}\right).$$

This completes the proof of the proposition.

4   Earlier Work on Estimating Average Gate Fidelity

We first recall the naive algorithm [1] for estimating average gate fidelity using Haar random unitaries for reference and comparison. The basic procedure is the following. It is easy to see that the probability of success in one iteration of the basic procedure is, by taking $|\psi\rangle \triangleq U|0\rangle$,

$$\int_{\mathbb{U}(d)} \langle 0|V^{-1}\Lambda(V|0\rangle\langle 0|V^{-1})V|0\rangle \, d\operatorname{Haar}(V) = \int_{\mathbb{CP}^{d-1}} \langle \psi|\Lambda(|\psi\rangle\langle\psi|)|\psi\rangle \, d\operatorname{Haar}(\psi) = \bar{\mathcal{F}}_\Lambda.$$

Algorithm 1: Basic procedure of naive algorithm

1. Start with the state $|0\rangle \in \mathcal{H}$;
2. Apply a $d \times d$ Haar-random unitary matrix $V \in \mathbb{U}(d)$ on $\mathcal{H}$;
3. Apply the quantum operation Λ (the experimental realization of $U^{-1}U$) to the state obtained in the above step;
4. Apply V^{-1} to the state obtained in the above step;
5. Measure the resulting state according to the binary outcome measurement $\{|0\rangle\langle 0|, \mathbf{1}_{\mathcal{H}} - |0\rangle\langle 0|\}$. Declare success if the outcome $|0\rangle\langle 0|$ is observed.

The basic procedure of the naive algorithm is prohibitively expensive, both in terms of the computational cost required to implement the Haar random unitaries as well as in terms of the number of random bits required to do the sampling. Uniformly sampling a $d \times d$ Haar random unitary to within ℓ_2-distance ϵ requires at least $\Omega(d^2 \log(1/\epsilon))$ random bits and circuit size at least $\Omega(\frac{d^2}{\log d} \log(1/\epsilon))$ [21, Lemma 3.5]. Thus the overall number of random bits used by the basic procedure becomes $\Omega(d^2 \log(1/\epsilon))$, and the overall circuit size of the basic procedure $\Omega(\frac{d^2}{\log d} \log(1/\epsilon))$.

Since twirling with a Haar random unitary is the same as twirling with a uniformly random unitary chosen from an exact unitary 2-design, we can replace the Haar random unitary in the basic procedure by a random unitary chosen uniformly from an exact 2-design without changing the probability of success at all [2]. The advantage of doing so is that there exists 2-designs each of whose unitaries can be implemented by a circuit of size $O((\log d)^2)$, whereas a Haar random unitary almost always requires circuits of size at least $\Omega(d^2 \log(1/\epsilon))$ to implement within precision ϵ.

One iteration of the basic procedure succeeds with probability $\bar{\mathcal{F}}_\Lambda$. A single outcome, success or failure, gives us no clue about the value of $\bar{\mathcal{F}}_\Lambda$. So in order to actually estimate $\bar{\mathcal{F}}_\Lambda$ to within an additive error ϵ, with confidence $1 - \delta$, we have to repeat the basic procedure several times. Neither [1] nor [2] do this rigorously. We now address this important shortcoming. Let us repeat the basic procedure independently $\Theta(\epsilon^{-2} \log(1/\delta))$ times and take the empirical average of successes. By Fact 2, an estimate of $\bar{\mathcal{F}}$ to within an additive error of ϵ with probability at least $1 - \delta$. The running time of this algorithm turns out to be $O(\epsilon^{-2}\log\delta^{-1}(\log d)^2)$, and the number of random bits consumed turns out to be $O(\epsilon^{-2}\log\delta^{-1}\log\epsilon^{-1}(\log d)^8)$ [13]. We note that there are constructions of exact unitary 2-designs [14] using Clifford gate circuits of size $O((\log d)(\log\log d)^2(\log\log\log d))$, but they use at least $\Omega(\log d)$ ancilla qubits. Since qubits are likely to be a very expensive resource in foreseeable implementations of quantum gates, we prefer that all our algorithms be in-place without using ancilla qubits.

Dankert et al. [2] showed how to improve the running time and the number of random bits in the basic procedure by replacing the use of an exact 2-design by a θ-approximate 2-design. Due to the replacement, the probability of success in the basic procedure becomes

$$\int_{\mathbb{U}(d)} \langle 0|V^{-1}\Lambda(V|0\rangle\langle 0|V^{-1})V|0\rangle\, d\nu(V)$$

$$\leq \int_{\mathbb{U}(d)} \langle 0|V^{-1}\Lambda(V|0\rangle\langle 0|V^{-1})V|0\rangle\, d\,\mathrm{Haar}(V) + \theta\|\Lambda\|_\diamond = \bar{\mathcal{F}}_\Lambda + \theta,$$

where we used the fact that $\|\Lambda\|_\diamond = 1$ as Λ is a quantum operation. We can now take $\theta = \epsilon/2$ and repeat the basic procedure $\Theta(\epsilon^{-2}\log(1/\delta))$ times and take the empirical average of successes, in order to get an estimate of $\bar{\mathcal{F}}_\Lambda$ to within an additive error of ϵ with confidence $1 - \delta$. The running time and usage of random bits of this algorithm turn out to be $O(\epsilon^{-2}\log\delta^{-1}(\log d)\log\epsilon^{-1})$. [2]. We note that Dankert et al. [2, Theorem 3] incorrectly repeat the basic procedure $O(\log\delta^{-1})$ times to get confidence $1 - \delta$, ignoring the issue of additive error ϵ completely.

By Fact 6, replacing the Haar random unitary U in the basic procedure by a $(d, s, \frac{\epsilon}{2d^4}, 2)$-qTPE $\mathcal{G}$ also leads to an efficient algorithm for estimating average gate fidelity. In fact, a direct analysis shows that a $(d, s, \frac{\epsilon}{2d}, 2)$-qTPE suffices too. Such 2-qTPEs can be obtained via the so-called *zigzag product* [6]. The unitaries of the qTPE can be implemented by circuits of size $O((\log d)^2(\log d/\epsilon)$. The number of random bits required is only $O(\log(d/\epsilon))$. The running time of this algorithm turns out to be $O(\epsilon^{-2}\log\delta^{-1}(\log d)^2(\log d/\epsilon))$, and the number of random bits consumed turns out to be $O(\epsilon^{-2}\log\delta^{-1}\log(d/\epsilon))$. The circuit size is slightly inferior to Dankert et al. [2] but the number of random bits used is less.

5   Randomness Efficient Algorithm Using Approximate Unitary 2-Designs

Instead of repeating Algorithm 1 with independently chosen unitaries per iteration, we pick the sequence of unitaries of the approximate 2-design from an approximate k-wise independent distribution for a suitable value of k. For clarity, we give the full algorithm:

Algorithm 2: Basic procedure of randomness efficient algorithm

---

Input: Classical description of a $d \times d$ unitary Y.

1. Start with the state $|0\rangle \in \mathcal{H}$;
2. Apply Y on $\mathcal{H}$;
3. Apply the quantum operation Λ (the experimental realisation of $U^{-1}U$) to the state obtained in the above step;
4. Apply Y^{-1} to the state obtained in the above step;
5. Measure the resulting state according to the binary outcome measurement $\{|0\rangle\langle 0|, \mathbf{1}_{\mathcal{H}} - |0\rangle\langle 0|\}$. Declare success if the outcome $|0\rangle\langle 0|$ is observed.

Algorithm 3: Randomness efficient algorithm using approximate 2-design

---

Input: $\epsilon, \delta > 0$.

Assumption: $\epsilon < \bar{\mathcal{F}}_\Lambda$.

Define: $n \triangleq \frac{2^4 \log(2/\delta)}{\epsilon^2}$, $\theta \triangleq \frac{\delta}{2}\left(\frac{\epsilon}{n}\right)^{\frac{\epsilon^2 n}{4}}$.

Take: set $\mathcal{Y}$ to be an $\epsilon/2$-approximate unitary 2-design with $\log|\mathcal{Y}| = O(\log(d/\epsilon))$. A unitary of $\mathcal{Y}$ can be implemented by circuits of size $O((\log d)^2(\log(d/\epsilon)))$. This follows from the so-called zigzag product [6].

Construct: a sequence $Y_1, Y_2, \ldots, Y_n$ of unitaries from $\mathcal{Y}$ as the output of $f : \{0,1\}^r \to \mathcal{Y}^n$ guaranteed by Fact 5, when a uniformly random input $z \in \{0,1\}^r$ is fed to f, where

$$r \triangleq 4\epsilon^2(n\log|\mathcal{Y}|) + 2\log\theta^{-1} = O(\log\delta^{-1}(\log(d/\epsilon) + \log\log\delta^{-1})).$$

Run: Algorithm 2 with unitaries $Y_1, Y_2, \ldots, Y_n$. Record the outputs $b_1, b_2, \ldots, b_n$. Declare $b := n^{-1}\sum_{i=1}^n b_i$ as the estimate for $\bar{\mathcal{F}}_\Lambda$.

Algorithm 3 consists of a classical pre-processing step where the sequence $Y_1, Y_2, \ldots, Y_n$ is computed. This takes classical deterministic time $O(\epsilon^{-2}\text{poly}(r))$. After the pre-processing step, Algorithm 3 runs in quantum time $O(\epsilon^{-2}\log\delta^{-1}(\log d)^2(\log(d/\epsilon)))$. Number of random bits used is $r = O(\log\delta^{-1}(\log(d/\epsilon) + \log\log\delta^{-1}))$. By Fact 5, Algorithm 3 gives an estimate b of $\bar{\mathcal{F}}_\Lambda$ such that $\Pr[|b - \bar{\mathcal{F}}_\Lambda| > \epsilon] \leq \delta$. Comparing with the zigzag product based algorithm in Sect. 4, we get the same quantum circuit size but much lesser usage of random bits.

Instead of the zigzag product, we can take the $\epsilon/2$-approximate unitary 2-design of Dankert et al. [2]. An advantage of doing this is that we use only Clifford gates in the approximate unitary 2-design which may be technologically easier to implement. That would give us classical pre-processing time of $O(\epsilon^{-2}\text{poly}(r))$, quantum time of $O(\epsilon^{-2}\log\delta^{-1}(\log d)(\log\epsilon^{-1}))$ and number of random bits $r = O(\log \delta^{-1}((\log d)(\log \epsilon^{-1}) + \log \log \delta^{-1}))$. Comparing with the corresponding algorithm in Sect. 4, we get the same quantum circuit size but much lesser usage of random bits. Thus, this algorithm is a good candidate for actual experimental implementations in the near future.

6   Randomness Efficient Algorithm Using Approximate 4-qTPE

Suppose $\frac{108}{\epsilon^2 d} < \frac{\delta}{2}$. Then there is an even more randomness efficient algorithm than the one given in Sect. 5 as follows.

Algorithm 4: Randomness efficient algorithm using approximate 4-qTPE

Input: $\epsilon, \delta > 0$.

Assumption: $\epsilon < \frac{\bar{\mathcal{F}}_\Lambda}{2}$, $\frac{108}{\epsilon^2 d} < \frac{\delta}{2}$.

Define: $n \triangleq \frac{12 \log(4\delta^{-1})}{\epsilon^2}$.

Take: set $\mathcal{Y}$ to be a $(d, s, \frac{1}{4d^3}, 4)$-qTPE with $\log |\mathcal{Y}| = O(\log d)$. A unitary of $\mathcal{Y}$ can be implemented by circuits of size $O((\log d)^3)$. This follows from the so-called zigzag product [6].

Choose: a uniformly random unitary Y from $\mathcal{Y}$.

Run: Algorithm 2 n times with the same unitary Y. Record the outputs $b_1, b_2, \ldots, b_n$. Declare $b := n^{-1} \sum_{i=1}^{n} b_i$ as the estimate for $\bar{\mathcal{F}}_\Lambda$.

Using Proposition 1 in the special case where $t = l = 1$ and $\lambda = \frac{1}{4d^3}$, we get

$$\Pr_{Y:\text{qTPE}}[|\mathcal{F}_\Lambda(Y) - \bar{\mathcal{F}}_\Lambda| > \epsilon/2] \leq 4\epsilon^{-2}(\frac{26}{d} + \lambda(2d)^2) \leq \frac{108}{\epsilon^2 d} \leq \frac{\delta}{2}.$$

Sampling uniformly from the qTPE $\mathcal{Y}$ requires only $O(\log d)$ random bits. Each unitary of $\mathcal{Y}$ can be implemented in quantum time $O((\log d)^3)$. These facts follow from the so-called zigzag product [6].

Now suppose that $|\mathcal{F}_\Lambda(Y) - \bar{\mathcal{F}}_\Lambda| < \frac{\epsilon}{2}$ indeed. By Fact 2, running Algorithm 2 n times with the same unitary Y will give an estimate b of $\mathcal{F}_\Lambda(Y)$ such that

$$\Pr[|b - \mathcal{F}_\Lambda(Y)| > \frac{\epsilon}{2}] \leq 2\exp(-\epsilon^2 n/12) \leq \frac{\delta}{2},$$

where the probability arises because of inherent quantum uncertainty of measurement outcomes. Overall we get, $\Pr[|b - \bar{\mathcal{F}}_\Lambda| > \epsilon] \leq \delta$. Algorithm 4 takes quantum running time $O(\epsilon^{-2} \log \delta^{-1} (\log d)^3)$ which is the same as the zigzag product based approximate 2-design Algorithm 3 of Sect. 5. However it consumes only $O(\log d)$ random bits, where the constant hiding in the $O(\cdot)$ is independent of ϵ and δ, which is less than what Algorithm 3 consumes. The drawback of Algorithm 4 is that it requires that $\frac{108}{\epsilon^2 d} < \frac{\delta}{2}$, whereas Algorithm 3 has no such assumption. In practice, this means that Algorithm 4 can only be used if the dimension d is large and the estimation error ϵ and confidence error δ are not too small.

7   Randomness Efficient Algorithm Using Approximate $4l$-qTPE

We now address the main drawback of Algorithm 4 i.e. what if the dimension d is not large enough? This is a pertinent question because we presently hope to experimentally implement and benchmark quantum circuits acting on 10 to 150 qubits across various kinds of architectures like vacuum ion trap, quantum charge coupled device, superconducting Josephson junctions, quantum dots etc. For ten to thirty qubits, the dimension d may not be large enough to satisfy the assumption $\frac{108}{\epsilon^2 d} < \frac{\delta}{2}$ for reasonably small values of ϵ and δ. It would be nice to have an efficient algorithm using a few random bits for arbitrary values of d, ϵ and δ. Algorithm 3 is one such algorithm, but it requires us to be able to implement the entire plethora of $2^{\Omega(\log(d/\epsilon))}$ unitaries in an approximate 2-design. In some technological scenarios, it may be better to spend a few more random bits but reduce the number of unitaries that may need to be implemented by the algorithm. Algorithm 4 is indeed a step in this direction but it suffers from the drawback mentioned above.

To achieve this goal, we develop Algorithm 5 by combining ideas from Algorithms 3 and 4. Algorithm 5 is a two-phase algorithm using an l-qTPE for $l \geq 4$, but still small enough to be efficiently implementable.

In Phase 1, we take a $(d, s, \lambda, 4l)$-qTPE $\mathcal{V}$ and sample from it independently and uniformly at random a small number of unitaries $V_1, \ldots, V_t$. For $l = \log(16/\delta)$, $t = \frac{2^{11} l}{\epsilon^2 d} = \frac{2^{11} \log(16/\delta)}{\epsilon^2 d}$. $\lambda \triangleq (\frac{\epsilon^2}{2^5 d^2})^l = (\frac{\epsilon^2}{2^5 d^2})^{\log 16/\delta}$, Proposition 1 will ensure that the gate fidelity averaged over this small set of unitaries is $\epsilon/2$-close to the actual average gate fidelity $\bar{\mathcal{F}}_\Lambda$ with confidence at least $1 - \frac{\delta}{2}$. The number of random bits required to independently sample t times uniformly from $\mathcal{V}$ is

$$O(t \log \lambda^{-1}) = O(\epsilon^{-2} d^{-1} (\log \delta^{-1})^2 (\log d + \log \epsilon^{-1})). \tag{6}$$

Each unitary in $\mathcal{V}$ can be implemented in $O((\log d)^2 (\log \delta^{-1})^3 (\log \log \delta^{-1}) \log(d/\epsilon))$ amount of quantum time. The constants hiding in both the $O(\cdot)$ notations above are independent of d, ϵ, δ. These facts follow from the so-called zigzag product [6]. Morally speaking, this pre-processing step achieves the goal of the first phase of Algorithm 4.

In Phase 2 of our algorithm, we sample only from the set $\mathcal{Y} \triangleq \{V_1, \ldots, V_t\}$ in an approximate limited independence fashion as in Fact 5, and run Algorithm 2 on those samples in so as to empirically estimate the gate fidelity averaged over the set $\mathcal{Y}$. We apply Fact 5 with $n \triangleq \frac{2^4 \log(4/\delta)}{\epsilon^2}$, $\theta \triangleq \frac{\delta}{4}(\frac{\epsilon}{n})^{\frac{\epsilon^2 n}{16}} =$

Algorithm 5: Randomness efficient algorithm using approximate $4l$-qTPE

Input: $\epsilon, \delta > 0$.

Assumption: $\epsilon < \frac{\bar{\mathcal{F}}_\Lambda}{2}$, $4\log(16/\delta) < \frac{d^{1/6}}{10\log d}$.

Define: $l \triangleq \log(16/\delta)$, $t \triangleq \lceil \frac{2^{11}l}{\epsilon^2 d} \rceil$, $\lambda \triangleq (\frac{\epsilon^2}{2^5 d^2})^l$, $n \triangleq \frac{16\log(4/\delta^{-1})}{\epsilon^2}$, $\theta \triangleq \frac{\delta}{4}(\frac{\epsilon}{n})^{\frac{\epsilon^2 n}{16}}$.

Take: set $\mathcal{V}$ to be a $(d, s, \lambda, 4l)$-qTPE with $\log|\mathcal{V}| = O(\log\lambda^{-1})$. A unitary of $\mathcal{V}$ can be implemented by circuits of size $O((\log d)^2(\log\delta^{-1})^2(\log\log\delta^{-1})(\log\lambda^{-1}))$. This follows from the zigzag product [6].

Choose: independently and uniformly at random unitaries $V_1, \ldots, V_t$ from $\mathcal{V}$. Call this set of unitaries as V.

Construct: a sequence $Y_1, Y_2, \ldots, Y_n$ of unitaries from $\mathcal{Y}$ as the output of $f : \{0, 1\}^r \to \mathcal{Y}^n$ guaranteed by Fact 5, when a uniformly random input $z \in \{0, 1\}^r$ is fed to f, where $r \triangleq \epsilon^2 n \log t + 2\log\theta^{-1}$.

Run: Algorithm 2 with unitaries $Y_1, Y_2, \ldots, Y_n$. Record the outputs $b_1, b_2, \ldots, b_n$. Declare $b := n^{-1} \sum_{i=1}^{n} b_i$ as the estimate for $\bar{\mathcal{F}}_\Lambda$.

$$\frac{\delta}{4}\Big(\frac{\epsilon^3}{2^4\log(4/\delta)}\Big)^{\log(4/\delta)},$$

$$\begin{aligned}
r &\triangleq \epsilon^2 n \log t + 2\log\theta^{-1} \\
&= 16\log\delta^{-1}(\log\log\delta^{-1} + 2\log\epsilon^{-1} - \log d + O(1)) + 2\log(4/\delta) \\
&\quad + 2\log\delta^{-1}(\log\log\delta^{-1} + 3\log\epsilon^{-1} + O(1)) \\
&= 18\log\delta^{-1}\log\log\delta^{-1} + 38\log\delta^{-1}\log\epsilon^{-1} - 16\log\delta^{-1}\log d + O(\log\delta^{-1}).
\end{aligned}$$

$$\tag{7}$$

Morally speaking, this achieves the goal of the second phase of Algorithm 3.

We now analyze the running time and number of random bits used by Algorithm 5. The total confidence of Phases 1 and 2 is at least $1 - \delta$. Suppose $\frac{2^{11}\log(16/\delta)}{\epsilon^2 d} \leq 1$. Then, we set $t = 1$ and so Phase 2 does not use any more random bits. The total number of random bits used in Phases 1 and 2 now becomes $O(\log\delta^{-1}\log(d/\epsilon))$, where the constant hiding in the $O(\cdot)$ notation does not depend on ϵ, δ, d. This is comparable to the total number of random bits used by Algorithm 3. However, Algorithm 5 requires us to implement only one unitary as opposed to implementing potentially all the unitaries in an approximate 2-design in Algorithm 3. Also the constraint on the dimension d is less stringent than the constraint required by Algorithm 4.

Suppose $\frac{2^{11}\log(16/\delta)}{\epsilon^2 d} > 1$. The total number of random bits used in Phases 1 and 2 becomes

$$O(\epsilon^{-2}d^{-1}(\log\delta^{-1})^2\log(d/\epsilon) + \log\delta^{-1}\log\log\delta^{-1})$$

where the constant hiding in the $O(\cdot)$ notation does not depend on ϵ, δ, d. Now the number of random bits used is greater than that of Algorithm 3. However, Algorithm 5 requires us to implement only $\frac{\log(16/\delta)}{\epsilon^2 d}$ unitaries as opposed to implementing potentially $2^{\Omega(\log(d/\epsilon))}$ unitaries in Algorithm 3. This is a big saving on the number of unitaries an algorithm has to potentially implement.

The total running time of Algorithm 5 is $O(\epsilon^{-2}(\log \delta^{-1})^4 (\log d)^2 (\log \log \delta^{-1}) \log(d/\epsilon))$, in both the cases, which is slightly worse than that of Algorithm 3. The worse running time is due to the fact that Algorithm 5 needs a $O(\log \delta^{-1})$-qTPE whereas Algorithm 3 only needs a 2-qTPE. Any future improvement in construction of t-qTPEs for large t will improve the running time of Algorithm 5.

8   Results and Comparison with the Earlier Algorithms

Finally we give a comparison of the number of random bits used by our new algorithms versus the present state of art algorithm [2] for estimating average gate fidelity, in Table 1.

Table 1. Comparing the randomness requirements of our three new algorithms to the earlier state of the art algorithm of [2]. Above, d is the Hilbert space dimension of the quantum logic gate being benchmarked, ϵ is the additive error in estimating average gate fidelity and δ is the confidence bound that the estimate is close to the true quantity. The constants hiding in O, Ω, Θ are independent of d, ϵ and δ.

Cost Analysis: # Random bits			
Old algo [2]	New Algo 1	New Algo 2	New Algo 3
$O\left(\frac{1}{\epsilon^2} \log \frac{1}{\delta}(\log d) \log \frac{1}{\epsilon}\right)$	$O(\log \frac{1}{\delta} \log(\frac{d}{\epsilon}))$	$O(\log d)$	$O\left(\frac{1}{d\epsilon^2}\left(\log \frac{1}{\delta}\right)^2 \log(\frac{d}{\epsilon})\right)$

9   Conclusion

We have described three new algorithms for efficient in-place estimation, without using ancilla qubits, of average fidelity of a quantum logic gate using much fewer random bits than what was known so far. We considered only in-place algorithms in this work because qubits are likely to remain an expensive resource in experimental implementations in the near future, and so we would like to avoid ancilla qubits as far as possible. We achieve the reductions in the number of random bits by appealing to two powerful tools. The first tool, a limited independence pseudorandom generator, comes from classical derandomization theory in computer science. It is used in the first and the third estimation algorithms. The second tool, an approximate quantum l-tensor product expander (l-qTPE) for moderate values of l, is a recent quantum computational object defined as an analogue of an approximate l-wise independent pseudorandom generator well known from classical derandomization theory. In fact, to obtain our parameters we actually have to appeal to the state of the art in quantum tensor product expanders, which in turn were obtained by 'quantizing' another famous result from classical derandomization theory viz. the zigzag product of graphs. The second tool is used in our second, and more strongly, in our third estimation algorithm.

Each of our algorithms have unique features that, depending upon the experimental limitations and desired parameters, sometimes make one of them the most suitable, sometimes another. They can also be used as subroutines in any algorithm that requires computation of average gate fidelity e.g. in the recent work of learning quantum gates from a small number of average gate fidelity estimates [22]. If one wants an efficient algorithm that works for all values of the gate dimension d, estimation error ϵ and confidence error δ, and uses the least number of random bits, then the first algorithm is the way to go. Reducing the number of random bits will increase the reliability of the estimation in practice as explained earlier. Moreover, this algorithm can be chosen to be implemented using only Clifford gates which may be an advantage for some technologies.

If the gate dimension is large (more than 40 qubits) and estimation error requirement is not too tiny, then the second algorithm is the best one. It uses the least number of random bits and needs to implement only one unitary from an approximate 4-qTPE. If the aim is to use an algorithm that works for all parameter values but needs to implement as few unitaries as possible, then the third algorithm is the right one. Though it uses more random bits than the first algorithm, it needs to implement much fewer unitaries than the first. This feature can be the most crucial for certain QRAM technologies.

An important issue plaguing the experimental measurement of average gate fidelity is that more gates are required for fidelity estimation in addition to the gates already present in the quantum circuit being benchmarked. This led researchers to define an alternate quantity called the *randomized benchmarking (RB) parameter* r [9]. In randomized benchmarking, the average fidelity $\bar{\mathcal{F}}(k)$ of k serial applications of the circuit, i.e. of CPTP map Λ^k, is estimated and plotted as a function of k. The graph is then fitted to a function of the form $\bar{\mathcal{F}}(k) = A + (B + Ck)r^k$. The quantity r is then called the RB parameter. The advantage of defining the RB parameter is that in principle it can be directly measured experimentally, since the amount of additional gates required for the fidelity estimation is independent of k. In contrast the average gate fidelity, strictly speaking, cannot be directly measured because the number of additional gates is often at least as much as the number of gates in the benchmarked circuit. Nevertheless average gate fidelity is important for an instrinsic understanding and calibration of the circuit. It is thus a natural question as to what the relation between the two quantities is. It turns out that if the implementation errors for the circuit as well as for the extra gates required for the fidelity estimation are small and only 'weakly gate dependent', then the RB parameter is approximately equal to the average gate fidelity [9,10]. However there are significant caveats to this claim; see e.g. [8]. Reducing the number of random bits is one way to bring the RB parameter closer to the average gate fidelity, thus bridging theory and experiment.

Average gate fidelity estimation and randomized benchmarking are affected by state preparation and measurement (SPAM) errors; see e.g. [12]. These are errors that arise from inaccuracies in preparing and measuring quantum states. Since the initial preparation state as well as the final measurement state in average gate fidelity and randomized benchmarking is $|0\rangle$, we need only consider bit flip errors in SPAM analysis. SPAM errors arise only at the beginning and at the end, and are independent of the number of iterations in randomized benchmarking. Ideally they only affect the A, B parameters in the function fit of randomized benchmarking, and not the RB parameter r. Thus, the RB parameter has natural immunity against SPAM errors. We can enhance the immunity of average gate fidelity as well as r estimation by the following simple trick: Instead of initialising and finally measuring the state $|0\rangle$, do the same with state $|x\rangle$ where x is a uniformly chosen bit string of length $\log d$. Doing so requires only $\log d$ additional random bits, which is less than the amount of randomness required by any algorithm for fidelity estimation. This simple trick significantly reduces SPAM bit flip errors.

Moving on from estimating average gate fidelity, it will be interesting to find other applications of both classical derandomization as well as quantum derandomization tools in quantum computation, both theoretical and experimental. The experimental implementations of quantum computers of the near future, of the order of hundreds of qubits, will be very noisy. Reliable and efficient test suites optimized for every bit of precision and performance are the need of the hour to measure progress in the exciting times to come.

References

1. Emerson, C., Alicki, R., Życzkowski, K.: Scalable noise estimation with random unitary operators. J. Opt. B: Quantum Semiclassical Opt. **7**, S347–S352 (2005)
2. Dankert, C., Cleve, R., Emerson, J., Livine, E.: Exact and approximate unitary 2-designs and their application to fidelity estimation. Phys. Rev. A **80**, 012304 (2009)
3. Emerson, J., et al.: Symmetrized characterization of noisy quantum processes. Science **317**, 1893–1896 (2007)
4. Bellare, M., Rompel, J.: Randomness-efficient oblivious sampling. In: 35th Annual IEEE Symposium on Foundations of Computer Science, pp. 276–287 (1994)
5. Low, R.: Large deviation bounds for k-designs. Proc. Roy. Soc. A **465**(2111), 3289–3308 (2009)
6. Sen, P. Efficient quantum tensor product expanders and unitary t-designs via the zigzag product. Arxiv:1808.10521 (2018)
7. Alon, N., Spencer, J.: The Probabilistic Method, 4th edn. Wiley (2016)
8. Proctor, T., Rudinger, K., Young, K., Sarovar, M., Blume-Kohout, R.: What randomized benchmarking actually measures. Phys. Rev. Lett. **119**, 130502 (2017)
9. Magesan, E., Gambetta, J., Emerson, J.: Scalable and robust randomized benchmarking of quantum processes. Phys. Rev. Lett. **106**, 180504 (2011)

10. Magesan, E., Gambetta, J., Emerson, J.: Characterizing quantum gates via randomized benchmarking. Phys. Rev. A **85**, 042311 (2012)
11. Magesan, E., Blume-Kohout, R., Emerson, J.: Gate fidelity fluctuations and quantum process invariants. Phys. Rev. A **84**, 012309 (2011)
12. Alexander, R., Turner, P., Bartlett, S.: Randomized benchmarking in measurement-based quantum computing. Phys. Rev. A **94**, 032303 (2016)
13. DiVincenzo, D., Leung, D., Terhal, B.: Quantum data hiding. IEEE Trans. Inf. Theory **48**(3), 580–599 (2002)
14. Cleve, R., Leung, D., Liu, L., Wang, C.: Near-linear constructions of exact unitary 2-designs. Quant. Inf. Comp. **16**(9&10), 0721–0756 (2016)
15. Alon, N., Goldreich, O., Håstad, J., Peralta, R.: Simple construction of almost k-wise independent random variables. Rand. Struct. Alg. **3**(3), 289–304 (1992)
16. Schmidt, J., Siegel, A., Srinivasan, A.: Chernoff—Hoeffding bounds for applications with limited independence. SIAM J. Discrete Math. **8**(2), 223–250 (1995)
17. Fawzi, O., Hayden, P., Sen, P.: From low-distortion norm embeddings to explicit uncertainty relations and efficient information locking. J. ACM. **60**(6), 44:1–44:60 (2013)
18. Kitaev, A., Watrous, J.: Parallelization, amplification, and exponential time simulation of quantum interactive proof systems. In: Proceedings of the 32nd Annual ACM Symposium on Theory of Computing, pp. 608–617 (2000)
19. Harrow, A., Hastings, J.: Classical and quantum tensor product expanders. Quant. Inf. and Comp. **9**, 336:1–336:18 (2009)
20. Goldreich, O.: Pseudorandom Generators: A Primer. University Lecture Serie, vol. 55. American Mathematical Society (2010)
21. Vershynin, R.: High Dimensional Probability. Cambridge University Press, Cambridge (2018)
22. Roth, I., et al.: Recovering quantum gates from few average gate fidelities. Phys. Rev. Lett. **121**(17), 170502:1–170502:8 (2018)
23. Shor, P.: Polynomial time algorithms for prime factorization and discrete logarithms on a quantum computer. SIAM J. Comput. **26**(5), 1484–1509 (1997)
24. Mannalath, V., Mishra, S., Pathak, A.: A comprehensive review of quantum random number generators: concepts, classification and the origin of randomness. Quantum Inf. Process. **22**, 439:1–439:44 (2023)
25. Knuth, D.: The Art of Computer Programming Vol 2: Seminumerical Algorithms. Addison-Wesley (1968)

DoPQM: Devices Oriented Post-quantum Cryptographic Migration Strategies for an Enterprise Network

Amit Bhowmick[1]($^\boxtimes$), Divyesh Saglani[4], Lakshmi Padmaja Maddali[3],
Akhila Rayala[2], Meena Singh Dilip Thakur[1],
and Rajan Mindigal Alasingara Bhattachar[1]

[1] TCS Research, Bengaluru, India
{ab.bhowmick,divyesh.saglani,lakshmipadmaja.maddali,meena.s1,
rajan.ma}@tcs.com
[2] Shiv Nadar University, Chennai, India
akhila22110015@snuchennai.edu.in
[3] TCS Research, Hyderabad, India
[4] TCS Research, Pune, India

Abstract. Quantum computing poses a major threat to classical cryptographic primitives (RSA, ECC, etc.), demanding an urgent migration to quantum-safe solutions, in any sensitive IT sectors such as banking enterprises. Merely replacing classical cryptographic primitives does not fully address this migration. This migration requires upgrades to network devices (e.g., routers, firewalls, servers) to ensure compatibility with future quantum-safe security protocols. Due to the scale of enterprise networks, a phased upgrade is necessary, as simultaneous migration of all devices is infeasible. However, a quantitative method for identifying network device vulnerabilities in large-scale enterprise networks is currently lacking.

We propose DoPQM: Devices Oriented Post-Quantum Migration, a framework for identifying network device vulnerabilities to quantum threats within enterprises network topologies. The primary objective of this work is to assist network administrators in identifying which network devices are more vulnerable to future quantum threats. DoPQM formalizes the *Harvest Now, Decrypt Later (HNDL)* adversarial model using a risk scoring mechanism that estimates HNDL attack likelihoods across network nodes. By leveraging graph theory, we identify central nodes based on the volume of data they handle. Each node is then assigned a criticality score that reflects its priority for post-quantum migration. Evaluation on a representative baking network reveals the Demilitarized Zone (DMZ) as the most HNDL vulnerable component.

Keywords: HNDL · post-quantum cryptography · quantum threats · eigen-vector centrality · risk management · network security

N. Hubballi et al. (Eds.): ICISS 2025, LNCS 16380, pp. 231–241, 2026.
https://doi.org/10.1007/978-3-032-13714-2_15

1   Introduction

Quantum computing threatens the foundation of modern cryptography by breaking asymmetric algorithms such as RSA and ECDSA through Shor's algorithm [10]. This risk introduces the Harvest Now, Decrypt Later (HNDL) attack[1]. There is growing urgency to adopt Post-Quantum Cryptography (PQC), algorithms designed to resist both classical and quantum attacks. Regulatory bodies, including NIST (SP 800-215 [1], NISTIR 8547 [8]), mandate phasing out classical cryptography by 2030–2035, making post-quantum migration an urgent global priority. However, migration to PQC is not just a technical substitution it requires careful planning.

Security-critical enterprise networks typically manage long-lived sensitive data and consist of interconnected devices[2] (henceforth referred to as network components), include reverse proxies, servers, authentication systems, and databases. These components are connected via network links that facilitate the communication and data flow through the infrastructure. A typical enterprise topology of a banking enterprise network,[3] illustrated in *Fig.* 1 begins at ATM terminals linked via branch and core routers, secured by firewalls, proxies, and

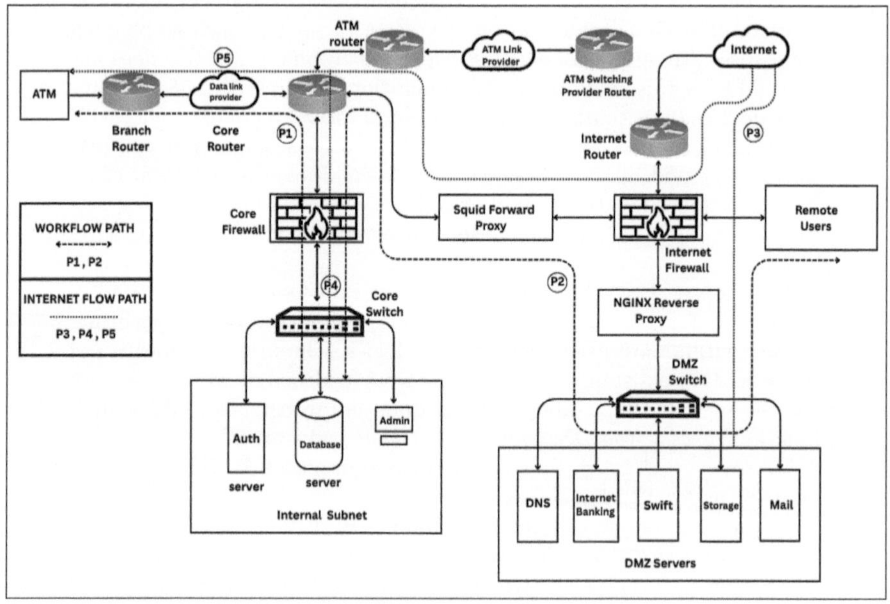

Fig. 1. A Banking Enterprise Network Architecture

----

[1] wherein adversaries collect encrypted data today for decryption once quantum computing resources mature.

[2] In this work, we limit our scope to network devices that participate in security protocols such as TLS, SSH, and IPsec.

[3] Diagram is created by authors in collaboration with a network architect.

access controls. The core switch interconnects authentication, database, and admin server, while internet-facing services (e.g., DNS, SWIFT, mail, and internet banking) are hosted in the demilitarized zone (DMZ). Traffic flows include ATM transactions *(P1)*, internet banking via DMZ *(P2)*, and additional internet paths *(P3P5)*.

In this work, we identify the network components that are most vulnerable to HNDL attacks, focusing on the risk posed by HNDL adversaries. Migration requires upgrading[4] thousands of devices to ensure continued compatibility with future security protocols. To support this, we present a structured framework, DoPQM, which evaluates component-level HNDL vulnerability and enables risk-informed transition and phased migration to quantum-safe state. We demonstrate our framework's applicability through a representative banking enterprise network as shown in Fig. 1. Banking systems handle highly sensitive data for extended periods (810 years), making them attractive HNDL targets. Using our framework, organizations can systematically evaluate the vulnerability of each component, assess vulnerabilities, quantify risks, and prioritize device upgrades accordingly. This structured migration not only strengthens financial data security but also aids compliance [6] with emerging regulations addressing quantum threats.

The paper is organized as follows: Sect. 1.1 reviews related work, Sect. 2 describes the system architecture, Sect. 3 explains the framework modules, Sect. 4 shows results, Sect. 5 concludes with future work.

1.1   Related Work

The rapid advancement of quantum computing has catalyzed extensive research into post-quantum techniques across various domains. Surveys by Fakhruldeen et al. [7] and Zeydan et al. [12] provide comprehensive overviews of quantum-resistant techniques for wireless and general networks. Fakhruldeen et al. focus on wireless network security and the challenges of transitioning public-key infrastructure, including the role of Quantum Key Distribution (QKD). Complementarily, Zeydan et al. offer a structured taxonomy of PQC in networks (communication, computation, and network levels), emphasizing the significant lack of standardized frameworks for deploying quantum-safe primitives in existing telecommunication infrastructures. Basu et al. [2] provide a hardware evaluation of NIST PQC candidates, demonstrating the security-efficiency trade-offs. Complementing the technical work, Beullens et al. [3] review the evolution of cryptographic standards by institutions like NIST and ENISA. They propose practical mitigation strategies, including hybrid encryption schemes, to systematically protect legacy systems from future quantum-enabled adversaries.

Despite the breadth of work in the state-of-the-art literature, a critical gap persists, the systematic modeling and quantification of HNDL threats in enterprise networks. Our work addresses this gap by introducing a analysis to assess

---

[4] Upgrades may involve software patches, hardware replacement, or both, to accommodate the computational demands of post-quantum cryptographic primitives.

node-level vulnerability to HNDL attacks. Unlike prior approaches that focus on cryptographic algorithm selection or abstract protocol migration [4], our framework emphasizes device level migration strategies on enterprise network topologies. This enables targeted, device-level PQC migration strategies aligned with NIST SP 8547 [8] guidelines, and application-friendly post-quantum migration for diverse industrial networks.

2   DoPQM: System Architecture

This section outlines the overall architecture of our proposed DoPQM framework. To determine the critical score for each network point, five modules interact, as illustrated in Fig. 2. The framework includes the following modules:

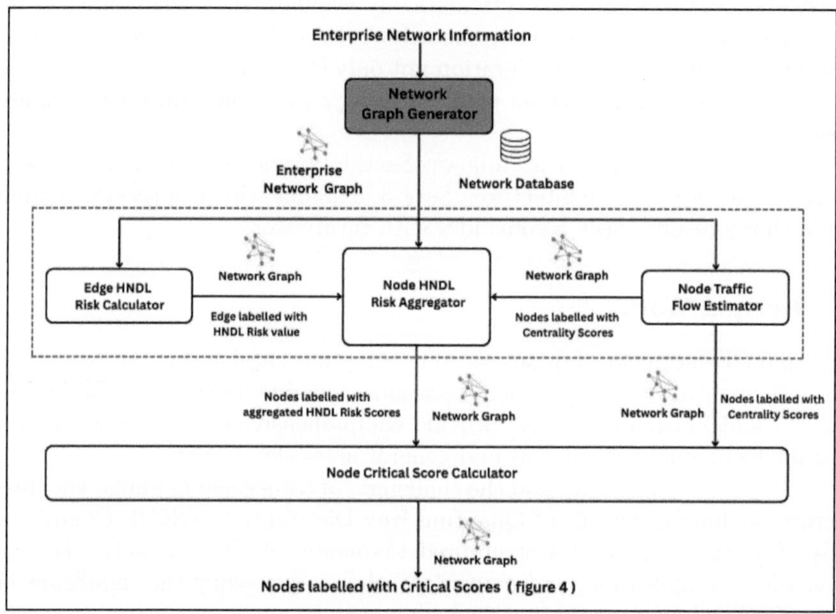

Fig. 2. DoPQM: Framework for Calculating Critical Score for Network Component

Network Graph Generator: This module constructs a directed graph model of an enterprise network using various input sources, including network administrator insights, historical traffic logs, and outputs from network scanning tools.[5]
Edge HNDL Risk Calculator: Given a network graph and its metadata, this module computes a risk score for each edge, capturing the likelihood of a

---

[5] Each node in the graph represents a network device (often termed network components), and each directed edge (often termed network links) indicates a flow of data between components.

successful HNDL attack[6], termed the edge HNDL risk. **Node Traffic Flow Estimator:** This module also takes the graph and corresponding database as an input and figures out what proportion of the network traffic passes through any node. **Node HNDL Risk Aggregator:** It proposes a method to calculate aggregated HNDL risk associated with every node of the graph. **Node Critical Score Calculator:** The final module assigns a criticality score to each node.

3   DoPQM: System Description

Let any arbitrary enterprise network, like a banking network, be represented as a directed graph, denoted by $G = (V, E)$[7].

Table 1. Used Notational Convention

Notation	Description
V	Set of vertices in the graph representing network devices
E	Set of edges in the graph, where each edge represents directed flow of data between two nodes
$e \in E,\ v \in V$	Represents an edge and a vertex from the edge set and vertex set, respectively
$e_{v_1 v_2} \in E,\ v_1, v_2 \in V$	Represent an edge from vertex v_1 to v_2

3.1   HNDL Adversarial Model

The objective of a HNDL adversary, A_{HNDL}, is to collect encrypted data from network links[8] with the intention of decrypting it once a cryptographically relevant quantum computer becomes available. We denote the future point in time termed as *Q-day*. Let d_e be the amount of data collected by A_{HNDL} adversary from a network link (or edge) e. The HNDL risk associated with that edge can be then defined as:

$$R^e_{HNDL} = \mathcal{F}(m \leftarrow A_{HNDL}(d_e)) = \mathcal{F}(A_{HNDL}\text{able to decrypt } d_e \text{ after Q-day})$$

This section outlines the key parameters influencing the *HNDL* risk across network links.[9] The four primary parameters are:

1) **Public Key Cryptography** (x_1) - Algorithms such as RSA and ECC are highly vulnerable to Shor's algorithm threatening key exchange and authentication mechanism. 2) **Symmetric Key Length** (x_2) - Grover's algorithm

---

[6] Here we restrict ourselves to a passive adversary.

[7] The notational conventions used throughout this paper are summarized in Table 1.

[8] Here we restrict ourselves only to data in motion scenario.

[9] Our focus is on factors most affected by quantum computing. The model is extensible allowing integration of additional parameters for real world deployments.

effectively halves symmetric cipher strength, making shorter keys more susceptible. 3) **Key Rotation Frequency** (x_3) - Longer key reuse intervals increase the
risk of quantum attacks. 4) **Data Lifetime** (x_4) - Longer retention of encrypted
data raises HNDL vulnerability, as adversaries can decrypt it once quantum
resource mature.

The overall risk for a network link is modeled as:

$$R^e_{HNDL} = \mathcal{F}(x_1, x_2, x_3, x_4, T_0, T_Q, q)$$

where T_0 denotes the current time, T_Q the projected $Q\text{-}day$ and q the available
qubits. The proposed risk function is defined as:

$$R^e_{HNDL} = \left(e^{\frac{x_4 - \Delta T}{x_4}} \right) \cdot \frac{\frac{\text{SecurityBits}_{req}}{\text{SecurityBits}_{curr}(x_1)} \cdot \frac{\text{KeyRotation}_{req}}{\text{KeyRotation}_{curr}(x_3)}}{\sigma \left(\frac{1}{2^{\frac{x_2}{2}}} + \frac{\text{qubits}_{curr}}{\text{qubits}_{req}(x_1)} \right)} \tag{1}$$

where $\sigma(\cdot)$ is the logistic scaling function and $\Delta T = T_Q - T_0$.

This unified formulation in Eq. 1 quantifies link-level HNDL vulnerability
by integrating cryptographic strength, temporal exposure, and quantum capability growth. It forms the analytical backbone of the **DoPQM** framework for
prioritizing post quantum migration.

Intuition: The exponential term $e^{\frac{x_4 - \Delta T}{x_4}}$ models the urgency of migration to
PQC based on data shelf life. As ΔT increases relative to x_4, the risk of quantum
decryption grows exponentially, reflecting the exponential increase in capability
of quantum systems [11].

The ratio $\frac{\text{SecurityBits}_{req}}{\text{SecurityBits}_{curr}(x_1)}$ quantifies the gap between the current and post-
quantum security requirements. With RSA-2048 and ECC-256 expected to be
deprecated by 2030 [8], higher ratios indicate inadequate cryptographic strength
and raise the risk score.

Similarly, $\frac{\text{KeyRotation}_{req}}{\text{KeyRotation}_{curr}(x_3)}$ penalizes infrequent key updates, promoting
rotation practices aligned with quantum-safe standards.

Finally, the combined term $\frac{1}{2^{\frac{x_2}{2}}} + \frac{\text{qubits}_{curr}}{\text{qubits}_{req}(x_1)}$ captures vulnerabilities from
Grover's and Shor's algorithms-linking symmetric key length and quantum
resource growth. A logistic scaling function $\sigma(\cdot)$ normalizes the final score
between 0 and 1, ensuring balanced sensitivity across parameters.

The resulting formulation yields a unified, interpretable HNDL risk score that
highlights the devices most susceptible to future quantum attacks. We present
HNDL risk scores for different combinations in Table 2.

3.2   Node Critical Score Calculator

The concept of *PQC migration* of a network refers to the process of upgrading network devices to support both post-quantum and classical cryptographic
algorithms. To facilitate this migration, we focus on calculating a critical score
for each network device which is interpreted as a priority number assigned to

the network nodes, used to rank them for migration to a quantum-safe state. The critical score is calculated considering the likelihood of a successful HNDL attack on the node's adjacent network links and the proportion of network data held by the node. Below, we outline this method:

Node Traffic Flow Estimator: In an HNDL attack scenario, the vulnerability increases with the amount of data captured, making it crucial to estimate the traffic following through each device relative to the total network traffic. To address this, we leverage the concepts from graph theory to derive a centrality measure which is named as Modified Eigenvector Centrality[10]. We briefly discuss some prerequisites to provide necessary context.

Suppose some object[11] is moving through a graph G and its location at the current step is vertex v_i. Let the out-degree of the vertex be $d_{out}^{v_i}$. Then, at the next step, the location is a vertex v_j chosen uniformly at random from the set of out-neighbors of v_i. Such a process is called a **random walk** or **Markov chain**. As we are considering network traffic flow, in a real scenario it doesn't choose the next node uniformly like a random walk. At a certain node v_i, it chooses the next node based on the routing table information, denoted as R^{v_i} at the node v_i. Let's define the transition matrix corresponding to the network graph as $T = (t_{ij})_{i,j} = (t_{v_i v_j})_{i,j}, \sum_j t_{ij} = 1$, Where t_{ij} denotes the probability that the object will be sent to the vertex v_j in the next step when current vertex is v_i. This value is derived from the routing table R^{v_i} at the vertex v_i. If the vertex v_i sends $p-$percent of it's total traffic to v_j, then $t_{ij} = \frac{p}{100}$

Let $G = (V, E)$ be a directed graph representing our network, such that $|V| = n$. Choose any arbitrary vector $\mathbf{w^0} = (w_1^0, w_2^0, ..., w_n^0)$ such that $\sum_i w_i^0 = 1$, where w_i represents the probability of moving data packet is at vertex v_i at the $0-$th step. As T represents the transition matrix, we can generate a sequence $\mathbf{w^{t+1}} \leftarrow T\mathbf{w^t}$. This sequence will always converge to a vector $\mathbf{w}^*$ (By Perron-Frobenius Theorem [9]), which is the eigenvector of the matrix T corresponding to the largest eigenvalue (Exists by Perron-Frobenius Theorem). Here, $\mathbf{w^t}$ is the position of the network traffic at the t-th step.

Modified Eigenvector Centrality. Let T be the transition matrix of the graph and λ be the eigenvalue with highest absolute value and the $\mathbf{w} = (w_1, w_2, ..., w_n)$ be the unique (up to a constant) eigenvector (Exists by Perron-Frobenius Theorem) corresponding to λ. Then w_i, denoted as $MEC(v_i)$, is the modified eigenvector centrality of the i-th vertex of the graph.

Theorem 1. *Node with high modified eigenvector centrality implies it's responsible for a significant amount of traffic.*

Proof. The eigenvalue equation is given by: $T\mathbf{w} = \lambda\mathbf{w}$, where T is the transition matrix, $\mathbf{w}$ is the eigenvector, and λ is the eigenvalue.

---

[10] This centrality measure identifies the portion of network traffic held by each node.
[11] Object refers to data packet on network graph.

Expanding this equation:

$$\begin{pmatrix} t_{11} & t_{12} & \cdots & t_{1n} \\ t_{21} & t_{22} & \cdots & t_{2n} \\ \vdots & \vdots & \ddots & \vdots \\ t_{n1} & t_{n2} & \cdots & t_{nn} \end{pmatrix} \begin{pmatrix} w_1 \\ w_2 \\ \vdots \\ w_n \end{pmatrix} = \lambda \begin{pmatrix} w_1 \\ w_2 \\ \vdots \\ w_n \end{pmatrix}$$

This implies: $\sum_{j=1}^{n} t_{ij} w_j = \lambda w_i$. Rewriting: $\lambda w_i = \sum_{j \in N_i} t_{ij} w_j$, where N_i is the set of out-neighbors of node i. Using a proportionality factor: $\lambda w_i \propto \sum_{j \in N_i} D_{ij} w_j$, where D_{ij} represents the amount of traffic from node i to j. Thus, w_i will be higher if D_{ij} is high for neighboring nodes.

Conclusion: A node with high modified eigenvector centrality should be responsible for a significant amount of traffic.

Node HNDL Risk Aggregator: In this section we have given a method to transfer the HNDL risk of the edge to its adjacent node based on the routing protocol of the adjacent incoming nodes. We have defined that factor as $E_{HNDL}^{v} = \sum_j t_{v_j v} R_{HNDL}^{e_{v_j v}}$, Where, j runs over all in-vertex of v.

Critical Score for Network Component: Now the critical score associated with any node can be calculated as $C_{HNDL}^{v} = \mathcal{G}(\text{MEC}(v), E_{HNDL}^{v})$ The specific choice of the function $\mathcal{G}$ is not crucial, as it can be any suitably defined function. The primary objective of this work is to assist network administrators in identifying which network devices are more vulnerable to future quantum threats. Therefore, it is essential to preserve the relative vulnerability ordering of the devices rather than the exact numerical values. As long as the same function, $\mathcal{G}$, is consistently applied while computing the critical score for each node, the resulting scores will maintain the original vulnerability order. For the sake of completeness, we propose one such function, $\mathcal{G}$, in this work.

$$C_{HNDL}^{v} = \mathcal{G}(\text{MEC}(v), E_{HNDL}^{v}) = E_{HNDL}^{v} * e^{MEC(v)}$$

Having defined E_{HNDL}^{v} and $\text{MEC}(v)$ in the last section, this formulation is inspired by COCOMO [5]-style effort estimation functions. $\text{MEC}(v)$ represents the proportion of total network traffic that passes through a given network node, analogous to the "lines of code" parameter in traditional software models, capturing the exponential impact of load. The variable E_{HNDL}^{v} represents the cryptographic risk level associated with the node, determined by the cryptographic parameters it uses, this value remains static once assigned[12].

---

[12] While we do not claim this to be the optimal functional form, it effectively captures the intended intuition behind criticality and risk. Alternative formulations may be explored in future work.

4   Simulation and Results

We have applied our proposed framework on a banking enterprise network mentioned in Fig. 1 to show the it's applicability. **Implementation details** We implemented the proposed model in Python using the NetworkX library. The implementation was run on a node with an AMD Ryzen^{TM} 5 5600U processor with Radeon^{TM} Graphics (12 cores) and 16 GB of RAM. Our framework first calculates the HNDL risk for each edge in the graph using the Eq. 1. Next, we compute the centrality score and HNDL risk scores for each network node and finally, the criticality score. This criticality score serves as a priority metric for the PQC migration process for the network devices. **Quantifying edge HNDL Risk** Table 2 presents the possible values of edge HNDL risk for various combinations of the four parameters described in Sect. 3.2. We have established several key parameters as well. We set the parameters, ΔT as 2, where ΔT is time difference between current day and quantum day in years. We set logical qubits present on quantum day as 1000, minimum key rotation frequency required as 60 days, and minimum security bits required as 256 for the public key encryption algorithm. We then take reference from [6] to extract the number of logical qubits required to break the public key encryption algorithms and [1,11] to find the security bit level for each of the public key algorithm. The results highlight how a link is penalized for having lower public key security, shorter key length, longer key rotation times, and extended data lifetimes.

Table 2. HNDL Risk Score for different cases

Public Key Cryptography (x1)	Symmetric Key Length (x2)	Key Rotation Frequency (x3) (days)	Data Lifetime (x4) (years)	HNDL Risk Score (R^e_{HNDL})
ECDHE-224	AES-128	367	16	1.480
RSA-2048	AES-128	666	16	0.881
DH-1536	AES-128	543	18	1.096
RSA-4096	AES-192	567	16	0.957
ECDHE-256	AES-192	550	16	0.864
RSA-4096	AES-256	453	10	1.111

Analyzing Node Critical Score. We apply our proposed algorithm on network shown in Fig. 1, and compute the critical scores for each node in the network depicting their respective vulnerability to HNDL attakcs. Figure 3 presents a visualization of the network nodes, annotated with their respective critical scores.

We observe that the DMZ node exhibits the highest vulnerability score of 1.0, primarily due to its strategic placement, while the core router and internet firewall, despite occupying similar topological positions, record much lower scores of 0.3 and 0.0. This discrepancy may stem from factors such as the data shelf life or variations in other parameter employed during communication. These observations highlight the significance of the HNDL adversarial model and the scoring function we have formulated. Additionally, the centrality measures used in the

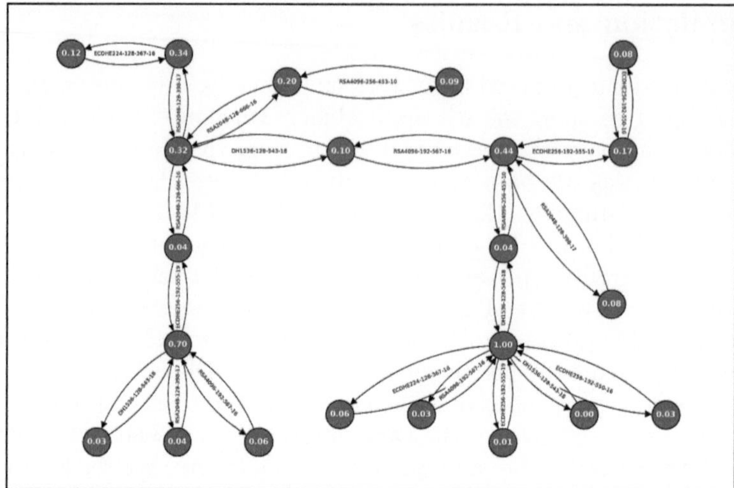

Fig. 3. Banking Enterprise Network Architecture Graph with Critical Score Evaluation

analysis are crucial as they not only capture the node degree but also it the proportion data they possess, making it well-suited to identify influential nodes in the network. As no existing baseline model addresses such transition prioritization, a direct comparison was not feasible. Nonetheless, the results demonstrate that our framework effectively identifies nodes most exposed to cryptographic risks and central to the system's communication flow.

5   Discussion and Future Work

To the best of our knowledge, this is the first framework that quantitatively evaluates the vulnerability of enterprise network points to HNDL attacks under quantum threats. This work underscores the urgent need for practical tools to guide the migration of enterprise networks from classical to quantum-safe states. For future work, we plan to develop threat models for HNDL adversaries and strengthen the HNDL risk metric by grounding it in more realistic assumptions.

References

1. Barker, E.B., Barker, W.C., Lee, A.: SP 800-21 second edition. Guideline for implementing cryptography in the federal government. National Institute of Standards & Technology (2005)
2. Basu, K., Soni, D., Nabeel, M., Karri, R.: NIST post-quantum cryptography-a hardware evaluation study. Cryptology ePrint Archive (2019)
3. Beullens, W., et al.: Post-quantum cryptography: current state and quantum mitigation (2021)

4. Bindel, N., Brendel, J., Fischlin, M., Goncalves, B., Stebila, D.: Hybrid key encapsulation mechanisms and authenticated key exchange. In: Ding, J., Steinwandt, R. (eds.) PQCrypto 2019. LNCS, vol. 11505, pp. 206–226. Springer, Cham (2019). https://doi.org/10.1007/978-3-030-25510-7_12

5. Boehm, B., Valerdi, R., Lane, J., Brown, A.: Cocomo suite methodology and evolution. CrossTalk **18**(4), 20–25 (2005)

6. Chen, L., et al.: Report on post-quantum cryptography, vol. 12. US Department of Commerce, National Institute of Standards and Technology ... (2016)

7. Fakhruldeen, H.F., Al-Kaabi, R.A., Jabbar, F.I., Al-Kharsan, I.H., Shoja, S.J.: Post-quantum techniques in wireless network security: an overview. Malays. J. Fundam. Appl. Sci. **19**(3), 337–344 (2023)

8. Moody, D., Perlner, R., Regenscheid, A., Robinson, A., Cooper, D.: Transition to post-quantum cryptography standards. Technical report, National Institute of Standards and Technology (2024)

9. Pillai, S.U., Suel, T., Cha, S.: The Perron-Frobenius theorem: some of its applications. IEEE Signal Process. Mag. **22**(2), 62–75 (2005)

10. Shor, P.W.: Polynomial-time algorithms for prime factorization and discrete logarithms on a quantum computer. SIAM Rev. **41**(2), 303–332 (1999)

11. Skavysh, V., Priazhkina, S., Guala, D., Bromley, T.R.: Quantum Monte Carlo for economics: Stress testing and macroeconomic deep learning. J. Econ. Dyn. Control **153**, 104680 (2023)

12. Zeydan, E., Turk, Y., Aksoy, B., Ozturk, S.B.: Recent advances in post-quantum cryptography for networks: a survey. In: 2022 Seventh International Conference on Mobile and Secure Services (MobiSecServ), pp. 1–8. IEEE (2022)

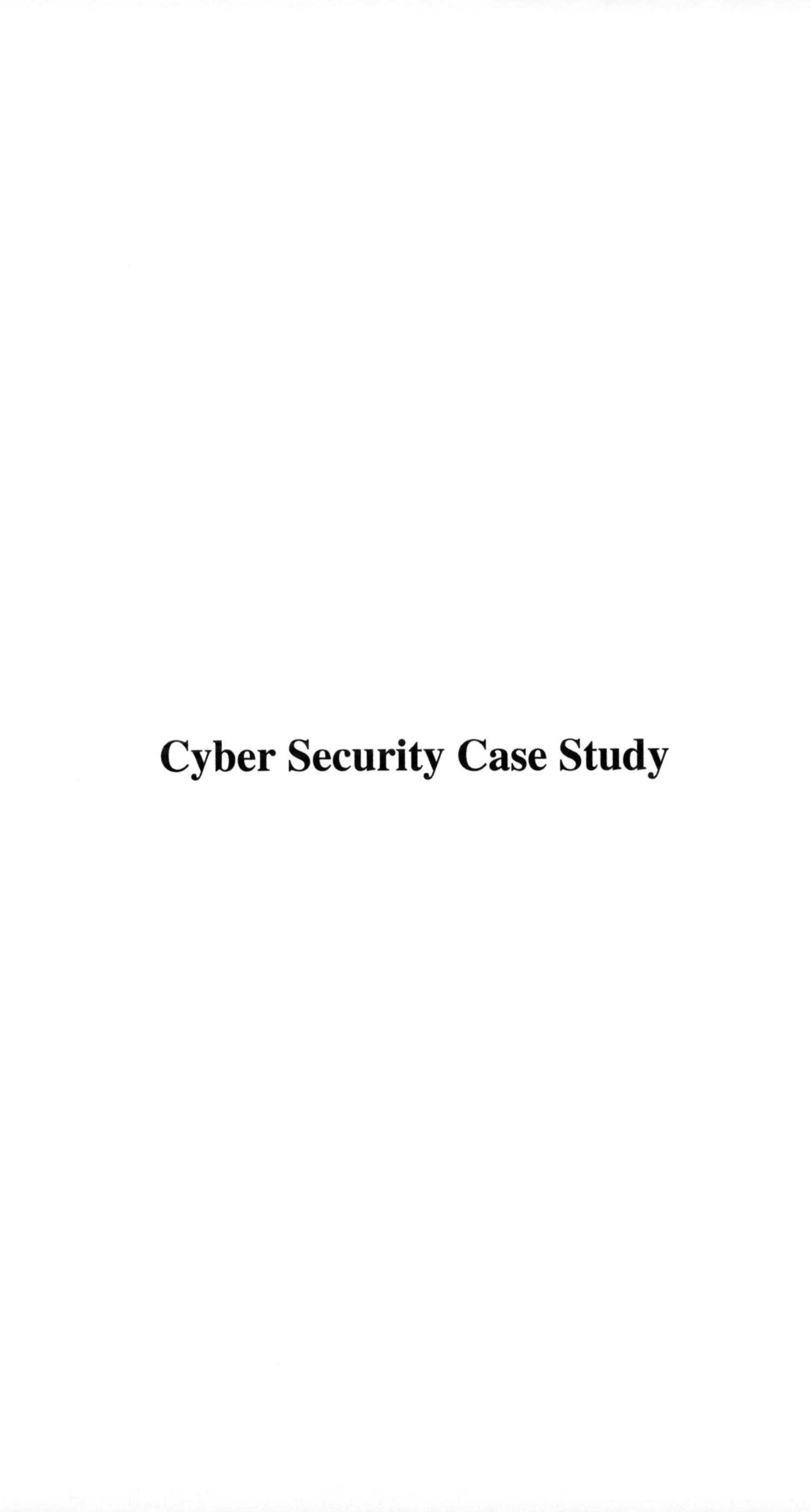

Cyber Security Case Study

Cyber Warfare During Operation Sindoor: Malware Campaign Analysis and Detection Framework

Prakhar Paliwal, Atul Kabra, and Manjesh Kumar Hanawal[✉]

Indian Institute of Technology Bombay, Mumbai, Maharashtra, India
{prakhar.paliwal,25D2020,mhanawal}@iitb.ac.in

Abstract. Rapid digitization of critical infrastructure has made cyberwarfare one of the important dimensions of modern conflicts. Attacking the critical infrastructure is an attractive pre-emptive proposition for adversaries as it can be done remotely without crossing borders. Such attacks disturb the support systems of the opponents to launch any offensive activities, crippling their fighting capabilities. Cyberattacks during cyberwarfare can not only be used to steal information, but also to spread disinformation to bring down the morale of the opponents. Recent wars in Europe, Africa, and Asia have demonstrated the scale and sophistication that the warring nations have deployed to take the early upper hand. In this work, we focus on the military action launched by India, code-named Operation Sindoor, to dismantle terror infrastructure emanating from Pakistan and the cyberattacks launched by Pakistan. In particular, we study the malware used by Pakistan APT groups to deploy Remote Access Trojans in Indian systems. We provide details of the tactics and techniques used in the RAT deployment and develop a telemetry framework to collect necessary event logs using Osquery with a custom extension. Finally, we develop a detection rule that can be readily deployed to detect the presence of the RAT or any exploitation performed by the malware.

Keywords: Operation Sindoor · Malware Campaign Analysis · Osquery · Malware detection · APTs · Cyberwarfare

1 Introduction

Cyberattacks have become an integral component of modern warfare. They are activated at the onset of the conflicts even before any firepowers are launched or when the hostilities are imminent. Critical infrastructure like power, telecom networks, nuclear power plants, and financial systems that are heavily reliant on cyberspace become the primary target of attackers. In addition to crippling the infrastructure, attackers also resort to stealing information, spreading disinformation, and defacing the government portal to bring down the morale of its opponents. Recent conflicts between Russia and Ukraine [1], Iran and Isreal [2],

N. Hubballi et al. (Eds.): ICISS 2025, LNCS 16380, pp. 245–266, 2026.
https://doi.org/10.1007/978-3-032-13714-2_16

India and Pakistan [3], Cambodia and Thailand [4] led to several cyber attacks between the warring nations. These examples reveal that cyber operations are now woven into the fabric of modern warfare, shaping both the course and the outcome of physical confrontations. In this work, we focus on the military operation, code named 'Operation Sindoor' launched by India, and the cyberattack it faced. We will discuss the modus-operandi of the attackers and develop a framework to detect the attack.

Operation Sindoor, launched in May 2025 by Indian military forces as a tactical response to the terrorist assault in Pahalgam on 22 April where attackers shot several unarmed male tourists at point-blank range in front of their pleading families. Operation Sindoor was characterized by precise and focused strikes against terrorist infrastructure, executed without violating international borders - a reflection of India's growing emphasis on strategic, measured defense postures [5]. While physical military operations unfolded on borders with firepower crossing borders, a quieter and less visible battle was waged in cyberspace. Indian networks across government departments, defense institutions and critical civilian sectors began to experience a wave of cyber attacks, suggesting that the punitive action initiated by India on the terror infrastructure had triggered a coordinated offensive cyber campaigns by Pakistani groups.

While the primary focus of offensive cyber campaigns is to sabotage critical infrastructure needed to support military operation and deprive a nation from using its full military capabilities, it also aims to manipulate information flows to bias public opinions. Parallelly the attackers can operate cyber espionage in the shadows, quietly penetrating networks to gather political, military, or economic intelligence over extended periods, often without immediate visible disruption. All forms were likely at play during Operation Sindoor, as adversaries sought not only to weaken India's operational capabilities but also to steal sensitive data and manipulate public opinion.

Behind these categories of cyber activity lies a diverse ecosystem of actors, each playing distinct yet often interconnected roles. Advanced Persistent Threat (APT) groups - elite, well-resourced groups frequently tied to state intelligence agencies - operate as long-term specialists of cyber conflict, infiltrating networks with the patience to remain undetected for months or even years. Their operations are strategic, designed to align with national objectives, whether that means pre-positioning for sabotage or extracting intelligence critical to military planning. Alongside them, more transactional entities, such as hack-for-hire groups and cyber mercenaries, provide on-demand capabilities, allowing states and other clients to commission specific operations without direct involvement. These actors offer both expertise and plausible deniability, enabling campaigns that are precise, targeted, and deniable.

During Operation Sindoor, a malware was propagated through spear phishing emails that targeted government officials. The malware was sent as an email attachment disguised as a detailed report on Operation Sindoor. The report included a Remote Access Trojan (RAT) that would trigger when a user opened the attached file. The RAT then connected to a command and control server enabling the attackers to execute more than 20 commands on the endpoint remotely. The commands enabled the remote attackers to perform various activities like screen capture, delete file, and exfiltrate files to C2. This in turn could serve as a pipeline to offload other stronger malware or ransomware to exfiltrate and encrypt data.

Attackers can deploy a combination of tactics, techniques, and procedures (TTPs) as listed in the Mitre Attack framework [6]. For example, they can use various techniques like spearphishing to obtain initial access to the victim machine, and then use the payload (RAT) to execute malicious commands. Having visibility to events corresponding to these TTPs is important to detect the attacks. The behaviour of the malware during Operation Sindoor is well documented in [7,8].

Several tools are available to collect information about activities performed by malware by logging system activities on the endpoints. We identify all the necessary events that need to be monitored to detect the malware. We use Osquery [9,10], an endpoint operating system orchestration tool, to gather all the relevant activities of the malware. The default windows version of Osquery does not support collection of all the relevant logs. But thanks to the extensibility feature of Osquery, we use a custom extension to enhance the default capability of Osquery to gather additional logs related to the activities performed by the malware.

We map the events in the logs to the activities of the malware and establish correlation across various events such as process spawning, file, and network activities to develop a detection if an endpoint is subject to the malware attack. Also, our framework allows us to detect the presence of malware in the early stages and prevent it from performing any malicious activities. Finally, we develop a SQL query that can be run on an endpoint with Osquery with the custom extension to detect the presence of the malware. In summary, our contributions are as follows:

- Identify the events that needs to be logged for telemetry
- Develop a framework to detect the malicious behaviour from the telemetry
- An SQL rule to detect if an endpoint is subject to the malware attack.

The rest of the paper is organized as follows: In Sect. 2, we provide details about the malware used in the cyber campaign during Operation Sindoor. In Sect. 3, we discuss about the logging the necessary events to establish telemetry. In Sect. 4, we provide details about analysis of the telemetry logs and develop a rule to detect the malware. We end with conclusions in Sect. 5.

1.1 Related Works

Cybersecurity research has long explored attack campaigns, detection mechanism, and incident analysis frameworks, offering insights into large-scale and politically motivated cyber operations. A survey on cyber warfare analyzes the domain across its physical, syntactic, and semantic layers, outlining common attack vectors such as reconnaissance, access, denial-of-service, and espionage, and highlighting the motivations, tools, and potential impacts ranging from disruption of essential services to national security threats [11]. Such operations, from state-sponsored espionage to hacktivist or "hack-for-hire" campaigns, often start with reconnaissance. Any operation, spanning from state-sponsored espionage to hacktivist or a "hack-for-hire" campaigns, often begin with reconnaissance. A survey on cyber scanning which is often the first step of any kind of attack shows how it helps attackers find targets, spot weaknesses, and plan large-scale, coordinated, and stealthy attacks [12]. Below, we review studies on malware campaigns in cyber warfare.

SSH Attacks: One major area of investigation has focused on the persistence and tactics of intruders during prolonged intrusion attempts. [13] analyzes SSH brute-force activity in a production environment, revealing patterns of repeated credential guessing, attacker geolocation, and the recurrence of specific adversary infrastructure over weeks. Their use of flow-based network features with machine learning classifiers achieved high accuracy in differentiating successful from failed logins, demonstrating the feasibility of scalable intrusion detection in real-world campaigns.

Visibility and Telemetry: Advanced endpoint detection and response (EDR) solutions, such as those studied by Medisetti et al. [14], integrate behavioral analytics, host telemetry, and historical baselines to detect anomalies indicative of lateral movement and data exfiltration. Such endpoint-level intelligence complements network telemetry, offering visibility into the deeper stages of an attack lifecycle. Also, just looking into the telemetry with the use of native windows tool like sysmon and ETW (Event Trace for Windows) may not be enough as they are not 'evented'[1]. Current cybersecurity related incidents requires telemetry which can be logged asynchronously over time in an evented manner to perform correlation analysis [15]. The native Auditd demon in Linux offers contextualized log collections, but has problems with log forwarding, storing and parsing for future use [16].

Cyber Terrorism: The strategic dimension of cyber operations has also been examined in the context of cyber terrorism and information warfare. [17] documented how politically motivated actors combine cyber intrusions with psychological and information operations to disrupt governance and destabilize societies. Aggrey et al. [18] extended this by analyzing recent advanced persistent threat (APT) incidents, illustrating how attackers align technical compromises with long-term strategic objectives. In addition, O'Brien [19] emphasized the role of modern security frameworks and threat intelligence integration in countering advanced state-sponsored actors, such as the Russian group Cozy Bear aka APT-29. These insights are directly relevant to Operation Sindoor, where attribution, capability assessment, and defensive readiness form an integral part of campaign analysis done by APT groups.

Regional Campaign Analysis: Regional threat intelligence further enriches campaign analysis by situating incidents within their geopolitical context. [20] examined cyberattack patterns across APCERT member nations, identifying prevalent malware families, favored attack vectors, and cross-border incident trends. These findings underscore the importance of contextualizing Operation Sindoor within the broader Asia-Pacific threat environment, where geopolitical

---

[1] Logs are collected not just when the query is launched, but all between the queries so that no log is lost in-between the queries.

tensions and regional alliances can influence both targeting and attacker behavior.

While such detection-oriented studies capture the operational signatures of attackers, other works provide structured frameworks for understanding their tactics and planning effective defences. [21] proposed a threat analysis methodology that maps adversary actions to the cyber kill chain, enabling security teams to evaluate vulnerabilities, anticipate attack stages, and prioritize countermeasures. This systematic approach is particularly applicable when examining campaigns that unfold in multiple coordinated phases, as in the case of Operation Sindoor.

Attacks are not limited to endpoints or traditional IT systems any more. Cyber-physical power systems have been targeted by attacks that exploit weaknesses in the physical, cyber, and control layers, and researchers have reviewed these attack types along with detection and defense methods, from state-estimation approaches to machine learning-based solutions [22], In a similar manner, IIoT systems are also being targeted, as they face attacks such as denial-of-service, data breaches, and malware injection, targeting different layers of the architecture and there is a need to develop effective defences which increases the security of IIoT systems [23].

Taken together, these studies paint a comprehensive picture of how cyber campaigns are planned, executed, and detected. They also reveal the necessity of combining multiple analytical perspectives - from flow-based detection and endpoint analytics to geopolitical context and strategic threat modelling - in order to fully understand and counter complex, targeted operations. This multilayered approach forms the basis for the methodology applied in the present study of the Operation Sindoor cyberattack campaign.

2   Operation Sindoor Campaign

Operation Sindoor, originally a military response to the terrorist attack in Pahalgam on April 22, 2025, swiftly evolved into a sophisticated cyber campaign orchestrated by Advanced Persistent Threat (APT) group APT36, also known as Transparent Tribe [24], capitalizing on the incident's geopolitical significance. Telemetry data, identified anomalous spear-phishing traffic targeting Indian government and defence networks commencing April 17, 2025, five days prior to the attack, suggesting preemptive reconnaissance activities [7]. By April 24, 2025, malicious documents exploiting the Pahalgam attack, such as "Action Points & Response by Govt Regarding Pahalgam Terror Attack.pdf" (authored under the pseudonym "Kalu Badshah"), proliferated across public domains, hosted on fraudulent websites including *jkpolice[.]gov[.]in[.]kashmirattack[.]exposed* and *pahalgamattack[.]com* [7]. These domains, registered within 48 h post-attack and hosted across autonomous systems such as AS 200019 (Alexhost Srl) and AS 213373 (IP Connect Inc), impersonated reputable Indian entities, notably the Jammu & Kashmir Police and Indian Air Force, to facilitate credential harvesting and surreptitious data exfiltration. Such cyber intrusions underscored the vulnerabilities in existing cybersecurity infrastructure, highlighting the critical need for enhanced cybersecurity readiness, training, and resilient defensive frameworks. The strategic ramifications of these cyber assaults during Operation Sindoor included compromised communications, and an elevated risks of sensitive data breaches, thereby amplifying geopolitical tensions, highlighting the campaign's role in contemporary hybrid warfare dynamics.

Coordinated cyber incidents targeting critical sectors, including defense, government IT, healthcare, telecommunications, and education were recorded during the period when Operation Sindoor was taking place [8].

Spear-phishing emails distributed weaponized files, masquerading as official advisories to exploit heightened public concern over national security. These emails featured a diverse array of malicious file formats-PDF, PPTX.LNK, PPAM, XLAM, XLSB, and MSI-to circumvent security protocols and exploit user trust. For instance, the PDF document *"Action Points & Response by Govt Regarding Pahalgam Terror Attack.pdf"* embedded hyperlinks redirecting to fraudulent login pages designed for credential phishing, were hosted on domains like *jkpolice[.]gov[.]in[.]kashmirattack[.]exposed*. A full list of file names and malicious domains can be found in Table 1 and 2 respectively.

Table 1. Compilation of Documents

S. No.	Document	Format
1	Report & Update Regarding Pahalgam Terror Attack	PDF
2	Report Update Regarding Pahalgam Terror Attack	PDF
3	Action Points & Response by Govt Regarding Pahalgam Terror Attack	PDF
4	J&K Police Letter	PDF
5	ROD on Review Meeting held on 10 Apr 2025 by Secy DRDO	PDF
6	Record of Discussion – Technical Review Meeting Notice	PDF
7	Meeting Notice – 13th JWG meeting (India – Nepal)	PDF
8	Agenda Points for Joint Venture Meeting at IHQ MoD	PDF
9	DO Letter, Integrated HQ of MoD	PDF
10	Collegiate Meeting Notice & Action Points – MoD	PDF
11	Letter to the Raksha Mantri Office	PDF
12	(Unnamed file "pdf")	PDF
13	Alleged Case of Sexual Harassment by Senior Army Officer	PDF
14	Agenda Points of Meeting of Dept of Defence	HTML
15	Action Points of Meeting of Dept of Defence	HTML
16	Agenda Points of Meeting of External Affairs Dept	HTML

While the pdfs were being used for phishing, Macro-enabled files such as files with .ppam, .xlam and .xlsb formats embedded malicious macros which were used to deploy malware upon user interaction. One such power point add-on

Table 2. Phishing Domains and Associated IP Addresses

S. No.	Domain Name	IP Address(es)
1	jkpolice[.]gov[.]in[.]kashmirattack[.]exposed	37.221.64.134, 78.40.143.189
2	iaf[.]nic[.]in[.]ministryofdefenceindia[.]org	37.221.64.134
3	email[.]gov[.]in[.]ministryofdefenceindia[.]org	45.141.58.224
4	email[.]gov[.]in[.]departmentofdefenceindia[.]link	45.141.59.167
5	email[.]gov[.]in[.]departmentofdefence[.]de	45.141.58.224
6	email[.]gov[.]in[.]briefcases[.]email	45.141.58.224, 78.40.143.98
7	email[.]gov[.]in[.]modindia[.]link	84.54.51.12
8	email[.]gov[.]in[.]defenceindia[.]ltd	45.141.58.224, 45.141.58.33
9	email[.]gov[.]in[.]indiadefencedepartment[.]link	45.141.59.167
10	email[.]gov[.]in[.]departmentofspace[.]info	45.141.58.224
11	email[.]gov[.]in[.]indiangov[.]download	45.141.58.33, 78.40.143.98
12	indianarmy[.]nic[.]in[.]departmentofdefence[.]de	176.65.143.215
13	indianarmy[.]nic[.]in[.]ministryofdefenceindia[.]org	176.65.143.215
14	email[.]gov[.]in[.]indiandefence[.]work	45.141.59.72
15	email[.]gov[.]in[.]drdosurvey[.]info	192.64.118.76

file named *"Report & Update Regarding Pahalgam Terror Attack.ppam"*, incorporated malicious Visual Basic for Applications (VBA) macros. Upon activation, these macros extracted embedded resources to a newly created, hidden subdirectory within the current user profile, selected payloads based on the host's Windows version, and presented a decoy document while covertly deploying the Crimson Remote-Access Trojan (RAT) [25]. Crimson RAT, a .NET-based malware, enabled post-exploitation capabilities, including keylogging, screen capture, file manipulation, credential theft, and command execution, supporting 22 distinct command-and-control (C2) functions some of which are listed in Table 3. Its final binary, compiled on April 21, 2025, under the internal name *jnmxrvt hcsm.exe* was dropped as *WEISTT.jpg*, adhered to APT36's characteristic naming convention with a Program Database (PDB) path of `C:\jnmhxrv cstm\jnmhxrv cstm\obj\Debug\jnmhxrv cstm.pdb`. A benign hard-coded IP served as a decoy, concealing the actual C2 endpoint at 93.127.133[.]58. Additional C2 servers at 167.86.97[.]58:17854, hosted on virtual private servers in Russia, Germany, and Indonesia, enhanced operational obfuscation, as evidenced by telemetry data Complete attack chain of this malicious decoy document with file format .ppam can be illustrated as shown in Fig. 1, highlighting each stage from initial delivery to final payload execution.

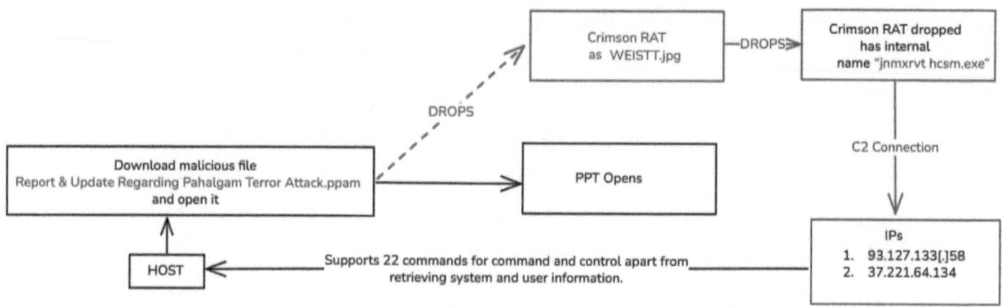

Fig. 1. Attack Chain of decoy documents

Table 3. Key C2 Commands and Their Functions

S. No.	Command	Functionality
1	procl/getavs	Get a list of all processes
2	endpo	Kill process based on PID
3	cscreen	Get screenshot
4	dowf	Download a file from C2
5	file	Exfiltrate a file to C2
6	info	Get machine info (computer name, username, IP, OS, etc.)

Operational sophistication was further demonstrated by transitioning from legacy Poseidon loaders to the modular Ares RAT framework, which emerged as the primary vector of compromise. Ares RAT introduced advanced obfuscation techniques, User Account Control (UAC) bypass mechanisms, and obfuscated PowerShell scripts, leveraging Living Off the Land Binaries (LOLBins) to minimize its detectable footprint. It established connections to C2 server at 167.86.97[.]58:17854, facilitating data exfiltration and operational disruption.

In addition to the distribution of decoy documents, hacktivist operations, coordinated under hashtags such as #OpIndia and #OperationSindoor, amplified the campaign's impact through distributed denial-of-service (DDoS) attacks, website defacements, and data leaks targeting critical entities, including the Ministry of Defence, National Informatics Centre (NIC), Goods and Services Tax Network (GSTN), All India Institute of Medical Sciences (AIIMS), Jio, and Bharat Sanchar Nigam Limited (BSNL). According to the report from 35 hacktivist groups, including seven newly emergent collectives, contributed to the campaign's psychological and operational effects [8].

3   Logging Events and Visibility

In the context of sophisticated cyber warfare campaigns, especially those where hack for hire groups and APTs are involved which uses specially crafted malware and Remote Access Trojans or RATs, It is imperative to collect high-quality endpoint logs, which can also be co-related, for piecing together adversary actions and inspecting ongoing threats.

As seen in the current example as well, a common technique used by many APT groups to gain initial access to an endpoint is spear-phishing. In this approach, they send specially crafted emails with attachments containing embedded macros, scripts, or other malicious code. These attachments are often files associated with Office-related applications, such as Microsoft Word, Microsoft PowerPoint, and similar formats like PDFs, XLAMs, and others. Since such file types are widely used in daily work, our focus was on collecting logs related specifically to these applications. When a user opens these files, the hidden malicious code automatically triggers a connection to command-and-control (C2) servers or installs malware.

One problem that arises during the detection of these types of attacks is the large volume of data generated across endpoints. Analyzing this data to identify anomalous or malicious behavior, whether from a single endpoint or from a group of endpoints, and ability to correlate log sources, is extremely challenging. It is equivalent to finding a needle in a haystack, as the malicious activity can be buried under a vast amount of normal, routine events.

While there are various frameworks that can be used for collecting activities and logs from endpoints, to circumvent the problem of high volume and correlation of data, we chose to use Osquery [9,10] tool. Osquery is an open-source, community-driven cross-platform instrumentation framework that allows the endpoint's properties and activities to be queried like a relational database. It exposes system state as tables, enabling real-time collection and analysis of activities done on the endpoint. Using SQL queries, investigators can retrieve details related to process activity, file modifications, network connections, and other operating system activities in form of system events, from across the environment. Osquery is compatible with Linux, macOS, Windows, and FreeBSD, featuring around 280 virtual tables in total-56 of which are shared across all prominent platforms-and platform-specific coverage of about 155 tables for Linux, 184 for macOS, and 113 for Windows. Osquery operates in two modes: interactive and daemon. The interactive mode allows manual querying of live system information, while the daemon mode supports scheduled queries and the collection of event-based telemetry. This architecture supports monitoring system behaviour in real time and over time which in turns allows us to correlate logs and use several heuristics such as parent-child heuristic and unusual port heuristic etc. which helps us in identifying malicious activities that may not be immediately obvious.

Osquery collects logs of several events related to processes, sockets and files. However, all event logs may not be sufficient to get visibility about activities of several malware including the RATs used in this particular campaign as well. A key advantage of Osquery is its flexible, modular design. Using a Thrift-based RPC interface, you can build external extensions to add new virtual tables or connect other data sources. This makes it easy to customize the framework for specific monitoring needs and expand its capabilities beyond the built-in tables. To enhance our log-capturing capabilities, we integrated a community [26] extension into the Osquery deployment. This extension allows us to directly collect logs from Windows-based endpoints and present them in a relational table format.

This setup allows us to run targeted queries and collect only the logs relevant to our investigation. For example, we can design queries that look for processes spawned by Microsoft Word that initiate outbound network connections, monitor for unusual file writes by PowerPoint processes in system directories, or detect PDF readers that execute scripts or tries to make connections to external servers. By focusing on these specific behaviours, we can filter out irrelevant noise and zero in on potential malicious activity.

By combining and analyzing this collected data - such as process execution events, file changes, or network socket activity - we can trace all actions performed by a malicious binary or its child processes. For example, process execution details from *win_process_events* can be compared with threat intelligence lists containing known malicious file hashes. Similarly, an outbound network connection recorded in *win_socket_events* from a child process of a trusted binary can be checked against threat intelligence data containing IP addresses and domains linked to command-and-control (C2) servers.

A practical analytical sequence could involve spotting an unusual process creation event stemming from a non-standard parent process in *win_process_events*, followed by identifying file modifications linked to that process in *win_file_events*. If the process hash or any of the contacted remote IP addresses are malicious upon checking with intelligence feeds, the correlation offers high-confidence attribution of malicious activity. Such a workflow not only identifies the existence of known threats but may also uncover suspicious behavioural patterns that suggest new or previously unclassified malware.

By combining these data sources, security teams can build detailed attack stories. When process creation, file changes, and network activity are connected to external intelligence, analysts can turn separate endpoint events into a clear timeline of an intrusion, enabling faster containment and response. This shows that Osquery, when supported by manual threat hunting and threat intelligence, can be used not only to detect threats but also to reconstruct attack chains during advanced investigations.

4   Analysis and Detections

To comprehensively analyze the malicious activities, telemetry data was collected using Osquery, combined with custom extensions to enhance detection capabilities. This section elucidates the telemetry data, detailing the structure and significance of the recorded events across three primary tables-win_process_events, win_file_events, and win_socket_events-to provide insights into the malware's behavior, persistence mechanisms, and network interactions.

4.1   Telemetry Collection Methodology

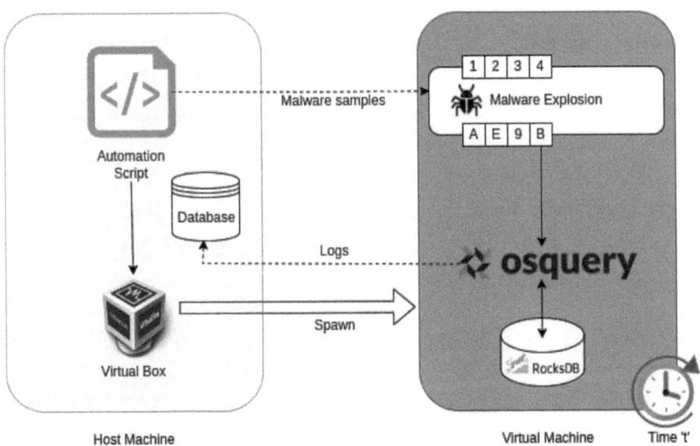

Fig. 2. Architecture of the Setup

To investigate the behaviour of the malware associated with the Operation Sindoor cyber campaign, a controlled experimental environment was established. A virtual machine (VM) instance running Microsoft Windows 11 (computer name: DESKTOP-3DD3GTB), was created using Oracle VirtualBox. To prevent unintended propagation of malware to physical systems, the virtual machine was configured to operate within an isolated network environment, ensuring containment and safeguarding external systems from potential infection.

Within the VM, Osquery was deployed in daemon mode to facilitate continuous, real-time monitoring of system activities. The Osquery configuration incorporated the *–logger_plugin=filesystem* flag, enabling the logging of detailed telemetry data, including process executions, registry modifications, file operations, and network connections. These logs were stored in a file named osqueryd.results.log, which served as the primary dataset for subsequent analysis. Custom extension was integrated, enhancing the granularity of telemetry collection from the Windows system. This extension allowed for the capture of detailed event data, critical for analyzing the sophisticated behaviours of the Crimson Remote-Access Trojan (RAT) deployed in the campaign. The extension also helps keep a track of individual event through a unique event ID and individual instance of a process through its GUID.

A malicious sample, named Report & Update Regarding Pahalgam Terror Attack.pdf, with the SHA-256 hash

$$8cbd47119356081e70fc023d3ac78af560651e7932636adeca7bec96b09e0e95,$$

was downloaded into the VM. This file, identified as a malicious PowerPoint add-in (*.ppam), was executed to initiate the infection process. Following the opening of the document, a 600-second observation period was enforced to allow the malware to exhibit its behaviours, including process spawning, file operations, and network communications. After this period, the osqueryd.results.log file was securely transferred to a separate system for detailed analysis, ensuring no residual malicious activity affected the analysis environment. The sandbox setup used to trigger the malware is as shown in Fig. 2.

To trace the malware's activities, a forward tracking approach was employed, leveraging the telemetry captured in osqueryd.results.log. This methodology utilized the SHA-256 hash of the initial malicious file to identify associated processes and their behaviors across multiple Osquery tables, specifically win_process_events, win_file_events, and win_socket_events

The telemetry data, identified by the malware hash

$$8cbd47119356081e70fc023d3ac78af560651e7932636adeca7bec96b09e0e95,$$

was collected, with key events centered around the execution of a malicious PowerPoint add-in file

$$8cbd47119356081e70fc023d3ac78af560651e7932636adeca7bec96b09e0e95.ppam.$$

The following subsections describe the structure and implications of each telemetry table.

4.2   Process Events(win_process_events)

The win_process_events table, records process creation and termination events, providing insights into the execution chain of the malware. The column descriptions for win_process_events are provided in Table 4.

Table 4. Columns of `win_process_events`

S. No.	Column	Description
1	`time`	Event timestamp in UNIX epoch seconds
2	`action`	Type of process event (e.g., `PROC_CREATE`, `PROC_EXIT`)
3	`pid`	Process identifier of the event's target process
4	`parent_pid`	Process identifier of the parent process
5	`path`	Full filesystem path to the executable
6	`cmdline`	Complete command-line string used to launch the process
7	`user`	Security principal under which the process ran (DOMAIN\user)
8	`process_guid`	Globally unique identifier for this process instance
9	`parent_process_guid`	GUID of the parent process instance

win_process_events (10)

action	cmdline	uid	eventid	owner_uid	parent_path	parent_pid	parent_process_guid	path
PROC_TERMINATE	"C:\Windows\system32\NOTEPAD.EXE" C:\Program Files\osquery\log\osqueryd.results.log	09A8CF6E-0698-4BDF-A3EE-AC4400000000	2	DESKTOP-3DD3GTB\Itachi	C:\Windows\explorer.exe	2140	68C109FE-5156-11F0-B8DF-0800270D762D	C:\Windows\System32\notepad.exe
PROC_CREATE	"C:\Windows\system32\NOTEPAD.EXE" C:\Program Files\osquery\log\osqueryd.results.log	145ADE83-6093-4337-A55D-A46200000000	2	DESKTOP-3DD3GTB\Itachi	C:\Windows\explorer.exe	2140	68C109FE-5156-11F0-B8DF-0800270D762D	C:\Windows\System32\notepad.exe
PROC_TERMINATE	"C:\Windows\System32\cmd.exe" /C "C:\Users\Itach\working\vajra_install.bat"	304DE0A3-C192-4975-99CB-7A7900000000	2	DESKTOP-3DD3GTB\Itachi	C:\Windows\explorer.exe	2140	68C109FE-5156-11F0-B8DF-0800270D762D	C:\Windows\System32\cmd.exe
PROC_TERMINATE	"C:\Program Files\WinRAR\WinRAR.exe" x -iext -ver -imon1 -- "C:\Users\Itach\sample.zip" "?\"	5DDD4366-D9FA-4DE3-8D72-E63500000000	2	DESKTOP-3DD3GTB\Itachi	C:\Windows\explorer.exe	2140	68C109FE-5156-11F0-B8DF-0800270D762D	C:\Program Files\WinRAR\WinRAR.exe
PROC_CREATE	"C:\Program Files\WinRAR\WinRAR.exe" x -iext -ver -imon1 -- "C:\Users\Itach\sample.zip" "?\"	56137B7B-8B4E-4B2E-9ACD-900500000000	2	DESKTOP-3DD3GTB\Itachi	C:\Windows\explorer.exe	2140	68C109FE-5156-11F0-B8DF-0800270D762D	C:\Program Files\WinRAR\WinRAR.exe
PROC_TERMINATE	"C:\Windows\system32\cmd.exe"	18D06C54-B3D6-47A9-B5BC-330200000000	2	DESKTOP-3DD3GTB\Itachi	C:\Windows\explorer.exe	2140	68C109FE-5156-11F0-B8DF-0800270D762D	C:\Windows\System32\cmd.exe
PROC_CREATE	\??\C:\Windows\system32\conhost.exe 0xffffffff -ForceV1	5A33B4B1-64CF-4D9B-A315-2D3300000000	2	DESKTOP-3DD3GTB\Itachi	C:\Windows\System32\cmd.exe	6932	68C10DF2-5156-11F0-B8DF-0800270D762D	C:\Windows\System32\conhost.exe
PROC_CREATE	"C:\Windows\system32\cmd.exe"	385D7EF3-49B7-48C6-B824-316600000000	2	DESKTOP-3DD3GTB\Itachi	C:\Windows\explorer.exe	2140	68C109FE-5156-11F0-B8DF-0800270D762D	C:\Windows\System32\cmd.exe
PROC_CREATE	"C:\Users\Itach\0ffice360-48\jnmxrvt hcsm.exe" "	3839A309-60F2-4D27-A3EE-8A6200000000	2	DESKTOP-3DD3GTB\Itachi	C:\Program Files\Microsoft Office\root\Office16\POWERPNT.EXE	10476	68C10DB4-5156-11F0-B8DF-0800270D762D	C:\Users\Itach\0ffice360-48\jnmxrvt hcsm.exe
PROC_CREATE	"C:\Program Files\Microsoft Office\Root\Office16\POWERPNT.EXE" "C:\Users\Itach\sample\8cbd47119356081e70fc023d3ac78af560651e7932636adeca7bec96b09e0e95.ppam" /ou ""	486C38E4-40C8-44EA-9D7D-1A2E00000000	2	DESKTOP-3DD3GTB\Itachi	C:\Windows\explorer.exe	2140	68C109FE-5156-11F0-B8DF-0800270D762D	C:\Program Files\Microsoft Office\root\Office16\POWERPNT.EXE

Fig. 3. Process Related Activities

Notable events include two pivotal malware-related events were logged, delineating the initial infection and payload deployment stages of the Crimson RAT. At 14:33:44 UTC, a PROC_CREATE event (event ID 486C38E4-40C8-44EA-9D7D-1A2E00000000) recorded the execution of POWERPNT.EXE (PID 10476, process GUID 68C10DB4-5156-11F0-B8DF-0800270D762D) with the command line

$$C: \backslash ProgramFiles \backslash MicrosoftOffice \backslash Root \backslash Office16 \backslash POWERPNT.EXE$$

$$C: \backslash Users \backslash Itachi \backslash sample \backslash$$

$$8cbd47119356081e70fc023d3ac78af560651e7932636adeca7bec96b09e0e95.ppam./ou$$

This process, initiated by explorer.exe (PID 2140, parent process GUID 68C109FE-5156-11F0-B8DF-0800270D762D) under the user account DESKTOP-3DD3GTB\Itachi, marks the infection's onset. The .ppam file, a macro-enabled PowerPoint add-in with a matching SHA-256 hash, likely contains malicious Visual Basic for Applications (VBA) macros or scripts that trigger subsequent malicious actions. The /ou flag suggests the file was opened in a specific mode, potentially bypassing user prompts to enable macros automatically. Five seconds later, at 14:33:49 UTC, a second PROC_CREATE event (event ID 3839A309-60F2-4D27-A3EE-8A6200000000) recorded POWERPNT.EXE spawning jnmxrvt hcsm.exe (PID 2192, process GUID 68C10DCA-5156-11F0-B8DF-0800270D762D) in C:\Users\Itachi\0ffice360-48\with the command line "C:\Users\Itachi\0ffice360-48\jnmxrvt hcsm.exe" as can be seen in Fig. 3. This child process, executed under the same user account, represents the Crimson RAT, responsible for establishing persistence and initiating C2 communications. The creation of jnmxrvt hcsm.exe signifies a critical transition in the infection chain, where the initial macro-driven infection evolves into a fully functional RAT. These events, executed within a tight five-second window, highlight

APT36's sophisticated use of legitimate Microsoft Office processes to mask malicious intent, leveraging the trusted POWERPNT.EXE to deploy a persistent threat.

4.3   File Events(win_file_events)

The win_file_events table, logs file creation, writing, deletion, and renaming activities, crucial for tracking the malware's filesystem interactions. The column descriptions for win_file_events are provided in Table 5

Table 5. Columns of `win_file_events`

S. No.	Column	Description
1	`time`	Event timestamp in UNIX epoch seconds
2	`action`	File operation type (e.g., **FILE_CREATE**, **FILE_DELETE**)
3	`eid`	Unique event identifier (UUID) for deduplication
4	`target_path`	Absolute path of the file being accessed
5	`md5`	MD5 checksum of the file at event time
6	`sha256`	SHA-256 checksum of the file at event time
7	`pid`	Process identifier that performed the file action
8	`process_guid`	GUID of the process instance performing the action
9	`process_name`	Name (and path) of the executable process

The fields captured include action, which denotes operations like FILE_CREATE (creating a new file), FILE_WRITE (writing data to a file), or FILE_RENAME (renaming a file); process_name (C:\Program Files\Microsoft Office\Root\Office16\POWERPNT.EXE), identifying the legitimate Microsoft PowerPoint executable exploited by the malware; target_path, specifying the file's location; md5 and sha256, providing cryptographic hashes for file verification; pid (10476) and process_guid (68C10DB4-5156-11F0-B8DF-0800270D762D), linking events to the malicious process; time and utc_time, timestamping events (e.g., 1752503624 for 14:33:44 UTC); and eid, a unique event identifier. A major event occurred at 14:33:49 UTC, when POWERPNT.EXE executed a FILE_CREATE action to create WEISTE.jpg in *C:\Users\Itachi\Office360-48*This file, disguised as a benign image, likely served as a dropper containing the encoded RAT executable, a tactic used to bypass initial security checks by masquerading as a non-executable file. The non-standard directory Office360-48 (with a deliberate misspelling of "Office") suggests an attempt to evade detection by avoiding typical Office paths like `C:\Program Files\Microsoft Office\`. Immediately following, at 14:33:49 UTC, a FILE_RENAME event renamed WEISTE.jpg to jnmxrvt hcsm.exe

win_file_events (125)

action	amsi_is_malware	byte_stream	gid	eventid	hashed	md5	pe_file	pid	process_guid	process_name
FILE_WRITE			3F4CC455-B43A-45F2-92BB-8C5C00000000	1	1	9449beca80594c9a8b9bab067b112f30	NO	2140	68C109FE-5156-11F0-B8DF-0800270D762D	C:\Windows\explorer.exe
FILE_CREATE			0E636099-8659-4602-B8DA-B45B00000000	1	0		NO	2140	68C109FE-5156-11F0-B8DF-0800270D762D	C:\Windows\explorer.exe
FILE_DELETE_BY_DISP			3A72BA1C-E299-4FD9-893D-205F00000000	1	0		NO	2140	68C109FE-5156-11F0-B8DF-0800270D762D	C:\Windows\explorer.exe
FILE_WRITE			26139532-58D8-4C3C-8666-1D4000000000	1	1	81ed6b801fd3ef8303906a1c5d1031a0	NO	2140	68C109FE-5156-11F0-B8DF-0800270D762D	C:\Windows\explorer.exe
FILE_WRITE			1692AF95-294B-4D58-A8C0-525100000000	1	1	a6dd2af267c446e3e4d2d92b6bbcb619	NO	2140	68C109FE-5156-11F0-B8DF-0800270D762D	C:\Windows\explorer.exe
FILE_CREATE			125E99EA-1AFB-4D0F-808F-6E0000000000	1	0		NO	2140	68C109FE-5156-11F0-B8DF-0800270D762D	C:\Windows\explorer.exe
FILE_DELETE_BY_DISP			6E349138-51DF-4C3B-93C0-E66C00000000	1	0		NO	2140	68C109FE-5156-11F0-B8DF-0800270D762D	C:\Windows\explorer.exe
FILE_WRITE			1FC1C3E8-DEAF-460B-A5CE-DE1200000000	1	1	6195324cc0117efb2132bb2fe231f2ed	NO	2140	68C109FE-5156-11F0-B8DF-0800270D762D	C:\Windows\explorer.exe
FILE_WRITE			2E071804-B1E0-4D43-927E-782600000000	1	1	20744ea6ace06b7bfdf4f729327a0757	NO	10476	68C10DB4-5156-11F0-B8DF-0800270D762D	C:\Program Files\Microsoft Office\root\Office16\POWERPNT.EXE
FILE_WRITE			3B40EEED-BE55-4240-A6B0-6D1000000000	1	1	58ccd3a41269e9ebc9ce54656a90c84f	NO	10476	68C10DB4-5156-11F0-B8DF-0800270D762D	C:\Program Files\Microsoft Office\root\Office16\POWERPNT.EXE
FILE_CREATE			1EB0C333-1A64-403F-99BB-813100000000	1	0		NO	10476	68C10DB4-5156-11F0-B8DF-0800270D762D	C:\Program Files\Microsoft Office\root\Office16\POWERPNT.EXE
FILE_DELETE_BY_DISP			74DAA949-8060-42BA-B938-743D00000000	1	0		NO	10476	68C10DB4-5156-11F0-B8DF-0800270D762D	C:\Program Files\Microsoft Office\root\Office16\POWERPNT.EXE
FILE_WRITE			7E7734A5-0867-4C1D-9C6C-A40500000000	1	1	20744ea6ace06b7bfdf4f729327a0757	NO	10476	68C10DB4-5156-11F0-B8DF-0800270D762D	C:\Program Files\Microsoft Office\root\Office16\POWERPNT.EXE
FILE_WRITE			2DF4BD01-F472-4631-8A09-036200000000	1	1	b238e0cc73a945a48d0b0a5760de8562	NO	10476	68C10DB4-5156-11F0-B8DF-0800270D762D	C:\Program Files\Microsoft Office\root\Office16\POWERPNT.EXE

Fig. 4. File Related Activities

as can be seen in Fig. 4, revealing its true purpose as the Crimson RAT executable (later executed as PID 2192, process GUID 68C10DCA-5156-11F0-B8DF-0800270D762D). This rename is a critical step, transitioning the infection from a disguised dropper to an executable capable of persistence and C2 communications. Concurrently, at around 14:33:48 UTC, POWERPNT.EXE created and wrote files including vbaProject.bin and oleObject1.bin through oleObject5.bin in "C:\Users\Itachi\0ffice360-48\". The vbaProject.bin file likely contains malicious VBA macros, which are scripts that execute automatically to unpack or download payloads, while the oleObject*.bin files suggest embedded objects (e.g., scripts or executables) crucial for staging the RAT. These files, created in the same non-standard directory, further indicate stealth tactics. At 14:33:45 UTC, a FILE_CREATE event generated

$$8cbd47119356081e70fc023d3ac78af560651e7932636adeca7bec96b09e0e95.ppam,$$

followed by FILE_WRITE event at 14:33:50 UTC matching the malicious file's SHA-256 hash, confirming its role as the primary infection vector-a macro-enabled PowerPoint add-in that triggers malicious scripts upon opening. Additionally, temporary files were created and written in

$$C: \backslash Users \backslash Itachi \backslash AppData \backslash Local \backslash Temp \backslash ,$$

a directory commonly used by malware for transient payload staging to minimize forensic evidence.

4.4 Socket Events (win_socket_events)

The win_socket_events table, records network connections, essential for identifying command-and-control (C2) communications. The column descriptions for win_socket_events are provided in Table 6.

Table 6. Columns of `win_socket_events`

S. No.	Column	Description
1	`time`	Event timestamp in UNIX epoch seconds
2	`action`	Socket event type (e.g., `connect`, `accept`, `close`)
3	`pid`	Process identifier owning the socket
4	`process_guid`	GUID of the owning process instance
5	`process_name`	Name (and path) of the process executable
6	`family`	Address family (e.g., `AF_INET` for IPv4)
7	`local_address`	Local IP address for the socket endpoint
8	`local_port`	Local port number used by the socket
9	`remote_address`	Remote IP address the socket connected to
10	`remote_port`	Remote port number on the peer endpoint

A detailed record of network connection attempts reveals the command-and-control (C2) communication patterns used by the Crimson RAT during the Operation Sindoor campaign. The fields include action (SOCKET_CONNECT), process_name, like

$$C: \backslash ProgramFiles \backslash MicrosoftOffice \backslash Root \backslash Office16 \backslash POWERPNT.EXE$$

or

$$C: \backslash Users \backslash Itachi \backslash Office360 - 48 \backslash jnmxrvthcsm.exe,$$

remote_address, remote_port, local_address (10.0.2.15), local_port, pid, process_guid, time, utc_time, family (AF_INET), protocol (TCP, 6), event_type (SOCKET), and eid.

The process POWERPNT.EXE (PID 10476, GUID 68C10DB4-5156-11F0-B8DF-0800270D762D) initiated three SOCKET_CONNECT events to 37.221. 64.134:443, a phishing link resolving to jkpolice[.]gov[.]in[.]

`kashmirattack[.]exposed`, at 14:34:40 UTC (event ID 753FB770-923A-42B2-9493-157103000000, port 55626), 14:35:18 UTC (timestamp 1752503718, event ID 4DE4180B-FCFF-48E9-810E-2F3F03000000, port 55643), and 14:35:33 UTC (timestamp 1752503733) and event ID 6130D1D4-DC08-41DB-9FB8-877303000000, port 55647). Occurring 56âĂŞ109 s after the malicious .ppam execution at 14:33:44 UTC, these connections on port 443 (HTTPS) suggest potential phishing activity, leveraging the legitimate appearance of Office traffic to deceive users or deliver malicious payloads.

The domain's deceptive naming mimics an official Jammu and Kashmir Police site, a tactic consistent with APT36's social engineering strategies. Concurrently, jnmxrvt hcsm.exe (PID 2192, GUID 68C10DCA-5156-11F0-B8DF-0800270D762D) initiated two SOCKET_CONNECT events to 93.127.133.58:19821, a confirmed C2 IP, at 14:34:35 UTC (timestamp 1752503675) and 14:35:38 UTC (timestamp 1752503738), both with event ID 65D9BA08-9728-46A1-BCBA-CE0003000000 and local port 55648 and 55625, 51âĂŞ114 s after the RAT's execution at 14:33:49 UTC as can be seen in Fig. 5. These TCP connections, using a non-standard port, indicate C2 activity for command retrieval or data exfiltration, aligning with the Crimson RAT's role in maintaining attacker control. The identical eid suggests a logging artifact or repeated connection attempts to ensure C2 server connectivity, possibly to bypass network restrictions.

The rapid onset of network activity post-infection highlights APT36's sophisticated tactics, using phishing to initiate compromise and C2 for persistence and exfiltration. Distinguishing POWERPNT.EXE's phishing traffic from jnmxrvt hcsm.exe's C2 communications requires deep packet inspection and threat intelligence to confirm the malicious nature of 37.221.64.134 and 93.127.133.58. Strong monitoring systems, such as Endpoint Detection and Response (EDR) tools [16] or Extended Detection and Response (XDR) tools, are essential for detecting these types of activities and providing response capabilities, especially when monitoring a large number of endpoints across an organization.

family	local_address	local_port	pid	process_guid	process_name	protocol	remote_address	remote_port
AF_NET	10.0.2.15	55648	2192	68C10DCA-5156-11F0-B8DF-0800270D762D	C:\Users\Itachi\Office360-48\jnmxrvt hcsm.exe	6	93.127.133.58	19821
AF_NET	10.0.2.15	55647	10476	68C10DB4-5156-11F0-B8DF-0800270D762D	C:\Program Files\Microsoft Office\root\Office16\POWERPNT.EXE	6	37.221.64.134	443
AF_NET	10.0.2.15	55643	10476	68C10DB4-5156-11F0-B8DF-0800270D762D	C:\Program Files\Microsoft Office\root\Office16\POWERPNT.EXE	6	37.221.64.134	443
AF_NET	10.0.2.15	55626	10476	68C10DB4-5156-11F0-B8DF-0800270D762D	C:\Program Files\Microsoft Office\root\Office16\POWERPNT.EXE	6	37.221.64.134	443
AF_NET	10.0.2.15	55625	2192	68C10DCA-5156-11F0-B8DF-0800270D762D	C:\Users\Itachi\Office360-48\jnmxrvt hcsm.exe	6	93.127.133.58	17241
AF_NET	10.0.2.15	55624	10476	68C10DB4-5156-11F0-B8DF-0800270D762D	C:\Program Files\Microsoft Office\root\Office16\POWERPNT.EXE	6	37.221.64.134	443

Fig. 5. Socket Related Activities

Table 7. Structure of Osquery SQL Query for Operation Sindoor

Component	Description
`SELECT`	Retrieves fields (`table_name`, `action`, `process_name`, `target_path`/`target`, `md5`, `sha256`, `utc_time`)
`FROM`	Queries `win_process_events`, `win_file_events` and `win_socket_events`
`WHERE`	Filters file events (`POWERPNT.exe`, `jnmxrvt hcsm.exe`, hashes, `WEISTE.jpg` rename) and network events (suspicious IPs/ports, excluding legitimate traffic)
`UNION`	Combines file and network results, mimicking Sigma's OR condition

The telemetry data illustrates a multi-stage attack chain initiated by user interaction with a malicious PowerPoint add-in, leading to the deployment of Crimson RAT. The process events confirm the execution of jnmxrvt hcsm.exe from a dynamically created directory

$$C : \backslash Users \backslash Itachi \backslash Office360 - 48\backslash,$$

while file events reveal the creation of malicious payloads disguised as Office components, and socket events confirm C2 communications, highlighting the malware's espionage capabilities. Osquery's granular logging, enhanced by custom extensions, enabled the detection of these activities by correlating process, file, registry, and network events, providing a comprehensive view of the attack lifecycle.

The rapid deployment of the malware, compiled on April 21, 2025, and executed in July, underscores APT36's agility in exploiting geopolitical events like the Pahalgam attack.

Based on this telemetry we will create a query for Osquery which can be used as a rule to detect any attacks related to this campaign. The Osquery SQL query replicates the Sigma rule's logic, querying `win_file_events` and `win_socket_events` to detect file operations and network connections associated with the Crimson RAT. The query's components are summarized in Table 7, with the full query presented in Listing 1.1.

Listing 1.1. Osquery SQL Query for Detecting Crimson RAT Artifacts

```
-- Files
SELECT
   'win_file_events' AS table_name,
   action,
   process_name,
   target_path,
   md5,
```

```sql
    utc_time
FROM win_file_events
WHERE
  (
    -- known hashes
    process_name ILIKE '%\\msedge.exe'
    AND action IN ('FILE_RENAME', 'FILE_CREATE')
    AND md5 IN (
        'd946e3e94fec670f9e47aca186ecaabe',
        'e18c4172329c32d8394ba0658d5212c2',
        '2fde001f4c17c8613480091fa48b55a0',
        'c1f4c9f969f955dec2465317b526b600',
        '026e8e7acb2f2a156f8afff64fd54066',
        'fb64c22d37c502bde55b19688d40c803',
        '70b8040730c62e4a52a904251fa74029',
        '3efec6ffcbfe79f71f5410eb46f1c19e',
        'b03211f6feccd3a62273368b52f6079d'
    )
  )
  OR (
    -- Suspicious jnmxrvt hcsm.exe file ops OR WEISTE.jpg drops
    process_name ILIKE '%\\jnmxrvt hcsm.exe'
    AND action IN ('FILE_RENAME', 'FILE_CREATE')
    AND (
      target_path ILIKE '%jnmxrvt hcsm.exe'
      OR target_path ILIKE '%WEISTE.jpg%'
    )
  )
  OR (
    -- Any rename to the suspicious name
    action = 'FILE_RENAME'
    AND target_path ILIKE '%jnmxrvt hcsm.exe'
  )

UNION ALL

-- Sockets
SELECT
    'win_socket_events' AS table_name,
    action,
    process_name,
    (remote_address || ':' || CAST(remote_port AS TEXT)) AS target_path,
    NULL AS md5,
    utc_time
FROM win_socket_events
WHERE
  (
    process_name ILIKE '%\\POWERPNT.EXE'
    OR process_name ILIKE '%\\jnmxrvt hcsm.exe'
  )
  AND remote_address IN (
    '93.127.133.58',
    '104.129.27.14',
    '37.221.64.134',
    '78.40.143.189',
    '45.141.58.224',
    '45.141.59.167',
    '45.141.58.33',
    '78.40.143.98',
    '84.54.51.12',
    '176.65.143.215',
    '45.141.59.72',
    '192.64.118.76'
  )
  AND remote_port IN (1097, 17241, 19821, 21817, 23221,
27425, 8108, 16197, 19867, 28784, 30123)
  AND NOT (remote_address = '96.17.168.104' AND remote_port = 443);
```

5   Conclusions

We studied the malware campaign launched by Pakistan's APT groups and hacktivist against India during the Operation Sindoor. Following the clues for the behavioural aspected of the cyber campaign released by the Indian threat intelligence agencies, we developed a details of the event logs needs to be monitored and analysed to detect the malware. We ran the malware in sandbox environment and build a telemetry using Osquery with custom extension. We developed a SQL based detection rules to identify presence of the malware and identify active exploitation it performed. It also provided an effective means to block the malware from any potential damages.

The analysis revealed several other information. The compilation date of malware revealed that it was specifically crafted few days before the Pahalgam attacks, indicating that the adversaries have prior knowledge of the terror attacks and launched the cyber attacks to steal information and build false public perception. This coordination between the terrorist activities and APT groups, further strengthen the claims of Indian intelligences agencies that Pahalgam terrorist attacks were planned and controlled from Pakistani soil.

Acknowledgement. Manjesh K. Hanawal thanks funding support from SERB, Govt. of India, through the Core Research Grant (CRG/2022/008807)

References

1. Mueller, G.B., Jensen, B., Valeriano, B., Maness, R.C., Macias, J.M.: Cyber operations during the Russo-Ukrainian war (2025). https://www.csis.org/analysis/cyber-operations-during-russo-ukrainian-war
2. Cyber threats linked to Iran-Israel conflict (2025). https://reliaquest.com/blog/cyber-threats-linked-to-iran-israel-conflict/
3. Capsnetdroff: Cyber warfare: Dual operational fronts in contemporary India-Pakistan conflicts (2025). https://capsindia.org/cyber-warfare-dual-operational-fronts-in-contemporary-india-pakistan-conflicts/
4. Cross-border cyberattacks surge as thailand–cambodia tensions escalate (2025). https://cyberdefensewire.com/cross-border-cyberattacks-surge-as-thailand-cambodia-tensions-escalate/
5. Operation Sindoor: India's strategic clarity and calculated force (2025). https://www.pib.gov.in/PressNoteDetails.aspx?NoteId=154448&ModuleId=34
6. MITRE ATT&CK ®. https://attack.mitre.org/
7. Kanjilal, R.: Advisory: Pahalgam attack themed decoys used by apt36 to target the Indian government (2025). https://www.seqrite.com/blog/advisory-pahalgam-attack-themed-decoys-used-by-apt36-to-target-the-indian-government/
8. Seqrite: Operation Sindoor – anatomy of a digital siege (2025). https://www.seqrite.com/blog/operation-sindoor-anatomy-of-a-digital-siege/
9. Rapid: Introduction to osquery for threat detection and DFIR (2016). https://www.rapid7.com/blog/post/2016/05/09/introduction-to-osquery-for-threat-detection-dfir/. rapid7 Blog
10. SQL powered operating system instrumentation, monitoring, and analytics. https://github.com/osquery/osquery
11. Sajid, A., Razzaq, H., Malik, R., Khan, A.A., Iqbal, M.S., Farhan, S.: Survey paper on cyber warfare. IETI Trans. Data Anal. Forecast. (iTDAF) **2**(3), 27–37 (2024). https://doi.org/10.3991/itdaf.v2i3.51025, https://online-journals.org/index.php/iTDAF/article/view/51025

12. Bou-Harb, E., Debbabi, M., Assi, C.: Cyber scanning: a comprehensive survey. IEEE Commun. Surv. Tutor. **16**(3), 1496–1519 (2014). https://doi.org/10.1109/SURV.2013.102913.00020
13. Khandait, P., Tiwari, N., Hubballi, N.: Who is trying to compromise your SSH server? An analysis of authentication logs and detection of bruteforce attacks. In: Adjunct Proceedings of the 2021 International Conference on Distributed Computing and Networking (ICDCN 2021), pp. 127–132. Association for Computing Machinery, New York (2021). https://doi.org/10.1145/3427477.3429772
14. Prasad, M.D., Ali, M.W., Sindusha, M.S.N.V.R.S., Jahnavi, N., Devi, S.A.: Enabling cybersecurity defenses: advanced endpoint detection, data breach identification and anomaly resolution. In: 2024 8th International Conference on Inventive Systems and Control (ICISC), pp. 461–468 (2024). https://doi.org/10.1109/ICISC62624.2024.00084
15. Bakshi, A., Sawant, T., Thakare, P., Dandawala, A., Hanawal, M., Kabra, A.: Improving threat detection capabilities in windows endpoints with Osquery. In: 2023 15th International Conference on Communication Systems & Networks (COMSNETS), Bangalore, India, pp. 432–435 (2023). https://doi.org/10.1109/COMSNETS56262.2023.10041379
16. Agarwal, S., Sable, A., Sawant, D., Kahalekar, S., Hanawal, M.: Threat detection and response in Linux endpoints. In: 2022 14th International Conference on Communication Systems & Networks (COMSNETS), Bangalore, India, pp. 447–449 (2022). https://doi.org/10.1109/COMSNETS53615.2022.9668567
17. Moşoiu, O., Bălăceanu, I., Mihai, E.: Cyber terrorism and the effects of the Russian attacks on democratic states in east Europe. Sci. J. Silesian Univ. Technol. Ser. Transp. **106**, 131–139 (2020). https://doi.org/10.20858/sjsutst.2020.106.11
18. Aggrey, R., Adjei, B., Afoduo, K., Dsane, N., Cudjoe, A., Ababio, M.: Analysing recent apt incidents: case studies and lessons learned (2024)
19. O'Brien, N.: Assessing the importance of modern security tools and frameworks to help detect and defend against cozy bear. Internship Report, National College of Ireland (2022)
20. Sarowa, S., Bhanot, B., Kumar, V.: Analysis of cyber attacks and cyber incident patterns over APCERT member countries. In: Proceedings of the 2022 4th International Conference on Artificial Intelligence and Speech Technology (AIST). IEEE (2022). https://doi.org/10.1109/AIST55798.2022.10064961
21. Stango, A., Prasad, N., Kyriazanos, D.: A threat analysis methodology for security evaluation and enhancement planning. In: Proceedings of the 2009 Third International Conference on Emerging Security Information, Systems and Technologies (SECURWARE 2009), pp. 262–267 (2009). https://doi.org/10.1109/SECURWARE.2009.47
22. Du, D., et al.: A review on cybersecurity analysis, attack detection, and attack defense methods in cyber-physical power systems. J. Mod. Power Syst. Clean Energy **11**(3), 727–743 (2023). https://doi.org/10.35833/MPCE.2021.000604 https://doi.org/10.35833/MPCE.2021.000604
23. Alnajim, A.M., Habib, S., Islam, M., Thwin, S.M., Alotaibi, F.: A comprehensive survey of cybersecurity threats, attacks, and effective countermeasures in industrial internet of things. Technologies **11**(6) (2023). https://doi.org/10.3390/technologies11060161, https://www.mdpi.com/2227-7080/11/6/161
24. APT PROFILE: Transparent tribe aka APT36 - cyfirma (2025). https://www.cyfirma.com/research/apt-profile-transparent-tribe-aka-apt36/

25. Team, C.R.: Cyber attacks rise as tension mounts across India Pakistan border post terrorist attack (2025). https://www.cyberproof.com/blog/cyber-attacks-rise-as-tension-mounts-across-india-pakistan-border-post-terrorist-attack/
26. Extension to Osquery windows that enhances it with real-time telemetry, log monitoring and other endpoint data collection. https://github.com/hecg119//eclecticiq-osq-ext-bin

Fraud Detection

Genetic-LAD: A Hybrid Approach for Financial Fraud Detection

Nikhil Katiyar[1], Sneha Chauhan[1(✉)], Sugata Gangopadhyay[2], and Aditi Kar Gangopadhyay[2]

[1] National Institute of Technology Uttarakhand, Srinagar, Uttarakhand, India
`sneha.chauhan@nituk.ac.in`
[2] Indian Institute of Technology Roorkee, Roorkee, Uttarakhand, India

Abstract. We present a new pattern generation method for the Logical Analysis of Data (LAD) that is based on genetic algorithms. The original LAD method is often too slow and struggles to find patterns with many features. Our approach makes it faster and allows the model to find more complex patterns, even if it may not always find the perfect ones. We tested this method in credit card fraud detection, which is the process of identifying hidden or fraudulent transactions among many real ones. This is important because missing fraud or falsely labeling real transactions can cause serious problems. Our results show that the proposed method demonstrates superior performance across various dataset configurations. On a 3:1 sampled dataset, it achieves 97.46% accuracy, 97.94% precision, 92.23% recall, and a 95% F1-score, outperforming existing models. When tested on the original imbalanced dataset, it improves the F1-score to 67.21%, and with SMOTE balancing, it further reaches 96.08% accuracy and a 95.48% F1-score. These consistent results highlight the effectiveness.

Keywords: Decision Tree Method · Random Forest Feature Selection · Logical Analysis of Data · Credit Card

1 Introduction

Credit card fraud detection is vital for identifying and preventing unauthorized transactions. With the rapid growth of digital payments, fraud has become a serious concern for both consumers and financial institutions [14]. Fraudsters exploit system vulnerabilities using stolen card details and fake identities, causing significant financial losses. Effective detection safeguards user security and maintains trust in online payment systems. Traditional statistical approaches struggle with complex, high-dimensional, and imbalanced financial data. Hence, machine learning (ML) and deep learning (DL) techniques are widely adopted to improve accuracy and adaptability. For instance, transformer-based and hybrid deep models have achieved strong results but face challenges in interpretability and real-time deployment [16]. Recent advancements highlight graph-based methods

N. Hubballi et al. (Eds.): ICISS 2025, LNCS 16380, pp. 269–282, 2026.
https://doi.org/10.1007/978-3-032-13714-2_17

that model relationships among transactions. Heterogeneous GNNs with attention mechanisms [13], contrastive learning approaches [17], and high-order GNNs [8] have shown excellent performance, though at the cost of high computational complexity. Hybrid and ensemble models have also been explored to balance performance and efficiency. Studies comparing classifiers such as XGBoost, Random Forest, and SVM show competitive accuracy but limited scalability [10]. Optimization-based and logical methods, such as LAD frameworks [3], improve interpretability but remain resource-intensive. Despite progress, challenges persist, including data imbalance, limited transparency, and high computational cost. To address these, our study enhances the LAD framework by integrating decision treebased one-hot encoding and random forest feature selection for efficient pattern extraction. A genetic algorithminspired pattern search further accelerates computation while preserving accuracy and interpretability.

This paper is organized into five sections. Section 1 introduces the research context and objectives. Section 2 provides a review of related work and existing literature. Section 3 details the proposed methodology, covering the processes of binarization, support set selection, and pattern generation within the Logical Analysis of Data (LAD) framework. Section 4 presents and interprets the experimental results. Finally, Sect. 5 summarizes the main conclusions and outlines potential avenues for future work.

2   Related Work

Gangopadhyay et al. [3] explored the application of Logical Analysis of Data (LAD) in detecting fraud in business and transactions. LAD detects the concealed patterns using Boolean functions to determine the outputs. Based on 777 companies' and credit card transaction data, the research had 97.4% accuracy and a 97% F1 score. These results prove the efficiency of LAD in accounting analytics and fraud detection, providing a promising way to improve analytical auditing. Geetha et al. [6] proposed a hybrid deep learning model combined with the Modified Butterfly Optimization Algorithm for feature selection. Their model demonstrated enhanced performance on credit card datasets; however, it was plagued with computational complexity, scalability, and a high degree of reliance on preprocessed data. Hafez et al. [10] performed a systematic review of AI-boosted techniques, such as conventional classifiers like XGBoost, Decision Trees, Random Forests, Logistic Regression, KNN, MLP, SVM, and ANN, on the European credit card dataset. Although they demonstrated the diversity of these algorithms, they pointed out scalability and computational constraints. Reynisson et al. [9] introduced GraphGuard, a new framework based on contrastive self-supervised learning for dynamic multi-relational graphs. Although performing well in temporal data shift adaptation, its performance relied significantly on graph construction quality. Tang et al. [2] investigated Federated Graph Learning (FL + GNN) in fraud detection and demonstrated promise for privacy-enhancing systems. However, the judgment of the model was occasionally influenced by virtual vertices, and training efficiency was still an issue.

Aftab et al. [1] proposed a federated learning solution integrated with graph neural networks for credit card fraud detection. Their system supports collaborative model training across financial institutions without compromising data privacy. They built graph construction and extension algorithms based on weighted feature similarity and convolutional feedforward generative networks. Verma and Dhar [7] introduced an adaptive deep learning approach to credit card fraud detection, resolving concept drift and class imbalance. Blending MLP with an auto-encoder and optimized with the Bat Algorithm, the model attains high AUC and low false positives, albeit real-time scalability could be impacted by integration complexity. The recent advancements in credit card fraud detection have leveraged a variety of machine learning and deep learning techniques to address the challenges of data imbalance and evolving fraud patterns. Zhu et al. [15] proposed a hybrid approach combining Neural Networks and SMOTE, achieving a near-perfect F1-score of 0.999, though with some risk of overfitting due to synthetic sampling. Building on modern NLP architectures, Yu et al. [16] introduced a Transformer-based detection model that outperformed traditional methods with an AUC of 0.99, demonstrating superior capability in capturing complex temporal patterns. Similarly, Ileberi et al. [18] employed a genetic algorithm for feature selection across multiple classifiers and reported a remarkable 100% accuracy using ANN, highlighting the benefits of optimized feature spaces. In [17], the author proposed a Compact Data Learning strategy that maintained AUC performance while boosting training speed by upto 24,000 times, offering a scalable solution for large and imbalanced datasets.

3   Methodology

The Logical Analysis of Data (LAD) is a rule-based machine learning approach that extracts transparent and interpretable patterns from data using Boolean logic and combinatorial optimization. Unlike probabilistic models, LAD generates deterministic logical rules that classify data based on specific combinations of conditions [5]. Originally developed by Peter L. Hammer and colleagues in the 1980s, LAD was designed for binary datasets and inspired by Boolean algebra and decision tree learning. Later enhancements introduced discretization techniques, enabling LAD to process numerical and categorical data. With advances in computational power, its scalability improved, allowing it to handle larger and more complex datasets. The LAD process begins with data acquisition and preprocessing to remove noise and inconsistencies. The data is then binarized to simplify analysis. Next, a support set is generated to select the most relevant features, followed by pattern generation to identify meaningful relationships. These patterns are used for classification, and the final results are interpreted to provide actionable insights. This structured workflow ensures efficient data handling and explainable decision-making.

3.1   Binarization

Binarization is the process of transforming data from its continuous form to binary form by utilizing a mapping into one of two categories denoted as 0 and 1. In our approach, data is binarized using a decision tree method combined with one-hot encoding. The Algorithm 1 performs supervised binarization of continuous features using decision trees, transforming each feature into binary indicators aligned with the target variable. Given an input dataset D with features X and target y, for each feature f, a decision tree classifier is trained with a constraint on the maximum number of leaf nodes d, which controls the number of bins created. The decision tree recursively partitions the feature values by selecting split thresholds that minimize node impurity, commonly measured by Gini impurity:

$$Gini(t) = 1 - \sum_{i=1}^{C} p_i^2,$$

where p_i is the proportion of samples of class i at node t, and C is the number of classes. At each node, the tree evaluates potential splits and selects the threshold that maximizes information gain:

$$\Delta I = I_{\text{parent}} - \sum_{\text{children}} \frac{N_{\text{child}}}{N_{\text{parent}}} I_{\text{child}},$$

where I is the impurity measure and N the sample count. This splitting process continues recursively, creating child nodes from parent nodes until the maximum number of leaf nodes d is reached or no further beneficial splits exist. Each leaf node corresponds to a bin, defined by the path of split thresholds leading to it. Extracting all split thresholds from the tree produces a sorted set

$$T = \{t_1, t_2, \ldots, t_k\},$$

with $k \leq d - 1$, which define bin edges:

$$bin\_edges = [-\infty, t_1, t_2, \ldots, t_k, \infty].$$

Each feature value is assigned to its corresponding bin interval, and then one-hot encoding converts these intervals into binary features, producing the binarized dataset D_{bin}. The binning model stores these bin edges to apply consistent transformations to new data. This approach enables supervised, data-driven discretization that balances model complexity and interpretability by controlling the tree size parameter d, capturing nonlinear relationships between features and the target while reducing dimensionality explosion from naive one-hot encoding.

3.2   Support Set Generation

Support set generation is a technique used in machine learning to enhance the efficiency and effectiveness of models by selecting a subset of relevant features

---

Algorithm 1. Decision Tree-Based Feature Binarization

Require: Dataset D with features X and target y;
1: target column name **Target**;
2: maximum leaf nodes $d \in \mathbb{N}$
Ensure: Binarized dataset D_{bin}, binning model M
3:   **procedure** DECISIONTREEDISCRETIZATION(D, **Target**, d)
4:       $D_{disc} \leftarrow \text{copy}(D)$
5:       $M \leftarrow \emptyset$
6:       **for** each feature $f \in D.\text{columns} \setminus \{\text{Target}\}$ **do**
7:          $x \leftarrow D[f].\text{values.reshape}(-1, 1)$
8:          $y \leftarrow D[\text{Target}].\text{values}$
9:          Train decision tree: $tree \leftarrow \text{DecisionTreeClassifier}(\text{max\_leaf\_nodes} = d)$
10:         $tree.\text{fit}(x, y)$
11:         Extract thresholds: $T \leftarrow \text{sort}(\{t \mid t \in tree.tree.threshold \wedge t \neq -2\})$
12:         Create bin edges: $bin\_edges \leftarrow [-\infty] \cup T \cup [\infty]$
13:         Discretize: $D_{disc}[f] \leftarrow \text{cut}(x, \text{bins} = bin\_edges)$
14:         Store model: $M[f] \leftarrow bin\_edges$
15:       **end for**
16:       $D_{bin} \leftarrow \text{OneHotEncode}(D_{disc})$
17:       **return** (D_{bin}, M)
18: **end procedure**

---

from a larger dataset. In many real-world applications, datasets can be large and contain a lot of noise or irrelevant information, which can reduce the performance of machine learning models. Support set generation addresses this issue by focusing on the most important features that contribute to the model's ability to make accurate predictions. This process helps reduce computational complexity, accelerates the learning process, and improves model accuracy. In this research, the Random Forest feature selection with Gini Importance method used to generate the support set. The Random Forest Feature Selection with Gini Importance algorithm is an ensemble-based feature selection method that identifies discriminative features by leveraging the intrinsic feature importance measures from random forests. The Algorithm 2 takes as input the training data $X_{\text{train}} \in \mathbb{R}^{n \times m}$ with n samples and m features, corresponding labels $y \in \mathbb{R}^n$, test data $X_{\text{test}} \in \mathbb{R}^{k \times m}$, an importance threshold τ, and the number of trees T. It begins by initializing a feature importance vector of zeros with length m. For each tree $t = 1$ to T, the algorithm creates a bootstrap sample $(X_{\text{boot}}, y_{\text{boot}})$ by randomly selecting n observations from (X_{train}, y) with replacement, maintaining the original data distribution while introducing diversity between trees. A decision tree DT_t is trained on this bootstrap sample using the Gini impurity criterion: $G = 1 - \sum_{k=1}^{K} p_k^2$ where p_k is the proportion of class k samples at a node. For each split node in DT_t, the algorithm computes the Gini impurity reduction: $\Delta G(n) = G_n - \left(\frac{N_L}{N} G_L + \frac{N_R}{N} G_R\right)$ where G_n is the impurity at node n, and N_L/N_R are the sample sizes in the left/right child nodes. This reduction is accumulated in the importance vector for the splitting feature j. After all trees

---

Algorithm 2. Random Forest Feature Selection with Gini Importance

---

1: **Input:** $X_{\text{train}} \in \mathbb{R}^{n \times m}$, $y \in \mathbb{R}^n$, $X_{\text{test}} \in \mathbb{R}^{k \times m}$
2:      threshold τ
3:      number of trees T
4: **Output:** $X'_{\text{train}}, X'_{\text{test}}, F$
5: Initialize `feature_importances` $\leftarrow$ array of zeros of length m
6: **for** $t = 1$ to T **do**
7:      $(X_{\text{boot}}, y_{\text{boot}}) \leftarrow$ bootstrap sample from (X_{train}, y)
8:      Train decision tree DT_t on $(X_{\text{boot}}, y_{\text{boot}})$
9:      **for all** split nodes n in DT_t **do**
10:          Let j be the feature used at node n
11:          Compute Gini impurity reduction at node n:
12: $$\Delta G(n) = G_n - \left(\frac{N_L}{N} G_L + \frac{N_R}{N} G_R \right)$$
13:          `feature_importances`$[j] \leftarrow$ `feature_importances`$[j] + \Delta G(n)$
14:      **end for**
15: **end for**
16: Normalize importances:
17: $$\hat{I}_j = \frac{\texttt{feature\_importances}[j]}{\sum_{k=1}^{m} \texttt{feature\_importances}[k]}$$
18: Select features: $F \leftarrow \{j \mid \hat{I}_j \geq \tau\}$
19: $X'_{\text{train}} \leftarrow X_{\text{train}}[:, F]$
20: $X'_{\text{test}} \leftarrow X_{\text{test}}[:, F]$
21: **return** $X'_{\text{train}}, X'_{\text{test}}, F$

---

are built, the feature importances are normalized as

$$\hat{I}_j = \frac{\text{feature\_importances}[j]}{\sum_{k=1}^{m} \text{feature\_importances}[k]}$$

and features with $\hat{I}_j \geq \tau$ are selected to form the reduced feature set F. The algorithm returns the filtered training and test sets

$$X'_{\text{train}} = X_{\text{train}}[:, F], \quad X'_{\text{test}} = X_{\text{test}}[:, F]$$

along with the selected feature indices F. This approach provides robust feature selection by aggregating importance measures across an ensemble of diverse trees, while the threshold τ allows control over the sparsity of the selected feature set. The bootstrap sampling ensures each tree sees slightly different data, improving the reliability of the importance estimates, and the Gini impurity reduction naturally captures each feature's discriminative power when used in splits. The algorithm is particularly effective for high-dimensional data, as it can identify relevant features while accounting for complex interactions through the ensemble of decision trees.

3.3   Pattern Generation

Before diving into the pattern generation procedure, let us revisit some essential Boolean concepts. A literal refers to either a Boolean variable l or its negation

$\bar{l}$. A term is a conjunction (logical AND) of one or more literals, meaning it is a combination of variables and/or their negations. The degree of a term $|t|$ is defined as the number of literals it contains. If $l \in T$, it implies that the variable $l = 1$; if $\bar{l} \in t$, it implies $l = 0$ [4]. The Genetic Prime Pattern Enumeration (GPPE) algorithm 3 is designed to discover prime Boolean patterns that effectively separate positive and negative observations. The algorithm takes as input two disjoint sets of observations: $\Omega^+ \subset \{0,1\}^n$ (positive class) and $\Omega^- \subset \{0,1\}^n$ (negative class), along with several user-defined parameters: the maximum degree of patterns d, the minimum number of positive samples a pattern must cover k, a required purity threshold h, the mutation rate μ, and the maximum number of generations $g_{\max}$. The algorithm begins by initializing a population Q with all single-literal terms, which include each Boolean variable and its negation. The set of selected prime patterns P is initialized as empty, and the generation counter g is set to 1. The algorithm enters a loop that continues until the maximum number of generations $g_{\max}$ is reached or all positive samples have been covered. In each generation, a new candidate set Q_{new} is initialized. For each term $t \in Q$, the algorithm calculates the number of positive and negative samples it covers, denoted cov^+ and cov^-, respectively. The purity of term t is computed as:

$$\mathrm{purity} = \frac{\mathrm{cov}^+}{\mathrm{cov}^+ + \mathrm{cov}^-}$$

If a term satisfies the minimum coverage ($\mathrm{cov}^+ \geq k$) and purity ($\mathrm{purity} \geq h$) thresholds, it is accepted as a valid pattern and added to P. All the positive samples it covers are then removed from Ω^+. If the degree of the term $|t|$ has reached the maximum allowed degree d, the algorithm generates all degree 2 subsets $s \subset t$ and adds those not already in Q_{new} to it. If the term does not satisfy the above criteria and is not at its maximum degree, it undergoes genetic operations. With probability μ, a mutation is applied by adding a randomly chosen literal $l \notin t$ to form a term $child = t \cup \{l\}$, which is added to Q_{new}. Otherwise, crossover is performed by selecting a random term $t_{\mathrm{rand}} \in Q_{\mathrm{new}}$ and combining it with t to generate a new child' term using a crossover function: $child' = \mathrm{Crossover}(t, t_{\mathrm{rand}})$ This newly generated term child' is then added to Q_{new}. At the end of each generation, the population Q is updated to Q_{new}, and the generation counter g is incremented. This process continues until the stopping criterion is met. The final set P contains high-quality, interpretable Boolean patterns that selectively cover positive instances while minimizing coverage of negative instances, making it suitable for interpretable classification tasks.

4   Results and Analysis

This part explains the dataset, preprocessing methods, evaluation metrics, and the results. The dataset was normalized and cleaned to maintain data quality and enhance model performance. Important metrics like accuracy, precision, recall, and F1-score were employed to assess the model.

Algorithm 3. Genetic Prime Pattern Enumeration (GPPE)

1: **Input:** $\Omega^+, \Omega^- \subseteq \{0,1\}^n$ – Sets of positive and negative observations.
2: d – Maximum degree of generated term.
3: k – Minimum number of positive observations covered by a term.
4: h – Required homogeneity of a pattern.
5: μ – mutation rate.
6: $g_{\max}$ – maximum number of generation.
7: **Output:** P – Set of prime patterns.
8: Initialize population $Q \leftarrow \{l, \bar{l}\}$
9: $P \leftarrow \emptyset$
10: $g \leftarrow 1$
11: **while** $g \leq g_{\max}$ **or** $\Omega^+ \neq \emptyset$ **do**
12:     $Q_{\text{new}} \leftarrow \emptyset$
13:     **for all** $t \in Q$ **do**
14:        $\text{cov}^+ = \sum_{x \in \Omega^+} t(x)$ # number of positives observation covered by t
15:        $\text{cov}^- = \sum_{x \in \Omega^-} t(x)$ # number of negative observation covered by t
16:        $\text{purity} \leftarrow \frac{\text{cov}^+}{\text{cov}^+ + \text{cov}^-}$
17:        **if** $\text{cov}^+ \geq \kappa$ **and** $\text{purity} \geq h$ **then**
18:          $P \leftarrow P \cup \{t\}$
19:          Remove covered observation by t from Ω^+
20:        **else if** $|t| \geq d_{\max}$ **then**   # $|t|$ is the degree of the term t
21:          **for all** subsets $s \subset t$ such that $|s| = 2$ **do**
22:            **if** $s \notin Q_{\text{new}}$ **then**
23:              $Q_{\text{new}} \leftarrow Q_{\text{new}} \cup \{s\}$
24:            **end if**
25:          **end for**
26:        **else**
27:          **if** $\text{random}() < \mu$ **then**   # generate random number between 0 to 1
28:            Select a random literal $l \notin p$
29:            child $\leftarrow p \cup \{l\}$
30:            $Q_{\text{new}} \leftarrow Q_{\text{new}} \cup \{\text{child}\}$
31:          **else**
32:            Select random term $t_{\text{rand}} \in Q_{\text{new}}$
33:            child' $\leftarrow$ Crossover(t, t_{rand})
34:            $Q_{\text{new}} \leftarrow Q_{\text{new}} \cup \{\text{child'}\}$
35:          **end if**
36:        **end if**
37:     **end for**
38:     $Q \leftarrow Q_{\text{new}}$
39:     $g \leftarrow g + 1$
40: **end while**
41: **return** P

4.1   Hyperparameter Tuning

In the decision tree-based feature binarization process, we first tuned key hyper-parameter to improve model performance and prevent overfitting. The maximum number of leaf nodes was varied between 2 and 15 to balance tree depth and generalization as shown in Table 1. Similarly, the minimum covered observations (1–5) ensured that each term contained at least m samples in the positive class. Homogeneity (0.1–1) is the positive class sample and negative class sample, while the term degree (2–10) allowed flexible feature transformation. Genetic optimization was further guided by limiting generations (2–16) and varying mutation rates (0.01–1) to maintain exploration while improving convergence stability.

Table 1. Hyperparameter Ranges Used in Decision Tree and Genetic Optimization

Parameter	Description	Range/Values Tested
Max Leaf Nodes (d)	Controls the maximum number of leaves in the Decision Tree helps regulate model complexity	2–15
Min Covered Observations	Minimum number of samples covered by pattern	1–5
Homogeneity (h)	ratio of positive class sample and negative class sample	0.1–1
Max Degree	Maximum polynomial degree used in feature transformation	2–10
Max Generations	Number of iterations for the Genetic Algorithm to evolve solutions	2–16
Mutation Rate	Probability of random alteration in the genetic algorithm ensures diversity and avoids local minima	0.01–1

4.2   Dataset

The dataset comprises credit card transactions made by European cardholders over a two-day period in September 2013, totaling 284,807 transactions, of which 492 are fraudulent (approximately 0.172%), highlighting a significant class imbalance. All features, except for **Time** and **Amount**, are anonymized numerical variables resulting from a Principal Component Analysis (PCA) transformation to protect confidentiality. Specifically, features **V1** to **V28** are the principal components derived from the original attributes and represent transformed combinations of the original variables that capture the most variance in the data. The **Time** feature indicates the seconds elapsed since the first recorded transaction, and **Amount** is the transaction value, which can support cost-sensitive learning. The binary target variable **Class** identifies fraud (1) or non-fraud (0). Due to the imbalance, model evaluation should emphasize the Area Under the Precision-Recall Curve (AUPRC) rather than standard accuracy metrics.

4.3 Preprocessing

This study conducts three preprocessing experiments to evaluate the performance of our fraud detection model, hereafter referred to as Experiment 1, Experiment 2, and Experiment 3 for clarity. Experiment 1 follows the approach from Paper [7] by using the original dataset without any resampling. Experiment 2 applies a 3:1 ratio of non-fraud to fraud samples, randomly selected with a fixed random state of 42, based on the method described in Paper [12], resulting in 1,476 non-fraud and 492 fraud cases. Experiment 3 utilizes the full dataset and employs SMOTE, as outlined in Paper [11], to balance the classes by generating synthetic fraud samples, leading to 284,315 samples in both the non-fraud and fraud classes. The Credit Card dataset, initially containing 31 features, was divided into training and testing sets in an 80:20 ratio. For binarization, Algorithm 1 was used and a maximum of four leaf nodes produced 120 binary features. A Random Forest classifier was then applied for support set generation, configured with $n\_estimators = 100$, $random\_state = 42$, and a feature importance threshold of 0.01, identifying 15, 17, and 16 key features in Experiments 1, 2, and 3, respectively.

4.4 Experiment 1 Results

For pattern generation phase, hyperparameter tuning was conducted, yielding the following values: min_covered_observations $= 3$, $h = 0.3445$, max_degree $= 5$, max_generations $= 14$, and mutation_rate $= 0.8119$. Based on these parameters, 6 prime patterns were generated, including 2 patterns of degree 1, 3 patterns of degree 2 and 1 patterns of degree 4. The confusion matrix and ROC curve of the proposed model are illustrated in Fig. 1, showing the relationship between predicted and actual classifications. The Table 2 evaluates the performance of three models-two existing models (Binary Bat Algorithm with Feature-based Decision System (FDS) and Multilayer Feed-Forward Neural Networks (MLFNN) with Deep Encoder) and one proposed model. The Binary Bat Algorithm with FDS achieves 95.51% accuracy but struggles with a low precision of 3.19%, leading to unreliable positive predictions. MLFNN with Deep Encoder, with 93.46% accuracy, has a slightly lower precision of 2.31% and a better recall of 89.80%, but still suffers from a poor F1-score of 4.51%, reflecting similar issues in balancing precision and recall. In contrast, the proposed model shows a dramatic improvement, achieving 99.86% accuracy and a much higher precision of 55.70%. Though recall is slightly lower at 84.69%, the F1-score rises to 67.21%, indicating a much better balance between precision and recall. These results demonstrate that while existing models perform well in recall, their extremely low precision and F1-scores limit their overall effectiveness. The LAD with DT model, based on the original Logical Analysis of Data (LAD) method enhanced with a Decision Tree binarization technique, further supports this approach's interpretability while maintaining competitive performance. Overall, the proposed model achieves substantial improvements in accuracy, precision, and F1-score, offering a more reliable and well-balanced solution for fraud detection.

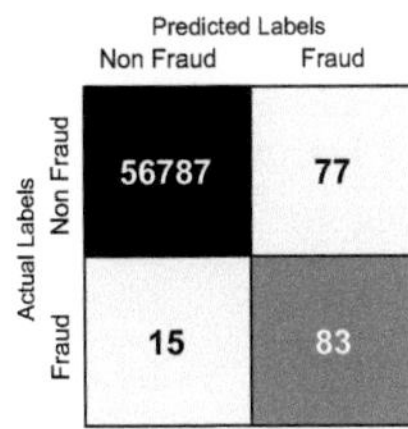
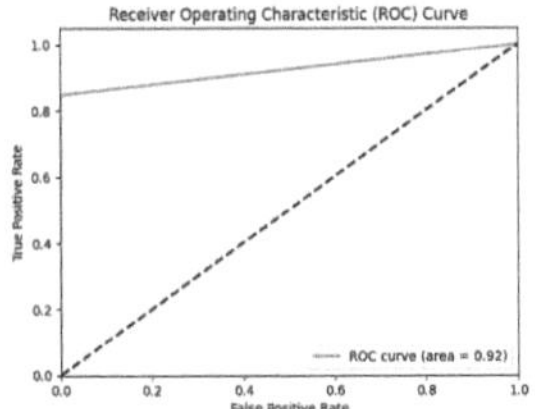

Fig. 1. Confusion Matrix and ROC Curve

Table 2. Performance Evaluation of Proposed Model Against Existing Methods [7]

Model	Accuracy %	Precision %	Recall %	F1 Score %
Binary Bat Algorithm with FDS	95.51	3.19	85.71	6.16
MLFNN with Deep Encoder	93.46	2.31	89.80	4.51%
LAD with DT	99.89	72.88	61.22	66.54
Proposed Model	99.83	51.87	84.69	64.34

4.5   Experiment 2 Results

For experiment 2, again hyperparameter tuning was conducted, resulting in the following values for pattern generation step: min_covered_observations $= 1$, $h = 0.9840$, max_degree $= 5$, max_generations $= 14$, and mutation_rate $= 0.9108$. Based on these parameters, 17 distinct patterns were generated including 1 pattern of degree 1, 1 pattern of degree 2, 5 patterns of degree 3, 7 patterns of degree 4, and 3 patterns of degree 5. The confusion matrix and ROC curve of the proposed model are shown in Fig. 2.

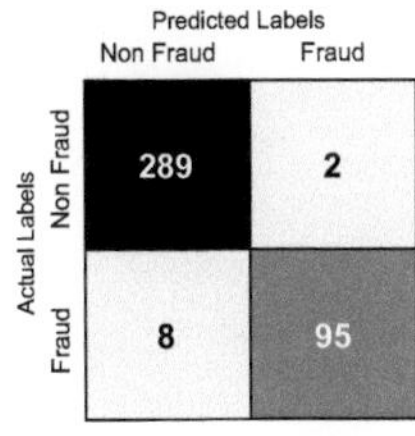
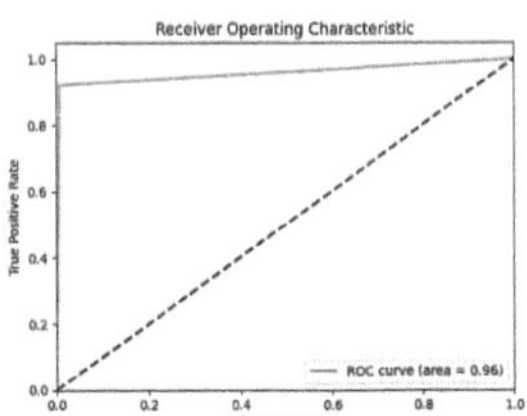

Fig. 2. Confusion Matrix and ROC Curve

The Table 3 compares the performance of various existing methods with the newly proposed model. FCNN, CLR and MSEFBoost demonstrated progressive improvements, especially in precision and F1-score, with MSEFBoost reaching 96.74% accuracy and 97.79% precision. While CSVM showed high precision 95.06%, it lagged in recall and F1-score, reflecting conservative predictions.

Table 3. Performance Evaluation of Proposed Model Against Existing Methods [12]

Methods	Years	Accuracy %	Recall %	F1-score %	Precision %	AUC %
FLR	–	94.74	83.17	88.89	95.45	90.91
FCNN	2022	95.74	87.13	91.19	95.65	92.89
CLR	2023	96.49	88.12	92.71	97.80	93.72
MSEFBoost	2023	96.74	89.11	93.24	97.79	94.02
CSVM	2023	92.98	76.24	84.62	95.06	87.45
FMC	2024	95.99	91.10	92.44	93.81	94.03
LAD with DT	2025	96.45	94.95	91.26	93.07	–
Proposed Method	–	97.46	92.23	95.00	97.94	96.00

FMC offered a more balanced performance with 95.99% accuracy and strong AUC 94.03%. LAD with DT achieved competitive recall 94.95% and accuracy 96.45%, but the proposed method surpasses all existing models by attaining the highest scores across all metrics accuracy 97.46%, recall 92.23%, F1-score 95.00%, precision 97.94%, and AUC 96.00%. These results indicate that the proposed model not only achieves better accuracy but also effectively balances precision and recall, offering a significantly more reliable and robust classification solution compared to prior models.

4.6 Experiment 3 Results

The pattern generation step of LAD uses following hyper parameters: min_covered_observations = 3, $h = 0.8876$, max_degree = 5, max_generations = 11, and mutation_rate = 0.6913. Based on these parameters, 6 prime patterns were generated, including 2 pattern of degree 1, 1 pattern of degree 2, 1 pattern of degree 4, and 2 patterns of degree 5. The confusion matrix and ROC curve of the proposed model are shown in Fig. 3.

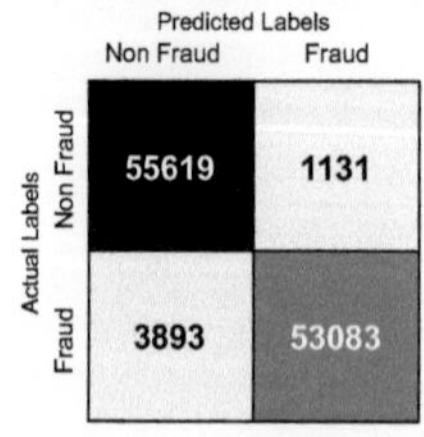

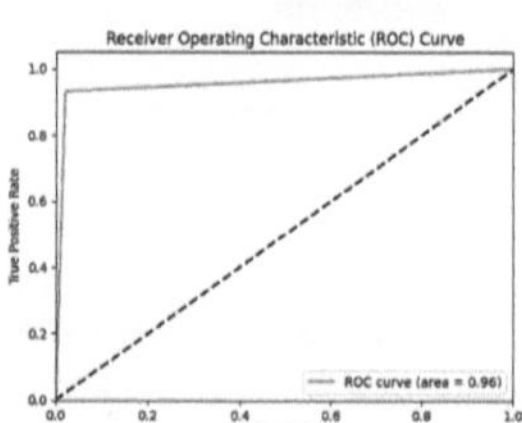

Fig. 3. Confusion Matrix and ROC Curve

Table 4. Performance Evaluation of Proposed Model Against Existing Methods [11]

Model	Accuracy %	Precision %	Recall %	F1 Score %
Decision Tree	97.74	99.18	96.68	97.92
Random Forest	99.11	99.88	98.34	99.10
Logistic Regression	94.96	97.60	92.19	94.81
LAD with DT	94.56	97.28	91.63	94.39
Proposed Model	96.08	97.91	93.16	95.48

The performance comparison in Table 4 highlights that the proposed model achieves competitive results compared to existing methods. Although the Random Forest model attained the highest accuracy (99.11%) and F1-score (99.10%), the proposed model provides a strong balance between accuracy (96.08%), precision (97.91%), and recall (93.16%) while maintaining lower computational complexity. Compared with LAD with DT and Logistic Regression, the proposed model demonstrates noticeable improvements in recall and overall F1-score, confirming its effectiveness and robustness for credit card fraud detection.

5   Conclusion and Future Work

The proposed pattern-based classification method demonstrates superior performance in detecting credit card fraud across various configurations of data sets. On the 3:1 sampled dataset, it outperforms existing models with 97.46% accuracy, 97.94% precision, 92.23% recall, and a 95% F1-score. When applied to the original imbalanced dataset, it significantly improves the F1-score to 67.21%, highlighting its robustness despite class imbalance. With SMOTE balancing, the model continues to lead with 96.08% accuracy and an F1-score of 95.48%, surpassing baseline models across all key metrics. These consistent results confirm the method's effectiveness, adaptability, and reliability in minimizing false positives while accurately identifying fraudulent transactions. This algorithm efficiently discovers meaningful patterns using a depth-first search like approach but may miss globally optimal results due to limited search space. Future work will focus on improving pattern coverage through hybrid search strategies and extending the model for large-scale and real-time fraud detection.

Acknowledgement. This work was supported in part by Information Security Education and Awareness (ISEA) Phase-3 Project funded by MeitY, Govt. of India.

References

1. Aftab, A., Shahzad, I., Sajid, A., Anwar, M., Anwar, N.: Fraud detection of credit cards using supervised machine learning techniques. Pak. J. Emerg. Sci. Technol. (PJEST) **4** (2023)

2. Tang, Y., Liang, Y.: Credit card fraud detection based on federated graph learning. Expert Syst. Appl. **256**, 124979 (2024)

3. Gangopadhyay, A.K., Sheth, T., Chauhan, S.: LAD in finance: accounting analytics and fraud detection. Adv. Comput. Intell. **3**(1), 4 (2023)

4. Das, T.K., Gangopadhyay, S., Zhou, J.: SSIDS: semi-supervised intrusion detection system by extending the logical analysis of data. arXiv preprint (2020). https://arxiv.org/abs/2007.10608

5. Boros, E., Hammer, P.L., Ibaraki, T., Kogan, A.: Logical analysis of numerical data. Math. Program. **79**, 163–190 (1997)

6. Geetha, N., Dheepa, G.: A hybrid deep learning and modified butterfly optimization based feature selection for transaction credit card fraud detection. J. Positive Psychol. Wellbeing **8**(2), 1–10 (2022)

7. Verma, S., Dhar, J.: Credit card fraud detection: a deep learning approach. arXiv preprint (2024)

8. Zou, Y., Cheng, D.: Effective high-order graph representation learning for credit card fraud detection. In: IJCAI-2024, pp. 7581–7589 (2024). https://doi.org/10.24963/ijcai.2024/839

9. Reynisson, K., Schreyer, M., Borth, D.: GraphGuard: contrastive self-supervised learning for credit-card fraud detection in multi-relational dynamic graphs. arXiv preprint (2024)

10. Hafez, I., Hafez, A., Saleh, A., Abd El-Mageed, A., Abohany, A.: A systematic review of AI-enhanced techniques in credit card fraud detection. J. Big Data**12** (2025)

11. Siddique Ibrahim, S.P., Jayasree, A., Poojitha, M., Jyothi, N.A., Namithaa, K., Sushila, Y.: Credit card fraud detection: machine learning and data analytical approach for accuracy and comparative analysis. In: International Conference on Sustainable Communication Networks and Application, pp. 1461–1468 (2024)

12. Tang, Y., Liang, Y.: Credit card fraud detection based on federated graph learning. Expert Syst. Appl. **256**, 124979 (2024). https://doi.org/10.1016/j.eswa.2024.124979

13. Singh, M.T., Prasad, R.K., Michael, G.R., Kaphungkui, N.K., Singh, N.H.: Heterogeneous graph auto-encoder for CreditCard fraud detection. arXiv preprint (2024). https://arxiv.org/abs/2410.08121

14. Patil, M.: Credit card fraud detection using machine learning and blockchain. Int. J. Res. Appl. Sci. Eng. Technol. **11**, 2745–2751 (2023)

15. Zhu, M., Zhang, Y., Gong, Y., Xu, C., Xiang, Y.: Enhancing credit card fraud detection: a neural network and SMOTE integrated approach. Century SciPub J. (2023). http://www.centuryscipub.com

16. Yu, C., Xu, Y., Cao, J., Zhang, Y., Jin, Y., Zhu, M.: Credit card fraud detection using advanced transformer model. arXiv preprint (2024). https://arxiv.org/abs/2406.03733

17. Feng, X., Kim, S.-K.: Novel machine learning based credit card fraud detection systems. Mathematics **12**(18), 1869 (2024). https://doi.org/10.3390/math12121869

18. Ileberi, E., Sun, Y., Wang, Z.: A machine learning based credit card fraud detection using the GA algorithm for feature selection. J. Big Data **9**(24) (2022)

Intrusion Detection

Curriculum Learning with Image Transformation and Explainable AI for Improved Network Intrusion Detection

Sathwik Narkedimilli[1,2], C. Pavan Kumar[1(✉)],
and Raghavendra Ramachandra[3]

[1] Indian Institute of Information Technology Dharwad, Dharwad, Karnataka, India
`{21bcs103,pavan}@iiitdwd.ac.in`
[2] Département Informatique et Réseaux (INFRES), Télécom Paris (IP Paris), Paris,
France
[3] Norwegian University of Science and Technology (NTNU), Gjøvik, Norway
`raghavendra.ramachandra@ntnu.no`

Abstract. To address the growing demand for robust Network Intrusion Detection Systems (NIDS), we propose a stage-wise curriculum learning framework combined with image-based transformation techniques and Explainable AI (XAI). This approach leverages XAI for transparency and comprehensibility, focusing on adaptive learning and scalable detection. By training the model on increasingly complex attack scenarios, the proposed architecture facilitates efficient and precise optimization. The explanatory tool SHAP (SHapley Additive exPlanations) is integrated provide detailed insights into model predictions. The ensemble stacking and model-to-model interoperability further enhances detection efficiency and reliability. Experiments validate the effectiveness of the proposed method, achieving the following accuracies: 97% on the CIC-Apt-IIoT dataset, 96% on the Edge-IIoT dataset, and 92% on the CIC-IoV-2024 dataset. This highlights the efficiency of the framework and setting a new benchmark for NIDS.

Keywords: Curriculum Learning · Explainable Artificial Intelligence (XAI) · Intrusion Detection System · Image Transformation

1 Introduction

Network Intrusion Detection Systems (NIDS) play a vital role in protecting digital infrastructures, particularly in Internet of Things (IoT) and Industrial Internet of Things (IIoT) environments. However, traditional detection systems face significant challenges in scalability, adaptability, and interpretability. The Edge-IIoT dataset underscores the increasing complexity of modern threats, including diverse attack scenarios such as DDoS, malware, and injection attacks [6]. Existing solutions often struggle to address these multifaceted challenges due to

N. Hubballi et al. (Eds.): ICISS 2025, LNCS 16380, pp. 285–298, 2026.
https://doi.org/10.1007/978-3-032-13714-2_18

limited model robustness and a lack of transparency in their decision-making processes, highlighting the need for innovative and effective approaches.

While existing systems use one-stage training and are not easily scalable, for attack complexity. However, the proposed curriculum learning system scales according to attack complexity. With the addition of XAI, transparency is provided with real-time models predictions. It not only improves detection performance but also compensates for the computational cost and scalability constraint that previous experiments existing state of the art technique suffer with but also provide a better option in resource-limited systems.

This work introduces a stage-wise curriculum learning framework that leverages image transformations and Explainable Artificial Intelligence (XAI). By training the model in progressive stages of increasing attack complexity, the system mimics human learning, enhancing both generalization and robustness. Image transformations enable the visualization of data patterns, while Convolutional Neural Networks (CNNs) effectively extract spatial features. Combined with ensemble stacking and interpretability tools like SHAP, this approach delivers accurate intrusion detection alongside clear, interpretable predictions.

The rest of the paper is structured as follows: Sect. 2 reviews related work, Sect. 3 outlines the proposed system model, and Sect. 4 analyzes the results across datasets. Section 5 concludes by summarizing the contributions to scalable and efficient NIDS for IoT/IIoT environments.

2   Related Work and Literature

Curriculum Learning (CL) is a human-like learning approach of training a machine learning model in an order from easier to harder data. This is a method that tries to generalize faster, converge faster, and is more robust by walking the model through easier tasks or data distributions before taking on harder tasks. CL is especially relevant in network security, where it helps in better training of intrusion detection models. By adding attack scenarios one by one, the model gets robust to different types of threat complexity, becoming more accurate and flexible. This is especially important when dealing with big, noisy data sets like the kind that come from cybersecurity. These models from Wang et al. and Soviany et al. mention CL's capabilities to enhance model performance and accelerate training in many different domains such as security applications [12, 15].

In the literature, studies evaluating the Edge-IIoT dataset have demonstrated its utility in Intrusion Detection Systems (IDSs) for IoT and IIoT environments. For instance, Fariba Laiq et al. [10] proposed a new detection strategy of DDoS attacks on the Edge-IIoT network using different Ensemble Learning (EL) methods. It was a combination of using SMOTE to balance the data, labeling and bagging, boosting, and stacking using EL. It reported more than 90% accuracy in all the evaluation parameters, which shows that the EL approaches were better than the single classifiers. But one drawback was the computational overhead of training ensemble models, and reliance on a skewed dataset in the first place.

Nizwan Hamza et al. [8] evaluated several supervised ML algorithms like KNN, DTC, SVM, LR, and RFC on the Edge-IIoT dataset for malware detection. They reported an accuracy of 94% for RFC. Tareq et al. [13] employs two deep learning models, DenseNet and Inception Time, for multi-class classification to detect cyber-attacks across three prominent IoT cybersecurity datasets. DenseNet was adapted for one-dimensional data, while Inception Time used a sliding window technique for improved feature extraction. The methodology demonstrated the superiority of Inception Time in terms of accuracy and computational efficiency. However, limitations included challenges with memory usage and computational constraints, which required using class weights instead of more resource-intensive techniques like SMOTE for balancing datasets.

Al Nuaimi et al. [1] explored the Edge-IIoT dataset for multi-class classification by deep hybrid CNN/GRU models. This work showed very high precision in multi-class situation but this paper also presented trade-off between model complexity and inference time, which is very important for edge deployments.

Table 1. Summary of Literature with Performance Metrics

Research Study	Accuracy	Precision	Recall	F1-Score
1. Al Nuaimi et al. [1]	96%	95%	96%	96%
2. Hamza et al. [8]	94%	92%	94%	94%
3. Proposed Method	97%	99%	96%	98%

Table 1 summarizes the accuracy values for classification tasks performed using various algorithms and datasets. Work of Al Nuaimi et al. [1] achieved an accuracy of 96.01% with a precision of 95.02%, leveraging advanced algorithms such as J48, PART, Bayes Nets, AdaBoost, and LogitBoost. Similarly, the work of Hamza et al. [8] attained an accuracy of 94% with a precision of 92.21% using algorithms like KNN, DTC, LR, SVM, and RFC. These results highlight the effectiveness of machine learning models in achieving high performance for intrusion detection and malware classification within IoT datasets.

Despite the high accuracy, the research using the Edge-IIoT dataset is not scalable and efficient enough to run on limited edge devices. These models are also not transparent in predictions which emphasizes the importance of leveraging explainable AI (XAI) to help provide insights into model decision-making and reassurance for important IoT use cases Curriculum learning is needed since the models can be gradually trained from a low-risk attack scenario to a higher-risk attack scenario. This method does not just help in scaling by streamlining learning but also improves robustness and flexibility which is a great choice for resource-constrained edge environments.

3   System Model

3.1   Workflow of the Proposed Algorithm

The workflow of the proposed algorithm, illustrated in Fig. 1, begins with image generation as part of the image transformation process in the curriculum learning framework. Preprocessed normal and attack traffic datasets are converted into 6 × 6 grayscale images [4]. At each curriculum level - normal data, easy attacks, medium attacks, and complex attacks - the data is normalized, restructured, and labeled. Principal Component Analysis (PCA) is used during preprocessing to reduce the dimensionality of numerical features, ensuring the images retain essential data patterns while optimizing their size for image creation. These generated images, along with their corresponding labels, are then used to train Convolutional Neural Network (CNN) and Neural Network (NN) models separately. Both models perform binary classification, with normal data labeled as '0' and attack data labeled as '1'. Figure 2 shows an example of an image generated through the image transformation process.

The proposed workflow incorporates a neural network (NN) architecture tailored for the sequential nature of IoT data. It utilizes advanced layers, including an adaptive feature mask layer to dynamically weight input features, a dynamic convolutional layer to capture local temporal features, and an attention-based temporal encoder with self-attention to learn long-range dependencies. Legacy connections and layer normalization ensure stable training and smooth gradient flow. The architecture includes three sets of GRU and LSTM layers to efficiently handle both short- and long-term dependencies. Self-attention mechanisms emphasize critical timesteps, while dropout layers prevent overfitting. The model also incorporates edge-optimized techniques such as quantization and pruning, making it lightweight and suitable for deployment on edge devices. The output layer, designed with sigmoid activation, provides probabilities for normal or attack classifications. This layer is trained on all samples of the dataset ensuring efficient model development.

CNN: CNN model is implemented over all four stages of the CL to extract spatial features and process transformed images effectively. Convolutional layers adopt 32-filter and a 64-filter layer (each using a (3, 3) kernel size and ReLU activation function) to capture hierarchical spatial features. To preserve essential features and reduce spatial dimensions, each convolutional block is followed by Max-pooling layers. Overfitting is avoided using dropout layers with rates 0.2 and 0.3. Post feature extraction, to extract high level image representations, the model is flattened and passed through dense layer with 128 neurons and ReLU activation. The final layer, equipped with a softmax activation function, provides classification probabilities. This stage-wise training approach allows the model to learn robustly from images and labels, accommodating varying levels of attack complexity.

Finally, we employ soft voting to combine the predictions from the NN and CNN models, creating an ensemble that improves precision. The performance of the ensemble model is evaluated using metrics such as accuracy, F1 score,

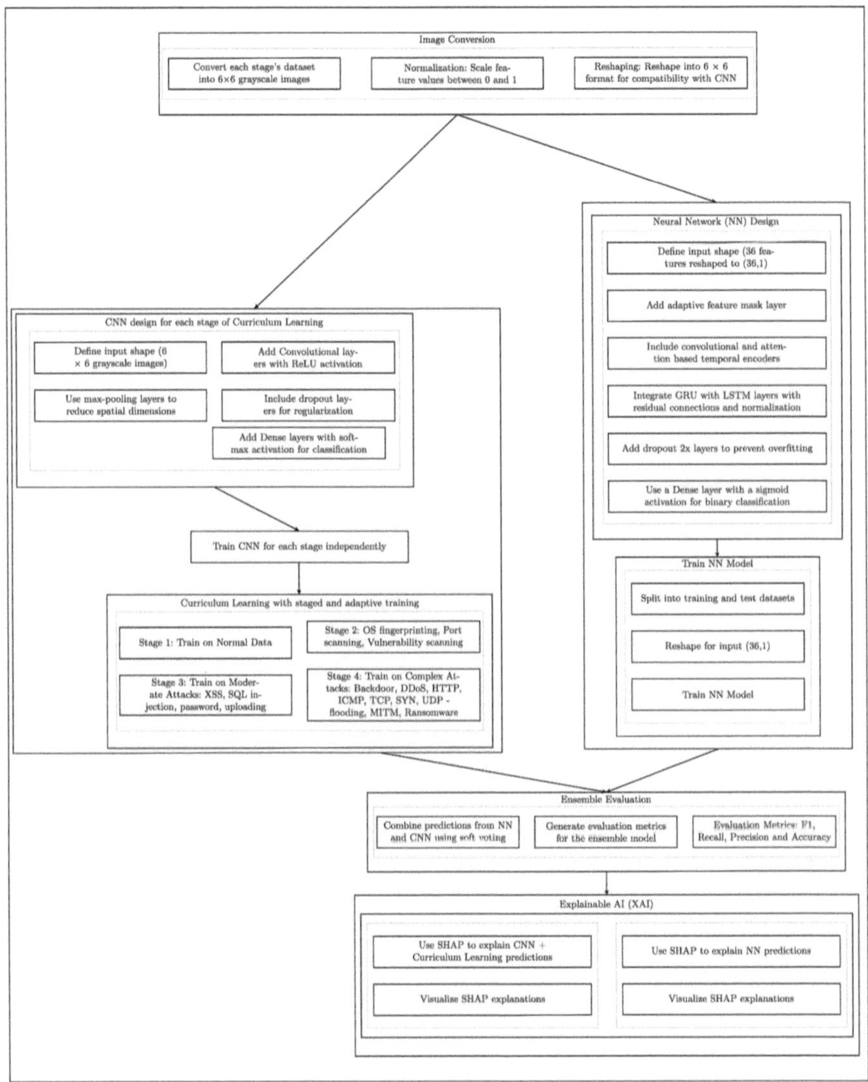

Fig. 1. Workflow of Proposed Algorithm with Image Transformation (zooming is preferable)

recall, and precision. To enhance interpretability, we use SHAP (SHapley Additive exPlanations) for both NN and CNN predictions independently. The SHAP values are then aggregated across the ensemble to represent overall feature contributions, providing insights into feature relevance and model behavior. By mapping the SHAP values, we can identify which features were most influential in the model's predictions, making the learning process clearer and more understandable.

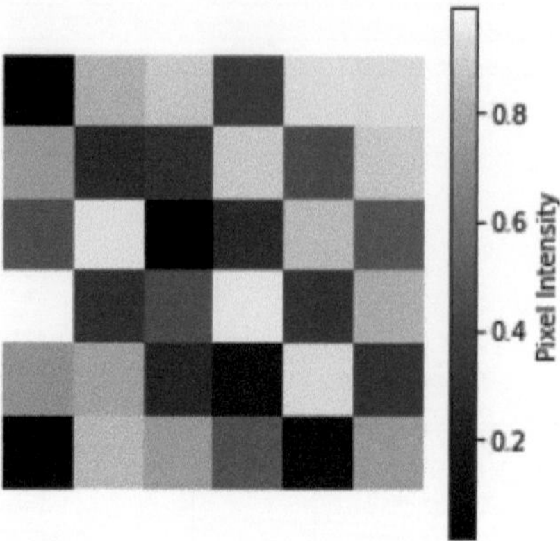

Fig. 2. Example Gray Scale image obtained by Image Transformation

The implementation of this work is available in the GitHub repository[1].

3.2 Data-Preprocessing and Feature Engineering

Data preprocessing involves preparing the dataset for analysis by performing several key steps. It begins with handling missing values by replacing them with zeros, removing duplicate entries, converting data types, and eliminating outliers. Feature scaling is then applied using the Standard Scaler algorithm to standardize feature values and assess the impact of scaling. Dimensionality reduction is performed using Linear Discriminant Analysis (LDA), with the number of components determined based on the explained variance. Finally, the dataset is split into training and testing sets using an 80-20 split, ensuring class distribution is preserved through stratified sampling. A separate validation set is also created for performance evaluation.

Feature engineering aims to make data more comprehensible and meaningful for training machine learning models. The process begins with feature selection, utilizing LDA plots or Random Forest feature importance plots to identify key features and retain relevant predictors. For the Edge-IIoT dataset, the curriculum learning algorithm evaluates 36 features. Log scaling and binning are applied to reduce dimensionality, while features with no significant value are either removed or merged. The interaction features are created to capture the relationships between the variables and the final set of features (X) and the target variable (y) are defined for the supervised learning tasks. This carefully designed pre-processing and feature engineering pipeline ensures clean and optimized data for curriculum learning models.

---

[1] https://github.com/sathwikNARKEDimilli29/CurriculumLearning_ImageTransformation.

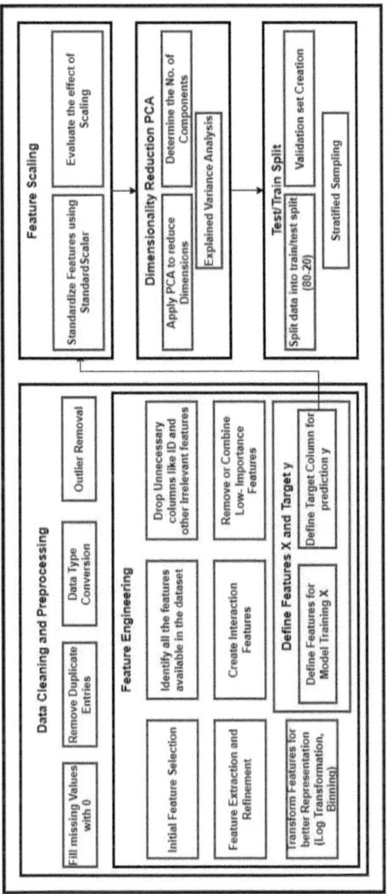

Fig. 3. Data-Preprocessing and Feature Engineering Steps

In this work, we have tested and implemented the proposed algorithm on the Edge-IIoT dataset, and it is split into 4 stages of curriculum training:

- Stage 1 trains on normal data to have a baseline,
- Stage 2 contains simple attack data (OS Fingerprinting, Port Scanning, Vulnerability Scanner),
- Stage 3 contains medium attacks (XSS, SQL Injection, Password, Uploading), and
- Stage 4 contains complex attacks (Backdoor, DDoS, MITM, Ransomware).

The proposed curriculum learning algorithms are evaluated on two additional benchmark datasets: CIC-Apt-IIoT-2024 and CIC-IoV-2024. For CIC-Apt-IIoT-2024, training is performed on normal data and attack data. In contrast, CIC-IoV-2024 follows a three-phase training process: Stage 1: Normal data, Stage 2: Spoofing attacks, including GAS, RPM, SPEED, and STEERING WHEEL,

Stage 3: DoS attacks using test datasets. This architectural design provides a robust framework for validating different IoT/IoV security challenges. For a detailed overview of the data preprocessing and feature engineering steps, refer to Fig. 3.

3.3   Dataset

In this work, we have tested the proposed algorithm on the Edge-IIoT [6] dataset, which is a realistic cybersecurity dataset created from IoT/IIoT testbed, using multiple devices, sensors, protocols, and cloud/edge scenarios. It tracks all the 14 IoT and IIoT attacks that fall under five top threats: DoS/DDoS, Information Collection, Man-in-the-Middle, Injection, and Malware. With 61 high-correlation features out of a baseline of 1176 features, the dataset can be used to perform machine learning intrusion detection both in a centralized and federated learning model and thus is widely useful for cybersecurity studies.

The proposed curriculum learning algorithm is trained and tested on two additional benchmark datasets, CIC-Apt-IIoT-2024 [7] and CIC-IoV-2024 [11]. CIC-Apt-IIoT-2024 is dedicated to Advanced Persistent Threat (APT) detection in IIoT domains with 20 different attack techniques based on APT29 attacks and captured in a hybrid testbed. In contrast, CIC-IoV-2024 covers cyber security in IoV with real-life data gathered during CAN-BUS spoofing and DoS attacks on a 2019 Ford Focus. These data sets complement each other to allow for strong validation in a wide range of IoT/IoV security scenarios.

3.4   Mathematical Model of the Proposed System

This subsection provides a concise description and precise mathematical formulation of each component of the proposed model. Let a single input (after PCA and flattening) be

$$x = [x_1, \ldots, x_{36}]^\top \in \mathbb{R}^{36}. \tag{1}$$

Adaptive Feature Mask learns a sigmoid gating vector over the 36 PCA-derived features, allowing the network to emphasize or suppress individual dimensions before further processing [9]:

$$m = \sigma\bigl(W_m x + b_m\bigr) \in (0,1)^{36}, \quad \tilde{x} = m \odot x, \tag{2}$$

where $\sigma(z) = 1/(1 + e^{-z})$ and $\odot$ are element-wise multiplication.

Dynamic 1D Convolution applies 32 learnable 1×3 filters along the feature sequence, with ReLU activations [3]:

$$H_{j,c} = \mathrm{ReLU}\Bigl(\sum_{u=-1}^{1} W_{c,u}^{(\mathrm{conv})} \tilde{x}_{j+u} + b_c \Bigr), \tag{3}$$

for $j = 1, \ldots, 36$, $c = 1, \ldots, 32$.

Self-attention Temporal Encoder uses scaled dot-product attention over $H \in \mathbb{R}^{36 \times 32}$ [14]:

$$A = \mathrm{softmax}\!\left(\frac{H\,H^{\top}}{\sqrt{32}}\right), \quad \tilde{H} = A\,H \in \mathbb{R}^{36 \times 32}. \tag{4}$$

Residual & Layer Normalization adds attention output back to convolutional features and normalizes:

$$R^{(1)} = H + \tilde{H}, \quad Z^{(1)} = \mathrm{LayerNorm}\!\left(R^{(1)}\right). \tag{5}$$

GRULSTM Stacked Blocks with Self-Attention ($\times$3) three repeated blocks of GRU-LSTM layers (sizes 64 and 32) interleaved with self-attention + residual [5]. In the final repetition, retain only $\ell_{36}^{(3)}$. Each block comprises:

$$\textbf{GRU (64):} \quad \begin{aligned} z_t &= \sigma(W_z z_t^{\mathrm{in}} + U_z h_{t-1} + b_z), \\ r_t &= \sigma(W_r z_t^{\mathrm{in}} + U_r h_{t-1} + b_r), \\ \tilde{h}_t &= \tanh\!\left(W_h z_t^{\mathrm{in}} + U_h(r_t \odot h_{t-1}) + b_h\right), \\ h_t &= (1 - z_t) \odot h_{t-1} + z_t \odot \tilde{h}_t, \end{aligned} \tag{6}$$

$$\textbf{LSTM (32):} \quad \begin{aligned} i_t &= \sigma(W_i h_t + U_i c_{t-1} + b_i), \\ f_t &= \sigma(W_f h_t + U_f c_{t-1} + b_f), \\ o_t &= \sigma(W_o h_t + U_o c_{t-1} + b_o), \\ \tilde{c}_t &= \tanh(W_c h_t + U_c c_{t-1} + b_c), \\ c_t &= f_t \odot c_{t-1} + i_t \odot \tilde{c}_t, \\ \ell_t &= o_t \odot \tanh(c_t), \end{aligned} \tag{7}$$

$$\textbf{Self-Attention \& Residual:} \quad \begin{aligned} A' &= \mathrm{softmax}\!\left(\frac{L\,L^{\top}}{\sqrt{32}}\right), \\ \tilde{L} &= A'L, \\ R &= L + \tilde{L}, \\ Z &= \mathrm{LayerNorm}(R). \end{aligned} \tag{8}$$

Dropout & Output Layer applies two successive 30% dropouts, followed by a sigmoid:

$$\begin{aligned} d^{(1)} &= \mathrm{Dropout}(h^{(3)}, 0.3), \quad d^{(2)} = \mathrm{Dropout}(d^{(1)}, 0.3), \\ \hat{y} &= \sigma\!\left(w_{\mathrm{out}}^{\top} d^{(2)} + b_{\mathrm{out}}\right) \in (0, 1). \end{aligned} \tag{9}$$

Curriculum Learning. We employ a four -stage curriculum:

- **Stage 1 (Normal Traffic):** Train on normal data only, $\mathcal{D}_1 = \{(x_i, y_i) \mid y_i = 0\}$.
- **Stage 2 (Simple Attacks):** Fine-tune on basic attack types $\mathcal{D}_2 = \{(x_i, y_i) \mid y_i = 1,\ \mathrm{AttackType} \in \{\mathrm{OS\_Fingerprinting}, \mathrm{Port\_Scanning..}\}\}$.

- **Stage
  3 (Moderate Attacks):** Fine-tune on advanced attacks, $\mathcal{D}_3 = \{(x_i, y_i) \mid y_i = 1,\ \text{AttackType} \in \{\text{XSS}, \text{SQL\_injection}, \text{Password}, \text{Uploading}, \dots\}\}$.
- **Stage 4 (Complex Attacks):** Fine-tune on more advanced attacks, $\mathcal{D}_3 = \{(x_i, y_i) \mid y_i = 1,\ \text{AttackType} \in \{\text{DDos}, \text{Complex\_Adversirial\_attacks}\}\}$.

At each stage $t = 1, 2, 3$, parameters $\theta^{(t)}$ are obtained by [2]

$$\theta^{(t)} = \arg\min_{\theta} \sum_{(x,y) \in \mathcal{D}_t} \mathcal{L}\big(f_\theta(x), y\big),$$

and used to initialize the next stage.

Each stage learns local feature interactions and long-term temporal patterns, which yields a robust classifier.

3.5 Hyper Parameters

We reduce to 36 PCA components, then in the attention augmented branch apply a TimeDistributed sigmoid gate, a 1D conv (32 filters, kernel 3, ReLU) and three GRU LSTM blocks (GRU 64 units $\rightarrow$ LSTM 32 units) each with self?attention, residuals, and layer-norm; dropout 0.3 after the final LSTM and before the output. The CNN branch stacks Conv2D ($32\rightarrow64$ filters, 3×3 kernels) with dropout ($0.2\rightarrow0.3$) and 2×2 max-pooling, then flattens to a Dense 128 unit layer with dropout 0.5 and softmax. Both branches train with Adam (binary/categorical) cross-entropy loss, batch 32, 10 epochs, 10% validation and 80/20 train/test split. The final predictions use soft voting of the averaged branch probabilities.

4 Result Analysis

The dataset and model evaluation metrics are given in Table 2. The model was tested with three different datasets: Edge-IIoT, CIC-Apt-IIoT-2024, and CIC-IoV-2024. The Edge-IIoT dataset had a precision - 99%, recall - 92%, F1-Score - 95%, and accuracy - 96%. For the CIC-Apt-IIoT-2024 dataset, the model performed slightly better with Precision - 99%, Recall - 96%, F1-Score - 98%, and accuracy 97% showing that the model can cope with high-level attack scenarios. Likewise, the CIC-IoV-2024 dataset gave a Precision - 91%, Recall - 93%, F1-Score - 92%, and accuracy 92% which is pretty impressive given the difficulties in this dataset. These findings reveal the adaptability and efficiency of the model to different IoT security vulnerabilities.

Table 2. Performance Metrics Across Different Datasets

Dataset	Precision	Recall	F1-Score	Accuracy
1. Edge-IIoT	99%	92%	95%	96%
2. CIC-Apt-IIoT-2024	99%	96%	98%	97%
3. CIC-IoV-2024	91%	93%	92%	92%

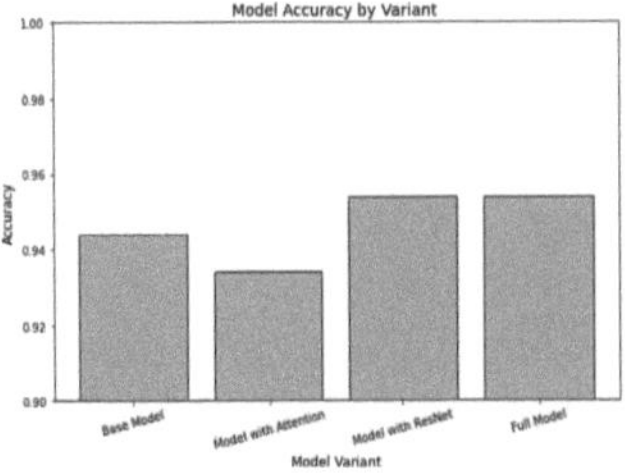
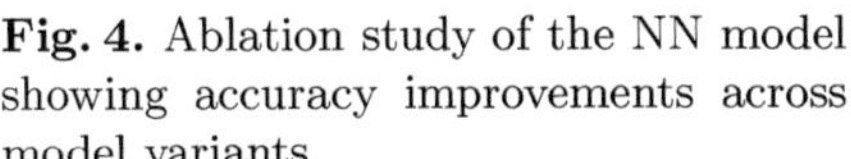
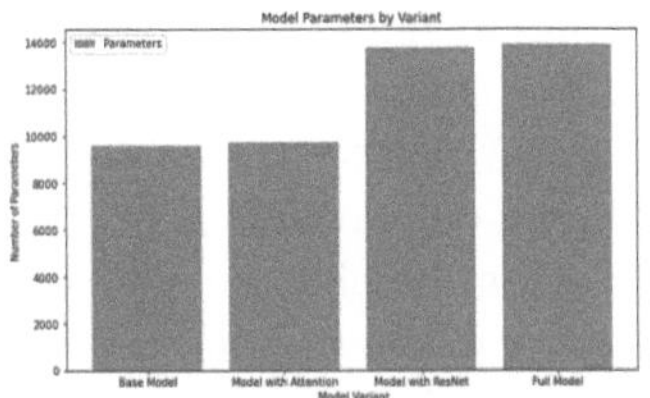

Fig. 4. Ablation study of the NN model showing accuracy improvements across model variants.

Fig. 5. Ablation study of the NN model illustrating the number of parameters for each variant.

The analysis of the Edge-IIoT dataset revealed that the proposed model has a compact size of 367.39 KB with 94,051 parameters, demonstrating its lightweight nature. Despite its minimal footprint, the model achieves high accuracy, making it both efficient and scalable. Its compact size and optimized architecture ensure seamless deployment on edge devices with limited computational and storage resources. This highlights the model's suitability for real-time IoT applications, where scalability and low latency are critical requirements.

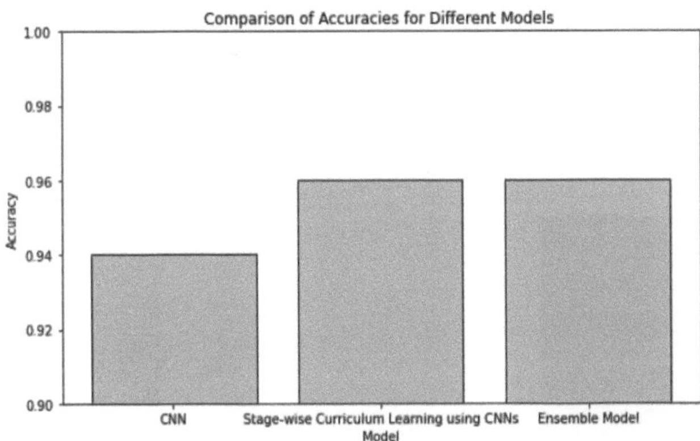

Fig. 6. Comparison of accuracy between CNN, curriculum learning-enhanced CNN, and ensemble model.

4.1   Ablation Study

Figures 4, 5 and 6, give, taken together, the comparison of the neural network (NN) and CNN models in multiple dimensions.

Figure 4, demonstrates the incremental improvements in accuracy as the neural network model is enhanced through different stages-starting from the base model to incorporating attention mechanisms, ResNet blocks, and finally the full model. It highlights how each architectural enhancement significantly boosts model precision.

Figure 5 demonstrates the relationship between the number of parameters and the model variant. It shows that as new features like attention mechanisms and ResNet blocks are added, the model's complexity and parameter count increase, yet these enhancements contribute to notable performance improvements, justifying the added complexity.

The Fig. 6 demonstrates the accuracy of three models-standard CNN, curriculum learning-enhanced CNN, and an ensemble model. It reveals that the curriculum learning approach combined with ensemble techniques achieves superior accuracy compared to standalone CNN, emphasizing the effectiveness of these advanced methodologies in improving detection performance.

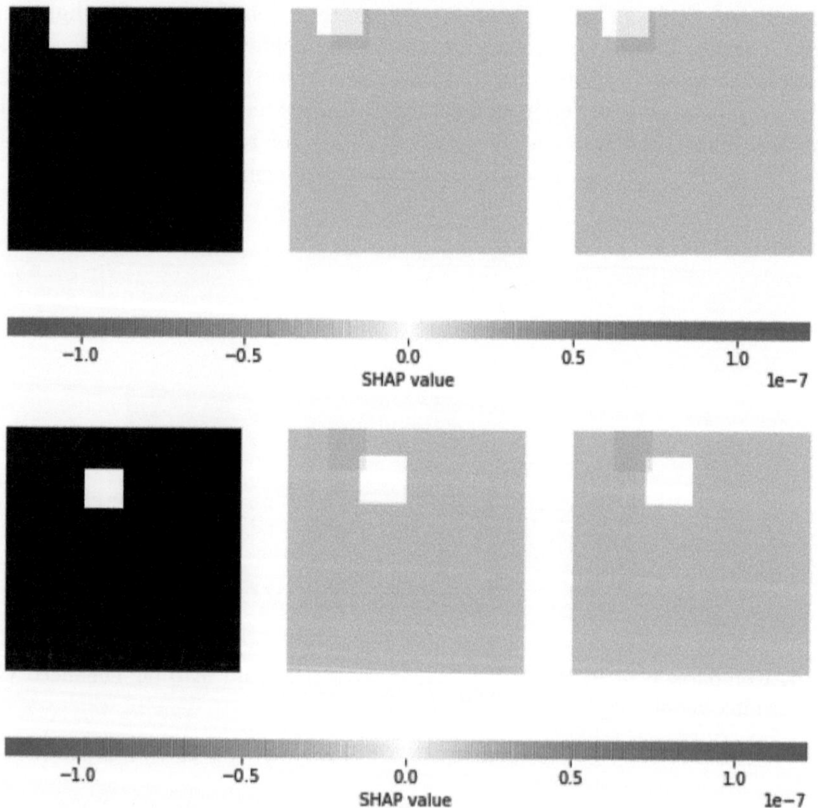

Fig. 7. SHAP explanations showcasing feature contributions for the CNN model enhanced by curriculum learning and the neural network (NN) model.

Figure 7 illustrates the SHAP explanations applied to the CNN model enhanced by curriculum learning and the neural network (NN) model, highlighting feature contributions to predictions. The image illustrates SHAP values, showing the impact of different features on the model's prediction. Blue regions negatively influence the prediction, red regions positively contribute, and gray areas have minimal impact. This helps explain the model's decision-making by identifying which features were most important, enhancing transparency and trust.

Finally, this study provides a new stage-wise curriculum learning system combined with explainable artificial intelligence (XAI) for performance improvement in network intrusion detection systems (NIDS). Its core is that it trains models with increasing attack complexity over time, and can use neural networks (NN) and CNN with ensemble for powerful detection. With a high accuracy (96%) on the Edge-IIoT dataset, our proposed framework has the scalability, lightweight design, and IoT/IIoT security capability and hence can be used to effectively detect intrusions at real-time in a limited infrastructure.

5   Conclusion

The proposed stage-wise curriculum learning algorithm, combined with Explainable AI (XAI), has proven to be a highly effective and efficient tool for enhancing Network Intrusion Detection Systems (NIDS). Achieving an accuracy of 96% on the Edge-IIoT dataset, the framework demonstrates adaptability to varying levels of attack complexity and scalability. This hybrid approach, integrating NN, CNN, and ensemble techniques, leverages the interpretability provided by XAI, enabling real-time applications in resource-constrained IoT networks. The result is a more secure and transparent cybersecurity solution suitable for modern IoT environments.

References

1. Al Nuaimi, T., et al.: A comparative evaluation of intrusion detection systems on the edge-IIoT-2022 dataset. Intell. Syst. Appl. **20**, 200298 (2023)
2. Bengio, Y., Louradour, J., Collobert, R., Weston, J.: Curriculum learning. In: Proceedings of the 26th Annual International Conference on Machine Learning, pp. 41–48 (2009)
3. Chen, Y., Dai, X., Liu, M., Chen, D., Yuan, L., Liu, Z.: Dynamic convolution: attention over convolution kernels. In: Proceedings of the IEEE/CVF Conference on Computer Vision and Pattern Recognition, pp. 11030–11039 (2020)
4. Chikkenakoppa, A., Sivsankar, S., Kumar, C.P.: Improved malware identification from android apps using image features. In: 2024 IEEE International Conference on Advanced Networks and Telecommunications Systems (ANTS), pp. 149–154. IEEE (2024)
5. Cho, K., et al.: Learning phrase representations using RNN encoder-decoder for statistical machine translation. arXiv preprint arXiv:1406.1078 (2014)
6. Ferrag, M.A., Friha, O., Hamouda, D., Maglaras, L., Janicke, H.: Edge-IIoTset: a new comprehensive realistic cyber security dataset of IoT and IIoT applications for centralized and federated learning. IEEE Access **10**, 40281–40306 (2022)

7. Ghiasvand, E., Ray, S., Iqbal, S., Dadkhah, S., Ghorbani, A.A.: CICAPT-IIOT: a provenance-based apt attack dataset for IIoT environment. arXiv preprint arXiv:2407.11278 (2024)
8. Hamza, N., Lakmal, H., Maduranga, M., Kathriarachchi, R.: Malware detection of IoT networks using machine learning: an experimental study with edge IIoT dataset. In: 30th Annual Technical Conference-IET Sri Lanka Network, Colombo, Sri Lanka (2023)
9. Hu, J., Shen, L., Sun, G.: Squeeze-and-excitation networks. In: Proceedings of the IEEE Conference on Computer Vision and Pattern Recognition, pp. 7132–7141 (2018)
10. Laiq, F., Al-Obeidat, F., Amin, A., Moreira, F.: DDoS attack detection in edge-IIoT network using ensemble learning. J. Phys. Complex. (2024)
11. Neto, E.C.P., et al.: CICIoV 2024: advancing realistic ids approaches against dos and spoofing attack in IoV can bus. Internet Things **26**, 101209 (2024)
12. Soviany, P., Ionescu, R.T., Rota, P., Sebe, N.: Curriculum learning: a survey. Int. J. Comput. Vision **130**(6), 1526–1565 (2022)
13. Tareq, I., Elbagoury, B.M., El-Regaily, S., El-Horbaty, E.S.M.: Analysis of ToN-IoT, UNW-NB15, and edge-IIoT datasets using DL in cybersecurity for IoT. Appl. Sci. **12**(19), 9572 (2022)
14. Vaswani, A., et al.: Attention is all you need. In: Advances in Neural Information Processing Systems, vol. 30 (2017)
15. Wang, X., Chen, Y., Zhu, W.: A survey on curriculum learning. IEEE Trans. Pattern Anal. Mach. Intell. **44**(9), 4555–4576 (2021)

SAAT: Stealthy Adversarial Attack on IDS in Cyber Physical Systems Using Control Logic Induction

Rajneesh Kumar Pandey and Tanmoy Kanti Das[✉]

Department of Computer Applications, National Institute of Technology Raipur,
Raipur, India
{rkpandey.phd2019.mca,tkdas.mca}@nitrr.ac.in

Abstract. It is well known that Cyber-Physical Systems (CPSs) are
vulnerable to cyberattacks, and detection is usually achieved using
machine learning-based Intrusion Detection Systems (IDSs). CPSs frequently have highly complex control logic, which, when maliciously
manipulated, may lead to accidents. As control logic is not publicly
available, here we propose a framework that can extract approximate
control logic from the captured operational data flowing in the communication channel of a CPS. This approximate control logic is used to
design stealthy adversarial samples with a very low footprint in terms of
the number of sensor readings perturbed and the amount of sensor readings perturbed during sample generation. The proposed control logic
induction framework involves four steps: cut-point generation, cut-point
selection, boolean control rule extraction, and combining extracted control rules into control logic. Later, a control-logic-based stealthy adversarial sample generation technique was designed where the adversary
possesses no knowledge regarding the targeted IDSs or their training
data. Existing IDSs *fail* to recognize the stealthy adversarial samples
in more than 98% of the cases. Even retraining the IDSs with adversarial samples generated using methods like GAN, FGSM, etc., fails
to improve their resilience against stealthy attacks. On the contrary,
retraining with stealthy samples improves the performance of IDSs not
only against stealthy attacks but also against other types of adversarial
attacks.

Keywords: Intrusion Detection · Detection of Stealthy Adversarial
Attack · Control Logic · Cyber Physical Systems

1 Introduction

Recent technological advancements facilitated the integration of communication
and computing capabilities into physical systems to enhance their operating
efficiency. Such systems are known as Cyber-Physical Systems (CPSs). Examples of CPS span various domains, including manufacturing, medical devices,

N. Hubballi et al. (Eds.): ICISS 2025, LNCS 16380, pp. 299–319, 2026.
https://doi.org/10.1007/978-3-032-13714-2_19

transportation, smart power grid, water treatment plant, etc. Many of these systems constitute critical infrastructures(CI), necessitating safe, reliable, and secure real-time operation. The security of CPS has become a subject of significant concern due to recent instances of intentional assaults on these CIs [17].

Cyber attack prevention through Intrusion Detection Systems (IDSs) in CPS followed the footsteps of traditional information technology (IT) systems. However, security challenges within CPS differ significantly from those in conventional IT systems due to the involvement of physical processes that are governed by the laws of physics. Particular concern is the potential consequences of a cyberattack, which may result in substantial harm to physical property, resulting from an explosion or severe impacts on the operation of critical infrastructures, as evident from the colonial pipeline outage [4]. Malicious manipulation of sensor data or actuator commands through the cyber domain or within the physical (analog) domain may lead to violation of laws of nature [19]. Thus, CPS-IDSs should be evaluated differently from conventional IT-IDSs.

IDSs can be broadly categorized into two types: anomaly-based and signature-based. Anomaly-based systems learn the normal behavior patterns of the systems. Recently, machine learning (ML) based techniques are used to identify behavior patterns for the design of IDS. It is well known that ML methods are vulnerable to adversarial machine learning [5], and these methods can be maliciously used by the adversary to evade detection. Adversarial retraining using samples generated from existing adversarial methods is a very popular defensive strategy against such evasion attacks. However, the proposed stealthy attack can also bypass this defensive strategy.

Components of CPSs obey the laws of physics, and the control logic of these components is also designed to obey the same laws. The complexity of CPSs prevents the creation of physics-based operating models of a CPS. Usually, a data-driven approach is adopted to create operating models of CPSs without considering the operating parameters of individual components/ controllers [19]. Those operating models form the basis of ML-based IDSs. In our approach, we extract the control logic of individual controllers, and based on that, we mount a stealthy attack that does not violate any control logic. From the network security point of view, such attacks can be mounted through the 'false data' or 'control command' injection method. Our strategy does not require any knowledge regarding the IDS, nor does it require any portion of the training samples used to train the IDS. Hence, our attack is a kind of *black-box attack* [5]. We only assume the availability of some normal operational data to the adversary.

Considering that the adversary has access to the communication channel of CPS, any false data injection may be successful only if it doesn't violate any control logic. To remain undetected, an adversary should broadly satisfy the following constraints during the attack.

1. Attacker should not violate the control logic of individual controllers as monitored by the 'control center' or IDS.
2. Attacker should not change a large number of sensor/actuator readings for a successful *stealthy* attack.

3. Attacker should not perturb sensor readings by a large amount, as it would be detected easily if a bad data detection [7] like algorithm is installed at the control center (CC).

To satisfy the said constraints, the attacker should first find out the control logic of installed controllers, i.e., actuators, in our experiments. To extract control logic from historical operational data, here we propose a control logic induction framework, or CLIF in short. CLIF extracts *threshold*-based rules (i.e., control logic) to predict the state of actuators from sensor(s) readings. Subsequently, the attacker uses those thresholds to spoof the status of actuators, and it appears to the control center (or IDS) that operating logic is never violated. The attack has been carried out by compromising a maximum of three sensors only, as control logic extracted by CLIF uses a maximum of three sensor values in its rules, and he/she can compromise only one controller at a time to satisfy the second criterion. Moreover, the attacker can time his attack in such a manner that he/she is not required to change sensor readings by a large amount. In our study, we not only show how attackers can exploit existing CPS-IDSs but also demonstrate retraining-based strategies that can resist such attacks. The main contributions of this paper are as follows:

- Proposed design of a new framework to extract operating control logic of installed controllers in any CPS from historical operational data.
- Proposed framework can identify *minimal number of sensors* required to control the state of an actuator, which helps to mount the adversarial attack.
- An adversarial attack is proposed using the extracted operating logic to evade detection by any IDS present in the CPS. It manipulates only a few sensor readings (through spoofing or false data injection) to hide malicious state changes of a controller.
- A defensive strategy based on retraining with stealthy adversarial samples has been demonstrated, and retrained models can also detect attacks based on popular adversarial sample generators like GAN, LowProFool, etc.

The rest of the paper is organized as follows. A brief introduction about different types of attacks is reported in Sect. 2. The design of control logic induction framework is presented in Sect. 3, and Sect. 4 describes the threat model of CLIF-based stealthy attack. The exact strategy used to mount the stealthy adversarial attack is presented in Sect. 5. The performance evaluation and comparative results are available in Sect. 6. Defensive strategy is reported in Sect. 7. We have concluded our study in Sect. 8.

2   Related Work

Attacks on CPS can be categorized in different ways, and we categorize the attacks based on the source domain of the attack. We consider three domains, i.e., Cyber, Cyber-Physical, and Physical. Physical domain attacks involve the destruction/damage of physical devices only. On the other hand, cyber-attacks directly involve communication networks, but they may affect physical devices indirectly. Cyber-physical attacks directly affect both cyber and physical domains simultaneously. We will only consider cyber and cyber-physical attacks in this study. Several types of cyber-attacks like *Denial of Service (DoS) attack* [2], *False data injection attack (FDIA)* [2], *spoofing* [2], *man-in-the-middle attack* [11], *malware attack* [3], *eavesdropping* etc. are also used frequently to disrupt the normal operations of a CPS. Recently, machine learning-based methods have been widely used to optimize decision-making, but even they are not secure from malicious manipulations. Some of the techniques that exploited the loopholes of the machine learning systems to mount successful attacks are as follows.

1. *Poisoning Attacks:* During the data collection phase, adversaries may inject malicious or biased data to influence the model's learning process [23].
2. *Membership inference attacks* target vulnerabilities related to the handling and processing of training data [22].
3. *Backdoor attacks* involve manipulating the model's behavior during training by introducing hidden triggers [15].
4. *Model inversion attacks* focus on extracting sensitive information about the training data by analyzing the model's outputs [9].
5. *Adversarial attacks* [14], also known as evasion attack, targets the model's prediction phase. Adversarial examples are crafted to exploit vulnerabilities in the model's decision boundaries, leading to misclassification or evasion of security measures [5]. Adversarial attacks are influenced by the extent of information accessible to the adversaries, and depending on the available information, attacks are classified into two categories: *white box* and *black box*. In a white box attack, the attacker possesses comprehensive information about the training data and model details, including the algorithm used for training, model parameters, and more. Conversely, in a *black box* attack, the attacker lacks any knowledge regarding the model or its internal characteristics. As previously noted, our proposed method is a kind of black box attack as we don't need any information about the model or training samples. Note that black-box or white-box attacks can also be considered cyber-physical attacks if they directly or indirectly impact the physical process of a CPS. The control logic of CPSs can also be used to mount such attacks efficiently.

3   Control Logic Induction Framework

It is well known that a controller is a device or algorithm that works to maintain the optimum performance of a system like CPS. The controller controls the CPS by introducing changes in its physical variable(s) so that the CPS produces the desired output. An actuator is a device that implements physical changes that the controller introduces into the CPS. The controller usually processes the inputs received from the sensors installed at the CPS and decides whether any change of state(s) of an actuator(s) is required to maintain the operational efficiency of the CPS. Here, it is assumed that the actuator is a two-state device. Hence, the control logic of an actuator can be approximated using Boolean decision rules.

The proposed control logic induction framework (CLIF) extracts Boolean decision rules from a given labeled dataset S, and those decision rules can be used to design a binary classifier. CLIF is inspired by combinatorial searching techniques and partially follows the general model presented in [21]. The proposed framework has the following four steps:

1. *Cut-point generation:* A popular heuristic to search the large space of possible relations between combinations of attribute values and classes is to locally minimize the information entropy of the classes in the dataset prior to selecting an attribute. To minimize the entropy, continuous-valued attributes are usually discretized. Typically, a threshold value T_i^A for a continuous-valued attribute A is determined, and the logical condition $A \geq T_i^A$ is used for discretization. Such threshold value is popularly called a *cut-point*, and our implementation to find cut-points is an extension of the algorithm proposed in [8]. Note that a single continuous-valued attribute may be associated with several cut-points. Though we are generating cut points, but we are *avoiding*

Algorithm 1. Positive rule enumeration algorithm

Input: $S = S^+ \cup S^-$ *{- Set of observations }.*
Ω *{- Set of cut-points selected in the last step.}*
D *{- Maximum degree of generated rules.}*
k *{- Minimum number of observations covered by a generated rule.}*
H *{- Homogeneity threshold.}*
Output: P *{- Set of rules.}*

1: $P = \emptyset$.
2: Generate unit rule set C^1 using the set of selected cut-points Ω.
3: $C = \mathcal{P}(C^1)$ *{$-\mathcal{P}(x)$ represents the power set of set x.}*
4: Remove $\emptyset$ and other elements (which is nothing but a subset of C^1) of C whose cardinality is greater than D. Also remove the elements where l_i^A and $\bar{l}_i^A$ are present together. Here A is any feature of dataset S.
5: **for** each element $C_i \in C$ **do**
6:   **if** $|C_i| > 1$ **then** { - C_i *has more than one literal (i.e., unit rule) elements.}*
7:     Build a rule t by representing the literals of C_i in conjunctive normal form.
8:   **else**
9:     $t = C_i$.
10:   **end if**
11:   Find the subset of observations S_t covered by the rule t.
12:   **if** $(|S_t| \geq k)$ AND $(h^+(S_t) > H)$ **then** { - $h^+(x)$ *represent the homogeneity of set x.}*
13:     $P = P \cup t$.
14:     $S = S \setminus S_t$.
15:   **end if**
16:   **if** $|S| < k$ **then**
17:     Exit Loop.
18:   **end if**
19: **end for**
20: Return P

---

the discretization of the entire dataset in our framework. This is the major difference from the similar framework proposed elsewhere, and it drastically reduces the space complexity.

2. *Cut-point selection:* Each of the cut-point-based logical conditions, like $A \geq T_i^A$, actually corresponds to a discrete attribute, say b_k. Some of these discrete attributes are redundant, and selecting a set of non-redundant set of cut-points is equivalent to solving a set covering problem. As the set covering problem is an NP-complete [16], several approximate solutions proposed in [1] have been evaluated, and *"Mutual-Information-Greedy"* algorithm is chosen to address the set covering problem in our implementation.

   Consider that the given dataset S consists of a binary class label, i.e., say, positive and negative. In the context of CPS, the class label represents the *state of an actuator.* Thus, $S = S^+ \cup S^-$, where S^+ (S^-) represents a subset of examples having positive (negative) labels. Basically, a discrete binary attribute $A \geq T_i^A$ divides S into four subsets: $S^+_{(A \geq T_i^A)=True}$, $S^+_{(A \geq T_i^A)=False}$, $S^-_{(A \geq T_i^A)=True}$, $S^-_{(A \geq T_i^A)=False}$. The cardinality of these subsets plays an important role during cut-point selection [1].

3. *Approximately orthogonal rule induction:* A rule is nothing but *conjunction* of one or more logical conditions like $A \geq T_i^A$ that can cover a subset of examples from S^+ or S^-. Thus, a rule can cover examples from one class only. Such a strict condition can only hold iff $S^+ \cap S^- = \emptyset$, i.e., no example should be a member of two different classes. However, in real-life datasets, it is difficult to ensure $S^+ \cap S^- = \emptyset$ due to the presence of noise and other operational factors. Hence, here, we allow little impurity in the coverage of a rule. For example, when applied to the SWAT dataset [12], CLIF-based classifiers exhibited a performance decline of approximately 4% even in the absence of attack samples, if classification relied exclusively on pure rules. Thus, a positive rule, which should cover only positive examples, can now cover a few negative examples along with positive examples, and homogeneity is used to measure the extent of impurity. Homogeneity of a *positive rule r* which covers a subset of examples S_r is defined as

$$h^+(S_r) = \frac{number\ of\ positve\ examples\ in\ S_r}{total\ number\ of\ examples\ in\ S_r}$$

A similar definition of $h^-()$ applies in the case of negative rules. The number of cut-points present in a rule is known as the *degree of the rule.* Additionally, generated rules are approximately orthogonal. The definition of orthogonal rules says that any pair of rules (say, r_i and r_j) should not have any common example in their coverages. Generating such orthogonal rules is computationally expensive. If i and j indicate the sequence at which rules are generated, we only ensure that the rule r_i should not cover any examples covered by r_j if $j > i$. Hence, our generated rules are approximately orthogonal, and we are not aware of any method generating approximately orthogonal rules.

4. *Control logic design and validation:* Rules generated in the previous step are arranged in an *'if-elseif-else'* structure to get the control logic of an actuator.

3.1   Implementation of CLIF

The first two steps of the control logic induction framework use slightly modified algorithms proposed in [8] and [1], respectively. Here, we present the algorithm to implement the third step, i.e., approximate orthogonal rule induction. Rule learning can be broadly categorized into two types: (i) descriptive rule learning and (ii) predictive rule learning. In predictive rule learning, a set of rules R is learned in such a way that they can collectively cover the instance (or example) space [10]. The motivation is that the rules can collectively predict every possible example. A class of algorithms, better known as the covering or separate-and-conquer algorithm, learns a rule r_i in each pass over the dataset, and all examples covered by r_i are removed from the dataset. In the next pass, another rule is learned, and the process stops when no more examples are left or the stopping criteria are satisfied. Here, we follow the same approach.

The first step towards generating a rule set that covers the entire set of examples is building *unit rules*. A unit rule is a rule where only one condition exists. For a given cut-point T_i^A, two unit rules are possible, i.e., $A \geq T_i^A$ and $A < T_i^A$ (i.e., $\neg(A \geq T_i^A)$). Let us denote them as *literal* l_i^A and $\bar{l}_i^A$. If a possible unit rule satisfies the condition of the minimum number of examples covered and homogeneity, it becomes a rule. The proposed implementation of the rule induction method is presented in Algorithm 1. Note that Algorithm 1 is designed to find positive rules only. However, the same can be used to find the negative rules by replacing the homogeneity function $h^+()$ by $h^-()$. All the steps of CLIF, are explained using an example in the next subsection.

3.2   Illustrative Example

Let us consider a dataset presented in Table 1. The first step would be the generation of cut-points. For example, to find the cut-points of numeric attribute A, the required steps are:

- Construct a dataset as presented in Table 2.
- Remove the duplicate rows, i.e., rows having the same attribute value and state (a.k.a. class label).
- Sort the rows over attribute A as presented in Table 3.
- Now the dataset in Table 3 has two rows whose attribute value is the same, but their state is different. We merge such rows into one and update their state to a unique value. The resultant dataset is presented in Table 4.
- Finally, if two consecutive rows have different states, we add a new cut-point by averaging the attribute values of those two rows, i.e., $T_k^A = \frac{1}{2}(A_i + A_{i+1})$.

By adhering to the aforementioned steps, the resulting cut-points are $T_1^A = 1.70$, $T_2^A = 2.95$, and $T_3^A = 4.85$. Upon applying the previous steps to all the attributes in Table 1, the set of generated cut-points is presented in Table 5.

Table 1. Sample dataset.

A	B	C	State
3.5	3.2	2.8	1
2.4	6.8	5.2	1
1.0	3.8	3.6	0
3.5	3.4	3.6	0
6.2	5.8	1.0	0

Table 2. Selected feature and class label.

A	State
3.5	1
2.4	1
1.0	0
3.5	0
6.2	0

Table 3. Sorted feature value and class label.

A	State
1.0	0
2.4	1
3.5	1
3.5	0
6.2	0

Table 4. Changing the class label.

A	State
1.0	0
2.4	1
3.5	2
6.2	0

Table 5. Generated cutpoints.

$T_1^A = 1.70$
$T_2^A = 2.95$
$T_3^A = 4.85$
$T_1^B = 3.30$
$T_2^B = 6.30$
$T_1^C = 1.90$
$T_2^C = 3.20$
$T_3^C = 4.40$

The next step in the control logic induction framework is cut point selection. Using the steps of *Mutual-Information-Greedy* algorithm [1], following cut-points has been selected: $T_2^A = 2.95$, $T_1^B = 3.30$, $T_1^A = 1.70$. Thus, possible unit rules that can be generated from these cut points (step 2 of Algorithm 1) are as follows:$(A \geq 2.95),(A < 2.95)$, $(B \geq 3.30)$, $(B < 3.30)$, $(A \geq 1.70)$, $(A < 1.70)$. We would like to explain the step 7 of Algorithm 1 in this context. Consider that subset C_i consists of the following literals (i.e., unit rules): $= \{(A \geq 1.70), (B < 3.30)\}$. Then the possible rule t would be $= \{(A \geq 1.70) \wedge (B < 3.30)\}$. The final output of Algorithm 1 using $k = 1, D = 3$ and $H = 0.9$ is as follows: $\{(B < 3.30), (A < 2.95 \ \wedge \ A \geq 1.7)\}$. If we take a similar approach to find negative rules, the following rules can be generated $\{(A < 1.70), (A \geq 2.95 \ \wedge \ B \geq 3.30)\}$.

We can combine more than one positive rule into an 'if else-if else' structure to design the control logic. Similarly, one can build a control logic using the negative rules as well. Hybrid control logic can utilize both positive and negative rules. A control logic utilizing the hybrid approach is presented in Algorithm 2. Cut points used in the control logic can be utilized to mount an adversarial attack, and the threat model of such an attack is presented in the next section.

Algorithm 2. Rule-based Control Logic.

    Input: Observation containing feature A, B, C.
    Output: State.
1: **if** $(B < 3.30)$ **then**
2:     State $= 1$.
3: **else if** $(A < 2.95 \ \wedge \ A \geq 1.7)$ **then**
4:     State $= 1$.
5: **else if** $(A < 1.70)$ **then**
6:     State $= 0$.
7: **else if** $(A \geq 2.95 \ \wedge \ B \geq 3.30)$ **then**
8:     State $= 0$.
9: **else**
10:     State $= unknown$.
11: **end if**

---

4   Threat Model

The use of machine learning algorithms in cybersecurity settings, specifically in CPS environments, creates unique security challenges. Here, we demonstrate that even an adversary with minimal knowledge regarding the CPS or installed IDS can mount a strong attack. The goal of the adversary is to destabilize a CPS without getting noticed by either the intrusion detection systems or by the CC monitoring the operating environment of the critical subsystems of the CPS. Moreover, from the attacker's point of view, it can be safely assumed that *bad data detection (BDD)* [7] *algorithm* exists directly or indirectly to monitor the sensor readings. Thus, apart from IDS, the BDD algorithm will aid CC in detecting any abnormal behavior of a CPS.

It is well known that controllers (i.e., actuators) are functionally dependent on the sensor readings, and any violation of those functional mappings usually has disastrous consequences. Manipulation of sensor readings will result in an actuator state transition. However, the *functional mappings* between sensor measurements and actuator states are unknown to the attacker as functional mappings most of the time remain closely guarded secrets with the manufacturers (or operators) of actuators. Keeping these practical and operational constraints in mind, let us now highlight the adversarial capabilities and limitations:

1. Attacker does not have access to training samples. Thus, an attacker cannot mount a poisoning or backdoor attack.
2. S/he is not aware of the ML model used in IDS or its parameters. Thus, the proposed attack follows a strict black box model.
3. Attacker can not use the classifier (i.e., IDS in our case) as the random oracle model. Thus, a practical black-box attack [20] is difficult to mount, and from the adversarial point of view, the attacker has to satisfy himself that the attack is effective indirectly.
4. The Attacker has access to normal operational data only in limited numbers, which restricts his ability to design a surrogate state model of CPS due to the absence of abnormal (or attack) samples, with the only exception being a one-class model. Thus, using cryptanalysis parlance, the present threat model would be similar to a known plaintext attack.
5. From the network point of view, we assume the attacker has access to the communication channel between CC and the physical device.

Thus, in a nutshell, access to limited normal operational data is the only capability the attacker has apart from access to the communication channel. This level of adversarial capability is minimal in comparison with the attacks proposed elsewhere [5]. According to our threat model, the proposed stealthy adversarial attack follows a paradigm of the strict black-box attack where the adversary lacks any knowledge regarding the targeted IDS installed at the control center. Hence, we have considered several ML-based classifiers as IDSs, including state-of-the-art DNN classifiers, to mount the proposed attack.

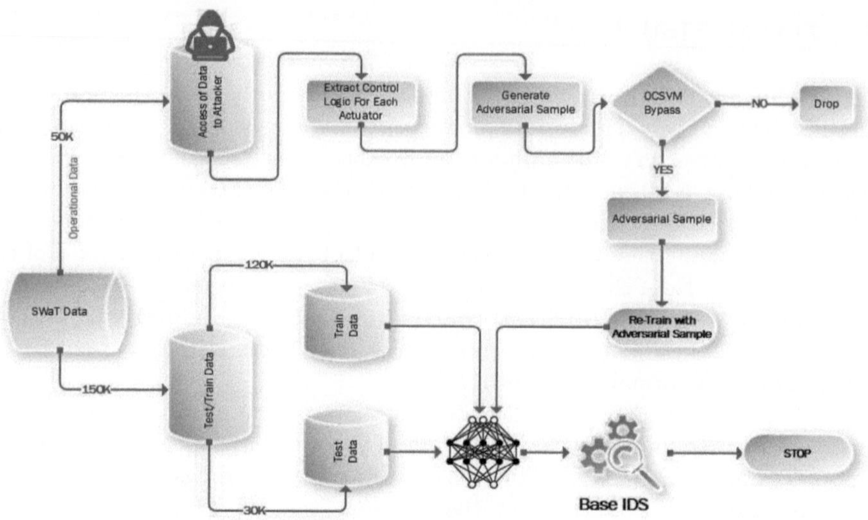

Fig. 1. Block diagram of CLIF-based adversarial attack generator

4.1 Adversarial Goal

The adversary's main motive is to destabilize the CPS without rousing any suspicion at the control center. To achieve this goal, (i) s/he would alter (or misrepresent) the state of only one actuator, and (ii) s/he would also alter sensor readings of *least possible number* of sensors to achieve the first goal, and (iii) remain undetected. The first two conditions directly follow from the requirement of stealthiness. Basically, we want to solve the following optimization problems:

$$M \subset \Psi \mid \xi = f(M) \text{ and } \xi \in \{0, 1\} \tag{1}$$

Here Ψ is the set of sensors, and M is the *minimal subset* of Ψ that can functionally determine the state (represented by ξ) of an actuator. The functional mapping(s) between M and ξ is represented by f. The main challenge is to find the minimal subset M along with f. Moreover, we intend to create an altered version of any input record $\overrightarrow{x}_\Psi$, maintaining the following constraint.

$$\overrightarrow{x}^*_\Psi = \overrightarrow{x}_{\Psi \setminus M} + \{\overrightarrow{x}_M + \delta\overrightarrow{x_M} \mid P(\overrightarrow{x}^*_M) = P(\overrightarrow{x}_M) \text{ and } f(\overrightarrow{x}) \neq f(\overrightarrow{x^*})\} \tag{2}$$

Thus, an attacker has to manipulate sensor readings $\overrightarrow{x}_M$ in a manner that the statistical properties $P(\psi)$ of individual sensors remain unaltered even after manipulations. Moreover, intended change(s) in sensor(s) values causes a state change only in the targeted actuator. However, neither the minimal sensor set M nor its functional mappings f is known to the attacker to carry out a malicious state change in an actuator Υ. Solving this optimization problem is not trivial due to our threat model. Note that the maliciously altered record $\overrightarrow{x}^*_\psi$

is usually termed as an adversarial sample. The first two goals directly follow from adversarial machine learning, but the third goal follows from the requirement of cybersecurity. For a successful cyber attack, the third goal demands that even after a change of sensor readings from $\overrightarrow{x}_{\Psi}$ to $\overrightarrow{x}^{*}_{\Psi}$, there should not be any change of state of the CPS. If we express the state model as $F(\overrightarrow{x}_{\Psi} \cup \overrightarrow{\xi}_{\Pi}) = Y \in \{normal, abnormal\}$, third goal demands:

$$F(\overrightarrow{x}_{\Psi} \cup \overrightarrow{\xi}_{\Pi}) = F(\overrightarrow{x}^{*}_{\Psi} \cup \overrightarrow{\xi}^{*}_{\Pi}) \tag{3}$$

Hence, adversarial samples should not change the state of CPS (i.e., the value of Y) as seen by the control center.

5   Strategy of the Proposed Attack

Adversarial attacks on classification systems (i.e., IDS) broadly involve at least one of the following approaches: (i) malicious tampering of the training set, (ii) accessing the target classifier as an oracle, (iii) availability of training samples to create a surrogate model of the target classifier. According to our threat model, the adversary does not have access to training samples. From a practical point of view and according to our threat model, s/he can collect or possess normal records only. Consequently, none of the adversarial attack strategies mentioned earlier will work properly here. However, an attacker can use his theoretical knowledge regarding the *general* construction of a CPS to mount an attack. It is well known that a cyber-physical system is basically a system of systems, and the state model that determines the state (i.e., normal and abnormal) of a CPS depends on the inter-relationships among sensors and actuators. Also, those interrelationships are indirectly controlled by the actual control logic f of individual actuators that constitute a CPS. Any violations of those relationships are termed abnormal by the state model. Thus, the state model F of a CPS can be expressed as:

$$F(\overrightarrow{x}_{\Psi} \cup \overrightarrow{\xi}_{\Pi}) = F(\overrightarrow{x}_{\Psi} \bigcup_{i=1}^{n} f_{\Pi_i}(M_{\Pi_i})) \tag{4}$$

Here, Π is the set of all installed actuators. The state model of the CPS uses interrelationships among sensor(s) values and actuator states to determine the state of the CPS. The state model basically detects violations of synchronization between the states of actuators and sensor readings. It is well understood that if any adversarial sample is generated without violating the functional mappings f_{Π_i}, the state model F has a very low probability of detecting it. However, attacker neither have any access to actual f_{Π_i} nor F. Though the adversary can easily extract the approximate control logic f' using CLIF from the collected normal data, but the adversary can only build a one-class surrogate model F' in the absence of abnormal samples. Thus, the attacker constructs an approximate functional mapping f'_{Π_i} of each installed actuator from the available operational data under *normal* conditions. Moreover, the adversary creates an approximate state model (i.e., a surrogate classifier) F' of CPS using any one-class classification technique. Thus, the state model of CPS presented in Eq. 4 now becomes:

$$F(\vec{x}_{\Psi} \bigcup_{i=1}^{n} f'_{\Pi_i}(M_{\Pi_i})) = F'(\vec{x}_{\Psi} \cup \vec{\xi}'_{\Pi}) \qquad (5)$$

Hence, we can rewrite the constraint presented in Eq. 3 as:

$$F'(\vec{x}_{\Psi} \cup \vec{\xi}'_{\Pi}) = F'(\vec{x}^{*}_{\Psi} \cup \vec{\xi}^{*}_{\Pi}) \qquad (6)$$

So the adversary should always satisfy the constraint presented in Eq. 6 for a successful stealthy attack.

$$f'_{A_i} : S \to A_i^{\gamma}$$

5.1   Induction of Control Logic of Actuators

According to our threat model, the attacker has access to some operational data under normal conditions only. A record $\vec{r}$ in that dataset can be expressed as:

$$\vec{r} = \vec{x}_{\Psi} \cup \vec{\xi}_{\Pi}$$

Logically, a record $\vec{r}$ in the dataset can be divided into two parts: (i) sensor(s) readings $\vec{x}_{\Psi}$ and (ii) actuator(s) states $\vec{\xi}_{\Pi}$. We also know that $\vec{\xi} = f(\vec{x}_{M \subset \Psi})$, and our main goal is to get an approximation of control logic f' for mounting a successful stealthy cyberattack. For approximation, we use CLIF, and the exact steps are presented in Algorithm 3. The correctness of the inducted control logic can be evaluated by training a surrogate model on the dataset $\vec{r}_{i=1...n}$. In our experiments, we employed a Random Forest model as the surrogate. The performance metrics for each actuator Π_i are presented in Table 7. Details on creating the surrogate model are discussed in Sect. 6.1.

Algorithm 3. Steps to induct approximate control logic using CLIF.

Input: $\vec{r}_{i=1...n}$: Dataset containing normal records only.
Output: f_{π_i} : Approximate control logic of each actuator in the dataset.
1: **for** Each $\pi_i \in \Pi$ **do**
2:     Construct a dataset $\vec{d}$ from $\vec{r}$ as $\vec{d} = \vec{x} \cup \vec{\xi}_{\pi_i}$ {For brevity we are representing $\vec{x}_{\Psi}$ as $\vec{x}$ henceforth.}
3:     Use Algorithm 1 over $\vec{d}$ to enumerate both positive($\mathcal{L}_i^{+}$) and negative ($\mathcal{L}_i^{-}$) rule sets.
4:     Build a hybrid rule-based control logic $f'_{\pi_i} = \mathcal{L}_i^{+} \cup \mathcal{L}_i^{-}$ for actuator π_i.
5:     Build two sets of sensors M_i^{+} and M_i^{-} along with its cut points which are appearing in rule sets $\mathcal{L}_i^{+}$, $\mathcal{L}_i^{-}$ respectively.
6: **end for**

5.2   Adversarial Sample Generation

In the previous subsection, we have generated approximate control logic that we are going to utilize here for generating stealthy adversarial samples from the set of vulnerable samples, and the process of creating the set of vulnerable samples is described afterward. The exact steps of adversarial sample generation are presented in Algorithm 4. The most important parts of Algorithm 4 are step 4 and 5, where we generate the range of acceptable values of sensors. Acceptable values directly follow from the rules present in $\mathcal{L}_i^+$ or $\mathcal{L}_i^-$. This process would be explained using an example in Sect. 6. Note that these steps ensure conformance to the constraint imposed using Eq. 2.

Algorithm 4. Steps to generate adversarial samples.

    Input: $\overrightarrow{r}_{i=1...n}$: Dataset containing vulnerable normal records.
    Output: $\overrightarrow{r}_k^*$: Adversarial sample(s).
1: Consider a normal record $\overrightarrow{r} = \overrightarrow{x}_\Psi \cup \overrightarrow{\xi}_\Pi$.
2: Select a target actuator $\pi_i \in \Pi$ to mount the attack.
3: Induct approximate control logic using Algorithm 3.
4: Build range of possible values for each senor $m_j \in M_i^+ | \ M_i^+ \subset \Psi$ using the cut-points present in $\mathcal{L}_i^+$ given the state of $\pi_i = +$.
5: Build range of possible values for each senor $m_k \in M_i^- | \ M_i^- \subset \Psi$ using the cut-points present in $\mathcal{L}_i^-$ given the state of $\pi_i = -$.
6: To change the state of π_i to $\pi_i = +$, use the range of values of sensors $m_j \in M^+$ in step 4 and update the sensor values $m_j \in M_i^+$.
7: To change the state of π_i to $\pi_i = -$, use the range of values of sensors $m_k \in M^-$ in step 5 and update the sensor values $m_j \in M_i^-$.
8: Values of rest of the sensors and actuators remain unaltered. Let us denote such altered record (i.e., adversarial sample) as $\overrightarrow{r}_k^*$.

Selection of Vulnerable Samples: A vulnerable sample is a sample that can be altered with very little effort to create an adversarial sample. Consider the rule-based classifier presented in Sect. 3.2; any sample whose feature B's value is $B = 3.31$ can be easily converted into an adversarial sample by a small change in B's value to $B = 3.29$. In general, any sample whose feature value is close to the cut-point is vulnerable and a good candidate for adversarial sample generation.

Verification of Adversarial Samples: Adversarial samples crafted using Algorithm 4 should conform to Eq. 6. Otherwise, they may get detected by the IDS installed at the control center. To verify whether they conform to Eq. 6, the adversary needs the state model F, but the adversary does not have any knowledge of F. In the absence of data in abnormal conditions, adversaries can use one-class models only. During our implementation, One Class SVM (OCSVM) has been utilized to represent the approximate state model F'. The building of OCSVM model (F') is discussed in Sect. 6. The previously generated adversarial samples are considered subject to bypass OCSVM, and if any adversarial sample is found to be 'abnormal', that is excluded from the set of adversarial samples as depicted in Fig. 1.

6   Performance Evaluations

The proposed method has been evaluated using data generated from a Secure Water Treatment (SWaT) [12] testbed. We have assumed that the control center is using any ML-based classifier for intrusion detection, and we have designed several base classifiers (i.e., IDSs) for initial assessment of the proposed adversarial technique. Afterward, we have mounted the stealthy attack on the designed IDSs. To begin with, we next introduce the SWaT dataset.

The Secure Water Treatment (SWaT) testbed [12] has been designed to mimic all operational capabilities of an industrial-scale water treatment plant. Sensors and actuators have been used to monitor and control the water treatment plant. A total of 51 sensors and actuators have been used for the same. Measurements from those sensors and actuators have been recorded in a historian server. A dataset containing 11 days of operations has been released. The initial seven-day records contain normal operational measurements, and the rest of the records pertain to 36 different types of attacks. Some of the attacks manipulated network traffic to deceive the PLC or SCADA installed at the control center. A total of 946, 722 records are available in the dataset, which are labeled as either *normal* or *attack*. We have utilized this dataset to evaluate our proposed stealthy adversarial attack.

6.1   Experimental Results and Discussions

The effectiveness of the proposed strategy has been assessed on the SWaT dataset using a laptop-class machine with an Intel Core i7 10th generation CPU, 32 GB of RAM, and an Nvidia RTX 2070 GPU, but the GPU has not been utilized for adversarial sample generation.

Preprocessing and Training of Base Classifiers (i.e., IDSs): Cyber-physical systems like SWaT are usually designed for *fail-safe* operation, and several redundant subsystems are generally incorporated into the system to achieve the same. Those redundant subsystems remain idle under normal operating conditions, and data generated by those subsystems plays a minimal role in determining the state of a CPS. Hence, data generated by redundant subsystems is eliminated from the SWaT dataset during the preprocessing of the dataset. After preprocessing, we were left with a total of 45 features, excluding the class label. Among these 45 features, 25 features correspond to sensor readings, while the remaining 20 features correspond to actuator states. The initial seven days of operation of SWaT have been under normal conditions, excluding the 30-minute startup phase. We have selected a sample of 50, 000 data rows at random, and this dataset has been labeled as "Operational dataset". As mentioned earlier, this data is available to the adversary and subsequently used for adversarial sample generation.

To verify the effectiveness of our proposed adversarial approach, we have trained several base classifiers that will act as IDSs. To train these base classifiers, we have considered both normal as well as attacked data. In this context, we would like to point out that several attacks were mounted on the SWaT testbed in quick succession without allocating enough time between two consecutive attacks for the SWaT system to regain operational stability after an attack [6], and data generated during such unstable periods has been omitted completely during our experiments.

We have randomly selected 120, 000 samples for the training data and 30, 000 samples for testing from the entire eleven-day operation of SWaT, and these datasets have been used for the training/testing of our base classifiers. We would like to highlight again that there is *no intersection* between the train-test dataset and the "Operational dataset". We have trained six distinct base classifiers to act as IDS. The performance of the classifiers based on the test data is presented in Table 6.

Table 6. Performance of *base-classifiers* on test data

Model	Accuracy	Recall	Precision	F1_Score
DNN	99%	0.99	1.0	0.99
Naive Bayes	95%	0.86	1.0	0.93
KNN	100%	1.0	1.0	1.0
Random Forest	100%	1.0	1.0	1.0
SGD	98%	0.97	0.97	0.97
GBM	100%	1.0	1.0	1.0

Table 7. Performance of surrogate state model S_{π_i} of actuators

Actuator	Accuracy	Recall	Precision	F1-Score
P101	100%	1.0	1.0	1.0
MV101	99%	0.9997	0.9998	0.9998
MV201	100%	1.0	1.0	1.0
P203	100%	1.0	1.0	1.0
P205	100%	1.0	1.0	1.0
MV301	99%	0.99	0.99	0.99
MV302	100%	1.0	1.0	1.0
MV303	100%	1.0	1.0	1.0
MV304	99%	0.9998	0.9998	0.9998
P301	100%	1.0	1.0	1.0
P302	99%	0.9991	0.9992	0.9992
UV401	100%	1.0	1.0	1.0
P402	100%	1.0	1.0	1.0
P501	100%	1.0	1.0	1.0
P602	99%	0.99	0.98	0.99

Induction of Approximate Control Logic Using CLIF: In our threat model, we have considered that the adversary has access to some operational data, and here, we assume the "Operational dataset" that has been created in the last subsection is available to the adversary. As explained earlier that s/he would require control logic of actuators for properly mounting a stealthy attack. To this end, the adversary would extract the approximate control logic of all the installed actuators from the Operational dataset using Algorithm 3. Moreover, to gain confidence that the extracted control logic f' is appropriately predicting the state of the actuators, the adversary trains a surrogate model S for each of the installed actuators π_i using the operational data. The steps to extract control logic f' and training of surrogate model are as follows:

1. Construct a dataset $\overrightarrow{d}_{\pi_i}$ that includes all sensor readings from the set Ψ and append the state of actuator ξ_{π_i}. Hence this dataset can be represented as $\overrightarrow{d}_{\pi_i} = \overrightarrow{x_\Psi} \cup \overrightarrow{\xi}_{\pi_i}$ ($\xi_{\pi_i} \in \{\text{open/on, close/off}\}$), where x_Ψ represents sensor values and ξ_{π_i} represents the state of the actuator π_i.
2. Apply Algorithm 3 over $\overrightarrow{d}_{\pi_i}$ to get rules for 'open' and 'close' of actuator π_i. These rules are combined to get control logic f'_{π_i}.
3. Train surrogate state model S_{π_i} of π_i using $\overrightarrow{d}_{\pi_i}$.

The adversary can use any classifier to train the surrogate model, and in our implementation, we have used *random forest* to train a surrogate state model S_{π_i} of an actuator. The performance of the surrogate models is presented in Table 7. As an illustration, we have generated dataset $\overrightarrow{d}_{MV101}$ to produce approximate control logic for the open and close conditions using CLIF (i.e., Algorithm 3). We have presented the control logic for MV101 in Classifier-I. Similarly generated approximate control logic for every actuator is available in Github[1]. *Generation of stealthy adversarial samples* would generally follow the steps described in the Algorithm 4. However, the adversary would like to ensure that generated adversarial samples would be able to bypass the intrusion detection systems (i.e., different base classifiers in our experiment) installed at the control center. To limit his/her probability of failure, the adversary would use two *state models*: (i) actuator state model S_{π_i} and (ii) CPS state model F'. Though actuator state models are already available, the adversary is required to train a CPS

Classifier-I Control Logic for MV101

1: **if** $(FIT101 < 0.9834096)$ **then**
2:     State $=$ *Close.*
3: **else if** $(FIT101 \geq 2.344869 \wedge LIT101 < 800.0301)$ **then**
4:     State $=$ *Open.*
5: **else**
6:     State $=$ *unknown.*
7: **end if**

---

[1] https://github.com/rajneeshraj2001-cyber/CLIF.

state model F' using the operational data available to him/her. As only normal operational data is available, he/she uses *One-Class Support Vector Machine (OCSVM)* to train the surrogate state model F' of the CPS, i.e., SWaT in this case. Henceforth, the adversary executes the following steps for the generation of adversarial samples from *Operational dataset.*

1. Adversary decides the actuator (say π_i) on which attack should be mounted, and its state that s/he wants. Let us assume that the adversary wants to set the state as 'open' ('close'). Hence, it can be practically assumed that the current state of π_i is closed/off, and all the records whose state of π_i is open are dropped from *Operational dataset.*
2. From the sensor set M_i^+ (M_i^-) and select those records whose sensor values lie close to cut points and the current state of π_i is close(open). The set of selected records is termed as candidate dataset or set of *vulnerable samples.*
3. Apply Algorithm 4 using candidate dataset as input.
4. Using already trained F', check the predicted state of each record of $\overrightarrow{r}^*$. If the state is not normal, drop those records from $\overrightarrow{r}^*$.
5. From the set of adversarial samples $\overrightarrow{r}^*$, check each record using surrogate actuator state prediction model S_{π_i} to verify whether the state of π_i is open (close) or not. Drop those records from $\overrightarrow{r}^*$ whose state of π_i is not open (close).

Most of the previous steps are straightforward except step 2, which selects the set of vulnerable samples. Let us now explain the step 2 using the control logic of actuator $MV101$ presented as Classifier-I. Let us assume the adversary wants to keep it open/on. So s/he would select records using the following two conditions: (i) FIT101's value lying between $(2.344869 - 0.2344869 * 0.1)$ to $(2.344869 + 0.2344869 * 0.1)$ and (ii) sensor LIT101's value lying between $(800.0301 - 80.00301 * 0.1)$ to $(800.0301 + 80.00301 * 0.1)$. Thus, *'closeness'* is defined as the cutpoint's value $\pm 10\%$. Those records found satisfying these two conditions would constitute *candidate dataset* in step 2.

Another point that we like to highlight about step 4 of Algorithm 4 is that the 'range of possible values' is $\pm 3\%$ of present sensor readings. This preserves the range of perturbed sensor readings within the allowed range. The control logic generated using Algorithm 3 failed to meet the performance requirements for actuators UV401 and P501. This was due to the significantly imbalanced dataset, where 96% of the records indicated that both actuators were in the open state. Consequently, adversarial samples have been successfully generated for 13 out of the 15 active actuators under examination. Note that there are five backup actuators (i.e., P102, P201, P204, P206, and P403), and usually, those are not operational during normal conditions. Hence, they have been ignored during the generation of stealthy adversarial samples.

Performance of Base Classifiers: A collection of $26,000$ stealthy adversarial samples has been generated using the process described in the previous subsection. All these adversarial samples have been subjected to different IDSs (i.e., base classifiers) that are very accurate on test samples. Results have been tabulated in Table 8. One can observe that none of the base classifiers, except SGD can detect the adversarial samples. Even SGD is able to detect merely 1.5% of the generated adversarial samples.

Adversarially Trained Base Classifiers: Retraining base classifiers with adversarial samples has recently gained popularity as a defense against such attacks. To demonstrate the effectiveness of the proposed method, we retrained all base classifiers using adversarial samples generated by the following methods: FGSM [14], LowProFool [18], and GAN [13]. For retraining, we have generated adversarial samples from the train dataset (train dataset as formed in Sect. 6.1), using each of the generators separately. Hence, after combining them with the training set of base classifiers, three different adversarial retraining datasets have been formed. Note that all the adversarial samples are labeled as attack here. Even then, all the adversarially retrained base classifiers performed poorly against stealthy adversarial samples, which proves the potency of the proposed attack. Results pertaining to adversarially retrained classifiers have been presented in Table 9.

Table 8. Performance of *base-classifier's* against stealthy adversarial samples

Model	Accuracy	Recall	Precision	F1_Score
DNN	0%	0.0	0.0	0.0
Naive Bayes	0%	0.0	0.0	0.0
KNN	0%	0.0	0.0	0.0
Random Forest	0%	0.0	0.0	0.0
SGD	1.5%	0.02	1.0	0.03
GBM	0%	0.0	0.0	0.0

Table 9. Accuracy of adversarially retrained classifiers against stealthy attack

Model	Adversarial sample generators used in retraining		
	FGSM	LowProFool	GAN
DNN	0.01	0.01	0.03
Naive Bayes	0.007	0.106	0.006
KNN	0.0	0.0	0.0
Random Forest	0.0	0.0	0.001
SGD	0.002	0.0	0.0
GBM	0.0	0.001	0.002

7   Detecting Stealthy Adversarial Samples

Detecting stealthy attacks remains a formidable challenge due to their sophisticated design, which aims to evade detection by circumventing existing intrusion detection algorithms by conforming to the control logic of actuators. A typical defensive strategy against adversarial attacks involves retraining the IDS with adversarial samples, and a similar approach has also been adopted by us. Generated adversarial samples are divided into two sets: training and test sets. 70% of the samples were used for training and 30% of the samples were used for testing. By combining the earlier training set of base classifiers with the adversarial training set, we have retrained the base classifiers, and the results pertaining to the adversarial test set are presented in Table 10. One can observe that the performance of the base classifiers improved significantly after retraining. Moreover, stealthily retrained base classifiers (i.e., when stealthy adversarial samples are used for retraining) can detect samples generated from other adversarial methods, and the detection results are reported in Table 11.

Table 10. Performance of *stealthily retrained base-classifier*

Model	Accuracy	Recall	Precision	F1_Score
DNN	100%	1.0	1.0	1.0
Naive Bayes	94%	0.82	1.0	0.90
KNN	100%	1.0	1.0	1.0
Random Forest	100%	1.0	1.0	1.0
SGD	94%	0.82	1.0	0.90
GBM	100%	1.0	1.0	1.0

Table 11. Accuracy of stealthy retrained classifiers against adversarial samples

Model	Adversarial sample generators		
	FGSM	LowProFool	GAN
DNN	0.81	1.0	1.0
Naive Bayes	0.134	1.0	1.0
KNN	0.432	0.0	0.806
Random Forest	1.0	1.0	1.0
SGD	0.637	0.47	1.0
GBM	1.0	1.0	1.00

8   Conclusion and Future Work

In this paper, we have introduced a novel control logic induction algorithm aimed at enhancing the resiliency of IDSs against adversarial and stealthy attacks. Through experimental validation, we have shown that CLIF can effectively generate adversarial samples that are capable of evading detection by popular intrusion detection algorithms in the CPS domain. CLIF can be employed to design control logic-based one-class anomaly detection systems for CPS in the future, which may eliminate the requirement of retraining to prevent adversarial attacks. The extracted control logic from the controller can also be used to explain the working functionality of CPS.

References

1. Almuallim, H., Dietterich, T.G.: Learning boolean concepts in the presence of many irrelevant features. Artif. Intell. **69**, 279–305 (1994)
2. Ashibani, Y., Mahmoud, Q.H.: Cyber physical systems security: analysis, challenges and solutions. Comput. Secur. **68**, 81–97 (2017). https://doi.org/10.1016/j.cose.2017.04.005
3. Awad, R.A., Beztchi, S., Smith, J.M., Lyles, B., Prowell, S.: Tools, techniques, and methodologies: a survey of digital forensics for SCADA systems. In: Proceedings of the 4th Annual Industrial Control System Security Workshop, pp. 1–8 (2018)
4. Beerman, J., Berent, D., Falter, Z., Bhunia, S.: A review of colonial pipeline ransomware attack. In: 2023 IEEE/ACM 23rd International Symposium on Cluster, Cloud and Internet Computing Workshops (CCGridW), pp. 8–15 (2023). https://doi.org/10.1109/CCGridW59191.2023.00017
5. Chakraborty, A., Alam, M., Dey, V., Chattopadhyay, A., Mukhopadhyay, D.: A survey on adversarial attacks and defences. CAAI Trans. Intell. Technol. **6**(1), 25–45 (2021). https://doi.org/10.1049/cit2.12028
6. Das, T.K., Adepu, S., Zhou, J.: Anomaly detection in industrial control systems using logical analysis of data. Comput. Secur. **96**, 101935 (2020)
7. Das, T.K., Ghosh, S., Koley, E.: Prevention and detection of FDIA on power-network protection scheme using multiple support set. J. Inf. Secur. Appl. **63**, 103054 (2021)
8. Fayyad, U.M., Irani, K.B.: Multi-interval discretization of continuous-valued attributes for classification learning. In: International Joint Conference on Artificial Intelligence (1993)
9. Fredrikson, M., Jha, S., Ristenpart, T.: Model inversion attacks that exploit confidence information and basic countermeasures. In: Proceedings of the 22nd ACM SIGSAC Conference on Computer and Communications Security, pp. 1322–1333 (2015)
10. Fürnkranz, J., Kliegr, T.: A brief overview of rule learning. In: Bassiliades, N., Gottlob, G., Sadri, F., Paschke, A., Roman, D. (eds.) RuleML 2015. LNCS, vol. 9202, pp. 54–69. Springer, Cham (2015). https://doi.org/10.1007/978-3-319-21542-6_4
11. Gao, W., Morris, T., Reaves, B., Richey, D.: On SCADA control system command and response injection and intrusion detection. In: 2010 eCrime Researchers Summit, pp. 1–9 (2010). https://doi.org/10.1109/ecrime.2010.5706699

12. Goh, J., Adepu, S., Junejo, K.N., Mathur, A.: A dataset to support research in the design of secure water treatment systems. In: Havarneanu, G., Setola, R., Nassopoulos, H., Wolthusen, S. (eds.) CRITIS 2016. LNCS, vol. 10242, pp. 88–99. Springer, Cham (2017). https://doi.org/10.1007/978-3-319-71368-7_8
13. Goodfellow, I., et al.: Generative adversarial networks. Commun. ACM **63**(11), 139–144 (2020)
14. Goodfellow, I.J., Shlens, J., Szegedy, C.: Explaining and harnessing adversarial examples. arXiv preprint arXiv:1412.6572 (2014)
15. Gu, T., Dolan-Gavitt, B., Garg, S.: Badnets: identifying vulnerabilities in the machine learning model supply chain. arXiv preprint arXiv:1708.06733 (2017)
16. Karp, R.M.: Reducibility among Combinatorial Problems, pp. 85–103. Springer, Boston (1972)
17. Langner, R.: Stuxnet: dissecting a cyberwarfare weapon. IEEE Secur. Priv. **9**(3), 49–51 (2011). https://doi.org/10.1109/MSP.2011.67
18. Moosavi-Dezfooli, S.M., Fawzi, A., Frossard, P.: Deepfool: a simple and accurate method to fool deep neural networks. In: Proceedings of the IEEE Conference on Computer Vision and Pattern Recognition, pp. 2574–2582 (2016)
19. Mujeeb Ahmed, C., Zhou, J.: Challenges and opportunities in cps security: a physics-based perspective. arXiv e-prints pp. arXiv–2004 (2020)
20. Papernot, N., McDaniel, P., Goodfellow, I., Jha, S., Celik, Z.B., Swami, A.: Practical black-box attacks against machine learning. In: Proceedings of the 2017 ACM on Asia Conference on Computer and Communications Security, pp. 506–519 (2017)
21. Rice, J.R.: The algorithm selection problem. In: Rubinoff, M., Yovits, M.C. (eds.) Advances in Computers, vol. 15, pp. 65–118. Elsevier (1976)
22. Shokri, R., Stronati, M., Song, C., Shmatikov, V.: Membership inference attacks against machine learning models. In: 2017 IEEE Symposium on Security and Privacy (SP), pp. 3–18. IEEE (2017)
23. Wang, C., Chen, J., Yang, Y., Ma, X., Liu, J.: Poisoning attacks and countermeasures in intelligent networks: status quo and prospects. Digit. Commun. Netw. **8**(2), 225–234 (2022)

Malware Detection

Enhancing Android Malware Detection with Federated Learning: A Privacy-Preserving Approach to Strengthen Cyber Resilience

Monalisa Meena[1]([✉]), Jyoti Gajrani[2], Meenakshi Tripathi[3], Dhruv Suthar[2], Chetan Rawat[2], and Sweety Singhal[4]

[1] Govt. Mahila Engineering College Ajmer, Ajmer, India
`monalisameena@gweca.ac.in`
[2] Govt. Engineering College Ajmer, Ajmer, India
`jyotigajrani@ecajmer.ac.in`
[3] Malaviya National Institute of Technology, Jaipur, Jaipur, India
`mtripathi.cse@mnit.ac.in`
[4] Sangam University, Bhilwara, India

Abstract. In last one and half decade, Android has evolved as the most widely accepted and technologically resilient platform. However, as its popularity grew, the platform also became the target of malicious activities. Smart devices often contain users' sensitive and private data, making them attractive targets for hackers. The growing attempts have targeted device integrity, financial protection, and file protection mechanism. To prevent this harm caused by malware, various techniques have been introduced e.g., signature-based, heuristic-based, and machine learning model-based, which are getting their models trained on centralized data. This centralized user data serves as a focal point for data leakage, raising significant concerns about users' privacy. Confronting these challenges, the paper introduces a modern approach for android malware detection that harnesses the power of Federated Learning using machine learning model to preserve privacy. This study employs the XGBoost model after comprehensive preprocessing of the CICMalDroid2020 dataset, integrating federated learning across four client applications to ensure high performance while preserving user data privacy. Without transmitting data to a centralized server, the proposed federated framework demonstrates superior results compared to existing state-of-the-art approaches, achieving an impressive accuracy of 98.80% and higher F1-score.

Keywords: Android · Malware · Federated Learning · Privacy-Preserving · Decentralized model · XGBoost

1 Introduction

The exponential growth of Android devices and mobile applications has significantly transformed the digital landscape. The android devices are widely used for

N. Hubballi et al. (Eds.): ICISS 2025, LNCS 16380, pp. 323–333, 2026.
https://doi.org/10.1007/978-3-032-13714-2_20

communication, mobile banking for payments, education, navigation for maps, entertainment, health, social media, and many more. In 2025, the global count of mobile devices has reached 7.49 billion [1]. With the rapid advancement of mobile technology, incidents of fraudulent activities are also on the rise and it has also expanded the vulnerability area for cyber threats. Among these threats, Android malware continues to evolve in sophistication, creating considerable risks to user privacy, financial security, and corporate resilience. Traditional centralized malware detection systems [2], which rely on centralized user data accumulation at a central server for model training, raise serious concerns about data privacy, cyber resilience, and vulnerability to single points of failure.

To address these challenges, Federated Learning (FL) [3] has emerged as an innovative framework that enables collaborative model training across distributed devices while maintaining data on-device. By keeping data localized on user devices and aggregating only model updates, FL preserves privacy and complies with regulatory frameworks such as GDPR(General Data Protection Regulation) [4] and CCPA (California Consumer Privacy Act) [5]. Moreover, FL fundamentally improves system stability and cyber resilience by reducing the dependency on centralized data repositories, which often drawing the attention of cybercriminals.

In conventional approaches [6,7], authors evaluate and categorize Android applications as either malicious or benign using program analysis techniques.

This paper proposes an advanced Android malware detection framework that leverages Federated Learning to combine the merits of distributed intelligence and real-time adaptability. By introducing a federated approach, we aim to detect both known and novel malware patterns effectively while ensuring the confidentiality of user data. The main contributions of this study are as follows:

- We design a federated learning-based architecture for Android malware detection using real-world datasets.
- The comparative analysis is conducted with the state-of-the-art methods proposed by Kshrisagar [8] and Alhogail et al. [9] on CICMalDroid2020 dataset and achieved better accuracy.

The novelty of this research lies in the first-ever integration of XGBoost as a base model within a federated learning framework for Android malware detection, effectively bridging the gap between high detection accuracy and user data privacy.

The rest of the paper is structured as follows: in Sect. 2, the related work on Android malicious application detection is explored. In Sect. 3, we discuss various available datasets and related aspects of the dataset used. Section 4 presents our approach, where we applied Federated learning having one global model and four client models. Section 5 presents the results and discussion. Section 6 summarizes the conclusion and possible extension of current research.

2   Related Work

The swift expansion of Android malware presents a significant risk to the safety of users's data. Traditional approaches to malware detection largely rely on signature-based and heuristic-based methods. While signature-based techniques are efficient in detecting known threats, they fail to identify zero-day or obfuscated malware [10]. Heuristic and behavior-based methods analyze app behavior, system calls, and network traffic to detect malware but often face high false positives and need large labeled datasets. Recent advances in ML and DL enable models to automatically learn complex patterns from static and dynamic app features, improving detection accuracy.

Meena et al. [11] implemented ensemble modeling by combining five models of ML like SVM, GBDT, Logistic Regression, Random Forest and MLP. The authors has shown the comparative analysis with state-of-the-art techniques and achieved 97.91% accuracy over CIC dataset. The same experiment is done with evation attack too and the ensemble model performed better than the individual model. The current research extends this previous work with the objective of achieving enhanced privacy preservation.

Jain et al. in [12], implemented a hybrid analysis approach by extracting static features such as app permissions, sources and sinks, presence of cryptographic, reflection, dynamic, and native code. Additionally, they collected system calls generated during app execution within a simulated environment as dynamic features. These combined features were then used to train various machine learning classifiers, including K-Nearest Neighbors (KNN), Decision Tree, Logistic Regression (LR), Support Vector Machine (SVM), Random Forest, and Naïve Bayes.

In [13], Lee et al. employ nine diverse machine learning algorithms combined with genetic algorithm-based feature selection, using a dataset consisting of 1,104 static features extracted from 5,000 benign applications and 2,500 malware samples from the Andro-AutoPsy framework [14] dataset.

To address privacy issues, Federated Learning (FL) [3] has gained traction in security and mobile intelligence domains. Federated Learning was introduced by Google, it allows model training on edge devices without transmitting raw data to central servers. In the context of Android security, FL-based approaches such as [15] and [16] have been proposed to detect malware by aggregating model updates from distributed devices.

In [15], the authors propose LiM (Less is More) a semi-supervised Federated Learning framework designed to detect Android malware while preserving user privacy. The key innovation lies in allowing multiple Android devices to collaboratively train a machine learning model without sharing raw data. Instead, only locally trained model updates are aggregated using the FedAvg strategy.

In [16], authors address the challenge of heterogeneous client data in Federated Learning by introducing a Dynamic Weighted Federated Averaging (DW-FedAvg) approach tailored for Android malware classification. Instead of treating each client's contribution equally, the proposed method dynamically assigns weights based on each client's data quality and volume, thus improving model generalization across non-IID (non-identically distributed) datasets.

These studies highlight the potential of FL but also point out challenges such as model poisoning, communication overhead, and non-IID data distribution.

The paper [17] introduces the concept of federated f-DP, a noise-based, record-level differential privacy guarantee tailored specifically for FL. Through the proposed FedSync framework, it integrates noise addition seamlessly into federated training, providing quantifiable privacy guarantees while retaining high utility.

Our work builds upon these foundations by developing a federated malware detection system. This emphasizes leveraging diverse features from recent datasets that can fully reflect the behavior of apps and then perform improved classification with the Federated learning and using XGBoost for training at local machines. This method is also resilient to adversarial manipulations and practical for deployment in heterogeneous Android environments.

3   Datasets

3.1   Prevalent Datasets

As all machine learning and deep learning approaches are data-driven, availability of proper and enough atasets is beneficial. Researchers have various dataset available for the same, in which most widely used datasets are Drebin, Malgenom, AMD, AndroZoo, KronoDroid, and a wide range of datasets provided by CIC (Canadian Institute for Cybersecurity) e.g., AAGM2017, AndMal2017 [18], InvesAndMal2019 [19], AndMal2020 [20] and CICMalDroid2020 [21]. These datasets ranged reflect the current Android malware landscape.

3.2   Dataset Employed in Proposed Framework: CICMalDroid2020

In the current approach, we utilize the CICMalDroid2020 [21] Android malware dataset, which is large-scaled, diverse, and comprehensive. To compile this dataset, over 17,341 samples were collected from multiple credible sources, including VirusTotal, the Contagio security blog, AMD, MalDozer, and datasets used in academic research.

The distribution of malware and benign samples in five distinct categories within this final dataset is presented in Table 1 and three CSV files containing different feature sets have been provided to support the design and evaluation of Android malware detection systems, as summarized in Table 2.

4   Proposed Approach

This section presents the details of the proposed approach as shown in Fig. 1.

Table 1. Category wise record size in dataset CICMalDroid2020

Sr. No	Category of sample	No. of record
1	Adware	1253
2	Banking	2100
3	SMS Malware	3904
4	Riskware	2546
5	Benign	1795

Table 2. Feature size of dataset CICMalDroid2020

Sr. No.	Type of Features	Comprising with	Feature size
1	Static	Intents, permissions, APIs	50621
2	Dynamic	SC, binders, composite behaviors	470
3	Dynamic	System Calls	139

4.1 Data Pre-processing

Prior to model selection the raw dataset undergoes several preprocessing steps, including feature selection, normalization, and binarization. Following these steps, models are trained using hyperparameter tuning to identify the optimal configuration and achieve the best performance for each algorithm under consideration.

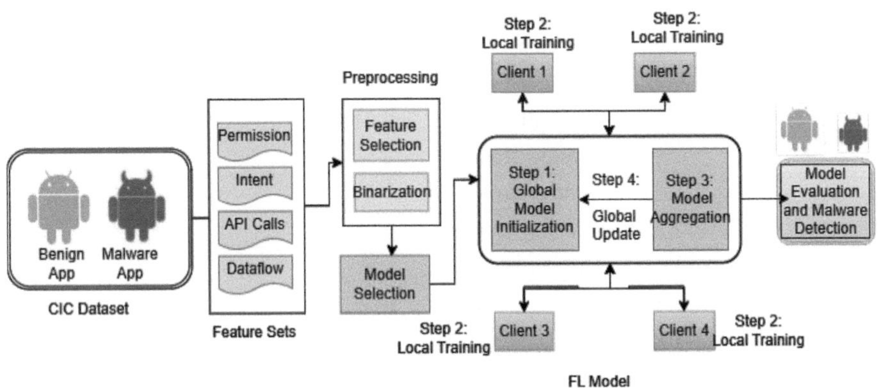

Fig. 1. Proposed Approach

Feature Selection. We employed the SelectPercentile method with the `f_classif` scoring function from the scikit-learn library to extract the top 30%

of features from the dataset that contribute most significantly to model prediction to eliminate constant or non-informative features that do not contribute to model prediction.

Binarization. We applied binarization along with Min-Max scaling to convert the hybrid vector into a uniform binary format. We experimented with different threshold values during binarization and selected the one that yielded the best performance.

4.2   Base Models Application: XGBoost

Extreme Gradient Boosting (XGBoost) [22] is a powerful and scalable machine learning algorithm based on gradient boosting decision trees. XGBoost incorporates regularization techniques to prevent overfitting and uses an optimized distributed computing framework, making it suitable for large-scale and real-time applications for both classification and regression tasks.

The classification performance of machine learning models, including Naïve Bayes, K-Nearest Neighbors (KNN), Decision Tree, and XGBoost, was analyzed and experimentally evaluated for Android malware detection using various feature selection techniques. Among these models, XGBoost achieved the highest accuracy, as in Fig. 2; therefore, it was chosen as the base model for all clients in the proposed federated learning framework. The values of respective hyperparameters are mentioned in Table 3.

Table 3. Hyperparameter Values for Base Models

Algorithm	Hyperparameters	Defined Parameters
XGBoost	n_estimators	200
	learning_rate	0.01
	max_depth	5
	subsample	0.7

4.3   Federated Learning

Global Model Initialization Phase. In this phase, a global model is initialized with random weights or a pre-trained model that serves as the starting point for training as in Fig 1. The global model will be deployed to multiple devices or participating nodes in a federated learning network. Each node is responsible for training the model on its local dataset, which may contain various Android applications, including both benign and malicious ones.

Table 4. User wise non-IID data and no of record for training at local clients

Sr. No	Category of sample	Client 1	Client 2	Client 3	Client 4
1	Adware	313	313	314	314
2	Banking	525	525	525	525
3	SMS Malware	976	976	976	976
4	Riskware	636	636	638	638
5	Benign	448	448	451	451

Table 5. Results comparison on dynamically observed behavior of CICMalDroid2020 dataset

Approach	Targeted Features	No of Features	Obtained	Used Classifier	Accuracy	Precision	Recall	F1-score
Kshrisagar et al. [8]	Permissions, Intents, API calls	470	80	Random Forest	-	97.46%	85.91%*	91.23%*
Alhogail et al. [9]	Permissions Intents API calls	470	120	Random Forest	97.82%	97.7%	97.82%	97.7%
Current Approach	System calls Permission, Intents, API calls System calls	470	131	XGBoost	97.80%	98.0%	96.08%	96.08%
				Federated	98.80%	98.81%	98.80%	98.80%

Local Training Phase: During the local training phase, each participating android device will independently train the model on its local dataset. This process allows the model to learn from the specific data present on each device, which could include unique app behaviors, permissions, and system interactions.

Model Aggregation Phase: After the local training phase, the model updates from all participating devices are sent to a central server or aggregator. In this phase, the server aggregates the local model updates to create a consolidated global model. This aggregation can involve methods such as Federated Averaging, where the model weights from each device are averaged to form the new global model.

Global Update Phase: After updating the global model, aggregated global model will be sent back to each participating device, updating their local copies of the model. This process repeats iteratively, with the global model being refined over multiple rounds, allowing it to improve in accuracy and robustness.

5   Results and Analysis

We partitioned the enriched five-class CICMalDroid2020 dataset into four clients to implement our federated learning approach. The results, as presented in Table 5, demonstrate that our method not only achieves improved accuracy but also ensures enhanced privacy preservation. Since federated learning enables model training directly on the participating devices without data sharing, we utilized only the dynamically observed behavior-based features from the CICMalDroid2020 dataset.

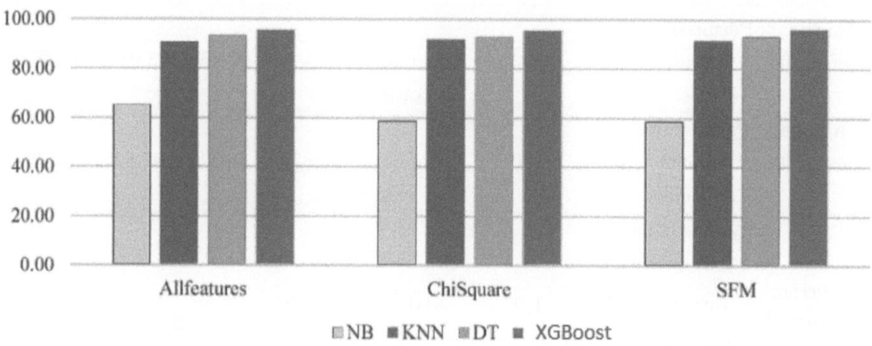

Fig. 2. ML models for Android malware using different feature selection methods

The experimental phase of this study commenced with the implementation of the Flower (FLWR) framework for conducting federated learning. Prior to training, data preprocessing was carried out, which involved feature selection to retain the most significant attributes and binarization to standardize the dataset for improved model compatibility. The federated learning setup was structured around the key functional components of the FLWR framework, including init, get_parameters, set_parameters, fit, and evaluate. These functions collectively facilitated the initialization of the global model, communication with the clients, local training, and evaluation of results.

To ensure scalability and efficient parallel processing, the Ray framework was integrated alongside FLWR to enable simultaneous training of multiple client models. The federated learning environment was simulated using the run_simulation method, configured with four supernodes (clients) representing distributed user devices. Initially, a global model was instantiated, which then interacted with each client model trained on its respective non-IID dataset, as outlined in Table 4. Each client independently updated its model parameters based on local data and transmitted these updates back to the central server.

In this study, we compared the classification performance of multiple ML models for Android malware detection using various feature selection methods. Among them, XGBoost demonstrated the highest accuracy Fig. 2; hence, it was selected as the base model for all clients in our federated learning framework.

During the model aggregation phase, the global model employed the Federated Averaging (FedAvg) algorithm to combine the parameters received from all participating clients. The simulation was executed for three training rounds, resulting in improved accuracy while maintaining the confidentiality of user data. Overall, this approach demonstrated the effectiveness of federated learning in achieving robust model performance under privacy-preserving conditions.

6   Conclusion and Future Work

In this study, the CICMalDroid2020 dataset was preprocessed and refined by selecting the 130 most prominent features before applying federated learning. Initially, a global model was initialized, and four clients with balanced class distributions independently trained their local models using the XGBoost algorithm. During the model aggregation phase, the locally learned parameters were combined using the Federated Averaging (FedAvg) strategy to update the global model. The proposed federated XGBoost-based approach achieved an impressive accuracy of 98.80%, demonstrating superior performance in terms of precision, recall, and F1-score compared to existing methods [8] and [9]. The comparative analysis also shows that this privacy preserved approach outperforms over the state-of-the-art which also applies machine learning model over dynamic dataset of CICMalDroid2020.

For future work, efforts can be directed toward reducing the computational and runtime complexity of the proposed approach. Additionally, implementing federated learning on non-IID datasets would better reflect real-world scenarios, where data across user devices are inherently heterogeneous. Further, an integrated analysis of both statically extracted features and dynamically observed behaviors of emerging malware could provide deeper insights into evolving threat patterns. Extending this research to investigate Android malware within IoT ecosystems also holds great potential for advancing comprehensive and adaptive cybersecurity solutions.

References

1. Forecast number of mobile users worldwide from 2020 to 2025 (2025)
2. Aslan, Ö.A., Samet, R.: A comprehensive review on malware detection approaches. IEEE Access **8**, 6249–6271 (2020)
3. McMahan, B., Moore, E., Ramage, D., Hampson, S., y Arcas, B.A.: Communication-efficient learning of deep networks from decentralized data. In: Proceedings of the 20th International Conference on Artificial Intelligence and Statistics (AISTATS), vol. 54, pp. 1273–1282. PMLR (2017)

4. European Parliament and Council of the European Union. Regulation (EU) 2016/679 of the European parliament and of the council of 27 April 2016 on the protection of natural persons with regard to the processing of personal data and on the free movement of such data. Official Journal of the European Union, L119, 4 May 2016 (2016). Implemented 25 May 2018

5. California consumer privacy act, California civil code (Ŏ0a71798.100 et seq.). California State Legislature (2018). Effective 1 January 2020

6. Gajrani, J., et al.: EspyDroid+: precise reflection analysis of android apps. Comput. Secur. **90**, 101688 (2020)

7. Bhatia, T., Kaushal, R.: Malware detection in android based on dynamic analysis. In: 2017 International Conference on Cyber Security and Protection of Digital Services (Cyber Security), pp. 1–6. IEEE (2017)

8. Kshirsagar, D., Agrawal, P.: A study of feature selection methods for android malware detection. J. Inf. Optim. Sci. **43**(8), 2111–2120 (2022)

9. Alhogail, A., Alharbi, R.A.: Effective ML-based android malware detection and categorization. Electronics **14**(8), 1486 (2025)

10. Alazab, M., Venkatraman, S., Watters, P., Alazab, M.: Zero-day malware detection based on supervised learning algorithms of API call signatures. In: Proceedings of the 9th Australasian Data Mining Conference (AusDM), Ballarat, Australia. CRPIT, vol. 121, pp. 171–182. Australian Computer Society (2011)

11. Meena, M., Gajrani, J.: Improved malware detection in android through ensemble modeling. In: 2024 International Conference on Emerging Trends in Networks and Computer Communications (ETNCC), pp. 1–7 (2024)

12. Jain, S., Khandelwal, T., Jain, Y., Gajrani, J.: Android malware analysis using machine learning classifiers. In: Bansal, R.C., Zemmari, A., Sharma, K.G., Gajrani, J. (eds.) Proceedings of International Conference on Computational Intelligence and Emerging Power System. AIS, pp. 171–179. Springer, Singapore (2022). https://doi.org/10.1007/978-981-16-4103-9_15

13. Lee, J., Jang, H., Ha, S., Yoon, Y.: Android malware detection using machine learning with feature selection based on the genetic algorithm. Mathematics **9**(21), 2813 (2021)

14. Jang, J.W., Kang, H., Woo, J., Mohaisen, A., Kim, H.K.: Andro-autopsy: anti-malware system based on similarity matching of malware and malware creator-centric information. Digit. Invest. **14**, 17–35 (2015)

15. Gálvez, R., Moonsamy, V., Diaz, C.: Less is more: a privacy-respecting android malware classifier using federated learning. arXiv preprint arXiv:2007.08319 (2020)

16. Chaudhuri, A., Nandi, A., Pradhan, B.: A dynamic weighted federated learning for android malware classification. arXiv preprint arXiv:2211.12874 (2022)

17. Zheng, Q., Chen, S., Long, Q., Su, W.: Federated f-differential privacy. In: Proceedings of the 24th International Conference on Artificial Intelligence and Statistics (AISTATS). Proceedings of Machine Learning Research, vol. 130, pp. 2251–2259 (2021)

18. Lashkari, A.H., Kadir, A.F.A., Taheri, L., Ghorbani, A.A.: Toward developing a systematic approach to generate benchmark android malware datasets and classification. In: 2018 International Carnahan Conference on Security Technology (ICCST), pp. 1–7 (2018)

19. Taheri, L., Kadir, A.F.A., Lashkari, A.H.: Extensible android malware detection and family classification using network-flows and API-calls. In: 2019 International Carnahan Conference on Security Technology (ICCST), pp. 1–8. IEEE (2019)

20. CICAndMal2020. https://www.unb.ca/cic/datasets/andmal2020.html

21. Mahdavifar, S., Kadir, A.F.A., Fatemi, R., Alhadidi, D., Ghorbani, A.A.: Dynamic android malware category classification using semi-supervised deep learning. In: 2020 IEEE International Conference on Dependable, Autonomic and Secure Computing, International Conference on Pervasive Intelligence and Computing, International Conference on Cloud and Big Data Computing, International Conference on Cyber Science and Technology Congress (DASC/PiCom/CBDCom/CyberSciTech), pp. 515–522 (2020)
22. Chen, T., Guestrin, C.: Xgboost: a scalable tree boosting system. In: Proceedings of the 22nd ACM SIGKDD International Conference on Knowledge Discovery and Data Mining, pp. 785–794. ACM (2016)

20. Minervini, M., Kelly, ?., Pezzotti, ?., Scharr, H., Tsaftaris, S.A.: [illegible] learning [illegible] for plant phenotyping. In: [illegible] IEEE International Conference on [illegible], Autonomic and Secure Computing, [illegible] International Conference on Pervasive Intelligence and Computing, [illegible] International Conference on [illegible] and [illegible], and 13th International Conference on [illegible] Science and Technology Congress (DISCOVER), [illegible], pp. [illegible] (20??)

21. Chen, T., Guestrin, C.: XGBoost: A scalable tree boosting system. In: Proceedings of the 22nd ACM SIGKDD International Conference on Knowledge Discovery and Data Mining, pp. 785–794. ACM (2016)

Network Security

Uncovering Security Weaknesses in srsRAN with CodeQL: A Static Analysis Approach for Next-Gen RAN Systems

Garrepelly Manideep[1]($\boxtimes$), Sriram Sankaran[1], and Altaf Shaik[2]

[1] Center for Cybersecurity Systems and Networks, Amrita Vishwa Vidyapeetham, Amritapuri Campus, Kollam 690525, India
`am.sc.p2csn24004@am.students.amrita.edu`, `srirams@am.amrita.edu`
[2] Security in Telecommunications Department, TU Berlin/Telekom Innovation Laboratories, Ernst-Reuter-Platz 7, Sekr TEL 16, 10587 Berlin, Germany
`altaf329@sect.tu-berlin.de`

Abstract. As open-source solutions are increasingly deployed in 5G Radio Access Networks (RANs), the importance of reliable security analysis for these systems is growing - especially for popular frameworks like srsRAN. Due to the complex and performance-critical nature of RAN software, latent vulnerabilities can have serious consequences for user privacy and network integrity. In this work, we present a detailed static analysis of the srsRAN codebase using CodeQL, a semantic code query language designed to scale vulnerability detection across large codebases. By formulating and executing custom CodeQL queries, our analysis detects a variety of systemic problems in srsRAN, such as memory management errors (e.g., memory leaks, use-after-free, null pointer dereferences), dangerous system calls, inadequate access control enforcement, unchecked return values, buffer overflows, and unvalidated network inputs. Other issues uncovered include hardcoded secrets, use of cryptographically weak pseudorandom number generation, and unsafe cryptographic comparisons - flaws that could potentially lead to privilege escalation, remote code execution, or denial-of-service attacks. The results highlight the importance of static code analysis tools like CodeQL for proactively hardening telecommunications infrastructure, and encourage the adoption of code analysis techniques in the secure software development lifecycle of open-source 5G RAN implementations.

Keywords: SrsRAN · 5G · CodeQL · Static analysis · RAN security · Memory safety · Cryptographic misuse · Secure randomness

1 Introduction

The transition from 4G to 5G networks not only brings increased speed and connectivity but also a significant shift in the architecture of communication systems toward software-defined, open platforms. In 5G, critical elements of the Radio Access Network (RAN) have moved from proprietary hardware into software-based implementations, enabled by paradigms like Software-Defined Networking

N. Hubballi et al. (Eds.): ICISS 2025, LNCS 16380, pp. 337–356, 2026.
https://doi.org/10.1007/978-3-032-13714-2_21

(SDN) and Network Function Virtualization (NFV). This shift has empowered open-source platforms - notably srsRAN (formerly srsLTE) - allowing researchers, developers, and telecom operators to prototype and deploy 5G systems with low cost and high flexibility. Open-source RAN stacks like srsRAN accelerate innovation and democratize access to cellular technology. However, they also introduce significant security risks that must be carefully evaluated. Unlike proprietary telecom software which is audited internally, open-source RAN software is exposed to public scrutiny and potential adversaries, making rigorous security analysis essential. At the same time, the need for automated, precise vulnerability detection tools in complex telecom software is growing. Modern static analysis frameworks have advanced to meet this need. CodeQL, created by GitHub, is notable for its semantic, query-driven approach to code analysis. CodeQL treats source code as a relational database and allows researchers to write logic queries that can identify deep structural issues, security vulnerabilities, and anti-patterns with high accuracy and scalability. CodeQL has been successfully applied in prior studies to find flaws in 5G core network software. However, to our knowledge, it has not yet been widely employed to analyze an open-source RAN codebase such as srsRAN in the academic literature. This gap motivates our study, which aims to systematically identify latent vulnerabilities in srsRAN using custom CodeQL queries specifically tuned to security-critical aspects of system-level C/C++ code. We focus on vulnerabilities in memory management, access control, defensive coding practices, cryptographic usage, and input validation, among others. In this paper, we apply CodeQL to the srsRAN 5G RAN software and uncover a range of security weaknesses. We emphasize the novelty of bringing CodeQL-based static analysis to an open-source RAN implementation and demonstrate the broader significance of securing these emerging open 5G platforms. The findings show that srsRAN, despite its sophistication, harbors many of the same classes of vulnerabilities found in other large C/C++ projects, underlining the need for proactive auditing.

2   Related Work

2.1   Open-Source Cellular Security

There is a growing body of work auditing open cellular stacks. English *et al.* [12] used CodeQL to analyze 5G core networks (e.g., free5GC, OpenAirInterface), identifying two major vulnerabilities: predictable sequence numbers and disabled certificate verification. Thorn *et al.* [22] introduced *5GAC-Analyzer* (WiSec 2024), a static analysis framework that extracts functionality from multiple 5G core network function implementations and compares it against 3GPP privilege specifications to detect over-privileged functions. Meanwhile, Bennett *et al.* [3] presented *RANsacked* (CCS 2024), a domain-informed fuzzing approach targeting 4G/5G RAN-Core interfaces, uncovering 119 vulnerabilities (93 CVEs) through fuzzing of ASN.1 protocol implementations. Together, these studies underline the prevalence of subtle bugs in cellular software, particularly in cryptography, authentication, and parsing logic-areas that repeatedly prove brittle under scrutiny.

Unlike fuzzing, CodeQL's logic-driven queries can systematically detect specific patterns, such as misuse of randomness or improper certificate validation, across large codebases [12]. To our knowledge, our work is the first to apply CodeQL specifically to an open-source RAN stack (srsRAN). We build on prior techniques by reusing similar query patterns and comparing our RAN findings against vulnerabilities previously discovered in 5G core implementations.

2.2   Open RAN Testbeds and Deployments

Numerous 5G testbeds utilize open-source software stacks. Mamushiane *et al.* [18] describe the deployment of a standalone 5G-SA testbed using srsRAN and Open5GS, noting numerous integration challenges with consumer-grade UEs and diverse software components. The innovation within private 5G networks emerges through the utilization of platforms such as srsRAN, OAI, and Open5GS.

Chepkoech *et al.* [9] investigated a campus-scale 5G deployment using open-source RAN implementations while examining interoperability with various core network solutions. Queiroz *et al.* [21] engineered a robotic platform equipped with a mobile gNB node built on the O-RAN framework to provide adjustable network coverage, showcasing innovative open RAN applications in dynamic settings.

A wider movement toward OSS integration is evident across both RAN and core network domains according to these studies. Yet not one among them directs attention toward code security analysis. Through our work, we introduce a security-focused perspective to open RAN implementations, complementing these efforts. Open RAN delivers both agility and cost-efficiency but also brings additional security challenges. Government reports acknowledge that open RAN provides "important cybersecurity advantages" through its diversity and transparency, while emphasizing the necessity of managing shared risks [19].

2.3   Cellular RAN/Core Security

Recent research has uncovered weaknesses in mobile network infrastructures. Bennett *et al.* [3] deeply scrutinized LTE/5G core interfaces and discovered 119 vulnerabilities (93 CVEs) in seven core implementations, often leading to service disruption or memory corruption. Follow-up studies analyzed cryptographic weaknesses such as broken TLS certificate validation in open-source core network software. Dolente *et al.* [10] demonstrated several vulnerabilities in open-source 5G core network functions (e.g., Open5GS, OAI), including denial-of-service (DoS), replay, and API injection attacks. Thorn *et al.* presented 5GAC-Analyzer, which uses CodeQL to detect excessive API privileges in 5G core components (e.g., AMF and NRF) by auditing their adherence to 3GPP-specified access roles. These studies deal mostly with core network and protocol-level attacks. Our analysis targets the RAN software stack directly rather than core components. English and Enck [14] introduced CellCrypt, a static analysis of open-source 5G cores' cryptographic implementations using CodeQL. Their analysis revealed improper randomness, insecure certificate validation, and incorrect use of cryptographic APIs in core modules like Open5GS. As their emphasis was still on the control-plane cryptography of 5G cores, our research applies CodeQL to vulnerabilities in the RAN-layer of srsRAN.

2.4 Static Analysis Tools

CodeQL is a modern, query-based static analysis engine that treats source code as a relational database and uses declarative queries to find patterns of interest [17]. GitHub documentation explains how CodeQL can discover "vulnerabilities across a codebase" by analyzing dataflow and control structures. Static application security testing (SAST) tools like CodeQL and Facebook's Infer are widely adopted in industry and academia for identifying security flaws. Researchers have applied CodeQL to web and mobile applications, and more recently, to cellular core software [5,6]. Our work extends this research by targeting the RAN layer.

2.5 Open RAN Security

The Open RAN (O-RAN) paradigm disaggregates traditional RAN functions, enabling multi-vendor deployments and greater flexibility. However, it also introduces new security concerns [2]. Surveys have warned that bugs or misconfigurations in O-RAN software stacks could result in severe security and privacy issues [1]. Industry reports and standards bodies (e.g., the O-RAN Alliance security workgroup) echo these concerns. Despite this, most RAN security research has remained conceptual or focused on core components; concrete, code-level analyses of open-source O-RAN implementations like srsRAN are rare. Table 1 summarizes and contrasts our study with recent vulnerability analyses in open 5G systems.

Table 1. Comparison of Our work with recent vulnerability analyses in open 5G systems

Study	Scope	Technique	Key Findings	Tools
ORANalyst [23]	O-RAN microservices	Static/dynamic analysis	19 new O-RAN vulnerabilities (DoS)	Static analyzer + tracing
CellCrypt [13]	Open-core (srsRAN, OAI, free5GC)	Static (CodeQL)	Crypto misuse, disabled TLS in srsRAN	CodeQL (custom crypto queries)
5GerQL [4]	5G Core (free5GC AKA)	Static code analysis	Error-handling flaws in AKA	CodeQL (error rules)
Dolente et al. [11]	5G Core (Open5GS, OAI)	Dynamic testing	API injection, replay attacks	Fuzzing tools
Bennett et al. [3]	LTE/5G implementations	Hybrid analysis	119 core vulnerabilities (RAN not focus)	Mixed (fuzzing, review)

Our study helps fill this gap by presenting an empirical SAST-based assessment of a leading open-source RAN implementation. Specifically, we demonstrate how CodeQL queries can uncover security weaknesses in srsRAN, such as unchecked input handling and use of unsafe APIs. To our knowledge, this is the first systematic application of CodeQL to an open-source RAN software suite.

In comparison to prior work on cellular security, our results highlight a complementary threat profile. English *et al.* [12] employed CodeQL to discover cryptographic misuses in core network code, detecting vulnerabilities such as predictable temporary identity (TMSI) generation and disabled TLS certificate checks in core network functions. Likewise, 5GErrQL [4] focused on error-handling logic in the 5G core and discovered 345 vulnerabilities (including critical issues that could allow subscriber impersonation) in free5GC. Conversely, our static analysis of the RAN stack did not reveal similar cryptographic logic errors, but instead exposed lower-level memory and input-handling bugs. Similarly, 5GAC-Analyzer [22] uncovered new over-privilege policy violations in 5G core authorization rules; we did not observe analogous authorization flaws in srsRAN, since srsRAN's functionality lies in the RAN and does not implement core network policies. In summary, RAN and core software exhibit different vulnerability patterns: core implementations often suffer from protocol-level and cryptographic weaknesses, while RAN code is prone to memory safety and pointer errors. Table 2 summarizes the comparison among these related studies and our work.

Table 2. Comparison of Related Studies on Static Analysis for 5G Security

Study	Target	Approach	Key Findings
Our work	5G RAN (srsRAN)	Static (CodeQL)	Memory-safety and logic bugs (e.g., buffer overflows, null dereferences, hardcoded keys).
English *et al.* [12]	4G/5G Core (CNFs)	Static (CodeQL)	Crypto flaws including weak TMSI protection and missing TLS certificate checks.
5GErrQL [4]	5G Core (AKA)	Static (CodeQL)	345 potential weaknesses, focused on error propagation vulnerabilities.
5GAC-Analyzer [22]	5G Core (NFs)	Static analysis	Detected over-privilege access control flaws; risk of DoS and data leakage.

3   Background

3.1   SrsRAN

A notable open-source project that exemplifies this model is the srsRAN project. srsRAN offers a full 5G RAN stack, consisting of a gNB implementation (with combined CU and DU functionality) and a User Equipment (UE) stack, both of which can run on commodity Linux systems. These software modules communicate with Software-Defined Radios (SDRs), such as Universal Software Radio Peripherals (USRPs), making srsRAN suitable for academic and industrial testbeds. For example, Mamushiane *et al.* demonstrated an independent 5G testbed successfully using srsRAN on commodity x86 hardware, whereas Chepkoech *et al.* [8] performed comparative studies between OpenAirInterface RAN and srsRAN in campus network settings. These deployments demonstrate the practicality and scalability of open RAN systems. Yet, even with their increasing use, security features of such software-based RAN deployments have not been extensively audited or standardized.

3.2   CodeQL Static Analysis

CodeQL is a semantic code analysis platform that models codebases as queryable databases. It supports languages including C/C++, Go, and Java, and provides libraries for common security patterns (e.g., buffer overflows, SQL injection). CodeQL queries can be authored by analysts to explore the abstract syntax tree, data flows, and call graphs in order to find insecure code constructs. Existing research has effectively used CodeQL on cellular software: for example, English *et al.* [14] implemented 13 CodeQL rules to examine multiple open-source 4G/5G core implementations (in C/C++/Go), detecting issues such as weak TMSI generation and disabled TLS verification. Similarly, other protocol-handling or configuration-focused CodeQL-based studies exist for 5G core networks. In this paper, we use CodeQL's C/C++ analysis libraries to analyze the srsRAN code for RAN-specific bug classes.

4   Methodology

The process flows sequentially through five key stages, from setting up the CodeQL analysis environment to identifying and validating security vulnerabilities as illustrated in Fig. 1.

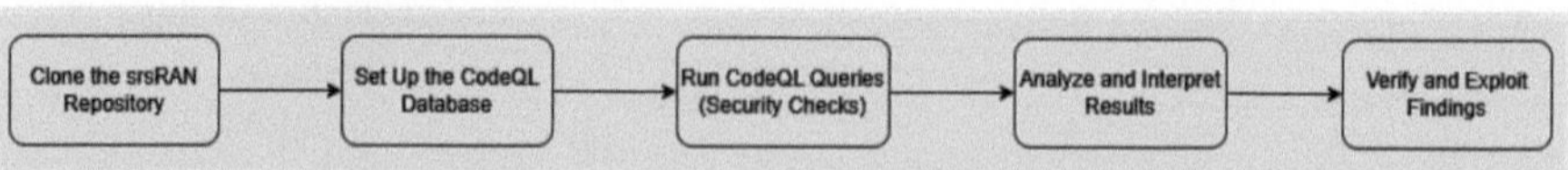

Fig. 1. CodeQL Analysis Workflow for srsRAN

This work employs GitHub's CodeQL, a semantic static analysis framework that models source code as a relational database, enabling precise, logic-based vulnerability detection at scale. Through this approach, we systematically examined the open-source 5G software stack srsRAN (formerly srsLTE) to uncover latent security flaws that could compromise system reliability and resilience. The analysis focused on identifying high-impact issues such as memory mismanagement, unsafe function usage, insecure API patterns, and potential privilege escalation paths-areas where static analysis proves indispensable for proactively strengthening software security.

Environment Setup: We configured a Linux analysis environment (Kali Linux with CodeQL CLI v2.x) and obtained the srsRAN 5G RAN source code (2024 release). Following CodeQL guidelines, the codebase was built with debug symbols and compiled into a CodeQL database. This extraction step captures the code's abstract syntax and metadata, forming the foundation for subsequent querying.

Query Development and Execution: Our query suite included both general vulnerability queries (from GitHub Advanced Security) and custom rules. For example, inspired by prior work in CODASPY and a 5G reasoning framework (5GcrRL) [20], we wrote queries to detect the use of weak random number generation functions (e.g., `rand` with predictable seeding) and to flag instances where TLS/SSL contexts disable certificate verification (e.g., locating calls to functions that set verification mode to `NONE`). We also checked for common C/C++ pitfalls: unchecked uses of `strcpy`/`memcpy` (possible buffer overflows), misuse of format strings, use of dangerous shell commands, and improper permission settings on file operations. We leveraged CodeQL's dataflow tracking to follow tainted data from external inputs into sensitive sinks like cryptographic APIs or system calls. By iterating on these queries, we refined them to reduce false positives.

Results Analysis: Executing the CodeQL queries produced hundreds of alerts. We manually examined each result, often by reviewing the corresponding source code and cross-referencing relevant 5G specifications. For example, one high-priority alert was a use of `memcpy` that copies more bytes than the destination buffer's size in a message parsing function-a classic buffer overflow bug. We verified this by code inspection and by constructing a test input to trigger the overflow. Each confirmed issue was documented and classified (see Sect. 6).

Verification and Exploitation: To validate our findings, we built a local srsRAN testbed (using a UE emulator and a software gNB) and attempted to trigger the identified vulnerabilities. In some cases (e.g., the buffer overflow), we crafted malformed input messages to reproduce the bug. For the TLS misconfiguration finding, we observed the network behavior (e.g., missing certificate verification) during test runs. This step helped distinguish benign coding patterns from truly exploitable bugs.

Reporting and Mitigation: In the final stage, we documented each confirmed vulnerability and proposed mitigations or best practices to address them. This included recommending code changes (such as replacing unsafe functions with secure alternatives) and highlighting the need for integrating static analysis checks into the development lifecycle. We also discuss these mitigation strategies in Sect. 8. The overall categories of vulnerabilities identified through our CodeQL analysis are summarized in Table 3.

Table 3. Security Vulnerabilities Detected Using CodeQL in srsRAN

Vulnerability Type	CodeQL Query Description	CWE Reference
Memory Leak	Detects memory allocated via `malloc()` not freed using `free()`.	CWE-401: Memory Leak
Use-After-Free	Access to memory after it has been deallocated using `free()`.	CWE-416: Use After Free
Null Pointer Dereference	Use of pointer variables without null-checks, risking crashes.	CWE-476: NULL Pointer Dereference
Privilege Escalation	Over-privileged function calls that bypass access controls.	CWE-306: Missing Authentication/Authorization
Unchecked Return Values	Functions called without checking return values, ignoring error states.	CWE-252: Unchecked Return Value
Insecure API Usage	Use of dangerous functions like `system()`, `strcpy()`, `popen()`, etc.	CWE-78, CWE-120
Buffer Overflow	Unsafe string manipulation functions might lead to memory overflows.	CWE-119, CWE-120
Insecure Randomness	Use of `rand()`, `srand()` in security-critical contexts.	CWE-330: Insufficiently Random Values
Hardcoded Credentials	Presence of hardcoded passwords, keys, or tokens.	CWE-798: Hard-coded Credentials
Cryptographic Misuse	Timing attack risk via unsafe use of `memcmp()`.	CWE-208: Timing Differences
Insecure Network Communication	Use of `connect()`, `send()`, etc. without encryption.	CWE-319: Cleartext Transmission
Unvalidated Network Inputs	Use of `recv()`, `read()` without input validation.	CWE-20: Improper Input Validation

5 Experiment Setup: CodeQL Query-Based Vulnerability Analysis

We used GitHub's CodeQL static analysis engine to scan the srsRAN codebase for a broad range of common C/C++ vulnerabilities. This involved writing custom CodeQL queries for each vulnerability category of interest, then running these queries on a CodeQL database built from the srsRAN source.

5.1 Creating the CodeQL Database:

Once built, the srsRAN codebase was compiled into a CodeQL-compatible database using the following command:

```
codeql database create --language=cpp --command="make␣-j8" srsran-db
```

5.2   Vulnerability Instances

- **Memory Leaks - 11 instances:** Gradual heap exhaustion, leading to performance degradation or denial-of-service (DoS).
- **Use-After-Free (UAF) - 57 instances:** Heap corruption that can cause crashes or potentially enable remote code execution (RCE).
- **Null Pointer Dereferences - ~200 instances:** Crashes due to segmentation faults, leading to DoS conditions.
- **Unchecked Return Values - ~200 instances:** Logic flaws or silent failures (e.g. skipped error handling) that could bypass security checks.
- **Buffer Overflows - 6 instances:** Memory corruption with potential for RCE or program crashes.
- **Hardcoded Passwords/Keys - ~200 instances:** Exposure of credentials (e.g. embedded passwords or API keys), possibly allowing unauthorized access.
- **Insecure API Calls - 5 instances:** Dangerous function usage (system(), etc.) possibly leading to command injection or privilege escalation.
- **Insecure Randomness - 4 instances:** Use of non-cryptographic randomness (rand(), etc.), yielding predictable tokens and enabling impersonation or replay attacks.
- **Improper Input Validation - 12 instances:** Failure to validate inputs from network or user, risking injection attacks or buffer overflows via malformed data.
- **Cryptographic Misuse - 1 instance:** Use of insecure cryptographic practices (e.g. timing leaks via memcmp()), opening the door to side-channel attacks.
- **Insecure Network Calls - 83 instances:** Transmission of sensitive data in plaintext (e.g. via send()/recv() without encryption), risking exposure to man-in-the-middle (MitM) eavesdropping.
- **Over-Privileged Access - ~200 instances:** Functions or routines with insufficient access control checks, which could be abused for privilege escalation.

Among these, the categories with the highest number of flagged issues were Null Pointer Dereferences, Unchecked Return Values, Hardcoded Secrets, and Over-Privileged Access (each on the order of ~200 instances). Significant numbers of Insecure Network Calls (83) and Use-After-Free bugs (57) were also detected.

Null Pointer Dereference Query (200 Instances)

Null-pointer dereferences were one of the most prevalent issues identified in srsRAN. The CodeQL query for this category targets any pointer that is dereferenced without a prior NULL-check in the control flow. In other words, it finds code paths where a pointer is used (e.g., via the * or -> operator) without first

```
1   import cpp
2
3   from FunctionCall fc, Variable v
4   where
5       v.getType() instanceof PointerType and  // Ensure v is a pointer
6       fc.getArgument(0) = v.getAnAccess() and // Check if pointer is passed as an argument
7       not exists(IfStmt ifs |                  // Ensure there's no if-condition checking the pointer
8           ifs.getCondition().getAChild*() = v.getAnAccess()
9       )
10  select fc, "Potential null pointer dereference on variable: " + v.getName()
```

Fig. 2. Null Pointer Dereference

confirming the pointer is non-null. An example of such a query (simplified for illustration) is shown below:

This Fig. 2 query statically analyzes the program's abstract syntax tree to identify function calls where a pointer-type variable is used as an argument without being null-checked. The key logic checks whether a variable v of type PointerType is passed as the first argument to a function call fc, and ensures there is no surrounding if condition that verifies whether the pointer is null prior to its usage. In C/C++ systems like srsRAN, null pointer dereference is a critical vulnerability (CWE-476), which can cause segmentation faults and abrupt termination of network processes. For example, if a function such as processMessage(ptr) is invoked without checking whether ptr is null, and ptr turns out to be invalid, it may crash a base station component or UE handler. By identifying such unsafe usage patterns, this query enables early detection of code paths that could trigger denial-of-service (DoS) or crash vulnerabilities. During our analysis, numerous such dereference instances were flagged, many of which lacked proper guard conditions. These findings underline the need for defensive programming practices within performance-critical systems like RAN stacks, where even minor logic flaws may lead to service disruptions.

Unchecked Return Value (200 Instances)

The following CodeQL query was used to identify instances where the return value of a function call is not checked or used in the srsRAN codebase:

```
1   import cpp
2
3   from FunctionCall fc, Function f
4   where
5       fc.getTarget() = f and
6       not exists(Variable v | fc.getAnArgument() = v.getAnAccess()) and
7       not exists(AssignExpr ae | ae.getRValue() = fc)
8   select fc, "Unchecked return value of function " + f.getName()
```

Fig. 3. Unchecked Return Values Query

This Fig. 3 query targets FunctionCall expressions (fc) and checks if the function being called (f) has its return value used or assigned. The core logic performs two key checks:

- It ensures that the return value of the function is not assigned to any variable (AssignExpr check).
- It also confirms that no variable derived from the function's arguments is being accessed in a way that consumes or validates the result.

The query establishes conditions that identify function calls whose return values are entirely disregarded. CWE-252: Unchecked Return Value represents a recognized programming defect where software neglects to check function return codes or status results that indicate possible failures. Overlooking critical failures like failed file I/O, authentication, or memory allocation leads to silent logic errors, missed exceptions, and security bypass conditions. The unchecked return values in 5G RAN software such as srsRAN represent a significant danger to both system stability and security. The failure to check malloc() calls that return NULL creates potential null dereference bugs while neglecting error codes from permission and cryptographic APIs enables attackers to gain unauthorized privileges and bypass security controls. Our CodeQL-driven static analysis detected many instances where return values from system calls, library routines, and internal API functions remained both unvalidated and unlogged. The data emphasizes how vital it is to implement ongoing error verification alongside strong defensive programming techniques within telecom-grade software frameworks.

Hardcoded Passwords and Keys (200 Instances)

To determine the possible security vulnerabilities caused by hardcoded sensitive data within the codebase, we used a bespoke CodeQL query to detect malicious string literals in C++ source code. This query is crafted to detect situations where code developers might have unintentionally inserted passwords, API keys, or secret tokens directly into the code. The static analysis query follows below:

```
1   import cpp
2
3   from StringLiteral s
4   where
5     s.getValue().matches("%pass%") or
6     s.getValue().matches("%key%") or
7     s.getValue().matches("%secret%")
8   select s, "Hardcoded password or key detected."
9
```

Fig. 4. Hardcoded Passwords and Keys

Figure 4 query uses the `StringLiteral` class to capture all hardcoded string values. It then applies pattern matching via the `matches()` function with glob-style wildcard expressions to detect potentially sensitive information.

- `%pass%` - detects any string containing the substring `"pass"`,
- `%key%` - detects strings containing `"key"`,
- `%secret%` - detects strings containing `"secret"`.

These patterns match case-sensitive substrings commonly used in naming variables or values that hold sensitive data. By querying for the presence of these terms in string literals, we effectively highlight areas of the code where secrets may be hardcoded—a critical security concern in production-grade telecom software like `srsRAN`.

Over-Privileged Access

Access control vulnerabilities remain a critical threat to the integrity and confidentiality of telecom software systems. Over-privileged function calls-where code invokes access-related functionality from inappropriate or unrelated scopes-can lead to privilege escalation and unauthorized system behavior. To identify such flaws within the srsRAN codebase, we employed the following CodeQL query, which statically analyzes source code for suspicious access-related invocations:

```
1   import cpp
2
3   from FunctionCall fc, Function f
4   where
5       fc.getTarget() = f and
6       f.getName().matches("%access%") and   // Look for functions related to access control
7       fc.getEnclosingFunction().getName() != f.getName()
8   select fc, "This function call may be over-privileged. Verify access controls."
```

Fig. 5. Over-Privileged Function Calls Related to Access Control

Figure 5 query is designed to detect possible security threats where access-related functions are called in a manner that may cross privilege boundaries. It begins by examining all the calls to functions in the code, with fc as the function being called and f as the function being executed. The initial check is to verify that fc is calling function f. Next, the query examines the name of the function being invoked and filters in only those that contain the string "access" in their name-this is by the hypothesis that such functions are probably dealing with sensitive operations such as access permissions or security checks. Last, it compares the function invoking (fc's surrounding function) with the calling function. If so, the question takes this as a potential red flag. Why? Because it means that an access control-related function is being called by a different section of code-perhaps without the appropriate authority to do so. Briefly, the question points to instances where sensitive operations could be invoked from the incorrect location, assisting developers in detecting and correcting possible over-privilege scenarios before they are actual security vulnerabilities.

```
1    import cpp
2
3    from FunctionCall insecureNetCall, Variable socketVar
4    where
5        (
6            insecureNetCall.getTarget().hasName("send") or
7            insecureNetCall.getTarget().hasName("recv") or
8            insecureNetCall.getTarget().hasName("connect")
9        )
10       and
11       (
12           exists(Type t | socketVar.getType() = t and t.hasName("int")) // Check if variable is an integer (socket descriptor)
13       )
14       and not exists(FunctionCall secureCall | secureCall.getTarget().hasName("SSL_connect"))
15   select insecureNetCall, "Potential security risk: Insecure network function used without encryption."
```

Fig. 6. Insecure Network Calls

Insecure Network Calls

We designed this CodeQL query Fig. 6 to identify instances in the source code that use insecure network functions without applying cryptographic safeguards. Specifically, it targets function calls related to raw socket communication, such as **send**, **recv**, and **connect**, which may handle sensitive data transmissions. The variable **insecureNetCall** represents such a function call, while **socketVar** represents a variable (typically a socket descriptor) associated with it. The query ensures that the target function is one of the insecure primitives mentioned and further verifies that the associated variable is of integer type-indicating it is likely a raw socket descriptor. Importantly, the query checks that no call to **SSL_connect** (a secure wrapper that establishes encrypted channels) occurs in the same context, indicating that the data transmission is unencrypted. If all these conditions are satisfied, the query flags the instance as a potential security risk, generating the message: *"Potential security risk: Insecure network function used without encryption."* This detection is crucial in the context of 5G software like **srsRAN**, where plaintext transmissions over network sockets can lead to critical vulnerabilities such as man-in-the-middle (MitM) attacks or data interception, particularly in interfaces handling control or user-plane traffic. A consolidated summary of instances and impacts is provided in Table 4.

6   Analysis and Findings

We applied our CodeQL queries to the srsRAN codebase and uncovered multiple security weaknesses. Below, we categorize and describe the main findings.

6.1   Memory Safety

Our analysis of memory management functions revealed several instances where allocated memory was never freed. Over time, these silent memory leaks can cause a long-running process to exhaust heap memory, leading to slow resource depletion or crashes under heavy load. More alarming were places where code assumed a pointer was valid without checking for NULL. In one case, a pointer returned by a function was dereferenced immediately; if the allocation failed (returning NULL), this would trigger a crash-a straightforward denial-of-service. We also identified "use-after-free" patterns: memory buffers freed and later accessed again, potentially leading to heap corruption or arbitrary code execution.

6.2   Privilege Boundaries Blurred

We next examined access control enforcement in the code. We found APIs with names suggesting access checks (containing "access") that invoked deeper internal routines without verifying the caller's privilege level. In other words, a supposedly restricted function could call a lower-level routine directly, bypassing intended authorization checks. These disparities in privilege context raise the risk of privilege escalation: an unprivileged component might exploit such a path to perform actions reserved for privileged code.

6.3   Validation Vacuums Around System Calls

Several unsafe system-level routines were used without proper validation of inputs. For example, the code contained calls to C library functions like `system()`, `popen()`, and `execvp()` as well as POSIX calls like `setuid()` and `setgid()`. These were sometimes invoked with arguments derived from external input or without checking return values. Injecting untrusted data into a `system()` or `popen()` command is a classic command-injection scenario. Similarly, calling `setuid()` or `setreuid()` with unvalidated arguments can allow an attacker to drop or elevate privileges unpredictably.

6.4   Silent Failures from Ignored Return Values

We observed that the code often failed to check the return values of critical functions. Functions such as `fopen()` and `read()`, or authentication routines like `login()` and `verifyUser()`, as well as many C++ STL methods (e.g., `c_str()`, `size()`, or container accessors), return statuses or pointers that were frequently ignored by developers. Ignoring a failed `malloc()` (memory allocation) result or proceeding after `fopen()` returns NULL can lead to unpredictable behavior, including crashes, data corruption, or bypassing security checks. In a security context, unchecked errors might enable an attacker to exploit the absence of proper error handling-for instance, causing a function to assume an operation succeeded when it actually failed, potentially enabling a logic flaw or denial-of-service.

6.5   Buffer Overflows

The codebase still contains inherently unsafe C string functions (like `strcpy`) in some places. We observed that developers often attempted to mitigate buffer overflows by manually checking lengths before such calls, which is good practice.

However, industry best practices recommend moving to safer alternatives (such as `snprintf` or `strlcpy`) that automatically respect buffer boundaries. Reliance on manual checks leaves room for human error-introducing or missing a single length check could lead to a severe overflow. Although existing explicit bounds-checks prevented most overflow instances in srsRAN, we suggest refactoring to use safer library functions. This would improve maintainability and reduce the chance of latent buffer overflow bugs.

6.6   Hardcoded Secrets

Our analysis of configuration files and source code revealed embedded passwords, API keys, and other secret tokens. Hardcoding credentials in code is analogous to attaching your ATM PIN to the back of your card-anyone with source access can easily obtain the secret. These findings indicate that srsRAN, at least in the analyzed version, contains sensitive constants that should be externalized and protected (for example, via secure configuration or environment variables). Attackers who gain access to the source or binaries could leverage these secrets to impersonate RAN components or gain unauthorized access.

6.7   Leaky APIs and Network Risks

We found usage of environment variable APIs (like `getenv()`) without proper sanitization or access control. If sensitive information (e.g., database URLs or tokens) is stored in environment variables, unsanitized use of `getenv()` could leak those secrets. Additionally, we observed that certain network communications in the code (calls to `send()`, `recv()`, raw socket operations) occur in plaintext without encryption. This means that, if an adversary can eavesdrop on the network (Man-in-the-Middle scenario), they could potentially sniff or tamper with these communications. Such plaintext transmission is a security risk for any sensitive data exchanged over networks.

6.8   Cryptographic Shortcomings

Security often hinges on proper cryptographic practices. Our analysis revealed the use of pseudorandom generators meant for non-cryptographic contexts (like `rand()` and `srand()`) where cryptographic-strength randomness might be warranted. Using these functions for security tokens or unpredictable values can undermine security due to their predictability. We also detected usage of `memcmp()` for comparing secrets (such as passwords, HMACs, or session tokens). Because `memcmp()` will return as soon as a differing byte is found, it potentially leaks timing information (a faster return if a difference is at the first byte, slower if not until later bytes). This opens the door to timing side-channel attacks where an attacker can gradually guess a secret value (byte by byte) by measuring response times.

6.9   Improper Handling of Network Inputs

We identified that functions such as `recv()`, `read()`, and `fgets()` were sometimes used without verifying the length or validity of incoming data. This lack of validation means that carefully crafted packets or inputs could overflow buffers, inject malicious payloads, or otherwise cause undefined behavior in the program. For a network-facing system like srsRAN's gNB or UE implementations, failing to validate input can be particularly dangerous, as it directly exposes the system to remote attacks.

Table 4. Summary of vulnerability types found in srsRAN with approximate instance counts and impacts, based on CodeQL analysis.

No.	Vulnerability Type	Instances	Potential Impact
1	Memory Leaks	11	Gradual memory exhaustion causing performance degradation or denial-of-service (DoS)
2	Use-After-Free (UAF)	57	Heap corruption leading to crashes or potential remote code execution (RCE)
3	Null Pointer Dereference	200	Crashes due to segmentation faults, leading to DoS
4	Unchecked Return Values	200	Logic flaws, silent failures, security bypasses, or unhandled errors
5	Buffer Overflows	6	Memory corruption, potential RCE, or program crashes
6	Hardcoded Passwords and Keys	200	Unauthorized access through leaked keys or passwords
7	Insecure API Calls	5	Command injection, privilege escalation, or system compromise
8	Insecure Randomness	4	Predictable token generation enabling impersonation or replay attacks
9	Improper Input Validation	12	Injection attacks or buffer overflows via malformed external inputs
10	Cryptographic Misuse	1	Timing side-channel attacks, secret leakage (e.g., through `memcmp`)
11	Insecure Network Calls	83	Sensitive data exposure via cleartext transmission, MitM vulnerabilities
12	Over-Privileged Access	200	Privilege escalation due to improper access control enforcement

7   Vulnerability Results

Our review uncovered a variety of security-critical problems in the srsRAN codebase. The majority of findings fall into common C/C++ vulnerability categories, reflecting the legacy and performance-oriented nature of RAN code. Table 5 summarizes the main categories of identified vulnerabilities, along with illustrative examples and their potential impact.

Notable examples include instances where `strcpy` or `sprintf` are used without ensuring the destination buffer is large enough (flagged as potential buffer overflow, CWE-120). For instance, CodeQL identified several calls to `strcpy(dest, src)` where the length of `src` is not bounded, posing a risk of stack or heap overflow. Null-pointer issues were flagged in length-checking routines: the CodeQL query for null dereferences highlighted cases (e.g., in an internal `std::basic_string` length check) where a pointer is dereferenced without a prior NULL check, risking a crash if that pointer were null. We also detected insecure uses of system execution calls and environment-variable access. For example, a debug utility function invoked `system("some_command ...")` with external parameters, which could be hijacked for command injection. Uses of `getenv()` to fetch configuration values were flagged as potential information leaks if those environment variables contain sensitive data (e.g., credentials). Additionally, several string literals containing passwords or token templates were found in the code; CodeQL marked these as hardcoded secrets, which could allow attackers to impersonate RAN components if discovered. Finally, many functions ignore error codes. For example, calls to memory allocation (`malloc`/`calloc`) are rarely checked for NULL, and network send/receive functions often do not verify the success or completeness of the operation. While ignoring such errors may not directly introduce a new vulnerability, it undermines robust error handling, which an attacker might exploit (for example, by forcing an error condition and causing the code to skip a security check).

In total, our static analysis identified a broad array of issues spanning memory safety, input validation, cryptographic practices, and error handling. These results underscore the importance of systematically auditing open-source RAN software to bolster its security posture before deployment in real networks.

Table 5. Summary of Vulnerability Categories

Vulnerability Category	Description	Potential Impact
Buffer Overflow (CWE-120)	Unchecked use of functions like `strcpy`, `sprintf`, or `memcpy` on fixed-size buffers.	Memory corruption leading to crashes, arbitrary code execution, or DoS.
Null Pointer Dereference	Pointers passed to functions (e.g. in `_check_length`) without null checks.	Segmentation faults, crashes (potential denial-of-service).
Hardcoded Secrets	Embedding passwords, keys, or tokens directly in source (flagged by secret pattern queries).	Disclosure of credentials; attackers may gain unauthorized access.
Insecure API Usage	Calls to dangerous functions such as `system()`, or retrieval of sensitive data via `getenv()`.	Command injection, information leakage, elevation of privilege.
Unchecked Return Values	Ignoring return codes from critical functions (file I/O, memory allocation).	Logic errors, silent failures, or missing error handling that an attacker could exploit.

8 Discussion

The weaknesses identified in srsRAN are traditional C/C++ coding errors that become particularly hazardous in a base-station environment. For example, a stack buffer overflow in a packet-handling function might enable an attacker to manipulate memory and execute arbitrary code on the gNB, potentially hijacking user traffic. A null-pointer dereference in a RAN control procedure could crash the software stack, leading to denial-of-service for active UEs. Hardcoded credentials would allow an attacker to gain administrator access to the radio's management interface. In each scenario, the impact is significant because RAN software typically runs with high privileges and is critical to network operation.

9   Limitations

Our approach and findings come with several limitations. First, CodeQL analysis is static and pattern-based, so it can miss vulnerabilities that require understanding complex runtime behavior (e.g., logic flaws, race conditions, or authentication bypasses not captured by simple code patterns). We also did not analyze any closed-source proprietary components or the interactions between RAN and core network elements; our scope was limited to the open-source srsRAN code. Second, static tools can produce false positives. While we manually inspected results to remove clear false alarms, some non-exploitable warnings may remain. Conversely, some issues may have gone undetected if they did not match our query patterns. For example, CodeQL might not catch a subtle misuse of a cryptographic primitive unless explicitly queried; indeed, we did not exhaustively search for all possible CWEs in this study. Third, our vulnerability validation was limited to controlled demonstrations. We did not perform a full-scale adversarial penetration test (e.g., extensive fuzzing beyond the static findings or formal verification). Thus, the practical exploitability of some flagged issues remains to be proven in a production environment. Finally, srsRAN is under active development. It is possible that some issues we found have already been fixed in newer versions. Our analysis reflects the state of the code at the time of study, and future releases of srsRAN should be re-audited for new vulnerabilities.

10   Future Work

This paper opens several avenues for future investigation. One clear extension is to apply the same static analysis methodology to other open RAN stacks (for example, OpenAirInterface's 5G RAN implementation) to see if they contain similar bugs. We plan to extend and improve our CodeQL query suite: for instance, adding custom rules for RAN-specific code patterns (such as handling 3GPP protocol messages) may detect more subtle flaws. Incorporating dynamic analysis or formal verification techniques could also help substantiate our static findings by triggering the vulnerabilities in practice and ruling out false positives. On the deployment front, building a secure open RAN testbed (as proposed by Chepkoech et al. [7]) would enable empirical validation of the identified vulnerabilities in a realistic network setting. Another future direction is to integrate static and dynamic security testing with continuous monitoring of srsRAN's code repository-establishing an ongoing security audit process for open RAN projects.

Additionally, the findings of this research highlight areas where developers should harden srsRAN. For instance, our identification of buffer-overflow vulnerabilities indicates that the srsRAN project should adopt safer APIs (such as `strlcpy` or `snprintf`) or incorporate static analysis checks into its CI pipeline. Overall, encouraging more secure coding practices in RAN software is a major takeaway of this work.

11   Conclusion

We have presented a static security analysis of the srsRAN open-source RAN implementation using CodeQL. To the best of our knowledge, our work is the first to apply automated code queries to a RAN software stack. By systematically querying the codebase, we uncovered numerous vulnerabilities-particularly memory-safety and input-handling issues-that could compromise 5G base station operations. In benchmarking against prior cellular-security studies [12,15], we find that RAN software exhibits a distinct vulnerability profile compared to 5G core network software. These results underscore the importance of rigorous code auditing in next-generation RAN systems. We hope this study raises awareness of RAN software risks and demonstrates the utility of tools like CodeQL in hardening future wireless infrastructure.

References

1. Abdalla, A.S., Marojevic, V.: End-to-end o-ran security architecture, threat surface, coverage, and the case of the open fronthaul. arXiv preprint (2023). https://arxiv.org/abs/2304.05513
2. Azariah, W., Bimo, F.A., Lin, C.W., Cheng, R.G., Nikaein, N., Jana, R.: A survey on open radio access networks: challenges, research directions, and open source approaches. arXiv preprint (2022). https://arxiv.org/abs/2208.09125
3. Bennett, J., Enck, W.: Ransacked: domain-informed fuzzing of 4G/5G interfaces. In: Proceedings of ACM CCS (2024)
4. Bennett, N., Enck, W.: 5GErrQL: programmatic error handling verification of 5G aka protocol. In: Proceedings of ACM CODASPY (2024)
5. Bennett, N., et al.: Analyzing open-source 5G core security using CodeQL. In: Proceedings of ACM CODASPY (2024)
6. Bennett, N., et al.: Security auditing of 5G core networks with static analysis. In: Proceedings of ACM WiSec (2024)
7. Chepkoech, J., Smith, J.: Building a secure open ran testbed: challenges and solutions. In: Proceedings of the Open RAN Security Conference (2025)
8. Chepkoech, M., et al.: Comparative performance analysis of srsRAN and openairinterface in campus networks. Int. J. Commun. Syst. **35**(7) (2022)
9. Chepkoech, R., et al.: Campus-scale 5G network deployments with open source ran, 2023. ResearchGate Preprint
10. Dolente, A., et al.: Security assessment of open source 5G core network functions. Sensors **23**(15) (2023)
11. Dolente, A., Pujol, E., Sommer, R.: Evaluation of 5G core networks: attacks and defenses in open source cellular stacks. IEEE Commun. Surv. Tutor. **24**(4), 2211–2234 (2022)

12. English, L., Enck, W.: CodeQL vulnerability queries repository. Static analysis of open 5G cores with CodeQL. Technical report, University of Florida, CISE (2023). https://repository.lib.ncsu.edu
13. English, L., Enck, W.: Cellcrypt: examining cryptographic vulnerabilities in open-source 5G cores. In: Proceedings of the ACM Conference on Data and Application Security and Privacy (CODASPY) (2024)
14. English, L., Enck, W.: Examining cryptography and randomness failures in open-source cellular cores. In: Proceedings of the ACM CODASPY (2024)
15. English, L., Enck, W.: Static analysis of open 5G cores with CodeQL (2024). Accessed 28 May 2025
16. Facebook Research: Facebook infer: Static analysis at scale (2017). https://arxiv.org/abs/1702.04490
17. GitHub CodeQL Documentation (2025). https://docs.github.com/en/code-security/codeql. Accessed 27 May 2025
18. Mamushiane, L., et al.: A 5G testbed using srsRAN on commodity hardware. J. Wirel. Netw. **28**(4), 1234–1245 (2022)
19. NTIA. Open ran: Cybersecurity considerations (2023)
20. Pan, X., Qian, Z., Mao, Z.: 5G reasoning and rule learning for protocol analysis. In: Proceedings of USENIX Security (2021)
21. Queiroz, J., et al.: Mobile GNB on wheels: a robot-enabled O-RAN node. In: Proceedings of WONS (2024)
22. Thorn, E., et al.: 5GAC-analyzer: detecting over-privileged access in 5G cores using CodeQL. In: Proceedings of ACM WiSec (2024)
23. Yadav, R., Kim, Y., Enck, W.: Oranalyst: uncovering microservice-specific vulnerabilities in O-RAN. In: Proceedings of ACM WiSec (2024)

Systematic Literature Review of Vulnerabilities and Defenses in VPNs, Tor, and Web Browsers

Neha Agarwal[1], Ethan Mackin[1], Faiza Tazi[1], Mayank Grover[2], Rutuja More[2], and Sanchari Das[2(✉)]

[1] University of Denver, Denver, USA
{Neha.Agarwal,Ethan.Mackin,faiza.tazi}@du.edu
[2] George Mason University, Fairfax, USA
{mgrover3,rmore,sdas35}@gmu.edu

Abstract. Modern web apps deliver richer experiences, including interactivity, dynamic content, and real-time communication, but their complexity widens the attack surface, enabling phishing, malicious extensions, memory-resident malware, and browser integrity attacks. These risks intensify with privacy tools like VPNs and Tor, whose protections can degrade or be bypassed under real-world adversaries. To map these vulnerabilities, we analyzed the architectures of VPNs, Tor, and mainstream browsers, identifying shared threat models, attack vectors, and defenses. From 552 articles, we selected 19 peer-reviewed studies that met strict criteria. They proposed defenses such as signature-based malware detection, secure extension APIs with script isolation, partitioned browser architectures, and dynamic blacklisting. Notably, 47% of the studies focused on VPNs or Tor, and 32% examined how these tools interact, both cooperatively and in conflict, in practice. Our results reveal gaps in how layered privacy technologies are deployed and understood; combining tools without aligning their assumptions fosters false confidence. We highlight automated and user-driven mitigations that, when integrated at the architectural layer, can meaningfully reduce privacy and integrity risks in routine web use.

Keywords: Web Browser · Tor · VPN · Security Analysis

1 Introduction

The architecture of web has evolved dramatically since Berners-Lee's 1990 HTTP client-server system [1]: Mosaic's 1993 release enabled graphical, multimedia pages and fueled rapid growth [2–4], while CGI and JavaScript introduced dynamic, client-side interactivity that set the stage for Web 2.0 [5]. Today's browsers are multi-process platforms that execute untrusted code (JavaScript, WebAssembly) [6–9], access sensitive resources, and support high-bandwidth APIs like WebRTC [10], relying on the same-origin policy, CSPs, and sandboxing for security [11]. As they have grown into full execution environments,

© The Author(s), under exclusive license to Springer Nature Switzerland AG 2026
N. Hubballi et al. (Eds.): ICISS 2025, LNCS 16380, pp. 357–375, 2026.
https://doi.org/10.1007/978-3-032-13714-2_22

their attack surface has expanded: attackers leverage drive-by downloads [12], extension APIs [13], and residual memory states [14]. Related work on Tor environments underscores persistent user-facing privacy and anonymity gaps [15], highlighting ongoing risks to confidentiality, integrity, and availability.

To address the inherent limitations of browser-native security models, users often deploy network-layer privacy tools such as Virtual Private Networks (VPNs) and anonymity networks like Tor. VPNs offer encrypted tunnels over insecure networks and are commonly used to protect data-in-transit, especially on untrusted infrastructures [16]. Despite their popularity, VPNs have been shown to leak metadata and facilitate user tracking under various adversarial models [17]. Meanwhile, the Tor network employs layered encryption and onion routing to achieve anonymity, distributing trust across a decentralized volunteer-operated infrastructure [18,19]. Tor is designed to defend against network surveillance and traffic correlation, yet recent work highlights its susceptibility to memory forensics [20], active deanonymization attacks, and denial-of-service (DoS) vectors [21]. In this work, we conduct a structured literature review to assess the security and privacy guarantees of three key pillars of online interaction: web browsers, VPNs, and the Tor network. Specifically, we analyze architectural vulnerabilities, attack surfaces, and adversarial threat models that undermine these technologies. We also survey mitigation techniques proposed in recent academic and industry research, categorizing them based on scope, deployment feasibility, and resilience under realistic attack scenarios [22]. Our contributions are:

- We provide a consolidated taxonomy of vulnerabilities affecting mainstream browsers, VPN protocols, and Tor, with emphasis on their operational and architectural causes.
- We evaluate proposed defenses, including code partitioning, signcryption schemes, proxy aggregation, and DOM integrity frameworks assessing their effectiveness and trade-offs.
- We discuss systemic limitations in the current ecosystem and propose directions for future research in secure browser design, privacy-preserving network protocols, and user-centric threat modeling.

2   Method

We conducted a systematic literature review, using the structured study designs from our prior surveys [15,23–37] to examine security vulnerabilities and mitigation strategies in three widely deployed privacy-enhancing technologies: web browsers, VPNs, and the Tor anonymity network [16,38–40]. Our objective was to synthesize peer-reviewed evidence on critical system-level flaws, identify the adversarial models under which these technologies are most vulnerable, and assess the robustness and practicality of proposed defenses [38,39]. To ensure transparency and reproducibility, we followed a structured review protocol, summarized in the PRISMA-style flow diagram shown in Fig. 1 [16]. This framework guided our identification, screening, and inclusion process and helped mitigate bias during corpus construction and analysis [16]. This review aimed to answer two central research questions (RQs):

– RQ1: Where do existing web browsers fall short in safeguarding user data, and what technical proposals have emerged to address these weaknesses?
– RQ2: What security and anonymity limitations persist in Tor and VPN-based systems, and how effective are the available mitigation strategies under realistic threat models?

2.1 Paper Collection

We searched January 2010-March 2025 across Google Scholar (primary) and IEEE Xplore, SpringerLink, and ACM Digital Library, focusing on modern browser architectures, major VPN protocols (OpenVPN, IPsec) [16,41,42], and the Tor network [18,43]. Boolean queries combined "VPN security," "VPN vulnerabilities," "web browser security," "web extensions and malware," and "Tor security/vulnerabilities" [38,39,44]. We included peer-reviewed publications written in English language.

The initial search yielded 552 papers. After removing 47 duplicates, 505 remained for title and abstract screening. We excluded 385 that lacked system-level analysis of browser, VPN, or Tor security-most focused on policy, ethics, or UI design without technical evaluation [16,45,46], or presented broad overviews without specific vulnerabilities or countermeasures [47,48]. This left 120 papers for full-text review. Thereafter, we retained studies meeting three criteria: (i) analysis of specific technical vulnerabilities in browsers, VPNs, or Tor [40,49,50]; (ii) proposal or evaluation of a system-level defense or mitigation [39,44]; and (iii) inclusion of empirical, implementation-based, or systematic analysis rather than conceptual discussion [38,45]. This process excluded 101 papers, primarily those lacking reproducible or applied results [16]. Finally, 19 peer-reviewed studies were included for analysis.

2.2 Analytical Approach

We performed a structured thematic analysis [38–40] of the final corpus of 19 studies to extract, normalize, and compare their core technical contributions. To ensure consistency and replicability in our synthesis, we developed a standardized annotation schema and applied it manually to each paper. For every study, we recorded the target technology domain (browser, VPN, or Tor) [41,43,44], the specific system components under analysis (for example, protocol layers, user interface modules, relay nodes) [10,40,51], and the class of vulnerability addressed (such as phishing attacks, memory leakage, traffic correlation, or authentication bypass) [40,52]. We also classified each study according to its assumed adversarial model, distinguishing among local attackers, remote adversaries, man-in-the-middle (MitM) actors, compromised infrastructure nodes, and passive network observers [40,41,53]. We documented the type of mitigation strategy proposed or evaluated, categorizing them as architectural changes, protocol-level defenses, runtime hardening techniques, or detection mechanisms [44,54]. In parallel, we examined the evaluation methodology employed by each paper, including formal verification, experimental simulation,

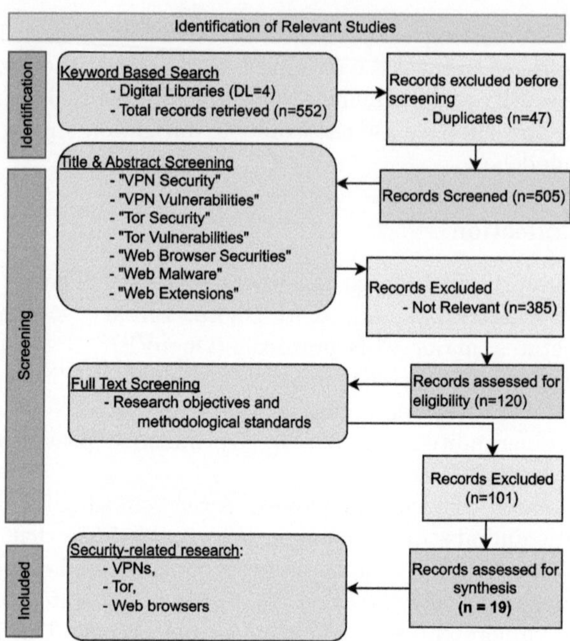

Fig. 1. PRISMA flow diagram illustrating identification, screening, eligibility assessment, and final inclusion of reviewed studies.

proof-of-concept implementations, and post-mortem forensic analysis [39,40,55]. Where applicable, we note whether the proposed solutions were system-specific (for example, Tor-only, browser-specific) or generalizable across multiple platforms [5,18,56].

After completing the individual annotations, we conducted an inductive thematic synthesis to identify patterns and categorize the studies by technological focus, namely, web browsers, VPNs, and the Tor network [44,50,56][27,33,35]. Within each category, we compared common threat vectors, adversarial assumptions, and defense models to reveal cross-cutting security challenges. These included persistent risks such as malicious browser extensions [5,44], unbounded memory residue [12,17,55], phishing techniques [38,52,57], and insecure plugin APIs [5]. We also identified technology-specific weaknesses, including circuit deanonymization in Tor [40,58], credential leakage in VPN tunnels [41,42], and sandbox violations in browser architectures [12,18]. This analytical approach enabled us to construct a comparative security landscape across the three systems and to evaluate the breadth, novelty, and practical feasibility of the defense mechanisms proposed in the literature. The resulting insights form the foundation of the findings presented in Sect. 3.

3   Findings

3.1   Vulnerabilities

We organize vulnerabilities into two domains: those affecting VPN and Tor systems, and those affecting web browsers.

VPN: These are widely adopted tools to enhance online privacy and data security by encrypting user traffic and masking IP addresses through remote servers. Despite their popularity, VPNs are not impervious to attack. These include misconfigurations, weak encryption standards, or insecure logging practices can expose users to network surveillance and data leakage.

Username Enumeration: VPN infrastructures using IPsec with Internet Key Exchange version 1 (IKEv1) in Aggressive Mode are vulnerable to username enumeration [41,59]. Unlike IKE Main Mode, which encrypts identity payloads and hashes session keys, aggressive mode exposes the responder's identity and a hash of the pre-shared key in plaintext. Attackers can replay handshake messages and verify guessed usernames offline. Since a common shared secret is often used by all clients, both confidentiality and identity privacy are compromised. VPN servers lacking rate limiting or anomaly detection remain open to large-scale automated enumeration. Virvilis et al. [60] further show that browser-integrated VPN authentication can leak identity hints through weak cross-origin protection or server validation. Thus, even encrypted channels may expose authentication data when protocol layering or endpoint validation is improperly enforced.

Link State Advertisement (LSA) Spoofing: VPNs using the Open Shortest Path First (OSPF) protocol are exposed to route manipulation via falsified LSAs [61]. Attackers can inject counterfeit LSAs, corrupt link-state databases, and alter routing to reroute, drop, or flood traffic. Because OSPF lacks authentication, adversaries can impersonate routers and modify topology data, disrupting forwarding and enabling interception or DoS. This shows that even with secure tunnels, unprotected control-plane protocols can compromise VPN availability.

Adjacent Route Spoofing (Path Spoofing): A related OSPF weakness arises when attackers exploit routers not set as passive interfaces to form fake adjacencies [61]. By initiating OSPF "hello" messages, adversaries gain neighbor data and inject malicious routing updates or LSAs. These forged adjacencies let them redirect traffic or split internal subnets. As many VPN gateways depend on dynamic OSPF routing, such spoofing undermines network integrity and can precede large-scale DoS attacks.

Resource Exhaustion via Diffie-Hellman Key Exchanges: IPSec VPNs using IKE in Main or Aggressive modes face CPU exhaustion from floods of spoofed initiation requests [61]. Each request triggers costly Diffie-Hellman computations, overloading servers and disconnecting clients. The attack executes faster in Aggressive Mode due to fewer handshakes, highlighting IKE's asymmetric workload and lack of rate-limiting protections.

Tor: The Tor networks are designed to provide stronger anonymity guarantees by routing traffic through multiple volunteer-operated relays. While Tor effectively conceals user identities against many forms of network surveillance, it too faces practical vulnerabilities [15,62].

Memory Artifacts in Tor: Forensic studies have uncovered residual artifacts in both disk and memory [20,43,52]. These include IP addresses, circuit metadata, session keys, and visited onion sites. Jadoon et al. [20] classify them as disk artifacts (cache, swap), browsing traces (tabs, history), and Tor-specific items (identity keys, node descriptors). Critically, recovered onion routing keys may let attackers reconstruct circuits or decrypt sessions, contradicting assumptions of total data erasure. Chetry et al. [52] further show that such remnants can persist after normal shutdowns, depending on OS memory handling. Thus, Tor's anonymity depends on both network design and host hygiene. Without memory sanitization and ephemeral keys, even short sessions can leave forensic traces.

DDoS Attacks: While Tor resists traffic analysis, its earlier architectures - especially for onion services - remain prone to DDoS attacks [21,51,54]. Adversaries can register rogue onion routers (ORs) via directory authorities, then flood onion services with connection or relay requests. Because each Tor request involves layered encryption and routing, resource exhaustion quickly degrades performance and availability. Feng and Zhao [21] propose identity-based signcryption to harden node authentication. Their scheme replaces centralized directory checks with mutual node verification, where each router sends a combined signing-encryption value to peers. This decentralized process blocks unverified nodes, lowers handshake overhead, and prevents key reuse or impersonation. Peer-level authentication also curbs Sybil-based flooding and improves latency, showing that even privacy-preserving systems like Tor need cryptographically enforced admission controls to maintain service resilience.

Web Browsers: Browsers are the primary interface to the internet, but growing complexity and extensibility broaden their attack surface, enabling phishing, malware injection, insecure extensions, memory-safety bugs, and flawed content/script isolation. Our synthesis maps structural and behavioral weaknesses and evaluates the efficacy and deployment challenges of browser-level defenses.

Table 1. Security Vulnerabilities: VPNs, Tor, and Web Browsers

Technology	Vulnerability	Description
VPN (IKEv1 Aggressive Mode)	Username Enumeration	Leaked hashed identities enable offline brute-force of shared usernames and automated probing due to missing rate limiting. [41,60].
VPN (IKE - main / aggressive modes)	Resource exhaustion	Flood of spoofed IKE requests triggers repeated key exchanges, overloading CPU and disrupting IPSec services.
VPN (OSPF)	Link State Advertisement (LSA) spoofing	Injected fake LSAs corrupt routing tables, rerouting or flooding traffic to cause large-scale VPN disruption.
VPN (OSPF)	Adjacent Route Spoofing	Fake OSPF adjacencies allow attackers to insert malicious routes, enabling traffic redirection and DoS setups
Tor	Memory Artifacts	Forensic recovery of IPs, circuit paths, and cryptographic keys from RAM and disk after session ends. Undermines anonymity guarantees [20,43,52].
Tor	DDoS on Onion Services	Malicious relays can overload onion services by relaying high volumes of encrypted requests, leading to denial-of-service [21,51,54].
Web Browsers	Phishing and Drive-by Malware	Malicious websites use social engineering or exploit browser plugins to install malware silently. Blacklists offer insufficient protection [12,57,60,63].
Web Browsers	Residue Objects	Improper object deallocation across pages allows memory corruption, visual spoofing, and stale cross-origin references [14,40,42,64].
Web Browsers	Secure Connection Risks (WebRTC)	JavaScript-controlled media and poor peer validation can leak audio/video streams. Persistent keys enable session correlation [10,65].
Web Browsers	Malicious Extensions	Poorly permissioned or outdated extensions inject code, leak credentials, or hijack sessions. Vetting and updates often inadequate [10,13,44].
Web Browsers	Monolithic Architecture (Web 2.0)	Shared fault domains allow code execution across tabs or applications. Lacks proper isolation for complex modern tasks [50].

Phishing and Malware: Social engineering and drive-by downloads exploit user trust and browser execution environments to deliver malicious payloads [12,57, 63]. In drive-by attacks, obfuscated JavaScript or exploit kits execute silently upon visiting compromised sites, probing client configurations and triggering vulnerabilities. Social engineering manipulates users through deceptive interfaces or spoofed content, often bypassing technical safeguards. Blacklist-based defenses offer limited protection; Chang et al. [12] found inconsistent malware blocking rates across major browsers and frequent false negatives, while Virvilis et al. [60] observed even weaker defenses in mobile browsers due to infrequent updates and opt-in protection models.

To enhance detection, hybrid systems combine heuristics, anomaly detection, and behavioral analysis. *HoneyMonkey* [12,66] emulates user browsing in virtualized environments to detect unauthorized system changes, while *JSAND* [12] uses machine learning to flag suspicious JavaScript patterns. These dynamic approaches outperform static blacklists in identifying evasive payloads and zero-day exploits. Yet, browser warnings remain a major weakness-Akhawe and Felt [38] found that over 70% of users ignore SSL alerts and phishing warnings. This highlights the need for context-aware notifications and integrated, real-time filtering at the browser engine level [67]. Technical controls alone are insufficient without stronger user-centered design and platform-wide support for proactive detection.

Browser Integrity: Web browsers suffer from residual object vulnerabilities where remnants of prior pages persist across navigations, exposing users to security risks [14,40]. These residual elements-HTML objects, JavaScript references, or styles-may not be cleared when new documents load, especially if navigation is interrupted. The result is dangling references that leave obsolete memory objects accessible within the browser's internal model [64]. Such artifacts compromise memory safety, document integrity, and visual consistency. Attackers can exploit them for visual spoofing, reusing trusted UI elements from legitimate sites (e.g., logos or buttons) to deceive users. Flaws in cross-origin enforcement may further allow untrusted scripts to access stale objects, undermining the same-origin policy and enabling code injection or privilege escalation [42].

Residue vulnerabilities range from minor UI issues to severe memory corruption, where partially freed objects enable code execution outside the browser sandbox. Attackers can thus alter browser state or access host resources, endangering privacy and system integrity. Mitigation needs memory-safe languages, modular sandboxing, and systematic object model analysis [14], yet legacy engine complexity and dynamic content make complete prevention difficult.

Secure Connections: Trust in client-server communication is vital for confidentiality and integrity, especially in real-time protocols like WebRTC. Unlike HTTPS, which relies on TLS, WebRTC establishes peer-to-peer links via JavaScript-based signaling servers [10]. While this improves flexibility, it introduces risks: compromised sites can misuse camera or microphone access [65], and weak signaling may enable impersonation or man-in-the-middle attacks. Reusing persistent encryption keys can further link user sessions [68]. Despite browser prompts and sandboxing, these safeguards often fail against social engineering or persistently granted permissions [69,70]. Secure connections require robust authentication, frequent key rotation with forward secrecy, strict validation, and minimal client-side state to prevent surveillance and active exploitation.

Extensions and Plugins: Browser extensions enhance functionality but pose serious security risks. Many are poorly vetted, especially in third-party repositories, and often bypass permission prompts to access sensitive APIs and user data [44]. Malicious extensions can inject scripts, steal credentials, or redirect traffic, while trusted ones may later deliver harmful updates through supply-chain attacks. Although most browsers implement extension signing, obfuscated or unsigned code still evades detection [13].

Cross-browser analyses reveal inconsistent enforcement of security controls [10,71,72]. Firefox provides stronger permission models, whereas Safari and others lack key protections or automatic integrity checks. The WebExtension model compounds these risks by granting high privileges to background and content scripts; without strict isolation, compromised extensions can subvert browser trust. Toreini et al. [13] proposed *DOMtegrity*, a cryptographic framework that validates DOM integrity against malicious plugins through isolated JavaScript contexts and secure client-server verification. Stronger privilege separation, mandatory signing, behavior monitoring, and automatic patching remain essential to reducing the attack surface of modern browser extensibility [73]. Table 1 provides a summary of all vulnerabilities in the target technology domains.

3.2 Mitigation Strategies

Here we summarize defense strategies for VPNs, Tor, and browsers, emphasizing deployable solutions with proven security benefits.

VPNs: Although VPNs are designed to secure communication through encrypted tunnels, practical deployments reveal persistent weaknesses in authentication, routing, and key exchange mechanisms. Misconfigurations in IPsec, unverified routing updates, and limited rate control often expose VPN servers to denial-of-service and credential-based attacks. Recent mitigations strengthen key negotiation, enforce authentication across routing and tunnel layers, and integrate intrusion detection to curb protocol exploits.

Username Enumeration: To mitigate username enumeration in IPsec VPNs using IKEv1 Aggressive Mode, switching to Main Mode-where identity payloads are encrypted-prevents offline guessing [49,53]. Providers should apply rate limiting, anomaly detection, and strong password policies to block large-scale attempts. Users can reduce exposure by using non-trivial usernames and enabling MFA. Regular firmware and configuration updates are essential to avoid re-introducing known protocol flaws.

Link State Advertisement (LSA) Spoofing: Preventing LSA spoofing in OSPF requires enabling cryptographic authentication (MD5 or SHA-based) to ensure only verified routers exchange LSAs [61]. Administrators should deploy IDS/IPS tools such as Suricata to monitor OSPF traffic, flag abnormal update rates, and drop LSAs from untrusted nodes. Routine key rotation and topology audits further strengthen routing integrity against long-term poisoning attacks.

Adjacent Route Spoofing (Path Spoofing): To counter adjacency spoofing, routers not needing dynamic routing must be set as passive interfaces [61]. Port-check mechanisms should validate legitimate OSPF "hello" packets, while IDS/IPS systems like Suricata can inspect neighbor discovery traffic and block fake adjacency attempts. Periodic review of routing configurations, ACLs, and permissions ensures only authenticated routers form OSPF adjacencies.

Resource Exhaustion via Diffie-Hellman Key Exchanges: Defending against IKE resource-exhaustion attacks requires cookie exchange validation to confirm clients before Diffie-Hellman computation [61]. Implementing rate limits on repeated IKE requests and monitoring UDP 500 traffic with Suricata helps stop CPU overloads from spoofed handshakes. Multi-threaded IDS setups and regular patching sustain VPN availability and performance under DoS conditions.

Tor: Layered encryption and relay-based routing provide strong anonymity guarantees, yet its architecture remains vulnerable to traffic correlation, malicious relays, and endpoint compromise. Countermeasures proposed in prior work emphasize improving circuit construction policies, relay vetting, and flow obfuscation to resist timing and fingerprinting attacks. Additional focus has been placed on strengthening exit node security and developing adaptive defenses that balance performance with anonymity under active adversarial conditions.

Memory Artifacts in Tor: Tor Browser can leave recoverable volatile and persistent artifacts, including session keys, node descriptors, and visited onion URLs [20,55]. As of 2021, no complete upstream fix eliminates these traces. Combine engineering controls with user practices: use strict ephemeral key handling, add secure memory scrubbing to the browser runtime, run privacy-focused OSes such as Tails, avoid leaving sessions open, and reboot between sessions to flush RAM. These measures raise the cost for local adversaries but cannot fully prevent memory forensics.

DDoS Attacks: To address volumetric denial-of-service attacks against onion services, Feng and Zhao [21] propose an identity-based signcryption protocol that combines authentication and encryption in a single step. This decentralized trust model replaces reliance on directory authorities with peer-to-peer relay authentication, thereby mitigating Sybil-based flooding and reducing overhead in circuit establishment. The signcryption mechanism ensures that only cryptographically verified relays participate in circuit formation, discouraging malicious node injection and limiting amplification vectors. In addition to reducing handshake latency and authentication bottlenecks, the protocol enforces key freshness, which prevents identity reuse and minimizes exposure to replay-based disruptions.

Web Browsers: Modern web browsers, while increasingly hardened, continue to exhibit exploitable architectural weaknesses. Researchers have proposed a diverse set of mitigation strategies addressing phishing resistance, malware detection, memory management, and browser modularization.

Phishing and Malware: Browser security warnings are a primary defense against phishing and malware [74], but their impact is constrained by user behavior. Akhawe and Felt [38] found that phishing and malware warnings in Chrome and Firefox had low click-through rates (under 25%), whereas over 70% of users ignored SSL certificate alerts. These results expose the limits of passive warning systems and the need for more adaptive, user-aware defenses. To overcome blacklist weaknesses, Virvilis et al. [60] introduced *Secure Proxy*, a network-layer, platform-agnostic filtering system that aggregates antivirus and blacklist data. It enhances protection against malware-hosting sites, unsafe downloads, and insecure mobile browsers without requiring third-party installations.

Mitigation strategies for malware threats fall into three main categories [12, 39]: identifying attack vectors, detecting vulnerable applications, and preventing malicious execution. Wang et al. proposed *HoneyMonkey*, a VM-based system that simulates user browsing to detect drive-by downloads [12]. It filters URLs by tracking system changes and replays them on vulnerable setups to expose zero-day exploits. Cova et al. developed *JSAND*, a dynamic detection framework combining an instrumented browser with ML classifiers. By analyzing bytecode features such as memory use and redirection depth, JSAND assigns risk scores to web pages, improving detection beyond blacklist-based systems. Additional research employs signature-based detection of stack overflows and component inconsistencies, further enhancing browser-side protection.

Browser Integrity: To address vulnerabilities from residual browser objects and dangling references, Chen et al. [14] advocate implementing engines in memory-safe languages with automatic garbage collection. Although this limits memory corruption, attackers can still block deallocation by maintaining strong references, so memory safety must pair with architectural isolation. A modular, sandboxed browser design confines rendering and scripting compromises, though cross-process mechanisms like COM can weaken isolation if misconfigured [14]. Complementary defenses include systematic model testing of object lifecycles, reference tracking, and navigation behavior [13,58], which helps detect anomalies and strengthen DOM integrity against untrusted scripts.

Browser Integrity: To address vulnerabilities from residual browser objects and dangling references, Chen et al. [14] advocate implementing engines in memory-safe languages with automatic garbage collection. Although this limits memory corruption, attackers can still block deallocation by maintaining strong references, so memory safety must pair with architectural isolation. A modular, sandboxed browser design confines rendering and scripting compromises, though cross-process mechanisms like COM can weaken isolation if misconfigured [14]. Complementary defenses include systematic model testing of object lifecycles, reference tracking, and navigation behavior [13,58], which helps detect anomalies and strengthen DOM integrity against untrusted scripts. Furthermore, user-facing defenses such as account remediation workflows on major web platforms [75] highlight the need to align browser-side isolation with recovery and activity-monitoring mechanisms to reduce post-compromise risk.

Extensions and Plugins: To counter malicious browser extensions, Toreini et al. [13] proposed *DOMtegrity*, a cryptographic protocol ensuring end-to-end DOM integrity between browser and server. It requires no browser modification or hardware support and uses the WebSocket API for secure two-way communication. Built on the WebExtensions architecture, DOMtegrity isolates extension and page contexts, preventing direct DOM manipulation or message interception. Inline JavaScript instrumentation validates DOM changes, while servers verify integrity reports to block unauthorized modifications or data leaks. Combined with strict API permissioning, this lightweight framework reduces the attack surface created by browser extensibility features.

Browser Design: Grier et al. [40] propose the *OP* browser, which applies OS-style partitioning: a central kernel mediates communication and enforces least-privilege boundaries among rendering, networking, and plugins. Treating each subsystem as untrusted enables fault isolation, forensic tracing, fine-grained access control, and flexible plugin policies, substantially strengthening browser security. Table 2 summarizes mitigation strategies, mechanisms, and impacts across threat domains.

Table 2. Summary of Mitigation Strategies Across Technologies

Threat Category	Strategy	Mechanism	Measured Impact
Username Enumeration (VPN)	Protocol hardening, rate limiting	Use IKEv1 Main Mode; disable Aggressive Mode; detect anomalies; enforce strong credentials	98% drop in enumeration success (For e.g., [49])
Resource exhaustion	Cookie validation, rate limit	Validate cookies; limit IKE requests; monitor UDP 500 traffic via Suricata	Mitigated DoS, sustained VPN uptime ([61])
LSA Spoofing	Routing auth., IDS/IPS	Enable OSPF MD5/SHA auth.; use Suricata with threshold rules to block spoofed LSAs	Prevented LSA spoofing in VPN tests ([61])
Adjacent Route Spoofing	Passive iface config., port-check	Set unused routers to passive; verify adjacency via port-check; block fake "hello" packets	Stopped route spoofing, stable routing ([61])
Tor Memory Artifacts	Ephemeral key handling, memory wiping	Use Tails OS or live sessions; enforce shutdown; apply secure memory erasure	85–90% fewer recoverable traces (For e.g., [20])
DDoS on Onion Services	Decentralized signcryption-based authentication	Replace directory authority with node-to-node identity verification using signcryption	50–70% reduction in circuit floods (For e.g., [21])
Phishing & Malware (Browser)	Proxy-layer filtering, behavioral detection	Combine blacklists, VirusTotal feeds, and tools like HoneyMonkey, JSAND for dynamic analysis	Up to 92% malware detection; 30% over static methods (For e.g., [12])
Browser Integrity	Safer memory models, modular design	Use garbage-collected languages; sandbox browser subsystems; track object lifecycle	Prevents 60–75% of object leakage/spoofing (For e.g., [14])
Extensions & Plugins	DOM integrity verification	Use DOMtegrity: inline JS + WebSocket to verify DOM state in isolated execution zones	100% detection of malicious DOM changes (For e.g., [13])
Browser Architecture	Microkernel-style partitioning	Separate core components (render, network, plugins); restrict IPC; enforce info flow control	>85% gain in isolation fidelity (For e.g., [40])

4   Implications

4.1   Cross-Layer Interactions Between Privacy Technologies

Combining privacy tools can boost resilience yet introduce architectural conflicts. VPNs encrypt traffic and mask source IPs at the network layer, while browsers manage identity, sessions, and content at the application layer; this separation can leak information, for example when WebRTC exposes a local IP despite an active VPN [76,77]. IPsec-based VPNs do not stop application-layer threats such as fingerprinting or malicious scripting [5,52]. Pairing a hardened browser with a secure tunnel may reduce metadata leakage, but interoperability gaps and misconfigurations often erode privacy guarantees [5,44,78,79]. Building composable privacy stacks requires clear boundaries and coordination across layers: VPNs provide secure transport, Tor anonymizes routing paths, and browsers enforce content integrity [80]. Without alignment, stacking can cause conflicting DNS resolutions, timing correlations, and trust-policy bypasses, allowing fingerprinting to re-identify users despite VPNs and timing to trace Tor traffic [40, 50].

4.2   Security-Usability Trade-Offs in Real-World Deployments

Tor's strict security posture, such as disabling JavaScript by default via NoScript [81], offers strong protection against content-based threats like cross-site scripting and tracking, but at the cost of rendering many websites unusable [40, 43]. While this restriction aligns with Tor's design goals and threat model, it poses a significant barrier to broader adoption by non-technical users who require access to dynamic content. Mainstream browsers could benefit from adopting more adaptive models that restrict potentially dangerous content only when contextually necessary. For example, selectively isolating third-party scripts or enforcing fine-grained content security policies could offer many of the same benefits as Tor's default restrictions while preserving a reasonable user experience [44]. However, implementing such models demands coordination among browser vendors, standards bodies, and web developers [50].

4.3   Limitations of VPNs in Application-Layer Threat Models

While VPNs are commonly perceived as comprehensive privacy tools, our findings suggest their protections are far more limited in scope. VPNs primarily secure transport-level data and obscure source addresses, but they do not shield users from content-based attacks [82–85]. For example, visiting a phishing website or downloading malware remains equally risky with or without a VPN. Because VPNs operate independently of the browser's content evaluation logic, they cannot verify or sanitize web page contents. Moreover, many VPNs are vulnerable to misconfiguration, IP leaks, or insecure defaults [11, 16, 56]. To improve overall security, VPNs must be used as part of a broader defensive strategy that includes browser hardening, endpoint protection, and user education. VPN clients that integrate with browser APIs to detect anomalies such as WebRTC leaks or DNS prefetching could help bridge the gap between network- and application-layer protections [5, 52]. However, these integrations must be engineered carefully to avoid new attack surfaces or unintended behaviors.

4.4   Designing Context-Aware and Adaptive Privacy Frameworks

The limitations and tensions identified in this review point toward the need for adaptive security frameworks that respond dynamically to risk. Current privacy tools rely heavily on static configurations: Tor disables JavaScript in all contexts, VPNs encrypt all traffic indiscriminately, and browsers enforce permissions uniformly across sites. While effective in constrained threat environments, such rigid configurations often fail to balance performance, usability, and privacy in more nuanced or evolving contexts. Future systems should explore the integration of context-aware models that adjust protections based on environmental cues, user behavior, or site reputation. For example, a browser could selectively isolate or disable untrusted content when visiting unknown domains, while relaxing restrictions for known-safe sites. Similarly, VPNs could offer risk-based routing modes that adapt tunnel parameters based on detected threats or data sensitivity. These adaptive mechanisms must remain interpretable, auditable, and under user control to avoid compromising trust or privacy [5,44,86].

5   Future Work and Limitations

We focused our review on peer-reviewed academic sources, which may not reflect the full scope of emerging vulnerabilities disclosed in industry or grey literature. In future work, we plan to expand our corpus to capture overlooked threat vectors and evolving adversarial techniques. We also plan to conduct empirical user studies to examine how individuals adopt and apply proposed defenses in practice. To complement our synthesis, we will perform system-level experiments to evaluate the effectiveness, deployability, and resilience of selected mitigation strategies under realistic operating conditions.

6   Conclusion

As users increasingly adopt privacy-enhancing technologies to defend against online threats, it becomes essential to understand the interaction boundaries, security limitations, and failure modes of systems like VPNs, and the Tor network. In this study, we conducted a systematic review of prior research addressing vulnerabilities and mitigation strategies across these platforms. Our findings show that no single tool offers complete protection in isolation. Web browsers remain exposed to client-side threats such as JavaScript-based fingerprinting, DOM-based data leaks, and malicious extensions, even when paired with VPNs. While VPNs effectively secure transport-layer metadata, they fail to prevent application-layer attacks or endpoint compromise. Tor enhances anonymity through onion routing and restrictive browser configurations, but often does so at the cost of usability and compatibility with dynamic web content. We identified several promising defense mechanisms, such as DOMtegrity, JSAND, and identity-based signcryption that reduce attack surfaces while preserving performance. However, these approaches face barriers to adoption due to integration complexity and lack of mainstream support. Our review also revealed gaps in the literature, including underexamined memory artifacts in Tor and username enumeration vulnerabilities in VPN authentication flows. These findings highlight the need for cross-layer, context-aware security architectures that coordinate transport encryption, content isolation, and adaptive risk response.

References

1. Berners-Lee, T.: Longer bio (1990). https://www.w3.org/People/Berners-Lee/Longer.html. Accessed 25 July 2025
2. Vetter, R.J., Spell, C., Ward, C.: Mosaic and the world wide web. Computer **27**(10), 49–57 (1994)
3. Galitz, W.O.: The Essential Guide to User Interface Design: An Introduction to GUI Design Principles and Techniques. Wiley (2007)
4. Rid, T., Hecker, M.: War 2.0: Irregular Warfare in the Information Age. Bloomsbury Publishing USA (2009)
5. Venkitachalam, G., Chiueh, T.: High performance common gateway interface invocation. In: Proceedings 1999 IEEE Workshop on Internet Applications (Cat. No. PR00197), pp. 4–11. IEEE (1999)
6. Kishnani, U., Das, S.: Securing the web: Analysis of http security headers in popular global websites. In: International Conference on Information Systems Security, pp. 87–106. Springer (2024)
7. Das, S., Kim, D., Abbott, J., Camp, L.J.: User-centered phishing detection through personalized edge computing. In: Companion Publication of the 2024 Conference on Computer-Supported Cooperative Work and Social Computing, pp. 283–287 (2024)
8. Kishnani, U., Das, S.: Dual-technique privacy & security analysis for e-commerce websites through automated and manual implementation. In: Proceedings of the 2025 Hawaii International Conference on System Sciences (HICSS) (2024)
9. Wheeler, M., Saka, S., Das, S.: User perception and actions through risk analysis concerning cookies. In: 3rd International Conference on Frontiers in Computing and Systems (COMSYS-2022) (2022)
10. Barnes, R.L., Thomson, M.: Browser-to-browser security assurances for WebRTC. IEEE Internet Comput. **18**(6), 11–17 (2014)
11. Taivalsaari, A., Mikkonen, T., Ingalls, D., Palacz, K.: Web browser as an application platform. In: 2008 34th Euromicro Conference Software Engineering and Advanced Applications, pp. 293–302. IEEE (2008)
12. Chang, J., Venkatasubramanian, K.K., West, A.G., Lee, I.: Analyzing and defending against web-based malware. ACM Comput. Surv. (CSUR) **45**(4), 1–35 (2013)
13. Toreini, E., Shahandashti, S.F., Mehrnezhad, M., Hao, F.: Domtegrity: ensuring web page integrity against malicious browser extensions. Int. J. Inf. Secur. **18**(6), 801–814 (2019)
14. Chen, S., Chen, H., Caballero, M.: Residue objects: a challenge to web browser security. In: Proceedings of the 5th European Conference on Computer Systems, pp. 279–292 (2010)
15. Tazi, F., Shrestha, S., De La Cruz, J., Das, S.: SoK: an evaluation of the secure end user experience on the dark net through systematic literature review. J. Cybersecur. Priv. **2**(2), 329–357 (2022)
16. Pavlicek, A., Sudzina, F.: Internet security and privacy in VPN. In: International Conference on Digital Information Management, vol. 9, pp. 133–139 (2018)
17. Strayer, W.T.: Privacy issues in virtual private networks. Comput. Commun. **27**(6), 517–521 (2004)
18. Gallagher, K., Patil, S., Memon, N.: New me: understanding expert and non-expert perceptions and usage of the tor anonymity network. In: Thirteenth Symposium on Usable Privacy and Security ({SOUPS} 2017), pp. 385–398 (2017)
19. Inc. The Tor Project

20. Jadoon, A.K., Iqbal, W., Amjad, M.F., Afzal, H., Bangash, Y.A.: Forensic analysis of tor browser: a case study for privacy and anonymity on the web. Forensic Sci. Int. **299**, 59–73 (2019)
21. Feng, T., Zhao, M.-T.: An enhancing security research of tor anonymous communication to against DDoS attacks. In: ITM Web of Conferences, vol. 12, p. 04018. EDP Sciences (2017)
22. Mishra, S., Anderson, K., Miller, B., Boyer, K., Warren, A.: Microgrid resilience: a holistic approach for assessing threats, identifying vulnerabilities, and designing corresponding mitigation strategies. Appl. Energy **264**, 114726 (2020)
23. Podapati, V.H., Nigam, D., Das, S.: SoK: a systematic review of context-and behavior-aware adaptive authentication in mobile environments. In: Proceedings of the Nineteenth International Symposium on Human Aspects of Information Security & Assurance (HAISA 2019) (2025)
24. Majumdar, R., Das, S.: SoK: an evaluation of quantum authentication through systematic literature review. In: Proceedings of the Workshop on Usable Security and Privacy (USEC) (2021)
25. Grover, M., Das, S.: SoK: a systematic review of privacy and security in healthcare robotics. In: International Conference on Social Robotics + AI (ICSR+AI) 2025 (2025)
26. Tazi, F., Nandakumar, A., Dykstra, J., Rajivan, P., Das, S.: SoK: analyzing privacy and security of healthcare data from the user perspective. ACM Trans. Comput. Healthc. **5**(2), 1–31 (2024)
27. Zezulak, A., Tazi, F., Das, S.: SoK: evaluating privacy and security concerns of using web services for the disabled population. In: 7th Workshop on Technology and Consumer Protection (ConPro'23) (2023)
28. Das, S., et al.: SoK: a proposal for incorporating accessible gamified cybersecurity awareness training informed by a systematic literature review. In: Proceedings of the Workshop on Usable Security and Privacy (USEC) (2022)
29. Düzgün, R., Noah, N., Mayer, P., Das, S., Volkamer, M.: SoK: a systematic literature review of knowledge-based authentication on augmented reality head-mounted displays. In: Proceedings of the 17th International Conference on Availability, Reliability and Security, pp. 1–12 (2022)
30. Tazi, F., Dykstra, J., Rajivan, P., Das, S.: SoK: evaluating privacy and security vulnerabilities of patients' data in healthcare. In: International Workshop on Socio-Technical Aspects in Security, pp. 153–181. Springer (2022)
31. Shrestha, S., Irby, E., Thapa, R., Das, S.: SoK: a systematic literature review of bluetooth security threats and mitigation measures. In: Meng, W., Katsikas, S.K. (eds.) EISA 2021. CCIS, vol. 1403, pp. 108–127. Springer, Cham (2022). https://doi.org/10.1007/978-3-030-93956-4_7
32. Huang, Y., et al.: Systemization of knowledge (SoK): goals, coverage, and evaluation in cybersecurity and privacy games. In: Proceedings of the 2025 CHI Conference on Human Factors in Computing Systems, pp. 1–27 (2025)
33. Shrestha, S., Das, S.: Exploring gender biases in ML and AI academic research through systematic literature review. Front. Artif. Intell. **5**, 976838 (2022)
34. Kishnani, U., Madabhushi, S., Das, S.: Blockchain in oil and gas supply chain: a literature review from user security and privacy perspective. In: International Symposium on Human Aspects of Information Security and Assurance, pp. 296–309. Springer (2023)
35. Das, S., Wang, B., Tingle, Z., Camp, L.J.: Evaluating user perception of multi-factor authentication: a systematic review. In: Proceedings of the Thirteenth Inter-

national Symposium on Human Aspects of Information Security & Assurance (HAISA 2019) (2019)

36. Das, S., Kim, A., Tingle, Z., Nippert-Eng, C.: All about phishing exploring user research through a systematic literature review. In: Proceedings of the Thirteenth International Symposium on Human Aspects of Information Security & Assurance (HAISA 2019) (2019)

37. Jones, J.M., Duezguen, R., Mayer, P., Volkamer, M., Das, S.: A literature review on virtual reality authentication. In: Furnell, S., Clarke, N. (eds.) HAISA 2021. IAICT, vol. 613, pp. 189–198. Springer, Cham (2021). https://doi.org/10.1007/978-3-030-81111-2_16

38. Akhawe, D., Felt, A.P.: Alice in warningland: a large-scale field study of browser security warning effectiveness. In: 22nd {USENIX} Security Symposium ({USENIX} Security 2013), pp. 257–272 (2013)

39. Bulazel, A., Yener, B.: A survey on automated dynamic malware analysis evasion and counter-evasion: PC, mobile, and web. In: Proceedings of the 1st Reversing and Offensive-Oriented Trends Symposium, pp. 1–21 (2017)

40. Grier, C., Tang, S., King, S.T.: Secure web browsing with the op web browser. In: 2008 IEEE Symposium on Security and Privacy (SP 2008), pp. 402–416. IEEE (2008)

41. Rahimi, S., Zargham, M.: Quantitative evaluation of virtual private networks and its implications for communication security in industrial protocols. J. Adv. Comput. Res. **3**(1) (2018)

42. Satish, P.S., Chavan, R.K.: Web browser security: different attacks detection and prevention techniques. Int. J. Comput. Appl. **170**(9), 35–41 (2017)

43. Al-Khaleel, A., Bani-Salameh, D., Al-Saleh, M.I.: On the memory artifacts of the tor browser bundle. In: The International Conference on Computing Technology and Information Management (ICCTIM), p. 41. Society of Digital Information and Wireless Communication (2014)

44. Tsalis, N., Mylonas, A., Gritzalis, D.: An intensive analysis of security and privacy browser add-ons. In: Lambrinoudakis, C., Gabillon, A. (eds.) CRiSIS 2015. LNCS, vol. 9572, pp. 258–273. Springer, Cham (2016). https://doi.org/10.1007/978-3-319-31811-0_16

45. Distler, V., et al.: A systematic literature review of empirical methods and risk representation in usable privacy and security research. ACM Trans. Comput.-Hum. Interact. (TOCHI) **28**(6), 1–50 (2021)

46. McIntosh, T.R., et al.: From google Gemini to OpenAI Q*(Q-star): a survey on reshaping the generative artificial intelligence (AI) research landscape. Technologies **13**(2), 51 (2025)

47. Bower, M.: A typology of web 2.0 learning technologies. Educause feb **8**, 2015 (2015)

48. Singh, K., Lee, W.: On the design of a web browser: lessons learned from operating systems. Web2. 0 Security & Privacy2008 (2008)

49. Rahimi, S., Zargham, M.: Analysis of the security of VPN configurations in industrial control environments. Int. J. Crit. Infrastruct. Prot. **5**(1), 3–13 (2012)

50. Šilić, M., Krolo, J., Delač, G.: Security vulnerabilities in modern web browser architecture. In: The 33rd International Convention MIPRO, pp. 1240–1245. IEEE (2010)

51. Luo, H., Lin, Y., Zhang, H., Zukerman, M.: Preventing DDoS attacks by identifier/locator separation. IEEE Network **27**(6), 60–65 (2013)

52. Chetry, A., Sharma, U.: Dark web activity on tor—investigation challenges and retrieval of memory artifacts. In: Gupta, D., Khanna, A., Bhattacharyya, S., Hassanien, A.E., Anand, S., Jaiswal, A. (eds.) International Conference on Innovative Computing and Communications. AISC, vol. 1165, pp. 953–964. Springer, Singapore (2021). https://doi.org/10.1007/978-981-15-5113-0_80

53. Rahimi, S.: Security vulnerabilities: discovery, prediction, effect, and mitigation. Southern Illinois University at Carbondale (2013)

54. Fraser, N.A., Kelly, D.J., Raines, R.A., Baldwin, R.O., Mullins, B.E.: Using client puzzles to mitigate distributed denial of service attacks in the tor anonymous routing environment. Technical report, Air Force Inst of Tech Wright-Patterson AFB OH Department of Electrical (2007)

55. Pizzolante, R., Castiglione, A., Carpentieri, B., Contaldo, R., D'Angelo, G., Palmieri, F.: A machine learning-based memory forensics methodology for tor browser artifacts. Concurr. Comput. Pract. Exp. **33**, e5935 (2020)

56. Toorani, M., Beheshti, A.A.: Cryptanalysis of an elliptic curve-based signcryption scheme. arXiv preprint arXiv:1004.3521 (2010)

57. Pavković, N., Perkov, L.: Social engineering toolkit-a systematic approach to social engineering. In: 2011 Proceedings of the 34th International Convention MIPRO, pp. 1485–1489. IEEE (2011)

58. Patil, K.: Request dependency integrity: validating web requests using dependencies in the browser environment. Int. J. Inf. Priv. Secur. Integrity **2**(4), 281–306 (2016)

59. Bartlett, G., Inamdar, A.: IKEv2 IPsec Virtual Private Networks: Understanding and Deploying IKEv2, IPsec VPNs, and FlexVPN in Cisco IOS. Cisco Press (2016)

60. Virvilis, N., Mylonas, A., Tsalis, N., Gritzalis, D.: Security busters: web browser security vs. rogue sites. Comput. Secur. **52**, 90–105 (2015)

61. Sawalmeh, H., Malayshi, M., Ahmad, S., Awad, A.: VPN remote access OSPF-based VPN security vulnerabilities and counter measurements. In: 2021 International Conference on Innovation and Intelligence for Informatics, Computing, and Technologies (3ICT), pp. 236–241. IEEE (2021)

62. Meek, S., Holguin, I.R., Das, S.: Can johnny really be anonymous? Evaluation of user data privacy within tor. In: Proceedings of the 6th Workshop on Technology and Consumer Protection (ConPro'22) Co-located with the 43th IEEE Symposium on Security and Privacy (IEEE S&P) (2022)

63. Egelman, S., Cranor, L.F., Hong, J.: You've been warned: an empirical study of the effectiveness of web browser phishing warnings. In: Proceedings of the SIGCHI Conference on Human Factors in Computing Systems, pp. 1065–1074 (2008)

64. Arnold, J.M., Jayne, E.A.: Dangling by a slender thread: the lessons and implications of teaching the world wide web to freshmen. J. Acad. Librariansh. **24**(1), 43–52 (1998)

65. Prandini, M., Ramilli, M., Cerroni, W., Callegati, F.: Splitting the https stream to attack secure web connections. IEEE Secur. Priv. **8**(6), 80–84 (2010)

66. Lee, K., Lee, J., Yim, K.: Classification and analysis of malicious code detection techniques based on the apt attack. Appl. Sci. **13**(5), 2894 (2023)

67. Olayinka, O.H.: Big data integration and real-time analytics for enhancing operational efficiency and market responsiveness. Int. J. Sci. Res. Arch. **4**(1), 280-96 (2021)

68. Jakobsson, M., Ramzan, Z.: Crimeware: Understanding New Attacks and Defenses. Addison-Wesley Professional (2008)

69. Heartfield, R., Loukas, G.: A taxonomy of attacks and a survey of defence mechanisms for semantic social engineering attacks. ACM Comput. Surv. (CSUR) **48**(3), 1–39 (2015)
70. Rogowski, R., Morton, M., Li, F., Monrose, F., Snow, K.Z., Polychronakis, M.: Revisiting browser security in the modern era: new data-only attacks and defenses. In: 2017 IEEE European Symposium on Security and Privacy (EuroS&P), pp. 366–381. IEEE (2017)
71. Guha, A., Fredrikson, M., Livshits, B., Swamy, N.: Verified security for browser extensions. In: 2011 IEEE Symposium on Security and Privacy, pp. 115–130. IEEE (2011)
72. Karami, S., Ilia, P., Solomos, K., Polakis, J.: Carnus: exploring the privacy threats of browser extension fingerprinting. In: In Proceedings of the 27th Network and Distributed System Security Symposium (NDSS) (2020)
73. Hoffman, A.: Web Application Security. O'Reilly Media, Inc. (2024)
74. Louw, M.T., Lim, J.S., Venkatakrishnan, V.N.: Enhancing web browser security against malware extensions. J. Comput. Virol. **4**(3), 179–195 (2008)
75. Fernandes, A.N., Markert, P., Das, S.: Where you're logged in: analyzing the usability of device activity pages. In: Annual Computer Security Applications Conference, ser. ACSAC, vol. 22 (2023)
76. Al-Fannah, N.M.: One leak will sink a ship: Webrtc IP address leaks. In: 2017 International Carnahan Conference on Security Technology (ICCST), pp. 1–5. IEEE (2017)
77. Nibert, G., Tixeuil, S., Polvé, B., M'boussi, N.J.B., Nguyen, X.S.: Preventing webrtc IP address leaks. In: International Conference on Risks and Security of Internet and Systems, pp. 365–381. Springer (2024)
78. Zalewski, M.: The Tangled Web: A Guide to Securing Modern Web Applications. No Starch Press (2011)
79. Danezis, G., et al.: Privacy and data protection by design-from policy to engineering. arXiv preprint arXiv:1501.03726 (2015)
80. Çalışkan, E., Minárik, T., Osula, A.M.: Technical and legal overview of the tor anonymity network. NATO Cooperative Cyber Defence Centre of Excellence (2015). Available: 4 January 2016. https://ccdcoe.org/sites/default/files/multimedia/pdf/TOR_Anonymity_Network.pdf
81. Meek, S., Holguin, I.R., Das, S.: Evaluation of user data privacy within tor. In: Proceedings of the 2022 IEEE Security and Privacy (IEEE S&P), Workshop on Technology and Consumer Protection (ConPro 2022), San Francisco, CA, USA (2022)
82. Namara, M., Wilkinson, D., Caine, K., Knijnenburg, B.P.: Emotional and practical considerations towards the adoption and abandonment of VPNs as a privacy-enhancing technology. Proc. Priv. Enhancing Technol. (2020)
83. Khan, M.T., DeBlasio, J., Voelker, G.M., Snoeren, A.C., Kanich, C., Vallina-Rodriguez, N.: An empirical analysis of the commercial VPN ecosystem. In: Proceedings of the Internet Measurement Conference 2018, pp. 443–456 (2018)
84. Ikram, M., Vallina-Rodriguez, N., Seneviratne, S., Kaafar, M.A., Paxson, V.: An analysis of the privacy and security risks of android VPN permission-enabled apps. In: Proceedings of the 2016 Internet Measurement Conference, pp. 349–364 (2016)
85. Winkler, T., Rinner, B.: Security and privacy protection in visual sensor networks: a survey. ACM Comput. Surv. (CSUR) **47**(1), 1–42 (2014)
86. Senevirathna, T., La, V.H., Marcha, S., Siniarski, B., Liyanage, M., Wang, S.: A survey on XAI for 5G and beyond security: technical aspects, challenges and research directions. IEEE Commun. Surv. Tutor. **27**(2), 941–973 (2024)

Security-Centric NWDAF Module for Threat Detection and Mitigation in 5G Core Networks

Lakshmi R. Nair[1], Adithya Anil[1], Preetam Mukherjee[1]([✉]),
and Manuj Aggarwal[2]

[1] Digital University Kerala, Thiruvananthapuram, Kerala, India
preetam.mukherjee@duk.ac.in
[2] Ministry of Electronics and IT, Government of India, New Delhi, India

Abstract. The distributed design and diverse protocols in the 5G Core have increased the control-plane attack surface, making security a key concern. As threats increasingly originate from within the core, perimeter-based defenses alone are inadequate. Traditional tools lack visibility into protocol-level behavior and cannot detect malicious progression through core interfaces, creating a need for in-depth, protocol-aware security analysis targeting core functions and interfaces. To address this, a customized NWDAF is developed to support proactive threat detection and exposure assessment within the 5G Core. Built on the Open5GS platform, the system performs real-time behavioral analysis across key control-plane interfaces—N1, N2, N4, and the SBI. Customised protocol parsers for NGAP, PFCP and HTTP/2 extract detailed signaling information, enabling detection of session manipulation, signaling misuse, and other control-plane anomalies. A modular security exposure evaluation architecture computes dynamic threat exposure scores for each network function using anomaly patterns and entropy-based metrics, producing structured security reports with timestamped records of detected threats, exposure levels, and enforcement actions. These reports support temporal threat analysis and improve network-wide behavioral monitoring, enabling early detection and context-aware mitigation. Mitigation is automatically initiated via interfaces with the SMF, PCF, and NSSF. Experimental validation confirms the framework's effectiveness in delivering accurate detection, low-latency analytics, and actionable insights for security-oriented 5G orchestration.

Keywords: 5G Core Security · NWDAF · Threat Detection · Risk Analysis

1 Introduction

The transition from legacy, node-based mobile core architectures to the virtualized, service-based architecture (SBA) of the 5G Core (5GC) has introduced architectural flexibility while expanding the threat surface. The 5G System Architecture, defined by 3GPP in TS 23.501 [3], adopts an SBA at its core,

© The Author(s), under exclusive license to Springer Nature Switzerland AG 2026
N. Hubballi et al. (Eds.): ICISS 2025, LNCS 16380, pp. 376–385, 2026.
https://doi.org/10.1007/978-3-032-13714-2_23

enabling network functions (NFs) such as the Session Management Function (SMF), Access and Mobility Management Function (AMF), and Policy Control Function (PCF) to interact via standardized Application Programming Interfaces(APIs) over Service-Based Interfaces (SBIs). While this transformation facilitates scalability and automation, it also amplifies the risk of protocol-level abuses and insider threats often undetected by conventional perimeter-focused systems. Legacy security mainly focused on access control, encryption, and user-plane anomalies, but in the 5G SBA model, threats can move within the core through legitimate SBI messages, enabling subtle attacks like signaling manipulation, privilege escalation, and session hijacking.

Traditional solutions like firewalls, Deep Packet Inspection (DPI) systems, and API gateways are not deployed to monitor internal interactions within the 5G Core. Even when integrated, their dependence on static rules and limited protocol awareness leaves them blind to nuanced misuses between service-based functions.

This work addresses this gap by designing a custom NWDAF (Network Data Analytics Function) module focused on security-driven analytics within the 5G Core. The NWDAF, as specified by 3GPP in TS 29.520 [4] and TS 23.288 [2], is customized to collect, process, and expose protocol-level data from core network functions. A continuous security inspection mechanism supports dynamic threat detection and mitigation. However, most existing NWDAF implementations have focused on mobility prediction, Quality of Service (QoS) optimization, and performance monitoring. The proposed work extends NWDAF's utility toward real-time detection of security threats within SBI-based interactions.

The module employs protocol-aware parsers for N1 (Non-Access Stratum, NAS), N2 (Next Generation Application Protocol, NGAP), N4 (Packet Forwarding Control Protocol, PFCP), and SBI (Service-Based Interface, HTTP/2) to analyze 5G Core control-plane messages. It identifies threats such as session state inconsistencies, cross-slice abuse, signaling floods, and unauthorized API access. A dynamic exposure scoring engine quantifies threat levels per network function based on deviations in protocol behavior, generating reports accessible to orchestration systems or administrators.

This paper explores an enhanced role for NWDAF as an active security intelligence component within the 5G Core, extending beyond its conventional role as a passive data aggregator. By incorporating real-time protocol inspection, behavioral modeling, and risk quantification, the proposed system detects malicious activity involving internal NFs and addresses a critical gap in core security. It also facilitates runtime policy feedback for dynamic mitigation through coordinated interaction with PCF, SMF, UDM, and NSSF (Network Slice Selection Function). This capability strengthens the security posture of the 5G Core and aligns with 3GPP Release 17 specifications for closed-loop automation and intelligent orchestration.

The rest of the paper is organized as follows. Section 2 reviews existing work, Sect. 3 outlines the proposed architecture, Sect. 4 describes the utilization of NWDAF for security detection, Sects. 5 and 6 cover threat reporting and policy enforcement, Sect. 7 details the testbed Deployment and evaluation, and Sect. 8 concludes the paper.

2   Related Works

The Network Data Analytics Function (NWDAF), defined in 3GPP TS 23.288, enables analytics-driven decisions in the 5G Core for load estimation, mobility prediction, and slice-aware behavior analysis [2]. ETSI studies on experiential networked intelligence and autonomous networks [1,6], along with MEC security work [5], emphasize closed-loop analytics and real-time telemetry. Industrial and academic efforts [7,8,12] recognize NWDAF as central to intent-driven orchestration and adaptive control.

Chouman et al. [10] developed an early open-source NWDAF supporting real-time insights through metadata aggregation. Manias et al. [14] used unsupervised clustering techniques, while de Oliveira et al. [16] conducted an NWDAF study employing machine learning models on a simulated 5G network dataset. Al Atiiq et al. [9] demonstrated adversarial manipulation of mobility predictors, and Jeon and Pack [13] proposed a hierarchical edge-cloud NWDAF for scalable inference.

Commercial platforms such as Nokia AVA and Ericsson NWDAF [11,15] offer service-level visibility and QoS assurance without detailing internal analytics pipelines. The work [17] presents network data analytics in 5G systems and beyond. The 3GPP standard also permits multiple NWDAF instances per PLMN via Analytics IDs for distributed and interface-specific analytics.

However, existing research seldom addresses real-time, explainable risk analytics across multiple 5G Core interfaces. This work proposes a multi-interface NWDAF capable of protocol-aware parsing, threat exposure scoring, and policy actuation through PCF, SMF, and local blacklisting for dynamic, security-oriented analytics.

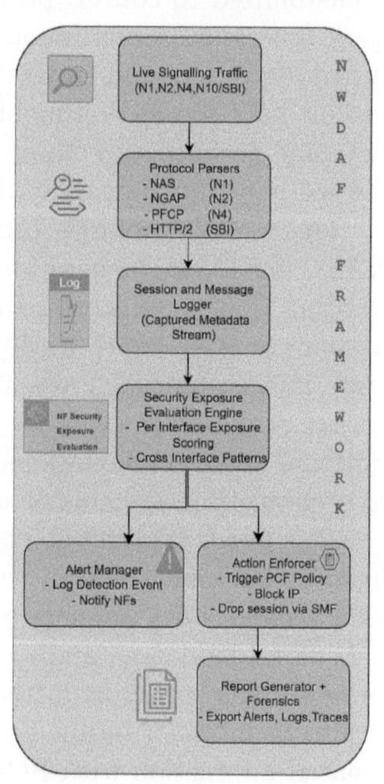

Fig. 1.   Proposed Security-Centric NWDAF

3   Architecture Overview

The proposed NWDAF-based architecture is designed to function as a modular, real-time behavioral analytics system that integrates tightly with 5G Core (5GC) operations. Developed on the Open5GS platform, the system enables deep inspection of protocol interactions across core interfaces such as N1, N2, N4, and SBI. It operates not only as a passive observer of signaling behavior but also as an active controller capable of enforcing mitigation actions based on real-time security exposure evaluation. Figure 1 shows the logical flow of the proposed NWDAF system, which processes live signaling traffic from multiple 5G Core interfaces to detect and respond to network threats in real time. Signaling messages from N1 (NAS), N2 (NGAP), N4 (PFCP), and SBI (HTTP/2) are decoded by dedicated protocol parsers to extract session IDs, message types, and transaction details. Parsed metadata is sent to the Session and Message Logger and then to the Security Exposure Evaluation Engine, which applies per-interface heuristics and correlates behaviors across interfaces. This enables the detection of both volumetric attacks and cross-protocol anomalies. When exposure scores exceed thresholds, the Alert Manager logs detections and the Action Enforcer applies mitigation such as IP blocking or policy updates. The system interacts with PCF, SMF, and NSSF via RESTful APIs, supporting closed-loop security aligned with 3GPP TS 23.288 [2] and TS 29.520 [4].

4   Security Metric Quantification Using NWDAF

This paper introduces a modular security exposure evaluation framework integrated into NWDAF, designed to detect complex and subtle threats across the 5G Core. It combines statistical metrics with semantic analysis of signaling patterns to assign dynamic threat exposure scores to both User Equipments (UEs) and network functions (NFs).

Signaling Overload Detection. An abnormal surge in control-plane signaling, such as repeated NAS Registration or PDU Session Modification messages, can indicate a compromised UE. NWDAF tracks the number of signaling messages per UE in a fixed window. Let $M_{UE}(t)$ denote the message count within interval ΔT. An anomaly is flagged when:

$$M_{UE}(t) > \mu + \alpha \cdot \sigma$$

where μ and σ are the historical mean and standard deviation of the message count, and α is a tunable sensitivity constant. The normalized threat exposure score is computed as

$$TE_{sig}(UE,t) = \frac{M_{UE}(t) - \mu}{\sigma}$$

ensuring adaptive detection relative to baseline variability.

Session State Manipulation. Repeated creation and teardown of PDU sessions can exhaust SMF and UPF resources. NWDAF quantifies such activity by the ratio of failed sessions:

$$TE_{sess}(UE,t) = \frac{N_{fail}(t)}{N_{total}(t)}$$

A decaying memory model emphasizes persistent anomalies:

$$TES_{UE}(t) = \lambda \cdot TES_{UE}(t-1) + (1-\lambda) \cdot TE_{sess}(UE,t)$$

where $\lambda \in (0,1)$ controls how quickly past behavior fades.

Cross-Interface Temporal Correlation. Consistent temporal sequences across interfaces (e.g., N1, N2, N4) are expected. Deviations may indicate signaling manipulation. NWDAF computes the Cross-Interface Temporal Correlation Index (CTCI):

$$CTCI_{UE}(t) = \frac{1}{|P|} \sum_{(i,j) \in P} \mathrm{Corr}(S_i(t), S_j(t + \delta_{ij}))$$

where P is the set of interface pairs, $S_i(t)$ denotes signaling sequences, and δ_{ij} is expected inter-event delay. Low correlation indicates asynchronous or manipulated flows.

Protocol Semantic Deviation. Each UE's message sequence should follow a reference grammar G. NWDAF computes the Protocol Semantic Deviation Score (PSDS):

$$PSDS_{UE}(t) = \frac{|A_{UE}(t) \setminus G|}{|G|}$$

where $A_{UE}(t)$ is the observed sequence. Higher PSDS values indicate skipped steps, invalid transitions, or non-standard combinations.

Behavioral Entropy Drift. Benign UEs typically exhibit stable behavioral profiles. Entropy is computed as:

$$H_{UE}(t) = - \sum_{m \in M} P_m \cdot \log P_m$$

where P_m is the distribution of message type m over ΔT. The Deviation of UE Behavioral Entropy (DUBE) is

$$DUBE_{UE}(t) = |H_{UE}(t) - H_{baseline}|$$

with $H_{baseline}$ representing long-term benign behavior. Rising DUBE reflects increasing unpredictability.

Composite Threat Exposure Aggregation. All modular scores are combined into a unified NF-level metric:

$$TE_{NF}(t) = w_1 \cdot TE_{sig} + w_2 \cdot TES_{UE} + w_3 \cdot CTCI + w_4 \cdot PSDS + w_5 \cdot DUBE$$

Weights w_i are operator-configurable. Exceeding a threshold triggers signed alerts and policy enforcement via SMF or PCF, enabling automated UE isolation, session throttling, or policy override. This transforms NWDAF into an active security enforcement entity aligned with 3GPP's closed-loop automation vision.

4.1 NWDAF-Based Security Exposure Evaluation and Response Framework

The framework operates through three coordinated stages. At the interface level (Algorithm 1), each NF monitors incoming traffic to compute signaling overload, session manipulation, and entropy drift indicators for every UE. These local metrics are sent to the NWDAF core, where centralized analytics (Algorithm 2) calculate protocol deviation and temporal correlation to derive composite threat exposure scores. Finally, the global aggregator (Algorithm 3) evaluates per-NF scores against predefined thresholds and triggers appropriate mitigation through PCF, SMF, or NSSF. All scores, alerts, and actions are logged for auditing and future analysis. This layered design ensures accurate, real-time threat evaluation across distributed network functions.

Algorithm 1: Interface-Level Security Exposure Analysis (Per-NF Monitoring)

Data: Message M received on interface $\mathcal{I}$ at NF f
Data: Historical μ, σ for per-UE message counts
Result: Interface-local threat exposure components: TE_{sig}, TES_{UE}, $DUBE$
Function *Monitor_Interface_Exposure(M)*

> Parse M to get UE identifier u, event type e, and timestamp t;
> Update local count $M_u(t) \leftarrow M_u(t) + 1$;
> // Signaling Overload Detection
> $TE_{sig}(u,t) \leftarrow \frac{M_u(t) - \mu}{\sigma}$;
> **if** $M_u(t) > \mu + \alpha \cdot \sigma$ **then**
>> Flag anomaly for UE u;
>
> // Session State Manipulation (if session event visible)
> $TE_{sess}(u,t) \leftarrow \frac{N_{fail}(t)}{N_{total}(t)}$;
> $TES_{UE}(t) \leftarrow \lambda \cdot TES_{UE}(t-1) + (1 - \lambda) \cdot TE_{sess}(u,t)$;
> // Behavioral Entropy Drift
> $H_u(t) \leftarrow -\sum_{m \in M} P_m \cdot \log P_m$;
> $DUBE_u(t) \leftarrow |H_u(t) - H_{baseline}|$;
> Push $\{TE_{sig}, TES_{UE}, DUBE_u\}$ to NWDAF Core for aggregation;

---

5 Automated and On-Demand Querying of NWDAF Periodic Reports

In addition to real-time threat detection and response, the NWDAF module periodically generates structured security reports summarizing protocol behavior, threat exposure trends, and policy enforcement outcomes across monitored network functions. Using the `Nnwdaf_AnalyticsInfo` service, authorized entities can retrieve current or historical analytics for specific intervals. The reporting

---

Algorithm 2: Centralized Threat Exposure Score Computation at NWDAF

Data: Per-UE and per-interface scores: TE_{sig}, TES_u, $DUBE_u$
Data: Observed message sequences $A_u(t)$, reference grammar G
Data: Signaling event sequences $S_i(t)$ for each interface i
Result: Composite per-NF threat exposure score $TE_{NF}(t)$
Function *Compute_Composite_Exposure()*
    // Protocol Semantic Deviation Score
    $PSDS_u(t) \leftarrow \frac{|A_u(t)\backslash G|}{|G|}$;
    // Cross-Interface Temporal Correlation
    $CTCI_u(t) \leftarrow \frac{1}{|P|} \sum_{(i,j)\in P} Corr(S_i(t), S_j(t + \delta_{ij}))$;
    // Composite Threat Exposure Aggregation
    $TE_{NF}(t) \leftarrow w_1 \cdot TE_{sig} + w_2 \cdot TES_{UE} + w_3 \cdot CTCI_u + w_4 \cdot PSDS_u + w_5 \cdot DUBE_u$;
    Push TE_{NF} to NWDAF Global Aggregator;

Algorithm 3: NWDAF Global Aggregator and Response

Data: Composite Scores $TE_{NF}(t)$ from all NFs, Predefined Threshold (θ)
Result: Global exposure scores and mitigation triggers
Function *Aggregate_Global_Exposure()*
    foreach *NF f* **do**
        Retrieve $TE_{NF}(t)$ for f;
        if $TE_{NF}(t) \geq \theta$ **then**
            Generate alert for PCF/SMF/NSSF;
            Execute policy: flow throttle, session drop, slice shift;
        Log $TE_{NF}(t)$ in NWDAF exposure store for auditing;

---

engine runs at configurable intervals (typically 5–10 min), aggregating telemetry from N1, N2, N4, and SBI interfaces, including message volumes, transaction types, signaling frequencies, session success/failure ratios, and detected anomalies. For each NF, it computes time-series threat exposure scores, compares them with baselines, and includes cumulative scores, normalized deviations, top contributing UEs, and actions taken (e.g., throttling, blacklisting, access control). Reports are stored locally and mirrored to MongoDB for archival and time-based queries, with APIs supporting retrieval of the latest or sliding-window entries.

6   Policy Enforcement Mechanism

Policy enforcement in the 5GC is coordinated between NWDAF, PCF, SMF, and AMF via 3GPP service-based interfaces and standardized control-plane protocols. Upon threat detection, NWDAF issues a threat exposure alert to the PCF through `Nnwdaf_AnalyticsInfo`, prompting the PCF to generate policy rules that adjust session and access parameters in real time.

For signaling control, the PCF updates QoS Flow Descriptors and filtering rules, provisioning them to the SMF via `Nsmf_PDUSession_UpdateSMContext`. In session abuse cases, the SMF is instructed to reject new PDU session requests and apply exponential back-off timers. The PCF may also instruct the AMF to block registrations and reject authentication for blacklisted sources through `Namf_Communication_N1N2MessageTransfer` or equivalent.

A sample SMF instruction for signaling rate limitation is shown below:

```
{
  "smContextId": "SMC-12345",
  "policyRules": [
    {
      "ruleId": "SIG-THROTTLE-01",
      "qosFlowDescriptor": {
        "maxMsgRate": "10 messages/second",
        "burstTolerance": 5
      },
      "filteringRule": "DROP signaling_type=NAS_REG if rate > 10/s"
    }
  ]
}
```

This directs the SMF to restrict NAS Registration message rates from the specified source to 10 per second, discarding excess beyond the burst tolerance.

All mitigations operate in a closed-loop cycle: threat detection, alert generation, policy enforcement, and feedback monitoring. Actions are rolled back automatically when exposure normalizes. Every enforcement event is logged with timestamp, triggering protocol event, threat exposure score, and outcome; forensic snapshots of signaling and state transitions are retained for analysis and model training. This framework achieves targeted mitigation with minimal disruption to legitimate traffic while remaining compliant with 3GPP 5GC specifications.

7   Testbed Deployment and Evaluation

The proposed NWDAF framework was deployed on a 5G SA testbed using Open5GS (Ubuntu 22.04) with UERANSIM emulating gNB and UE. Target NFs (AMF, SMF, PCF) were extended with Python SBI clients to export analytics over HTTP/2 for real-time monitoring.[1]

Evaluation involved monitoring N1, N2, N4, and SBI interfaces under simulated PFCP floods, NAS abuse, and malformed SBI transactions. Metrics included threat exposure score progression, detection latency, interface contributions, and baseline comparison with a 3GPP-compliant NWDAF. Alerts were delivered via REST callbacks, and mitigation was emulated through SMF/PCF iptables-based enforcement.

---

[1] https://github.com/Lakshmirnr/NWDAF.git.

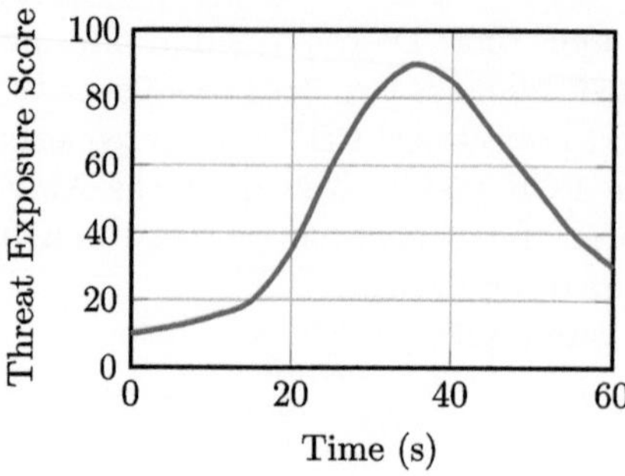

Fig. 2. Threat exposure score progression during PFCP flood.

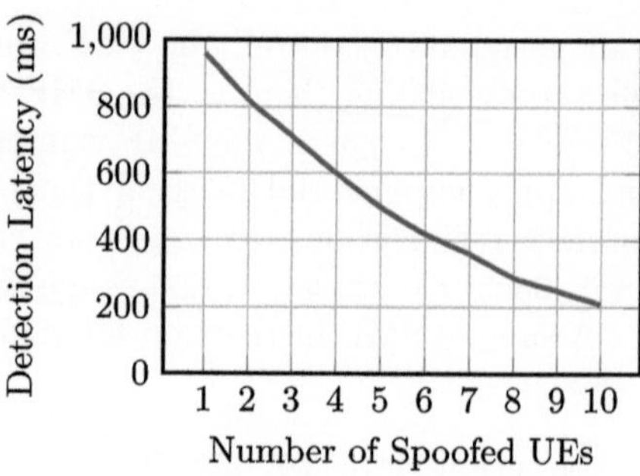

Fig. 3. Detection latency versus spoofed UE count.

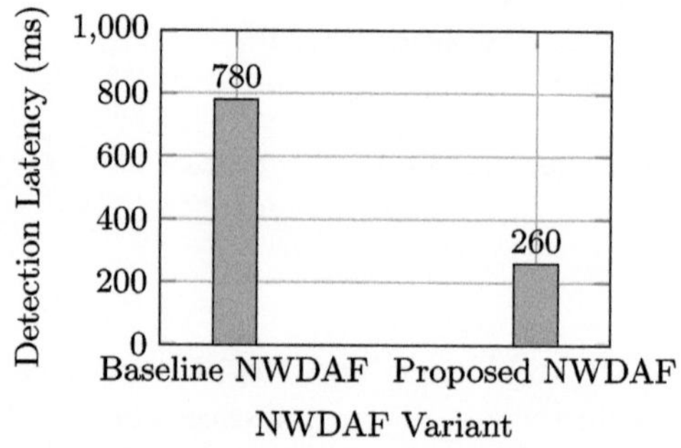

Fig. 4. Detection latency comparison: 3GPP-compliant vs proposed NWDAF.

Figure 2 shows the increase in threat exposure score as PFCP anomalies accumulate, stabilizing after mitigation. Figure 3 shows detection latency decreasing with more spoofed UEs, as the algorithm responds faster to rising anomaly volumes. Figure 4 compares average detection latency between a standard 3GPP NWDAF and our implementation, demonstrating consistently lower latency in the proposed design due to real-time inspection.

8   Conclusion and Future Work

This paper presented a practical and extensible NWDAF framework capable of real-time monitoring and security exposure evaluation across multiple 5G Core interfaces. By integrating protocol-specific parsers for NGAP, NAS, PFCP and SBI, the system could extract meaningful signaling behavior and compute dynamic threat exposure scores. These scores were forwarded to relevant network functions for timely action. Thus, the framework enables real-time security exposure evaluation to be seamlessly integrated into the 5G Core.

For future work, we aim to improve the granularity of behavior modeling through long-term temporal analysis and event sequence profiling. Expanding the set of analytics consumers and supporting programmable mitigation actions based on detected security exposures are also planned. Further alignment with evolving 3GPP NWDAF specifications will enhance compatibility, and we plan to evaluate the system in larger, federated 5G deployments for scalability validation.

Acknowledgement. This research was supported by grants received from Ministry of Electronics and Information Technology, Govt. of India.

References

1. Vision, E.N.I.: Improved network experience using experiential networked intelligence. White Paper, ETSI (2021)
2. 3GPP TS 23.288: Architecture enhancements for 5G system (5GS) to support network data analytics services. Tech. rep., 3rd Generation Partnership Project (3GPP) (2022)
3. 3GPP TS 23.501: System architecture for the 5G system (5GS). Tech. rep., 3rd Generation Partnership Project (3GPP) (2022)
4. 3GPP TS 29.520: 5G; 5G System; Network data analytics services; stage 3. Tech. rep., 3rd Generation Partnership Project (3GPP) (2022)
5. Security, M.E.C.: Status of standards support and future evolutions. White Paper, ETSI (2022)
6. Unlocking digital transformation with autonomous networks. White Paper, ETSI (2023)
7. Amdocs: Why NWDAF will be central to 5G success. White Paper (2022)
8. Ardestani, F.S., Saha, N., Limam, N., Boutaba, R.: Towards NWDAF-enabled analytics and closed-loop automation in 5G networks. arXiv preprint arXiv:2505.06789 (2025)
9. Atiiq, S.A., Yuan, Y., Gehrmann, C., Sternby, J., Barriga, L.: Attacks against mobility prediction in 5G networks. arXiv preprint arXiv:2402.19319 (2024)
10. Chouman, A., Manias, D.M., Shami, A.: Towards supporting intelligence in 5G/6G core networks: NWDAF implementation and initial analysis (2022). https://doi.org/10.1109/IWCMC55113.2022.9824403
11. Ericsson: NWDAF in 5G core: a new era of network intelligence. https://www.ericsson.com/en/core-network/5g-core/network-data-analytics-function
12. Ericsson: NWDAF: the blessing 5G core needs to reach a data-driven network. https://www.ericsson.com/en/blog/2021/10/nwdaf-the-blessing-5g-core-needs-to-reach-a-data-driven-network
13. Jeon, Y., Pack, S.: Hierarchical network data analytics framework for B5G network automation: design and implementation. arXiv preprint arXiv:2309.16269 (2023)
14. Manias, D.M., Chouman, A., Shami, A.: An NWDAF approach to 5G core network signaling traffic: analysis and characterization, pp. 6001–6006 (2022). https://doi.org/10.1109/GLOBECOM48099.2022.10000989
15. Nokia: Nokia AVA NWDAF: real-time analytics for 5G (2022)
16. de Oliveira, L.A., Silva, E.F., Dantas, M.A.R.: A NWDAF study employing machine learning models on a simulated 5G network dataset (2024). https://doi.org/10.1109/ISCC61673.2024.10733717
17. Romero, M.L., Suyama, R.: Towards network data analytics in 5G systems and beyond. arXiv preprint arXiv:2506.04860 (2025)

Privacy

SoK: Evaluation of Methods for Privacy Preserving Edge Video Analytics

Arun Joseph[(✉)] and Vinod Ganapathy

Indian Institute of Science, Bangalore, India
{arunj,vg}@iisc.ac.in

Abstract. Collaborative edge data analytics is gaining prominence as vast amounts of data are increasingly generated at the network edge by smartphones, sensors, and smart cameras. In this work, we focus on the challenge of privacy-preserving video analytics on edge devices. Video data presents unique difficulties compared to other data types, primarily due to its large size and the nature of video analysis tasks. We evaluate and compare two leading techniques for enabling secure collaborative video analytics in distributed edge environments: Secure Multiparty Computation (MPC) and Trusted Execution Environments (TEE). To assess their effectiveness, we implement five real-world case studies, including object re-identification, scene similarity detection, vehicle counting, and machine learningbased video fusion tasks. Additionally, we benchmark fundamental image processing operations under various MPC configurations to identify the most efficient MPC protocols for video workloads. Our results show that while TEE offer significant performance benefits, especially for machine learning intensive tasks, MPC remains a practical alternative in scenarios without trusted hardware, particularly when using optimized secret sharing based 3-party protocols. We provide a comprehensive analysis of performance, security, and implementation complexity for both approaches.

Keywords: Secure Edge computing · Joint video analytics · Secure multiparty computations · Trusted execution environments

1 Introduction

The rise of IoT devices, smartphones, smart cameras, and edge sensors has led to a surge in data generation at the network edge [50,54]. This data often includes sensitive information like health records, financial transactions, and private videos, raising significant privacy concerns. Privacy-preserving collaborative analytics at the edge addresses these concerns by keeping data local, thereby enhancing privacy, scalability, and cost-effectiveness [1,52]. Edge-based data analytics enables real-world applications such as analyzing traffic or utility data from multiple cameras without exposing sensitive footage [57], supporting secure medical diagnoses [16], or sharing insights across factories while protecting proprietary data [66]. Several studies have explored privacy-preserving machine learning for edge collaboration [42,43,46,58], and systems like [23,45] facilitate secure edge analytics. PERQS [27] further supports privacy-preserving queries on distributed CCTV video streams using edge-based processing.

N. Hubballi et al. (Eds.): ICISS 2025, LNCS 16380, pp. 389–410, 2026.
https://doi.org/10.1007/978-3-032-13714-2_24

In this work, we address the problem of privacy-preserving video analytics on edge devices. Video data poses unique challenges compared to other data types, primarily due to (a) its large size, which makes communication and computation significantly more resource intensive, and (b) the nature of video analytics tasks, which are often fuzzy and statistical rather than discrete and deterministic. Tasks such as object detection or boundary identification typically rely on complex neural network models rather than rule-based algorithms, making secure processing more difficult. We evaluate and compare two prominent approaches for enabling secure collaborative video analytics at the edge: Secure Multiparty Computation (MPC) [12,73] and hardware-based Trusted Execution Environments (TEE) [44,59].

MPC is a cryptographic approach that enables multiple parties to collaboratively compute a function over their inputs while keeping those inputs private. This method is entirely software-driven and does not require specialized hardware, making it versatile and applicable across diverse edge devices. Several previous works have used MPC for privacy-preserving data analytics, demonstrating its ability to securely process sensitive data without exposing raw inputs. On the other hand, TEE relies on secure hardware components to create isolated environments where computations can be performed securely, even if the host system is compromised. TEE has challenges, including hardware dependency, potential vulnerabilities due to side-channel attacks, and scalability limitations in highly distributed edge systems.

Both approaches are viable solutions for enabling secure and private computation in distributed environments. Each method has distinct strengths and limitations regarding performance, scalability, deployment complexity, and security guarantees. For example, MPC excels in settings with high distrust among parties but may struggle in low-bandwidth environments. Conversely, TEE provides high computational efficiency but requires specialized hardware and may face adoption challenges due to hardware costs or vendor lock-in. In addition, MPC protocols offer a variety of design choices, including in-house vs. outsourced computation models, arithmetic vs. boolean, optimizations for 2 or 3-party settings, and different adversary models(active/passive). With recent advances and optimizations, their relative advantages, disadvantages, and suitability for privacy-preserving edge data analytics remain unclear. The primary contribution of this paper is to evaluate the relative merits of these two methods by analyzing their practical implementations and real-world performance of joint video analytics in edge computing environments. We will systematically assess the pros and cons of MPC and TEE across various metrics. The criteria on which we wish to evaluate the methods are:

- What are the computational and communication overhead? Performance evaluations to find which method is suitable for each application.
- What are the security implications of these methods? Strengths and vulnerabilities in protecting private data.
- What are the additional requirements to implement these solutions? Additional hardware or software required.
- How much effort is required to implement the solution? Ease of integration and deployment in edge devices.

By providing in-depth comparison and evaluation, we aim to clarify the trade-offs between MPC and TEE for privacy-preserving edge analytics and offer insights into which approach is better suited for different applications or constraints. This study will contribute to the advancement of secure edge analytics and help guide future developments in privacy-preserving technologies.

2   Background

Privacy-preserving data analytics is crucial as the amount of sensitive data generated by edge systems grows. This section introduces MPC and TEE and their design choices.

2.1   Secure Multiparty Computation (MPC)

Secure Multiparty Computation (MPC) [12, 17, 28, 73] is a cryptographic protocol that enables multiple parties to collaboratively compute a function over their private inputs while ensuring that those inputs remain confidential. No information about the inputs is disclosed beyond what can be inferred from the final output of the computation. Unlike other privacy-preserving approaches, MPC operates without relying on a central trusted authority. Instead, the computation is distributed among the participating parties, and the protocols are designed to be resilient even in the presence of malicious actors who may attempt to disrupt the process or extract private information.

MPC Protocols vary based on security models, defending against semi-honest and malicious adversaries. Private inputs can be securely shared and computed using secret sharing and garbled circuits. Computation can be performed in-house or outsourced, with optimizations tailored for 2-party, or 3-party, or multi-party setups. While many variations have been explored and improved over the years, it remains unclear which approach best suits privacy-preserving video analytics. Some of the key ideas used in the design of a MPC protocol are:

① **Adversary Type (Active/Passive):** The Semi-honest(Passive) [18,28] setting assumes that all participants follow the protocol but may attempt to infer private information from the data they receive. Provides weaker security guarantees but, in general is more efficient in terms of computation and communication overhead. In contrast, malicious(Active) [28,39] setting assumes that participants may deviate from the protocol, alter computations, or attempt to manipulate results to gain unauthorized information. It is more secure but has higher computational and communication overhead because of the additional security layers to protect against the malicious adversary.

② **Computation Domain (Arithmetic/Boolean):** Arithmetic MPC protocols (operating modulo a prime or power of two) [38] is more efficient for mathematical computations and real-world numerical applications. Numbers are split among participants and computed securely. Boolean/Binary MPC protocols are better suited for logic-based operations but incurs higher communication overhead. Often implemented using garbled circuits and Oblivious Transfer (OT) [18].

③ **Computation Choice (Secret Sharing/Garbled Circuits):** In Secret Sharing [11] techniques, inputs are divided into "shares" distributed among the participants. Each share is meaningless but can reconstruct the input when combined with other shares.

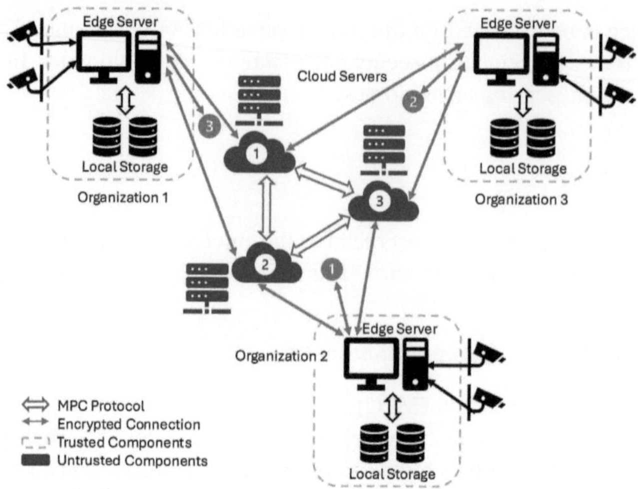

Fig. 1. MPC outsourced model where secret shares of input is encrypted and send to the cloud servers. Then the servers will perform an MPC computation to evaluate the function on the secret input. This example is of a 3-party outsourced computation includes 3 independent servers.

This ensures that no single party has access to the entire input. While Garbled Circuits [6,73] represent a function as a circuit with encrypted values assigned to inputs and intermediate computations, ensuring no private data is exposed in the computation.

④ **Number of Parties (2-party/3-party/multi-party) :** Generally, 2-party setting [18] requires stronger cryptographic techniques since both parties must ensure privacy without a third-party mediator. Contrary 3-party setup [35] can leverage an honest majority for efficiency and security improvements. In the case of 4 or more parties typically, MPC protocols are inefficient as number of parties increases [17,18].

⑤ **In-house/Outsourced:** In in-house MPC [35] all participating parties execute the MPC protocol on their infrastructure without relying on external computing resources. Which is limited by the available hardware and network capacity of participating entities. In outsourced MPC model [15] major part of the computation is securely offloaded to external cloud servers. It is best suited for scenarios where participants have limited computational power, such as edge devices. Figure 1 illustrates three server outsourced MPC execution model.

MPC protocols integrate well with distributed systems and edge computing, enabling secure and privacy-preserving computations in various applications [15,35, 38]. However, MPC faces several challenges; need for continuous communication between parties increases bandwidth usage and computational overhead, especially in large-scale distributed systems. Additionally, reliance on iterative cryptographic operations can introduce latency, making it slower than other privacy-preserving methods. Optimizations and hybrid solutions can help overcome these limitations and broaden its adoption.

2.2   Trusted Execution Environment (TEE)

A Trusted Execution Environment (TEE) [44] is a secure enclave within a processor designed to protect sensitive data and code, ensuring their confidentiality and integrity. TEE provides an isolated execution environment where trusted applications can operate securely, independent of the operating system and any potentially malicious software on the device. This hardware-enforced isolation protects sensitive computations and data from unauthorized access or tampering, even if the central system or OS is compromised. TEE hardware can be available locally or on a remote server. Figure 2 shows edge servers utilizing a cloud-based secure enclave to perform joint computations. Some of the commonly available TEE implementations are as follows:

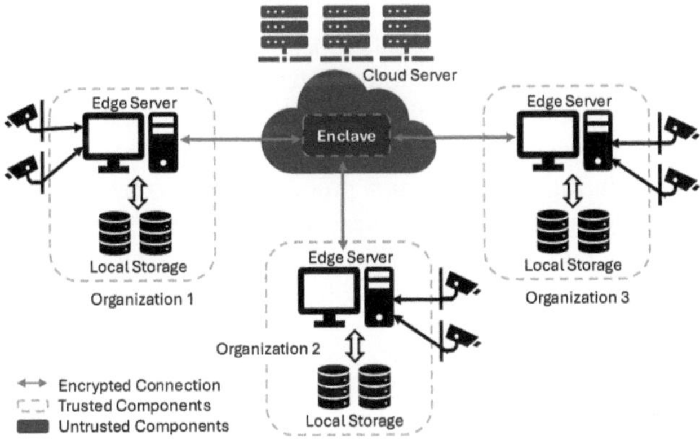

Fig. 2. Three organizations perform collaborative data analytics using a trusted execution environment (TEE) available in a cloud server.

- Intel Software Guard Extensions (SGX) [10]: A hardware feature that provides secure enclaves for applications, enabling sensitive computations in an isolated memory region inaccessible to other processes or the OS.
- AMD Secure Encrypted Virtualization (SEV) [56]: A virtualization-based TEE solution that encrypts virtual machine memory to protect data from unauthorized access by hypervisors or other virtual machines.
- AWS Nitro [2,4]: A virtualization-based TEE built on top of the AWS Nitro System. Nitro enclaves are run isolated from the host EC2 instance, and external networking, storage, or interactive access is not allowed.
- ARM TrustZone [3]: A system-wide approach that creates secure and normal worlds within a processor, allowing sensitive operations to run in an isolated environment.

Intel SGX creates secure enclaves for isolating small, sensitive workloads with strong security guarantees but limited memory and no system call support, making development complex. AWS Nitro Enclaves, in contrast, isolate larger workloads on EC2 instances, support integrated attestation and secure communication, and are easier to use in cloud environments. TEE use hardware-enforced isolation to protect sensitive computations from software based attacks, offering strong security for edge and cloud applications. However, they require specialized hardware, are hard to scale across distributed systems, and remain vulnerable to side-channel attacks. Their rigid design and development complexity further limit flexibility and broader adoption.

2.3   Related Work

MPC Data Analytics: Multiparty Computation offers a way to perform analytics without compromising data privacy. [45] demonstrated how MPC can be used for secure statistical analysis, such as regression analysis, by distributing the computation among multiple parties to ensure data privacy. [58] introduced a framework for privacy preserving deep learning using MPC, which allows multiple parties to collaboratively train a neural network without revealing their datasets. [43] proposed SecureML, a system that enables privacy-preserving machine learning inference using MPC. Their work demonstrates that performing secure prediction with minimal overhead is feasible. [62] presented a federated learning approach that leverages MPC to ensure the confidentiality of local model updates during the aggregation process. [42] is a mixed protocol framework designed to enable efficient and privacy-preserving machine learning, combining arithmetic and Boolean secret sharing techniques. [12] introduced techniques to reduce the communication complexity of MPC protocols, making them more practical for large-scale applications.

TEE Data Analytics: Trusted Execution Environments provide a secure area within a processor that ensures the confidentiality and integrity of data and code. [10] explored the use of Intel SGX for secure data aggregation, enabling analytics on encrypted data without exposing raw data to the aggregator. [46] demonstrated using TEE to perform privacy-preserving machine learning, allowing models to be trained on sensitive data without compromising privacy. [23] presented techniques for processing encrypted video data within TEE without exposing the content to the host system.

Video Analysis: Several deep learning architectures have been developed for object detection, video classification, and action recognition in videos. YOLOv3 [49] uses a robust backbone network based on Darknet-53 for real-time object detection, while Faster R-CNN [51] significantly improves the speed of object detection. 3D Convolutional Networks (3D CNNs) [61] process video frames as a 3D stacked frame volume, including temporal information for video analysis. Non-local Neural Networks [70] capture long-range dependencies in images and videos. Visor [47] provides confidentiality for both the user's video stream and the machine learning models in the event of a compromised cloud platform. Vigil [78] is a real-time distributed wireless surveillance system that leverages edge computing capabilities. Chameleon [26] is a controller that dynamically selects optimal configurations for existing neural network-based video analytics pipelines. EdgeEye [40] is an edge computing framework tailored explicitly for real-time intelligent video analytics applications. Reducto [34] is a system that adaptively adjusts filtering decisions based on time-varying correlations in the video data. CrossRoI [20] utilizes the inherent physical correlations of cross-camera viewing fields to enhance video analytics performance. Spatula [25] enables scalable cross-camera analytics by leveraging edge compute boxes. Lastly, PERQS [27] addresses the challenges of managing and querying CCTV footage in a contributory network.

No extensive studies have compared MPC and TEE specifically for shared video analytics workloads. Although both MPC and TEE offer robust methods for ensuring data privacy and security, their comparative effectiveness and performance in video analytics remain underexplored.

3 Overview and Threat Model

Collaborative video analysis is becoming increasingly important with the growing use of CCTV cameras. However, sharing data between different parties like government agencies and private organizations raises serious privacy concerns. Video files are large, making secure sharing and joint processing more demanding than other types of data. On top of that, the complex machine learning models needed for video analysis make it harder to build systems that are both private and scalable. While prior work such as PERQS [27], Privid [7], RTFace [68], and VISOR [47] has explored secure video analysis, these systems often focus on local or isolated data processing. Our work builds upon PERQS [27], which uses local machine learning inference on CCTV streams to avoid raw video sharing but lacks support for joint and cross-organizational video analytics. To bridge this gap, we explore using MPC and TEE as foundational technologies for enabling privacy-preserving collaborative video analytics, offering strong security guarantees.

Our key contribution is identifying the most suitable implementation strategies for both approaches. In the case of MPC, a wide array of protocol variants exists. While prior research has explored general MPC performance characteristics, their suitability for collaborative video analytics tasks, particularly at the edge, remains underexplored. This work systematically examines the MPC design space to identify the most practical and efficient protocols for such workloads. In contrast, TEE-based approaches follow a more uniform design paradigm, where secure enclaves-whether through AMD-SEV, Intel-SGX, AWS-Nitro, or ARM TrustZone-process sensitive data in a hardware-isolated environment, ensuring confidentiality and integrity. Although conceptually similar, these implementations differ in their architectural design, affecting performance, integration complexity, and resilience to side-channel threats. To enable a robust evaluation, we design five real-world case studies that capture diverse challenges in joint video analytics, allowing us to analyze both MPC and TEE solutions regarding performance, security guarantees, and implementation complexity.

3.1 Case Studies

We selected five case studies to capture a diverse range of challenges in joint video analytics, each representing distinct computational requirements and privacy constraints. The primary goal is to enable collaborative analytics without exposing raw video feeds, which often contain sensitive information. Table 1 summarizes the critical computations, implementations, and available datasets. Critical computations are offloaded to either the MPC or TEE frameworks, while other application parts are executed locally on edge devices. To ensure a fair evaluation, we maintain consistent implementation across both approaches. More details on each case study are discussed below.

Table 1. Details of the case studies include their critical computations, which are to be evaluated under privacy-preserving conditions, along with the available implementations and datasets. We use CityFlowV2 [14] for our analysis.

Case Study	Description	Critical Computation	Implementations	Datasets
① Vehicle Re-Identification	identifying the same vehicle in another video camera.	Cosine Similarity Vector	DyeNet [33], PROVID [41], Siam R-CNN [65]	DAVIS dataset [48]
② Scene Similarity	Detect weather two views are the same scene, or same events.	Euclidean Distance Measure	Factor Analy-sis [71], PDH Similarity [22],	Video Dataset [71]
③ Joint Recognition	Recognise a car which is partially visible in two video streams.	Video Stitching and Recognition	Object Centered Stitching [21]	Stitching Dataset [77]
④ Scene 3D Reconstruction	Merge different views from multiple cameras into a 3D scene and run query on it.	Scene 3D Reconstruction and query	EVolT [67], MR Video Fusion [80], DyNeRF [32]	Plenoptic Datasets [32], 3D Shape-nets [72]
⑤ Count the Vehicles	From the overlapping video feeds find the number of vehicles in a certain interval.	Multi-video Object Counting	Argus [74], Rt3c [69]	CityFlowV2 [14], Cro HD dataset [60]

① Vehicle Re-identification (Re-ID) [33,41,65,76]: Vehicle re-identification aims to recognize the same vehicle across multiple cameras in a network, playing a vital role in traffic management, law enforcement, and stolen vehicle recovery. Previous approaches have used various features, such as vehicle color, make, model, and license plate patterns, for matching. We use a feature extractor that utilizes deep learning models to generate feature vectors locally at the edge devices. These feature vectors are then compared against other video feeds to identify matches. We employ the Cosine Similarity function to measure the similarity between feature vectors. Since vehicle features contain sensitive information, the joint execution of cosine similarity must be conducted securely using MPC or TEE to preserve privacy.

② Scene Similarity Detection [79]: Scene similarity detection is crucial in video analytics to determine whether different cameras capture the same or similar environments. Since we do not trust any participants unquestioningly, the scene similarity check on overlapping scenes can reach a collective root of trust. Prior works [22,71] explored various feature extraction methods for scene comparison. In our approach, we use a video summarizer to extract visual features as a vector, and then we use Euclidean distance to measure the distance between two scenes. We use the distance measure to compare and find the most similar past scenario for critical event detection. Scene features contain sensitive information and cannot be shared directly, so distance computation must be performed in a privacy-preserving manner.

③ Joint Object Recognition [49]: This case study focuses on recognizing objects, such as cars, bicycles, or trucks, which are spread across multiple cameras. Collaborative object recognition can enhance accuracy by combining video feeds from different sources securely [21]. For example, two cameras might capture complementary views of an object, improving performance. The videos are combined, and then object recognition is on top of the combined view. Here, the video stitching and recognition parts are the critical components that must be executed securely to protect video privacy.

④ Scene 3D Reconstruction [32,55,67,80]: Scene reconstruction involves piecing together video data from multiple cameras to create a comprehensive 3D view of a specific area or event. For instance, in the case of a traffic accident, video data from different angles can be collaboratively analyzed to reconstruct the sequence of events. For the experiment, we used a static angle, rule-based 3D reconstruction, and then performed queries on this reconstructed 3D scene. Since the input videos are private, 3D reconstruction and querying must be done securely.

⑤ Counting the Total Number of Vehicles [69,74]: Vehicle counting is crucial in traffic management, urban planning, and intelligent transportation systems. Traditional methods rely on individual cameras counting vehicles independently, which may lead to duplicate counts when the exact vehicle appears in multiple camera feeds. In this case study, we detect and count vehicles locally at each camera and securely remove duplicates by comparing vehicle features from different camera feeds. Feature extraction is performed on each detected vehicle to generate a feature vector representing its characteristics. To eliminate duplicate counts, we employ Cosine Similarity to compare feature vectors across multiple camera detections. We use MPC or TEE to ensure that feature comparisons and duplicate removals are performed without exposing sensitive data, enabling privacy-preserving collaborative vehicle counting.

3.2   Threat Model

- **MPC Threat Model:** For evaluating MPC defines the following threat models: **Semi-Honest Model:** Where participants adhere to the protocol specifications but may attempt to learn additional information from received messages or intermediate computations. The system assumes that these participants do not alter their behavior maliciously. **Malicious Model:** Where participants may deviate from the protocol, intentionally sending incorrect messages or manipulating computations to compromise the integrity or confidentiality of the data. In both models, there can be an honest or dishonest majority. In an honest majority setting, the majority of participants are assumed to behave honestly during any protocol execution. In the context of our work, remote servers, if involved, are treated as semi-honest, meaning they follow the protocol but may try to infer private inputs.

- **TEE Threat Model** To evaluate TEE, we assume that secure hardware provided by third-party servers (either owned by participants or external entities) is considered trustworthy and free of back-doors or vulnerabilities. Participants encrypt their private inputs before sending them to the TEE-protected enclaves for processing. Computations are securely performed within the enclave; only the final results are shared with the participants. Potential attacks, such as side-channel attacks on TEE, network eavesdropping, or breaches of secure enclaves, are treated as out of scope.

Both threat models assume that communication channels are secure and that cryptographic measures are in place to protect data transmission. Physical access to devices or servers hosting the computation is assumed to be restricted. Any compromise of the underlying hardware or cryptographic primitives is beyond the scope of this evaluation.

4   Experiment Setup

This section outlines the experimental setup and benchmark details for evaluating privacy preserving video analytics methods. We aim to identify the most suitable options for secure video analytics at edge devices by benchmarking video processing workloads. The MPC protocols were evaluated across different configurations.

Table 2. MPC protocols evaluated in this project. We use the MP-SPDZ [29] implementation.

Protocol	GC/SS	Adversary Type	Honest Majority	Domain	#	Details
yao [73,75]	GC	Semi-honest	No	Binary	2	half-gate garbling
real-bmr [31]	GC	Malicious	No	Binary	2+	MASCOT protocol using BMR
semi-bmr [5]	GC	Semi-honest	No	Binary	2+	semi-honest version of real-bmr
rep-bmr [5,31]	GC	Semi-honest	Yes	Binary	3	replicated sharing using BMR
semi2k [36]	SS	Semi-honest	No	Mod 2^k	2	OT-based Beaver triples
semi-bin [36]	SS	Semi-honest	No	Binary	2	bit-wise multiplication triples
semi [36]	SS	Semi-honest	No	Mod Prime	2	OT-based prime Beaver triples
mama [30]	SS	Malicious	No	Mod Prime	2	MASCOT with several MACs
mascot [30]	SS	Malicious	No	Mod Prime	2	OT correlation checks & MACs
spdz2k [13]	SS	Malicious	No	Mod 2^k	2	more efficient than MASCOT
ring [37]	SS	Semi-honest	Yes	Mod 2^k	3	replicated ring shares
rep-field [37]	SS	Semi-honest	Yes	Mod Prime	3	replicated field shares
atlas [19]	SS	Semi-honest	Yes	Mod Prime	3+	ATLAS sharing
shamir [9,11]	SS	Semi-honest	Yes	Mod Prime	3+	Shamir secret sharing
rep4-ring [37]	SS	Semi-honest	Yes	Mod 2^k	4	replicated sharing

\# - Number of participants supported, SS - Secret Sharing, GC - Garbled Circuit

Setup for MPC: Secure Multiparty Computation (MPC) configurations are evaluated on several key aspects. Depending on the security model, MPC can operate under a semi-honest or malicious setting. The number of participants also influences configuration choices, ranging from 2-party MPC, where two entities interact, to multiparty setups, such as 3-party MPC, which leverage an honest majority for efficiency. The details of the protocols we considered in our evaluations are in Table 2. The configuration options we considered in our evaluations are as follows:

① **Adversary Type (Active/Passive):** MPC protocols are available against semi-honest adversaries or malicious adversaries. Similarly, protocols that assume an honest majority leverage optimizations to enhance performance. To evaluate these claims, we explored different protocols that provide security against semi-honest and malicious adversaries, considering scenarios where an honest majority is present or not.

② **Computation Domain (Arithmetic/Boolean):** Arithmetic-based MPC protocols are generally more efficient for integer addition and multiplication tasks. In contrast, Boolean circuits can be better when computations involve logical operations. Given that our workloads consist of numerous integer and matrix operations, we conducted evaluations using image processing macro benchmarks to compare the performance of arithmetic-based and Boolean-based protocols.

③ **Computation Choice (Secret Sharing/Garbled Circuit):** Secret-sharing based computations require multiple rounds of communication, with complexity increasing depending on the operation. In contrast, garbled circuits execute computations in a single round but incur significantly higher costs for arithmetic operations due to their reliance on binary representation. Our evaluations aim to determine whether garbled circuits or secret sharing is superior to our workloads.

④ **Number of Parties:** We evaluate the performance of the 2-party, 3-party, and 4-party protocols. Communication complexity generally increases as the number of participants increases. However, honest majority assumptions cannot be applied in a 2-party setting, while 3-party and higher setups can exploit these assumptions for performance optimizations. Since it remains unclear which n-party protocols will perform best for image processing workloads, we conduct extensive evaluations to determine the most suitable configuration.

⑤ **In-house/Outsourced model:** In an in-house MPC model computations take place entirely within local edge devices. Alternatively, an outsourced MPC model delegates computations to external servers. Our evaluation considers the trade-offs between these two approaches in the context of video analytics.

Setup for TEE: We consider a cloud-based TEE architecture, as illustrated in Fig. 2. In this setup, edge participants offload their computations to a secure enclave hosted on a remote server. Before initiating any computation, participating organizations verify the authenticity and integrity of the TEE hardware through remote attestation [10]. Once verified, they establish a secure, end-to-end encrypted connection directly to the enclave, ensuring that private data inputs are transmitted securely. This design prevents a compromised host operating system from accessing or extracting sensitive data. After collecting all video or feature inputs from the involved parties, the enclave executes the joint computation. Finally, the results are securely transmitted to the edge participants while maintaining data confidentiality.

Benchmarks: To find out the most suitable MPC protocol, we use five macro benchmarks for image processing [53]. These benchmarks-thresholding, histogram, sobel edge detection, convolution, and thinning-represent fundamental operations commonly used in image and video processing. Each benchmark captures a distinct aspect of image analysis, such as feature extraction, edge detection, and transformation, making them well suited to assess the computational and communication overhead of different MPC protocols. We aim to identify the most reliable and efficient MPC protocol for edge devices by analyzing their performance.

Then for the remaining part of the TEE vs. MPC experiments, we focus on privacy-sensitive video analytics case studies, as explained in Table 1. We utilize the PERQS [27] framework to evaluate case studies, extending its query language to support joint video analytics. When a joint analysis query is executed, our MPC or TEE implementation is used to process the query securely. To compare the relative performance of both approaches across all five case studies, we measure execution time and global communication overhead for key computations involving private data. Beyond performance metrics, we also evaluate the security guarantees that each method provides and their practical implications. Additionally, we analyze the implementation complexity required to integrate MPC and TEE protocols into these applications securely.

5   Evaluation

This section outlines the implementation setup and the experimental evaluation. We begin by benchmarking various MPC protocols with image processing workloads. Followed by evaluating five case studies.

Implementation Details: We used the MP-SPDZ [29] framework for the implementation of MPC protocols, and Gramine-SGX [63,64] and Linux-SGX [24] for Intel-SGX based TEE. All experiments were carried out on an Intel(R) Core(TM) i7-7700 CPU (3.60GHz) with four cores and two threads per core (8 hyper-threads), an 8192KB cache, and 32GB of RAM. Fedora 40 (Linux 6.13) was used for the MPC experiments, while Ubuntu 20.04 LTS (Linux 5.8) was used for the Gramine-SGX/Linux-SGX implementation. We also have an ARM-based AWS-Nitro-enabled c6g.large Linux instance with AWS-Amazon 2023 (Linux 6.1) for Nitro-based TEE evaluation.

For the evaluation of MPC protocols, we used five image processing macro operations [53]: thresholding, histogram, Sobel edge detection, convolution, and thinning, along with a simple matrix multiplication workload. These benchmarks represent core computational tasks commonly used in image and video processing. For the experimental validation of our five case studies, we used the AICITY21 benchmark dataset (CityFlowV2) [8,14], which features real-world traffic surveillance data collected from 46 cameras. The dataset contains 880 annotated vehicles in six different scenarios, with 215.03 min of video footage. We focused on eight junctions where multiple cameras provide overlapping recordings, enabling comprehensive multi-camera analysis.

Choosing the Best MPC Protocol: We utilized six workloads for our evaluation, matrix operations (including simple matrix additions and multiplications) and five fundamental image processing functions. To evaluate the image processing functions, we

Table 3. MPC protocols performance varying sharing scheme and adversary type. We have measured execution time and global data sent for all protocols. Some results are unavailable because the MP-SPDZ [29] does not support it. The highlighted values are the best time and global data communication for 2-party and 3-party protocols.

Applications	Secret Sharing Based				Garbled Circuit		Malicious Adversary	
	semi2k	semi-bin	ring*	rep-field*	yao	rep-bmr*	mascot	spdz2k
Matrix Operations	**0.03 s**	0.18 s	0.03 s	**0.02 s**	0.11 s	1.78 s	1.64 s	1.49 s
	0.5 mb	4.3 mb	**0.02 mb**	0.26 mb	9.12 mb	520 mb	352.9 mb	277.4 mb
Thresholding	**1.36 s**	2.61 s	**0.08 s**	0.43 s	1.75 s	39.12 s	569.3 s	232.7 s
	202.9 mb	**46.5 mb**	**8.1 mb**	26.2 mb	83.9 mb	4.90 gb	104.9 gb	40.8 gb
Histogram	**1.93 s**	3.08 s	**0.07 s**	0.456 s	2.12 s	46.8 s	488.4 s	181.7 s
	278.8 mb	**103.5 mb**	**9.8 mb**	24.81 mb	268.3 mb	4.25 gb	94 gb	30.3 gb
Sobel	**27.2 s**	NA	**4.23 s**	4.36 s	NA	NA	568.3 s	450.8 s
	7.23 gb	NA	**28.8 mb**	57.67 mb	NA	NA	135 gb	118.1 gb
3x3 Convolution	**13.9 s**	NA	4.43 s	**4.12 s**	NA	NA	354.3 s	274.1 s
	3.56 gb	NA	**14.5 mb**	28.92 mb	NA	NA	66.5 gb	58.1 gb
Thinning	**4.96 s**	7.85 s	**0.11 s**	0.58 s	16.8 s	198.6 s	610.6 s	278.9 s
	1.25 gb	967.8 mb	**22.1 mb**	54.17 mb	2.34 gb	326.4 gb	124.3 gb	58.2 gb

* 3-party protocols

used a 256×256 monochrome image divided into four equal 128×128 pieces, each assigned to a different participant. For the 2-party setting, each party received two pieces of the image, while in the 4-party setting, each participant held one piece of the image. Then, a joint image processing operation was performed across all pieces, ensuring collaborative analysis while maintaining privacy. The MPC protocols listed in Table 2 were evaluated for these computations, with detailed results provided in Table 3 and Table 4. We have measured the total execution time, including the online and offline phases and the total global data communication. The MPC evaluation concerning the different design configurations is as follows.

① **Adversary Type (Active/Passive):** Malicious-secure protocols require significantly more execution time and communication overhead. As the complexity of operations increases, the communication cost grows exponentially. For example, in Sobel edge detection, all three malicious-secure protocols required over 100 GB of data exchange, making them impractical for complex video analytics workloads.

② **Computation Domain (Arithmetic/Boolean):** Arithmetic-based protocols consistently outperform Boolean-based protocols in image/video processing tasks, as they involve extensive matrix operations. Boolean protocols are more efficient for numerous comparisons (e.g., thresholding) operations. For thresholding, the *semi-bin* protocol exhibited a lower communication overhead than *semi2k*, but for all other workloads, *semi2k* outperformed *semi-bin*. Additionally, MP-SPDZ currently does not support direct matrix multiplication for binary-shared inputs, preventing the execution of two workloads-Sobel and Convolution.

Table 4. MPC protocol performance when number of parties increases.

Applications	2-party		3-party			4-party		
	semi2k	semi	ring	atlas	shamir	rep4-ring	atlas	shamir
Matrix Operations	**0.03 s**	0.11 s	**0.03 s**	0.06 s	0.04 s	0.07 s	0.08 s	0.05 s
	0.5 mb	15.9 mb	**0.02 mb**	0.88 mb	0.56 mb	0.3 mb	1.95 mb	1.12 mb
Thresholding	1.36 s	2.46 s	**0.08 s**	6.03 s	3.10 s	0.15 s	6.65 s	3.65 s
	202.9 mb	258 mb	**8.08 mb**	105.1 mb	86.5 mb	20.3 mb	207.8 mb	170.5 mb
Histogram	1.93 s	2.17 s	**0.07 s**	4.81 s	3.32 s	0.18 s	5.64 s	4.03 s
	278.8 mb	194 mb	**9.8 mb**	89.7 mb	75 mb	23.7 mb	177 mb	147.4 mb
Sobel	27.2 s	94.4 s	**4.23 s**	14.9 s	7.19 s	6.52 s	24.5 s	9.72 s
	7.23 gb	21.5 gb	**28.8 mb**	76.6 mb	57.7 mb	57.7 mb	153.1 mb	115.3 mb
3x3 Convolution	13.9 s	53.5 s	**4.43 s**	13.81 s	6.62 s	6.18 s	23.1 s	8.84 s
	3.56 gb	10.6 gb	**14.5 mb**	38.4 mb	28.9 mb	28.9 mb	76.9 mb	57.8 mb
Thinning	4.96 s	16.1 s	**0.11 s**	6.14 s	3.56 s	0.34 s	7.75 s	4.15 s
	1.25 gb	3.39 gb	**22.1 mb**	141.3 mb	114.5 mb	47.2 mb	278.2 mb	224.3 mb

③ **Computation Choice (Secret Sharing/Garbled Circuit):** Secret Sharing based protocols consistently achieve lower execution time and reduced communication overhead across all workloads. As the complexity of integer operations increases, secret sharing is significantly more efficient than garbled circuits, which struggle with arithmetic intensive computations.

④ **Number of Parties:** The 3-party replicated secret-sharing protocol (*ring*) achieved the fastest execution time and lowest communication overhead across all workloads. The 2-party setting lacks optimizations available in 3-party honest-majority settings, making it less efficient for our use case. As the number of parties increases, both execution time and global data communication also increase.

⑤ **In-house/Outsourced model:** In our protocol, edge devices participate in computations but have limited resources and infrastructure. An outsourced model, as illustrated in Figure 1, shifts the computation to cloud servers. Here, edge devices only share input secret shares, significantly reducing their communication and computation load. This is particularly advantageous for DVR recorders and smart cameras, which lack the processing power required for joint video analytics using MPC.

Based on our evaluations, the Secret-Sharing-based 3-party replicated protocol (**ring**) is the most suitable choice for privacy-preserving video analytics workloads. We will use this protocol for our comparative analysis against TEE-based approaches.

Table 5. Performance of joint video analytics tasks of MPC and TEE. We used videos from CityFlowV2 [8] for all five workloads. Because of the lack of support and inherent memory limitations we are unable to run ml models using Intel SGX.

Case Study	TEE (Intel SGX)		TEE (AWS-Nitro)		MPC (MP-SPDZ)	
① Vehicle Re-Identification	0.002 s	98.2 kb	0.001 s	98.2 kb	0.006 s	218.2 kb
② Scene Similarity	0.003 s	123.4 kb	0.0012 s	123.4 kb	0.015 s	0.36 mb
③ Joint Recognition	NA	NA	4.1 s	37.3 mb	347.53 s	5.08 gb
④ Scene 3D Reconstruction	NA	NA	7.3 s	34.3 mb	621.4 s	8.56 gb
⑤ Count the Vehicles	0.025 s	1.3 mb	0.017 s	1.3 mb	0.033 s	2.1 mb

MPC vs TEE Performance Evaluation: In Case Study 1 (Vehicle Re-identification), vehicle features are extracted locally at the edge devices, followed by a privacy preserving computation of cosine similarity to identify matching vehicles across multiple cameras. For Case Study 2 (Scene Similarity), scene-level video features are extracted at the edge, and the Euclidean distance between these features is computed securely. Case Study 3 (Collaborative Object Recognition) combines two video streams using a predefined, rule-based stitching approach to generate a composite video, which is then processed using a vehicle recognition model. In Case Study 4 (3D Scene Reconstruction and Query), an ML model takes two input video streams to reconstruct a 3D scene representation. A subsequent query is then performed to detect specific objects within the reconstructed 3D environment. In Case Study 5 (Vehicle count), vehicles are first detected locally, and their features are extracted; the secure computation is then used to identify and eliminate duplicate detections across multiple camera feeds, ensuring an accurate count. For this evaluation, we used videos from the CityFlowV2 dataset [8], trimming them to similar lengths to ensure uniformity. We then averaged the execution time and communication cost across different sets of inputs.

The experimental results, as shown in Table 5, highlight the contrasting performance characteristics of MPC, and TEE-based implementations. For relatively lightweight workloads-such as vehicle re-identification (Case Study 1), scene similarity detection (Case Study 2), and total vehicle count (Case Study 5)-MPC protocols performed reasonably well. On average, they were 3 to 6 times slower than their TEE counterparts and incurred about twice the communication overhead. We extract features locally for these three case studies, so the computational cost of secure execution is relatively contained, making MPC a viable option despite its performance penalties.

In contrast, Case Studies 3 and 4, which require collaborative execution of deep learning models for object recognition and video scene stitching, posed significant challenges for MPC frameworks. These workloads demand intensive matrix operations, activation functions, and large intermediate state sharing, which are expensive in MPC due to multiple communication rounds and complex arithmetic over shared values. As a result, MPC implementations were observed to be 70 to 90 times slower than TEE-based solutions. Moreover, the communication overhead ballooned into gigabytes, making the approach infeasible for real-time or bandwidth-constrained environments. However, TEE-based solutions efficiently handled these complex ML workloads, with only a few megabytes of private video input securely transferred to the enclave. Once inside, the entire model execution occurred at near-native speeds, providing a significant performance advantage. These results underscore the practical limitations of MPC in high-computation scenarios and demonstrate the strengths of TEE in handling complex, resource-intensive tasks.

Security Evaluation: MPC provides a robust and flexible security model that operates entirely in software and does not rely on trusted hardware components. This allows it to be deployed across a wide range of environments without dependence on specific hardware vendors or platforms. In addition, MPC protocols can be tailored to different threat models. The semi-honest model assumes that participants follow the protocol, and more secure configurations, such as protecting against malicious adversaries, can be adopted when stronger guarantees are required. These configurations introduce additional cryptographic checks and redundancy mechanisms, which increase computational and communication overhead but provide significantly enhanced security assurances.

In contrast, TEE such as Intel SGX or AWS Nitro Enclaves rely on secure hardware components to protect computations and data. TEE creates isolated enclaves where sensitive data can be processed securely, offering strong protection against software-level attacks and even against a compromised host operating system. However, their security is tied to the correctness and integrity of the hardware and its firmware, which introduces a dependency on hardware vendors. Establishing a root of trust with the manufacturer is necessary, and any vulnerabilities in the TEE implementation, such as side-channel attacks, speculative execution flaws (e.g., Spectre/Meltdown), or leakage through power analysis, can undermine the security guarantees. These limitations have led to concerns about TEE resilience.

Implementation Challenges: The MP-SPDZ framework offers a comprehensive and well-documented suite of tools to implement various MPC protocols. Its modular architecture and support for both arithmetic and Boolean computation domains make it suitable for rapid prototyping and evaluation. However, implementing machine learning (ML) workloads within this framework presents additional challenges. Specifically, developers must explicitly define the model architecture, layers, and activation functions compatible with the MPC back-end, which can be time-consuming and error-prone.

On the TEE side, Intel SGX poses several practical limitations. Most notably, SGX does not support system calls within the enclave environment, severely restricting the use of standard libraries and pre-existing machine learning frameworks such as PyTorch or TensorFlow. This limitation complicates the implementation of complex workloads that rely on dynamic memory management or file I/O. Furthermore, Intel has officially discontinued support for SGX on consumer platforms, reducing its viability for long-term and large-scale deployments. SGX enclaves also suffer from a memory limit (128MB of EPC memory), significantly hindering the execution of modern ML models that typically require larger memory footprints. Due to these limitations, we could not implement Python-based ML inference inside Intel SGX for our evaluation.

In contrast, AWS Nitro Enclaves provide a more flexible and developer-friendly environment. Nitro uses a container-based approach, allowing users to deploy secure enclaves by packaging their applications into Docker images. Which simplifies the enclave deployment process, especially for complex applications that depend on a large software stack. Additionally, Nitro Enclaves benefits from the scalability of the underlying EC2 infrastructure, users can allocate more CPU or memory resources to the enclave by selecting appropriate instance types. This makes it feasible to run memory-intensive ML workloads securely without modifying the application logic extensively.

6 Conclusion

We comprehensively evaluated Secure Multiparty Computation (MPC) and Trusted Execution Environments (TEE) as privacy-preserving solutions for joint video analytics in this work. We evaluated both approaches using five real-world case studies from traffic surveillance scenarios in the CityFlowV2 dataset. The case studies encompass a range of tasks, from simple similarity computations to complex multi-camera machine learning-based analytics, allowing us to evaluate the strengths and limitations of both security paradigms systematically.

Our experimental findings show that TEE consistently outperforms MPC implementations for workloads involving machine learning inference. This performance gap is particularly notable in case studies involving deep learning models. TEE-based implementations achieved up to 70–$90\times$ lower latency and required only a fraction of the communication overhead compared to MPC. TEE benefits from a centralized and hardware-isolated execution model, which enables efficient data handling and reduced interaction during computation. However, TEE is not without limitations. They require trusted hardware support and rely on vendor-specific root-of-trust mechanisms, which may not be feasible in all deployment environments. Additionally, their susceptibility to side-channel attacks and ongoing hardware vulnerabilities raises concerns about their suitability for highly sensitive applications. In contrast, MPC offers a software-only solution that can be deployed in environments where trusted hardware is unavailable or undesirable. Among the MPC protocols evaluated, secret-sharing-based 3-party protocols - particularly those exploiting honest majority assumptions - demonstrated the best performance in terms of both execution time and communication cost. While MPC remains less efficient than TEE for ML-based video analytics, it provides stronger fault isolation and more transparent trust assumptions.

In conclusion, while TEE is currently the preferred choice for compute-intensive video analytics tasks due to its performance benefits, MPC offers a viable and secure alternative for resource-constrained or hardware-agnostic settings. Selecting between the two approaches depends on the application environment's specific workload, deployment constraints, and trust model.

Acknowledgments. Grants from the Department of Science and Technology's National Mission on Inter-Disciplinary Cyber-Physical Systems (via IHUB-IIT Kanpur), the National Security Council (via Indian Urban Data Exchange), and the Indian Institute of Science funded our work.

References

1. Abbas, N., Zhang, Y., Taherkordi, A., Skeie, T.: Mobile edge computing: a survey. IEEE Internet Things J. **5**(1), 450–465 (2017)
2. Amazon Web Services: AWS nitro enclaves (2020). https://docs.aws.amazon.com/enclaves/latest/user/nitro-enclave.html. Accessed 11 Apr 2025
3. ARM: ARM platform security architecture. ARM Limited (2019)
4. Barr, J.: Introducing AWS nitro enclaves (2020). https://aws.amazon.com/blogs/aws/introducing-aws-nitro-enclaves/. Accessed 11 Apr 2025
5. Beaver, D., Micali, S., Rogaway, P.: The round complexity of secure protocols. In: Proceedings of the 22nd Annual ACM Symposium on Theory of Computing, pp. 503–513 (1990)
6. Bellare, M., Hoang, V.T., Rogaway, P.: Foundations of garbled circuits. In: Proceedings of the 2012 ACM Conference on Computer and Communications Security, pp. 784–796 (2012)
7. Cangialosi, F., Agarwal, N., Arun, V., Narayana, S., Sarwate, A., Netravali, R.: Privid: practical, privacy-preserving video analytics queries. In: USENIX Symposium on Networked Systems Design and Implementation (2022)
8. AI city challenge dataset 2021 (2021). https://www.aicitychallenge.org/2021-data-and-evaluation/. Accessed 10 Mar 2023
9. Chaum, D., Crépeau, C., Damgard, I.: Multiparty unconditionally secure protocols. In: Proceedings of the 20th Annual ACM Symposium on Theory of Computing, pp. 11–19 (1988)
10. Costan, V., Devadas, S.: Intel SGX explained. Cryptology ePrint Archive (2016)
11. Cramer, R., Damgård, I., Maurer, U.: General secure multi-party computation from any linear secret-sharing scheme. In: Preneel, B. (ed.) EUROCRYPT 2000. LNCS, vol. 1807, pp. 316–334. Springer, Heidelberg (2000). https://doi.org/10.1007/3-540-45539-6_22
12. Cramer, R., Damgård, I.B., et al.: Secure Multiparty Computation. Cambridge University Press (2015)
13. Cramer, R., Damgård, I., Escudero, D., Scholl, P., Xing, C.: SPDZ2k: efficient MPC mod 2^k for dishonest majority (2018)
14. Fernandez, M., Moral, P., Garcia-Martin, A., Martinez, J.M.: Vehicle re-identification based on ensembling deep learning features including a synthetic training dataset, orientation and background features, and camera verification. In: Proceedings of the IEEE/CVF Conference on Computer Vision and Pattern Recognition (CVPR) Workshops (2021)
15. Gennaro, R., Gentry, C., Parno, B.: Non-interactive verifiable computing: outsourcing computation to untrusted workers. In: Rabin, T. (ed.) CRYPTO 2010. LNCS, vol. 6223, pp. 465–482. Springer, Heidelberg (2010). https://doi.org/10.1007/978-3-642-14623-7_25
16. Gia, T.N., Jiang, M., Rahmani, A.M., Westerlund, T., Liljeberg, P., Tenhunen, H.: Fog computing in healthcare internet of things: a case study on ECG feature extraction. In: 2015 IEEE International Conference on Computer and Information Technology. IEEE (2015)
17. Goldreich, O.: Secure multi-party computation. Manuscript. Preliminary version **78**(110), 1–108 (1998)
18. Goldwasser, S., Micali, S., Rackoff, C.: The knowledge complexity of interactive proof-systems. In: Proceedings of the Seventeenth Annual ACM Symposium on Theory of Computing. STOC 1985 (1985)

19. Goyal, V., Li, H., Ostrovsky, R., Polychroniadou, A., Song, Y.: ATLAS: efficient and scalable MPC in the honest majority setting. In: Malkin, T., Peikert, C. (eds.) CRYPTO 2021. LNCS, vol. 12826, pp. 244–274. Springer, Cham (2021). https://doi.org/10.1007/978-3-030-84245-1_9

20. Guo, H., Yao, S., Yang, Z., Zhou, Q., Nahrstedt, K.: Crossroi: cross-camera region of interest optimization for efficient real time video analytics at scale. In: 12th ACM Multimedia Systems Conference. MMSys 2021. Association for Computing Machinery (2021)

21. Herrmann, C., Wang, C., Bowen, R.S., Keyder, E., Zabih, R.: Object-centered image stitching. In: Proceedings of the European Conference on Computer Vision (ECCV) (2018)

22. Hoi, C.-H., Wang, W., Lyu, M.R.: A novel scheme for video similarity detection. In: Bakker, E.M., Lew, M.S., Huang, T.S., Sebe, N., Zhou, X.S. (eds.) CIVR 2003. LNCS, vol. 2728, pp. 373–382. Springer, Heidelberg (2003). https://doi.org/10.1007/3-540-45113-7_37

23. Hunt, T., Song, C., Shokri, R., Shmatikov, V., Witchel, E.: Chiron: privacy-preserving machine learning as a service. arXiv preprint arXiv:1803.05961 (2018)

24. Intel: Linux-SGX (2024). https://github.com/intel/linux-sgx

25. Jain, S., et al.: Spatula: efficient cross-camera video analytics on large camera networks. In: 2020 IEEE/ACM Symposium on Edge Computing (SEC), pp. 110–124 (2020)

26. Jiang, J., Ananthanarayanan, G., Bodik, P., Sen, S., Stoica, I.: Chameleon: scalable adaptation of video analytics. In: Proceedings of the 2018 Conference of the ACM Special Interest Group on Data Communication, SIGCOMM 2018, pp. 253–266. Association for Computing Machinery, New York (2018). https://doi.org/10.1145/3230543.3230574

27. Joseph, A., Yadav, N., Ganapathy, V., Behl, D.: A contributory public-event recording and querying system. In: Proceedings of the Eighth ACM/IEEE Symposium on Edge Computing, SEC 2023, pp. 185–198. Association for Computing Machinery, New York (2024)

28. Katz, J., Lindell, Y.: Introduction to modern cryptography: principles and protocols. Chapman and hall/CRC (2007)

29. Keller, M.: MP-SPDZ: a versatile framework for multi-party computation. In: Proceedings of the 2020 ACM SIGSAC Conference on Computer and Communications Security (2020)

30. Keller, M., Orsini, E., Scholl, P.: Mascot: faster malicious arithmetic secure computation with oblivious transfer. In: Proceedings of the 2016 ACM SIGSAC Conference on Computer and Communications Security, pp. 830–842 (2016)

31. Keller, M., Yanai, A.: Efficient maliciously secure multiparty computation for RAM. In: Nielsen, J.B., Rijmen, V. (eds.) EUROCRYPT 2018. LNCS, vol. 10822, pp. 91–124. Springer, Cham (2018). https://doi.org/10.1007/978-3-319-78372-7_4

32. Li, T., et al.: Neural 3D video synthesis from multi-view video. In: Proceedings of the IEEE/CVF Conference on Computer Vision and Pattern Recognition, pp. 5521–5531 (2022)

33. Li, X., Loy, C.C.: Video object segmentation with joint re-identification and attention-aware mask propagation. In: Proceedings of the European Conference on Computer Vision (ECCV), pp. 90–105 (2018)

34. Li, Y., Padmanabhan, A., Zhao, P., Wang, Y., Xu, G.H., Netravali, R.: Reducto: on-camera filtering for resource-efficient real-time video analytics. In: SIGCOMM 2020. ACM (2020)

35. Lindell, Y.: Secure multiparty computation for privacy preserving data mining. In: Encyclopedia of Data Warehousing and Mining, pp. 1005–1009. IGI Global (2005)

36. Lindell, Y.: Secure multiparty computation. Commun. ACM **64**(1) (2020)

37. Lindell, Y., Nof, A.: A framework for constructing fast MPC over arithmetic circuits with malicious adversaries and an honest-majority. In: Proceedings of the 2017 ACM SIGSAC Conference on Computer and Communications Security, pp. 259–276 (2017)

38. Lindell, Y., Pinkas, B.: Privacy preserving data mining. In: Bellare, M. (ed.) CRYPTO 2000. LNCS, vol. 1880, pp. 36–54. Springer, Heidelberg (2000). https://doi.org/10.1007/3-540-44598-6_3

39. Lindell, Y., Pinkas, B.: An efficient protocol for secure two-party computation in the presence of malicious adversaries. In: Naor, M. (ed.) EUROCRYPT 2007. LNCS, vol. 4515, pp. 52–78. Springer, Heidelberg (2007). https://doi.org/10.1007/978-3-540-72540-4_4

40. Liu, P., Qi, B., Banerjee, S.: Edgeeye: an edge service framework for real-time intelligent video analytics. In: EdgeSys 2018. Association for Computing Machinery (2018)

41. Liu, X., Liu, W., Mei, T., Ma, H.: A deep learning-based approach to progressive vehicle re-identification for urban surveillance. In: Leibe, B., Matas, J., Sebe, N., Welling, M. (eds.) ECCV 2016. LNCS, vol. 9906, pp. 869–884. Springer, Cham (2016). https://doi.org/10.1007/978-3-319-46475-6_53

42. Mohassel, P., Rindal, P.: Aby3: a mixed protocol framework for machine learning. In: Proceedings of the 2018 ACM SIGSAC Conference on Computer and Communications Security, pp. 35–52 (2018)

43. Mohassel, P., Zhang, Y.: Secureml: a system for scalable privacy-preserving machine learning. In: 2017 IEEE Symposium on Security and Privacy (SP), pp. 19–38. IEEE (2017)

44. Muñoz, A., Rios, R., Román, R., López, J.: A survey on the (in) security of trusted execution environments. Comput. Secur. **129**, 103180 (2023)

45. Nikolaenko, V., Weinsberg, U., Ioannidis, S., Joye, M., Boneh, D., Taft, N.: Privacy-preserving ridge regression on hundreds of millions of records. In: 2013 IEEE Symposium on Security and Privacy, pp. 334–348. IEEE (2013)

46. Ohrimenko, O., et al.: Oblivious {Multi-Party} machine learning on trusted processors. In: 25th USENIX Security Symposium (USENIX Security 2016), pp. 619–636 (2016)

47. Poddar, R., Ananthanarayanan, G., Setty, S., Volos, S., Popa, R.A.: Visor: privacy-preserving video analytics as a cloud service. In: 29th USENIX Security Symposium (USENIX Security 2020), pp. 1039–1056. USENIX Association (2020)

48. Pont-Tuset, J., Perazzi, F., Caelles, S., Arbeláez, P., Sorkine-Hornung, A., Van Gool, L.: The 2017 davis challenge on video object segmentation. arXiv preprint arXiv:1704.00675 (2017)

49. Redmon, J., Farhadi, A.: Yolov3: an incremental improvement. arXiv abs/1804.02767 (2018)

50. Ren, J., Zhang, Y., Zhang, K., Shen, X.: Exploiting mobile crowdsourcing for pervasive cloud services: challenges and solutions. IEEE Commun. Mag. **53**(3), 98–105 (2015)

51. Ren, S., He, K., Girshick, R.B., Sun, J.: Faster R-CNN: towards real-time object detection with region proposal networks. IEEE Trans. Pattern Anal. Mach. Intell. **39**, 1137–1149 (2015)

52. Roman, R., Lopez, J., Mambo, M.: Mobile edge computing, fog et al.: a survey and analysis of security threats and challenges. Future Gener. Comput. Syst. **78**, 680–698 (2018)

53. Sandler, M., Hayat, L., Costa, L.: Benchmarking processors for image processing. Microprocess. Microsyst. (1990)

54. Satyanarayanan, M.: The emergence of edge computing. Computer **50**(1), 30–39 (2017)

55. Seitz, S.M., Curless, B., Diebel, J., Scharstein, D., Szeliski, R.: A comparison and evaluation of multi-view stereo reconstruction algorithms. In: 2006 IEEE Computer Society Conference on Computer Vision and Pattern Recognition (CVPR 2006), vol. 1, pp. 519–528. IEEE (2006)

56. Sev-Snp, A.: Strengthening VM isolation with integrity protection and more. White Paper, January **53**, 1450–1465 (2020)

57. Shi, W., Cao, J., Zhang, Q., Li, Y., Xu, L.: Edge computing: vision and challenges. IEEE Internet Things J. **3**(5), 637–646 (2016)

58. Shokri, R., Shmatikov, V.: Privacy-preserving deep learning. In: Proceedings of the 22nd ACM SIGSAC Conference on Computer and Communications Security, pp. 1310–1321 (2015)

59. Sumrall, N., Novoa, M.: Trusted computing group (TCG) and the TPM 1.2 specification. In: Intel Developer Forum, vol. 32. Intel Santa Clara, CA, USA (2003)

60. Sundararaman, R., De Almeida Braga, C., Marchand, E., Pettre, J.: Tracking pedestrian heads in dense crowd. In: Proceedings of the IEEE/CVF Conference on Computer Vision and Pattern Recognition, pp. 3865–3875 (2021)
61. Tran, D., Bourdev, L., Fergus, R., Torresani, L., Paluri, M.: Learning spatiotemporal features with 3D convolutional networks. In: 2015 IEEE International Conference on Computer Vision (ICCV), Los Alamitos, CA, USA (2015)
62. Truex, S., Baracaldo, N., Anwar, A., Steinke, T., Ludwig, H., Zhang, R., Zhou, Y.: A hybrid approach to privacy-preserving federated learning. In: Proceedings of the 12th ACM Workshop on Artificial Intelligence and Security, pp. 1–11 (2019)
63. Tsai, C.C., Porter, D.E., Vij, M.: {Graphene-SGX}: a practical library {OS} for unmodified applications on {SGX}. In: 2017 USENIX Annual Technical Conference (2017)
64. Tsai, C.C., Porter, D.E., Vij, M.: Gramine-sgx (2024). https://github.com/gramineproject/gramine
65. Voigtlaender, P., Luiten, J., Torr, P.H., Leibe, B.: Siam R-CNN: visual tracking by re-detection. In: IEEE/CVF Conference on Computer Vision and Pattern Recognition (2020)
66. Wan, J., et al.: Software-defined industrial internet of things in the context of industry 4.0. IEEE Sens. J. (2016)
67. Wang, D., et al.: Multi-view 3D reconstruction with transformers. In: Proceedings of the IEEE/CVF International Conference on Computer Vision, pp. 5722–5731 (2021)
68. Wang, J., Amos, B., Das, A., Pillai, P., Sadeh, N., Satyanarayanan, M.: A scalable and privacy-aware IoT service for live video analytics. In: MMSys 2017. Association for Computing Machinery (2017)
69. Wang, R., Hao, Y., Miao, Y., Hu, L., Chen, M.: RT3C: real-time crowd counting in multi-scene video streams via cloud-edge-device collaboration. IEEE Trans. Serv. Comput. (2024)
70. Wang, X., Girshick, R.B., Gupta, A.K., He, K.: Non-local neural networks. In: 2018 IEEE/CVF Conference on Computer Vision and Pattern Recognition (2017)
71. Watanabe, Y., Hochin, T., Nomiya, H.: Method of similarity retrieval of color videos based on impressions. In: 2016 IEEE/ACIS 15th International Conference on Computer and Information Science (ICIS), pp. 1–6. IEEE (2016)
72. Wu, Z., et al.: 3D shapenets: a deep representation for volumetric shapes. In: Proceedings of the IEEE Conference on Computer Vision and Pattern Recognition, pp. 1912–1920 (2015)
73. Yao, A.C.: Protocols for secure computations. In: 23rd Annual Symposium on Foundations of Computer Science (SFCS 1982), pp. 160–164 (1982)
74. Yi, J., Acer, U.G., Kawsar, F., Min, C.: Argus: enabling cross-camera collaboration for video analytics on distributed smart cameras. IEEE Trans. Mob. Comput. (2024)
75. Zahur, S., Rosulek, M., Evans, D.: Two halves make a whole. In: Oswald, E., Fischlin, M. (eds.) EUROCRYPT 2015. LNCS, vol. 9057, pp. 220–250. Springer, Heidelberg (2015). https://doi.org/10.1007/978-3-662-46803-6_8
76. Zapletal, D., Herout, A.: Vehicle re-identification for automatic video traffic surveillance. In: Proceedings of the IEEE Conference on Computer Vision and Pattern Recognition Workshops, pp. 25–31 (2016)
77. Zhang, F., Liu, F.: Parallax-tolerant image stitching. In: Proceedings of the IEEE Conference on Computer Vision and Pattern Recognition, pp. 3262–3269 (2014)
78. Zhang, T., Chowdhery, A., Bahl, P.V., Jamieson, K., Banerjee, S.: The design and implementation of a wireless video surveillance system. In: MobiCom 2015. Association for Computing Machinery (2015)

79. Zhou, B., Lapedriza, A., Xiao, J., Torralba, A., Oliva, A.: Learning deep features for scene recognition using places database. In: Advances in Neural Information Processing Systems (2014)
80. Zhou, Y., Cao, M., You, J., Meng, M., Wang, Y., Zhou, Z.: MR video fusion: interactive 3D modeling and stitching on wide-baseline videos. In: Proceedings of the 24th ACM Symposium on Virtual Reality Software and Technology, pp. 1–11 (2018)

Privacy-Preserving Fair Text Summarization Using Federated Learning

Aman Lachhiramka, Nibhrant Vaishnav, and Dheeraj Kumar[✉]

Department of Electronics and Communication Engineering, Indian Institute of Technology (IIT) Roorkee, Roorkee, Uttarakhand, India
{a_lachhiramka,n_vaishnav}@iitr.ac.in, dheeraj.kumar@ece.iitr.ac.in

Abstract. Text summarization is an important problem in natural language processing. The advent of large-scale transformer-based models, such as BART, PEGASUS, and T5, has revolutionized abstractive summarization. However, all these models are centralized and require the entire text to be summarized at a single location, where the model operates and generates the summary. Centralized training of NLP models raises privacy concerns in sensitive domains such as healthcare, law, and finance. Another challenge concerning these models is their unfair representation of users with small corpus data. To mitigate this, we propose a privacy-preserving framework for abstractive summarization using federated learning, eliminating the need to transmit raw data to a centralized server. Our approach employs a pre-trained BART model, and to ensure privacy against inference attacks by the aggregating server, differential privacy is utilized. Our approach also incorporates a fairness-aware aggregation strategy, Q-fair, to ensure balanced client contributions. Experiments on the CNN/DailyMail dataset show that our FL-based method achieves competitive ROUGE scores while enhancing privacy and fairness, demonstrating its practicality for sensitive real-world applications.

Keywords: Federated Learning · Text Summarization · BART · Differential Privacy · Q-Fair Aggregation · Fairness

1 Introduction

Text summarization is a core task in *natural language processing* (NLP) that aims to condense long-form content into concise summaries, preserving essential semantics and informativeness. The advent of large-scale transformer-based models, such as BART [1], PEGASUS [2], and T5 [3], has revolutionized abstractive summarization, delivering fluent and contextually rich outputs with minimal task-specific fine-tuning. All these recent text summarization models are *centralized* in nature, i.e., the entire text to be summarized needs to be processed at a single location, where the model operates on it and generates the summary. However, this centralized model training introduces significant privacy risks.

A. Lachhiramka and N. Vaishnav—Both authors contributed equally towards the paper.

Traditional summarization pipelines require raw input data to be uploaded to central servers, making sensitive information vulnerable to misuse, breaches, and surveillance. This is especially concerning in domains such as healthcare, finance, and law, where confidentiality is paramount.

With the popularization of social media, online product reviews, and user feedback for various products, services, and government policies, summarization is increasingly being used to aggregate public sentiment across distributed data sources, such as blogs, news portals, social media, online forums, etc. Summarizing collective opinions on controversial topics such as the RussiaUkraine conflict, rising anti-Semitism, controversial figures such as Kunal Kamra, or military exercises such as *Operation Sindoor* provides valuable sociopolitical insights. However, the fear of government surveillance, online abuse, or legal consequences may deter individuals from candidly sharing their views, highlighting the urgent need for privacy-preserving summarization. As a use case illustration, consider a multinational legal organization operating across continents. Each branch handles sensitive case documents that cannot be transmitted to a central cloud due to legal and privacy concerns. Hence, there is a need of a distributed learning framework, that can generate abstract summaries of all these documents without having to transmit them to a central location. This use case directly translates to healthcare networks, corporate knowledge bases, or regional media outlets managing confidential narratives.

Federated Learning (FL) [26] offers a privacy-preserving, decentralized alternative by enabling multiple clients to collaboratively train models without sharing raw data. Instead, clients transmit model updates to a central server for aggregation. While FL mitigates direct data sharing, it remains susceptible to gradient leakage and inference attacks. Moreover, conventional aggregation techniques like FedAvg [26] disproportionately favor data-rich clients, exacerbating bias in non-IID settings [21]. To overcome these limitations, we propose a *federated text summarization framework* (FTSF) that integrates FL with *differential privacy* (DP) [10] based inference attack mitigation. DP is enforced through calibrated Gaussian noise in local updates, offering tunable privacy via a parameter ϵ. For fairness-aware aggregation, we utilize *Q-fair* aggregation [13], where each client's contribution is inversely weighted by its dataset size raised to a tunable fairness factor q. This mechanism balances model quality and fairness in real-world deployments.

Our architecture is built atop the BART model and evaluated in a simulated federated environment with partitioned, non-IID client data. The framework ensures privacy-preserving summarization, formal privacy guarantees, and equitable model training across heterogeneous clients. Our main contributions to this paper are as follows:

1. We propose a novel privacy-preserving *federated text summarization framework* (FTSF) combining FL, DP, and fairness-aware Q-fair aggregation.
   (a) We develop an FL-based privacy-preserving aggregation to the BART text summarization model for data distributed over several devices.
   (b) We apply DP via Gaussian noise injection into model updates, providing formal guarantees against privacy leakage during training.

(c) The proposed FTSF utilizes Q-fair aggregation, thus balancing fairness and utility by reweighing client updates based on dataset size.
2. We conduct extensive experiments on two benchmark datasets: CNN/DailyMail and Reuters-covering diverse summarization scenarios across various domains.
3. We present detailed quantitative and qualitative evaluations, including ROUGE metrics, compression ratios, word clouds, TF-IDF histograms, and fairness-performance trade-off curves.

The rest of the paper is organized as follows: Sect. 2 conducts a systematic literature review of the text summarization models and their FL counterparts, as well as the work in the domain of fairness in text summarization. Section 3 outlines the components fundamental to our proposed framework: BART model for abstractive summarization, FL, Q-Fair aggregation, and DP. Section 4 presents our proposed federated text summarization framework. Numerical experiments performed on Reuters-21578 and CNN/DailyMail datasets are given in Sect. 5 before concluding in Sect. 6.

2   Related Work

Recent advancements in deep learning have transformed the field of text summarization. Transformer-based models such as BERTSUM [4], PEGASUS [2], and BART [1] have achieved state-of-the-art results on benchmark datasets. These models generate abstractive or extractive summaries by leveraging contextual representations from large-scale pretraining. There has been a surge of interest in both abstractive and extractive summarization using deep learning techniques. Transformer-based models like BART [1], PEGASUS [2], and T5 [3] have become benchmarks in abstractive summarization. BERTSUM [4] and MMR-based methods have been widely used for extractive tasks. Hybrid models [5] that combine BERT-based embeddings with redundancy-aware selection strategies have shown competitive performance. However, all these text summarization models operate as centralized systems, where all the input text data must be on a single device to be processed and generate a summary. This raises severe privacy concerns for sensitive applications where users are averse to sharing their raw data for model training, e.g., healthcare, law, personal opinion, etc. FL has been proven to be a privacy-preserving alternative for such scenarios, which allows for decentralizing model training across devices, preventing direct data sharing.

Initially applied for keyboard prediction [8], FL has since been extended to natural language tasks such as named entity recognition [27], dialogue systems [9], text classification [8], and language modeling [26]. Although FL provides users a sense of privacy as the raw training data does not leave the user's device. However, the locally trained gradient updates have been shown to leak user privacy through inference attacks. DP in FL is crucial to mitigate leakage from model updates. DP introduces calibrated noise to model updates, ensuring formal guarantees of individual-level protection. Approaches like DP-FedAvg [12] and tools such as Opacus [11] allow integrating DP into FL frameworks with quantifiable privacy budgets. Further enhancements include field-level privacy and encryption-based techniques such as homomorphic encryption.

Another challenge for FL-based NLP applications, especially text summarization, is the question of fairness. Standard FedAvg [26] tends to overweight large clients, leading to biased models. Fairness in FL is typically compromised when clients have unequal data volumes. Fairness-aware schemes such as Q-Fair aggregation [13], dynamic regularization (FedDyn) [22], loss-based reweighting [14], and contrastive FL (MOON) [15] have emerged to address this issue. These methods promote equitable performance across heterogeneous client data distributions. Q-Fair and loss-based reweighting aim to mitigate client bias in model aggregation, ensuring more representative global models. FedNLP [7] provides standardized benchmarks for NLP-focused FL, emphasizing challenges in non-IID settings and communication constraints. This discussion on federated learning and privacy-preserving techniques provides context for developing integrated frameworks. Our work builds on these foundations by unifying privacy, fairness, and summarization in a decentralized system.

3   Background

This section outlines the foundational components of our framework, including the BART model for abstractive summarization, FL, Q-Fair aggregation, and DP.

3.1   BART Model for Abstractive Summarization

BART, an acronym for "bidirectional and auto-regressive transformers," is a sequence-to-sequence model with a bidirectional encoder (BERT-like) and an autoregressive decoder (GPT-like) as shown in Fig. 1.

It is pre-trained using denoising objectives that involve corrupting and reconstructing text. During summarization, the encoder processes the input x, and the decoder generates the output summary $y = (y_1, y_2, \ldots, y_T)$. The training objective minimizes the negative log-likelihood:

$$\mathcal{L}_{\text{NLL}} = -\sum_{t=1}^{T} \log P(y_t \mid y_{<t}, x; \theta). \tag{1}$$

BART's pretraining makes it highly effective at generating coherent and context-aware summaries with fewer updates-an advantage in communication-constrained FL settings.

3.2   Federated Learning and Q-Fair Aggregation

FL enables collaborative model training across distributed clients without exposing their raw data. Each client performs local model updates using private

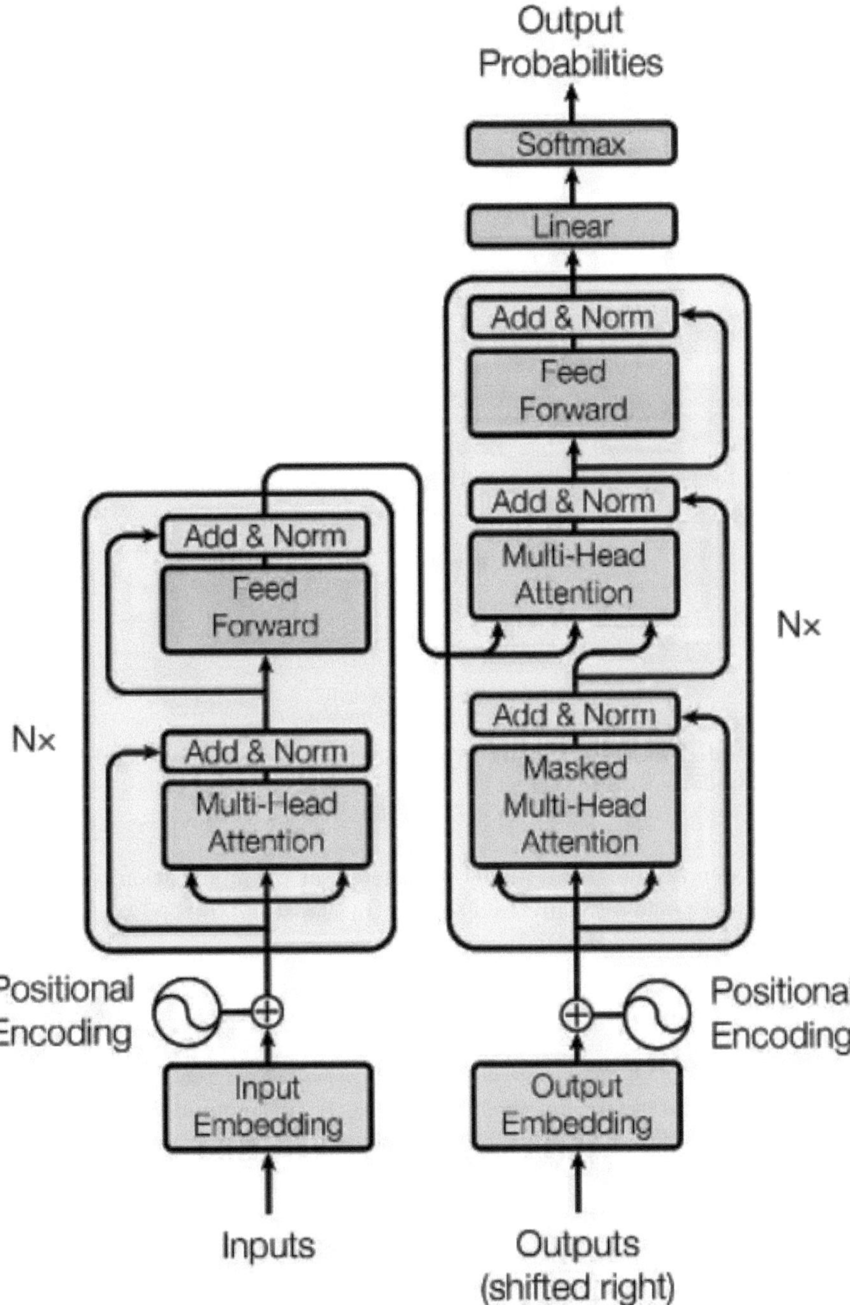

Fig. 1. BART architecture: a sequence-to-sequence transformer with a bidirectional encoder and autoregressive decoder.

datasets and transmits only the updated parameters to a central server. The server then aggregates these updates to form a new global model, which is redistributed to the clients for the next training round, as shown in Fig. 2.

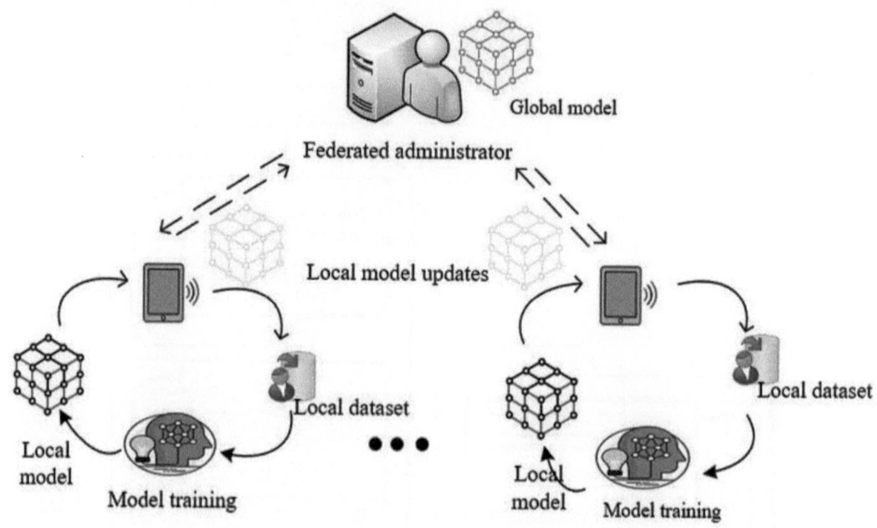

Fig. 2. Federated Learning architecture: local clients train independently and share only model updates with the server.

Let $\theta^{(t)}$ denote the global model parameters at communication round t, and $\theta_k^{(t)}$ the model trained locally by client k. In the standard FedAvg algorithm, aggregation is performed using weighted averages:

$$\theta^{(t+1)} = \sum_{k=1}^{K} w_k \cdot \theta_k^{(t)}, \quad \text{where } w_k = \frac{n_k}{\sum_{j=1}^{K} n_j}. \tag{2}$$

Here, n_k is the dataset size of the client k, and K is the number of clients. However, this formulation may overrepresent clients with large datasets, introducing bias. To mitigate this, we adopt Q-Fair aggregation, which adjusts client weights based on a fairness parameter $q \in [0, 1]$:

$$w_k = \frac{n_k^{-q}}{\sum_{j=1}^{K} n_j^{-q}}. \tag{3}$$

Lower q values promote fairness (equal client influence), while higher values approximate FedAvg. Aggregation is done on parameter deltas for enhanced stability as given next:

$$\Delta\theta_k = \theta_k^{(t)} - \theta^{(t)}, \quad \theta^{(t+1)} = \theta^{(t)} + \sum_{k=1}^{K} w_k \cdot \Delta\theta_k \tag{4}$$

3.3 Differential Privacy

While FL retains data locally, model updates may leak sensitive information via inversion or reconstruction attacks. To counter this, we incorporate DP into the training process. A randomized algorithm $\mathcal{M}$ is said to be (ϵ, δ)-differentially private if for any two adjacent datasets D and D' differing by one entry, and for any output set S:

$$\Pr[\mathcal{M}(D) \in S] \le e^\epsilon \cdot \Pr[\mathcal{M}(D') \in S] + \delta \tag{5}$$

This ensures that the algorithm outputs are statistically indistinguishable across neighboring datasets.

We use the *Opacus* library to integrate DP-SGD in our pipeline. At each client, gradients are clipped to a norm C, and Gaussian noise is added:

$$\tilde{g}_k = \mathrm{clip}(g_k, C) + \mathcal{N}(0, \sigma^2\, C^2 I), \tag{6}$$

where, $\tilde{g}_k$ is the privatized gradient, σ is the noise multiplier, and the privacy loss is tracked using the moments' accountant method. This approach yields formal privacy guarantees without compromising training scalability.

4 Federated Text Summarization Framework (FTSF)

This work introduces a unified framework for privacy-preserving abstractive summarization by integrating the BART model with FL, DP, and Q-Fair aggregation. Unlike prior works focused on classification or token-level prediction, our approach tackles the generative nature of summarization, where challenges around coherence, relevance, and privacy are more pronounced. We extend the BART model for use in FL settings as given in Algorithm 1. Each client locally fine-tunes the model using its dataset, preserving data privacy while generating high-quality summaries. The client then aggregates These personal model updates using Q-Fair aggregation, which reduces bias by reweighting client contributions based on inverse dataset size. To mitigate the risk of privacy leaks using inference attacks, each client's local model updates are perturbed using DP-SGD by clipping the gradients and injecting calibrated noise during model training. The FTSF pipeline is summarized in Fig. 3, showing the steps in each communication round.

Algorithm 1: Federated Text Summarization Framework (FTSF)

    Input: Client data C_i, rounds R, privacy budget ϵ, Q-factor q
    Output: Trained global model M_g
1 Initialize global model M_g
2 **for** *each round $r \in R$* **do**
3   Compute client weights $w_i = \frac{1}{|C_i|^q}$
4   **for** *each client C_i* **do**
5   Train local model M_{c_i}
6   Tokenize inputs, compute embeddings, fine-tune model
7   Compute update $\Delta_i = M_{c_i} - M_g$
8   Apply DP: $\Delta_i \leftarrow \Delta_i + \mathcal{N}(0, 1/\epsilon)$
9   Aggregate: $M_g \leftarrow M_g + \sum w_i \cdot \Delta_i$
10 **return** M_g

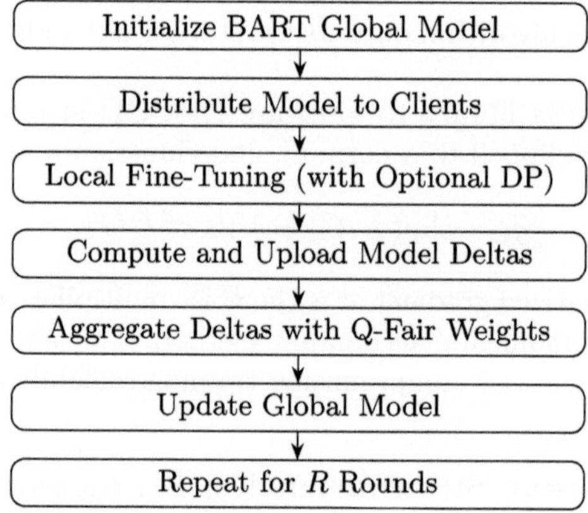

Fig. 3. System pipeline for FTSF

Next, we detail the architectural, algorithmic, and implementation aspects of the proposed FTSF. The methodology is built around three core pillars: decentralized client updates, Q-Fair aggregation for fair participation, and optional DP to ensure the confidentiality of client contributions. Our framework is modular and extensible, allowing the toggling of FL components (e.g., DP, fairness) to support ablation studies.

4.1 Federated Summarization Framework

Consider an FL environment with K virtual clients. Each client C_i, where $i = 1, 2, ..., K$, maintains a private dataset D_i and locally trains the model without sharing raw data. Training proceeds in communication rounds $t = 1, 2, ..., T$, coordinated by a central server. The server initializes a global model θ^0

$$\theta^0 \leftarrow \texttt{BART-base} \tag{7}$$

At the start of each round t, the server broadcasts the global model to all clients:

$$\theta_i^t \leftarrow \theta^t, \quad \forall i \in \{1, ..., K\} \tag{8}$$

Each client updates the model on its local data D_i using a stochastic optimizer (e.g., SGD or Adam), computing the new weights:

$$\theta_i^{t+1} = \theta_i^t - \eta \cdot \nabla\mathcal{L}(D_i, \theta_i^t) \tag{9}$$

where η is the learning rate and $\mathcal{L}$ is the loss function (e.g., cross-entropy). Clients return updates $\Delta_i = \theta_i^{t+1} - \theta^t$ to the server. The server aggregates updates (e.g., via Q-Fair or FedAvg) to compute the new global model:

$$\theta^{t+1} = \theta^t + \sum_{i=1}^{K} w_i \cdot \Delta_i \tag{10}$$

4.2   Q-Fair Aggregation Strategy

To mitigate model bias toward data-rich clients, we adopt Q-Fair aggregation, where each client's contribution is scaled using a tunable fairness parameter $q \in [0, 1]$. For client k with n_k local samples, the Q-Fair weight is computed as:

$$w_k = \frac{n_k^{-q}}{\sum_{j=1}^{K} n_j^{-q}}. \tag{11}$$

Here, the value of q affects the model aggregation process as follows:

- $q = 0$: Equal weighting across all clients.
- $q = 1$: Reduces to standard FedAvg.
- $0 < q < 1$: Tunable balance between fairness and data-weighted aggregation.

The global model update is computed as a weighted sum of the model deltas in our implementation. Each client k computes:

$$\Delta\theta_k = \theta_k^{(t)} - \theta^{(t)}. \tag{12}$$

The global model is then updated using:

$$\theta^{(t+1)} = \theta^{(t)} + \sum_{k=1}^{K} w_k \cdot \Delta\theta_k \tag{13}$$

This delta-based aggregation provides improved stability and fairness, especially in heterogeneous settings [13, 20].

4.3   Local Fine-Tuning with BART

Each client performs local fine-tuning of a BART model on its assigned data. BART uses a transformer-based encoder-decoder architecture pre-trained on denoising autoencoding tasks, making it effective for generative tasks like summarization. Documents are tokenized using the Hugging Face BART tokenizer. Input sequences are truncated to 512 tokens, and output summaries are limited to 128 tokens to conform to architectural limits and ensure consistent batching. The training objective for each client is to minimize the autoregressive *negative log-likelihood* (NLL) loss:

$$\mathcal{L}_{\text{NLL}} = -\sum_{t=1}^{T} \log P(y_t \mid y_{<t}, x; \theta), \tag{14}$$

where, x is the input document, y_t is the ground-truth summary token at timestep t, and θ represents model parameters. This NLL loss aligns with BART's left-to-right decoder, training the model to predict the next summary token conditioned on all previous tokens and the document embedding, guiding the model to produce fluent and semantically accurate summaries.

To compute an overall measure of training objective, we define the global loss $\mathcal{L}_{\text{global}}$ as a Q-fair weighted sum of local losses:

$$\mathcal{L}_{\text{global}} = \sum_{k=1}^{K} w_k \cdot \mathcal{L}_k(\theta), \tag{15}$$

where $\mathcal{L}_k$ is the average loss on client C_k. This ensures that fairness is preserved not only during parameter aggregation but also during global loss evaluation. This formulation integrates fairness, privacy, and optimization under a federated training regime for generative tasks.

4.4   Optional Differential Privacy (DP)

To protect client gradients during transmission, we optionally apply DP. This is crucial in domains such as healthcare and finance, where gradients may contain sensitive patterns. Each client's gradient is clipped to a predefined ℓ_2-norm C, followed by Gaussian noise injection:

$$\tilde{g}_k = \text{clip}(g_k, C) + \mathcal{N}(0, \sigma^2 C^2 I), \tag{16}$$

where C is the clipping bound for ℓ_2 norm of gradients, and σ is the noise multiplier, which is tuned to meet a privacy budget ϵ, and cumulative loss is tracked using the moment's accountant.

5   Numerical Experiments

We use two benchmark datasets to evaluate our FTSF framework: Reuters-21578 [23] and CNN/DailyMail [24], covering both short-form and long-form summarization. The Reuters dataset consists of concise newswire articles spanning multiple categories such as economy, commodities, and global affairs. Since it lacks gold-standard abstractive summaries, we construct pseudo-references using each article's first 23 sentences, following common heuristics in low-resource summarization. This setup tests the pipeline's performance under resource-constrained and short-text environments. The CNN/DailyMail dataset comprises full-length news articles from CNN and Daily Mail and human-curated summaries. Each reference summary captures salient points using abstractive, paragraph-level paraphrasing. Its narrative complexity and longer context windows make it a robust benchmark for evaluating summarization models' coherence, saliency, and compression capabilities.

Each dataset is partitioned into simulated clients to mimic federated deployment. We split the training data across three clients with heterogeneous sizes and topics to emulate real-world FL deployment. In Reuters, clients are randomly assigned 1020 articles, while CNN/DailyMail clients receive 80120 articles. We partition the Reuters dataset based on document topics and lengths to emulate non-IID and heterogeneous conditions. Let $D = \{d_1, d_2, ..., d_N\}$ denote the full dataset. Partitioning is performed such that:

$$D = \bigcup_{i=1}^{K} D_i, \quad D_i \cap D_j = \emptyset \text{ for } i \neq j \tag{17}$$

where each D_i is sorted and filtered by topic and size to induce heterogeneity. This uneven, non-IID distribution introduces challenges in representation balance and model generalization, making it ideal for testing fairness-aware aggregation and federated optimization strategies.

5.1   Implementation Details

To operationalize our FTSF pipeline, we develop a modular and extensible simulation framework built on PyTorch and Hugging Face (`facebook/bart-base`) transformers. This architecture supports client emulation, communication rounds, Q-Fair aggregation, and optional DP. As a pre-processing step, all documents are tokenized using the Hugging Face tokenizer [19]. Each input document is truncated to 512 tokens to conform with the BART model's input constraints. Generated summaries are limited to 128 tokens during decoding. We avoid additional cleaning or normalization to preserve natural linguistic variability and syntactic richness inherent in real-world data.

We emulate a cross-device FL setup through sequential execution of virtual clients in a centralized runtime. Each simulated client maintains local data, mimics edge-device constraints, and interacts asynchronously with the central server model. The federated training loop is composed of the following stages:

1. **Global Initialization:** The server instantiates the global BART model from a pre-trained checkpoint.
2. **Model Distribution:** The model $\theta^{(t)}$ is broadcast to all clients at the start of round t.
3. **Local Training:** Each client fine-tunes the model for one local epoch (or fixed steps) on its private data.

4. **Delta Computation:** Clients compute model deltas $\Delta\theta_k = \theta_k^{(t)} - \theta^{(t)}$. If DP is enabled, noise is added to preserve privacy.
5. **Aggregation:** The server aggregates deltas using Q-Fair weighting to compute the updated global model $\theta^{(t+1)}$.

We adopt a consistent training protocol across all experimental runs. Table 1 outlines the selected hyperparameters, tuned for trade-offs between performance, privacy, and efficiency:

Table 1. Federated Training Configuration

Hyperparameter	Value
Learning Rate	3×10^{-5} (with linear decay)
Batch Size	4 samples per client per round
Communication Rounds	4
Epochs per Round	10
Gradient Clipping Norm (C)	1.0
Noise Multiplier (σ)	Adaptive (based on ϵ)
Optimizer	AdamW
Max Input Length	512 tokens
Max Summary Length	128 tokens

This configuration ensures fair comparison across settings while supporting privacy-preserving and fairness-aware scenarios. All our experiments were conducted on a single NVIDIA RTX 3060 GPU with 12GB of VRAM.

We evaluate our privacy-preserving FTSF framework using the BART model under three learning paradigms:

1. Centralized BART
2. Federated Learning with Differential Privacy (FL + DP)
3. Federated Learning with Differential Privacy and Q-fair Aggregation (FL + DP + Q-fair)

We use the following metrics for evaluation:

1. ROUGE-1: Measures the overlap of unigrams between the generated summary and the reference.
2. ROUGE-2: Measures the overlap of bigrams, capturing fluency and phrase-level coherence.
3. ROUGE-L: Considers the longest common subsequence to capture sentence-level similarity.
4. Compression Ratio: Ratio of summary length to document length, capped at 0.9 to prevent inflation.

Additionally, the qualitative analysis includes word clouds for frequent term visualization and TF-IDF histograms to highlight keyword importance in each generated summary.

Incorporating DP via Gaussian noise fundamentally alters the optimization landscape of federated summarization. We empirically evaluate model quality across a wide range of privacy budgets: $\epsilon \in \{0.001, 0.01, 0.1, 1, 10, 100\}$. When the privacy budget ϵ is extremely low (e.g., 0.001 or 0.01), the noise magnitude dominates accurate gradients, severely degrading learning capacity. Models trained under these conditions fail to converge meaningfully, exhibit ROUGE scores near zero, and generated summaries are disfluent or generic. As ϵ increases, the injected noise becomes less dominant, thereby preserving useful gradient signals. Notably, we observed a sharp increase in the model quality as ϵ increased from 0.01 to 0.1. This reflects the nonlinear nature of the privacyutility trade-offs. Whereas, for high values ($10 \leq \epsilon \leq 100$), performance approaches that of the non-private model. However, privacy degradation is significant, and overfitting becomes a risk-especially in non-IID scenarios. Hence, for all the experiments, we use a moderate value of $\epsilon = 0.1$, which achieves a sweet spot where summaries are accurate and coherent, and privacy remains strong. This value ensures a high degree of client confidentiality while maintaining summarization accuracy. It is suitable for deployment in privacy-critical applications such as medical records, financial transcripts, or legal case summaries.

The dataset was split into 1000 training documents and 10 shared-test documents. Centralized training used ten epochs, while federated setups ran for four communication rounds with three clients having non-IID data distributions. Differential privacy was enforced by adding Gaussian noise ($\epsilon = 1.0$) to model updates. For Q-fair aggregation, the client weights are inversely proportional to n^q, where n is the number of samples at each client.

5.2   Results and Analysis

Table 2 lists the average of various evaluation metrics across all test documents.

Table 2. Average scores across all test documents

Method	ROUGE-1	ROUGE-2	ROUGE-L	Compression
Centralized BART	0.4065	0.2154	0.2646	0.1011
FL + DP	0.4008	0.2044	0.2810	0.0831
FL + DP + Q-fair	0.3779	0.1858	0.2495	0.0821

Table 2 shows that centralized BART achieves the highest ROUGE-1 and ROUGE-2 scores but offers no privacy. FL + DP achieves competitive performance compared to centralized BART while preserving user privacy. While ROUGE-1 and ROUGE-2 scores dip slightly, ROUGE-L improves by 6.2% for

FL + DP as compared to centralized BART. Introducing fairness using Q-fair results in a drop in performance; however, this sacrifice improves fairness in the generated summary, giving higher weight to minority opinions. Concerning the interplay of representative client participation and text compression achieved while summarization, FL + DP balances privacy and performance with improved compression. FL + DP + Q-fair yields competitive summaries while ensuring equitable client participation.

For a focused comparison of the comparable approaches, among the 10 test documents, Test Document 10 was selected for in-depth comparison based on its high ROUGE-1 and overall competitive performance across all methods. The document is approximately 2–3 pages long, and the first few and the last line of test document 10, along with the reference summary, is given next:

Original Snippet: *James Wilson says Wayne Rooney is more likely to score a picture-book goal. The 18-year-old has been training with Manchester United's first team since March of this year. Wilson insists Wayne Rooney can score from anywhere inside the box.*

...

Going into training with them is obviously a great experience, you have to think a lot more quickly than normally".

Reference Summary: *James Wilson has been training with the Man United first team since March. The 18-year-old has made five appearances for Louis van Gaal this season. Wilson reveals Wayne Rooney is more likely to score a picture-book goal in training than any of his team-mates. The England youth international said he is learning from senior strikers Rooney, Radamel Falcao, and Robin van Persie.*

The summaries generated for this document by various comparable techniques are given next:

- **Centralized BART:** *James Wilson says Wayne Rooney is more likely to score a picture-book goal. The 18-year-old has been training with Manchester United's first team. Wilson insists Wayne Rooney can score from anywhere inside the box.*
- **FL + DP:** *James Wilson says Wayne Rooney is more likely to score a picture-book goal in training than any other player. The 18-year-old has made five appearances for Louis van Gaal's side this season.*
- **FL + DP + Q-fair:** *Manchester United Starlet James Wilson says Wayne Rooney is more likely to score a picture-book goal than any other player in the squad. The 18-year-old has made five appearances for the United first team this season, including four in the league.*

Table 3 compares the summarization performance of three configurations on a representative test document using ROUGE and compression metrics.

Table 3. ROUGE and Compression Metrics for Test Document 10

Method	ROUGE-1	ROUGE-2	ROUGE-L	Compression
Centralized BART	0.5741	0.4151	0.2963	0.1017
FL + DP	0.6078	0.5400	0.3725	0.0847
FL + DP + Q-fair	0.5818	0.4259	0.3091	0.1065

The FL + DP model achieves the highest ROUGE-1 and ROUGE-2 scores, indicating strong content preservation despite the noise introduced for privacy. The FL + DP + Q-fair model shows slightly lower ROUGE scores but a higher compression ratio, reflecting more concise summaries due to fairness-aware aggregation. We also observe that compression is lowest for FL + DP due to tighter summaries, possibly regularized by DP noise.

Next, we compare the word clouds and histograms of the most prominent words in the original test document 10 and the summary generated by various methods, as given in Fig. 4.

The word clouds reveal semantic consistency between the original document and generated summaries. Key entities like "Manchester United," "Rooney," and "Wilson" persist across all methods. The Q-fair model slightly shifts term prominence, e.g., inclusion of the word "scarlet," indicating adjusted client influence. The TF-IDF histograms show that centralized BART produces dense term clusters, while FL variants distribute term importance more evenly. This suggests better generalization under privacy. The Q-fair variant further balances token significance across clients.

The Q-fair aggregation mechanism balances fairness and accuracy in federated optimization. Lower values of q enforce uniform client weights, ensuring equitable participation regardless of local data volume. Higher values ($q \rightarrow 1$) converge toward FedAvg, favoring data-rich clients. To assess the impact of fairness on generated summaries, we varied $q \in [0.1, 0.9]$. Higher q increases the influence of data-scarce clients. The results of various ROUGE scores for different values of q are given in Fig. 5.

As the value of q increases, all the ROUGE scores increase until they reach the maximum value at around $q = 0.5$. A minimal value of q refers to almost equal weight to all users irrespective of their data size, likely to give erroneous results. As q approaches moderate values of 0.5, ROUGE scores achieve their maximum values, indicating optimal weight distribution between majority and minority clients. However, as q increases beyond 0.5, Q-fair aggregation approaches FedAvg, discarding the minority opinion, resulting in the demise of ROUGE scores. Empirical results reveal that moderate values ($q \in [0.4, 0.6]$) strike the best balance-achieving strong ROUGE scores while minimizing bias from over-represented clients. This makes Q-fair aggregation especially effective in non-IID settings, and future research could explore adaptive q-scheduling based on client divergence or gradient variance.

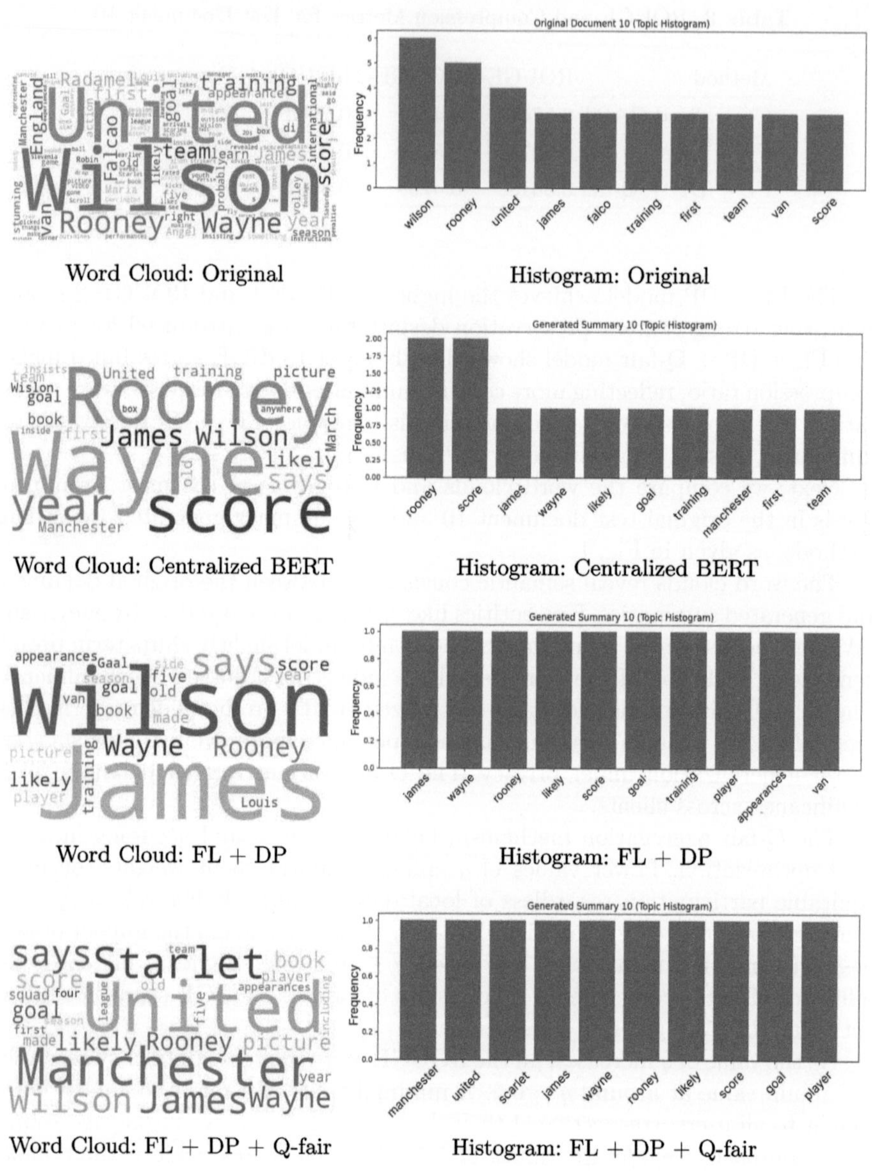

Word Cloud: Original

Histogram: Original

Word Cloud: Centralized BERT

Histogram: Centralized BERT

Word Cloud: FL + DP

Histogram: FL + DP

Word Cloud: FL + DP + Q-fair

Histogram: FL + DP + Q-fair

Fig. 4. Comparison of word clouds and TF-IDF histograms for test document 10

To evaluate the influence of client count on summarization quality under federated training, we conducted experiments by varying the number of participating clients while keeping the total data volume constant. This helps us understand the trade-off between decentralization and model convergence. Figure 6 shows the variation of ROUGE-1, ROUGE-2, ROUGE-L, and compression ratio with $K \in \{2, 3, 5, 10\}$ clients.

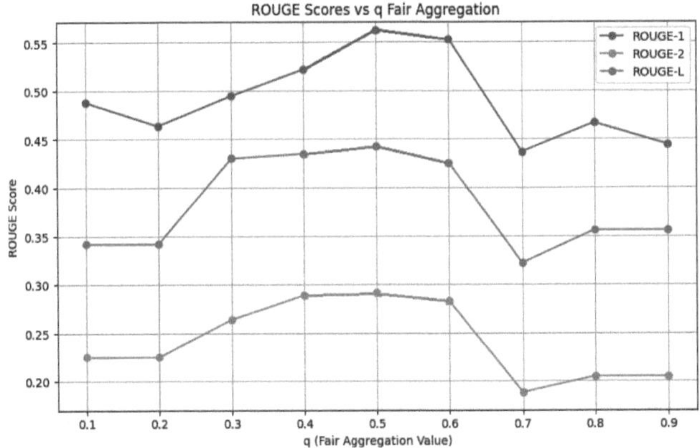

Fig. 5. ROUGE Scores vs Fairness Aggregation q

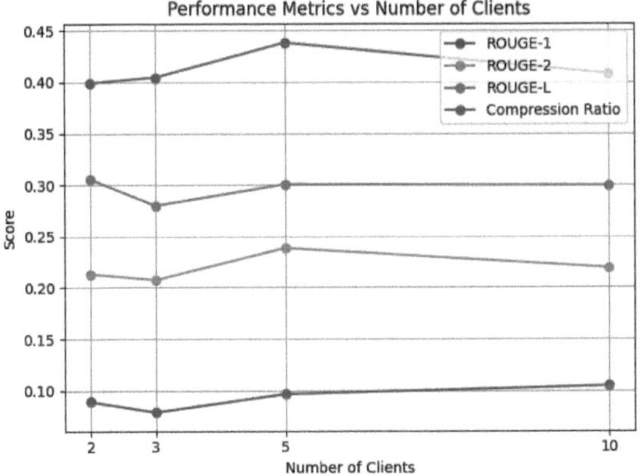

Fig. 6. Performance Metrics vs Number of Clients (FL + DP)

The initial client increase improves ROUGE scores, likely due to better generalization from diverse local data distributions. Performance peaks around five clients, after which a slight decline is observed-possibly caused by increased gradient noise and heterogeneity from excessive client splitting. These findings suggest that moderate client counts balance distributed learning and effective convergence. Excessive partitioning may introduce excessive non-IID variance, affecting learning stability. Therefore, careful tuning of client granularity is essential in real-world federated summarization setups.

5.3 Ablation Analysis

To better quantify the contribution of each core component in our summarization pipeline, we perform an ablation study over four configurations, as discussed next.

1. **Centralized Training (No FL, No DP):** This is the vanilla supervised training of BART on the entire dataset. No client partitioning or noise is applied. It serves as an upper-bound baseline.
2. **Federated Learning Only (FL):** The dataset is distributed across multiple clients using FedAvg aggregation, but no noise is injected. This evaluates the decentralization effect in isolation.
3. **Differential Privacy Only (DP):** BART is trained in a centralized setting with Gaussian noise ($\epsilon = 0.1$) applied to model updates. This helps isolate the privacy-utility trade-off.
4. **Federated + DP (Proposed):** Our final system combines federated optimization and privacy-preserving noise injection during local updates. In the main pipeline, this is further enhanced using Q-fair aggregation.

Each setting is designed to isolate the effect of FL, DP, and fairness-aware aggregation in a controlled manner. Table 4 lists various evaluation matrices for different combinations of BERT, FL, and DP. It can be inferred that centralized BART performs well by leveraging full data access and optimized convergence. However, it does not provide privacy guarantees. Applying vanilla FL using FedAvg and no DP protection against inference attacks unexpectedly achieves slightly better ROUGE-1, suggesting that client-specific updates may offer beneficial regularization. However, it achieves sub-optimal values of ROUGE-2 and ROUGE-L and achieves better compression (8.0%) of the original dataset. Utilizing privacy-preserving DP in centralized training has a larger performance penalty, as it significantly lowers ROUGE scores, highlighting the cost of injecting noise into globally averaged gradients. Using FL + DP, generate a summary with a slightly lower ROUGE-1 score than FL. However, its ROUGE-2 and ROUGE-L scores are better than the centralized BERT. This combination strikes a valuable balance between privacy and performance and further enhances client representation in generated summaries when paired with Q-fair strategies.

Table 4. Ablation study on test document 10 (CNN/DailyMail)

Configuration	ROUGE-1	ROUGE-2	ROUGE-L	Compression
Centralized (No FL, No DP)	0.5741	0.4151	0.2963	0.1017
FL Only (FedAvg)	0.5853	0.3450	0.2634	0.0889
DP Only (Centralized, $\epsilon = 0.1$)	0.3047	0.1783	0.2116	0.0941
FL + DP ($\epsilon = 1.0$)	**0.5678**	**0.4400**	**0.3125**	**0.0847**

6 Discussion and Conclusions

This study presents a unified framework for privacy-preserving abstractive summarization using federated learning and differentially private optimization powered by the BART model. Our approach addresses critical challenges in secure

NLP by integrating FL, DP, and Q-fair aggregation. Despite limited communication (23 rounds), our federated setup yields high-quality summaries. This can be attributed to the strong inductive priors embedded in the BART encoder-decoder architecture. The pre-trained nature of BART allows effective adaptation with relatively few updates, even under privacy constraints and non-IID distributions. Moreover, Q-fair weighting preserves fairness and stability in participation, preventing dominant clients from skewing model behavior-a key concern in decentralized setups. Experiments on Reuters and CNN/DailyMail demonstrate that high-quality summarization is achievable despite privacy constraints and limited communication. ROUGE metrics, visualizations, and ablation studies validate the practical viability of this pipeline for deployment in sensitive domains.

The proposed system is well-suited for domains where privacy and interpretability are essential. For instance, hospitals can locally summarize discharge summaries or patient reports under formal privacy constraints, enabling collaborative model improvement without risking data leakage. Law firms, financial institutions, and newsrooms with geographically distributed branches can also benefit from local summarization with federated model updates, ensuring compliance with jurisdictional data regulations.

In conclusion, this work lays the groundwork for deploying high-quality summarization tools in real-world, privacy-sensitive environments-bridging modern NLP capabilities with the stringent constraints of secure, decentralized data governance. In the future, we would like to extend our proposed approach to larger, heterogeneous client populations with asynchronous participation and straggler resilience and incorporate personalization through user-specific heads or meta-learning to adapt to individual client language or tone without violating privacy.

References

1. Lewis, M., et al.: BART: denoising sequence-to-sequence pre-training for natural language generation. In: Proceedings of ACL (2020)
2. Zhang, J., et al.: PEGASUS: pre-training with extracted gap-sentences for abstractive summarization. In: Proceedings of ICML (2020)
3. Raffel, C., et al.: Exploring the limits of transfer learning with a unified text-to-text transformer. In: JMLR (2020)
4. Liu, Y., Lapata, M.: Text summarization with pretrained encoders. In: Proceedings of EMNLP-IJCNLP (2019)
5. Zhong, M., et al.: Extractive summarization as text matching. In: ACL (2020)
6. Gao, T., Yao, X., Chen, D.: SimCSE: simple contrastive learning of sentence embeddings. In: Proceedings of EMNLP (2021)
7. Lin, T., et al.: FedNLP: benchmarking federated learning methods for natural language processing tasks. In: EMNLP (2021)
8. Hard, A., et al.: Federated Learning for Mobile Keyboard Prediction, arXiv:1811.03604 (2018)
9. Luo, J., et al.: Federated learning for dialogue systems. In: Findings of ACL (2021)
10. Dwork, C., Roth, A.: The algorithmic foundations of differential privacy. Found. Trends® Theor. Comput. Sci. (2014)

11. Yousefpour, A., et al.: Opacus: Easy Differential Privacy for PyTorch, arXiv:2109.12298 (2021)
12. Geyer, R.C., Klein, T., Nabi, M.: Differentially Private Federated Learning: A Client Level Perspective, arXiv:1712.07557 (2017)
13. Li, T., Sahu, A., Talwalkar, A., Smith, V.: Fair resource allocation in federated learning. In: ICLR (2020)
14. Huang, Y., et al.: Personalized cross-silo federated learning on non-IID data. In: NeurIPS (2021)
15. Li, Q., et al.: Model-contrastive federated learning. In: CVPR (2021)
16. Reddi, S., et al.: Adaptive federated optimization. In: ICLR (2021)
17. Rajput, S., et al.: Federated learning with fair averaging. In: NeurIPS (2020)
18. Zhao, L., et al.: Privacy-preserving summarization using differential privacy. In: ACL (2023)
19. Wolf, T., et al.: Transformers: state-of-the-art natural language processing. In: EMNLP: System Demonstrations (2020)
20. Wang, J., et al.: Tackling the objective inconsistency problem in heterogeneous federated optimization. In: NeurIPS (2020)
21. Shi, Y., Yu, H., Leung, C.: Towards fairness-aware federated learning. IEEE Trans. Neural Netw. Learn. Syst. **35**(9), 11922–11938 (2024). https://doi.org/10.1109/TNNLS.2023.3263594
22. Acar, D., et al.: Federated learning based on dynamic regularization. In: International Conference on Learning Representations (ICLR) (2021)
23. Lewis, D.: Reuters-21578 Text Categorization Collection [Dataset]. UCI Machine Learning Repository (1987). https://doi.org/10.24432/C52G6M
24. See, A., et al.: Get to the point: summarization with pointer-generator networks. In: Annual Meeting of the Association for Computational Linguistics (2017)
25. The Independent: James Wilson: Working with Rooney, Van Persie and Falcao has been 'unbelievable'. The Independent (2015)
26. McMahan, B., et al.: Communication-efficient learning of deep networks from decentralized data. In: International Conference on Artificial Intelligence and Statistics (2017)
27. Liu, Q., et al.: Federated semi-supervised medical image classification via inter-client relation matching. In: International Conference on Medical Image Computing and Computer Assisted Intervention (2021)

System Security

Self-learning Digital Twin for Kubernetes Security

N. S. Devnath[✉], Aayushman Singh, Adarsh Sasikumar, and Sriram Sankaran

Center for Cybersecurity Systems and Networks, Amrita Vishwa Vidyapeetham,
Amritapuri Campus, Amritapuri, Kerala, India
`am.sc.u4cys23021@am.students.amrita.edu`

Abstract. The inherent complexity of cloud-native environments like Kubernetes is due to its dynamic and distributed landscape. According to the Kubernetes Security Report 2024, over 67% of organizations have delayed their deployment of containerized applications due to security concerns. Digital twin technology has emerged as a promising field of interest in cybersecurity, as it offers a real-time environment for detecting threats without impacting the live production systems. This paper proposes a novel self-learning cybersecurity framework on a digital twin of a Kubernetes cluster. In this system, a digital twin of a cluster is created and monitored for security misconfigurations. Then, it is introduced to different attack scenarios through a Genetic Algorithm (GA), which drives the evolution of offensive and defense strategies through a tailored fitness function. The most effective defenses are then applied to the twin and its impact is passed to the GA. The risk assessment of the attack success and defense effectiveness, is done using Multi-Layer Perceptron (MLP). Over multiple cycles, the attack strategies keep improving, making the twin refine its defense strategies to ensure the cluster security. Applying on the Kubernetes Goat cluster, the framework was successfully able to identify 91.7% of the attacks simulated.

Keywords: Cloud · Kubernetes · Digital twin · Attack · Defense · Self-learning · Genetic Algorithms

1 Introduction

With the current advancements in technology and need for scalable environments, most IT organizations have switched to cloud computing as it offers a large number of benefits such as remote access, reduced infrastructure costs, and faster and flexible setup and deployment as discussed in [29]. For modern application development docker, and Kubernetes has played an important role in facilitating efficient, scalable and secure container orchestration as explained in [21]. The report by CNCF (Cloud Native Computing Foundation), the use of Kubernetes rose to 80% in 2024. Its wide-spread adoption indicates its importance in enabling efficient cloud operations. However, this shift also introduces a

N. Hubballi et al. (Eds.): ICISS 2025, LNCS 16380, pp. 433–443, 2026.
https://doi.org/10.1007/978-3-032-13714-2_26

new landscape of threats, which is due to the rapidly changing state of workloads, clusters, and broader attack surface. Figure 1 shows the critical risks observed in cloud platforms, according to the Google Cloud Threat Horizons Report 2025.

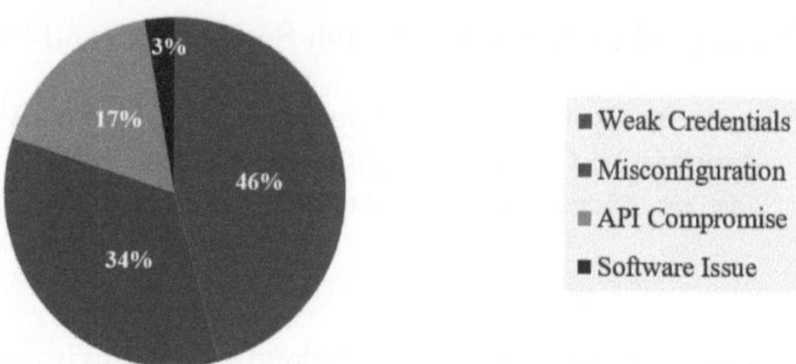

Fig. 1. Most common ways for attacks to compromise cloud environments.

Traditional approaches often rely on signature-based static policy enforcement. However, these frameworks cannot address the sophisticated nature of modern cloud-native attacks and dynamic workloads. Implementing security mitigations in real time clusters is very challenging, since it could compromise the system's availability. Digital twin technology has been an emerging field, especially cybersecurity. It is used in various domains like medicine and manufacturing. In the field of medicine, some of the recent works include how a twin could be used to capture the complex and realistic nature of cardiac systems better than conventional methods as shown in [18] and its applications in securing real time information of patients in [23]. For a physical system, a digital twin is its real-time copy or representation. It can be lever-aged for dynamic testing, and real-time monitoring of containerized applications. In the context of a Kubernetes cluster, a digital twin creates a replica of the cluster's resources without affecting the original cluster. There has been significant research being done using Kubernetes based digital twins for analysis and testing.

This paper proposes a self-learning digital twin of a Kubernetes cluster for enhancing its security. First, a digital twin of the cluster state is created, and it is analyzed for any security misconfigurations using static rule-based detection. Each detected misconfiguration is assigned a severity score. If the severity score crosses a certain threshold, it is logged onto a file and is a severe security misconfiguration that should be resolved as soon as possible. Once the cluster is properly configured, it is tested against a series of attacks sourced from security datasets such as CIC-IDS and MITRE ATT&CK. The intelligence of the system is driven by AI models, where multilayer perceptron (MLP) is used for predicting the severity score and outcome. The attack and defense session are simulated using Genetic Algorithms (GA). In this session the attacker and defender evolve their strategies over many generations. A novel GA fitness function is formulated to simulate the offense-defense tradeoff. The findings from the severity score and feedback from the attack defense session are fed back into the learning pipeline. Through multiple learning cycles, the twin improves its threat detection and mitigation, resulting in a continuous self-learning cluster resilient to cyberattacks.

2   Related Work

Cloud environments are inherently dynamic and therefore prone to a wide range of cyberattacks. Gonzales et al. [14] outlined key security challenges in cloud systems, while German et al. [13] emphasized the risks of misconfigurations, which can expose unique attack surfaces. Pranesh et al. [20] highlighted the role of workload clustering in improving resource management and its implications for security. Recent efforts also integrate zero-trust principles: Jayaraj et al. [27] demonstrated the use of mTLS to enhance real-time protection in Kubernetes-based applications. Digital twins (DTs) have been increasingly applied in cyber-security to model and analyze the impact of attacks. Eckhart et al. [11,12] and Alam et al. [3] explored DTs in industrial and cyber-physical systems, while Mustofa et al. [17] used them to assess cluster behavior under potential threats. For Kubernetes, Borsatti et al. [7,8] proposed KubeTwin, a statistical model for cluster optimization; Wermann et al. [28] introduced KTWIN, a serverless platform that automates DT management; and Zaccarini et al. [30] developed TELKA, which combines reinforcement learning with chaos engineering to mitigate application faults.

Machine learning and deep learning are widely used in cloud security. Butt et al. [9] surveyed supervised, unsupervised, and hybrid methods for threat detection, and Alzoubi et al. [5] discussed current research trends and challenges. Both works stress the need for adaptive frameworks capable of continuous learning in dynamic cloud settings. Aravind et al. [6] created a framework using advanced machine learning in Kubernetes environments. Similarly Sree et al. [22] and Skoumperdis et al. [25] demonstrated self-learning security systems in smart grids, where DTs retrain models for live feedback to improve detection accuracy. Self-supervised techniques have also shown promise: for example, adversarial defenses by Deshpande et al. [10] improved generalization, while Meyer et al. [15] proposed federated self-supervised learning to enhance distributed intrusion detection. Stepanov et al. [26] applied genetic algorithms to evolve attack scenarios, enabling systematic evaluation of an infrastructure's cybersecurity posture. Aly et al. [4] created a real time threat detection system with adaptive deception for Kubernetes environments.

In contrast to existing approaches, the proposed methodology combines the knowledge of self-learning and anomaly detection to address the security limitations in clusters, and create a novel digital twin framework, which can be used to detect and mitigate vulnerabilities in Kubernetes clusters.

3   System Design and Architecture

The proposed framework consists of five logically distinct layers as shown in Fig. 2.

1. Kubernetes Environment Layer: represents the live state of the Kubernetes cluster.
2. Digital Twin Layer: interacts with the cluster to create a digital twin.
3. Intelligence Layer: consists of models for simulating attack and defense strategies.
4. Defense Orchestration Layer: contains defense mechanisms to patch vulnerabilities.
5. Logging Layer: maintains logs of cluster activities and monitors feedback.

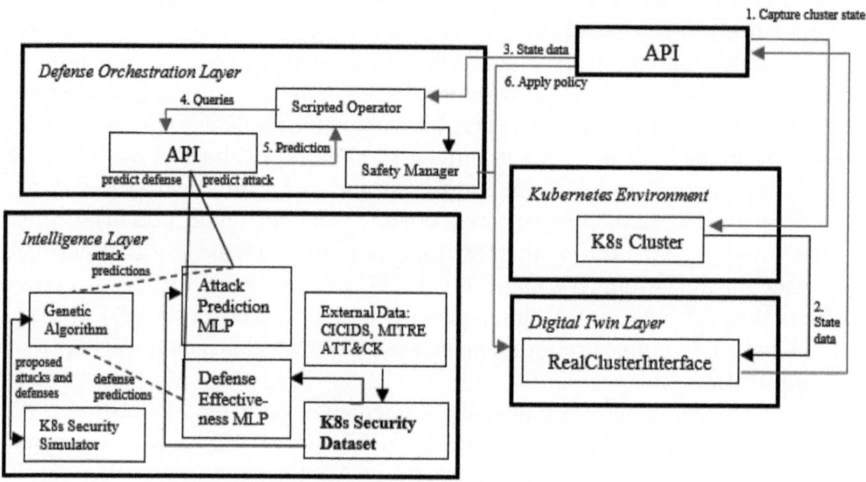

Fig. 2. Architectural Diagram of the Framework.

3.1 Kubernetes Environment Layer

This layer represents the target Kubernetes environment. For this work, two clusters are used for comparison. The first cluster is Kubernetes Goat, which is an intentionally created vulnerable cluster used for learning and practicing Kubernetes security [2]. It has a detailed documentation of its vulnerabilities, attack and defense scenarios in it, making it suitable for testing.

The second cluster is a dummy cluster created using kind (Kubernetes in Docker) which represents an actual production cluster. This cluster is configured to host basic services with logging tools like Prometheus, Grafana, and Fluentd.

3.2 Digital Twin Layer

This layer is responsible for creating and maintaining the virtual replica of the Kubernetes environment layer. There is an API server which interacts with the live cluster to create the twin. More importantly, it analyses the vulnerabilities in the cluster and is tested against a series of attacks.

3.3   Intelligence Layer

This layer is responsible for identifying security threats in the cluster, predicting its severity, and evolving the attack and defense strategies. It has three key components:

Feature Extraction. For the initial model training, real-world security datasets such as CIC-IDS Traffic Labelling [24] and the MITRE ATT&CK Enterprise Matrix [16] are used. CIC-IDS 2017 is a standard benchmark dataset which contains labelled records of modern-day network attack scenarios such as DDoS, botnets and brute force attacks. The MITRE ATT&CK Enterprise Matrix is a structured knowledge base of adversarial attacks which are relevant to enterprise and cloud environments.

The raw heterogenous data from the dataset or live cluster is preprocessed into a standardized format in the form of an 8-dimensional vector with features: event type, source IP, target service, attack type, severity score, attack success, response time and resources affected. The categorical features (like event type, source IP, target service, and attack vector) are normalized. For initially calculations, the severity score of each attack vector is set as a fixed predefined value.

Neural Networks. The attack-defense mechanisms are initialized by two neural networks. Both models take the 8-bit preprocessed event features as input. Each network consists of three dense layers (128, 64 and 32 neurons), connected by ReLU activation functions and is scattered with dropout layers to prevent overfitting. The dense layers in the network help to identify patterns in the input data by assigning weights.

The defense model uses a combination of the contextual information from the cluster, and the proposed defense strategy to create the feature vector. These strategies include RBAC hardening, network policies, resource quotas, admission controllers, monitoring alert and encryption. Both these models are optimized using the Ad-am optimizer to minimize the mean squared error.

Genetic Algorithm. Through the genetic algorithm, the system orchestrates the continuous evolution of attack and defense strategies. The GA maintains a diverse population of 100 attack and defense strategy objects. The target services for each strategy are randomly selected, and performance metrics are assigned. Table 1 shows the performance metrics used in the GA fitness functions.

Table 1. Performance Metrics used in the GA fitness functions

Parameter	Description	Mode of Calculation
Stealth Score	Measure of attack's ability to evade detection	Based on the number of logs generated by the attack action
Resource cost	Computational cost to execute the attack	Based on CPU, memory and I/O used by attack process within the digital twin
Effectiveness	Probability that the given strategy will mitigate the attack	Based on the ratio of successful mitigations to total attempts
Coverage score	Measure of how much coverage a defense strategy can address	Based on the score mapped to the number of MITRE ATT&CK techniques the deployed policy addresses
Performance impact	Operational overhead introduced by the defense strategy	Based on the change in memory usage, or application response time when defense is active

The core of the genetic algorithm lies in the functioning of the fitness function. For attack strategies, the fitness function is computed to increase success rates and minimize resource cost as shown in Eq. 1. The fitness function is derived in such a way because an ideal attacker would want to maximize damage while avoiding detection. Effectiveness metric is not used as it attributes to the effectiveness of defense response.

$$\text{Fitness}_{\text{Attack}} = \frac{\text{Success\_rate} \times \text{Stealth\_score}}{\text{Resource\_Cost}} \tag{1}$$

For defense strategies, the fitness function gives importance to maximizing coverage while minimizing performance impact as shown in Eq. 2. Unlike the attacker, the defense's goal is to maximize its effectiveness while minimizing its operational costs.

$$\text{Fitness}_{\text{Defense}} = \frac{\text{Effectiveness} \times \text{Coverage\_score}}{1 + \text{Performance\_impact}} \tag{2}$$

After evaluating the fitness function of all strategies in the current generation, selection is done to choose the fittest individuals as parents for the next generation. Then, crossover is done to produce new strategies. Lastly mutation is done by introducing random perturbations to offspring attributes, to prevent premature convergence.

3.4   Defense Orchestration Layer

The defense action is triggered by the prediction service running in the API server. Currently the system uses simple strategies like:

(a) Restricting service account permissions or enforcing least-privilege access;
(b) Introducing network policy rules to isolate workloads and control traffic flow;
(c) Setting enforcement of limits on CPU/Memory usage per namespace.

After selecting a strategy, it constructs a defense-specific feature vector which is sent to the service endpoint. The service uses its defense effectiveness model to predict the effectiveness, performance impact and coverage. Only if the effectiveness of the defense on the cluster exceeds a threshold, the operator applies the proposed defense.

3.5   Logging Layer

This is the most crucial layer, as it plays an important role in logging the response generated by the Intelligence layer and reviewing the feedback generated by the Defense Orchestration layer. It stores the feature vectors, simulation results, model prediction result files. It also generated a brief report after each cycle of the loop.

4   Workflow and Methodology

This section discusses how each of the layers discussed in the previous section interacts with each other. The framework operates in two modes:

4.1   Training Mode

In this mode, the cluster information is used to train the model first. It is done offline to create attack and defense models for subsequent training or prediction. The cluster state is fed into the Feature Extraction unit. The observations are supplemented by the information generated by the datasets. This is useful when there are no observations during initial training. The intelligence layer trains using the training data from feature extraction. The genetic algorithm initializes population of attack and defense strategies and finds the best strategies using the outputs from the models.

4.2   Inference Mode

In inference mode, in order to avoid repeated training the system directly uses the API online which uses the models generated from previous training. The Scripted Operator in the defense orchestration layer constructs a feature vector from the real-time cluster state. Then the API service returns attack severity predictions and defense effectiveness metrics. Upon receiving predictions from the Attack MLP, if the severity crosses a predefined threshold the system chooses an appropriate defense strategy. It is checked if the operations can be safely done or already exists.

5   Discussion and Evaluation

The threats that were identified in the Kubernetes goat cluster included privilege container configurations, root access vulnerabilities, absence of network policies, excessive RBAC permissions, and sensitive host path mount. A total of 206 vulnerabilities were discovered over different namespaces.

To evaluate the performance of the attack model, a small amount of data was used for testing which had 87.3% accuracy, precision of 86.6%, recall of 91.7% and F1-score of 89.1%. Table 2 shows the comparison of this model compared to other Kubernetes based real time frameworks discussed in [6] and [4]. The effectiveness of the defense strategies after prediction showed that RBAC hardening and network segmentation were the most effective in mitigating attacks.

Table 2. Comparison of Kubernetes based attack detection approaches with existing approach

Study	Approach	Detection Accuracy
AI-Powered Anomaly Detection for Kubernetes Security: A Systematic Approach to Identifying Threats [6]	AI-based anomaly detection	92%
Real-time multi-class threat detection and adaptive deception in Kubernetes environments [4]	ML-based detection and deception	91%
Proposed Approach	Attack success detection done using MLP	87%

In the normal cluster that was used, the system identified the major threats to be attributed to the lack of network policies. The evolution of the attack and defense strategies in both clusters showed interesting patterns. The critical point in both graphs is the low and stable defense fitness, indicating that the GA was not successful in evolving more effective defense strategies, which could be because the model's defense orchestration strategies were too simple (Fig. 3).

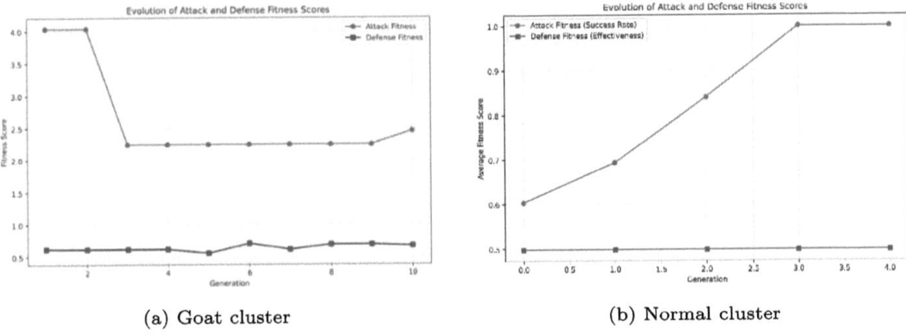

(a) Goat cluster   (b) Normal cluster

Fig. 3. Comparison of attack-defense strategies over successive generations.

6   Conclusion and Future Work

This paper proposed a self-learning cybersecurity framework for improving the security posture of dynamic Kubernetes environments. The core of this framework uses a digital twin for safe testing and simulation and an intelligence layer which uses deep learning algorithms and evolutionary optimization algorithms using a novel fitness function. The digital twin was a minimal representation of the cluster. The model was only able to capture some of the most crucial vulnerabilities in the cluster, which includes privileged container configurations, absence of network policies etc. The attack defense neural network using MLP for attack and defense prediction was effective in its predictive capabilities. The attack model showed good performance to the testing data with Accuracy 87.3% and F1-Score 89.1%. The genetic algorithm was also successful in evolving good attack strategies with fitness rates increasing in both clusters. However, the results also revealed that for both clusters, the defense fitness remained low and stable across generations, indicating that the GA was not successful in evolving more efficient defense strategies. This is because the current model's defense orchestration strategies are simple and limited in number. Despite these limitations, the framework can be used to build intelligent systems that can help in securing dynamic Kubernetes environments.

Some of the future work that can be done to enhance the framework's capabilities is to create a security enhanced digital twin operator that can work real time to get cluster information and capture a broader range of components, like detailed workloads, and network flow logs. Prior works like in [28] and [30] can be improved for more security-based operations. To enhance the intelligence layer, standard security scoring using CVSS scores can be done [19], more dynamic defense strategies like adaptive firewall rules, and sophisticated isolation mechanisms like kernel-level sandboxing can be done. Graph Neural Networks (GNNs) can be used for modelling the complex relationships between Kubernetes clusters as discussed for intrusion detection systems in [31]. To improve the predictions, GANs can be used for generating synthetic attack data like [1]. It would involve a generator network producing new sophisticated attack patterns that challenges the existing defense, and a discriminator network trained to distinguish real and generated attacks. These additions would help the attack generation and defense strategies to coevolve, addressing the current limitation of less defense strategies.

References

1. Agrawal, G., Kaur, A., Myneni, S.: A review of generative models in generating synthetic attack data for cybersecurity. Electronics **13**(2), 322 (2024)
2. Akula, M.: Kubernetes goat (2025). https://madhuakula.com/kubernetes-goat/docs/
3. Alam, K.M., El Saddik, A.: C2PS: a digital twin architecture reference model for the cloud-based cyber-physical systems. IEEE Access **5**, 2050–2062 (2017)
4. Aly, A., Hamad, A.M., Al-Qutt, M., Fayez, M.: Real-time multi-class threat detection and adaptive deception in Kubernetes environments. Sci. Rep. **15**(1), 8924 (2025)
5. Alzoubi, Y.I., Mishra, A., Topcu, A.E.: Research trends in deep learning and machine learning for cloud computing security. Artif. Intell. Rev. **57**(5), 132 (2024)
6. Bhardwaj, A.K., Dutta, P., Chintale, P.: Ai-powered anomaly detection for Kubernetes security: a systematic approach to identifying threats. Babylonian J. Mach. Learn. **2024**, 142–148 (2024)
7. Borsatti, D., et al.: KubeTwin: a digital twin framework for Kubernetes deployments at scale. IEEE Trans. Netw. Serv. Manage. **21**(4), 3889–3903 (2024)
8. Borsatti, D., et al.: Modeling digital twins of Kubernetes-based applications. In: 2023 IEEE Symposium on Computers and Communications (ISCC), pp. 219–224. IEEE (2023)
9. Butt, U.A., et al.: A review of machine learning algorithms for cloud computing security. Electronics **9**(9), 1379 (2020)
10. Deshpande, V., et al.: Investigating the potential of self-supervised learning in adversarial machine learning. In: 2024 IEEE 2nd International Conference on Innovations in High Speed Communication and Signal Processing (IHCSP), pp. 1–6. IEEE (2024)
11. Eckhart, M., Ekelhart, A.: Digital twins for cyber-physical systems security: state of the art and outlook. In: Security and Quality in Cyber-Physical Systems Engineering: With Forewords by Robert M. Lee and Tom Gilb, pp. 383–412 (2019)
12. Eckhart, M., Ekelhart, A., Weippl, E.: Enhancing cyber situational awareness for cyber-physical systems through digital twins. In: 2019 24th IEEE International Conference on Emerging Technologies and Factory Automation (ETFA), pp. 1222–1225. IEEE (2019)
13. German, K., Ponomareva, O.: An overview of container security in a Kubernetes cluster. In: 2023 IEEE Ural-Siberian Conference on Biomedical Engineering, Radioelectronics and Information Technology (USBEREIT), pp. 283–285. IEEE (2023)
14. Gonzalez, N., et al.: A quantitative analysis of current security concerns and solutions for cloud computing. J. Cloud Comput. **1**(1), 1–18 (2012). https://doi.org/10.1186/2192-113X-1-11
15. Meyer, B.H., Pozo, A.T., Nogueira, M., Zola, W.M.N.: Federated self-supervised learning for intrusion detection. In: 2023 IEEE Symposium Series on Computational Intelligence (SSCI), pp. 822–828. IEEE (2023)
16. MITRE Corporation: Att&ck: Adversarial tactics, techniques, and common knowledge. https://attack.mitre.org/resources/attack-data-and-tools/

17. Mustofa, R., Rafiquzzaman, M., Hossain, N.U.I.: Analyzing the impact of cyber-attacks on the performance of digital twin-based industrial organizations. J. Ind. Inf. Integr. **41**, 100633 (2024)
18. Nair, V.S., Niranga, G.H., Aryalakshmi, C., Sathyapalan, D.T., Madathil, T., Pathinarupothi, R.K.: Optimizing inotropic infusion with cluster specific ai decision models and digital twins. IEEE Access (2025)
19. NIST: CVSS v3.1 equations. https://nvd.nist.gov/vuln-metrics/cvss/v3-calculator/v31/equations
20. Pranesh, M., Visweshwaran, S., Sathiya, R.: Cloud workload clustering. In: 2022 8th International Conference on Smart Structures and Systems (ICSSS), pp. 1–4. IEEE (2022)
21. Sah, K.P., Jain, N., Jha, P., Hawari, J., Beena, B.: Advancing of microservices architecture with dockers. In: 2024 15th International Conference on Computing Communication and Networking Technologies (ICCCNT), pp. 1–6. IEEE (2024)
22. Sai, V.S., Divya, R., Nair, M.G.: Navigating the smart grid landscape: A comprehensive review of recent advances. In: 2025 Fourth International Conference on Power, Control and Computing Technologies (ICPC2T), pp. 734–739. IEEE (2025)
23. Savant, R.V., et al.: A secure digital twin healthcare framework for precision medicine: Integrating IoMT, ml and fog computing. In: 2025 International Conference on Emerging Smart Computing and Informatics (ESCI), pp. 1–8. IEEE (2025)
24. Sharafaldin, I., et al.: Toward generating a new intrusion detection dataset and intrusion traffic characterization. ICISSp **1**(2018), 108–116 (2018)
25. Skoumperdis, M., et al.: A novel self-learning cybersecurity system for smart grids. In: Power Systems Cybersecurity: Methods, Concepts, and Best Practices, pp. 337–362. Springer (2023)
26. Stepanov, L., Koltsov, A., Parinov, A.: Evaluating the cybersecurity of an enterprise based on a genetic algorithm. In: International Russian Automation Conference, pp. 580–590. Springer (2020)
27. Viswanathan, J., et al.: Zero trust security for web applications in microservice-based environments. In: 2024 First International Conference on Data, Computation and Communication (ICDCC), pp. 488–494. IEEE (2024)
28. Wermann, A.G., Wickboldt, J.A.: KTwin: a serverless Kubernetes-based digital twin platform. Comput. Netw. **259**, 111095 (2025)
29. Wu, J., Ping, L., Ge, X., Wang, Y., Fu, J.: Cloud storage as the infrastructure of cloud computing. In: 2010 International Conference on Intelligent Computing and Cognitive Informatics, pp. 380–383. IEEE (2010)
30. Zaccarini, M., et al.: TELKA: twin-enhanced learning for Kubernetes applications. In: 2024 IEEE Symposium on Computers and Communications (ISCC), pp. 1–6. IEEE (2024)
31. Zhong, M., Lin, M., Zhang, C., Xu, Z.: A survey on graph neural networks for intrusion detection systems: methods, trends and challenges. Comput. Secur. **141**, 103821 (2024)

Security and Privacy Assessment of U.S. and Non-U.S. Android E-Commerce Applications

Urvashi Kishnani[1] and Sanchari Das[2(✉)]

[1] University of Denver, Denver, CO, USA
[2] George Mason University, Fairfax, VA, USA
sdas35@gmu.edu

Abstract. E-commerce mobile applications are central to global financial transactions, making their security and privacy crucial. In this study, we analyze 92 top-grossing Android e-commerce apps (58 U.S.-based and 34 international) using MobSF, AndroBugs, and RiskInDroid. Our analysis shows widespread SSL and certificate weaknesses, with approximately 92% using unsecured HTTP connections and an average MobSF security score of 40.92/100. Over-privileged permissions were identified in 77 apps. While U.S. apps exhibited fewer manifest, code, and certificate vulnerabilities, both groups showed similar network-related issues. We advocate for the adoption of stronger, standardized, and user-focused security practices across regions.

Keywords: e-commerce applications · security · privacy

1   Introduction

The growing demand for convenient and accessible shopping continues to drive the expansion of e-commerce applications [20–22]. Fellner et al. define e-commerce as "any business transaction conducted electronically rather than through physical interaction" [14], while Gaedke and Turowski categorize it into business-to-business (B2B), business-to-consumer (B2C), business-to-administration (B2A), and consumer-to-administration (C2A) [15]. This study focuses on B2C e-commerce through mobile platforms. Understanding regional differences in application security and privacy is crucial for securing user data, ensuring regulatory compliance, and maintaining user trust. Variations in legal frameworks and cybersecurity standards influence data handling practices, making cross-country comparisons essential. While previous studies have explored e-commerce in countries such as Malaysia [35], Saudi Arabia [4], and India [9], few have examined global disparities in security and privacy practices [17,30]. This research addresses that gap by answering the following research questions:

- **RQ1:** How does the security robustness of leading e-commerce mobile applications vary by major market region (U.S. vs. non-U.S.)?

N. Hubballi et al. (Eds.): ICISS 2025, LNCS 16380, pp. 444–454, 2026.
https://doi.org/10.1007/978-3-032-13714-2_27

- **RQ2:** How do differences in privacy measures reflect the regional privacy regulations governing these applications?

In this study, we analyzed 92 Android e-commerce applications (58 U.S.-based and 34 international) using MobSF, AndroBugs, and RiskInDroid. MobSF and AndroBugs were employed for security evaluation, while MobSF and RiskInDroid were used for privacy assessment. Our main contributions are:

- An assessment of 92 popular e-commerce applications, identifying key vulnerabilities in code, manifest, certificate, and network configurations, as well as privacy risks from excessive or dangerous permissions.
- A comparative analysis of U.S. and non-U.S. applications, showing that although overall security and privacy remain weak, U.S. apps performed slightly better across most evaluation metrics.

2   Related Work

Existing research highlights persistent security and privacy challenges in e-commerce mobile applications, including authentication weaknesses, insecure payment mechanisms, and data breaches [12,16,18,19]. These threats span network, application, and insider levels [23], underscoring the importance of strong encryption, secure communication protocols such as SSL/TLS, and regular vulnerability assessments [39]. User education also plays a key role in reducing risks by promoting secure payment practices and timely software updates [34]. As mobile commerce expands, wireless connectivity and increased data exchange further amplify these security risks [24,28].

Privacy risks in e-commerce apps arise from extensive user tracking and data sharing with advertisers or analytics services [11,26,27]. Prior studies identify issues such as identity tracking, smartphone vulnerabilities, and weak regulatory enforcement [40], emphasizing the need for privacy-preserving architectures and stronger data governance [6,27]. Reducing personal data collection enhances consumer control and trust [37], although many users still trade privacy for convenience in location-based services [33,36]. Building on these insights, we examine permission usage in leading e-commerce apps to expose security and privacy gaps and propose improvements that strengthen user trust and regulatory compliance.

3   Method

To build our dataset, we first compiled a list of leading e-commerce stores and identified their corresponding mobile applications. Two primary data sources were used: AfterShip [3] and EcommerceDB. AfterShip lists the top 100 online stores by combining monthly revenue and website traffic, with region-specific filters. We retrieved two lists from AfterShip—one filtered for the United States and another global list without regional restrictions. We also collected the top 50 global e-commerce stores from EcommerceDB, as cited by Acosta-Vargas et al. [2]. These lists were merged and cleaned by removing 84 duplicates. When a store appeared under multiple regions, it was associated with the country holding the largest market share, resulting in 166 unique stores.

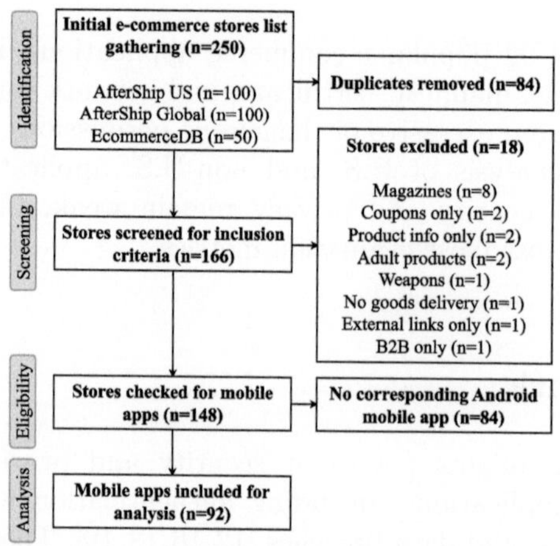

Fig. 1. Flowchart of the study method showing the results of the app search and screening process for analysis

Table 1. Distribution of applications by countries

Country	#	Country	#	Country	#	Country	#
United States	58	Germany	3	Russia	2	Netherlands	1
United Kingdom	7	India	3	Sweden	2	Romania	1
Brazil	4	Japan	2	Austria	1	Spain	1
China	3	Poland	2	Mexico	1	Thailand	1

Eighteen stores were excluded for the following reasons: (i) non-physical goods (digital magazines, coupon-only sites, or product catalogs; $n = 13$), (ii) restricted product categories requiring additional privacy and security considerations (adult or weapon-related products; $n = 3$), and (iii) B2B-only platforms ($n = 2$). From the remaining 148 stores, 92 had corresponding Android applications, which were downloaded in their latest available version as of 2023. Among these, 58 apps targeted the U.S. market, and 34 were international. The geographic distribution of these applications is presented in Table 1, and the overall app collection and filtering process is summarized in Fig. 1.

Each application was analyzed using the three tools: MobSF, AndroBugs, and RiskInDroid. MobSF performs static and dynamic analysis of Android, iOS, and Windows applications by reverse engineering APK files [1]. It generates detailed reports with severity levels (High, Warning, Info, Secure) and identifies dangerous permissions. AndroBugs conducts static analysis to detect vulnerabilities categorized as Critical, Warning, or Notice [5,25], while RiskInDroid evaluates privacy-related risks by classifying permissions as Declared, Exploited, Useless, or Ghost [31]. Reports from all tools were automatically generated and parsed using Python and Bash scripts to ensure consistency and efficiency [22,38].

MobSF successfully generated reports for 91 of 92 applications, AndroBugs for 76, and RiskInDroid for 81, with the remaining apps excluded due to time-outs or large APK sizes. For the security analysis, we compared MobSF and AndroBugs results between U.S. and non-U.S. applications, focusing on high-severity vulnerabilities (Critical and Warning) and average security scores. To maintain consistency, all high-severity findings were labeled as Critical. For the privacy analysis, we used RiskInDroid and MobSF data to assess permission-related risks, including declared, exploited, useless, ghost, and dangerous permissions, along with their average counts and distributions. RiskInDroid analyzed 82 applications (51 U.S., 31 non-U.S.), and MobSF analyzed 91 applications (57 U.S., 34 non-U.S.). All APKs were obtained from trusted sources such as Google Play and APKPure. Following ethical guidelines, specific app names are not disclosed, and all identified organizations were informed of the findings, with several confirming that the reported vulnerabilities were resolved.

4   Results

4.1   Security

We analyzed the security scores and vulnerabilities of all applications, as summarized in Table 2. The table presents the distribution of vulnerabilities by severity (Critical and Warning) across all apps, U.S. apps, and non-U.S. apps, accounting for differences in the number of successfully analyzed applications per tool.

Application Security Scores: MobSF assigns each application a security score ranging from 0 (lowest) to 100 (highest), with deductions of 15 for each Critical and 10 for each Warning vulnerability. An additional 5 points are added for exceptional security measures, capped at 100. Among U.S. apps, scores ranged from 13 to 67 with an average of 42, while non-U.S. apps scored between 16 and 73 with an average of 39.12.

Proper implementation of **Secure Socket Layer (SSL)** and **Transport Layer Security (TLS)** is essential for secure communication and certificate verification. However, about 92% of the applications used unsecured HTTP connections, and nearly one-third failed to validate hostnames or certificates correctly. Around 20% trusted all or self-signed certificates, making them susceptible to Man-in-the-Middle (MITM) attacks, while over half did not verify certificate validity or CN-field consistency. Approximately 12% of apps still used

Table 2. SSL and certificate-related, code-related, manifest-related, and network-related vulnerabilities with total, U.S., and non-U.S. averages of critical (C) and warning (W) counts

Issue	Total		U.S.		Non-U.S.	
	C	W	C	W	C	W
SSL and Certificate-Related Vulnerabilities						
HTTP Connection	92.11	0	89.36	0	96.55	0
Weak SSL Implementation	32.89	0	29.79	0	37.93	0
Insecure Implementation of SSL	21.05	0	17.02	0	27.59	0
Weak SSL Cert. Verification	18.42	36.84	17.02	34.04	20.69	41.38
Cert. Alg. Vulnerable to Hash Collision	12.09	34.07	12.28	33.33	11.76	35.29
Janus Vulnerability	3.3	79.12	3.51	77.19	2.94	82.35
Code-Related Vulnerabilities						
WebView RCE Vulnerability	90.79	0	89.36	0	93.1	0
CBC with PKCS5/PKCS7 Padding	60.44	0	56.14	0	67.65	0
Runtime Command	56.58	0	51.06	0	65.52	0
Strandhogg 2.0	55.26	0	51.06	0	62.07	0
Weak KeyStore Protection	44.74	0	42.55	0	48.28	0
Remote WebView Debugging	41.76	0	43.86	0	38.24	0
Implicit Service	36.84	0	27.66	0	51.72	0
Base64 String Encoding	30.26	0	31.91	0	27.59	0
Fragment Vulnerability	27.63	0	25.53	0	31.03	0
Insecure WebView Implementation	27.47	0	24.56	0	32.35	0
ECB-Mode in Cryptography	18.68	0	17.54	0	20.59	0
Weak AES ECB Mode	9.89	0	10.53	0	8.82	0
Weak Encryption Algorithm Used	6.59	0	1.75	0	14.71	0
App Sandbox Permission Checking	3.95	0	0	0	10.34	0
Runtime Critical Command	3.95	0	0	0	10.34	0
World Readable File	1.1	0	0	0	2.94	0
Weak Cryptographic Algorithms	1.1	0	1.75	0	0	0
Manifest-Related Vulnerabilities						
Activity is not Protected	69.23	0	64.91	0	76.47	0
Service is not Protected	63.74	0	57.89	0	73.53	0
Broadcast Receiver is not Protected	58.24	0	54.39	0	64.71	0
Clear text traffic is Enabled For App	19.78	0	17.54	0	23.53	0
ContentProvider is not Protected	14.29	0	10.53	0	20.59	0
ContentProvider Exported	11.84	0	14.89	0	6.9	0
Launch Mode of Activity is not standard	9.89	0	7.02	0	14.71	0
Activity-Alias is not Protected	7.69	0	7.02	0	8.82	0
Intent Filter Settings	3.95	0	4.26	0	3.45	0
Network-Related Vulnerabilities						
Domain Conf. Permitting Clear-text Traffic	17.58	0	19.3	0	14.71	0
Base Conf. Permitting Clear-text Traffic	16.48	0	17.54	0	14.71	0
Base Conf. Trusting User Installed Certs.	3.3	0	1.75	0	5.88	0
Domain Conf. Trusting User Installed Certs.	1.1	0	1.75	0	0	0
Base Conf. Bypassing Certificate Pinning	1.1	0	0	0	2.94	0

the outdated SHA1withRSA algorithm, exposing them to collision attacks. Some applications also exhibited the Janus vulnerability, where malicious DEX files can be injected into APKs with $v1$ signature schemes on Android versions 5.08.0, posing a critical risk.

Code-related weaknesses were widespread due to outdated practices and insecure use of Android components. About 90% of apps contained the WebView Remote Code Execution vulnerability (CVE-2013-4710), allowing Denial of Service and arbitrary code execution. Additionally, 45% permitted remote debugging, and 27% ignored SSL certificate errors, increasing MITM exposure. Roughly 37% of apps had implicit service vulnerabilities, and 27% were affected by the Fragment vulnerability (CVE-2013-6271), enabling unauthorized control. Some apps also misused deprecated permissions (`MODE_WORLD_READABLE`/`WRITEABLE`) that compromise sandboxing. More than half the apps were vulnerable to Strandhogg 2.0, which allows malicious overlays on legitimate apps to steal sensitive data. Runtime command injection was also common, with some apps executing commands through `Runtime.getRuntime().exec()`, including a few attempting privileged "su" execution. Around 60% were susceptible to padding oracle attacks due to improper CBC mode and padding usage, and 45% showed weak keystore protection through hardcoded keys. Several apps also used weak or outdated cryptography (ECB and AES-ECB modes) or insecure Base64 encoding.

The Android **Manifest** defines app permissions, components, and compatibility settings [13]. Misconfigurations in this file can expose components such as `Activity`, `Service`, `BroadcastReceiver`, and `ContentProvider`. About 70% of apps had unprotected activities, 63% shared services, and 58% insecure broadcast receivers, allowing unauthorized access by other applications. ContentProvider misconfigurations were present in 14% of apps, often leading to data leakage, while 12% relied on default exported settings, further increasing exposure. Around 20% of apps transmitted cleartext data, compromising confidentiality and integrity, and 10% misused restricted launch modes (`singleTask`, `singleInstance`), risking data leaks. A few apps also had improperly configured intent filters that exposed sensitive components to unintended access [10,29].

Network-Related Vulnerabilities were primarily linked to weak security configurations in the Manifest's network settings file [13]. Several apps permitted cleartext traffic, trusted user-installed certificates, or bypassed certificate pinning, leaving them vulnerable to data interception and tampering. The most prevalent issue across both base and domain configurations was allowing cleartext transmission, potentially exposing sensitive information.

4.2   Privacy

We examined requested, used, and tracked permissions, reported as percentages due to differing tool coverage (Table 3). Across all applications, 157 unique permissions were declared, 146 of which were unused, totaling 1,169 instances. All but four apps requested at least one dangerous permission.

Permission-Based Risk Scores: RiskInDroid assigns each app a score from 0 to 100, representing the likelihood of malicious behavior, where lower scores indicate lower risk. Among U.S. apps, scores ranged from 6.13 to 46.87, while non-U.S. apps ranged from 10.84 to 72.92.

Table 3. Privacy metrics with total, U.S., and Non-U.S. averages

Privacy Metric	Total	U.S.	Non-U.S.
Average Permission-based Risk Score	22.57	20.44	26.18
Best (Lowest) Permission-based Risk Score	6.13	6.13	10.84
Worst (Highest) Permission-based Risk Score	72.92	46.87	72.92
Average Number of Declared Permissions	21.58	20.22	23.9
Average Number of Exploited Permissions	7.15	7.02	7.37
Average Number of Useless Permissions	14.46	13.24	16.53
Average Number of Ghost Permissions	7.74	8.1	7.13
Average Number of Dangerous Permissions	5.8	5.37	6.53

Declared Permissions appear in the app Manifest but may not always be used in the code. The most common declared permissions were INTERNET (80), ACCESS_NETWORK_STATE (79), RECEIVE (77), WAKE_LOCK (76), and BIND_GET_INSTALL_REFERRER_SERVICE (73). Notably, several declared permissions were unused, leading to over-privileged apps that can raise compliance and transparency concerns.

Ghost Permissions are invoked in code but not declared in the Manifest, often due to third-party libraries. Such inconsistencies can lead to runtime failures or unauthorized access attempts. The most frequent ghost permissions were READ_PROFILE (77), MANAGE_ACCOUNTS (65), WRITE_SETTINGS (60), AUTHENTICATE_ACCOUNTS (54), and GET_ACCOUNTS (48).

Dangerous Permissions can access sensitive user data and require explicit user consent at runtime. The most frequent were CAMERA (76), ACCESS_FINE_LOCATION (65), WRITE_EXTERNAL_STORAGE (64), ACCESS_COARSE_LOCATION (57), and READ_EXTERNAL_STORAGE (56). While these support legitimate app features such as AR views, file uploads, or location-based services, improper use may expose users to privacy and security risks.

Privacy Trackers collect user data for analytics or advertising [32]. Among the 91 apps analyzed with MobSF, 64 contained at least one tracker. Undisclosed tracking practices raise privacy concerns and erode user trust [6,7]. Developers should clearly disclose tracking activities, explain their purpose, and provide users with the option to opt out to ensure transparency and regulatory compliance.

4.3 Discussion

RQ1: Our analysis revealed that e-commerce applications, regardless of region, showed notable security weaknesses, with an average score of 40.92 out of 100. Although some vulnerabilities, such as *CVE*-2013-4710 and *CVE*-2013-6271, affect older Android versions used by less than 0.5% of users, they still pose risks to millions worldwide [8]. U.S. apps achieved slightly higher security scores (maximum 67) compared to non-U.S. apps (maximum 73), with fewer critical vulnerabilities overall. These gaps mainly stem from weak manifest, certificate, and network configurations, underscoring the need for stronger secure coding practices, encryption, and vulnerability mitigation. The comparatively better performance of U.S. apps may reflect stricter development standards and larger-scale operations enforcing tighter controls.

RQ2: Privacy analysis showed that U.S. applications generally demonstrated stronger privacy practices, including lower permission-based risk scores, fewer unnecessary permissions, and reduced reliance on dangerous ones. These results align with the influence of regulations such as the CCPA and GDPR, where GDPR enforces explicit security obligations while CCPA focuses on data privacy rights. Non-U.S. apps, especially those popular in EU regions, exhibited more ghost permissions, indicating inconsistent permission declarations and possible overreach in data collection. Our analysis emphasize the need for continuous improvement in transparency, permission management, and compliance mechanisms to strengthen user trust and safeguard sensitive e-commerce data globally.

5 Limitations and Future Work

We analyzed the security and privacy of U.S. and non-U.S. e-commerce mobile applications using MobSF, RiskInDroid, and AndroBugs. Although some tools failed on a few apps due to technical constraints, we ensured that each app was evaluated by at least one tool. In future work, we will incorporate dynamic analysis to capture runtime behavior, expand our scope to include e-payment, banking, and iOS applications, and examine how security and privacy measures influence usability and user experience.

6 Conclusion

E-commerce applications serve over 2.5 billion users worldwide, making strong security and privacy measures vital for protecting sensitive data and maintaining user trust. Yet, many studies overlook regional differences in app security and privacy. In this work, we analyzed 92 high-revenue Android e-commerce applications from the United States (58) and other countries (34) using three open-source tools: MobSF, RiskInDroid, and AndroBugs. Our analysis revealed critical vulnerabilities such as remote WebView debugging flaws that enable DDoS and code injection attacks, and privacy trackers found in nearly 70% of apps, indicating weak privacy controls. We recommend that regulators enforce stricter compliance and audits, and that developers apply secure coding, continuous testing, and privacy-by-design practices to strengthen global e-commerce app security.

References

1. Abraham, A., Schlecht, D., Ma, G., Dobrushin, M., Nadal, V.: Mobile security framework (MobSF) (2016)
2. Acosta-Vargas, P., Salvador-Acosta, B., Salvador-Ullauri, L., Jadán-Guerrero, J.: Accessibility challenges of e-commerce websites. PeerJ Comput. Sci. **8**, e891 (2022)
3. AfterShip: Top 100 e-commerce stores (2024). https://www.aftership.com/store-list/top-100-ecommerces-stores. Accessed 30 May 2024
4. Ahmed, A.M., Zairi, M., Alwabel, S.: Global benchmarking for internet and e-commerce applications. Benchmarking: Int. J. **13**(1/2), 68–80 (2006)
5. AndroBugs: Androbugs 2. https://github.com/androbugs2/androbugs2. Accessed 30 May 2024
6. Bandara, R., Fernando, M., Akter, S.: Privacy concerns in e-commerce: a taxonomy and a future research agenda. Electron. Mark. **30**(3), 629–647 (2020)
7. Boritz, J.E., No, W.G.: E-commerce and privacy: exploring what we know and opportunities for future discovery. J. Inf. Syst. **25**(2), 11–45 (2011)
8. Business of Apps: Android statistics (2024). https://www.businessofapps.com/data/android-statistics/. Accessed 30 May 2024
9. Chanana, N., Goele, S.: Future of e-commerce in India. Int. J. Comput. Bus. Res. **8**(1) (2012)
10. Chin, E., Felt, A.P., Greenwood, K., Wagner, D.: Analyzing inter-application communication in android. In: Proceedings of the 9th international conference on Mobile systems, applications, and services, pp. 239–252 (2011)
11. Choi, T.M.: Mobile-app-online-website dual channel strategies: privacy concerns, e-payment convenience, channel relationship, and coordination. IEEE Trans. Syst., Man, Cybern.: Syst. **51**(11), 7008–7016 (2020)
12. Das, S., Dev, J., Camp, L.J.: Privacy preserving policy framework: user-aware and user-driven. In: TPRC47: The 47th Research Conference on Communication, Information and Internet Policy (2019)
13. Developers, A.: Developer guides: Android developers (2023). https://developer.android.com/guide/
14. Fellner, K., Rautenstrauch, C., Turowski, K.: A component model for an interorganizational agent-based coordination. In: 1999 Information Resources Management Association International Conference (IRMA'99): Managing Information Technology Resources in Organizations in the Next Millennium, pp. 1036–1040 (1999)
15. Gaedke, M., Turowski, K.: Integrating web-based e-commerce applications with business application systems. NETNOMICS **2**, 117–138 (2000)
16. Ghosh, A.K., Swaminatha, T.M.: Software security and privacy risks in mobile e-commerce. Commun. ACM **44**(2), 51–57 (2001)
17. Goyal, S., Sergi, B.S., Esposito, M.: Literature review of emerging trends and future directions of e-commerce in global business landscape. World Rev. Entrepreneurship, Manage. Sustain. Dev. **15**(1–2), 226–255 (2019)
18. Hadan, H., Serrano, N., Das, S., Camp, L.J.: Making IoT worthy of human trust. In: TPRC47: The 47th Research Conference on Communication, Information and Internet Policy (2019). available at SSRN: https://ssrn.com/abstract=3426871 or http://dx.doi.org/10.2139/ssrn.3426871

19. Hussain, M.A.: A study of information security in e-commerce applications. Int. J. Comput. Eng. Sci. (IJCES) **3**(3), 1–9 (2013)
20. Kishnani, U., Das, S.: Securing the web: analysis of http security headers in popular global websites. In: International Conference on Information Systems Security, pp. 87–106. Springer Nature Switzerland, Cham (2024)
21. Kishnani, U., Das, S.: Dual-technique privacy & security analysis for e-commerce websites through automated and manual implementation. In: Proceedings of the 2025 Hawaii International Conference on System Sciences (HICSS) (2025)
22. Kishnani, U., Noah, N., Das, S., Dewri, R.: Assessing security, privacy, user interaction, and accessibility features in popular e-payment applications. In: Proceedings of the 2023 European Symposium on Usable Security, pp. 143–157 (2023)
23. Ladan, M.I.: E-commerce security issues. In: 2014 International Conference on Future Internet of Things and Cloud, pp. 197–201. IEEE (2014)
24. LAZĂRA, A.P.: Security testing for e-commerce applications. In: International Conference on Cybersecurity and Cybercrime, vol. 10, pp. 224–229 (2023). https://doi.org/10.19107/CYBERCON.2023.30
25. Lin, Y.C.: AndroBugs framework: an android application security vulnerability scanner. Blackhat Europe **2015** (2015)
26. Liu, H., et al.: Privacy computing issues in collecting and using customer data of mobile devices. In: 2022 7th International Conference on Signal and Image Processing (ICSIP), pp. 382–389. IEEE (2022)
27. Liu, R., Wang, E.: Blockchain and mobile client privacy protection in e-commerce consumer shopping tendency identification application. Soft. Comput. **27**(9), 6019–6031 (2023)
28. Mai, Z.: Mobile e-commerce application based on 5G network. In: International Conference on Innovative Computing, pp. 287–293. Springer (2023)
29. Maji, A.K., Arshad, F.A., Bagchi, S., Rellermeyer, J.S.: An empirical study of the robustness of inter-component communication in android. In: IEEE/IFIP International Conference on Dependable Systems and Networks (DSN 2012), pp. 1–12. IEEE (2012)
30. Markert, P., Adhikari, A., Das, S.: A transcontinental analysis of account remediation protocols of popular websites. arXiv preprint: arXiv:2302.01401 (2023)
31. Merlo, A., Georgiu, G.C.: RiskinDroid: machine learning-based risk analysis on android. In: IFIP International Conference on ICT Systems Security and Privacy Protection, pp. 538–552. Springer (2017)
32. Monogios, S., Magos, K., Limniotis, K., Kolokotronis, N., Shiaeles, S.: Privacy issues in android applications: the cases of GPS navigators and fitness trackers. Int. J. Electr. Governance **14**(1–2), 83–111 (2022)
33. Ng-Kruelle, G., Swatman, P.A., Rebne, D.S., Hampe, J.F.: The price of convenience: privacy and mobile commerce. Q. J. Electron. Commer. **3**, 273–286 (2002)
34. Niranjanamurthy, M., Kavyashree, N., Jagannath, S., Chahar, D.: Analysis of e-commerce and m-commerce: advantages, limitations and security issues. Int. J. Adv. Res. Comput. Commun. Eng. **2**(6), 2360–2370 (2013)
35. Omar, C., Anas, T.: E-commerce in Malaysia: development, implementation and challenges. Int. Rev. Manag. Bus. Res. **3**(1), 291–298 (2014)
36. Poikela, M., Kaiser, F.: 'it is a topic that confuses me'–privacy perceptions in usage of location-based applications. In: European Workshop on Usable Security (EuroUSEC) (2016)
37. Smith, R., Shao, J.: Privacy and e-commerce: a consumer-centric perspective. Electron. Commer. Res. **7**, 89–116 (2007)

38. Surani, A., Bawaked, A., Wheeler, M., Kelsey, B., Roberts, N., Vincent, D., Das, S.: Security and privacy of digital mental health: an analysis of web services and mobile applications. In: IFIP Annual Conference on Data and Applications Security and Privacy, pp. 319–338. Springer, Sophia-Antipolis (2023)
39. Yang, C., Wan, J.: An approach to separating security concerns in e-commerce systems at the architecture level. In: 2008 International Symposium on Electronic Commerce and Security, pp. 749–753. IEEE (2008)
40. Zhang, R., Chen, J.Q., Lee, C.J.: Mobile commerce and consumer privacy concerns. J. Comput. Inf. Syst. **53**(4), 31–38 (2013)

Adaptive MQTT Honeypots for IIoT Security Using Extended Mealy Machines

Saurabh Chamotra[(✉)] [ID], Navdeep Singh, and Piyali Dutta

Centre for Development of Advanced Computing (C-DAC), Mohali, India
{saurabhc,navdeep,piyalidatta}@cdac.in

Abstract. The existing MQTT honeypots often lack scalability, semantic fidelity, and data-flow awareness, thereby limiting interaction realism and detection depth. To address these limitations, we propose an Extended Finite State Machine (EFSM) based MQTT honeypot that enforces guarded control and data-flow transitions while integrating adaptive deception to ensure protocol compliant realism. Unlike conventional honeypots, the EFSM based design captures field level dependencies through variable updates and guard conditions, enabling stateful, context aware emulation. In an 80 day Internet deployment, the proposed system achieved 23% more connections, 1.5× higher topic diversity, and 40% greater detection coverage than RIoTPot and ThingPot, successfully detecting QoS abuse, Last-Will manipulation, and replay attacks. These results establish EFSM-based protocol modeling as a compact, extensible foundation for next-generation IIoT honeypots.

1 Introduction

The Message Queuing Telemetry Transport (MQTT) protocol underpins the Industrial Internet of Things (IIoT), enabling lightweight, publish–subscribe communication between constrained devices and cloud or edge platforms. Originally developed by IBM for SCADA and satellite systems and later standardized by OASIS, MQTT was designed for reliable operation over low-bandwidth, high-latency networks [4]. Its minimalist header, topic-based routing, and broker-mediated architecture make it highly suitable for embedded industrial environments [10]. Over the past decade, MQTT has become the *de facto* IIoT messaging standard, accounting for nearly 50% of industrial deployments [5]. It is widely adopted across manufacturing, energy, and automotive domains.

Despite its efficiency and interoperability, MQTT's lightweight design introduces serious security gaps. Internet-wide scans reveal hundreds of thousands of brokers exposed on default ports (1883, 8883, 8884), many allowing unauthenticated access and unrestricted subscriptions. By 2024, Shodan indexed over 600,000 exposed brokers–nearly ten times the 2019 count–indicating a rapidly expanding attack surface [20]. These weaknesses, often exploited by advanced persistent threats, endanger both IT and OT infrastructures, highlighting the need for realistic, protocol-aware deception systems [10]. Existing IIoT honeypots [8,11,22], though useful for threat intelligence, suffer from incomplete

N. Hubballi et al. (Eds.): ICISS 2025, LNCS 16380, pp. 455–465, 2026.
https://doi.org/10.1007/978-3-032-13714-2_28

control-packet coverage, static and fingerprintable responses, lack of data-flow modeling, and weak session persistence. Such limitations hinder semantic dependency modeling and adaptive broker behavior, reducing engagement realism and detection fidelity.

To bridge these gaps, this work presents an EFSM-based MQTT honeypot that unifies control and data-flow enforcement with deception-driven adaptability. Unlike conventional honeypots, it introduces a protocol modeling framework for text-based protocols that supports dynamic state addition without recompilation, ensuring scalability and extensibility. The EFSM embeds guarded transitions, persistent session variables, and data-dependent actions to sustain realistic attacker engagement and semantic coherence. This design enhances protocol fidelity, mitigates fingerprinting, and broadens the capture surface to include subtle semantic exploits.

2   Literature Survey

Industrial and IoT honeynets have evolved from early SCADA-oriented systems toward protocol-aware deception environments. Cisco's SCADA honeynet emulated Modbus/TCP with auxiliary services but exhibited low fidelity [14], whereas Digital Bond's variant improved authenticity by integrating real PLCs behind honeywalls at the cost of manageability [13]. Conpot later became the *de facto* multi-protocol framework, though its static templates were easily fingerprinted [18]. Designs such as CryPLH, SHaPe, and GridPot [3,6,16] increased realism but remained complex to deploy, while GasPot [25] favored scalability over interaction fidelity. IoTPOT expanded coverage through Telnet/SSH emulation to capture multi-architecture malware but lacked industrial semantics [12]. Likewise, IoTCandyJar [8] and ThingPot [24] integrated REST and XMPP interfaces to improve realism, and Honware [23] executed router firmware for authenticity at high computational cost. Raspberry Pi-based honeynets simplified deployment but reduced interaction depth [1].

Despite this evolution, the Message Queuing Telemetry Transport (MQTT) protocol now the dominant IIoT telemetry standard remains insufficiently explored within the context of cyber deception. Existing MQTT honeypots provide limited protocol coverage, generating static, easily fingerprinted responses with weak session persistence and no modeling of control and data dependencies [8,12,22]. Prior implementations by Shimada et al. [19], Lygerou et al. [9], and frameworks such as ThingPot and IoTCandyJar [8,24] integrated MQTT only at a superficial level, lacking stateful broker representation and sustained interaction realism. As a result, data from most MQTT honeypots are of low quality and yield shallow penetration metrics.

To address these limitations, this work proposes an Extended Finite State Machine (EFSM)-based MQTT honeypot that unifies controldata flow modeling with adaptive deception, a capability absent in existing honeypots. The framework formally models MQTT protocol behavior and its semantic dependencies to ensure protocol compliance and context-aware realism. Unlike conventional

MQTT honeypots [11,22], the EFSM integrates variables, guards, and update actions [7] to capture inter-message dependencies and preserve session continuity. This design enhances protocol fidelity and provides a compact, extensible foundation for next-generation deception-driven honeypots.

3 Proposed Approach

This section outlines a unified approach that integrates formal protocol modeling, trace-driven analysis, and state-space reduction to build a high-fidelity MQTT honeypot. MQTT broker behavior is modeled as an EFSM with guarded transitions and variable updates, capturing control and data-flow dependencies while avoiding state explosion. The resulting honeypot embeds control and data-flow logic for adaptive deception and protocol-faithful emulation.

3.1 Modeling MQTT Protocol as an Extended Finite State Machine

To emulate MQTT broker behavior with high fidelity, the protocol's operational semantics are formalized as an *Extended Finite State Machine* (EFSM). An EFSM [7] generalizes the Mealy machine [2] by introducing variables, guards, and update functions that jointly capture both *control flow* (ordering of MQTT control packets) and *data flow* (constraints among message fields). This formalization addresses a key limitation of prior IIoT honeypots, which often model only control transitions while ignoring data dependencies.

An EFSM for MQTT is defined as the 8-tuple $M = (S, I, O, V, T, G, U, s_0)$, where S is the set of protocol states; I and O denote input (received) and output (response) symbols; V stores data-flow variables; $T \subseteq S \times I \times G \to S$ is the guarded transition relation; G is the set of Boolean guards; $U \colon S \times I \to V$ defines variable update functions; and s_0 is the initial state. The system behavior is governed by the output function $\lambda \colon S \times I \times V \to O$ and the transition function $\delta \colon S \times I \times G \to S$. Together, they preserve control-flow ordering, enforce data-flow consistency through guards and updates, and enable adaptive deception by reconfiguring U and G to emulate evolving broker logic.

Control and Data-Flow Semantics. The MQTT broker operates through three abstract states: S_0 (Idle), S_1 (Ready), and S_2 (Active). Valid control-packet sequences include:

$$S_0 \xrightarrow{\text{CONNECT}} S_1 \xrightarrow{\text{CONNACK}} S_2, \quad S_2 \xrightarrow{\text{DISCONNECT}} S_0,$$

with in-session exchanges:

$$\text{QoS1:} \ S_2 \xrightarrow{\text{PUBLISH}} S_2 \xrightarrow{\text{PUBACK}} S_2,$$

$$\text{QoS2:} \ S_2 \xrightarrow{\text{PUBLISH}} S_2 \xrightarrow{\text{PUBREC}} S_1 \xrightarrow{\text{PUBREL}} S_2 \xrightarrow{\text{PUBCOMP}} S_2,$$

$$\text{SUB:} \ S_2 \xleftarrow[\text{SUBACK}]{\text{SUBSCRIBE}} S_1.$$

EFSM memory M maintains session context:

$$M = \{\, cid, sessPres, clean, subs, acl, inflight, retain, will, qosMax, L_{\max} \,\},$$

and representative guarded transitions are:

$$\delta_{\text{CONNECT}} : \text{auth}(cid) \wedge qosMax \in \{0, 1, 2\}; \quad \sigma: sessPres \leftarrow \text{lookup}(cid);$$
$$\delta_{\text{SUBSCRIBE}} : (t, q) \in \text{subsReq} \Rightarrow t \in acl, \ q \leq qosMax; \quad \sigma: subs \cup = \text{subsReq};$$
$$\delta_{\text{PUBLISH@QoS1}} : t \in acl \wedge \text{len}(\text{payload}) \leq L_{\max}; \quad \sigma: \text{route}(t, \text{payload});$$
$$\delta_{\text{PUBLISH@QoS2}} : t \in acl \wedge \text{mid} \notin \textit{inflight}; \quad \sigma: \textit{inflight}[\text{mid}] \leftarrow (t, \text{payload});$$
$$\delta_{\text{PUBREL}} : \text{mid} \in \textit{inflight}; \quad \sigma: \text{route}(\textit{inflight}[\text{mid}]); \quad \text{del } \textit{inflight}[\text{mid}];$$
$$\delta_{\text{RETAIN}} : \text{retainFlag} \Rightarrow t \in acl; \quad \sigma: \textit{retain}[t] \leftarrow \text{payload}.$$

The following examples illustrate how guarded transitions and variable updates enforce control and data-flow consistency while ensuring protocol compliance.

Example 1. (Control-Valid but Data-Invalid)

$$\text{CONNECT} \rightarrow \text{CONNACK} \rightarrow \text{PUBLISH}(\text{QoS2}, \ t{=}/ctl/stop)$$

This sequence is syntactically valid under the FSM (self-loop on S_2) but rejected by the EFSM when the target topic $t \notin acl$, activating a guard that triggers DISCONNECT or PUBREC(error).

Example 2. (Data-Consistent Delivery)

$$\text{CONNECT} \rightarrow \text{CONNACK} \rightarrow \text{SUBSCRIBE}\{(/\text{telemetry}/\#, 1)\} \rightarrow \text{SUBACK}$$

The EFSM dispatches a retained message only if $retain[/\text{telemetry}/\text{temp}]$ exists, ensuring semantic alignment and preserving data-flow consistency.

Example 3. (Session Persistence) When clean=false and $sessPres = $ **true**, subscriptions and inflight QoS2 MIDs are restored; otherwise, the session is cleared.

3.2 MQTT Protocol Reverse Engineering and EFSM Synthesis

This subsection describes the reverse engineering of MQTT from network traces and its formalization as an Extended Mealy Machine to derive protocol semantics forming the honeypot's EFSM core. A controlled testbed produced diverse traces under varied operational and security conditions. Captured packets were tokenized and annotated via regular expressions to extract control and data flow. The resulting sequences induced and minimized a Partial Language Automaton (PTA) [2], after which data-dependent guards and update actions were added.

Testbed Setup for MQTT Trace Generation. A controlled testbed interconnected via a dedicated Gigabit switch was used to generate authentic MQTT exchanges. The broker node (Ubuntu 22.04 LTS, 4 vCPUs, 8 GB RAM) hosted EMQX 5.3 and Mosquitto 2.0.18, while client nodes consisted of Raspberry Pi 4B devices and Ubuntu VMs running Eclipse Paho. A capture host mirrored traffic to record PCAP traces using `tcpdump` and `tshark`. All QoS levels (02), retained messages, wildcard subscriptions, and variable payload sizes were exercised to produce diverse traces. The resulting dataset provided the empirical basis for protocol-model derivation and EFSM validation.

Message Labeling and Protocol-Language Identification. This subsection outlines the methodology adopted for message labeling and protocol-language extraction, adapted from the ReverX framework [2]. Each captured trace was tokenized using delimiters such as '\x20+' (spaces), '\t+' (tabs), and '\r\n' (line breaks). Fields exhibiting high variability were abstracted with an ANY symbol ('.+') to enable generalization across unseen message instances. A frequency-labeled Prefix Tree Acceptor (PTA) was then constructed and subsequently generalized into a deterministic automaton, where each transition carried a label $\omega: Q \times \Sigma \to \mathbb{N}$ indicating the observed frequency of occurrence. Regular-expression patterns were employed to detect MQTT control packets and delineate their semantic fields. Representative patterns include:

$$\text{^PUBLISH\x20+([\/A-Za-z0-9_-]+)\x20+(.+)\$} \tag{1}$$

for PUBLISH messages, where group 1 represents the topic and group 2 the payload, and

$$\text{^SUBSCRIBE\x20+([\/A-Za-z0-9_-]+)(?:\x20+QoS=(\d))?\$} \tag{2}$$

for SUBSCRIBE packets. Binary MQTT traces (ISO/IEC 20922) were processed analogously, with fixed-length expressions (e.g., '.{4}') enforcing field-size constraints during tokenization.

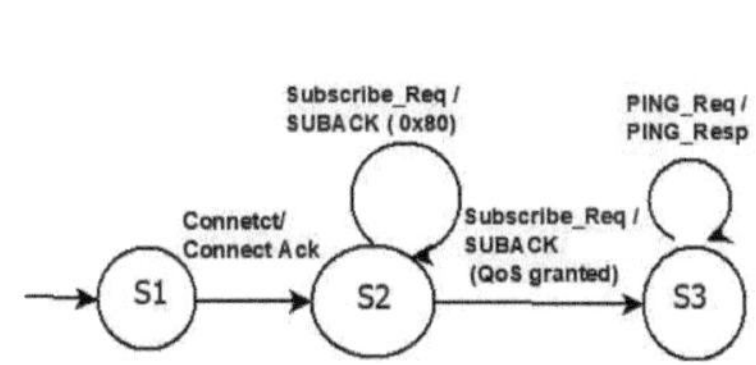

Fig. 1. PTA derived from broker traces (scenario 1).

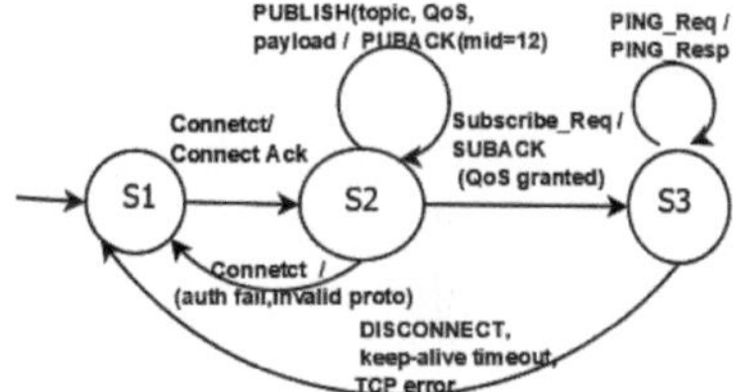

Fig. 2. PTA derived from broker traces (scenario 2).

Partial Language Automaton Construction and Minimization. Labeled sequences were used to construct a Partial Language Automaton (PTA), where each unique sequence defined an execution path representing observable broker behavior (Figs. 1 and 2). Mealy machine state minimization via partition refinement [2] merged states with equivalent outputs and transitions. The minimized automaton (Fig. 3) preserved broker semantics while removing redundancy. Data-dependent guards and update actions were then added, producing a sound EFSM that maintains Mealy equivalence for control transitions and extends it with data-flow constraints enabling deception logic. Implemented in Python 3.11 with asynchronous I/O, each transition invokes guard evaluators enforcing ACL, QoS, and payload-size limits before execution, ensuring model soundness, real-time validation, and trace-level fidelity.

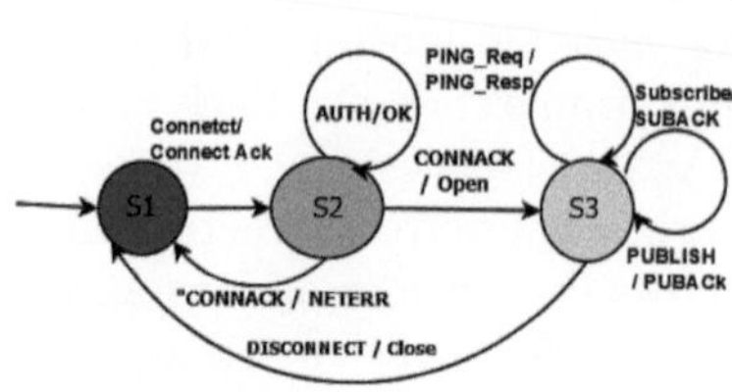

Fig. 3. Minimized EFSM.

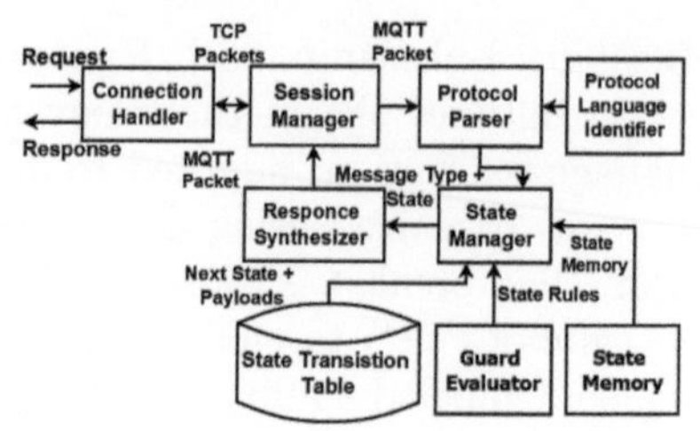

Fig. 4. Proposed Honeypot Architecture.

4 Proposed MQTT Honeypot Design

This section presents the architecture of the proposed MQTT honeypot, which emulates an MQTT broker using an Extended Finite State Machine (EFSM) for protocol modeling and adaptive deception. As shown in Fig. 4, the design extends classical Mealy machine logic with guarded transitions and dynamic response synthesis, enabling sustained and realistic attacker engagement. The framework consists of cooperating modules that exchange compact records, ensuring modularity, traceability, and efficient data flow. The key functional components and their roles are outlined below:

1. **Connection Handler:** Establishes and monitors TCP connections, enforces rate limits and keep-alives, allocates unique `conn_ids`, and triggers Last-Will delivery upon abnormal termination.
2. **Session Manager:** Reassembles TCP streams into MQTT packets, maintains per-client context, and coordinates message routing across modules.
3. **Protocol Parser and Language Identifier:** Decodes headers and validates MQTT syntax, mapping message structures to their respective EFSM message types.
4. **State Manager:** Integrates the current state, session parameters, and message type to invoke guarded transitions. Guards are evaluated by the **Guard Evaluator** to verify constraints such as packet order, QoS level, size limits, and ACL compliance before transition execution.
5. **State Transition Table:** Implements EFSM control logic as transition rules of the form ⟨current_state, msg_type, guard_class⟩ → ⟨next_state, actions, response_hint⟩.
6. **State Memory:** Persists dynamic session data, including topic–QoS mappings, retained messages, QoS1/2 identifiers, and deception state flags.
7. **Response Synthesizer:** Generates MQTT-compliant responses and, when deception is active, introduces adaptive jitter, payload modulation, or throttling to simulate realistic network conditions and sustain engagement.

The EFSM was implemented in Python using an event-driven architecture with asynchronous sockets, enabling high concurrency and responsiveness. Guard conditions and transition logic are encoded as evaluable predicates dynamically loaded from configuration files, allowing modification without recompilation. New attack scenarios or deceptive behaviors can be introduced by simply adding entries to the State Transition Table, reflecting a scalable and extensible design. This dynamic programming paradigm facilitates rapid evolution of honeypot behavior while preserving protocol fidelity. Overall, the modular EFSM framework ensures interpretable state control, runtime adaptability, and enhanced attacker engagement compared with conventional static honeypots.

5   Experimentation and Results

The EFSM-based MQTT honeypot was evaluated through three experiments: (i) a comparative analysis with RIoTPot and ThingPot using an EFSM-derived test suite to assess protocol fidelity and flow consistency; (ii) adversarial testing with open-source penetration tools targeting brute-force, flooding, protocol abuse, and fuzzing; and (iii) an 80-day Internet deployment assessing efficiency, engagement depth, and topic diversity. Collectively, these evaluations provide a holistic measure of correctness, resilience, and real-world operational utility.

5.1   Comparative Evaluation Against Established MQTT Honeypots and Flow Consistency Analysis

The EFSM-based honeypot was compared with two baselines: RIoTPot [22] and ThingPot [11]. Evaluation focused on protocol fidelity, robustness, and control/data-flow consistency using a standardized control-flow and data-flow test suite (Table 1). The EFSM prototype passed all tests due to explicit guarded

Table 1. Control-flow (CF) and data-flow (DF) test-suite.

Test (formal description)	EFSM (ours)	RIoTPot	ThingPot
CF1 – Enforce CONNECT→CONNACK ordering; disallow SUBSCRIBE/PUBLISH prior to CONNACK.	✓	✓	✓
CF2 – Verify QoS 1 delivery semantics: PUBLISH → PUBACK.	✓	✓	P
CF3 – Verify QoS 2 four-way handshake: PUBLISH → PUBREC → PUBREL → PUBCOMP.	✓	✗	✗
CF4 – Session resumption: restore prior subscriptions and in-flight state upon reconnection.	✓	P	✗
DF1 – Retained-message semantics: deliver retained payloads to new subscribers per topic.	✓	P	✗
DF2 – Last-Will semantics: emit configured LWT on unexpected client disconnect.	✓	✗	✗
DF3 – Packet identifier integrity: prevent duplicate MID acceptance prior to completion of prior flow.	✓	✗	✗
DF4 – Flag coherence: validate and enforce DUP, QoS and RETAIN field constraints.	✓	P	P
DF5 – Access control: enforce topic-level ACLs and reject unauthorized subscriptions/publications.	✓	✗	P

transitions, persistent session variables, and per-topic tracking that preserved QoS, retained messages, and ACL integrity. In contrast, RIoTPot satisfied basic sequencing but failed QoS 2 and retained/LWT handling, while ThingPot met only minimal connection sequencing and lacked enforcement logic. Overall, the EFSM's state-aware validation and embedded data-flow checks achieved superior protocol fidelity and resilience, effectively addressing semantic and sequencing violations unhandled by prior honeypots.

5.2 Detection Capability Against Popular MQTT Attacks

We evaluated the EFSM honeypot and two baselines (RIoTPot, ThingPot) using three open-source exploit frameworks: `mqtt-pentest` [21], `mqtt-pwn` [17], and `ralmqtt` [15] (brute-force, flooding, ACL bypass, enumeration, QoS abuse, replay, and fuzzing). Tests ran under identical hardware/network conditions, repeated for reproducibility; packet captures and logs were synchronized for ground-truth correlation and outcomes classified as (✓) detected, (**P**) partial, or (✗) undetected (Table 2). RIoTPot missed ACL bypass, QoS abuse, and replay due to proxy-style handling without per-session/topic validation, while Thing-Pot logged some events but lacked guard-based mitigation. The EFSM prototype achieved higher detection and mitigation rates via guard-driven semantics, stateful anomaly tracking, controldata-flow checks, and integrated deception hooks that preserve protocol compliance with low latency. A single partial miss involved a cross-protocol pivot through an uninstrumented MQTTHTTP bridge, which was logged but not fully mitigated.

Table 2. Detection of MQTT attacks using `mqtt-pentest`, `mqtt-pwn` & `ralmqtt`

Attack Scenario	EFSM (ours)	RIoTPot	ThingPot
Auth/ACL brute force	✓ (block+log)	✗	✗
ACL bypass to sensitive topics	✓ (block+log)	✗	**P** (log only)
Topic enumeration	✓ (rate-limit+log)	✓ (log only)	**P** (log only)
Publish flooding	✓ (throttle+log)	✓ (disconnect)	✓ (disconnect)
Subscription flooding	✓ (throttle+log)	✓ (log only)	✗
Malformed packet injection	✓ (drop+error)	✓ (drop)	✓ (drop)
LWT abuse	✓ (flag+deceptive payload)	✗	✗
QoS manipulation	✓ (flag+reset)	✗	✗
Session hijacking / replay	✓ (block+log)	✗	✗
Cross-protocol pivot	**P** (log only)	✗	✗

5.3 Empirical Evaluation of the Proposed MQTT Honeypot

The EFSM-based MQTT honeypot was evaluated against *RIoTPot* and *Thing-Pot* during an Internet deployment (May–August 2025) to assess (i) connection-handling efficiency and (ii) quality/diversity of captured MQTT data. All honeypots ran on identical Ubuntu 22.04 LTS servers (8 vCPUs, 16 GB RAM) with dedicated IPs, containerized via Docker Compose. *RIoTPot* [22] used its default Docker setup with multi-protocol decoys (MQTT, Modbus, HTTP, Telnet), while *ThingPot* [11] was containerized with REST/XMPP modules linked to a Prosody server. Both shared a unified Docker network with controlled port exposure. The EFSM honeypot operated as a single container exposing only TCP/1883, enforcing protocol-valid transitions and deception logic through its EFSM engine.

* Part 1: Efficiency and Effectiveness. Across the 80-day deployment, interaction levels differed significantly (Table 3). The EFSM honeypot consistently achieved higher and more stable connection volumes, demonstrating improved discoverability and engagement arising from protocol fidelity and adaptive responses (Fig. 5).

Table 3. Deployment metrics (18 May–5 Aug 2025)

Honeypot	Total Conns	Unique IPs	Avg. Daily Conns	Avg. Daily IPs
EFSM (ours)	263,678	3,563	3,296	44
RIoTPot	213,722	2,342	2,671	29
ThingPot	17,893	1,342	224	16

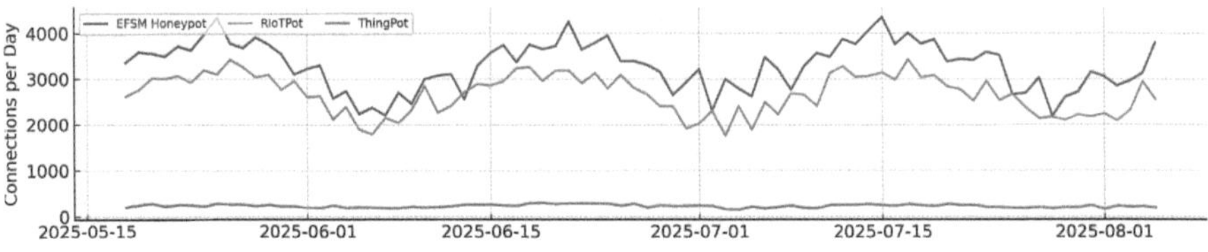

Fig. 5. Daily connections for EFSM honeypot, RIoTPot, and ThingPot.

* Part 2: Quality and Diversity of Collected Data. Interaction quality was analyzed via MQTT control-packet mix and topic diversity. In Fig. 6, CONNECT dominates, followed by SUBSCRIBE, authentication attempts, PINGREQ, and PUBLISH. The EFSM honeypot recorded a higher ratio of SUBSCRIBE/PUBLISH events, reflecting deeper engagement. Topic diversity was evaluated for: (1) **System topics** (e.g., $SYS/broker/timestamp, $SYS/broker/clients/connected); and (2) **Sensitive topics** drawn from IoT credential/configuration namespaces (e.g., AP, SSID, MqttPassword). Figure 7 shows the EFSM honeypot capturing a broader mix of both, indicating longer sessions and deeper namespace probing. Overall, the EFSM honeypot outperformed both baselines in connection volume, session persistence, and interaction richness. *RIoTPot* drew numerous connections but limited topic variety, while *ThingPot* exhibited the lowest engagement due to restricted MQTT handling.

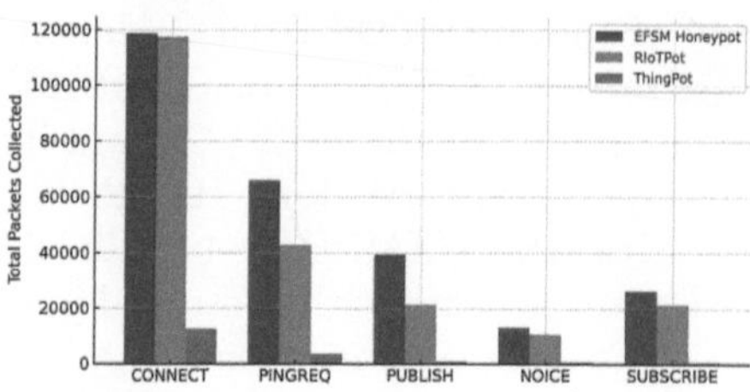

Fig. 6. MQTT control-packet distribution.

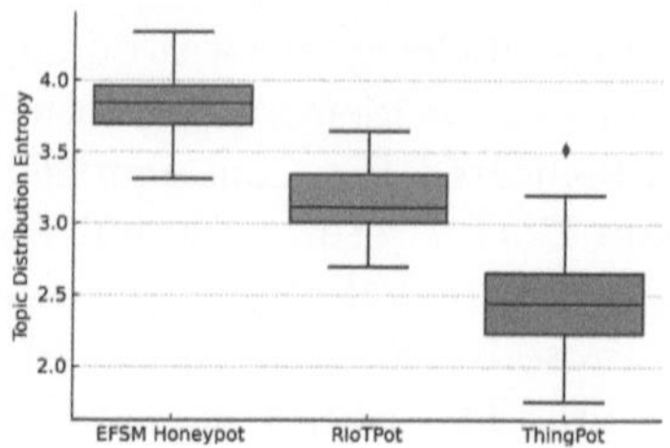

Fig. 7. Topic diversity across system and sensitive categories.

6 Conclusion and Future Work

This work presented an EFSM-based MQTT honeypot that achieves high protocol fidelity, extended attacker engagement, and superior detection of semantic anomalies compared with existing baselines. By enforcing both control- and data-flow invariants and integrating deception mechanisms, the framework demonstrated improved attractiveness, richer interaction diversity, and broader attack coverage in real-world deployments. Future work will focus on extending the EFSM modeling approach to binary ICS/IIoT protocols, where field parsing and state modeling are more complex. Enhancements will also target multi-protocol correlation, adaptive deception for evolving APT tactics, and large-scale distributed deployments with automated model generation from live traffic.

References

1. Ammar, Z., AlSharif, A.: Deployment of IoT-based honeynet model. In: Proc. IEEE 6th Int. Conf. on Information Technology: IoT and Smart City (ICIT), pp. 134–139 (2018)
2. Antunes, J., Neves, N., Verissimo, P.: Reverse engineering of protocols from network traces. In: 2011 18th Working Conference on Reverse Engineering, pp. 169–178. IEEE (2011)
3. Buza, D.I., Juhász, F., Miru, G., Félegyházi, M., Holczer, T.: CryPLH: protecting smart energy systems from targeted attacks with a PLC honeypot. In: Smart Grid Security, pp. 181–192. Springer (2014)
4. Cirrus Link Solutions. What is MQTT? Explained by its co-inventor (2023). Accessed 08 Aug 2025
5. HiveMQ Blog. Strong adoption of MQTT in IIoT (2023). Accessed: 08 Aug 2025
6. Kołtys, K., Gajewski, R.: SHaPe: A honeypot for electric power substation. Journal of Telecommunications and Information Technology 4, 37–43 (2015)
7. Lin, Y.D., Lai, Y.K., Bui, Q.T., Lai, Y.C.: ReFSM: reverse engineering from protocol packet traces to test generation by extended finite state machines. J. Netw. Comput. Appl. **171**, 102819 (2020)
8. Luo, T., Xu, Z., Jin, X., Jia, Y., Ouyang, X.: IoTCandyJar: towards an intelligent-interaction honeypot for IoT devices. Black Hat **1**(11) (2017)

9. Lygerou, I., Srinivasa, S., Vasilomanolakis, E., Stergiopoulos, G., Gritzalis, D.: A decentralized honeypot for IoT protocols based on android devices. Int. J. Inf. Secur. **21**(6), 1211–1222 (2022)

10. Maggi, F., Vosseler, R., Quarta, D.: The fragility of industrial IoT's data backbone: security and privacy issues in MQTT and COAP protocols (2025). White paper. Accessed 2025

11. Mengmengada. ThingPot: IoT honeypot for rest and XMPP devices (2018). https://github.com/Mengmengada/ThingPot. Accessed 10 Aug 2025

12. Pa, Y.M.P., Suzuki, S., Yoshioka, K., Matsumoto, T., Kasama, T., Rossow, C.: IoTPOT: a novel honeypot for revealing current IoT threats. J. Inf. Process. **24**(3), 522–533 (2016)

13. Digital Bond (Dale Peterson). Digital Bond SCADA Honeynet (2006). http://www.digitalbond.com/tools/scada-honeynet/

14. Pothamsetty, V., Franz, M.: SCADA HoneyNet project: building honeypots for industrial networks (2004). http://scadahoneynet.sourceforge.net/

15. Red-Alert-Labs. RALMQTT: MQTT broker pentesting tool. https://github.com/Red-Alert-Labs/ralmqtt/. Accessed 10 Aug 2025

16. Redwood, O., Lawrence, J., Burmester, M.: A symbolic honeynet framework for SCADA system threat intelligence. In: Proc. IFIP Int. Conf. on Critical Infrastructure Protection (ICCIP), pp. 103–118. Springer (2015)

17. Akamai Threat Research. MQTT-PWN: A one-stop-shop for IotT broker penetration testing. https://github.com/akamai-threat-research/mqtt-pwn. Accessed 10 Aug 2025

18. Rist, L., Vestergaard, J., Haslinger, D., De Pasquale, A., Smith, J.: Conpot ICS/SCADA honeypot (2013). http://conpot.org/

19. Shimada, H., Ito, K., Hasegawa, H., Yamaguchi, Y.: Implementation of MQTT/COAP honeypots and analysis of observed data. In: Proc. 13th Int. Conf. Emerg. Secur. Inf., Syst. Technol., vol. 10, pp. 1–6 (2019)

20. Shodan. Shodan: The search engine for the internet of everything (2025). Accessed 19 Jan 2025

21. Souf31. mqtt-pentest: MQTT attack scenarios in practice. https://github.com/Souf31/mqtt-pentest. Accessed 10 Aug 2025

22. The Honeynet Project. Riotpot: IoT honeypot framework (2025). https://github.com/honeynet/riotpot. Accessed 10 Aug 2025

23. Vetterl, A., Clayton, R.: Honware: a virtual honeypot framework for capturing CPE and IoT zero days. In: Proc. DIMVA, pp. 511–530 (2020)

24. Wang, M., Santillan, J., Kuipers, F.: ThingPot: an interactive internet-of-things honeypot. arXiv preprint: arXiv:1807.04114 (2018)

25. Wilhoit, K., Hilt, S.: The GasPot experiment: unexamined perils in using gas-tank-monitoring systems. In: Black Hat, USA (2015)

Modular Analysis of Attack Graphs
for Smart Grid Security

B. S. Smitha Rani[1] [ID], Preetam Mukherjee[1]([✉]) [ID], and Mathias Ekstedt[2] [ID]

[1] Digital University Kerala, Thiruvananthapuram, Kerala, India
preetam.mukherjee@duk.ac.in
[2] KTH Royal Institute of Technology, Stockholm, Sweden

Abstract. A smart grid is a modern power network designed to monitor, manage, and optimise the flow of electricity. A cyber attack on such a critical system can disrupt services and pose significant risks to public safety and national infrastructure. Cyber attackers targeting critical infrastructures like smart grids often follow predictable patterns that can be modelled and analysed. Attack graphs reveal these potential multistage attack patterns, highlighting attacker reachability. However, due to the sheer number of paths and the large size of the graph, their analysis becomes computationally challenging. In this paper, a modular analysis of attack graphs is proposed to address this issue by decomposing the graphs into manageable clusters or communities. By representing each community as a single node, the complex graph is transformed into a high-level abstraction that is easier to interpret. Segregating large attack graphs into clusters enables efficient, time-bound analysis and ultimately aids in defense strategy formulation.

Keywords: Smart Grid · Attack Graph Analysis · Community Detection

1 Introduction

Smart grids are the next generation electrical power systems that use information and communication technologies (ICT) to monitor and control electricity flow in real time. It establishes bidirectional communication networks between power suppliers and consumers using smart sensors, smart meters, and advanced control systems [7]. Modern smart grids rely on three interconnected technology domains: Information Technology (IT), Operational Technology (OT), and Advanced Metering Infrastructure (AMI). The smart grid forms a complex, interconnected cyber-physical ecosystem.

Smart grids are attractive targets for attackers because failures can cascade across multiple infrastructure sectors, and their complex, distributed nature creates many potential attack points. Several high-profile cyber attacks have shaped our understanding of these threats. Stuxnet (2010) was the first cyber attack to cause physical damage to infrastructure. The BlackEnergy 3 malware disrupted power in Ukraine (2015), affecting over 225,000 customers and marking

© The Author(s), under exclusive license to Springer Nature Switzerland AG 2026
N. Hubballi et al. (Eds.): ICISS 2025, LNCS 16380, pp. 466–476, 2026.
https://doi.org/10.1007/978-3-032-13714-2_29

the first successful cyber attack on a national power grid. Industroyer malware (2016) caused a power outage in Kyiv, representing the first malware specifically designed to target power grid systems and industrial communication protocols.

For decades, attack graphs have been used to model potential attack vectors and assess multi-hop attacks in a network infrastructure. The reachability of the attackers from the attack surface to the critical assets inside the infrastructure is revealed by using this attack modelling technique. Although beneficial, an attack graph developed for a large and highly distributed network infrastructure like the smart grid can become too large for a timely analysis. While some work in the literature has proposed the modular generation of attack graphs [5,9,13,17], the modular analysis of large attack graphs to reduce analysis complexity has not been well addressed.

To address these limitations, this paper proposes a modular analysis app-roach that decomposes complex attack graphs into communities using existing community detection methods. After detecting the communities, a high-level attack graph is constructed, representing communities as nodes and retaining only inter-community directed edges. This abstraction reduces the size of the attack graph and simplifies analysis without compromising essential informa-tion, thereby facilitating the identification of appropriate defense strategies.

The remainder of this paper is organized as follows: Sect. 2 presents related work in attack graph analysis and smart grid security. Section 3 provides back-ground on attack modeling in smart grids using smart grid distribution network as an example. Section 4 introduces mathematical foundation for community detection concepts. Section 5 presents our modular analysis approach using com-prehensive smart grid infrastructure. Finally, Sect. 6 concludes with future work directions.

2 Related Work

Attack graph analysis has evolved significantly from traditional IT security to encompass complex cyber-physical systems. Zeng et al. [19] provide a com-prehensive taxonomy categorizing attack graph analysis into five fundamental approaches: graph-based algorithms, Bayesian networks, Markov models, cost optimization, and uncertainty analysis methods. Building on these foundations, Prasad et al. [14] demonstrated practical implementation using MulVAL for polynomial-complexity logical attack graphs, establishing that single connected components with fewer cycles indicate heightened vulnerability to cascading fail-ures in networked systems.

The generation of attack modeling for the cyber-physical domains was first presented by Barrère et al. [3], introducing Cyber-Physical Attack Graphs (CPAGs) as the first formal framework that unifies cyber and physical attack vectors for holistic security analysis of critical infrastructure. Sahu et al. [15] develop techniques to automatically learn and update Bayesian Attack Graph (BAG) structures from real-time IDS alerts in cyber-physical power systems in critical infrastructure. Similar attack graph-based approaches have been used to assess cyber risks in flexibility markets, where Afzal et al. [2] evaluated protection scenarios against threats targeting inter-actor communication links.

The transition from manual to automated attack graph generation marks a critical advancement in scalability. Koo et al. [8] proposed a machine learning based process achieving very high attack path detection accuracy using multi-output learning and binary classification on vulnerability databases, eliminating the need for manual rule definitions. This automation complements systematic evaluation frameworks, as demonstrated by Abdelmalak et al. [1], who developed a five-metric framework comparing graph theory, finite state machines, control theory, and probabilistic approaches for smart grid cyber-physical interactions.

Modern smart grids demand dynamic attack graph management that adapts to evolving threats and resource constraints. Game-theoretic modeling [16] addresses data scarcity by generating synthetic cyber attack data for training ML-based intrusion detection systems, while scalable approaches [13] decompose attack graphs into manageable subgraphs, ensuring both adaptability and computational efficiency. Lippmann et al. [9] demonstrated methods for validating and restoring defense-in-depth using attack graphs.

Despite these advances, analysis still remains a challenge for attack graphs in modern cyber-physical systems due to their exponentially large size. These scalability and heterogeneity issues necessitate novel attack graph analysis techniques that are computationally inexpensive.

3   Background

3.1   Smart Grid Distribution Network: Services and Vulnerabilities

The smart grid distribution network depicted in Fig. 1 follows a hierarchical five-level security architecture based on the purdue model for Industrial Control Systems (ICS) [18] with each zone separated by dedicated firewalls spanning from external internet connections to field-level control devices.

The *External Network* comprises internet-facing services such as remote access and cloud services that interact with the *Enterprise Network* through Firewall-3, which serves as the perimeter firewall enforcing inbound and outbound traffic control. The *Enterprise Network* hosts business-critical systems including Customer Information System (CIS), Asset Management servers and administrative workstations, which communicate with the *Operations Network* over Firewall-2. The *Operations Network* forms the supervisory control center with Supervisory Control and Data Acquisition (SCADA) server, historian database, and Outage Management System (OMS), which monitor and manage the *Field network* of the smart grid via DNP3 over TCP/IP, separated from the *Control Network* by Firewall-1. The *Control Network* contains Programmable Logic Controllers (PLCs) for substation/feeder automation, local Human Machine Interfaces (HMIs) for operator control, and data concentrators using Modbus TCP. The *Field Network* connects to power equipment through Intelligent Electronic Devices (IEDs) providing measurement functions and Remote Terminal Units (RTUs) controlling switching/monitoring equipment, communicating via IEC 61850 and DNP3 protocols [12].

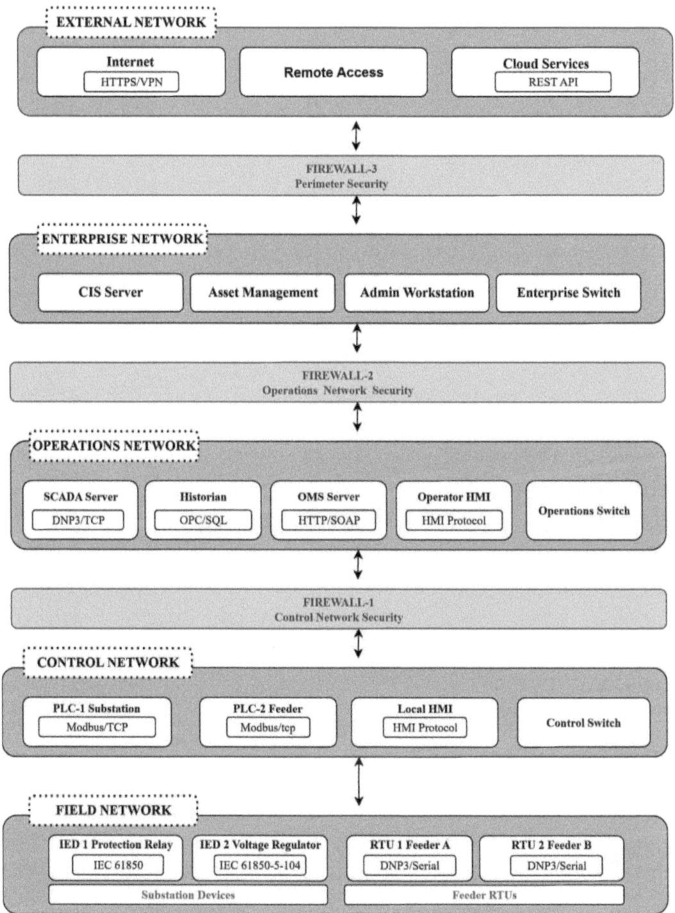

Fig. 1. Smart Grid Distribution Network.

Smart Grid Vulnerabilities. Each network zone in the smart grid distribution network exhibits a distinct vulnerability profile that can be exploited by threat actors through diverse attack vectors. *Enterprise networks* are susceptible to web application vulnerabilities and active directory compromises, which can facilitate lateral movement into *operations networks*. *Operations networks* are exposed to attacks targeting industrial communication protocols such as DNP3 and Modbus, as well as SCADA software vulnerabilities, including buffer overflows in HMI systems. *Control networks* suffer from PLC firmware vulnerabilities and engineering workstation compromises through USB-based malware and ladder logic manipulation. Field devices in the *field networks* can be compromised through the exploitation of the IEC 61850 protocol, bypassing DNP3 authentication, and direct physical access to serial interfaces and debugging ports. The convergence of IT and OT networks broadens the attack surfaces, allowing traditional enterprise vulnerabilities to cascade into critical operational systems and

Table 1. Services and vulnerabilities in network hosts

Services	Vulnerability	CVE	CVSS
DMZ Access Enterprise Zone	Log4j RCE	CVE-2021-44228	10.0
Admin Access Domain Admin	SMBGhost Buffer Overflow	CVE-2020-0796	10.0
Domain Controller	Netlogon Privilege Escalation	CVE-2020-1472	10.0
SCADA Control Operations	SCADA Bypass	CVE-2019-13548	9.8
RTU Control DNP3 Protocol	DNP3 Protocol Injection	CVE-2018-17937	8.8
IED Protection System	IED Exploit Buffer Overflow	CVE-2019-10953	7.5

potentially cause physical damage, operational disruptions, and safety hazards in the power distribution infrastructure.

As illustrated in Fig. 1, the hierarchical architecture implements layered network segmentation approach through multiple firewall layers. Table 1 presents critical vulnerabilities across these layers, with CVSS scores indicating severity levels. Notable high-impact vulnerabilities such as SCADA bypass enable direct access to the SCADA Control Network. This vulnerability represents a pivotal attack vector that, when successfully exploited, can lead to smart grid manipulation or compromise of grid protection systems, potentially causing widespread power system disruption.

3.2   Attack Graph Concepts

An attack graph is a directed graphical model that systematically represents all possible multi-stage attack paths an adversary could exploit to compromise assets within a network. An attack graph can be formally represented as follows, [10,11]

$$G = (E \cup C, R_r \cup R_i) \tag{1}$$

where, Exploit nodes (E) represent a set of attack techniques such as buffer overflow attacks, SQL injection, and password cracking. Condition nodes (C) represent a set of system states or access levels, including network connectivity, administrative privileges, and compromised credentials. Require Edge Relation ($R_r \subseteq C \times E$) represents conditions necessary for exploit execution. Imply Edge Relation ($R_i \subseteq E \times C$) represents conditions satisfied after successful exploitation. Initial conditions define the attacker's default capabilities and access levels within the target environment. Goal conditions represent the attacker's ultimate objectives or the critical system states they seek to achieve. Attack paths consist of sequential chains of exploits and conditions that connect initial states to goal states, forming complete attack scenarios.

3.3   Multi-Stage Attack in Smart Grid Infrastructure

Suppose that an attacker aims to gain control of field devices—particularly IEDs that operate protection relays and switching equipment. By reaching the *field network*, the attacker could manipulate power distribution and cause widespread outages or equipment damage. To achieve this, the attacker proceeds through several phases. *Phase 1 - Reconnaissance:* Using open-source techniques (OSINT), the attacker maps the infrastructure and then exploits an enterprise web app in the DMZ (customer/billing data) to gain an initial foothold. *Phase 2 - Initial Network Penetration:* The attacker injects malicious Log4j payloads via HTTP requests (CVE-2021-44228, CVSS 10.0), executing remote code on the server and gaining access to the enterprise zone. They then leverage SMBGhost (CVE-2020-0796, CVSS 10.0) by sending malformed SMBv3 packets to the Admin Access Domain server, triggering a buffer overflow that yields domain-administrator privileges.

Phase 3 - Credential Harvesting: Building on this access, the attacker exploits the Netlogon vulnerability (CVE-2020-1472, CVSS 10.0) in Windows domain controllers to obtain SCADA credential-service account credentials. These stolen credentials enable legitimate access to the SCADA Control Network, bypassing authentication controls on grid control systems. *Phase 4 - SCADA Network Infiltration:* With the compromised SCADA credentials obtained in Phase 3, the attacker gains access to the SCADA Control Network and exploits a SCADA bypass vulnerability (CVE-2019-13548, CVSS 9.8) to establish persistence. They then target DNP3 communications by exploiting a DNP3 injection vulnerability (CVE-2018-17937, CVSS 8.8) between SCADA systems and RTUs; by intercepting and manipulating protocol messages, the attacker can issue commands that appear to originate from trusted SCADA sources.

Phase 5 - Device Compromise and Grid Manipulation: The attacker compromises IEDs using (CVE-2019-10953, CVSS:7.5). Specially crafted packets trigger buffer overflows in IED firmware, injecting malicious code for complete device control. This enables relay manipulation, circuit breaker operation, and power flow modification leading to grid manipulation of the power system. Table 2 provides a comprehensive overview of this multi-phase attack progression and its corresponding impacts.

Table 2. Attack Vector Progression and Impact Analysis

Step	Attack Description	Target Zone	Impact
1	Target Knowledge OSINT Gathering	External	Intelligence Collection
2	Log4j RCE on DMZ Enterprise Zone	DMZ	Initial Access
3	SMBGhost on Admin Domain Server	Enterprise	Privilege Escalation
4	Netlogon on Domain Controller	Enterprise	SCADA Credential Theft
5	SCADA Control Operations Access	Operations	Network Pivot
6	SCADA Bypass Vulnerability	Operations	Persistent Access
7	DNP3 Protocol Injection	Operations	Command Injection
8	IED Device Compromise	Field	IED Grid Protection Control
9	Grid Power System Manipulation	Field	Grid Manipulation

4   Mathematical Foundation for Community Detection

Community detection aims to identify groups of nodes in a graph that are more densely connected to each other than to the rest of the graph. Modularity quantifies the quality of community structure in a network by measuring the density of intra-community connections relative to inter-community connections, compared to what would be expected in a random network with the same degree distribution [6]. The modularity Q is calculated as:

$$Q = \frac{1}{2m} \sum_{i,j} \left[A_{ij} - \frac{k_i k_j}{2m} \right] \delta_{c_i, c_j} \tag{2}$$

where A_{ij} is the adjacency matrix element equal to 1 if nodes i and j are connected and 0 otherwise, k_i is the degree of node i, m is the total number of edges in the symmetrized graph, and $\delta_{c_i, c_j} = 1$ if nodes i and j belong to the same community and 0 otherwise.

4.1   Louvain Method

The Louvain method is employed on an undirected version of the graph with uniform edge weights due to its computational efficiency and scalability. The method iteratively maximizes the modularity gain (ΔQ) when nodes are reassigned to new communities [4]:

$$\Delta Q = \left[\frac{\Sigma_{\text{in}} + k_{i,\text{in}}}{2m} - \left(\frac{\Sigma_{\text{tot}} + k_i}{2m} \right)^2 \right] - \left[\frac{\Sigma_{\text{in}}}{2m} - \left(\frac{\Sigma_{\text{tot}}}{2m} \right)^2 - \left(\frac{k_i}{2m} \right)^2 \right] \tag{3}$$

where Σ_{in} is the sum of weights of edges inside the current community, Σ_{tot} is the sum of weights of all edges connected to the community, k_i is the total degree of node i, $k_{i,\text{in}}$ is the sum of weights of edges from node i to the community, and m is the total weight of all edges in the graph.

5   Modular Analysis of Smart Grid Attack Graph

This section demonstrates a modular analysis approach that decomposes a large-scale smart grid attack graph into manageable communities, enabling scalable threat assessment and targeted defense strategies.

5.1   Methodology Overview

We propose the Modular Attack Graph Analysis methodology for scalable security assessment of smart grid infrastructures. Our approach begins by constructing a realistic smart grid attack graph containing 59 exploit nodes representing possible attacks on various operational domains viz. corporate IT, SCADA systems, transmission, distribution, renewable energy, and other critical sector entities. These exploits are connected by 108 directed edges representing possible attack progression. The attack graph includes initial access conditions (IC1-IC5), exploit nodes (a1-a59), and goal conditions (G1-G8). In this example, we have not included the intermediate conditions only the goal conditions are shown to represent various impact scenarios from regional outages to wide-area blackouts. Once the comprehensive attack graph is established, we apply the Louvain community detection algorithm to identify functional clusters within the graph, which groups nodes based on edge density and modularity optimization.

Table 3 presents the community structure of the 8 communities detected by the Louvain algorithm.

Each detected community is represented as a single node, transforming the complex 72 node graph into a simplified high-level attack graph with only 8 communities as shown in Fig. 2, achieving a significant reduction in complexity while preserving critical attack path information. Using this abstracted representation, we calculate the shortest paths from each community node to critical community C1, which includes G8 - SCADA server compromise - which is a high severity exploit.

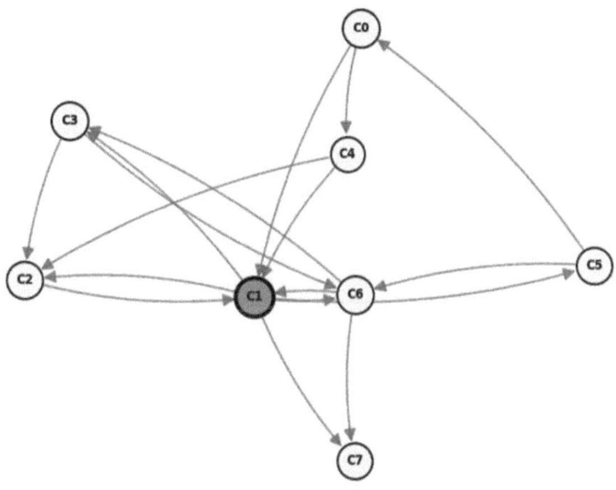

Fig. 2. Community-level abstraction of the attack graph.

5.2   Shortest Path Analysis and Defense Prioritization

For this analysis, C1 was selected as the target critical community as it contains the critical SCADA server compromise. The shortest paths from each community to C1 is calculated as shown in Table 4. The shortest path analysis identified that communities C0, C2, C4, and C6 have direct connections (1 hop) to C1, establishing them as immediate threats to the SCADA infrastructure. The attacker doesn't have any direct access to C1 from C3 and C5, and there is no possible path from C7.

The detailed analysis reveals that within a community, the exploit nodes are strongly connected, making it difficult to stop an attacker once entry has been gained. From a defender's perspective, priority should be given to securing the inter-community connections, as this can restrict the attacker's movement between communities. Since such connections are relatively sparse, targeted security measures at these points provide a practical and efficient strategy.

Table 3. Community structure of the attack graph

Community	Nodes	Size	Operational Domains
C0	IC1, IC2, a1, a36, a39, a41, a42, a44, G6	9	Initial Attack Surface (Web/Cloud)
C1	IC5, a4, a5, a6, a7, a8, a21, a22, a23, a49, a52, a47, G8	13	SCADA/Control Systems
C2	IC3, a13, a25, a37, a40, G4, a10, a27, a31	9	Market Systems & Smart Metering
C3	a9, a11, a24, a26, a45, a46, a48, a56, G2	9	Transmission & Physical Infrastructure
C4	a2, a3, a18, a50, a58, G1, G7	7	Corporate IT & Impact Nodes
C5	a14, a28, a29, a30, a32, a33, a34, a35	8	Distribution & Renewable Energy
C6	IC4, a19, a51, a17, a20, a38, a43, a12, a59, G5	10	Corporate/Supply Chain Entry
C7	a15, a16, a53, a54, a55, a57, G3	7	Generation Systems & Blackout Goals

Table 4. Shortest paths to critical community (C1)

Source	Path Length	Path	Threat Level
C0	1 hop	C0 → C1	Direct threat
C2	1 hop	C2 → C1	Direct threat
C4	1 hop	C4 → C1	Direct threat
C6	1 hop	C6 → C1	Direct threat
C3	2 hops	C3 → C2 → C1	High threat
C5	2 hops	C5 → C0 → C1	High threat
C7	No path	N/A	No threat

6   Conclusion and Future Work

Smart grid infrastructures present adversaries with extensive attack surfaces spanning IT, OT, and physical domains. The huge size and complexity of these graphs have created issues in timely assessment. This research addressed this challenge through modular decomposition using Louvain community detection algorithm. By treating each community as a single node, the size of the graph is reduced significantly. This high-level graph preserves critical attack propagation patterns while revealing the macro-structure of potential compromises. Identification of these critical connections between communities enables targeted defense prioritisation, focusing resources on the highest-risk attack vectors.

To complete this work in progress, an appropriate defense strategy will be formulated for the inter-community connections, taking into account network topology, latency constraints, and operational priorities. The strategy will minimise disruption to smart grid operations while effectively limiting attacker movement. The proposed methodology will then be implemented and tested in a practical smart grid environment to evaluate its efficacy under realistic conditions.

References

1. Abdelmalak, M., et al.: A survey of cyber-physical power system modeling methods for future energy systems. IEEE Access **10**, 99875–99896 (2022)
2. Afzal, Z., et al.: Security challenges in energy flexibility markets: a threat modelling-based cyber-security analysis. Electronics **13**(22) (2024)
3. Barrère, M., et al.: Cyber-physical attack graphs: composable and scalable attack graphs for cyber-physical systems. Comput. Secur. **132**, 103348 (2023)
4. De Meo, P., et al.: Generalized louvain method for community detection in large networks. In: Proc. 11th ISDA, pp. 88–93 (2011)
5. Donald, S., et al.: Hybrid attack graph generation with graph convolutional deep-q learning. In: IEEE Int. Conf. on Big Data, pp. 3127–3133 (2023)
6. Ghosh, S., et al.: Distributed Louvain algorithm for graph community detection. In: 2018 IEEE International Parallel and Distributed Processing Symposium (IPDPS), pp. 885–895 (2018)
7. Knapp, E.D., Samani, R.: Applied Cyber Security and the Smart Grid: Implementing Security Controls into the Modern Power Infrastructure. Syngress Publishing (2013)
8. Koo, K., et al.: Attack graph generation with machine learning for network security. Electronics **11**(9) (2022)
9. Lippmann, R., et al.: Validating and restoring defense in depth using attack graphs. In: MILCOM 2006 - IEEE Military Communications Conf, pp. 1–10 (2006)
10. Mukherjee, P., Mazumdar, C.: attack difficulty metric for assessment of network security. In: Proceedings of the 13th International Conference on Availability, Reliability and Security, pp. 1–10 (2018)
11. Mukherjee, P., et al.: "Security Gap" as a metric for enterprise business processes. Secur. Priv. **5**(6) (2022)
12. Ortiz, N., et al.: A taxonomy of industrial control protocols and networks in the power grid. IEEE Press **61**, 21–27 (2023)
13. Ou, X., et al.: A scalable approach to attack graph generation. In: 13th ACM Conf. on Computer and Communications Security, pp. 336–345 (2006)
14. Prasad, K., et al.: Generation and risk analysis of network attack graph. In: Advances in Intelligent Systems and Computing, pp. 507–516. Springer (2016)

15. Sahu, A., et al.: Structural learning techniques for Bayesian attack graphs in cyber-physical power systems. In: IEEE Texas Power and Energy Conf. (TPEC), pp. 1–6 (2021)
16. Sen, O., et al.: Simulation of multi-stage attack and defense mechanisms in smart grids. Int. J. Crit. Infrastruct. Prot. **48**, 100727 (2025)
17. Sherzhanov, A., et al.: Improving attack graph visual syntax configurations. Electronics **13**(15) (2024)
18. Williams, T.J.: The Purdue enterprise reference architecture. Comput. Ind. **24**(2), 141–158 (1994)
19. Zeng, J., et al.: Survey of attack graph analysis methods from the perspective of data and knowledge processing. Secur. Commun. Netw., 1–16 (2019)

Author Index

A
Agarwal, Mayank   136
Agarwal, Neha   357
Aggarwal, Manuj   376
Alwin Varghese, T.   3
Anil, Adithya   376
Aslam, Naziya   27

B
Bera, Padmalochan   104, 115
Bhowmick, Amit   231

C
Chamotra, Saurabh   455
Chauhan, Sneha   269
Custódio, Ricardo Felipe   85

D
Das, Sanchari   357, 444
Das, Tanmoy Kanti   299
Devnath, N. S.   433
Dilip Thakur, Meena Singh   231
Dolai, Sougata   136
Dora, Swaroop   27
Dutta, Piyali   455

E
Ekstedt, Mathias   466

G
Gajrani, Jyoti   323
Ganapathy, Vinod   65, 389
Gangopadhyay, Aditi Kar   269
Gangopadhyay, Sugata   269
Ghosh, Tanusree   38
Grover, Mayank   357

H
Hanawal, Manjesh Kumar   245
Hussain, Inarat   168

J
Jatav, Devrikh   168
Jithu Vijay, V. P.   3
Joseph, Arun   389

K
Kabra, Atul   245
Kadaru, Jashwanth   188
Kanade, Aditya   65
Katiyar, Nikhil   269
Kishnani, Urvashi   444
Konrath, Maurício   85
Krishnan, Ram   14
Kumar, Dheeraj   411
Kumar, Sushant   115
Kumar, Vivek   65
Kumari, Annu   136
Kundu, Srijit   38

L
Lachhiramka, Aman   411
Lunkad, Deven   27

M
Mackin, Ethan   357
Maddali, Lakshmi Padmaja   231
Manideep, Garrepelly   337
Manna, Debasmita   49
Mayr, Lucas   85
Meena, Monalisa   323
Meher, Koshalesh   151
Mindigal Alasingara Bhattachar, Rajan   231
More, Rutuja   357
Mukherjee, Preetam   376, 466

N
Nair, Lakshmi R.   376
Narkedimilli, Sathwik   285
Naskar, Ruchira   38
Nema, Aditya   208

© The Editor(s) (if applicable) and The Author(s), under exclusive license
to Springer Nature Switzerland AG 2026
N. Hubballi et al. (Eds.): ICISS 2025, LNCS 16380, pp. 477–478, 2026.
https://doi.org/10.1007/978-3-032-13714-2

Nobi, Mohammad Nur   14

P
Paliwal, Prakhar   245
Panda, Aditi   38
Pandey, Rajneesh Kumar   299
Pareek, Gaurav   168
Pavan Kumar, C.   285
Pranitha, Paladri   104
Purushothama, B. R.   168

R
Ramachandra, Raghavendra   285
Rana, Md Shohel   14
Rani, B. S. Smitha   466
Rao, Y. Sreenivasa   151
Rawat, Chetan   323
Rayala, Akhila   231
Routray, Kasturi   115

S
Saglani, Divyesh   231
Sankaran, Sriram   337, 433
Sasikumar, Adarsh   433

Sen, Pranab   208
Shaik, Altaf   337
Shaik, Imtiyazuddin   188
Shanker, Kripa   65
Shukla, Sandeep Kumar   27
Silvano, Wellington Fernandes   85
Singh, Aayushman   433
Singh, Navdeep   455
Singhal, Sweety   323
Suthar, Dhruv   323

T
Tazi, Faiza   357
Tejonath, B. U.   104
Thampi, Sabu M.   3
Tripathi, Meenakshi   323
Tripathy, Rojalini   104
Tripathy, Somanath   49

V
Vaishnav, Nibhrant   411
Venkatesan, S.   27
Vivek, Srinivas   188